D1443352

More Meditations
on the
NEW TESTAMENT
AND
PSALMS

More Meditations
on the
NEW TESTAMENT
AND
PSALMS

George H. Morrison

AMG
PUBLISHERS
Chattanooga, TN 37422

More Meditations on the New Testament and Psalms
© 1996 by AMG Publishers
All rights reserved.

ISBN: 0-89957-215-4

Printed in the United States of America.
03 02 01 00 99 98 –R– 7 6 5 4 3 2

Contents

Meditations on Acts

Waiting

And while they looked steadfastly toward heaven as he went up, behold, two men stood by them in white apparel; which also said, Ye men of Galilee, why stand ye gazing up into heaven?—Acts 1:10, 11.

Our lesson begins with the narrative of the Ascension, and the reader will remember that this is the *second* account of the departure of Jesus into heaven. The Gospel of Luke closes with the story, and now the Acts of the Apostles opens with it. The event that ends the earthly ministry of Jesus begins the ministry upon the throne. We are not to think of Jesus' work in heaven as something quite different from His work on earth. All He accomplished here was but the beginning (v. 1) of a service that He shall carry on forever. Now the Ascension is the link between the two. It is the passage of the unchanging Lord from the lower to the higher sphere of service. Hence Luke concludes his Gospel with it and then puts it in the forefront of the Acts. Note, too, in the descriptions given by Luke, how *sober and subdued* the coloring is. When Luke tells of Pentecost, he is thrilled with excitement. He is vivid and picturesque, almost dramatic, when he relates the healing of the lame man at the Gate Beautiful. But a few simple and very quiet words are all that he uses for the Ascension, yet to *us* that seems the greatest wonder in the world. Two thoughts are suggested by Luke's simple statement. The first is, how *Christlike* the Ascension was. He who came down like rain on the mown grass, and who would not strive nor cry nor lift up His voice in the streets, will not go home with any sound of trumpet. And the second is, how *natural* it seemed to the little company who went forth to Olivet. They had always felt that Jesus lived in heaven.

Could they be greatly surprised when He went there? The disciples *were* astounded at the cross. Death seemed so alien from the life of Jesus. But they were *not* astounded at the Ascension. They worshiped, and went to the city with great joy.

So the little company returned to Jerusalem, and we read that they went up into an upper room (v. 13). There can be little question that it was the very room that was already fragrant with memories of Jesus. Here, on the night on which He was betrayed, the bread had been broken and the cup had been drunk. Here they had sat, with the doors barred for fear of the Jews, when Jesus had appeared in their midst on the Lord's day. Probably from this very room they had gone forth to witness the Ascension upon Olivet. They were *not* forgetting the things that were behind when they returned under the familiar roof. The past was blending with the future for them; the agony, with the words "until He come." Try to imagine the company gathered there. There are the women who had ministered to Jesus and had held fast to Him when everyone else had fled. There is Mary, His mother, and this is the last glimpse we get of Mary, and she is worshiping the Son she once had nursed. His brethren are there, and only six months before (John tells us) they did not believe in Him. It was not so long ago since these very brethren had sought to have Him arrested as a madman. And now, for the ten days between Ascension and Pentecost, that company continues in united prayer. Their hearts are changed; their doubts have passed away; the command of Jesus is of supreme importance now. They are waiting for the promise of the Father, for the impending baptism of the Holy Ghost.

But one preparatory act still remained to be done. The number of the disciples was not complete. The little band must be at its full strength when the Spirit of God touched them with sevenfold power. So Peter rises—the same, and yet how changed! How different from the impulsive, boisterous Simon! He is spokesman yet (such men are chieftains always), but a great fall has bowed him to the dust, and a great love has set him on a rock, and there is a quiet dignity of sweet restraint about him now that makes him ten times the man he was in Galilee. He would have hurled hard names at Judas once. *Now* Judas "was guide to them that took Jesus." He would have pictured his doom in fiery colors once. *Now* Judas has just gone "to his own place." If ever a man came out of the darkness glorified, I think that man was gallant Simon Peter. At Peter's request, then, and after a brief sermon, a disciple was chosen to fill the place of Judas, and we may note these two features of the action. Firstly, everyone present had a hand in it. They all prayed and all gave forth their lots. Secondly, the qualification of the disciple was twofold—he must have companied with the Lord Jesus from His baptism, and he must have been a witness of the Resurrection. Matthias was chosen. The lot fell on Matthias. Can the reader cite instances of the lot from the Old Testament? It was entirely discarded after Pentecost, and I think that the Moravians are the only body of Christians who still practice the casting of the lot.

1. God Does Not Want Us to Be Always Gazing. The disciples would have stayed on the *Mount of Transfiguration,* but a demoniac boy was waiting at the foot. The women would have lingered *where their Lord was laid,* but they were bidden to depart with the glad news that Christ was risen. So *here* the two men in white apparel said, "Ye men of Galilee, why stand ye gazing?—have you no duties to fulfill at home, and do you not know that Christ will come again?" *2. There Are Unknown Disciples.* No man on earth knows who Matthias was. There is not a trace of him in any Gospel; we never meet him in history again. Yet he had been with Jesus since His baptism and seen Him after His rising from the dead, and now it is the unknown follower who is chosen to take the honored place of a disciple. God, then, has many hidden servants. We do not know them, but the Master does. If they are faithful in the toil that no one sees, they shall have the ten cities by and by. *3. There Is Purpose in God's Delay.* For ten days the disciples had to wait. God did not send the Holy Spirit at once. It must have been hard to abide in that upper room and keep the glorious secret Ascension. Yet the ten days were educative days. The power of fervent prayer was realized; the company were knit into a surer brotherhood upon their knees; the glory of Christ shone on them more transcendently. There was a deep purpose in that delay of God. He had a fatherly meaning in His tarrying. And whenever in *our* life the delays of heaven seem hard, we do well to remember that upper room.

The Sabbath Day's Journey

The mount called Olivet, which if from Jerusalem a Sabbath day's journey—
Acts 1:12.

A Sabbath day's journey with the Jews was a quite exact and definite expression. It was a journey of about three-quarters of a mile. In the Exodus, you will remember, the tabernacle was in the center of the camp. On every side of it were ranged the tribes of Israel. From the tabernacle to the farthest tent was a distance of about three-quarters of a mile and *that* was a Sabbath day's journey. Such was the technical import of the word, but like other words, it got a vaguer meaning. It came to mean a short and easy journey, a journey such as anyone might take. And it will help us to understand our text and some of the wealth of meaning in it if we keep that looser significance in mind.

As most of you doubtless are aware, though it may not often be present to your thought, the division of our Bible into chapters is a comparatively modern device. In the ancient Greek Testament there are no chapters. Now unquestionably, on the whole, the division into chapters is a help; yet there are cases where it is not a help but, on the contrary, obscures the meaning. One such unfortunate division bears directly on the Mount of Olives. At the end of the seventh chapter of St. John we read, "Then every man went away to his own house." At the beginning of the next chapter, "Jesus went to the Mount of Olives." And it is only when we take these two together and let them lie together in the mind that we feel what the writer wanted us to feel, the spiritual loneliness of Christ. Every man went unto his own house; Jesus went unto the Mount of Olives. It haunts the memory, that

6

lonely figure, homeless when all the company went home. And then, deepening the feeling greatly and throwing light on the loneliness of Christ, we are told here that the Mount of Olives *was but a Sabbath day's journey from Jerusalem.*

Now loneliness is of many kinds, just as love is of many kinds. And there are many pictures of loneliness in Scripture, that perfect mirror of the human heart. There is the loneliness of Cain when he was driven out from the face of living men. There is the loneliness of Abraham when he went out not knowing whither he went. And there is the loneliness of the apostle John when he was an exile on the isle of Patmos where in the evening, when the sun was setting, he could perhaps sit by the sad waves on the seashore. All these were far away from friends and kindred. They were separated from all the ties of home. Their eyes looked out on unfamiliar scenes where was no form of comrade or of brother. But the loneliness of Christ was of another kind. It was the loneliness of Olivet, and Olivet was but a Sabbath day's journey from Jerusalem. Not far away from Him were happy homes. He saw the sunshine flashing on the walls. In the still evening He could hear the voices of the children who were playing in the marketplace. His was a loneliness amid familiar scenes and not far distant from familiar faces where men were toiling and cottage fires were smoking and mothers were rocking their little ones to sleep.

Perhaps we better recognize the truth of this when we compare our Savior with the Baptist. The Baptist was a very solitary figure. The Baptist withdrew himself from human companionship—retired to the solitude of deserts—moved apart from men, far from the markets, where the lonely reeds were shaken by the wind. And yet the Baptist, for all his desert-solitude, does not touch one with such a sense of loneliness as Christ who moved among the haunts of men. The one was a recluse and dwelt apart; the other the friend of publicans and sinners. The one was a harsh and rigorous ascetic; the other was infinitely genial. And He loved the children, and He went to marriages, and He moved in the traffic of the village street; and yet I wonder if in all the centuries there has ever been such loneliness as Christ's. The loneliness of John was desert loneliness; it was the loneliness of isolation. But the loneliness of Christ was not like that. His was the loneliness of Olivet.

And is it not the case that loneliness like that is very often the most intense of all? It is not those who are alone who are most lonely.

> There is a pleasure in the pathless woods.
> There is a rapture by the lonely shore.
> There is society where none intrudes,
> By the deep sea, and music in its roar.

But often there is a loneliness unutterable in the crowded city where the street are thronged and the windows are brilliantly lighted in the evening. That is the loneliness of every city, it is the loneliness of every Christmas, where love and life and sympathy and comradeship may be so near and yet so far away. And that, too, was the loneliness of Olivet where Jesus went when everyone went home, only a Sabbath day's journey from Jerusalem.

Secondly, let us recall how the Mount of Olives is associated with agony. It is there that we find the agony of Christ; you remember the story of that agony? When the supper was ended they sang a hymn together, and then they went out to the Mount of Olives. They went down to the valley and across the brook and so upward to that place where was a garden. And there, under the silvery olive trees, with the light of the harvestmoon making them beautiful, our Savior was sorrowful even unto death. There He wrestled in spirit with His cross till his fastfalling sweat was red as blood. There He fought His battle for the crown. There He conquered the shrinking of the flesh. And all this anguish which has redeemed the world was experienced upon the slope of Olivet, only *a Sabbath day's journey from Jerusalem.*

Now as with loneliness, so is it too with agony. There is agony of many kinds in Scripture. There is every sort of human anguish there in that immortal mirror of mortality. There is the agony of Abraham when he climbed Moriah to sacrifice his son. There is the agony of Hagar out in the desert with her little Ishmael. And you must take such agonies as these and compare them with that under the olive trees to understand the agony of Christ. The agony of Abraham was on the lonely mountain where never a sound was heard except the calling wind. That of Hagar was in a dreary desert where could not be heard the beating of another heart. But the agony of Christ was in a garden, a garden under the shelter of Mount Olivet, and Olivet was but a Sabbath day's journey from Jerusalem. All that anguish, not on the lonely

8

moor, but known in its bitterness under the olive trees; amid familiar scenes where folk were moving and where the bridles rang upon the path, and Jerusalem but a little distance off, where mothers watched and little children dreamed, where some were toiling and some were making merry and some were brokenhearted.

Now does it not occur to you, my friend, that that is an illuminating thought? The greatest and most poignant sufferings—are they not always near the haunts of men? Men fly to the wilderness and suffer there as many a hermit and anchorite has done. Men scale the snowy cliffs and suffer there as in heroic adventure on the Alps. Yet perhaps the sorest and most bitter suffering is not the suffering of distant solitudes, but that which (like the Lord Himself) is not far away from anyone of us. It is suffering within hail of home and in the midst of familiar faces. It is the suffering of love despised, of friendship broken, of service unrewarded. It is the suffering being true to God in daily duty and at every cost; it is the suffering of fatherhood and motherhood. Such agony is not a distant thing; it is not like that of Abraham or Hagar. It is near at hand, amide the lives we cling to, within the sound of voices that we love. It is the anguish not of Mount Moriah where everything was desolate and still. It is the anguish of the Mount of Olives.

In the third place, and lastly, I observe that the Mount of Olives is associated with triumph: it was the scene of the Ascension of the Lord. It is not often that farewells are victories; very often they are tragedies. Had we:

> Never met or never parted,
> We had ne'er been brokenhearted.

But the farewell of our Lord was not a tragedy; it was the crowning hour of all that He had lived for, "who for the joy set before him, endured the cross, despising the shame." That hour was the coronation of His work. It was the completion of His career of service. It was the victorious ending of His toil and tears, of His humiliation and His sacrifice. And to me it is beautiful that all this happened, not in some remote and shadowy region, but *within a Sabbath day's journey of Jerusalem.*

Compare, for instance, the going home of Christ with the going home of Moses. One feels the difference between Christ and Moses by a comparison like that. Moses went home upon a lonely height far from the pleasant stir of human life. It was a desolate and dreary spot where

God unlocked the gate and took him in. But Christ went home amid familiar scenes and with the voices of those He loved around Him, not far away from the city of His ancestry. The eagle was wheeling and the wind was calling when "God kissed Moses, and he slept." His work was over, his splendid service finished, and the scene was far and desolate and lonely. But the triumph of Christ was of another kind. He went to the liberty of heaven from Olivet, and Olivet—a Sabbath day's journey from Jerusalem.

Now did it ever suggest itself to you how exquisitely beautiful that was? Christ triumphed then where He has triumphed always, near to the ordinary home and ordinary heart. There is a triumph of the lonely student keeping his vigil separate from men. There is a triumph of the Arctic traveler when he wins at last the silence of the pole. But every victory that Christ has won has been wrought out where men and women are, amid those hopes and fears and passions and affections which are the warp and woof of all humanity. It is Christ who has transfigured home and the lot of childhood and the love of motherhood. It is Christ who has ennobled common life, touching it with the glory of the infinite. He has won His victories where He was lonely; found His triumphs where He found His agony, not far away in any voiceless wilderness, but within sound of the voices of the city. That is why we can turn to Him tonight, certain that He is not far away. That is why we can say with glowing hearts, "I triumph still, if Thou abide with me." And that, I take it, is why He passed victorious into that heaven where His Father dwells from a familiar little hill called Olivet, which is but a Sabbath day's journey from Jerusalem.

Filled with the Spirit

And when the day of Pentecost was fully come, they were all with one accord in
one place—Acts 2:1.
Be filled with the Spirit—Eph. 5:18.

That the day of Pentecost was a great day for the Church is one of the plainest facts in Christian history. It is described, and not ineptly, as the Church's birthday. Up till that hour we were separate individuals putting their trust in the Lord Jesus Christ. We have Nicodemus and Zacchaeus and Martha and Mary and the Magdalene. But now in the outpouring of the Holy Spirit, we have separate individuals drawn together into the fellowship of faith and worship.

But if Pentecost means a great deal for the Church, it also meant much for the disciples. There is a true sense in which we may regard it as the great day, even the birthday, of their lives. Just as for Paul there ever stood out one day when he had met with Christ on the Damascus road, just as for Luther there ever stood out one day when there had rung on his ear that "the just shall live by faith," so for the disciples, through all their after-history with its journeyings, its persecutions, its service, and its martyrdom, there stood out clear and definite the day of Pentecost. And it was not the excitement of the day that made it memorable, for they had passed through many an hour of high excitement. Nor was it the outward miracle of tongues of fire, for they had witnessed far greater miracles than that. What made it memorable was the profound overwhelming change within them that had been wrought by the ascended Christ when He filled them with the Holy Spirit.

11

We are to notice, then, that this filling with the Spirit was not the beginning of discipleship. These men had been disciples, loyal disciples, long before the day of Pentecost. With one exception, they had all been called by Christ in the days of His humiliation. And they had heard the call, and followed Him, and shared in the unspeakable blessing of His intimacy. And they had gone apart into a desert place with Him and listened to all the riches of His wisdom, and then on that night on which He was betrayed, they had sat as His guests at the communion table. Nay, more, they had seen Him in His resurrection, and He had breathed on them the Holy Spirit then. He had come among them in the upper chamber and said, "Receive ye the Holy Ghost." And yet with all that wonderful experience of Christ as Teacher, Savior, and Friend, they were still waiting for a larger blessing. That blessing came to them beyond all question, and our text tells us when it came. It came when the day of Pentecost arrived, and they were all filled with the Holy Ghost. It was then that they were changed down to the depths, and it was then that everything was changed for them. They were new men, in a new universe, after the filling with the Holy Spirit.

Now one cannot look abroad upon the Christian Church today without becoming conscious of the fact that multitudes of men and women have never reached the experience of Pentecost. They too, like the disciples, have heard the call of Christ, and, like the disciples, have obeyed the call. And He has taught them, and He has breathed upon them, and they own Him sincerely as Prophet, Priest, and King. And yet, with all their allegiance to the Lord and all their trust in Jesus as Redeemer, they have never known that Pentecostal blessing that makes a man in Christ a new creation. They have never been filled and flooded by the Spirit. They have never been mastered by the living Christ. They have never felt themselves as empty vessels into which Christ was pouring grace and power. And so their lives, however loyal and dutiful and however blessed in their willing service, are not the Christ-filled and Christ-empowered lives that are the peculiar creation of the Gospel. For Pentecost, as I understand the Scripture, is not a mere matter of Church history. It is a privilege which every believer ought to claim. It is a blessing which every believer ought to have. Pentecost is the filling with the Spirit, and we are commanded in Scripture to be filled with the Spirit, just as plainly as we are commanded there to believe on the Lord Jesus Christ.

With that remark, then, I proceed to ask what change did Pentecost work in the disciples, and in the first place we shall observe how mightily it changed their spirit. As a simple matter of historical fact, that hour in the upper chamber of Jerusalem gave a new heart and a new outlook to every member of the company. It was not that it led them to believe in Christ; they had believed in Christ for many a day. It was not even that it led them to love Christ; for one had cried, "Thou knowest that I love Thee." But it was that in the filling with the Spirit, everything was so vitalized and vivified that old beliefs seemed shadowy as dreams, and they felt themselves new men in a new world. Before Pentecost they had been uncertain; after Pentecost they bore unfaltering witness. Before Pentecost they had been dimly groping; after Pentecost they were in full assurance. Before Pentecost they had been afraid and gathered in silence not knowing what might happen; and after Pentecost, like Christian knights, they were ready for battle with the world. When you contrast that quiet upper chamber with its door shut against intruding feet, with its seclusion, with its shrinking from publicity, with its avoidance of the big and bitter world, when you contrast that scene with the scene that immediately follows it of men aflame and fearless and heroic facing the crowd, lifting up their voices, coveting the opportunity of preaching—I say when you contrast these scenes and think that both belonged to the same day, you know that something mighty had occurred. And it was not anything outward or spectacular, such as a shaken house or tongues of fire. It was the promised fullness of the Holy Spirit filling every nook and every cranny of these rich natures that had been prepared for it by faith in Christ and fellowship and prayer.

So when to any man who names the name of Christ there comes in the goodness of God the hour of Pentecost, in him there is repeated this old miracle and he knows himself a new creature in Christ Jesus. He does not become a believer, for he had believed through many a cloudy day. Nor does he then begin to love his Savior, for he has truly loved Him and striven to obey Him. But, filled now with the Spirit of Him who lives, everything is energized and vitalized, and his old faith, in which he sought to serve, seems shadowy and unsubstantial as a dream. Now comes the time of which the apostle speaks in that magnificent chapter, the eighth of Romans, "The law of the Spirit of life in Jesus Christ hath made me free from the law of sin and death." So the old conflict is practically ended, and peace reigns and liberty and joy, "Not by might and not by power but by my Spirit, saith the Lord." All this, in a magnificence no words can utter, is the purchased inheritance of every Christian. No man who names the name of Christ should rest till he receives the fullness of the Holy Ghost. And sometimes God leads His children by strange ways, and by dark and devious and humbling paths, that He may bring them in His infinite mercy to the full blessing of the day of Pentecost.

The second thing we must observe is this, and it is equally evident with what I have now said. It is how mightily the day of Pentecost changed the disciples' apprehension of the truth. Not only did it affect their nature, but it had a profound effect on their comprehension of the truth. Now we should have expected that it would be so, for they had the promise of Jesus that it would be so: "When he, the Spirit of truth, is come he shall guide you into all truth"; and again, as if to interpret that great promise, "He shall take of mine and show it unto you"—He shall take of what you have all seen and heard in Me and shall show you what it really means. If ever a promise was literally fulfilled, brethren, it is that promise of the Lord Jesus Christ. For, as a simple matter of historical fact, that is precisely what Pentecost achieved. It did not teach the disciples any new truth, but it brought to their remembrance all the old; it so quickened it and showed its meaning that it became a gospel for the world. You read the sermon that Peter preached on the morning of the day of Pentecost, and there is not a thought in it but you shall find embraced in the teaching and the life and death of Jesus. And yet to think of Peter preaching *that* before his filling with the Holy Spirit is a thing that is utterly incredible. Think of John not knowing what spirit he was of, then go and read the Epistles of St. John. Think of Peter crying, "I go afishing," and then go and read the First Epistle of Peter. Something has happened—something mighty and wonderful has happened. And that something so mighty and so wonderful is the promised fullness of the Holy Ghost.

And so when a Christian man comes to his Pentecost, he too shares in the promise of his Lord. The Spirit not only makes him a new creature, but He guides Him into all truth. In that great experience of blessing, a man is not taught what he did not know before. The life of Jesus, His death, His resurrection—all that he has long known and studied.

But when the promised Spirit is vouchsafed, all that, and all the doctrine it involves, becomes so living and so intensely real that it is grasped as it never was before. The Spirit witnesseth with our spirit, and in that twofold witness we have a great assurance. Taught by the Holy Ghost, we apprehend what intellectually we failed to grasp. We find in our own experience the truth of what we had read for many a year in Scripture, and reading, had striven humbly to believe, on the authority of the Word of God. Now we no longer struggle to believe. Now, to disbelieve would be impossible. The outward witness of the Word of God is confirmed by the inward witness of the Spirit. And we need no argument to prove the truth nor any commentary to explain it to us. It is within us a living, mighty thing through the blessed indwelling of the Holy Ghost. What does a man want with an infallible church who has that infallible witness in his heart? The only infallible church is in the soul which is illuminated by the Holy Spirit. Let a man seek the authority of councils when he is still groping and wandering in darkness. He will never seek it, and he will never need it, when God in His mercy has brought him to his Pentecost.

And then, lastly, I ask you to observe what is also equally and singularly evident. It is how Pentecost, coming to the disciples, mightily changed them in their power for service. Not only did it revivify their natures; not only did it illuminate their minds; it gave them an actual power for service such as they had never had before. Of course they had all been used before; they had been used from the hour when they were called. From the very beginning of their following of Jesus they had been honored to be the Master's instruments. Long before a man has come to Pentecost he may have faith as a grain of mustard seed, and Christ has told us what a man can do if he has a faith like that. Let not a syllable fall from my lips to disparage the earlier toils of these disciples. Would God that you and I were found as faithful as they were in the Galilean ministry. And yet think of that earlier ministry, and then compare it with the later ministry, and it is all as moonlight unto sunlight and as water unto wine. Think of the mighty effects of Peter's sermon—three thousand were converted in one day. Think of the churches that sprang up and grew in the teeth of the most terrific oppositions. Think of the Gospels and letters that they wrote that came with such power to a dying world and which the

15

world will not willingly let die. My brother, it was not the atonement that did it. It was not the resurrection or ascension. It was the Holy Spirit taking the atonement and making it a mighty living thing. It was the day of Pentecost that gave the power, and that too had been foreseen by Christ, for "Tarry ye here," He said to the His disciples, "till ye receive power from on high."

The Pentecostal Blessing

Every man heard them speak in his own language—Acts 2:6.

Let us reverently try to understand what happened on that day of Pentecost. It is rightly called the birthday of the Church. Ten days before the Savior had ascended. He had passed into the presence of the Father. He had left His little band of faithful followers to be witnesses for Him. And yet the strange thing is that though they trusted Him and were perfectly convinced that He was risen, they were not ready yet to be His witness-bearers. All of them believed in Jesus, but for witness-bearing something more was needed: some new power and fullness in their lives that would carry conviction to the world. And *that* is what the disciples got at Pentecost—that new power and fullness of the Spirit which changed them from convinced believers into equipped witnesses for Christ. Without it they would have returned to Galilee, "the world forgetting, and by the world forgot." Without it, in daily fellowship with Christ, they would quietly have lived and died. With it there was a spiritual power about them that was mightier than any argument. They were witness-bearers to the living Christ. The Pentecostal blessing was equipment. It was adequacy for vocation. It was endowment for the stupendous task of the evangelization of the world. And of all this the sound as of the wind and the appearance as of tongues of fire were but the vivid and evanescent symbols.

We may illustrate the day of Pentecost from the experience of the Lord Himself. He, too, born of the Holy Ghost, had to tarry for power from on high. For thirty years He lived at Nazareth. It was a life of the most perfect beauty. In every thought, in every word and deed, He was beautiful, were for the Redeemer waiting years. He was tarrying for power from on high. *That* was given at His baptism when the Holy Spirit descended like a dove. Then was He endowed with power from God for His stupendous vocation of redemption. And like that moment in the life of Jesus when the fullness of the equipping Spirit rested on Him was Pentecost to the earliest disciples. It was not the hour when they were born again. They were saved men long before that morning. They would have won their crown and had their welcome though the day of Pentecost had never dawned. Pentecost was power for witness-bearing. It was equipment for vocation. It was the needed and adequate endowment for the evangelizing of the world.

It is thus we see the very deep significance of the first expression of that adequacy. They began to speak, we read, with other tongues as the Spirit gave them utterance. Parthians, Medes, and Elamites were there, men from every country under heaven, of different languages and diverse cultures, separate as the East is from the West; and the first glorious effect of Pentecost was to make every man and woman know that here was something sent of Heaven for *them.* Somehow, through the power of God, they were listening to familiar accents. The message was for *them;* they understood it; it broke its way through every racial barrier. Avenues were opened, ways cleared, entrances instantly discovered to hearts which before Pentecost were sealed. Later on, in the letters of St. Paul, we read about another gift of tongues. I want you very carefully to notice that that was different from this of Pentecost. *That* was impassioned and ecstatic utterance which was unintelligible save for an interpreter; *this* was speaking to be understood. No need at Pentecost for an interpreter. The Holy Spirit Himself was the interpreter. He gathered an audience out of every country to typify the universal heart. And then He so inspired those earliest witnesses that everybody who heard them understood and felt that the message was for them.

Now I take it that in its literal form that miracle will never be repeated. I never heard of any foreign missionary receiving by sudden gift a foreign language. Yet I profoundly feel that whenever to the Church there comes a time of Pentecostal blessing, this evidence is manifestly present. Take an inspired man like Mr. Spurgeon. Think of the crowds in Mr. Spurgeon's tabernacle. What an infinitely varied audience drawn from every section of society. The rich and poor, the gentleman and beggar, the saint and the sinner—and yet everybody heard in his own tongue. Filled with the Holy Ghost he spoke his message, and God in His infinite wisdom did the rest, touching the message with some familiar chords for lives that were as separate as the poles. And whenever there comes to the Church a time of Pentecost, *that* is one seal of its appointed ministry—everybody hears in his own tongue. Men do not say "I cannot understand. The preacher's tongue is alien from mine." The witness-bearing breaks through every barrier, and deep begins calling unto deep. Clothed with grace, the universal Gospel is spoken in a universal language: "not by might nor power, but by *My Spirit,* saith the Lord."

Cure of the Lame Man

And a certain man, lame from his mother's womb, was carried, whom they laid daily at the gate of the temple which is called Beautiful, to ask alms of them that entered into the temple—Acts 3:2.

It is perhaps wrong to call this the first miracle after Pentecost, though it is generally thought of in that way. The boldness of the disciples after the fiery baptism, the conviction wrought upon the hearts of thousands, and the adding to the church, after one sermon, of a great multitude of men and women—all these, for such as have the eyes to see, are as truly miraculous and supernatural as the healing of the lame man. We are very apt to confine the word *miracle* to things that we can see and touch and hear. We forget that the conversion of a soul is as truly miraculous as the curing of an ailment. It takes the power of God to change a life as surely as to make a lame man leap. This miracle, then, was *not* the first after Pentecost. But it was so remarkable, so unexpected, so fully in line with the ministry of Jesus, that it made an instant and profound impression. Everyone of us knows the story well. There is not a more graphic chapter in the Bible. It will be best then to leave the scene alone and to find one or two lessons in the verses.

First, then, let us note *the contrast between the beggar and the Beautiful Gate*. The Beautiful Gate was of Corinthian brass. Like the wonderful gates of the Baptistery at Florence (that Michaelangelo said might have served for Paradise), it was adorned with very perfect skill. It represented all that art could do. It was the masterpiece of the workmanship of man. When the sun glanced on it the people would cry "Beautiful," until at last it got that as its name. Yet here beside it was a lame man begging.

He lay in the shadow of the finest art. He was lame and helpless, poor and needy, and the wonderful gate was not a yard away. Are there no contrasts like that in our great cities? Is there nothing like that in New York or in London? Beautiful gates opening on beautiful homes, and very near to them outcasts such as this?

Or we might view it quite another way: *the Beautiful Gate was very near the sufferer.* Of all the gates into the sanctuary, *this* gate was the finest and the fairest, and just because this man was poor and helpless he found himself beside that fairest gate. Had he been strong, he would never have been there. He would have been out in the streets earning his livelihood. Who knows but he might have been an idle rioter had he been vigorous and whole like other men. But he was lame—the hand of God had touched him. He had a heavy cross to carry every day. And just because he had that cross to bear, his life was spent close to the Beautiful Gate. Have you a lame brother or a weak sister? There is a beautiful gate very near that sufferer, too.

Once more observe *what the kindness of friends can do.* It was friends who brought him to the spot where he was healed. The man was helpless. He could not move a step. He would have lain in his garret all his days, unaided. But the poor are very kind to the poor, and every morning he got a friendly *lift.* You see they were doing far more than they ever thought of. We *always* do more than we think, when we are kind. They carried their poor comrade to beg a few coins, but the day came when (thanks to them) the man got healed. Did you ever give anyone a hand towards a gate beautiful? Did you ever bring any lonely neighbor to your beautiful home or to your beautiful church? It seems a small and simple thing to do, yet who can tell what the results shall be?

Again, this shines out clearly in the story, *our choicest opportunities come unsought.* Peter and John were not bustling through Jerusalem saying, "I wonder if we can find anyone to help." Peter and John were quietly going to pray as they had been taught to do long since at home. Had they neglected church that afternoon, they would have lost a great deal more than an hour's worship. They would have lost the glorious opportunity of finding what an ascended Lord could do. The fact is, God takes us by surprise. Our great hours come when we never look for them. We are busy toiling at an ordinary task, when out of the infinite the angel comes. If you want to be famous, never think of fame. If you wish to be great, forget all about greatness. Like Peter and John, hold fast to common duty (even in the dull and sleepy afternoon), and some day you shall find your lame man at the gate.

Then note, *Christ gives us more than we expect.* There is an overflow in all His gifts. One of the great words of the Bible is *abundantly,* and in Christ's dealings there is great abundance. This poor man at the gate looked for an alms. He would have been perfectly satisfied with a few coins. But instead of a few coins, he got health and strength, and that is the generous way of Jesus Christ. The man who was let down through the cottage roof got his sins forgiven as well as his palsy healed. The prodigal would have lived contentedly in the kitchen; but instead of that he had the robe and ring. One thing let everyone of us be sure of: Jesus will do more for us than we expect, and none knew that better than the lame man here when he begged for a little coin and got a cure.

Then, lastly, *it is quite natural to leap at first.* The man went walking and leaping, praising God. It takes a little time to find one's feet after a great experience like that. Give the man ten or twenty years of city life, and he will walk as sedately as any other citizen. *First* they shall mount up with wings as eagles, says the prophet; *then* they shall run (as children always do); and *then,* when time and experience have wrought their sobering work, they shall walk and (thank God) shall not faint. Do not object to preliminary leaping. Do not be hard on a little wild enthusiasm in the man who has really been healed by Christ. Time will convert that spiritual electricity into a driving and illuminating power. Emotion will be translated by the years into the strength of action and of character.

Peter and John Before the Council

The priests, and the captain of the temple, and the Sadducees, came upon them, being grieved that they taught the people, and preached through Jesus the resurrection from the dead. And they took knowledge of them, that they had been with Jesus—Acts 4:1, 2, 13.

An old writer has said that a miracle was like the bell before the sermon, it caught the attention of the people and brought them together for the preaching of the Word. Now that was true of the miracle at the Gate Beautiful. As with the summons of some clear-toned bell, it brought a vast congregation to the disciples. And in the closing part of the third chapter, we have the sermon that Peter preached to them. But the miracle and the discourse which followed it were very abhorrent to the ruling powers. They thought that they had triumphed over Jesus, and here was His cause more visible than ever. Peter and John were apprehended instantly. They were going to the Temple and were taken to prison instead. I think that Peter and John sang hymns that night as lustily as Paul and Silas did at Philippi. Then in the morning they were led before the rulers. The council of state was set, and they were stationed in the midst of it. And they were asked (as if the questioners did not know) by what authority or name they had done this. Peter, briefly, respectfully, and manfully, declared that the power had been the power of Jesus. He showed his auditors how prophecy was fulfilled. He declared that there was no salvation out of Christ. And though to the hearers this was hateful doctrine and though they would willingly have silenced it forever, yet there was the lame man—lame no more—among them, and *that* was an argument not to be gainsaid. What could be done? Was there no help for it? Could none devise means for stopping the rising tide? That most august and venerable council revealed their impotence in the course they took. They laid a charge on Peter and on John that the name of Jesus was not to pass their lips. They might as well have charged the breaking sea to cease its thundering when the tempest blew. Peter and John were bound to disobey. Even as Jews, must they not be loyal to God? So they were loosed, and being loosed, they went (as well all do) to their own company (v. 23).

Now the first thing that arrests us here is this, *how ready we are to envy others' influence.* You would have thought that the Pharisees and priests, having the interests of their land at heart, would have been heartily glad to get a lame man healed. You would have thought that they might have argued like this, "Whoever did it is a secondary matter; the great thing is that suffering has been ended, so let us all give thanks to God for that." Instead of that we read that they were grieved. They were heart-harassed; they were quite sick with envy. If one of their *own* rank had wrought the miracle, it had been well. But it was all wrong when Peter and John did it. Do you think that that spirit has quite died away? Sometimes we call that spirit party-spirit, but in its essence it is nothing less than envy. It would have been sweet if we could have done this or that, but someone else has done it and it is torture. We must remember that God has many instruments. We must pray and struggle for a new humility. We must take as our spiritual motto that "God fulfills Himself in many ways."

The next thing that we observe is this, *there is no mistaking one who has been with Jesus.* When they saw the boldness of Peter and of John, they took knowledge of them that they had been with Jesus. That is not the mere statement of a fact of history. It does *not* mean that it dawned on the council then that these men had been in Jesus' company. John was on friendly terms with the authorities, and I fancy that all of them had heard of Peter. It means that when they saw the boldness of the two, they recognized the spirit of Jesus Christ. Like a flash, the demeanor of Christ upon His trial rose up before them; it was He who spoke through the two prisoners. There is no mistaking one who has been with Jesus. He may speak out as Simon Peter did, or like John he may not open his lips, but the world has an instinct for the

Master's presence and can tell when a man has truly been with Christ. I dare say you have all heard the eastern story of the lump of clay that exhaled an exquisite fragrance. And when someone asked it how it smelled so sweet, it replied that it had been lying near a muskrose for days. There is an unmistakable fragrance in a life that dwells continually near the Rose of Sharon.

Again this noble truth breaks from these verses, that *loyalty to God is our first duty*. It must have been hard for Peter to disobey the council. I think it would be harder still for John. They were both Jews, both steeped in Jewish feeling, nor had they lost their reverence for Jewish rule. Now comes the moment of crisis in their history. They are faced by the greatest choice to which a man is called. On the one hand is the past—the world—authority. On the other hand is the clear will of God. We know what Peter and John chose in that hour. It was very simply and very quietly done. Yet the future would have been far different for them both, and the story of Christendom would have been altered, had they swerved from the will of God in that decision. We can never tell the issues of our choices. They reach far further than we ever dream. We only know that when we choose as Peter did, we may leave the future with John's and Peter's Lord. The scene reminds us of Luther at the Diet, refusing to comply or to retract, and saying, "Here stand I. I can do nought else. God help me. Amen."

Lastly, we mark this in the story, *the great arguments for a risen Christ are facts*. It was not the preaching of Peter that silenced the council. It was the presence of the man who had been healed. It was a *man*, touched by the power of heaven, who was the sure witness of an ascended Lord. It is by facts that we prove the resurrection. It is by the long history of Christendom. It is by the experiences of countless hearts that are inexplicable save for a living Christ. Men may deny that rising from the dead. They may think it is but an idle tale. But when they behold the man who has been healed, like the Jews they can say nothing against it.

Elective Affinity

And being let go, they went to their own company—Acts 4:23.

The healing of the lame man at the Gate Beautiful of the Temple had stirred an intense excitement in Jerusalem. Like the church bell which summons people to church, it had attracted a crowd to the disciples. And Peter, who never saw a crowd but he longed for the opportunity to preach to it, began to preach—there were about five thousand gathered—and many of his hearers were converted. The priests and the captain of the Temple and the Sadducees were very indignant at this powerful doctrine. They put an arrest on Peter and John and committed them to prison for the night, and the next day they had them out and examined them on their authority for this miracle. We know how bravely and nobly Peter answered: what a change from that night of denial before Calvary! We know into what a sorry pass the council came: they threatened Peter and John, and let them go. So by the narrative of facts we reach our text, "And being let go, they went to their own company."

I wish, then, to spiritualize our text, for it seems to me to be full of rich suggestion. It hints at facts which lie very near to us, and which are worthy of our observation. None of us are prisoners in a literal sense. We are not immured in the dark or damp of dungeons. The age of persecution in its barbaric forms has fled from our land of liberty forever. But for all that there are shackles which still bind us, and we are under many constraints from day to day, and it is true of us as of Peter and John that being let go, we go to our own company. Like the carrier pigeon which, freed from its cage, wheels for its bearings and then starts

26

for home; like the mountain stream which the little child may dam but which when released goes hurrying to the sea—so all of us are subject to constraint, but being let go, we go to our own company. That is the thought on which I wish to dwell.

First, then, I think of the constraint of home. It is the earliest pressure which we know. In the years when we are climbing towards maturity, we are in the sweetest of all earth's imprisonments. We are engirdled by love then and by a father's ordering. We have to yield our wills up to another's will. It is not the child who chooses or decides; it is the father and the mother who do that. But the day comes when a young man leaves home. Like Peter and John in our story, he is let go. He has to face the world now on his own resources, and the day of authority and of command is over. It is in such a time, when the restraints are gone which were the safety and the strength of home, that a man steadily goes to his own company. What were the thoughts that were smoldering and burning under the gentle but firm constraint of home? What kind of life was being lived in secret under the quiet routine and through the family worship? What sort of ideal was glimmering and forming of which the mother knew absolutely nothing? It is not their liberty that wrecks men— what we call wreck is often revelation—it is the kind of life which they have led in secret before the hour of liberty arrives. The bonds of authority are broken now. There is no will to consult but a man's own. So being let go, with many a "God bless you," and hidden tears and prayers to a father's God, for all that is noblest or for all that is poorest, men go to their own company.

You know the parable of the prodigal son by heart. Did you ever think of the story in this light? I am sure you would never have guessed how vile that youth was if you had seen him living with his father. But no man becomes a prodigal in one swift hour. If he went to the harlots he had been dreaming of them. There was not a hillside and there was not a field at home but could have told stories of his unclean heart. Then came the tales of his wild life abroad, and his brother said, "I could not have believed it." But in the sight of God the riot was revelation; being let go, he went to his own company.

And you have often read of Jesus in the Temple. Did you ever think of *that* story in this light? Has it not been preserved for us out of these voiceless years because of its exquisite glimpse into that boyish heart? I doubt not that, as the companies turned homeward, other sons besides Jesus were missing from the crowd, and other mothers besides Mary of Nazareth went back to Jerusalem to look for them. And one would find her son among the soldiers, and another would find her son in the bazaars; Mary alone found *her* son in the Temple. As naturally as the sunflower to the sun, the heart of Jesus turned to that holy place. There was nothing on earth of such concern to Him as to ask and hear about eternal things. His mother thought that her dear son was lost, and she knew not where amid the crowds to find Him; but being let go, He had gone to His own company.

Again, I think of the constraint of work. There was a little book published some time ago with the attractive title *Blessed be Drudgery*, and I think that most of us, as the years pass, learn gladly to subscribe to that beatitude. What moods and whimsies does our work save us from! How it steadies us and how it guards us! If it were not for that bondage of our toil, how intolerable some of us should be to live with! I have known busy men who through the week would have scorned the very suggestion that they ailed, yet somehow they often ailed on Sundays. Of course there come seasons when such bondage irritates. We have all known how difficult it is in the summertime. When the cloudless mornings come and the shimmer of heat, and we hear the calling of field and lake and river, it is not easy then with quiet heart to get to the study and the office desk. But for all that, work is a wise constraint and a happy circumscription of God's finger, a narrowing of our way with such a hedge as will blossom into beauty by and by.

But being let go, we go to our own company. Every evening in a great city explains that. Men are imprisoned all day in the routine, but when the evening comes, they gravitate to their own. Here are three young fellows who work at the same desk. They are fellow clerks in the same city office. You will find all of them at the desk during the day; but the question is, where will you find them at night? You will find one of them in the dancehall, that most uninspiring of all haunts. You will find one at home with his few prized books around him, superbly happy in his Shakespeare or his Stevenson. You will find one down in the mission-hall, enthusiastic over his Boys' Brigade. What is your company? Where do you gravitate? When you can follow your own sweet will, where will it lead? Say to yourself when work is done tomorrow, "Being let go, I go to my own company"—and then thank God for it, or be ashamed.

Once more, and touching on more delicate matters, I think of the constraint of our self-interest. I speak of the bondage which everybody knows and which arises from our social system. No man is free, in an intricate society, to say and do exactly what he pleases. The most uncharitable people I ever met were the people who took pride in being candid. I grant you that in the heroic nature the thought of self-interest has hardly any place. But I am not talking about heroes now; I am talking of the average man in the average Christian city. And what I say is that he is so interlocked in this great mechanism which we call society that something of the rough and vigorous and outspoken liberty which characterized our forefathers is gone. It is expensive for the average citizen to speak out his whole mind. There are accommodations and compliances and silences that are well understood on every exchange and market. And one of the hardest tasks for any man is to keep a clean conscience and an unsullied heart while bowing to those restraints of self which society or wise self-interest demands.

But that bondage is not a perpetual bondage. All are released from it in various ways. If action be fettered, thought at least is free, nor is there any veil by the fireside at home. Or it may be that when a man has made his fortune he feels that at last he can dare to be himself, for he no longer depends for his advancement on the kindly offices of any brother. The question is what are you *then?* What judgments do you pass by the fireside? Are you less courteous and kindly now that you are *made,* than in the years when your career was making? Being let go from social entanglement and from the grim and ceaseless pressure of self-interest, steadily and silently and surely men go like the apostles to their own.

Again I think of the constraint of evil habit. One of the most arresting of Christ's miracles is the curing of the Gadarene demoniac. In his isolation and in his lonely misery the man is a type of sin's separating power. He had been very happy once in Gadara; his wife had loved him, and so had his little children. He was well thought of in his little village, and the evenings were pleasant there when work was done. Then fell on him the curse that ruined him, wrecking his intellect and all his happiness and driving him apart from those he loved until that hour when he was faced by Christ. In that great hour it was farewell to bondage. His fetters were broken and he was a man again. Fain would he have followed his deliverer and shared the fortunes of his Galilean healer. But Jesus said to him, "Go home again. Thy wife has been praying for thee and thy children love thee." So being let go from the tyranny of sin, the poor demoniac went to his own company.

And that is always one of the plagues of sin. It separates a man from his own company. We may be under the same roof as our own company, and yet be a thousand miles away from them. There is a burst of temper, and then misunderstanding, and then the pride which will never ask forgiveness—and hearts that were fashioned in eternity for one another go drifting apart like ships upon the sea. Sin separates the father from the son. Sin separates the mother from her child. From all that is ours by birthright of humanity we are barred out by the tyranny of evil. And then comes Christ and gives us spiritual freedom, rescuing us from the bondage of the years, and being let go we go to our own company. For the *best* is our true company and not the worst. We were made for goodness; we were not made for evil. It is love and tenderness and purity and light which are the true society of a God-created spirit. So when a man is released from sin's imprisonment by the word and present power of his Redeemer, being let go, he hastens to his own.

Then lastly, I think of the constraint of life, for there is a deep sense in which this life is bondage. We are the children of immortality and not of time, and here we are cribbed and cabined and confined. Nothing is perfect here, and nothing rounded. We are not built to the scale of three score years. There is no such thing as ultimate success here; the only success is not to give over striving. So are we fettered and hampered and imprisoned, and the bird is beating its wings against the bars; but when death comes, the spirit is set free, and being let go, it travels to its own. Did you ever think of eternity like that? It is an arresting and an awful thought. It is far wiser to think of it like that than to go about saying you do not believe in hell. I never read that even Judas went there. I read that Judas went *to his own place*. Being let go by his own act of suicide, he went to his own company—the rest is silence. God grant us all such love for what is good, such kinship of heart with the brave and the pure and the lowly, such secret comradeship with all who are wrestling heavenward in the living fellowship of Jesus Christ, that when death comes and the prison doors are opened and we go to our own company at last, we may go to be forever with the Lord.

Philip and the Ethiopian

And the angel of the Lord spake unto Philip, saying, Arise and go toward the south unto the way that goeth down from Jerusalem unto Gaza, which is desert—Acts 8:26.

Philip was in the full tides of work for Christ when the message came from God that he must leave it. He had been preaching in Sebasté, the old city of Samaria, and his preaching had been crowned with wonderful success when suddenly there came the angel of the Lord with this summons to get southward towards Gaza. It was a strange command, swiftly and well obeyed. There was nothing of the spirit of Jonah about Philip. Perhaps Philip remembered Jesus in the desert and thought he was going to meet his Master there. Then came the hour when the chariot rolled by. It was a very picturesque and lordly equipage. Its occupant was the chancellor of the Nubian exchequer, and he was reading aloud, as the Eastern custom is. A few broken syllables fell on Philip's ear in the brief respites of the jolting and jarring, and Philip (to whom the Old Testament was doubly precious now) recognized the priceless chapter of Isaiah. Did he remember the prophecy of the psalms, *"Ethiopia soon shall stretch out her hands to God"* (Psalms 68:31). Here was the stretched-out hand of Ethiopia, and God had so ordered it that it was not stretched in vain. Philip ran up to the side of the chariot—it was going very slowly on that rough desert road. He asked the courtier if he understood the chapter. The answer came, "How can I, without a guide?" And the passage closes with the preaching of a Savior; and with the conversion, baptism, and joy of this true seeker from afar for God.

Note then *the value of a single soul*. It must have seemed very strange and dark to Philip that he should be summoned from his Samaritan work. The tide was with him; enthusiasm was heightening; vast crowds were moved by the preaching of Christ crucified. It would have been hard to leave all that through sickness; it was doubly hard to do it when well and strong. Could no one else be found for that desert work? Was it right to leave the thousands in Samaria for the single chariot of a southern courtier? I am sure that Philip had many a thought like that, for he was a man of like passions with ourselves. Then gradually it would grow very clear to him that a single soul must be very dear to God. He would remember how the shepherd had left the ninety and nine that the one sheep in the desert might be found. From that hour on to the day he died, Philip held fast in all his work for Christ to the infinite worth, in the eyes of Christ, of *one*. We must never forget that in a busy city. Where God is, we are not lost in any crowd. We are separately precious and separately sought. In the love of Jesus we all stand alone. One by one we are found and led and humbled till the day break and the shadows flee away.

Again observe that *the earnest do not despair when disappointed.* There is something very noble in this courtier. There is a touch of true greatness in the man. In a heathen court and with everything against him, his life had grown into a great cry for God. Somehow, he had got his hands on the Old Testament. Never a Jewish trader came to Meroe but the chancellor had earnest converse with him until at last nothing would ease his heart but the resolve to journey to Jerusalem. The Temple was there, and the priests and scribes were there—would he not learn all that he craved for there? And now he is returning homeward, a weary, baffled, disappointed man. He had craved for bread—they had given him a stone. He had cried, like Luther when he first saw Rome, "Hail, Holy City"; and the holy city had brought no solace to him. How many a man, in such a disappointment, would have cast his Scripture to the winds of heaven? But the eunuch was of another mold than that. He was too great a heart to nurse despair. He must still seek; he must still read; he must still study. He was deep in Isaiah on that desert road. And it was in that hour when his journey seemed so useless and his hope was quenched and his heart was sick and weary—it was *then* that he stepped into the light of Christ. We must remember there are disappointments in all seeking. There come times when we all seem baffled in our quest. We are tempted to ask, What is the use of it? Is it worth while? Had we not better give in? We are often brought to the point of losing heart. In such moods recall the Ethiopian. He would still hold to it in spite of all failure. And on the day when everything seemed vain, the footsteps of the dawn were on the hills.

Then lastly, *God is behind many a chance meeting.* I think that the driver of this Nubian chariot was not a little startled to see Philip; it was an unlikely place to light on any traveler. And when he got home to the stables of his master and told the story by the fire at night, all would agree that this accidental meeting had been one of the strange chances of the road. But *we* know that the meeting was not that. The hand of God had ordered and prepared it. It had been arranged for in the plans of heaven, though it seemed an accident to the dusky charioteer. We must believe that it is often so. Our friendships and comradeships do not begin haphazard. We seem to be thrown across each other's path, but the hand of God has been ordering the way. Two people meet—we call the meeting chance. But life will be different evermore for both. It were well to strike out *chance* from our vocabulary, and in its place to put the will of God.

The Revelation of Duty

Arise, and go into the city, and it shall be told thee what thou must do—Acts 9:6

The first thing to be taught us in these words is how duty is gradually revealed. Our blessed Lord, in His knowledge of our hearts, never overloads His revelations. It is characteristic of the great apostle that he should instantly react on his experience. Vitality is measured by reaction—when we fail to react, then we are growing old—and Paul, vital to his fingertips, instantly reacted to the Lord—"Lord, what wouldst Thou have me to do? Tell me now. Make my future plain. Show me the service I can render Thee, and I shall do it even to the death." And it was then that Jesus answered him, "Arise and go into the city, and it shall be told thee there what thou must do." Suddenly was Paul converted. Gradually he learned what that involved. Paul found that illumination of the soul is different from illumination of the future. Step by step, duty after duty, each faithfully taken and performed, was the road to his service and his victory.

That lesson which the apostle learned is one secret of victorious living still. The next duty is the key to everything. When the future is dark to us as it was dark to him, when we cannot discern the larger will of God, when we want to be used and cannot find the road, when we are dubious of our capacities, always for us as for this great apostle there is a present and commanded duty on the doing of which everything shall hinge. Often it is a very lowly duty, and that is where so many people fail. Dreams may be spun upon the looms of God, but remember that dreams may be our traitors. We dream of voices, heavenly voices, crying to us, "Arise, do big things worthy of your powers";

and the voice on the Damascus road is crying, "Arise and go into the city." Had Paul not gone, he would never have learned his mission. He learned it by obedience. He learned it by unquestioning acceptance of the first dull thing that was demanded. And whatever the particular service be that God has in store for anyone of us, we learn it just as the apostle did. Service is gradually given. Duty is gradually shown. Do the thing that is demanded now, and out of that the vision shall emerge. It was a poor, dull thing for that illumined soul to go tramping on another mile or two, but it led him to the service of his life.

The other profound lesson of the words is that new vision is for old environment. Converted, changed in his whole being, Paul has to step out on the old road. To Damascus the apostle had been journeying when he set out to persecute the Church. Then came the flood of new life within him and the overwhelming experience of conversion. And the beautiful and Christlike thing is this, that Paul was not swept into any new surroundings but bidden to hold on the old road. Wert thou making for Damascus, Paul? To Damascus thou art still to go. There is no new path for thee across the hills. There is nothing but the old familiar highway. Resume it. Set thy face to it again. Take up and prosecute they interrupted journey. The new vision is for the old environment.

Now that is a lesson we do well to learn if we want to handle life aright. For the old roads never seem so dusty as after some great stirring of the heart. There are long periods when we are content. We are happy in the daily round. We are satisfied with our nutshell, unlike Hamlet, because we have no dreams. But then some day to us there comes the vision—the light that never was on sea or land—and there is born the passion to escape. It may come when the glow of youth is burning, or when the beauty of the world has caught us, or when love has wakened with its divine unsettlement, or when the chair is empty and the grave is full. Who has not felt in seasons such as that the longing that arises in the heart to have done with the road that is leading to Damascus? It is not easy to go quietly on then. It is not easy to get back to duty. We hate the drudgery—it is intolerable—we crave a more congenial environment. And it is then that to our restless hearts Christ comes as He came that noonday to St. Paul, saying, "Arise and go into the city." He does not offer us a new environment. Vision is not given for new environment. It is given that the common round, the irksome and unceasing drudgery, may be illuminated and transfigured.

The Blindness of Vision

When his eyes were opened, he saw nothing—Acts 9:8.

Blinded by the flash of light from heaven, the apostle was flung prostrate on the ground. It was then that the Savior said to him, "Saul, Saul, why persecutest thou me." For a little space his eyes were shut, as eyes instinctively shut in self-defense. That flash of light from heaven would have blinded him had it burst on the unguarded eyeball. And then in a moment or two the apostle rose and looked around him and scanned the heavens above him, and *when his eyes were opened, he saw nothing*. Half an hour before he had seen everything: the road, the palms, the gleaming city walls. Now he saw nothing—no human face nor form—no battlement—no cloud upon the sky. And the singular thing is that this loss of vision, this forfeiting of the sweet sight of things, came to him when his eyes were opened.

Now that is a very remarkable conclusion; we are tempted to say it is absurd. It is so different from what we might have expected as a consequence of the opening of the eyes. There was a young man once, in Old Testament times, who was sorely frightened by an Assyrian army. And the prophet, in pity for him, prayed to God, "Lord, open the young man's eyes that he may see." And when the eyes of that young man were opened he saw a sight to make any coward brave, for the mountain was full of the chariots of the Lord. That is the fitting consequence of vision. It reveals to us what we never saw before. It shows us in common hearts unlooked-for things and in common scenes an undiscovered glory. But here, on the road to Damascus, and at midday, it is the very opposite which meets us; when his eyes were opened he saw nothing. The question is, in our own life's experience is there anything analogous to that? Is there any opening of the eyes which leaves us with a vision forfeited? That is worthwhile pondering a little.

In the first place, let us think of nature and of all that the world of nature meant to men once. There was a bygone time when nature was alive; when every wood had its dryad or its faun:

> Rough satyrs danced, and fauns with cloven
> heel
> From the glad sound would not be absent
> long.

Such was the outlook of man on nature once. It was all haunted by mysterious life, in every spring, in every whispering forest, in every glade where shadows lay and lengthened. The great god Pan was moving with his music where the brooklets and the summer winds were calling, and sometimes he was nearer than they knew. Well, all that of course had had to go. Increase of knowledge has banished it forever. No school child believes in fairies now. And I suggest, to those who have ears to hear, that there are thousands for whom a little knowledge just means that when their eyes were opened *they saw nothing.*

Putting the matter in another light, suppose we think of the little frets of life, of the little pinpricks and unkindnesses which most people experience as they journey. There are folk who brood upon such things as these, until they practically see nothing else. They tend and water all their little grievances till their blossoms would take prizes at a show. And what I have noticed of such folk is this, that when through the mercy of God their eyes are opened, of all these little pinpricks they see nothing. Their eyes have been opened to what real suffering is. They were only playing before at being miserable. Their eyes have been opened to that larger life which is always given us in Christ. And the beautiful thing about that life is this, that worries which were overwhelming yesterday, somehow have vanished so that we cannot see them in the love commended on the cross. Every rock and ridge is clear and glistening in the Highland burn when it is low. But when the summer rain falls or the winter snow, then they become invisible. And I have found it so in many a man's life when a new tide of being has possessed him; things that were sharp and hard and hurt him yesterday, somehow have become invisible today. "Son, why hast thou thus dealt with us."–they felt the sting of it and thought that He was unfilial. But when their eyes were opened *they saw nothing;* that filial ingratitude had vanished. So when we see, many a thing vanishes; many a thing which hurt and fretted us, and met us everywhere, and barred the sunshine out, and silences all the music in the dwelling.

Does not the same thing often happen also with that opening of the eyes which the years bring? We experience it in many different ways. Here, for instance, is a child who thinks the world of a certain picture. It hangs on the wall of the nursery at home and is perfectly beautiful to him. It is only a rough and inartistic daub–a crude, gaudy, glaring oleograph–but to the child it is a joy forever. Then the years pass, and the little brain is educated, and these two little eyes are taught to see–taught to distinguish what is really beautiful from what is only a travesty of beauty–and then the child comes back to that old oleograph which long ago was a very heaven of gladness, and now that its eyes are opened *it sees nothing.* We can mark our progress by our growing vision. We can also mark it by our growing blindness. Not only do we see more as the years pass; if we are spending them rightly, we see less–less in certain books we thought the world of and in certain societies we held delightful and in certain characters we thought ideal. How many a madly infatuated girl had had the experience of our text. In spite of the warnings of a mother's love, she insisted on idealizing somebody. And perhaps she married him, and then her eyes were opened in the long dusty highway to Damascus, and when her eyes were opened *she saw nothing*–nothing of the manhood she had dreamed, nothing of the strength that she had conjured; nothing but selfishness where she had looked for service; nothing but coldness where she had looked for love. May heaven be very merciful to such on the desert-road when the ideal has vanished, for it is always a perilous season on life's journey.

Then our text, as it seems to me, applies again to many of those messages with which the world is ringing. There are faiths and philosophies which vanish when you see. When the sun is shining on you and the world is beautiful, you go, for instance, to hear a certain preacher. You have never been plunged into the depths yet and have never felt your utter need of Christ. And the man is artistic, or he is intellectual, or he has the fire and passion of the orator, and you feel as if you would never want another message. My brother, if the sun were always shining, it may be that that message would suffice you. But this is a strange, grim world, with lightning flashes and storms that cry havoc and waves that cruelly beat. And when these days come and you feel your need of Christ and of an arm to lean on and a hand to save you, no charm of speech—no intellect nor artistry—can reach and grip and satisfy the soul. You want a power to hold you out of hell. You want a love that goes unto the uttermost. You want a heart on which to lean securely though the whole universe should fall in ruin. And whenever through trial and suffering and sorrow your eyes have been opened to see that, then in the fine artistic preaching *you see nothing*. Nothing to pluck you from the miry clay. Nothing commensurate with sin and hell. Nothing that can be heard across the battle, like the voice of the trumpet summoning to victory. That is why your old and chastened saints who have suffered and struggled, battled, conquered, fallen, feel sometimes that there is not a word for them in preaching which may be exquisite as music.

I want also to say in passing that our text has got another application. It applies to the recognition which we give to men—too late. I think of two, long centuries ago, who were joined by a third as they journeyed to Emmaus. And though He opened the Scriptures to them till their hearts were burning, their eyes were holden and they did not know Him. And then they invited Him in to share their evening meal, and in the breaking of the bread their eyes were opened, and they knew Him and He vanished from their sight. When their eyes were opened they saw nothing. The One who was all the world to them was gone. *There* was the cup He had drunk from in their company, and there the couch on which He had reclined. Thou son or daughter, here in this church tonight, with a mother who loves thee with all a mother-love, see that thy recognition of her presence be not a gazing at vacancy like that. Thou takest her as a matter of course this evening. Thine eyes are holden; thou dost not recognize. Thou dost not dream what pleasure thou cloudst give by a little self-sacrifice for her who loves thee so. I bid thee awaken, while the days are flying, lest when it is all too late and thou are motherless, thine eyes should be terribly opened and *see nothing*.

I close by suggesting that in the case of Paul, and in the case of many a man since Paul, this is what happens when through the Holy Ghost our eyes are opened to see that we are sinners. There was a Pharisee once who came up to the Temple, and he thanked God he was not as other men. He fasted and was an exemplary person; he was proud of all he was and all he did. And in that same temple was a publican whose eyes had been opened by the grace of God, and when his eyes were opened, *he saw nothing.* Nothing of all his fasting and his tithing; nothing of all he had ever striven to do. His best was sinful. His life had been a failure. "God be merciful to me a sinner." My brother, when you see nothing, you see Christ. When you see that your best is rags, you see His riches. When you see at last that you have nothing to plead, you are ready for all the gladness of His grace.

Aeneas and Dorcas

And it came to pass, as Peter passed throughout all quarters, he came down also to the saints who dwelt at Lydda—Acts 9:32.

When the fierce fires of persecution had died out, Peter set forth on a tour of visitation. He was eager to find how the churches had been faring; Jesus was whispering to him, "Feed my lambs." He went from town to town and village to village, comforting, cheering, and inspiring; and it was in this tour that Jesus led him to the bedside of the palsied disciple in Lydda. Lydda was some thirty miles from Jerusalem on the high road from the capital to the coast. It is a little town that has had a strange and checkered history; its story is full of sieges and assault. Tradition tells us that St. George was born there—St. George, who fought with the dragon; but it is not through St. George, it is through St. Peter, that the name is so familiar to our ears. Aeneas, then, lived in Lydda, and Peter found him there (v. 33)—*found* him, I take it, because he was looking for him. It is the things we look for that we are quick to see, and Peter had won the eyes of Jesus now. If a Jewish merchant had come down to Lydda, he would have discovered much, but never Aeneas. It took a Christian missionary, filled with love, to find this sickbed and show it to the world. What do *you* find when you go to a strange place? What do *you* see when you travel in foreign countries? Is it only the mountains and the waterfalls and castles and the dresses so different from those at home? A Christ-touched spirit will see far more than that—it will see the need of saving and of healing. The man of science finds new species of plants; the explorer finds strange customs and observances; but the apostle finds a certain man

43

who has been eight years bedridden with the palsy. The boys who read Homer or Virgil have heard of another Aeneas. He was the hero and the champion of Troy. And once, when *that* Aeneas had been wounded, he was healed by the intervention of the gods. All that is fable; but *this* story is no fable. Peter said to Aeneas, "Jesus Christ maketh thee whole." And his palsy left him that very hour, and he arose immediately.

A few miles from Lydda lay the town of Joppa, and Joppa was the seaport of Jerusalem. Those who have read Charles Kingsley's *Heroes,* and who remember how Perseus rescued Andromeda, will be interested in knowing that the old world believed that it was at Joppa that Andromeda was chained. It was here that the materials were landed which were used in the building of the Temple. And it was from the port of Joppa that Jonah sailed when he thought to fly from the presence of the Lord. Here, then, lived Tabitha called Dorcas, and Tabitha means *gazelle.* The gazelle was one type of beauty for the Jew. And whether Tabitha was beautiful in face or not, we all know that she was beautiful in character. Probably she had been a fine seamstress as a girl; but in her girlish days it would be fancy work. The fancy work never became real work till the pity of Jesus touched her womanly heart. She was not a speaker; she never addressed meetings. I dare say she envied the ladies who could speak. But she learned that there was a service quite as good as that, and that was the service of a consecrated needle. In the glimpse which our verses give of Tabitha, we see how deeply and sincerely she was mourned. And we can picture the joy of many a home in Joppa when the news came that Tabitha lived again. The tidings traveled through all the town, we read, and many believed in the Lord. And then our passage closes with telling us that Peter lived for a long time with the tanner Simon. Do you know why the Bible tells us Simon's occupation? It is because the Jews thought tanning disgraceful work. No rigid and formal and self-respecting Jew would ever have demeaned himself by lodging *there.* And the narrative wishes to show us Peter's mind and how he was rising above Jewish prejudice, and how he was getting ready for the vision that we shall have to consider in our next lesson.

Now let us note the close resemblances between the raising of Tabitha and the raising of Jairus' daughter. Peter had never forgotten that memorable hour, and *now* he could not follow his Lord too closely. Peter had been boastful and self-willed and impetuous once; he had loved to suggest and dictate and take the lead. But *now,* with all the past graven on his heart his passion is to follow in Jesus' steps. Had Jesus put all the mourners from the room? Then Peter must be alone with Tabitha. Had Jesus said *Talitha cumi?* Then Peter will say *Tabitha cumi.* Had Jesus taken the maiden by the hand, and given her back again to her rejoicing friends? Then Peter will present Tabitha alive. The one point of difference that I find is this: our verses tell us that Peter knelt down and *prayed.* In that one clause there lies the difference between the work of Jesus and that of His disciple. For the power of Peter was delegated power. It was Christ who was working, and to Christ he must cry. But Jesus was acting in His inherent sovereignty. In His own right He was Lord of life and death.

Three minor lessons shine out from these incidents.

(1) *We may witness for Christ even in making a bed.* The first sign of power demanded of Aeneas was that he should arise and make his bed. Now the words may not quite mean what we understand by them. *His* bed was a carpet and had to be stowed away. But they *do* mean that in a little act like that—the rolling up and disposing of a rug—a man may show that Christ has dealt with him. You remember the servant girl who was asked by Mr. Spurgeon what evidence she had to show that she was a Christian, and she replied that she always swept under the mats now. I dare say she never thought about Aeneas, but the two arguments for Christ are close akin. (2) *The sight of a man may be better than a sermon.* "All that dwelt in Lydda *saw* him, and turned to the Lord." And (3) *We must help with our hand as well as with our prayer.* When Peter was left alone beside dead Tabitha, we read that he kneeled down and *prayed.* Had he not prayed, he had not wrought the miracle. But when Tabitha sat up, wrapped in her strange garments that hampered her limbs and made it hard to move, then Peter gave her his *hand* and lifted her up. I wonder if he remembered how Jesus had said, "Simon, Simon, I have *prayed* for thee," and then, on that wild night upon the lake, had put forth His *hand* and held him up? The heart and hand of Jesus had saved Peter. The heart and hand of Peter won back Dorcas. And it takes both the heart that prays and the hand that helps to bring the kingdom even a little nearer.

Peter and the Angel

And behold, an angel of the Lord came upon him, and a light shone in the prison; and he smote Peter on the side, and raised him up, saying, Arise quickly. And his chains fell off from his hands—Acts 12:7.

At the time when Christianity was spreading and getting its first welcome in the pagan world, Herod Agrippa I, grandson of Herod the Great, began to persecute the disciples in Jerusalem. James, one of the three whom Jesus had drawn closest to Him, was sent to be with Christ (which is far better); and then to conciliate the Jews, who were mightily annoyed at Peter's traffic with the Gentiles, Herod had an arrest laid upon Peter also. Now Peter had broken prison before. It would never do that that should happen again. Sixteen soldiers were thereupon sent off to watch him, between two of whom (taken in turn) Peter was chained. Everything looked very black for Peter then. His execution after Easter seemed inevitable. The king was against him, and the guard of soldiers, and the thick walls and bolted gates of the prison. What could a little band of well-wishers effect in the teeth of great worldly powers like these? Had they been faithless, they would have taken to *plotting;* but being faithful, they took to *praying* instead. We can often accomplish a great deal more by prayer than by all the plots and plans that seem so clever. For on the night before his execution Peter was sleeping, and dreaming perhaps of heaven in the morning, when suddenly the ward was filled with light, and Peter stood up to find himself at liberty. The angel of the Lord had come to him; it all seemed like a dream to Peter. They passed out under the open sky, and after going through one street, the angel left him. And then the passage closes in the house of Mary, and I am sure that no one in that house of Mary would ever doubt the power of prayer again.

First note, then, that *there is no squandering of divine power in any miracle.* When Peter rose up, his chains fell from his hands. It took the power of heaven to do that. And as he passed from the first ward to the second and through the iron gate into the street, the way was opened by divine assistance. Peter was powerless to achieve his liberty, and God did what Peter *could not do.* Still, there were many things that Peter *could* do, and heaven did not interfere in these. He had to gird himself and bind on his own sandals and cast his garment about him and step out. God was ready to do His proper work, but nobody but Peter must do Peter's. Now, the point I want the reader to observe is the economy of power in Bible miracles. That is one mark of the authentic miracle in contrast with the cheap marvels of a corrupted Church. At Cana, Jesus used the water pots and called on the servants who were standing there. In raising Lazarus the stone had to be rolled away, but no word of Jesus made the stone remove. At the feeding of the thousands on the hillside, the provisions of the young lad were taken, and the food was distributed by human hands. No one could have supplied the wine but Jesus; no one else could have brought Lazarus to life; no one could have fed the famished thousands—if these things are to be done, Jesus must do them. But there, as here, there is much that man can do. There are helping touches that human powers may give. And in the very heart of every miracle where the divine power is most signally in exercise, we find that these human powers are employed. That is the spiritual side of the old proverb that God helps those who help themselves.

Next, note that *the angels depart whenever their work is done.* The angel led Peter out of the prison ward; he was too dazed to grope his way in the dark corridors. And then they passed on through one street together under the first flushings of the Easter sunrise. Meanwhile the chill air was striking on Peter; he was coming to himself in the still street. He heard his own footfall echoing in the stillness; he recognized this house and that. It took the swift walk through one street to do it— *swift,* for I don't think that angels ever lag. But by the time one street was traversed, Peter was cooled and steadied, and forthwith the angel departed from him (v. 10). Now, sometimes the angels leave us, for our *sin*. It would stain the whiteness of their wings to walk with us. We live so meanly and have such unworthy thoughts that we are not fit company for angels. But there is another doctrine of the departing angel. They leave us as they left Peter, for our *good*. It would be very sweet to walk beside an angel. We should be certain never to take the wrong turn. We should move on through all the streets of life with never a tremor, under that angel guidance. But then—why has God given us our faculties? And what is our reason for, and what our will? You may depend upon it these would never waken, nor grow into their strong and godlike fullness if the white wings were always on ahead. If manhood is to come, childhood must go. There is no liberty where the angel is. It is where the spirit of the Lord is that there is liberty. So we all pass out of that angel street, to think ourselves alone in the chill morning. But we are not alone. for God is with us; and we shall reach the door we are seeking as did Peter.

Last, note that *even our gladness may become a hindrance.* When Samuel heard the voice of God in the sanctuary, he got up in the morning and opened the Temple doors. But when Rhoda heard the voice of Peter, she left the door shut in Peter's face. Was she afraid to open at that hour? Like the sister in *Comus,* she was too innocent to fear. She opened not the door *for gladness.* It was her joy that kept her from her duty. Joy, then, may sometimes hinder duty. Do we ever read of joy hindering *faith?* When the disciples were gathered together within closed doors and suddenly the risen Jesus stood in their midst, Luke tells us that they believed not for joy (24:41–45). Now, joy is a serious and holy thing. Christ wants us all to be sharers in His joy. But remember there is a joy that sometimes hinders duty, and there is a joy that sometimes hinders faith. May not that be the reason why in our spiritual life God sometimes has to take our joy away? It is so supremely essential that we do our duty; it is so imperative that we believe. Perhaps some mother, glancing at this page, thinks of the child she used to call "my joy." It may be a little plainer to her now why the flower was transplanted to the brighter garden.

The Angel and the Sandals

And the angel said unto him, Gird thyself, and bind on thy sandals. And so he did—Acts 12:8.

There is a vividness of detail about this story which assures us that facts are being recorded. No imagination, however lively, could have conceived the scene that is presented here. When a man has played a part in some great hour or been an eyewitness of some memorable action, there is a note in his telling of it, no matter how he blunders, which is better than all the periods of historians. And unless we be blinded by a foolish prejudice which deadens the literary as well as other faculties, we cannot but distinguish that note here. Peter had been in prison once before, and once before he had escaped miraculously. Now, having in their hands again this prison-breaker, the authorities were determined there should be no more miracles. But when prayer arises like a continual incense and when God puts out His mighty arm to help, "stone walls do not a prison make, nor iron bars a cage." Behold, the angel of the Lord came upon Peter, and a light shined in the darkness of the prison. And he smote Peter on the side and raised him up, and the chains fell off from his hands and he was free. Then dazed with the sudden light as Peter was, thinking he dreamed and that his dream was idle, the angel said to him, "Gird thyself, and bind on thy sandals."

These words are rich in spiritual suggestion. In the first place, they are the angel's argument that what had happened was actually true. Peter was fast asleep when the light shone; asleep, and it was the night before his execution. A man must have a very good conscience, or a

49

very dead one, to be able to sleep on such a night as that. Then in a moment the cell was all resplendent, and the glory of it pierced the sleep of Peter; and he opened his eyes, and the visitant was there, and he was dazed and "dark with excessive bright." Was this a dream, and waking would be vain?—"Peter, bind on they sandals, gird thyself. Art thou in doubt as to whether it is real? Employ the light I bring to tie thy shoe-latchet. Do not seek to handle me; do not inquire my name. Do not wait there wondering if it is all a dream. Gird up thy mantle and bind thy sandals on, and thou wilt speedily discover all is true." I do not think that Peter, however long he lived, would ever forget that lesson of the angel. Every morning as he stooped to tie his sandals he would say, "Even this may be an argument for liberty." Not by remarkable and striking proofs nor by the doing of anything uncommon, not in such ways was Peter made to feel that all that had happened to him was reality. It was by doing an ordinary deed—girding his cloak and putting on his shoes—but doing it now in the light the angel brought, a light that "never was on land or sea."

Now I think that that angel-argument with Peter is one that ought to be powerful with us all. There is no such proof that the new light is real as just the use of it for common deeds. We are all tempted to put things to the test in ways that are remarkable and striking. We want to say to the puddle, "Be thou dry," as Bunyan did in his untutored youth. But the voice of the angel says to us, "Not so; but buckle thy mantle and bind thy sandals on, and prove in the quiet actions of today that the vision which shone on thee was not a dream." It may be a mighty proof of a man's patriotism that he is willing to drain his veins for his dear country; but to fight for that country's welfare day by day, in the face of abuse and slander, is a greater. It may be a mighty argument for love that one would lay himself down and die for Annie Laurie but to be courteous and kind to Annie Laurie daily is the kind of argument that all the angels love. (I refer of course to the refrain of the exquisite and anonymous song, "Annie Laurie"—"And for bonnie Annie Laurie; I'd lay me down and dee.") Seekest thou great things for thyself? Seek them not. Use the light to tie the sandal on. Be a better father among your growing children. Be a better sister to your provoking brothers. I think that Peter would always have such thoughts when he recalled all that had happened in the prison.

Then once again our text suggests what I might call the divine economy of power. "Gird thyself; do not expect me to do it; what thou *canst* do for thyself, that thou must do." It was not pride that kept the angel from that service. Things we would scorn to do are done by angels gladly. If it was not beneath Christ to wash the feet of Peter, it was not beneath an angel to tie his shoe-latchet. But the angel refrained (as angels always do), in that economy of strength which is divine, from doing for Peter in his hour of need what it was in his power to do himself. Let Peter strive all night, he cannot loose his chains, and therefore it is the angel who does that. No beating of Peter's hands will burst the gate, and therefore it is the angel who unbars it. But "gird thyself, and bind thy sandals on"—even when God is at work there is something thou canst do; and that *something*, which is within thy compass, will never be performed by heavenly visitant.

We see this same economy of power when we study the miracles of Jesus Christ. It is an added evidence for Jesus' miracles that the miraculous is kept down to the lowest point. He makes the wine, but will not fetch the water; it is in the power of the servants to do that. He feeds the famishing thousands on the hill, but the disciples must bring the bread and distribute it. The hand of man must roll away the stone when Lazarus is to be summoned from the grave, and when the breath of life has been bestowed, it is for others to unwrap his cerements.

Do you see the meaning of that divine procedure? It makes us fellow workers with the Highest. Peter needed the angel for his rescue, but for the rescue the angel needed Peter. "Gird thyself and bind thy sandals on; do the little thou *canst* do to help me"—so Peter was lifted out of mere passivity and made a fellow laborer with God. I think of this text when I see the harvest field where men are busy amid the golden grain. The ministry of God has given the harvest, and now the ministry of man must bring it home. I think of it when I see men struggling heavenward, wrestling towards heaven "just a little 'gainst storm and wind and tide." It is God who has wrought in them to do His will, and now they must work out their own salvation. Do we not sometimes wonder why it should be so hard to win the crown which God delights to give? Redeemed by blood, why should we have to fight so, why struggle in deadly fashion to the end? And the answer is that thus we are ennobled and called into fellowship with the divine and raised to be sharers in that work of grace which rests on the satisfaction of Christ Jesus. All that you cannot do, God will do. All that you can do, God will never do. Trust Him to free you by bursting iron doors and leading you triumphantly from prison. But gird thyself; do not ask God to do it. Do not wait for the angel to tie on the sandal. It is only a fool who would be idle because he was assured the light had come.

Lastly, the text suggests to me a certain leisureliness in God's procedure. The angels are always bent upon their ministry, but we never find an angel in a hurry. We know the kind of man that Peter was and how ardent and impulsive was his nature. He was always swift to speak and swift to act, too often without any reckoning of consequence. But had the calmest and most phlegmatic spirit been the tenant of that apostle's breast, it might well have been stirred into feverish haste that morning. Every moment was precious, and every moment perilous. Another instant and the soldiers might awake. Alive to his danger and to his opportunity, can you wonder if Peter clean forgot his sandals? And then the angel, calm amid that tumult, with a calmness born of fellowship with God, said "Gird thyself and put thy sandals on." I wonder if the girdle was ever so rebellious as on that morning in the prison house. I wonder if his sandals were ever so refractory as when every moment meant life or death to Peter; but there was something imperious about this angel, and Peter had no choice but to obey. It seemed an age to Peter while he stooped in his great agony of apprehension. What mattered the securing of his cloak when every moment was infinitely precious? But when Peter came to look back upon it all, he would see the meaning of the angel's conduct and learn the lesson (which is so hard to learn) that there is no hurry in the plans of God.

The Departing of the Angel

And they went out, and passed on through one street; and forthwith the angel departed from him—Acts 12:10.

In the verses that precede our text we have the familiar story of Peter's release from prison. Perhaps the story would have been still more familiar, and would have impressed itself still more vividly on Christendom, had it not been overshadowed by that other scene when Paul and Silas sang in the jail at Philippi. The world would have been a great deal poorer but for its prisons. We owe more to our prisons than we think. Shining virtues have been developed in them; miracles of heaven have been wrought in them; immortal literature has been written in them, and these are things we could ill do without. And we could not do without that word of Jesus either—Sick and in prison, and ye visited Me.

Peter, then, had been imprisoned by Herod. He had been cast into the inmost ward. You can hear door after door shut behind him with a re-echoing clang. And then, to make assurance doubly sure, he is chained to two soldiers as Paul was, afterwards, in Rome. Perhaps Herod thought that if Peter's Master when He was left for dead had burst from the sealed grave, it were well to make assurance doubly sure when the prisoner was one of Jesus' henchmen. But there were some truths that Herod had yet to learn. And one of them was that when God Almighty works, "stone walls do not a prison make, nor iron bars a cage." Behold the angel of the Lord came upon Peter, and a light shined in the prison. You can shut out a man's nearest and dearest from him, but no authority can shut the angels out. And the

53

angel touched Peter, and the chains fell off him. And the angel led him out from ward to ward. And the iron gate swung back upon its hinges, and Peter was out under the stars again. And the angel and Peter passed on through one street, we read, and forthwith the angel departed from him.

Now, do you see why the angel left the disciple then? There is strong doctrine in the departing of the angel. Sometimes the angels leave us for our sin. We are so coarse, and evil-inclined and worldly, it would stain and sully their white robes to walk with us. They try it for one street—for we have all our chance—but it does not prove "the street which is called Straight." There is always a dying out of vision when a man or woman loses the childlike heart, and the dying of vision is the departing angel. Sometimes then, the angel leaves the soul—the brightness fades, the heavenlies disappear, the presence of white-robed purity is lost—and all because a man is growing worldly.

But that was clearly not the case with Peter. Right to the end, through all the struggle and the storm of life, Peter preserved, as only the greatest do, the great heart of a little child. If every child has got its guardian angel, I do not think that Simon's would be lacking. Yet for all that, when they had passed through one street, forthwith the angel departed from Simon Peter. And I think it is not difficult to see why. The angel's work was done; that is the point. There was no more need for the ministry of miracle. Peter was a man among men now; in the familiar streets, freed from his shackles, and with friends to go to—it was at that point the angel went away. There was the presence of Christ for Simon Peter now; there was God in His eternal law and love; but there was no need for the angel any more. His task was over when the chains were snapped, and the last gate between Peter and liberty swung wide.

I wonder if you grasp, then, what I should venture to call the helpful doctrine of the departing angel? I think it is a feature of God's dealing that has been somewhat neglected in our thought. It means that in extraordinary difficulties we may reasonably look for extraordinary help. It means that when we are shut in prison walls and utterly helpless to extricate ourselves, God has unusual powers in reserve that He is willing to dispatch to aid His own. But when the claimant need goes, so does the angel. In the open street, under the common sky, do not expect miraculous intervention. It was better for Peter's manhood, and it is better for yours, that only the hour of the dungeon should bring that. The angel departs, but the law of God abides. The angel departs, but the love of Christ remains. And I think that all God's leading of His people and all the experience of the Christian heart might be summed up, with not a little gain, in the departing angel and the remaining Lord.

I want then to take that suggestion and bring it to bear on various spheres of life. And first we shall think of Israel in the wilderness. There was a helplessness about Israel in the wilderness like the helplessness of Peter in the prison. It was a terrible journey through that gloomy desert, twice terrible for these newly emancipated slaves. There were mighty barriers between them and Palestine quite as impassable as any prison doors. They would all have perished but for angelic help. Hungry, the flight of quails came from the sea, and the ground was covered, in the red dawn, with manna. Thirsty, there flowed a stream of water from the rock, and they drank of the spiritual rock which followed them. The Red Sea became a highway for their feet, and they found a road right through the swellings of Jordan. It was the angel of God smiting their fetters off. It was the angel of God bursting the gates before them. Out of the dungeon and prison house of Egypt they were carried by the constraint of irresistible power. But then, when they reached Canaan and had, as it were, passed through one street of it, forthwith the angel departed from them. The manna ceased to fall after one harvest. They drank no more of the water from the rock. There came days when they were hunted down by enemies, yet the Jordan never stayed its flood again. Jehovah was with them still in love and law; the mystical presence of Jesus was their shield. But the need was past; the prison gates were broken, and they learned the doctrine of the departing angel.

Or we might think of the history of the Christian church in this light. We might compare Pentecost with after centuries. There was a radiance and a spiritual glory about Pentecost that remind us at once of Peter and the angel. There were tongues, as it were of fire, on every head; the doors of that upper room were opened wide; the bonds of that little company were loosed; they were filled with joy, and they got new gifts of speech. It was a season of wonder and of miracle; it was the intervention of heaven for an hour. And then the church passed on through one street mystical, and forthwith the angel departed from them. Could Justin or Jerome or Augustine work miracles? Does God give any missionary *now* the gift of tongues? Can we heal the lame with a word as Peter did? Can we shake off the serpent as Paul did at Malta? There are some men who would have us believe we can; and there are more who, knowing that we cannot, think it impossible that it was ever done. I beseech you to avoid these two mistakes. Remember the doctrine of the departing angel. We are out in the streets now under the stars of heaven; miraculous ministries would simply ruin our manhood. Once, when there were prison gates to open, the angel came and gave the church her liberty. But now the Lord is our shepherd and our stay; the grace of an abiding Christ suffices. The angel has been summoned home to God.

I think, too, that we become conscious of this truth in the unfolding of our individual life. There comes a time in the life of every one of us when, not for our sin but for our deepest good, the angel leaves us as he left Simon Peter. In childhood we were very near the angels; we heard the beating of their wings sometimes when the world was hushed and everything was dark. We never thought of law or will or character; we lived in a dreamland, and the great dream was God. "Heaven lies about us in our infancy." In my church in the far north—and a beautiful church it was—we had curtains on each side of the pulpit. The way into the pulpit was through the curtains. And I often used to notice a tiny girl gazing at these curtains with very eager eyes. It was quite clear it was not the minister she was looking at. It was whenever the curtains moved that she would start and stare. I found out afterwards what all the interest was. The little child thought that heaven was behind the curtains. It was only a wilderness of joists and planks, but she thought that Christ was these; she thought that God was there; she thought that the minister stepped out from God into the pulpit, and every time the curtain rustled—little heart, little eager, beating heart—who could tell but thou mightst catch the shimmer of an angel there? Ah, well, she has passed on through one street since then, and forthwith the angel has departed from her. She will never mistake an organ-loft for heaven again. She never expects to see the gleam of wings now. And it may be that she looks back half wistfully to the day of glory in the grass and splendor in the flower. But my point is that the angel must depart if we are to walk the street of life in our true dignity. We are not here to dream that heaven is near us; we are here so to live that heaven shall be within us. And if at every turn the angel met us and the vision of a dream enchanted us, we should lose heart and nerve and power for the struggle and be like the lotos-eaters in ignoble quietude. The angel may go, but duty still remains. The vision may disappear, but truth abides. We never understand what *will* is, we never realize what we can do, we never feel the worth of personality moved by the spirit of an ascended Lord, till the hour when the angel goes away. Therefore, in the interests of highest and holiest manhood, we shall thank God for the angel-atmosphere of childhood, and thank Him nonetheless that when we have passed through one street, forthwith the angel has departed from us.

I think, too, we may swing this thought like a lamp over the dark chamber of the grave. In a great congregation there are always mourners, and I do not like to close without a word for them. It may be there is someone here who, looking backward, remembers an angel presence. Perhaps it was a mother, perhaps a sister; but they were so gracious, so gentle, and so patient, that you see now it was of heaven, not of earth. And you thought it was going to be a lifelong comradeship; you would travel on through all life's streets together. But you only passed on through one street, and forthwith the angel departed from you. And you are not yourself yet, any more than Simon was. The streets seem strangely unreal; how the wind bites! But like Peter when he came to himself, you too shall say, "It was the Lord who sent His angel to deliver me." There was some work to do, and it was done. There was some help to give, and it was given. There were chains to break and prison doors to open, and you can bear witness that it was all accomplished. Remember the doctrine of the departing angel when the heart is empty and the grave is full.

Rhoda

And as Peter knocked at the door of the gate, a maid came to hearken, named Rhoda. And when she knew Peter's voice, she opened not the gate for gladness, but ran in, and told how Peter stood before the gate—Acts 12:13, 14.

In visiting a sickroom where there is so much that speaks of suffering, one is often met by a single spot of brightness. It is a flower that has been brought by loving hands to gladden and refresh the weary sufferer. The room is darkened to shut out the sunlight which might beat too fiercely on the aching head. The nurse as she moves upon her tender ministry does so with a noiseless footstep. Everything is quiet and subdued, suggestive of days and nights of anguish, save it may be one rose of perfect loveliness that opens its petals beside the sufferer's couch.

In some such way in this chapter of the Acts do we light on Rhoda, and Rhoda means a rose. She blossoms here in the presence of much suffering and glows like a flame of brightness in the gloom. The chapter opens with the death of James and with the imprisonment of Simon Peter. It closes with the tragic death of Herod when he was smitten of God in the midst of his great pomp. And it is in that environment of gloom, with the shadow on it of suffering and death, that we light on Rhoda—that is, Rose—and whose name is fragrant as a rose until this hour. Rhoda is no great lady playing a mighty part. We never hear of her before or after. And yet I think that God has set her here and given her an immortality she never looked for, not for her own sake but for ours, that we might be better because she has been.

In the first place, then, we shall observe that she shared in the devotions of the family. She was as eagerly interested in Simon Peter as anyone who was in the house that night. It is probable that Mary was in comfortable circumstances and that her home was a roomy and well-appointed one. She was the aunt of Barnabas, and Barnabas was a wealthy man who had had great possessions in the isle of Cyprus. And then we read that on this eventful night there was a large company in Mary's house, and that would point to it as a roomy dwelling, as of one who was in comfortable circumstances. We may take it, then, that in the home of Mary, Rhoda was not an only servant. She was one of several; she held an inferior place; it is likely that the other slaves would all be men. Yet here we find her at worship with the household, taking a share in their unceasing prayers, and overborne by a very tide of gladness when she heard the voice of Peter at the gate.

Now there is one thing we must be on our guard against when we think of slavery in the ancient world. We must never carry into our thoughts of Jewish slavery the stories we have read of Greek and Roman slavery. A Roman was often very cruel to his slaves; it was very seldom that a Jew was that. There lingered in Jewry the older and kindlier feeling of the household of patriarchal times. And yet granting all that, as we must grant it if we have an eye for the hand of God in history, do you not think we have here in Mary's household a trace of the growing influence of Jesus? It is only eleven years since the resurrection, yet what a beautiful Christian home is this one. The mistress is still the mistress in the dwelling and the slave has not yet ceased to be a slave. Yet something of a common sisterhood has touched them; in their deepest and dearest they are united now; they have sat at the Table of the Lord together, and together they have prayed through the long night. That is how Jesus handled social problems. He was never a wild and reckless revolutionary. He never came to Mary and said, "You must let Rhoda go: it is against the law of God to have a slave." What He did do was to draw into sweet sisterhood the mistress and the menial at her gate; to fill up the gulf with His redeeming love until you find them on their knees together.

Once more let us notice about Rhoda that she was not above her common duties. It was her task, as we say in Scotland, to mind the door, and our story tells us that she did it faithfully. In Jewish households, let me say in passing, it was generally a female slave who had this work to do. In our wealthier homes, I know not why, this duty is generally given to a manservant. But even among the wealthiest of the Jews and when every other servant was a man, the office of attending to the door was invariably entrusted to a woman. Even in the High Priest's palace it was so, as Simon Peter knew so bitterly. Was it not the maid who kept the door there who had taunted him into his base denial? How different was that porteress from Rhoda, for she had known him by his voice and spurned him, but Rhoda when she heard it was so glad that she was powerless in the very joy of it.

That, however, is by the way. What I want you to note just now is something different. It is how Rhoda, in spite of her new sisterhood, was still active in her menial duty. Do you not think she felt in these eleven years how the spirit of that home was altering? Was she not conscious of a new kindness and regard as for a little sister for whom Jesus died? Yet in spite of that and of the place it gave her and of the new liberties that clustered round it, she was just as faithful to her humble task as in the old days when she was nobody. Whatever her emancipation did, it did not make her fretful at her post. She did not think that she could play the mistress because for her and her mistress the one blood was shed. Rather I think did Rhoda realize now, as she had never realized before, that the very stamp and seal of Christian character is that one should be faithful in the least. It is never a mark of a true Christian liberty that it makes us discontented with our duty. It makes us discontented with ourselves, but never with the task that God has given us. Nay, on the contrary, it glorifies that task, treats it as something that can be done for Christ's sake, and never forgets that the Master whom it serves could find a kingdom in a mustard seed.

Now I think, friends, there are few truths that need to be more pressed home today than that. If we need a great deal more of Mary's love, we need a great deal more of Rhoda's service. I heard of a theater manager the other day who was talking to a friend about his difficulties. And he said that one of the greatest of his difficulties was this, to get people who would throw themselves into the humbler parts. He could always get actors to take the leading roles and who thought themselves perfectly competent to do it, but what troubled him was to get those who would do well in obscure and insignificant positions. That is a complaint we hear on every hand—a widespread unwillingness to do the lowlier services. And men lay the blame of it on education and on the new ideas that have followed education. But what we want is not less education: we shall never go back, please God, in that direction. What we want with all progress and all emancipation is more of the spirit of the Lord Jesus Christ. Do you think that there ever dwelt upon our earth one with a grander outlook than our Lord had? You recall how He said, "The Son shall make you free," and how He added, "Then are ye free indeed." And yet with all that freedom which was His, that largeness of heart as the sand of the seashore—how lovingly and how patiently He toiled in the lowly ministry of Galilee. That is the spirit we still need if we are to be saved from the perils of today. The boundaries of the past are being trampled on. The fences around the fields are breaking down. And you may depend upon it that with that enlargement there will be growing restlessness and trouble, unless we learn from Christ as Rhoda learned the sacredness of common duty. Samuel on the morning following his call opened the doors of the House of the Lord as usual. Rhoda returned to the duty of the slave though lifted up in Christ to be a sister. And Jesus, knowing that He came from God and went to God, knowing His past and future on the throne, did what? He took a towel and girded Himself and washed His disciples' feet.

But that is not the whole truth about Rhoda, though it is true and we do well to ponder on it. The fact remains that though not above her duty, yet she forgot her duty in her gladness. Like a cautious maid she did not open at once. That would have been perilous at such an hour. Someone was knocking and was knocking lustily, and she went to see if it was friend or foe. And it was then she recognized the voice of Peter, and it filled her with such an overmastering gladness that she was back in an instant with the news, and left the door barred in Peter's face. There was something, I take it, in Peter's voice that haunted the memory of those who heard it. And Rhoda knew it well. Had she not heard him preaching? Had she not often let him in before? And Peter would always have a word for her and always a smile of greeting when he passed, all which I have a shrewd suspicion had been the means of leading her to Christ. No wonder that her heart was rent in twain when she heard that Peter was at the point of death. No wonder she was ecstatically glad when she recognized his voice out in the street. And it is one of those touches which none could ever counterfeit and which in themselves are worth a score of arguments—to read that in the delirium of her joy she quite omitted to let Peter in.

Now, brethren, joy is a holy thing and gladness is a commanded duty. "Rejoice in the Lord always," says Paul, and, "again I say, Rejoice." There is a vast deal in the Gospel we profess that tends to foster a glad and joyous spirit. It is glad to be loved, and we are loved in Christ with a love that triumphs over sin and death. Yet in all gladness when it is overflowing do we not recognize a certain peril—the peril of forgetting just as Rhoda the voices that are calling from without. People whose lives are uniformly happy are very rarely generous in their sympathy. They do not understand; they have no eyes to see; they have no ears to hear the voice that cries. It takes the touch of sorrow to give that, and the bearing of burdens heavy to be borne, and the shadow that seems to bar the sunshine out and yet is the shadow of the wing of God. I think that God would give us far more happiness if He were only sure that we would use it well. If we would only use it to make others happy we should have it in full measure, running over. But there is something of Rhoda in us all, a tendency to forget for very gladness, and so we can thank God as in the hymn we sang, that our joys are touched with pain.

In closing shall we not notice this of Rhoda, that she was not to be laughed out of her conviction. Let them say what they would of the stranger at the gate, she constantly affirmed that it was Peter. It was very strange they should have disbelieved her, for this was the very thing they had been praying for. By night and day their prayers had been ascending that Peter might be restored to them again. Yet when their prayers were answered and he knocked and Rhoda came running to say that it was Simon, the only thanks she got from that prayer meeting was to be plainly told that she was mad. You see that people who attend prayer meetings can be pretty hasty in their judgments sometimes. It was not courteous and it was not kindly: what is more important still, it was not true. But we do not read that Rhoda lost her temper or left the room peeved because they doubted her. She constantly affirmed that it was so. She couldn't argue and she didn't try to. She showed her wisdom when she didn't try to. It is not for a maid to argue with her mistress, or for a mistress to argue with her maid. But mad or not mad, one thing Rhoda knew, and that was that she had heard the voice of Peter, and I honor her for the firm and steadfast way in which this girl adhered to her convictions. There is another voice that some of us have heard. It is the voice not of Peter, but of Peter's Lord. Long ago it may be, He stood at the door and knocked, and we knew His voice and opened and let Him in. God give us all something of Rhoda's courage, that we too may be steadfast and immoveable, though every man and woman whom we meet with should mock at us just as they mocked at her.

The Grace of Continuance

But Peter continued knocking—Acts 12:16.

It is perilous to judge a person by one action. Life is too complex and intricate for that. It is as if one were to judge a countryside by a single and isolated clump of trees. Ruskin has it that if out of a Turner landscape you cut a quarter of an inch of sky, within that single quarter of an inch you would feel the infinity of heaven; and it may be there are lives like that, so penetrated with purpose or with passion, that wherever you touch them you get the real character. As a general rule, however, it is a perilous thing to judge a man by a single action. in his great hours he may be greater than himself; possibly he may be less than his true self. And always it is wisest, if you would judge a person not by the tenor of his life but by an action, to take an action of a usual kind. There was an hour, for instance, when Peter drew his sword and cut off the ear of the priest's servant with it. There was another hour—never to be forgotten—when, panic-stricken, he denied his Lord. But if I wished to know the real Peter, I should not turn to either of these hours; I should rather choose an action such as this—*Peter continued knocking.* Shall I tell you what it reveals in the apostle? Three things that are well worth observing.

In the first place, this common act shows Peter's *courage.* It makes that unmistakable. Whoever it was who stood there in the street, it was not a panic-stricken man. When Peter broke prison we know what hour it was; it was the fourth watch of the night, between 3 and 6 in the morning. This indicates that it was no longer dark; the day was beginning to glimmer in the east. And the smoke of the household fires was mounting heavenward, and the first footfalls were echoing on the pavements, *and Peter continued knocking.* Shrouded in the darkness of the third watch, he might have been reasonably safe out in the street. But in the fourth watch, when the sun was rising, it was at his peril that he delayed a moment. Yet Peter, who had once been panic-stricken and in an agony of fear denied his Lord, was evidently not panic-stricken now. It was a very usual thing to do, and yet it was a courageous thing to do; far more courageous than that whirling passion which plucked the sword out of the scabbard once. And it sprang from the certainty that God was with him, and having rescued him would not desert him now. "The Lord will perfect that which concerneth me."

Now that is a lesson we would do well to learn about the essential quality of courage. Just to continue knocking patiently may be braver than the most gallant deed. I grant you there come moments in our lives when courage may flash into dramatic splendor. There are hours for men of crowded life which are worth an age without a name. When the soldier dismounts to save a wounded comrade—when the fireman risks his life to save a child, there is something in that which strangely moves the heart. But that is the courage which is thrilling rather than the courage which is telling. The truest courage in this life of ours is seldom momentary or spectacular. It moves in the shadow of the dreary street; dwells in the dull seclusion of the home; continues doing things, with quiet heart, when the natural impulse would be to turn and flee. Just to get up each dull and dreary morning and say, "Please God I shall play my part today"; just to go out and do it quietly in the teeth of weariness and ingratitude; just to shut our ears to calling voices and bear our daily cross victoriously, is the finest heroism on this side the river. No man is ever far from the heroic who has learned to do things when he feels least like them. There is little hope for a man in this strange world who surrenders to his whimsies every morning. To trample under foot all moods and feelings—to get to our duty and our cross in spite of them—to do that summer and winter till we die is the one road to the music and the crown. That was pre-eminently true of Christ. His was the courage of continuance. Through ridicule, through obloquy, through suffering, Christ continued knocking.

In the second place, this common action reveals to us Peter's *understanding.* Clearly he did not misinterpret what was happening within the house. Contrast him, for instance, with Naaman. When Naaman was bidden go and wash in Jordan, he thought that the prophet was making light of him. So Naaman turned and went away in a rage because he misinterpreted the prophet. And if Peter had misinterpreted like that, he too would have gone away in a great rage; but *Peter continued knocking.* We are always ready for misinterpretation when we knock or ring at a door and no one answers; doubly ready when we see peering faces behind the glass of the door or through the blind. And that is precisely what Peter had to bear, for Rhoda came and looked and went away again, and yet Peter understood it perfectly. The fact is he understood their feelings by what had happened that morning to himself. That is always how we understand people; by the kind of thing which has happened to ourselves. Half an hour earlier Peter had seen an angel, and he had been dazed and thought it was a ghost; and now *they* think that Peter is a ghost, and Peter instantly grasps the situation. That is why he did not grow indignant. That is why he did not stalk away. He understood from his own stupefaction how terrified they would be for a few moments. And so he stood there, out in the street at daybreak, and continued knocking and showed by his action that he understood.

Is it not usually in that way that people come to know we understand them? "Though I speak with the tongue of men and of angels, and have not charity, it profiteth me nothing." To be misunderstood is a true grief. It is a grief which Christ experienced to the full. A man is never himself—never at his best—when he is surrounded by misunderstanding. But when a man feels that he is understood, he casts aside reserve and is himself, and he generally feels that through common touches. There are people who would give their bodies to be burned, and yet you never feel they understand. There are others who do no splendid services, and yet have a genius for understanding. By a kindly question, by a homely word, by a little deed of kindness light as gossamer, men waken to find that they are understood. All great leaders of men have had that gift. It is really the secret of personal attraction. No power of organizing mighty armies will ever explain Napoleon, for example. Along with that must be the touch which tells and the mystic sympathy that breaks down strangerhood if dying legionaries are to cry "My Emperor." If thou canst serve in great and splendid ways, then go and serve thus, and the Lord reward thee. If thou hast genius or if thou hast wealth, consecrate them all to noble causes. But if thou canst only do quite common kindnesses, do not neglect them while the days are hurrying, for they tell men that they are understood.

Then, in the third place, this common action reveals to us Peter's *consecration*. He stood there knocking—and half an hour before he had been in the royal company of angels. It is all very well for a beggar to stand and knock. But Peter had had an experience that morning which had lifted him up into the courts of heaven. He had been made a little lower than the angels, for he had had an angel for his visitor: and yet in the dawn out in the common street *Peter continued knocking*. A little while before, that very morning, Peter had come to a great iron gate. And at a single touch of the angelic finger that gate had opened to let Peter through. And now he was at no massive iron gate, but at the humble door of a very humble dwelling—and he continued knocking. Had this chapter been a medieval legend, you would have had that cottage door fly open also. But the Book of Acts is no Arabian Nights: it is true to experience, and it is true to character. For sometimes the massive gates which we have dreaded fly open at the touch of God when we reach them, and the little doors are the hardest to get through. That is why I say a touch like this shows Peter as a consecrated man. He had been exalted up to heaven, and difficulties had vanished from his path. And now he was back again among life's obstacles, and the street doors that everybody knows—and he continued knocking.

Now unquestionably, as it was with Peter, so is it with every one of us. There is no such certain mark of consecration as just to return like that to common levels. We too, like Peter, have our hours of vision. We have our seasons when the heavens are opened. We have our mornings when we see the angels in the light that never was on sea or land. It may be in church—it may be in the country; it may be when love comes in and sings her music; it may be when someone very dear is taken, and the heart is emptier than the home. In such an hour as that we are like Peter. The angels are never far away. In such an hour as that, whether for weal or woe, we see our visions and we dream our dreams. And then we have to go back to common doors where there is no mystery of blood upon the lintel, and the question is what shall we do then? There are some who are too unsettled to do anything. They could have knocked yesterday; they cannot knock today. They have lost all interest in common tasks, and the dreary round of duty is unbearable. But he who is consecrated as Simon Peter was through the pardoning and restoring love of Christ—he *will continue knocking.* He will be a better father to his children. He will be a more chivalrous brother to his sisters. Deepened by sorrow, purified by love, he will go with a faithful heart to his day's drudgery. He will continue knocking till the door shall open, and faces that he has loved will answer his in a fellowship where time and space are not.

The Stoning of Paul

And when there was an assault made . . . ,They were aware of it, and fled unto Lystra and Derbe, cities of Lycaonia, and unto the region that lieth round about; and there they preached the gospel—Acts 14:5 a, 6, 7.

Driven from Antioch by the outbreak of persecution, Paul and Barnabas moved on to Iconium. There was a distance of some ninety miles between the two towns, and now they might reasonably hope to be at peace. Iconium was a fine strategic point. The Roman roads between east and west ran through it. Many a morning Paul would be wakened from sleep by the noise of some caravan under his window as it rolled westward with its eastern merchandise. And again it would be the tramp of Roman legions as they marched eastward along the military way. All this would set the heart of Paul a-throbbing. Might not his word reach to the end of the world from Iconium? Paul might have settled at Iconium for years if God had not said to him, "This is not your rest." That is one purpose which persecution serves. It is God's way of bidding His soldiers march. Jesus was thinking of far more than personal safety when He bade His disciples flee from city to city (Matt. 10:23). Just as the gale beats on the falling rain and drives it away till it falls on distant fields, so persecution, striking on the Gospel, carries it to unexpected spots. Paul and Barnabas had to fly from Iconium. It was the Jews who stirred up trouble again. The apostles were learning, in a very bitter way, how man's foes are they of his own household. There is no foe so dangerous or so relentless as an old friend who has turned dead against us.

About forty miles from Iconium lies Lystra in the wild and dreary plain of Lycaonia. Lycaonia means the Land of Wolves, and we can picture the desolate region by the name. I think that when Paul crossed the marches of that wolf-land he would remember the saying of his Master, "Behold I send you forth as sheep in the midst of *wolves*, be ye therefore wise as serpents and harmless as doves" (Matt. 10:16). To Lystra, then, Paul and Barnabas fled, and there they preached. And at Lystra, by the power of Jesus, Paul healed the cripple. You could tell that the writer (Luke) had been a doctor by the fond minuteness with which he describes the disease. Most writers would just have said that the man was lame. But the physician made a much fuller diagnosis. The man was impotent in both his feet; he had been so from birth; he had never walked. Do you see how all the training we have had can be used in the long run towards glorifying God? Luke never thought of that when he was studying medicine; but the miracle is doubly vivid just because he studied. So every interest we ever had, and every pursuit we were ever zealous over, and every hobby that once fascinated us, no matter how childish or slight it may have been—all these, when we are Christ's, shall prove of service. It is the vessel full of water that becomes wine.

Now there was a legend very well known in Lystra, for the scene of it was that very region—it was the legend of Baucis and Philemon. The Lystran children used to gather around their mothers and beg for the story of Baucis and Philemon. Baucis and Philemon were two humble cottagers to whom Jupiter and Mercury had come disguised. The gods had knocked in vain at every other door, but these two lowly souls gave them a welcome. It is a sweet story, exquisitely told by Ovid; it was devoutly believed in the homes of Lystra. Many a mother would call her son Philemon with the prayer that Jupiter might come again. Who, then, were these two strangers in the town who had healed the lame man in such a marvelous way? Was not one of them august and kingly and the other all life and activity and eloquence? It ran like wildfire through the marketplace that here were Jupiter and Mercury returned. Paul did not understand what all the stir was. The excited people fell back on their own dialect. He felt as helpless as a Londoner would feel in the middle of a crowd all speaking Gaelic. But when a solemn procession halted before his lodging, and he saw the oxen with garlands on their heads, it flashed on him in a moment what was happening, and he and Barnabas sprang out to stop the blasphemy. Had it been

Jews whom Paul was called to speak to, you would have had plenty of texts from the Old Testament. Had the crowd been an *Athenian* crowd, there would have been swift appeals to history and art. It shows the infinite tact of the apostle that with these rude folk he argued from the rain (v. 17). It was a sore disappointment to excited Lystra; the current of feeling very swiftly changed. We are not surprised a few days later to find Paul stoned and left for dead.

Now note, first, *the keen eyesight of a saint* (v. 9). Paul saw in a twinkling that the cripple had faith. There was something in the face of this poor sufferer that told the apostle that true faith was there. Our Savior was always on the outlook for faith, and Paul had caught this secret from the Master. There is nothing like love and fellowship with Christ for revealing the best points in a poor beggar's face. Next note, *there is a meaning even in a raindrop* (v. 17). It had often spoken to Paul of the Creator. And, lastly, mark (we cannot learn it too young) that *today's sacrifice may be tomorrow's stoning.* One day, with Jesus, it was "Hosanna"; a little afterwards, "Crucify Him, Crucify Him." And one day, with Paul, it was "He is a god"; a little afterwards, "Stone him and cast him out." Now I want no one to become cynical. The world is a kindly and happy and pleasant place. We are amazed as we struggle on through manhood at the loyalty and love that ring us round. All that I want my readers to do is to set their affections on things which are above, not to rate very highly human praise, not to be greatly depressed by human censure. Had Paul been desperately anxious to *please* Lystra, I fancy that that stoning would have killed him.

The Baffling of the Spirit

They assayed to go into Bithynia: but the Spirit suffered them not—Acts 16:7.

Paul was on his second missionary journey when he was hindered thus by the Spirit of his Lord. He had made up his mind to go northward to Bithynia when somehow he was divinely checked. How the door was thus shut on him we are not told: it is one of the wise reticences of Scripture. Perhaps he was warned by some prophetic voice or visited by irresistible conviction. On the other hand, if one prefer it so, we may think of the pressure of circumstance or health, for Paul would never have hesitated to find in these the checking power of the Holy Ghost. Whatever form the prohibition took, you may be sure it was very dark to the apostle. Paul was not at all the kind of man who took a delight in being contradicted. When he had set his heart on going northward, not selfishly, but in the service of his Lord, it was a bitter experience to be so checked and to have the door shut in his face.

But the point to note is that though it was dark for Paul, it is bright as the sunshine of a summer morn for us. He was never more wisely or divinely guided than in the hour when he thought that he was baffled. What would have happened to him had the door been opened, and he suffered to go into Bithynia? He would have turned away home again through lonely glens with his back to the mighty empires of the West. He would never have landed on the shore of Europe, never have lifted up his voice in Athens, never have preached the riches of his Savior beside the Roman palace of the Caesars. Paul was a true Jew in this respect: he had no ear for the calling of the sea. He would a thousand times rather have lived in inland places than by the surge and thunder of the ocean. And it was only when every other path was barred that he was pushed unwillingly to Troas where for him and for Europe everything was changed by the vision of the man from Macedonia. He was checkmated, and yet he won the game. He was thwarted, and it led him to his crown. Eager to advance with his good news, there rose before him the divine "No Thoroughfare." And yet that hour when he was hindered so was the hour when God was honoring him wonderfully and leading him to such a mighty service as at his highest he had never dreamed.

Now I think there is something in that thought on which it would do us good to dwell a little, for all of us, like the apostle Paul, are sometimes baffled that we may not be beaten. It is very pleasant to have an open road and to accomplish what our hearts are set upon. We can all be grateful when our toil is crowned, and the dreams we have cherished for years are realized. But when our plans are thwarted and our wishes crushed and all we have assayed is proved impossible, it is not so easy then to hear the music or to cherish the spirit of the little child. I think there are few things sadder on this earth than what we call a disappointed man. He is so cheerless and apt to be so bitter; there is such lack of luster in his life. And the pity is, it is not his disappointments that have made him a disappointed man, it is the way in which he has brooded on them and let them sink into his heart and soul. There are people whom no bafflings can tame, people whom no thwartings can embitter. They believe in a love divine that disappoints and may be exquisitely kind in disappointing. And so when they are barred from their Bithynia and led to the cold shore where the waves break, they can be happy and expectant like a lover, as trusting that their service lies that way.

Now I shall try to illustrate that truth by thinking of some of the spheres in which God baffles us. And in the first place, let us dwell a moment upon the baffling of our childish dreams. Do you remember what you were going to be when you were a happy child in your old home? It was to be nothing commonplace, I warrant you, like the commonplace occupation of your father. There were seas in it and desperate adventure and distant lands and daring and excitement. There is not a ragged child in any street but has his childish vision of Bithynia.

Ah well, the years have come and gone since then, and somehow or other *that* door has been shut. You are not a sailor, not a wild adventurer: you are a respectable and quiet-living citizen. And the point is that with the passing years you were never suffered to realize your dream, just that you might be led, almost unwillingly, to the very place where you could be of use. 'Twould be a poor world without the dreams of children. 'Twould be a poorer, if they were fulfilled. For everything splendid there would be a thousand candidates. For everything ordinary, not a single one. So we assay to go into Bithynia, and the Spirit suffers us not; and thus are we carried to those common tasks which build up character and help the world.

Or think again of our maturer hopes, born when childish things are put away. It is easy to be glad when they are reached; it is less easy when the way is barred. Sometimes it is a matter of the health. It is the body that becomes the barrier. I have known an artist whose arm was paralyzed when he was on the verge of his career. I have known those who would have given anything to go and preach the Gospel to the heathen; but when they assayed to go into Bithynia, the Maker of their frame would not allow them. Sometimes it is a matter of plain duty. A man must yield his hopes for those he loves. All he has hoped for and striven for and longed for must go by the board at once for others' sakes. A father has died, or there have been reverses, and the preparatory years are now impossible, and a man has to turn himself to other work which is far away from the calling of his dreams. There is always something noble in the man who takes these hours quietly and well. His very life was in those cherished plans, and he is laying down his life when he discards them. And yet remember that if God be God, ordering and opening and shutting, it is along the pathway of such baffling that you shall come to your place and to your power. You do not know yourself—God knows you thoroughly. He knoweth your frame and remembereth that you are dust. There are some characters that need the heightening of success. There are others that need the deepening of denial. So you assayed to go into Bithynia, and God—not fate, not chance—suffered you not; and for you as for Paul, life has been far richer since the bridle-road across the hills was blocked.

Again I like to apply our text to the bafflings of our attempts at self-expression. How much there is that we desire to utter, yet in every effort to utter it, are thwarted. It may be some thought that swiftly flashed on us, thrilling us with a truth unfelt before. It may be some comfort we are fain to give to those who are sorrowful and weary-hearted. Or it may be some deep experience of God when He meets us in the secret of the soul and in His lovingkindness speaks to us in another voice than He uses to the world. How powerless we have all felt in times like these to give expression the thoughts within us. We cannot grasp them or clothe them in fit speech or body them forth that others may be helped. And what I want to impress on you is this: that in such baffling of our desire for utterance there may be more than the stammering of the tongue; there may be the wisdom and the love of heaven. If a man could tell abroad all that he felt, before long he would cease to feel. It would be very perilous if we had the power to voice all that is deepest in the soul. For God has His secrets with every human heart, and in the silence of that heart they must be cherished, nor will He ever suffer us to utter them lest they should be tarnished in the telling. Never be discouraged if you can find no words to tell all that is deepest in your being. When you are baffled in your attempt to reach it, it may be God who keeps you from Bithynia. For in the deepest life there must be silence—the silence as of the mountain and the glen—and the awaiting of that perfect fellowship which shall be ours in the gladness of eternity.

Once again, may we not trace our text in the bafflings of the cravings of the heart? There are people whose whole life is little else than a hunger and a thirst for love. They do not want to be rich—they do not envy the kind of life they see among the rich. They do not want to be famous—they have never felt "that last infirmity of noble mind." They are not troubled with intellectual questioning; for them the one thing real is the heart, and all they ask of God and life is this—someone on whom to lavish all their love. The strange thing is how often they are baffled in that divinest of divine desires. And the years go by, and they have many friends; but the one friend of their dreaming never comes. And that is always a very bitter thing no matter how it be fought against in secret, for while an unsatisfied intellect is sore, a heart unsatisfied is sorer still. They have assayed to go into Bithynia, but somehow the pathway has been barred for them. Others have reached the sunshine on the hill; for them there has been no highway thitherward. And yet how often, for all its hidden loneliness, that ordering is found to be of God who trains His nobler children very sternly that they may come at last to rest in Him. Paul never would have heard that cry from Europe had he been suffered to go where he desired. It was when he was thwarted in his longings that "Come over and help us" rang upon his ear. And there are many of God's servants still who never would have had their call to serve had the Spirit not darkly barred to them the way which led to the Bithynia of the heart.

In closing, may we not take our text of the bafflings of our desires for rest? For as life advances rest becomes more sweet, and the comfort and the peace of life more dear. We ask for less and less as the years pass. That is always one sign of growing older. The land that we long for now is not a mountain-land; it is a land of quiet peacefulness and comfort. So we assay to go into Bithynia where we shall be comfortable and contented, and then comes God and bars the journey thither and says to us, "This is not your rest." He does it sometimes by the hand of sickness falling on the children whom we love. He does it sometimes by the hand of death, shattering the contentment of our days. He does it by conscience keeping us uneasy; by fear of tomorrow in our most sure estate; by the shame which visits us when we see other lives so strenuous and so gallant to the end. God uses all that to drive us from Bithynia and to send us onward to the shore at Troas. He blocks our way when we would settle here and urges us mightily to the beyond until at last a man lifts up his heart to things that are eternal and unshaken, and finds his rest where there is no more death and where Christ is at the right hand above.

The Gospel in Europe

And a vision appeared to Paul in the night; there stood a man of Macedonia, beseeching him, and saying, Come over into Macedonia, and help us—
Acts 16:9.

It was in the second missionary journey of St. Paul that the passage was made to our own coast of Europe. Kings have made the crossing with great armies; peoples have come pushing westward over the sea; but no irruption of Asiatic hordes, and no army bent on a world-conquest, has made such a change upon the life of Europe as did this traveler of our lesson. I think we all know how Paul found himself at Troas, and how, when there, the vision appeared to him. I think that among all the men mentioned in the Bible, there is none more familiar than this man of Macedonia. And then the voyage and the visit to Neapolis and the preaching at the riverside at Philippi—have we not known all that since we knew anything?—there is no page of history that we love more. What little beginnings the mightiest issues have! How insignificant is the start of mighty movements! It is good to think of Western Christendom today with its long record of saintly men and women, with its vast cathedrals and its countless churches, with its hospitals and infirmaries and asylums, with its innumerable charities, with its homes for the aged and the children, all of which owe their existence to the Gospel—it is good to think of that wonderful and rich life with its thousand activities that we call the Christian life, and then remember that we can trace it back to these few travelers on the quay at Troas. Do not despise the smallness of beginnings. The fate of a continent may be in one little boat. Behold how great a matter a little fire kindleth.

Now three truths arrest me in this story. First, *it is only when we obey that visions come.* Scholars have disputed about the "region of Galatia" (v. 6), whether it is a great territory or a small one. But there is no dispute about a much more important thing, namely, that *two* wills are seen at work right through these verses. On the one hand there is the will of Paul saying, "I think I should go here; I must go there." On the other hand there is the will of God closing this door and that before the apostle. Of course there was no physical force exerted. If Paul had been weak enough to be an obstinate man, he could have got to Asia or to Bithynia nicely. But Paul recognized that the say must lie with heaven, and he yielded himself up in freest self-surrender. He was willing that his own plans should be shattered and that his schemes and dreams should vanish if God bade, and it was *thus* that he was led to Troas, and it was *then* he had his vision in the night. Now that just means that if we are ever to have visions we must walk along the path of self-surrender. We shall never see the best and brightest things unless (as Jesus says) we are pure in heart. If we are blindly and obstinately set on our own way, the likelihood is that God will let us have it. We shall go away into half-wild Bithynia, and perhaps we shall never be heard of again. But it is when we hold our own plans very lightly and are ready to yield them up to God, if need be—it is *then* that we reach our Troas and get our vision of a larger service than we had ever dreamed of.

Next, *the vision must be followed by endeavor.* There is one great word in the vocabulary of the Bible that would make an excellent study for our leisure. It is the word *immediately.* There were no laggards among the Bible heroes. Life was a great thing, and time was very precious. When the trumpet sounds and the call from heaven comes—look in the next verse and you will find *immediately.* So it was here. Paul was asleep when he had his vision at Troas. Self-surrender makes an easy pillow. It was in a dream that the man of Macedonia appeared, crying "Come over to Macedonia and help us." And I think I see Paul leaping from his couch, in the burning certainty that God had spoken, and sending Luke post-haste down to the harbor to see when the next ship was likely to set sail. "Immediately we endeavored to go into Macedonia." The vision must be carried out in action. All effort must be made loyally to fulfill what had come to Paul in the glory of the night. Now what does that mean for us? It just means this. We must interpret our bright gleams in instant duty. All that is highest comes to us in vision, and we must translate it into the common task. When we awaken to God, that is a vision; it is a vision when we first see Jesus as our Savior. It is in a vision that we first see life's possibilities and the way ahead of us and the cross we shall have to bear. And all life, if we mean to live it well, will be little else than the endeavor to carry out that vision through the dust and dreariness and song and sunshine of the years that are going to be our life.

Lastly, *the endeavor often seems to contradict the vision.* You note that it was a *man* who appeared to Paul. It was a *man's* voice that summoned him to Europe. And in the man's words there was a great appeal; it was as if Macedonia hungered for the Gospel. Yet there is no trace that Neapolis welcomed Paul. And the first convert was a woman, not a man. The first *men* whom we read of in the story are the angry masters of the poor neurotic girl. I have often wondered if Paul was disappointed. The work was so utterly different from the dream. He had seen in his vision the hands of Macedonia stretched out, and now they were indeed stretched out, but only to lead him to the inner prison at Philippi (v. 24). It was a strange and startling contradiction. A weakling would have been tempted to deny the vision. But Paul was far too faithful to despair, and we see now that God was in it all. So when the vision of Jesus comes to us, and we set out to do some little service for Him, there will not be a task and there will not be a day in which the vision will not be contradicted. Our service may not turn out as we hoped; our prayers may not be answered as we wished; we may get no welcome from those who seemed to call us; we may look for liberty and find a prison house. But God makes no mistake. The work is His. He can transmute our failures into tomorrow's triumphs. When the dawn of the cloudless morning breaks above us, we shall waken to find He hath done all things well.

Unconscious Ministries

And the prisoners heard them—Acts 16:25.

Strangers in a strange city, Paul and Silas had very violent treatment. They were seized and, without semblance of a trial, were thrust into the inner prison. It was a gloomy and miserable place and might have appalled the spirits of the bravest. Men had been known in that dark cell to curse and some, in black despair, to kill themselves. But never, since these walls had been embattled, had any prisoner been known to sing there, and yet at midnight Paul and Silas sang. It was dark, and yet all bright to them. It was exceeding loathsome, and yet beautiful. Stone walls did not a prison make for them, nor iron bars a cage. And so they sang like the lark at heaven's gate—although for them it was a prison-gate—and as they sang, *the prisoners heard them.* Probably some of these prisoners became Christians afterwards. It was they who told the story to the Church: told how at dead of night, dull and despairing—hark—the sound of music! And one would recall how it held his hand from suicide, and another how it revived his hope, and another perhaps how it brought back the memory of his mother and his childhood and his home. Of all that service the men who sang knew nothing. They were totally unconscious of such ministry. They sang because Christ was with them and was cheering them. They sang because they could not help but sing. And all the time, although they never dreamed of it, they were serving others better than they knew, touching old tendernesses, reviving courage, making it easier to suffer and be strong.

Now something of that kind we all are doing. We all of us exercise unconscious ministries. When we never dream we are affecting anybody, we are touching and turning others all the time. We fret, and others feel our fretting, though never a syllable has passed our lips. We play the game, and just because *we* play it, folk we have never heard of play it better. We sing at midnight because God is with us and will never leave us nor forsake us, and prisoners in other cells are cheered. One of our writers, a man of genius—yet a man whose moral character was vile—has told us how, when in the grip of shame, somebody took off his hat to him. It was only a custom of familiar courtesy—the instinctive action of a gentleman—yet to him it was a gleam of heaven in his hell. We never know what we are doing when we do it. Our tiniest actions are touched to finest issues. Like Faithful, in the Valley of the Shadow, we lift up our voice because our heart is strong. And some poor Christian, stumbling on behind us on his way also to the Celestial City, thanks God and takes courage at the music. Be quite sure that the very humblest life is full of beneficent unconscious ministries. There is not a note of song we ever raise but the ear of some other prisoner will catch it. Words that we utter and then quite forget—a smile in passing—the clasp of hands in comradeship—have got their work in God's strange world to do and will meet us in the rosy-fingered dawn.

This unconscious human helpfulness is one of the chiefest ministries of happiness. Happiness is sometimes selfishness; but happiness is also sometimes service. He who resolves at all costs to be happy is generally a very miserable person. In this wide world the things we set our hearts on are so often the things we never get. But when anyone is genuinely happy, with a heart at leisure from itself, then happiness is unconscious benediction. One of the most beautiful poems of Robert Browning is a wonderful thing that he calls *Pippa Passes*. It is a story of murder and of guilt, portrayed with the passion and the truth of genius. And then below the house of all this vileness where vows are treachery and kisses shame, in the exquisite summer morning, Pippa passes. She is only an innocent girl, supremely happy, and because she is happy, as she goes she sings. She has no thought of doing good to anybody. She is quite oblivious of listeners. And yet that simple song of girlish happiness, entering the open casement of the house, comes with the very ministry of heaven. Happiness will sometimes do what bitterest reproach can never do. The man who can sing at midnight because God is with him is doing something for others all the time. To be happy—to be serene and radiant—when the shadows deepen and the cross is heavy is one of the finest of life's unconscious ministries.

A similar unconscious service is the sweet and tender helpfulness of childhood. Childhood never dreams that it is helping, yet its benedictions are incalculable. A well-known writer has told us that after anxious days he completed a certain book he had in hand. It had cost him much laborious research, and now it was completed. And all the joy of that completed toil, he tells us, was nothing to the gladness he experienced in the pattering footsteps of some little children whom he had taught to love him. Do you remember what they wrote upon the tombstone of a little girl who had gone home? They wrote her name and then beneath it this—*It was easier to be good while she was with us.* And that is what little ones are always doing—they are making it easier to be good. How many a man has been true to what is pure through the constraining influence of his children. How many a selfish heart has grown considerate when the mystery of motherhood has come. Those eyes of innocence, those pattering feet, those lips that are only still when they are sleeping, have done more to beautify and bless the world than all the legislation of the sages. There is no more real ministry than that, and the wonderful thing is it is unconscious. No child awakens on a summer morning and says, "Today I am going to be a blessing." He *is* a blessing and he never knows it. He plays in the marketplace and Christ is gladdened. He sings like Paul because he cannot help it—*and the prisoners hear.*

The same unconscious ministry, again, is often a beautiful feature of the sickroom. Patient suffering may be finest service. It is told of Dr. Norman Macleod that on one occasion he went to pay a visit to a Sunday school scholar of his own. He found him stretched upon a sorry bed, for the lad—an invalid—was dying amid scenes of crime and destitution. Norman Macleod was not a great preacher; Norman Macleod was a great human. Stooping over the bed he said, "My poor lad, I'm afraid you're very weak." "Yes, sir," was the reply, "I'm very weak, *but I'm strong in Him.*" The following Sunday, Dr. Macleod told that story from the pulpit. It was published in religious newspapers both in England and America. And by and by, from Scotland, England, and from far-off villages of the United States, came testimonies that the story had been blessed. Out in the High Street other lads were serving. Men and women were toiling for the Master. Here in the garret, above the crowded street was a sufferer who would never serve again. Yet, like Paul and Silas in the dungeon, he sang in his midnight because God was with him, and far away the other prisoners heard. I have heard women lamenting they were useless because they could never leave their little room. Others were out and active in the world; they were nothing but cumberers of the ground. And yet that little chamber was a Bethel, and to enter it was to feel that God was there, and through the streets one walked a better man because of that patient, beautiful endurance. Never forget that among life's many ministries, the finest may be the unconscious ministry. There is an exquisite service of passivity as surely as a service of activity. When the lights are low, when the strong ones bow themselves, when the silver cord is at the point of breaking, you may be serving better than you know.

This too is the real value of genuine and unaffected goodness. It is exercising every day a beautiful unconscious ministry. A man may forget all that his mother told him. He will never forget all that his mother *was*. He may lose count of all his father's counsel, but never of his father's character. It is not the things which we can utter glibly—it if often things we have no power to utter—that fall on other lives with benediction. When Sir Walter Scott was building Abbotsford in England, he put the lawn in a peculiar place. And at one corner of it he built a little summerhouse where he might sit in the evening after dinner. And he told Lockhart why he built it there; was it because the view was beautiful? Not so, but that he might sit there and listen to the evening worship of his coachman. Old Peter was a real old Scottish servant. He would not have talked religion for the world. But every nightfall in the year he took *The Book,* and "waled a portion wi' judicious care." And then a psalm was sung, and traveling heavenward to Him who understands the Scottish reticence, Sir Walter heard it, and hearing it, was comforted. Old Peter was preaching better than he knew. He was preaching when he never thought to preach. That is what all of us are doing constantly, though we were never in a pulpit in our lives. There are Spurgeons in unlikeliest places, apostles who are cheering all the prison, and they never know that they are doing anything.

Indeed, I believe that much of our Christian service must always be of that unconscious character. When that is lacking, the other is formality.

I trust that when this hurrying life is over, you and I shall each have the "Well done." That is the only thing worth living for. It is the only welcome which I want. But I have sometimes thought that if I ever hear it, one of the great surprises of the dawn will be the kind of thing for which it is given. Perhaps all these sermons at which I have daily toiled will never be mentioned in that summer morning. And certain ministries of which I knew not anything as I went in and out among you in the shadows here, will waken the trumpets on the other side. Men who do their best always do more though they be haunted by the sense of failure. Be good and true, be patient; be undaunted. Leave your usefulness for God to estimate. He will see to it that you do not live in vain.

He Called for Lights

Then he (the Philippian jailer) called for lights (R. V.), and sprang in, and came trembling—Acts 16:29.

That call of the Philippian jailer is the deepest call of every human heart. It distinguishes man from the dumb beasts. Give a beast its food, it is content. It asks for nothing more; it never questions. It never tries to understand its instincts. Its farthest horizon is present satisfaction. But man is always calling out for light. What is history but the call for light? What is science but the call for light? What is philosophy, with all its groping, but the call for light in the darkness of the prison? On every problem, on every unsolved riddle, on every mystery of earth and heaven, we call for light like the Philippian jailer. Why do men risk their life to reach the Poles—what lures them to the top of Everest—why does the thought of a place unexplored draw men as a magnet draws the steel? It is the human heart protesting against darkness as something alien from its deepest being. It is the call for light of the Philippian jailer.

It should be noted that this call for light came after the moment of the earthquake. The jailer called when everything was shaken. At midnight, generally, men are content with darkness. They are weary; their craving is for sleep. Look down the street when the clock is striking midnight, and well-nigh every window is in shadow. But let there come the rumbling of explosion, or the cry of fire, or uproar in the street, and lights are flashing from a hundred windows. So was it in the jail at Philippi. On ordinary midnights no one wanted lights. It was when things were shaken, and solid walls were rocking, that the Philippian jailer called for light. And never is the call for light so urgent in the lives of men and in the tale of history as when familiar things begin to reel and tremble. Do you remember the last great war? It was an earthquake worse than that of Philippi. It broke suddenly into our ordered life like some terrific catastrophe of nature. And instantly, from a thousand human hearts, as from the lips of the Philippian jailer, there was a call for light. Why did God permit the war? Could He be sovereign and suffer this to be? Was progress a chimera? Was Christianity only a veneer? Such questions were scarcely vital questions in the quiet and settled years before the war—but after the earthquake came the call for light.

You will remember, too, this call was made by a man who was within an inch of death. A moment before he was on the point of suicide. Death was very near to him that night. He had been standing on the margin of the grave. He thought to shuffle off this mortal coil. He faced the grim extremity. And it is when death is near and knocking at the door, or when the open sepulcher is at our feet, that we call for light like the Philippian jailer. What mother did not call for light when her dear boy went off to war? What father did not call for light when his beautiful child was lying in its coffin? More than anything—more than the heaviest cross or the bitterest reverse of fortune—it is the fact of death that inspires the call for light. What does it mean, this silence and this darkness—this bourne from which no traveler returns? Are powers given never to be perfected? Are we never to look on our dear dead again? The ceaseless questionings, the dim surmisings; these, of which dumb animals are ignorant, are the crown and title of humanity. We are great because we call for light. We are better than dumb, driven cattle. We want to know; we yearn to understand; we crave to penetrate the mystery. If from darkness we came, darkness would content us. Gloom and shadow would be our native air. But God has made us, and we call for light, and so tell of the Light which is our home.

I close by noting in this thrilling story that when the jailer called for lights, he got them. Cannot you see them flashing through the corridors? Who brought them we are not informed. It is one of the ministries of nameless people. Nameless people may do far more good than those whose names come ringing down the centuries. He called, and he was given. He called, and in the darkness torches flashed. He called, and servants heard the call and answered. Now, did you never hear of One who took on Him the form of a *servant?* Who willingly came down into our prison-house and was among the prisoners as one who serveth? And do you think, if these Philippian servants heard the call for lights and flashed their torches, that *this* Servant would not do the same? He flashed His torch on suffering. He flashed His torch on sin. He flashed it on the hidden heart of God and on the age-long mystery of death. Let not your heart be troubled, neither let it be afraid; in My Father's house are many mansions. He who has that light wants no other light. It casts its radiance on the murkiest passages. He may still tremble like the Philippian jailer, but in that light he has the power to spring. He has light for duty and for disappointment now; light on the heart of God and on the grave. "I am the Light of the world; he that followeth Me shall not walk in darkness."

The Attraction of Agnosticism

I found an altar with this inscription, TO THE UNKNOWN GOD—
Acts 17:23.

Not very long ago in Glasgow there was a criminal trial which attracted much attention, not only by reason of its peculiar circumstances, but also because of certain observations of the judge. When the prisoner was being examined by counsel one of the questions asked was, "Are you an atheist?" That was a very unusual question to be put in a modern court of law. No one, therefore, was very much surprised when Lord Guthrie, in giving the charge to the jury, dwelt with undisguised severity on that unusual interrogation. Now had the learned lord done nothing more than that, the aspect of things would have been entirely legal. But your true Scot is a theologian born—especially if he be born a Guthrie. And so we had a little discourse on theology in which we were very wisely told that there are no atheists nowadays— only agnostics. I was struck by the very widespread notice which was given to that dictum of the judge. It found its way into all sorts of papers and was commented upon from every point of view. And so I have thought this might be a fitting time to say one or two words about agnosticism.

Now I venture to think there are few who do not know the meaning of these words. An atheist is one who denies that there is a God; an agnostic one who denies that we can know God. The word agnostic is quite a modern word. It was coined, if I remember rightly, by Professor Huxley. It was suggested by that verse in the Acts of the Apostles which tells of the altar raised to the unknown God. It is very significant that

88

the view of things which utterly denies all revelation should have had to borrow its title from the Bible. An atheist has the courage of conviction. He lifts up his eyes and says there is no God. For him, heaven is a vacant place, and there is no eternal Personality. But the agnostic does not deny there is a God. All he asserts is that we are so constituted intellectually that to know God is utterly impossible.

You will observe that this agnostic attitude has nothing in common with Christian humility. It does not spring from the majesty of God, but from the limitations of our finitude. There are octaves of sound, in high and sunken registers, which no human ear is capable of hearing, yet to say that a thousand tones are imperceptible is not at all to say that man is deaf. And so the Christian reverently holds that there are heights and depths in God he cannot know, and yet he is convinced that God is knowable. "Now we know in part and see in part"; there is an agnosticism which is apostolic. There is a reverent veiling of our mortal gaze under the burning mystery of heaven. But to hold, as every Christian holds, that there are depths in God beyond our fathoming is not to assert that God cannot be known. On the contrary, for the Christian consciousness, there is no such intense reality as God. He is nearer than breathing, closer than hands and feet, more subtly present than any summer morning; and this though logic be powerless to reach and argument ineffectual to demonstrate Him, and life, in all the seeming tangle of it, too intricate a riddle to reveal Him. "And when I saw him," says John, "I fell at his feet as dead"; there were depths in the Infinite which overwhelmed him. Yet that same John—with what triumphant certainty does he ring out the clarion cry, *We know*. And this is the glory of our Christian faith that, with the fullest confessions of great ignorance, it can yet lift up its voice out of the darkness and say, *I know whom I have believed.*

It is significant, let me say in passing, that the wheel of antagonism has now come full circle. This last subversal of the Christian faith is the intellectual negation of the first. When the new Gospel was fighting for its life, it had one foe more deadly than others. Some of you probably have never heard its name, though the later epistles are full of references to it. It was more deadly than any Jewish hatred. It was more subtle than any pagan ridicule. It wrought more havoc in the infant Church than the most cruel and bloody persecutions. Across

89

the Empire, from Ephesus to Lyons, there was not a Christian community but suffered from it. It sapped the spiritual life of congregations and blighted the promise of countless catechumens. And this so subtle and insidious enemy, with which the infant Church fought for its life, was called by the forgotten name of *gnosticism*. Now the word gnostic, as students are aware, means exactly the opposite of agnostic. The gnostic is a man who says *I know;* the agnostic a man who says *I don't know.* And the singular thing is that the Christian faith, which began by battling against a spurious knowledge, should now have to battle against a spurious ignorance. I regard this as a very hopeful sign for the ultimate triumph of the Gospel. There is less hope for the man who says that he knows everything than for him who thinks that he knows nothing. For the one is unteachable, and in a world like this to be unteachable is to be condemned; but the other has at least the aspect of humility. That is why in early gnosticism the prevailing temper was one of scornful arrogance. And that is why in our modern agnosticism we can so often detect a note of wistfulness. It is always a humbling thing to say, I do not know; doubly so to a keen and brilliant intellect; trebly so when the things it does not know are known to the humble farmers in the glen.

Indeed it is this last fact, when you consider it, that makes the attraction of agnosticism so remarkable. It contradicts the deepest of all instincts: yet it is acceptable today. That there is a God, and that that God is knowable, is the universal verdict of humanity. That there is a God, and that that God is knowable, is the instinct and affirmation of the soul. Yet when agnosticism throws out its challenge and repudiates these universal witnesses, it finds a welcome in the modern mind. That is a very remarkable phenomenon, well worthy of our consideration. At gnosticism we all smile today; but at agnosticism no one thinks to smile. And what I suggest is that this is only explicable on the ground of a certain specious affinity between the negative creed of the agnostic and the general spirit of the age. Professor Lecky has taken pains to show that it is not argument which kills beliefs. It is rather those slow and subtle changes which gradually permeate the spirit of a people. But not only do these slow and subtle changes explain the destruction of ancient superstition; they explain also the emergence of beliefs. Every creed demands its fit environment as absolutely as does the Alpine flower. Without that environment it will never flourish though it be preached with genius and passion. And I want to show you how the agnostic creed, which once would have been treated with derision, has found a fitting environment today.

Agnosticism, for instance, seems to answer readily to our altered thought of the dwelling-place of man. "What is man, that thou art mindful of him" has meaning for us the psalmist never knew. So long as man deemed that the world which he inhabited was the great and glorious center of the universe, so long was it natural for him to hold that he was important in the eyes of heaven. But if his dwelling place be but an atom flying through boundless space where worlds are numberless, then things assume a different complexion. Now that is exactly what modern science has done. It has dislodged our world from its centrality. It has robbed us of our cosmical importance and made us the creatures of a tiny planet. And it was inevitable that this altered thought, which has so profoundly influenced man's attitude to nature, should have influenced also his attitude to God. It was natural to believe that God was knowable when just beyond the clouds He had His throne. But heaven has gone very far away now, and we sweep the depths of space and cannot find it. And so having learned, on evidence unquestioned, the actual insignificance of earth, we begin to doubt the significance of a man. It is to that temper agnosticism comes. It is the creed which answers that suspicion. It is not presumptuous as was atheism. It does not dare to say there is no God. It only says that for creatures such as we are, fashioned of the dust of a little distant planet, the proper attitude is one of ignorance.

But if men would only think a little, they would see the fallacy of that appeal. There is a little cottage down in Ayrshire to which pilgrims turn with tender hearts. It has no grandeur as of marble staircase nor spacious rooms with decorated ceiling. Yet he who was born there would have been no greater had he been cradled in a kingly palace, nor was he less a genius because a cottage-child. It is not the dwelling place that makes the man; it is the man that makes the dwelling place. There may be depths of meanness in the lordliest home and moral grandeur in the poorest mountain hut. And to argue that man must be a cipher because the world is not a lordly dwelling place is like arguing that Burns was not a genius because he was a cottage-child. On the contrary, it seems to me that the evidence is the other way. For it is not in palaces nor lordly manors that moral and spiritual worth is oftenest found. It is in humble homes with lowly roofs which have no beauty that we should desire them and which never obtrude themselves upon the passerby. Search through Scotland for the men who know, and you will not find them in the grandest dwellings. It is not in the castles of Dumbartonshire that you find the students who know Shakespeare. And so to argue that God cannot be known unless the world be the castle of the universe is to move contrary to all experience.

But there is another attraction of agnosticism which helps to explain its prevalence today. It is in apparent harmony with an age that cannot brook the accent of finality. To say *I do not know* is not dogmatic, at least it does not seem to be dogmatic, and so it answers to that prevailing spirit which cannot tolerate the thought of dogmatism. Probably we are suffering today for the overdogmatism of the past. You will very generally find an age of doubt after an age of overconfident assertion. And it may be that the preaching of a former generation, which was so absolutely confident of everything, has given us an age which is confident of nothing. Whatever the cause be, this at least is plain, that men today are not in love with dogmatism. They may have a wistful yearning for the Christ; but they are easily irritated at the creed. They do not accept the sufficiency of formulas. They are no longer held by orthodox beliefs. They are impatient at the suggestion of finality. That there is a nobler side to this impatience, I think it is only fair to recognize. It is always the characteristic of an age that is trembling on the verge of discoveries. And that we are now trembling on the verge of such discoveries as will revolutionize our life and thought, I have not the shadow of a doubt. Now whenever there is such expectancy abroad, the one intolerable standpoint is finality. To be dogmatic in a world of mystery is to seal the eye so that it cannot see. And any creed which cuts as with a saber into the heart of all dogmatic doctrine is certain to receive a kindly welcome. There have been ages when a teacher had no audience unless he could lift up his voice and say *I know*. But today a far more powerful appeal is to lift up the voice and say *I do not know*. And that is the attraction of agnosticism to an age that is a little weary of dogmatics and is beginning to feel again, in countless ways, the wonder and the mystery of things.

But the curious thing is that agnosticism has proved itself the most intolerant of dogmatisms. Professing to be the foe of all finality, it is itself the most final of all creeds. Through all the ages the Gospel has maintained itself with an infinite and living power of adaptation. It has responded to all the growth of knowledge and never forfeited its central verities. But agnosticism in these past forty years—and what are forty years to twenty centuries—has only saved itself from utter ruin by the very dogmatism which it scorns. To say we have no evidence for God may sound like intellectual humility. It may seem to indicate a very different temper from the blatant atheism of fifty years ago. But when you are dealing not with things but with *persons,* to say that you have no proof of their existence is really to deny that they exist. There might be gold under the snows of Greenland though we had no evidence that gold was there. But if there were little children in a home, would they not be certain to betray their presence? And if you found no nursery nor cot, no picture books nor fragmentary toys, would not that mean there were no children there? That would be the verdict of the briefest visit: but what if you lived for years within the dwelling? What if you lived there day and night for years and never found one proof that there were children? You see in a moment that to find no evidence is to be driven to deny their being; and as with little children, so with God. If even a shipwrecked sailor on an island leaves unmistakable traces of his presence, how much more the Creator of the universe.

Now that is where agnosticism fails. It has never been able to maintain itself. It has not been able, like the faith of Christ, to stand foursquare to every wind that blew. It has either gravitated far nearer atheism than Lord Guthrie would allow us to admit, or it has crept back to the feet of God again. I confess I have no faith in any creed that cannot maintain itself for forty years. I have a strong suspicion that the truth must lie with one that has stood the storm and shock of centuries. And when I find it meeting my deepest need and answering the crying of my heart, by it I am content to live and die. For character is not built upon negations, nor does life come to its victories that way. Life is too difficult and dark and terrible to be fought out by what I do not know. It is when I can say after the strain of years, *I know whom I have believed,* that my feet are planted on the rock.

The Perils of Unsettlement

None of these things move me—Acts 20:24.

Paul was journeying to Jerusalem when he spoke the words of our text. They were addressed to the elders of Ephesus whom he had summoned to meet him at Miletus. It was a journey attended by much hazard, and Paul was aware how hazardous it was. The spirit of prophecy, in every city, had testified to the hardships that awaited him. Yet though bonds and imprisonment were in his prospect, and perhaps a shadow darker than imprisonment, the apostle was able to say in all sincerity that none of these things moved him. With an unwavering and undaunted heart he held to the route that he had planned. Like his master, in a still darker hour, he set his face steadfastly towards Jerusalem. In other words, this great apostle had overcome the perils of unsettlement, and it is on the perils of unsettlement that I should like to speak for a little while this evening.

Now no one can read the New Testament without observing that this was one of the deadliest perils of the apostolic church. However fiercely other evils tried them, this one seems to have had peculiar power. The early Christians, like the Elizabethan mariners, had broken into an untraveled sea. They were beyond the experience of the ages. They lived in the daily hope that Christ was coming. And all this wrought such a ferment in their hearts, and seemed to release them so from common obligations, that with all its victories and all its virtues the early church was a-quiver with unsettlement. Men threw their tools down and refused to work. They studied everything save their own business. Why should they take provident care against tomorrow when at

94

sunrise tomorrow Christ might come again? So did there spread through apostolic days a spirit of unquiet and unrest, and men, through the very wonder of it all, were prone to be unbalanced for a little.

But though circumstances are very different now, this peculiar danger has not vanished. Today, not less than in the days of Pentecost, we are beset by the perils of unsettlement. I am not speaking of the characteristics of the age, though it is the fashion to call this an unsettled age. I take it that every age which has had life in it has been an unsettled and unsettling age. I speak rather of these large experiences which befall each of us upon our journey when I say that we are still exposed to the swift and subtle perils of unsettlement. Sometimes they reach us through a staggering sorrow which lays the palace in ruins at our feet. Sometimes through the thrilling of good news, or the excitement or variety of travel. Sometimes through the calling of the summertime, with its mystery of light and beauty, touching our hearts and strangely stirring them with cravings which we cannot well interpret. In such ways, and in other ways as evident, are we all in danger of unsettlement. We lose our grip on what we used to cling to. We begin to drag our anchors unexpectedly. We are restless and know not what we want, and we lack the unity that makes for power, and so do we learn out of our own experience the perils which the apostle mastered.

Indeed, the very concentration of today leads to the intensifying of this danger. When life is narrowed into a dull routine, unsettlement is very easily wrought. In the old days, when life was larger, men were less ready to be thrown off their balance. Familiar with a wider range of circumstance, they were not so lightly moved away by novelty. But now when that large liberty is gone, and men have to concentrate unceasingly, they have lost the power of responding quietly to what is new or strange or unexpected. They are more easily cast out of their reckoning than men who traveled across a larger field. When life is monotonous, even a little incident has the power of disturbing greatly. And so the very monotony of labor, which is so characteristic of today, makes it an easier thing to be unsettled.

Let me say in passing that this is a peril from which no man can hope to be exempted. No quiet sheltering of home or task will ward off the inroad of unsettlement. It is true that as life advances it grows less. With the passing of years comes the passing of unrest. In the fullness of its disturbing strength, unsettlement is the pain and privilege of youth. Yet God has so ordered this strange life of ours that into every lot, however sheltered, sooner or later there break out of the infinite those things which are mighty to unsettle. There are perils which we can shun in prudence. We can shape our course so as to avoid them. But this is a peril which we cannot shun, though we had all the wisdom of Athena. Suddenly a great sorrow is upon us, or the thrilling of unexpected joy, or we waken to hear, with hearts that burn within us, the calling of another summertime. From such disturbance there is no escape. We cannot expel the angels when they visit us. We must open the door to them and bid them welcome, and say, "Come in, thou blessed of the Lord." Only thus can we hope to use for good that recurring disturbance of the heart which falls upon us all, in diverse ways, amid the joys and sorrows of humanity.

Well now, let us consider one or two of the evils of unsettlement, and the first and most evident perhaps is this, that it makes our work harder to perform. For most men work is hard enough, even when they give to it an undivided mind. It takes every power and faculty which they possess to be honest toilers in the sight of heaven. But work becomes doubly hard for all of us, and to certain natures grows wellnigh impossible when these powers are inwardly distracted and will not answer the summons of the hour. It is not easy to do the common duty under the shadow of overwhelming sorrow. It is not easy to ply the daily task under the new glow of a great joy. It is not easy to take the burden up and to go quietly to our familiar place when the glad and open world is calling us. That is the commonest peril of unsettlement, and I take it there is no one here but knows it. Labor grows irksome; duty becomes irritating; drudgery is wellnigh intolerable. And yet this drudgery, for every one of us, from the dullard to the loftiest genius, is the one road that leads, o'er moor and fen, to the sunrise and the welcome and the crown.

Another peril of unsettlement is this, that it relaxes the hold of our good habits. We come to find, in our unsettled hours, that they do not hold us so firmly as we thought. Most of us are the creatures of habit in a far larger measure than we think. If it is to them that we owe many a weakness, it is to them also that we owe many a virtue. There are few men who can look back upon their lives, with gratitude to God that they have done a little, without recognizing what a debt they owe to one or two habits which were early formed. Such habits may be very simple, yet they have a wonderfully redeeming power. They redeem every day from being wasted and every energy from being ineffectual. If a bad habit is the worst of curses and leads by the road of bondage to the dark, a good habit, through the grace of God, is one of our surest and most priceless blessings. Now it is always one peril of unsettlement that it relaxes the hold of our good habits. It lifts us out of the embrace of good ones and throws us into the embrace of evil ones. For always, when we lose our self-control, sin, as the Scripture says, coucheth at the door waiting to call us to what we practiced once but have long through the grace of God forsworn. All men have a hunger for the good, but all men have a bias to the evil. It is that bias which the devil uses in the season of a man's unsettlement. Torn from his center by unexpected incidence, caught into new and strange environment, a man is in peril because his grip is weakened on the steadying and simple habits of his past.

And especially, will you let me say in passing, is this true of the sweet habits of the interior life. Unsettlement is the peculiar enemy of regularity in private prayer. I take it that most men pray in secret. I trust I am not mistaken in so thinking. It may be only a few words—it may be very formal—yet is it better than no prayer at all. But who does not know how this interior grace, which we may have learned beside a mother's knee, is apt to be shed off like an old garment when the hour of unsettlement arrives. I grant you that in a great catastrophe there is an instinct in the heart to pray. It is often then, when all the deeps are broken, that the pride which never prayed is broken too. But in all the lesser unsettlements of life when there is disturbance only, not catastrophe, there is the constant peril of forgetting the sweet and secret exercise of prayer. I have known men who prayed through years of drudgery, and who ceased it when great good fortune came. I have known men who prayed right through the winter, yet somehow in summer they forgot to pray. I have known men—yes, and women too—who would never have dreamed of omitting prayer at home, who yet omitted it, not once only, amid the excitement and the stir of foreign travel. That is a grave peril of unsettlement. There is not one of us but is exposed to it. It is appalling how lightly we are held by the secret habits of the interior life. A glimpse of liberty, a day of sunshine, a stroke of luck, a touch of one we love, and it may be—God only knows—that we shall throw ourselves upon a prayerless bed tonight.

Now it is always one mark of a great character not to be easily or lightly moved. A certain quiet and fine stability is generally one of the hallmarks of the noble. When Saul was chosen to be king of Israel and when the people shouted "God save the king," we could scarce have wondered if that swift elevation had unsettled him and turned his head a little. And it has always been held as a proof of Saul's nobility that he passed with a quiet heart through that great hour, and with the cry of the people in his ears went back to guide his father's plow again. Of course there are natures more prone than others to yield to the pressure of unsettlement. There are dogged natures and responsive natures, and there always shall be till the trumpet sounds. Still speaking broadly and generally, we may say that to be unsettled lightly is a bad sign, and that one mark of nobility of character is a quiet and resolute continuance. The question is then how we, not being great, can hope to attain to that continuance. How can we organize into victory the common perils of unsettlement?

Let me say first, and in a negative way, that it is but a sorry victory to stand aloof. It is not thus, as I understand my Bible, that God would have his children live. There are men who never take a holiday, they are so filled with dread of its disturbances. Knowing how certainly it will unsettle them, they prefer to forego it altogether. And while in the aged or in the infirm of body such a reluctance is easily understood, with others it is a road to peace that is perilously near to cowardice. We were never meant to live our lives so. We were never meant to bar the gates like that. To shut the summer out, and to shut love out, is not victory, it is defeat. In many of the choicest gifts of God there is a terrible power of unsettlement, and a Christian was never meant to reject the gift because of the unsettlement it brings. There was once a philosophy which wrought along these lines. It was called the Stoical philosophy. It sought to achieve serenity of life by steeling the soul against the passions. And do you know what happened as a fact of history? Well, I shall tell you what actually happened—one of two results was found in life. Sometimes men won the serenity they craved, but they won it at a tremendous cost. For love was banished and the charm of things and the touch of sympathy that makes us brothers. And some-times in the very hour of victory, nature, trampled on, rose to her rights again and in her passionate and overmastering way swept down the de-fenses they had built. It is no use fighting against nature. It is worse than useless fighting against God. We are not here to stand aloof from things and to steel our hearts against disturbances. We are here to wel-come whatever God may send, whether it be sunshine or be sorrow, and somehow out of all unsettlement to wrest the music of our tri-umph-song.

Well now, one great help to that is learning to see things in their true proportions. Without a certain feeling for perspective, we can never be quiet in the thick of life. You remember what Dr. Johnson said to a friend who was worrying about a trifle? *"Think, sir,"* he said in his wise way, *"think how little that will seem twelvemonth hence."* And if we only practiced that fine art of thinking how little many a thing will seem twelvemonth hence, we should be freed from much unsettlement today. It is good to know a big thing when we see it. It is not less good to know a little thing. There are people to whom the tiniest burn is as swift and dangerous as the Spey. And always when you have people of that nature who have never taken the measurements of life, you have people who live on the margin of unsettlement. Next to the grace of God for throughbearing, there is nothing more kindly than a little humor. To see things in a smiling kind of way is often to see them in the wisest way. For as there are things, and always shall be things, that strike to the very heart of human destiny, so are there things, and al-ways shall be things, that are so trifling as to be ridiculous. It is amazing how many worthy people seem never to have learned that simple les-son. You would think they had never heard the words of Jesus about swallowing the camel and straining at the gnat. And so are they always in peril of unsettlement, *not* because their experience is exceptional, but because they have never learned in life to see things in their true proportions.

But the greatest help of all is this, it is to see the hand of God in everything. When a man has come to see the hand of God in every-thing, he touches the secret of the weaned heart. I have noticed among domestic servants one very common reason of unsettlement. It is that they do not know who is the mistress and have to take orders from half a dozen people. And all of us are servants in God's house and always in our service we shall be irritable unless there be one voice we must obey and one will which gives us all our orders. That was the meaning of the peace of Job. He saw God always, and he saw Him everywhere. "The Lord hath given, and the Lord hath taken away," said Job, "blessed be the name of the Lord." It was not God today and fate tomorrow. It was not heaven in the morning and blind chance at night. Through light and shadow it was *God* to Job, and that was one secret of his rest. So is it with us all. To have many masters is always to be restless. "I have set the Lord always before me," said the Psalmist, "therefore I shall not be moved." To see *His* hand in the least and in the greatest, in the burden no less than in the blessing, is the sure way, amid all life's unsettlement, to have the heart at leisure from itself.

Paul Before His Judges

But after two years Porcius Festus came into Felix's room; and Felix, willing to show the Jews a pleasure, left Paul bound—Acts 24:27.

After being five days at Caesarea, Paul was formally indicted by the Jewish party. The case against him was conducted by Tertullus who was as unscrupulous as he was eloquent. Felix was no stranger to the matters in debate; he had lived long enough among the Jews to grow conversant with them. He therefore refused to decide the matter offhand; he would wait till his captain from Jerusalem came down. Now, whether the captain was unwilling to come or whether he got a broad hint not to hurry, is a question we need not trouble to decide. The fact remains that we have no trace of his visit during Paul's two years of confinement at Caesarea. What was the apostle doing all that time? We cannot be certain that he wrote any epistles. Do you think he was fretting? Or worrying over his churches as he paced his prison battlements by the blue sea? We may be absolutely certain he was doing nothing like that—he was growing and ripening in his own inward life. For twenty years he had been fighting for Christ amid the excitement and stress of a glorious campaign. New views of Christ had been borne upon his heart; new aspects of the Gospel had arrested him. It wanted leisure now to focus everything, and God bestowed that leisure at Caesarea. Compare the letters that were written *after* these years with the letters which we know were written before them. Note the richness and depth and glory of the later ones—their exaltation of the Lord Jesus Christ; their fresh insistence upon spiritual union; their recognition of the possibilities of sainthood; their method of bringing the most majestic doctrines to bear on the common duties of every day—and you will see what these two years did for Paul. I dare say the soldiers thought him very idle. Had you asked them, they would have said he was doing nothing. Yet all Christendom is deeply in God's debt for making Paul come apart and rest awhile.

Only one incident has been enshrined for us out of these two years at Caesarea. It is the scene with which our passage opens when Paul was brought before Felix and Drusilla. Drusilla was the youngest daughter of King Herod Agrippa I. She was a beautiful young Jewess of some eighteen years of age. But there were dark shadows lying across her path that would have marred the fairest womanhood. It was not God who had made her Felix's wife. She had a home already when Felix cast his bad eyes on her. And it may be that a guilty conscience and a torn heart and a mind that could not forget urged her to hear the Gospel of this prisoner. Do you observe what Paul was asked to speak about? He was asked to speak "concerning the faith in Christ." And do you note what Paul *did* speak about? He reasoned of righteousness and self-control and judgment. Righteousness—and Felix was a promise-breaker and had procured the murder of the High Priest Jonathan. Self-control—and there at his side, eagerly listening, sat beautiful Drusilla. Judgment—that was the very thought that haunted Felix, only it was the judgment of his emperor, not of his God. No wonder Felix trembled. He had the soul of a slave, says Tacitus, and the power of a sovereign. He would hear no more; Paul was dismissed; "when I have a convenient (not *more* convenient) season, I will call for thee."

About the year 60, Felix was recalled and was succeeded in the governorship by Porcius Festus. Festus seems to have been a better ruler, and probably he was a better man than Felix, but, like a Roman, he cared little for religion and could not understand religious earnestness. He was perplexed about this Jewish prisoner; it occurred to him that he might try the case at Jerusalem; and it was then that Paul, apprehending the danger he was in, took the great step of appealing to Caesar. That is not in the passage to be read, but it must be touched on to illuminate the passage. For it was not till Paul had appealed to Caesar that Agrippa and Bernice came to Caesarea. Might not *they* be able to unravel Festus' difficulties? They were Jews and understood the points at issue. Festus arranged that a court should be convened at which Agrippa and Bernice might be present. It was then that Paul made that most noble defense which is recorded in the twenty-sixth chapter. He told the story of his conversion again, for his greatest defense of all just lay in that. And our passages take up the narrative at the point where Paul has touched on resurrection and has been rudely silenced by Festus crying out in a loud voice, "Paul, thou art mad!" Paul instantly, and without losing self-command, repels the charge. He appeals to Agrippa on the grounds of Jewish prophecy. And Agrippa replies in these memorable words, "Almost thou persuadest me to be a Christian." Do we know what Agrippa really meant? He did *not* mean "I am almost persuaded." The Greek words that have been translated so are not capable of bearing such a sense. What Agrippa meant was "Paul, do you think that with a little persuasion you are going to persuade *me* to be a Christian? It is a far harder task than you imagine."

Now let us note three simple lessons, and first *the peril of tomorrow.* Someone has said that today has two great enemies—the one is yesterday, the other is tomorrow. Are we not reminded of that whenever we think of Felix whose evil past was such a burden on him and who talked of a convenient time—which never came. Next mark *how history reverses human judgments.* Peter and the other disciples were despised, because they were ignorant and unlettered men. Paul was put to scorn by Festus for just the opposite reason—he had learned too much. Men thought the prophets of Israel raved. They said of Jesus that He was beside Himself. Is there any one *now* who would harbor such a thought? Lastly, see the *perfect courtesy of the apostle*—"I would you were altogether as I am except these bonds." "Courtesy," says St. Francis of Assisi, "is the sister of charity, which quencheth hate and keepeth love alive." Never forget that God's mighty missionary was one of the truest gentlemen who ever breathed.

Paul's Voyage and Shipwreck

And when it was determined that we should sail for Italy, they delivered Paul and certain other prisoners unto one named Julius, a centurion of Augustus' band—Acts 27:1.

All of us love stories of voyages and shipwrecks, and our lesson of today deals with these themes. I do not know any chapter in the Bible that is more alive with thrilling interest. So far, we have seen Paul in many perils; we have followed him through many strange adventures; but just as the hero in the schoolboys' storybooks is never quite perfect till he has suffered shipwreck, so is it with this traveler and missionary. Can we briefly outline the fascinating story? Well, Paul embarked at Caesarea under the guard of a centurion, Julius. The vessel was only a coasting-vessel; they would have to change if they were to get to Rome. Fortunately, at Myra in Asia Minor, a corn-ship from Alexandria was in the harbor. It was bound for Rome to distribute its cargo there, and Julius and his prisoners got a passage. But the season was late, and the winds were getting stormy; it was with great difficulty that they made a port in Crete. Here they would have remained throughout the winter had they hearkened to the advice of Paul. But who was Paul that he should be attended to? Had not the captain made this voyage twenty times? The prospect of wintering in Crete was quite intolerable when the stir and gaiety of Rome were waiting them. So the harbor was left; the sails were trimmed again; a favoring breeze gave every one new heart when suddenly the ship was caught in a typhoon—one of the wild and dangerous storms of the Mediterranean. The boat was hoisted on board; the sails were furled; stout ropes were passed round the body of the ship; not a glimpse of the sun could be got and not a star was visible;—for fourteen days they drove on under bare masts. Then at midnight there arose the cry of "Land!" Soundings were taken; the water was getting shallower. Four anchors were cast out of the stern; they held, and the ship rode safely till the morning. Then as the light dawned and outlines became visible, a little bay among the cliffs was seen. The cables were cut, and a desperate effort was made to beach the vessel on the rock-engirdled sand. It partly failed, the currents were so strong. The ship was driven ashore and sorely battered. But though she soon went to pieces, and everything was lost, "it came to pass that they escaped all safe to land."

Now among the many lessons of this chapter, note first *that the hour reveals the man*. When Paul stepped on board, he was one of a batch of prisoners. Neither captain or sailors would give two thoughts to him. They had carried all manner of desperadoes Romeward, and there was nothing striking about this little Jew. But gradually, as the voyage became more perilous, Paul moved out from the darkness to the light. It was he who advised and encouraged and commanded. It was he who put new heart and hope in everybody. He went on board an unregarded prisoner, but the hour of need struck, and he stood supreme. Do not such hours come to all of us when for weal or woe we stand in our true colors? "There is nothing hid, but shall be revealed." It was Paul's years of reliance upon God and of secret prayer and of steadfast loyalty that broke into the rich blossom of this hour. Will there be such secrets to reveal in us?

Note next *how faith in God keeps a man calm*. Perhaps that is the most notable feature in this story. Amid a scene of excitement and of terror, we are arrested by the quietude of Paul. The sailors, panic-stricken, were for fleeing; the soldiers were crying out to kill the prisoners; but the apostle was cool, collected, confident, and he was so because of his faith in God. Men used to feel that, too, about General Gordon. There was something mysterious in his calmness in moments of peril. Those who had fought in many a desperate battle and witnessed many shining deeds of heroism would say there was something in the courage of Gordon that was unlike anything they had ever seen. We know now what that "something" was. It was living and glowing and conquering trust in God. It was the same faith as gave Paul the quiet mastery in the confusion and panic of the storm.

Again, we must not omit to notice here *that many may be saved for one man's sake.* When the ship was driving westward before the wind, an angel of God, we read, appeared to Paul. And the message which the angel brought was this: "Fear not, Paul, thou must be brought before Caesar; and lo, God hath given thee all them that sail with thee"—that means that for the apostle's sake every man on board the vessel would be saved. How little any of them ever dreamed of their obligation to this despised Jew! In after days when the sailors told the story of the wreck, they would say it was a miracle they were not lost. But the only miracle was the will of God in choosing their vessel for His servant's journey. And we are like these sailors in this one respect. We all owe debts where we little dream of it. A father's example and a mother's prayer, the presence of good men and women in our childhood, the spirit of Jesus breathing in the world and falling on us like the blowing of the wind, these influences mold us when we never know of it and may save us in our hours of gale and storm.

Then, lastly, it is not enough to wish for the day (v. 29); *there are some anchors that we all should cast.* One of them is *faith;* another is *a good conscience.* Without these, says Paul, some have made shipwreck (1 Tim. 1:19). A third is *hope:* "which hope we have as an anchor of the soul" (Heb. 6:19). We are all voyaging on a dark and boisterous sea. Our hearts and our eyes should ever be toward the morning. Meantime let us thank God that we have anchors by which the weakest may ride out the night.

The Life of Drift

When the ship was caught, and could not bear up into the wind, we let her drive—Acts 27:15.

It is interesting to remember some of the causes that make vessels drift. Often it is a breakdown in the engine room. So long as the engines are in perfect order the vessel holds to its appointed course. But let the shaft snap, as sometimes happens, and immediately the ship begins to drift. And as it is with ships, so is it not infrequently with lives; they drift because of interior breakdown. It may be a breakdown in morality, though no one knows anything about it yet. It may be a breakdown in the will, for the will is the shaft of life. It may be a breakdown in some sweet and simple piety like that of prayer in the secret place—and the ship goes drifting on the sea. There is a story of an officer in the Great War who went drifting and was finally cashiered. He came back again to his old home and entered the little bedroom of his boyhood. Then, turning to his mother, "Mother," he said, "the whole thing began when I stopped praying as a lad beside that bed."

Again, we must not forget that boats may drift because of the rising of the tide. One has had that experience on summer holidays. You draw the rowboat high up on the shore, and you leave it there, thinking it is safe. But the night is the night of a spring tide, and concurring with the tide there blows a gale. And in the morning you go to get the boat, only to find that it is gone: the spring tide has come and set it drifting. That is often how young people go drifting. Youth is the spring tide of life. Passions awake, tempestuous and turbulent; new thought and knowledge lap around the gunwale. And lives that once

107

were safe, beached in the securities of childhood, go drifting like ships upon the sea. That often happens when a lad goes to college out of an orthodox and godly home. He enters a new world of thought and gains a new conception of the universe. And the ship that was so safe once amid the unquestioning pieties of home, finds itself drifting on the deeps. Spring tide has come, and spring tide is of God. God is in the flow as in the ebb. Lives that drift like that can be recaptured. There is One who is out to seek and save. I find a perennial and profound significance in a Savior who could walk upon the sea. Drifting stops when He is taken aboard.

It is well to note, too, that a drifting ship is always a danger to the other shipping. Every captain would corroborate that. You can chart a quicksand or a reef, and having them on the chart you can avoid them. But nobody can chart a drifting ship; it may be on you in a moment in the night. It is well to remember that in that regard a drifting life is like a drifting vessel; it is fraught with peril and disaster. When a man drifts from his anchorage in Christ, he affects a hundred others lives. No one can tell the hurt that he may bring when he drifts into indifference and worldliness—spoiling the fair name of Christ, damping the zeal of zealous, eager people, making it always easier to be skeptical and always harder to be true. One of the signals of a drifting iceberg is a rapid lowering of the temperature. Drifting lives are just like drifting icebergs: wherever they drift there is fall in temperature. They chill the church. They chill the congregation. They chill the eager loyalties of youth, not because they are notoriously bad, but just because they are drifting.

That is one reason why our blessed Lord is always dead against the life of drift. He condemns it in a score of instances. Think how He describes the days of Noah. According to Genesis the earth was full of violence; but our Lord says nothing about violence as the precursor of calamity. He says that in the days before the flood men were eating, drinking, merrymaking, marrying—and then, suddenly, the flood came. Noah was a man of action, of swift decision, of determination. The others went drifting on from day to day, thoughtless, heedless, irresistible. It is the Lord's warning against the life of drift as leading to disaster, and He is always insisting upon that. The man of the one talent took no risks. He forfeited everything for doing nothing. The man who built his house upon the sand found that in the drift was his destruction. The man who worshiped God today and tomorrow was the slave of mammon was intolerable in the eyes of Jesus. Christ calls for action, for decision, for determination of the will. If thy right eye offend thee, pluck it out; if thy right hand offend thee, cut it off. Nobody knew better than our Savior that we are here not to drift but to decide if we are ever to have the music and the crown.

And how beautifully is that exemplified in His own so perfect life! Scoffers said He drank, but no one ever said He drifted. By a magnificent energy of faithful will He put from Him all the kingdoms of the world. He chose the long, hard trail and held to it, though His feet were bleeding and His heart was breaking. Far off He saw the cross in its agony and shame and ridicule, and He set His face steadfastly towards Jerusalem. Nothing could divert Him nor break the steady power of His purpose, no tempting friends nor cheering multitudes nor bitter desertion nor betrayal. The great word in the life of drift is *may,* but the great word in the life of Christ is *must,* and *must* is the last triumph of the will. No man can share His spirit who lives on in aimless indecision. Nobody can have His joy who shrinks from full surrender. The life of drift never reaches harbor. It reaches the quicksand and the reef—from which may God in His mercy save us all.

Social Consequences of Individual Faith

Wherefore, sirs, be of good cheer; for I believe God—Acts 27:25.

It might seem as if what a man believed were no concern to anybody else. That is his own affair and his alous, and straight, and it does not socially matter what his creed is. Others are not the better for his faith nor the worse for his want of it. One hears frequent expression of that view, and sometimes it is buttressed by the text, "Hast thou faith? Have it for thyself." As a matter of fact, what a man believes has profound and pervasive social consequence. It affects the lives of all he comes in contact with. It inspires or depresses them. And all this is more beautifully illustrated in the story of the shipwreck of St. Paul than perhaps in any other piece of Scripture.

We note, for instance, how the faith of Paul made him intensely and practically useful. One is reminded of the exclamation "What practical fellows these great mystics are." We could well imagine somebody dilating on the compelling preaching of St. Paul, but quite certain that in storm and shipwreck he would be altogether useless. And yet in such an hour, when things were darkest, Paul was the most useful man on board, and he was so because he believed God. The same thing is profoundly true of Jesus who lived in a perfect and unwavering faith. That did not make Him an ineffectual dreamer; it made Him intensely and socially useful. It filled the nets, and fed the hungry folk, and restored the withered arm to service, and brought joy and singing to the home at Bethany.

We help people by what we do. Perhaps we help them more by what we are. We prove ourselves useful when we give our money. We are still more useful when we give ourselves. And no man has his whole self to give, in all the expansion of his possibilities, until he has aligned himself with God.

We note again how the faith of the apostle brought new hope to everyone on board. These despairing souls were saved by hope. One moment there was not a star in all their sky. They were drifting on to certain death. The best of them would be crying to their gods; the worst would fall to cursing and blaspheming. And then, like the first faint flushings of the dawn, hope came stealing into every heart because there was one on board who believed God. Things were just as dark as they had been before. There was no cessation of the raging storm. They were still drifting on to an iron shore, their ship the sport and plaything of the elements. But one man believed God and because of that was radiant and serene, and it brought hope into the heart of everybody. What does it not matter what you believe? Is faith entirely devoid of social consequence? It mattered supremely for these despairing sailors. It matters every time. Have faith in God—have it for yourself—be strong and quiet and confident because of it, and everybody on shipboard is affected.

For that is always one of the fruits of faith. Faith radiates the atmosphere of hope. The presence of a strong and living faith calls out the music of a thousand hearts. A son may be a prodigal, and everybody may think him past redemption. But his mother never thinks him past redemption because of the faith in her big mother-heart. And because of the faith in the heart of the Lord Jesus, hope has dawned on twice ten thousand people who, like these shipwrecked sailors, were despairing. It is a great thing to give weary people hope. It is like sowing grass on a parched and arid land. And in all our weakness, one sure way to do it is the old sweet way of Jesus and of Paul. Have faith in God. Live it out in storms. Be strong and quiet when others cry in terror. And in mysterious ways we cannot trace hope will dawn upon the hearts of men.

Not only did the faith of Paul give hope; it also gave the blessing of good cheer. It brought the comfort of a happy confidence to every desponding heart on board. I have read somewhere of an ocean liner caught in the fury of a terrific storm. Men were panic-stricken—women screamed—and then the captain smiled. And the faith that lay behind that smile, that the ship he knew so well would weather through, brought good cheer to every soul on board. So was it with St. Paul. He believed God and he could smile. When others were terror-stricken and beside themselves, he could give thanks and quietly take his breakfast. And men, seeing it, forgot their fears and plucked up heart again and became cheerful—and all because one person believed God. It is a fine thing to do kindly, helpful deeds. It is one of the very finest in the world. But there is something finer than the helpful hand; it is the helpful heart. To be brave and radiant when things are darkest has an impact upon everybody, and for *that* one must believe God. My dear reader, longing to cheer others, begin by having faith in God. Fix the one point of your compass there, and let the other sweep as widely as you will. A strong faith is the secret of all helpfulness. Nothing can ever take the place of that. *This* is the victory that overcomes the world—even your faith.

The Broken Things of Life

Some on broken pieces of the ship . . . escaped . . . safely to land—Acts 27:44.

Among the broken things of life one would think first of broken time. Time, says Benjamin Franklin, is the stuff of life: it is a stuff which is very easily tattered. When a man is eagerly plying his own work, interruptions are intensely irritating. Sometimes they are inevitable; at other times they spring from thoughtlessness. And one of the lessons everyone must learn who wants to achieve anything in life is how to hold to things through recurring interruption. That is how the worker comes ashore. That is how most of the world's work is done; *not* by men of an unbroken leisure—is very rarely fruitful. It is done by men who have to seize their hours, rescue and redeem their opportunities, gather up the fragments that remain. I think of Shakespeare with all a player's worries; of Milton burdened with the cares of State; of Spurgeon founding colleges and orphanages yet preaching those magnificent discourses. They seized their hours, rescued their opportunities, toiled on in the teeth of interruptions, and on broken pieces of the ship they came ashore.

Again, the words have comforting suggestion for those who are suffering from broken health. Doubtless there are some of my readers in that category. Once they were strong, vigorous, and tireless; now they are very easily tired. Once it was a great, glad thing to live; now it is rather a burden to be borne. There is so much that they would gladly do if only they had the strength to do it. It is so very bitter to feel useless. My dear friends, health is a priceless blessing. Rubies and diamonds are nothing to it. Without it, castles and carriages are vanity;

with it, the tiniest cottage is a kingdom. But never forget that with a little courage and trust in God and patient, quiet endurance, you may get ashore on broken pieces of the ship. Think of Calvin with his sickly body; of Pascal, all his life an invalid; of Richard Baxter tortured by disease; of Mrs. Browning on her couch. Think of the great Apostle to the Gentiles with his ophthalmia and his malaria. *They* never knew what perfect health was; they did not sail in any golden galleon; they did not waken in the morning singing, feeling as if they were capable of anything. But they did their work, wrote immortal literature, altered Europe, changed the course of history, clinging to the broken pieces of the ship. I knew an invalid in quite a humble home who used to lament to me that she was useless. Her brothers and sisters were in splendid health; she was only a burden to them all. And yet no wages that the sisters earned brought such an enriching to that home as the presence of her who thought that she was useless. Her gentleness was like the rain from heaven—her patience a rebuke—her happy smile for everybody was gladdening as the sunshine in November. She earned no wages, wrote no poems, never made a dress nor cooked a dinner—and yet on broken pieces of the ship she came ashore.

Now I want to go a little deeper, from a shattered body to a shattered faith. There are many in the world today whose early faith is very sorely broken. Trained in Christian homes, there was a time when they accepted things. They prayed; they read their Bibles; they attended Sunday school; they went to church. And now the years have gone, and everything is different, and the old, sweet assurance has departed, and clouds and darkness are around the Throne. Once their faith was like a gallant vessel with the sails set and the flags flying. They thought, once, that they would reach the harbor so—and now that gallant vessel is a wreck. And I want to tell them, quietly and earnestly, for I fervently believe that it is true, that on broken pieces of the ship they can make shore. Much is lost; something yet remains, something they can cling to in the dark—something they cannot doubt, divine and unalterably true. And I say that if they only cling to that, like the shipwrecked sailor to a spar, it will buoy them up and bring them to the shore. There are those who make the haven gloriously. They have a prosperous and sunny voyage. Their love is burning, and their faith is bright; they live and die in the fullness of assurance. But I thank God that men can reach the haven *clinging to a spar,* for the Lord God is merciful and gracious. Trembling on the borders of agnosticism, questioning the fatherhood of God, uncertain of the authority of Scripture, critical of the Church and of its ministry, let them grip Christ, the little bit they know of Him; let them tell Him that they will not let Him go, and He will pluck them out of the deep waters.

Lastly, and in a word or two, I apply the words to broken character, to those whose character is sorely broken and who today are on the margins of despair. I think of the prodigal son in the far country; his conduct had disgraced the name of son. I think of Peter when he denied his Lord, and his whole life seemed toppling to ruin. I think of Rahab in her life of sin that must have crushed all that was fairest in her. I think of the woman who was called the Magdalene. Not perfect characters, very far from that; rent and torn by the fury of their passions; characters that sin had battered as the storm had battered the vessel of St. Paul. And then, thanks to the grace of God that is able to save unto the uttermost, on broken pieces of the ship they came ashore. The prodigal came home again, and there was music and dancing in the house. The Magdalene was drawn out of the mire into the garden of a saintly womanhood. Some who read this have been living carelessly, and their character has gone to pieces in the dark. Thank God that there is still a shining hope for them as for the shipwrecked comrades of St. Paul.

Kindness at Melita

And when they were escaped, then they knew that the island was called Melita—
Acts 28:1.

When at last the shipwrecked company reached shore, they learned that the island on which they were cast was Melita. There can be no reasonable doubt that Melita was the island known to us as Malta. Though small, it is of the highest importance. It is an important island in the Mediterranean. Its fortifications are extraordinarily strong. It is one of the most thickly populated islands in the world, and the natives love it—they call it "the flower of the world"; and in springtime at least, when it is carpeted with blossom, one would not readily quarrel with the name. Do boys know what a Maltese cross is like? And have they ever heard of the Knights of Malta? These names remind us of the part that Malta played in the inspiring and yet tragic story of the Crusades. It was on this island, then, that Paul was cast and found himself in the midst of a barbarous people. Now we must not think from that word *barbarous* that the Maltese were wild and dangerous savages. A barbarian was just a man whose speech was like "bar-bar-bar"—there was no sense in it to a Greek or Latin. Today the natives speak a corrupt Arabic with a strong flavor of Italian in it. But perhaps in Paul's time it would be a debased Phoenician dialect, and that would just be "bar-bar-bar" to the apostle.

Now the first thing to impress me in this story is *how thoroughly God fulfills His promises.* His care did not cease nor His loving-kindness vanish when the peril of the breakers was removed. You remember what God had whispered in the storm? He had promised to give to Paul the lives of all on board (27:24). And in the strict sense that promise was fulfilled when the whole company got safe to land. But what if the island had been a desert island? Or what if the natives had attacked the crew? The rescue from the wild surf in St. Paul's Bay would have been of little service if it had led to that. It is when I read of the kindness of the islanders, and of their hospitable welcome to the shipwrecked, that I see what a large and liberal interpretation we should always give to God's promise of protection. When Jesus had passed through the storm of His temptation, angels came and ministered unto Him. It was a desert place, the haunt of ravening beasts, yet even there God had His angels ready. So here when the peril of the sea was over, there are ministering hearts and hands upon the shore. It is always wise to take the words of God, not at their lowest but at their highest value. We need never hesitate to pour a wealth of meaning into the simplest and briefest of His pledges. As Paul looked back on this exciting voyage and traced the action of God's hand in it, he must have felt that God had done for him far above what he could ask or think.

Once more this lesson admirably illustrates the proverb that *it's an ill wind that blows nobody good.* This was an ill wind for the Alexandrian corn-ship. I dare say it almost broke the heart of the good captain. He had carried so many cargoes safe to Rome that this sudden calamity was overwhelming. Sailors are often very superstitious, and they were invariably so in the old world. They never dreamed of starting on a voyage without offering sacrifices and taking auspices. What was the meaning, then, of this ill-wind? Were the gods offended, or were they simply mocking? I think we see now that the furious gale was blowing a blessing upon heathen Malta. There would be much corn washed up on the shore. The beach would be covered with the grain from Africa. But it was not food like *that* that was the storm's best gift for the islanders who knew not God. It was the message of Christ that the apostle preached to them; it was the prayers which were offered in the name of Jesus; it was the healing of the sick and the diseased. There was not a sailor but muttered, "What an ill wind is this," yet it was blowing untold good to Malta. Can we recall, from the Bible or from history, any other great storms that blew a blessing anywhere? There are two that will suggest themselves at once. One was the tempest on the Lake of Galilee that so enriched the disciples in their knowledge of Christ. The other was the storm which fell on the Armada and drove it asunder and dashed it on wild rocks—an ill wind, but a wind which saved our country and wrought incalculable good for Europe.

Again our lesson shows us this, that *even a viper may help on the Gospel.* We all know the story of the viper. It is one of the Bible scenes we never forget. We see the creature torpid in the brushwood; we watch it stirring as the heat of the fire gets at it; and then—irritated—it grips the apostle's hand and is shaken off into the fire. You see that if Paul had let *others* tend the fire, he would have escaped this sudden peril. But it is always nobler to run the risk of vipers than to sit idle and let others do the work. And then what happened? Every eye was fixed on Paul. He came to his own rightful place at once. They thought that he was a murderer; then that he was a god. The captain and mate and crew took a second place. Paul would be spoken of that night in a hundred cottages, and before morning Publius would know of him. The viper was the bell before the sermon. It stirred up interest and centered it on Paul. He would not have to wait for an audience now when he began (through an interpreter) to preach. Note then that even poisonous creatures may be used to advance the message of Christ Jesus. It is a great thing to believe that we serve a Lord who can turn even a snake into an argument. No man ever gave himself up to what was highest without stirring up the venom in the firewood; but as the world looks back upon these noble lives, it sees that all things were working for their good.

Then lastly, the great lesson of these verses is *the sure reward that follows a kindly welcome.* We have all heard of the Cornish wreckers and of the heartless cruelty that characterized them. A wreck was an act of God not to be interfered with, and strange stories are told of how men were left to die. Such wreckers were true barbarians (though they called themselves Christians), and no blessing ever followed their vile gains. How different is this scene at Malta! The islanders gave the shipwrecked a kind welcome; they did it instinctively, looking for no reward. But when their fevered were cured and their diseased were healed, they found they had got far more then they gave. No generous welcome is ever thrown away. Kindnesses, not less than curses, come home to roost. Writ large, over all the passage, is the golden text, "Be not forgetful to entertain strangers, for thereby some have entertained angels unawares" (Hebrews 13:2).

Romans and 1 and 2 Corinthians

The Saving Power of Hope

We are saved by hope—Rom 8:24.

It is not difficult as one looks out on life to recognize the saving power of hope. One thinks, for instance, to what a large extent it is hope which saves humanity from idleness. When a student faces an examination, it is his uncertainty that makes him toil. Were he perfectly sure that he would fail or pass, that would take all the zest out of his studies. Hope is the kindly instrument of God for rescuing mankind from inactivity, and inactivity is sister to stagnation. It is in hope that the writer wields his pen; it is in hope that the sower casts his seed. Search deep enough into the springs of action—you always catch the whispering of hope. In a large sense, we are saved by hope from the tragedy of doing nothing in a world where there is everything to do.

Akin to that is the great fact of life that we are saved by hope from giving in. For the great multitude of men hope lies at the back of perseverance. That may not be true of elect natures. It was not true of Marcus Aurelius, for instance. Never was there a more hopeless man than he, yet how magnificently he persevered. But for the rank and file of ordinary mortals on whom the Gospel always keeps its eye, hope is essential to holding on. One thinks of the story of the little lame boy who was "hoping to have wings some day." He could not race nor leap like other boys, but he was hoping to have wings some day. It was that hope which helped him to endure and taught him to bear the burden of his lameness, and so it is largely in this life of ours. From giving in when things are very difficult, from breaking down just at breaking point, from losing heart when all the lights are dim and the clouds return after the rain, in deep senses we are saved by hope.

Equally true is it of life, that we are often saved by hope from losing faith. Think, for instance, how often that is true of our Christian hope of personal survival. When his friend Arthur Hallam died, Tennyson was plunged into the depths. It seemed as if the foundations were destroyed and the moral universe had fallen in ruins. And then, as one may read in *In Memoriam,* morning broke with the singing of the birds through the shining Christian hope of immortality. Nothing could be more dreary than the inscriptions on old pagan tombs, but pass to the catacombs and everything is different: they are radiant with trust in God. What millions have been saved from loss of faith in the hour when the heart was desolate and empty by the burning hope of a blessed immortality. "My soul, hope thou in God." His name is love, and love demands *forever.* "Forever" is engraven on the heart of love as Calais was engraven on the heart of Mary. When life is desolated by the hand of death so that faith in Fatherhood is very difficult, multitudes have been upheld and comforted by the saving power of hope.

Now, it is very beautiful to notice how our Savior utilized that saving energy. Think how often He began His treatment by kindling the flame of hope within the breast. One might take the instance of Zacchaeus, that outcast from the commonwealth of Israel. He had been taught there was no hope for him, and he believed it till the Lord came by. And then, like the dawn, there came the quivering hope that his tomorrow might differ from his yesterday, and in that new hope the saving work began. Often hope is subsequent to faith. The Scripture order is "faith, hope, charity." But it is equally true, in the movements of the soul, that hope may be the forerunner of faith. And our Lord, bent on evoking faith, that personal trust in Him which alone saves, began by kindling hope within the breast. That is how He often begins still. He does not *begin* by saying, "Trust in Me." He begins by kindling these hopes of better things that are lying crushed in every human heart. Despair is deadly. It is blind. It cannot see the arm outstretched to help. Our Lord begins with the quickening of hope.

One reads, too, in the Gospel story, of the pains He took just to keep hope alive. That, I think, is most exquisitely evident in His handling of Simon Peter. One would gather that Peter had a nature very prone to access of despair. He was the kind of man to climb the mountaintop and then swiftly to drop into the valley; and the pains, the endless pains that Jesus took to keep hope alive in Peter's breast, is one of the most beautiful things in history. One day he had to call him Satan. What darkness and anguish that must have brought to Peter! He would move through the crowding duties of the day saying despairingly, "The Master called me Satan." And then, within a week, when our Lord went up the Mount of Transfiguration, He said, "Peter, I want *you* to go with Me." It was not Peter's faith that needed strengthening. Peter trusted the Lord with all his heart. It was Peter's hope that needed to be strengthened, crushed by that terrific name of Satan. And then one remembers how on resurrection morning after the black hour of the denial, the angel (commissioned by the Lord) commanded, "Go, tell the disciples *and Peter.*" The Lord had to wrestle with the despair of Peter. He had a mighty work to keep his hope alive. He had that same work with Luther and with Bunyan and perhaps with many a one who reads these lines. All of whom, rescued from despair by the divine hopefulness of Christ, understand what the apostle meant when he wrote that we are saved *by hope.*

The Separating Power of Things Present

Things present—Rom. 8:38.

It is notable that in his enumeration of things which might dim the love of God to us, the apostle should make mention of things present, and by things present I take it that he means the events and trials of the present day. Many of us know how things to come may tempt us to doubt the love of God. The anxieties and forebodings of tomorrow often cloud the sunshine of today. But Paul, who knew all that as well as we do, for his apostleship gave no exemptions, knew also the separating power of things present. The task in which we are presently engaged, the thronging duties of the common day, the multitude of things we must get through before we go to bed at night, these, unless we continually watch, are apt to blind us to the great realities and to separate us from the love of God in Christ.

In part that separating power arises from the exceeding nearness of things present. Things which are very near command our vision and often lead to erroneous perspective. When I light the lamp in my quiet study, the moon may be riding through the sky, the stars may be glittering in heavenly brilliance, proclaiming that the hand which made them is divine. But the lamp is near me, at my side, and I read by it and write my letters by it, and most often the stars are quite forgotten. Things present are things near, and near things have a certain blinding power. You can blot the sun out with a penny if you only hold it near enough to the eye. And yet the sun is a majestic creation, beautifier and conserver of the world, and the penny is but a worn and trifling

126

coin. For most of us each day that dawns brings its round of present duties. They absorb us, commanding every energy, and so doing may occasionally blind us. And that is why, in busy crowded lives where near things are so swift to tyrannize, we all require moments of withdrawal. To halt a moment and just to say "God loves me"; to halt a moment and say "God is here"; to take the penny from the eye an instant that we may see the wonder of the sun, that, as the apostle knew so well, is one of the secrets of the saints, to master the separating power of things present.

Another element in that separating power is *the difficulty of understanding present things*. It is always easier to understand our yesterdays than to grasp the meaning of today. Often in the Highlands it is difficult to see the path just at one's feet. Any bunch of cowberries may hide it or any bush of overarching heather. But when one halts a moment and looks back, generally it is comparatively easy to trace the path as it winds across the moor. So we begin to understand our past, its trials, its disappointments, and its illnesses; but *such things are very hard to understand in their actual moment of occurrence,* and it is *that,* the difficulty of reading love in the dark characters of present things, which constitutes their separating power. Many a grown man thanks God for the discipline of early childhood. But as a child it was often quite unfathomable, and he doubted if his mother loved him. And we are all God's children, never in love with the discipline of love, and in that lies the separating power of things present.

Another element of that separating power is found in the distraction of things present. *"Life isn't a little bundle of big things: it's a big bundle of little things."* I read somewhere of a ship's captain who reported that a lighthouse was not shining. Inquiries were made, and it was found that the light was burning brightly all the night. What dimmed the light and made it as though it were not to the straining eyes of the captain on the bridge was a cloud of myriads of little flies. "While thy servant was busy here and there, the man was gone." What things escape us in our unending busyness! Peace and joy, and the power of self-control, and the serenity that ought to mark the Christian. And sometimes *that* is lost, which to lose is the tragedy of tragedies—the sense and certainty of love divine. Preoccupied, it fades out of our heaven. The comfort and the calm of it are gone. The light is there "forever, ever shining," but the cloud of flies has blotted out the light. Nobody knew better than the apostle did, in the cares that came upon him daily, the separating power of things present.

Of spiritual victory over present things, the one perfect example is our Lord. It is He who affords to us a perfect picture of untiring labor and unruffled calm. He gained the conquest over things to come. When Calvary was coming, He was joyous. He set His face steadily towards Jerusalem where the bitter cross was waiting Him. But, wonderful though that victory was over everything the future had in store, there was another that was not less wonderful. Never doubting the love of God to Him, certain of it in His darkest hour, through broken days, through never-ending calls when there was not leisure so much as to eat, not only did He master things to come, but He did what is often far more difficult—He mastered the separating power of things present. Do not forget He did all that for us. His victories were all achieved for us. In a deep sense we do not win our victories: we appropriate the victories of Christ. That is why the apostle in another place says, "All things are yours—*things present,* or things to come—and ye are Christ's and Christ is God's."

Maintaining the Glow

Maintaining the spiritual glow—Rom. 12:11 (Moffatt).

All of us have hours in the interior life when we are conscious of the glowing spirit. Our hearts burn within us as we journey. Sometimes these hours reach us unexpectedly; sometimes after periods of prayer. The wind bloweth where it listeth, and so is every one born of the Spirit. But when such hours come, the inward life grows radiant, and in the light of heaven we see light. In such hours we learn a great deal more than we ever gained from unillumined study. In such hours heaven is very near. In such hours, as by unseen fingers, the veil is taken from the face of Scripture, and the Word, that was marred more than any man, now shines on us as altogether lovely. We have caught the spiritual glow. We are in heavenly places with Christ Jesus. There steals on our ear the distant triumph song. We behold Satan as lightning fall from heaven. Such glowing hours of spiritual warmth and radiance come with greater or with lesser frequency to everybody who is stepping heavenward.

But the great difficulty in the interior life is to maintain that spiritual glow. The problem is not to catch it, but to keep it. Seasons come when we are overwrought and when the keepers of the house do tremble. We may have overdriven "our brother the ass," as St. Francis used to call his body. Or it may be, in the providence of God, that for long days we have to take our journey through a dry land where no water is. It is easy to lose the glow in such experiences. It fades into the light of common day. The Bible loses its fragrancy and dew. Heaven recedes; we miss the golden ladder. And yet the divine command is laid on us, poor unstable mortals though we be, that our duty is to maintain the spiritual glow. It can be ours in spite of feeble health. It can be ours whatever be our temperament. It is not given for rare or precious moments. It is meant for every mile of the long journey. And just there the difficulty lies, of maintaining, through dark and dreary days, the radiance and the warmth of hours of insight. He who does that is victor. Having done all, he stands. He "makes a sunshine in a shady place." In weakness he is strong. And we may be certain that when God commands a thing, He never mocks us with impossibilities. When He commands, He gives the power to do.

For what we must always bear in mind is this, that the spiritual glow is not a luxury. If it were that and nothing else than that, it would never reach us as a divine *command*. There are tasks that no man will accomplish unless he be gifted with a glowing spirit. There are victories that call for radiance. They never can be accomplished in cold blood. To come victorious out of this present life, unembittered by its tears and tragedies, is beyond the compass of the stoic heart. "No virtue is pure that is not passionate." The song of the Lord must sound above the sacrifice. For the campaign of life we need the song just as surely as we need the sword. Those who have conquered and are robed in white do not flash the glittering sword in heaven. They sing the song of Moses and the Lamb. *That* is why the inspired volume bids us to maintain the spiritual glow. It is not that we may be happy all the time. It is that we may be triumphant all the time. There are valleys we shall never cross unscathed, and there are temptations we shall never master without a certain glow within the soul.

Now it is just there that we thank God afresh for the unspeakable gift of the Lord Jesus. *To love Him gives the glow.* Nobody ever has a glowing heart because he is ordered to do certain things. Paul never found that *his* big heart was glowing when he struggled to obey the ten commandments. But when the ten commandments are incarnate in a living Lord whom we can love, then obedience is set to music. Love is the fulfilling of the law. Love is law translated into melody. Love laughs at difficulties, just as it is said to laugh at locksmiths. And when, right at the center of our being, there is real love for Him who died for us, cold and heavy obedience is gone—it is replaced by the spiritual glow. Thus to continue glowing is to continue in the love of Christ. It is to live in

130

the experience of His great love for us and in continual response to that experience. The one way to maintain the spiritual glow is to maintain fellowship with Christ, and that is possible for everybody. Every day we may open our hearts anew to receive anew the Holy Spirit. We may begin each day, however dark and dreary, by saying, "Even so, come, Lord Jesus." So maintaining, through heavenly supply, our loving personal fellowship with Him, we maintain (and yet not we) the glowing heart.

The Things That Make for Peace

Let us therefore follow after the things that make for peace–Rom. 14:19.

Peace! There is a benediction in the word! It is one of the fairest words in human speech. All that is brightest and happiest in life is associated with peace. There is a substance known as ambergris which is found floating in the ocean. Absolutely odorless itself, its use is to enrich the scent of odors. And peace has a quality like ambergris; it heightens and enriches every blessing. What is a congregation without peace; what without peace a home? It may have money, art, refinement, luxury, but if peace is wanting everything is wanting. All that wealth can give is but a mockery, all that art can furnish but a show, without the beatitude of peace. It was of peace the angels sang when Christ was born in Bethlehem. It was a message of peace that was first breathed from the lips of the risen Savior. And the sum and substance of all Gospel blessings, wrought out for sinful man by the Redeemer, is the peace of God that passes understanding. No wonder then that our Lord pronounced His blessing on the peacemakers. No wonder that the Scripture urges us to seek peace and ensue it. No wonder that this great apostle, who had known the havoc of dissension, cannot close his letter without this: "Follow after the things that make for peace."

You will notice in our text that social peace is pictured as a goal. It is a thing to be followed after. It is a thing to be lived for, to be striven for, to be followed through ill report and good report. It is the end, not the beginning, of endeavor. That is in keeping with the peculiar form which our Lord gave to His beatitude. He did not say, "Blessed are the peaceable"–He said, "Blessed are the peacemakers." Social peace was a thing that must be made. There are some blessings that we do not make. They are freely given us by God. We do not make the sunshine or the grass or the summer evening or the sea. But in all the greatest spiritual blessings, you and I are workers with the Infinite. They are bestowed, and yet we have to make them. It is so with love, so with every talent, so with the nobility of Christian character. We are saints from the hour of our electing mercy, and yet to the end, a thousand leagues from sainthood. And as it is in all these highest blessings which make life strong and beautiful and rich, so it is with peace. We do not start with social peace; in a fallen world like this we start with enmity. To the seeing eye this world is all a battlefield, and every living creature is in arms. And then there falls the blessing of the peacemaker, and we see that peace is something to be striven for; the goal, the difficult and distant goal, of the struggle and the anguish of the ages. Remember that when there is not peace at home. Remember it when there is war in the world. We have not really lost what once was ours. We have failed to achieve the infinitely difficult. Social peace is a thing we follow after. It is not the beginning but the end, the long last goal that we are making for, through Nazareth and the desert and Gethsemane.

I remark in passing that this is an end that everybody can set before himself. The Master's blessing on the peacemaker is a blessing within the reach of all. I remember a sentence in Dr. Bonar's diary to this effect. "God has not called me," he writes, "as He calls Dr. Chalmers, to do great service for Him: He calls me to walk three or four miles today to be a peacemaker in a disunited family." My Christian friend, God may not have called you to follow the things that make for power. And only rarely amid life's multitudes does He call men to follow the things that make for fame. But there is nobody, whether old or young, whether mother or business man or child, but is called to follow the things that make for peace. For social peace, one of the choicest blessings, can be ruined by the most trifling of causes. It is like a delicate and jeweled watch that is disordered by a single hair. A word will do it, or a fit of temper, or a suspicion, or the discovery of falsehood—how great a matter a little fire kindleth! You may destroy the lute by breaking it in two, and there are hearts and homes that lose their peace that way. But a little crack within the lute makes all the music mute. And it is just because the things that make for peace lie so largely among life's common elements that this is a calling that everyone can share.

One of the first things that makes for social peace is a watchful and a charitable silence. No man or woman can ever be a peacemaker who has not learned to put a bridle on his lips. Every student of Christ must have observed the tremendous emphasis He puts on words. Of every idle word, He tells us, in the day of judgment we are to give account. And if you want to understand aright the passion and the depth of that, you will remember the beatitude, "Blessed are the peacemakers." Think of the infinite harm that can be wrought by a malicious or a thoughtless tongue; think of the countless hearts it lacerates; think of the happy friendships which it chills. And sometimes there is not even malice in it—only the foolish desire to be speaking, for evil is wrought by want of thought as well as want of heart. There is no more difficult task in life than to repeat exactly what someone else has said. Alter the playful tone, you alter everything. Subtract the smile, and you subtract the spirit. And yet how often do we all repeat things that are almost incapable of repetition and so give pain that never was intended. You can say good-bye in such a tone that it is a dismissal of contempt. And yet how seldom do we think of tone, of voice, of eye, of smile, of personality when we pass on the word which we have heard. There are times that call for all outspokenness. No man ever denounced like Christ. "Woe unto you, scribes and Pharisees." "Go, tell that fox." All that I know, and yet the fact remains that as we move along life's common ways, one of the mightiest things that makes for social peace is a wise and charitable silence. Not to believe everything we hear, not to repeat everything we hear, or else believing it to bury it unless we are called by conscience to proclaim it, that is a thing that makes for social peace, a thing within our power today, and it may be along that silent road lies our "Blessed are the peacemakers."

Another thing that makes for social peace is the possession of a happy conscience. Conscience not only makes cowards of us all: it overshadows our society. He who walks with an uneasy conscience because he is unworthy or unfaithful is an unfailing source of social upheaval. I need not remind you how the Gospel insists upon wholeheartedness. Whatsoever thy hand findeth to do, it says, do it with all thy might. And it insists on this not only because all honest labor makes the doer happy, but because—so interwoven are our lives—it brings happiness and peace to others too. Here is a man, for instance, who comes home at evening after a day of honest, manly toil. He has done his work, faced his difficulties, resisted temptation when it met him. Such a man, when evening falls, not only enjoys serenity himself; he also spreads serenity around him. He feels a kinship with the children's merriment. There is that *in* him which augments the merriment. His wife has been toiling patiently all day—there is nothing to reproach him there. His happy conscience is a source of peace not only to himself, but to everyone with whom he comes in contact. Contrast with him another man who has squandered the precious hours of the day, who has not faced his work as a man should, who has yielded weakly to solicitings: such a man when he goes home at evening is not only unhappy in himself, he is also a source of unhappiness to others. He is almost certain to be irritable. He is very likely to be quarrelsome. On bad terms with himself, he is ready to be on bad terms with everybody. Like those widening ripples on the lake which the stone makes when cast into its stillness are the outward goings of the heart. None is so ready to foment a quarrel as he who has a quarrel with his conscience. None is so angry with the innocent as the man who is angry with himself. Half of those brutalities which shock us when the drunken ruffian beats his wife are but the outward sign of that dumb rage which the poor wretch feels against himself.

It therefore needs to be very clearly said, and it needs to be constantly remembered, that one of the things that makes for social peace is the possession of a happy conscience. Happy people are very rarely quarrelsome. They are not often abettors of turmoil. How often have I seen some newborn happiness act like magic on a bitter tongue. And there is no happiness in life more real, none that is more deserving of the name, than that of the task that is well done, of the cross that is well borne. Let any man so live his life then, and he shall not miss the blessing of the peacemaker. He may never know it. He may never dream of it. He may never interfere in any quarrel. Yet all the time in that brave way of his, he may be spreading the sunshine as he goes, and that is one of the things that makes for peace.

Then there is another thing that makes for social peace on a larger and a grander scale. It is righteousness. It is the passion, the long endeavor, on the part of the individual or the nation, to be unfalteringly true to what is right. Very often to a hasty judgment it is the opposite that seems the truth. There is not one of us here but has been tempted to secure peace at the expense of righteousness, and many succumb to that temptation. There is indeed one temperament which is peculiarly exposed to that temptation—not the temperament of the hero, but that of many most delightful people—the temperament that loves all human kindliness—is courteous, deferential, genial—that shrinks from struggle and from contradiction. To such a temperament, a text like ours may come as a positive temptation. It is tempted to follow the things that make for peace at the expense of things more glorious than peace. Yet is it not alone in being tempted so. When a child is tempted to a lie rather than confess and bear its punishment, when a mother is tempted to wink at disobedience rather than have the sorrow of chastising, when a man dishonors his convictions, when a nation takes refuge in neutrality, then righteousness and peace seem far apart. My Christian friend, they are not far apart. They are eternally, inextricably one. Freedom from pain and struggle is not peace. Freedom from struggle may be the devil's peace. That momentary calm, that short escaping, that lull that is possible where truth is forfeited, is but a travesty of peace as we have learned it from the lips of Christ. Do you think that child knows anything of peace that has secured exemption by a lie? Do you think that mother knows anything of peace who has secured it by being false to duty? Do you think that land knows anything of peace that has taken refuge in a base neutrality when the voice of the feeble which is the voice of Christ is crying out for protection in its ears? That is not peace. That is ignoble quiet. That is the stillness which betokens death. That is not the peace of Him who followed it through Gethsemane and Calvary. He knew—He had a righteousness, and that neither for man or nation is there peace unless it be broad-based on that. My Christian friend, lay it to your heart that cowardice can never make for peace, neither can lying, whether in man or nation, neither can neutrality. Such peace is but the quivering of moonlight. Such peace is but a sleep and a forgetting. Such peace is a dream from which a man awakes to find he has lost the angels and the stars.

I close by suggesting in a word—I should be false to my calling if I omitted it—I close by suggesting that there is one thing more that contributes most wonderfully to social peace. It is the experience of being reconciled to God. And so pervasive is the eternal spirit, so really does it determine everything, that so long as man is out of touch with God he cannot be in perfect touch with anything. Then through the Spirit of the Lord Jesus Christ, a man is reconciled to God. All the love that has been waiting for him flows in a tide into his life. And then at last, in harmony with God, he feels himself in harmony with everything, with bird and beast, with sunset and with hill, with every brother-man and sister-woman. There is no experience in life that makes for peace so steadily as that. Drawn into loving unity with God, we are drawn to a new brotherhood with everybody. That is how our Savior is our Peace. That is how He, Himself, has been the peacemaker. And that is how every man who really knows Him follows after the things that make for peace.

Joy and Peace in Believing

Now the God of hope fill you with all joy and peace in believing—
Rom. 15:13.

It is a question we ought to ask ourselves, in our quiet hours of meditation, whether we really know the joy and peace which are the benediction of our text. It is a great thing to be resigned amid the various buffetings of life. Resignation is better than rebellion. But resignation, however good it is, is not peculiarly a Christian virtue; it marks the stoic rather than the Christian. The Christian attitude towards the ills of life is something more triumphant than acceptance. It has an exultant note that resignation lacks. It is acceptance with a song in it. It is such a reaction to experience as suggests the certainty of victory—the victory that overcomes the world. It is a searching question for us all, then, whether we truly know this joy and peace. Does it characterize our spiritual life? It is evident in our discipleship? And that not only on the Lord's day and in the sanctuary, but in our routine dealings with the world.

Contrast, for instance, joy and peace in believing with joy and peace in working. Many who read this are happily familiar with joy and peace in working. It is true that work may be very uncongenial; there are those who hate the work they are engaged in. There are seasons, too, for many of us, when our strength may be unequal to the task. But speaking generally, what a good deal of joy and peace flow into the lives of men and women in prosecuting their appointed task. Again, think of joy and peace in loving; how evident is that in many a home. What a peaceful and happy place a home becomes when love

138

lies at the basis of it all. The splendid attitude of children, their glad-ness that makes others glad, spring not only from the heart of child-hood, but from the love that encircle them at home. Now Paul does not speak of joy and peace in working, nor does he speak of joy and peace in loving. His theme here is different from these: it is joy and peace in believing. And the question is, do we, who know these other things, know *this* in our experience of life and amid the jangling of our days.

Think for a moment of the men and women to whom St. Paul orig-inally wrote these words. Their cares and sorrows were just as real to them as our cares and sorrows are to us. They were called to be saints, and yet they were not saints. They were very far from being saints. Some were slaves, and some were city shopkeepers, and some were mothers in undistinguished homes. Yet Paul, when he writes to them, makes no exceptions. This blessing was for everyone of them. It never occurs to him that there might be anybody incapacitated for this joy and peace. We are so apt to think that an inward state of mind like this can never be possible for *us*. We have anxieties we cannot banish; we have temperaments we cannot alter. But just as Paul never dreamed there were exceptions in the various temperaments he was addressing, so the Holy Spirit who inspired the words never dreams there are ex-ceptions now. This is for me. It is for you. It is for everybody who knows and loves the Lord. Not rebellion—not even resignation when life is hard and difficult and sorrowful—but something with the note of triumph in it, a song like that which Paul and Silas sang, a peace that the world can never give—and cannot take away.

Lest anyone should misread this inward attitude that is the peculiar possession of believers, note how here, as elsewhere in the Scripture, joy and peace are linked together. There is a joy that has no peace in it. It is feverish, tumultuous, unsettled. It is too aggressive to be the friend of rest; too wild to have any kinship with repose. Its true companion-ship is with excitement, and, like other passions, it grows by what it feeds on, ever demanding a more powerful stimulus and at last de-manding it in vain. There is a peace that has no joy in it. "They make a solitude and call it peace." It is like a dull and sluggish river moving through an uninteresting country. But the beautiful thing is that on the page of Scripture as in the experience of the trusting soul, joy and peace are linked in closest union. The Kingdom of Heaven is not meat and drink; it is righteousness and joy and peace. The fruit of the Spirit is not love and joy alone; it is love and joy and peace. And our Lord in His last great discourse, when He declares His legacy of peace, closes with the triumphant note of joy. "These things have I spoken unto you" (and He had been speaking of His peace) "that your joy might be full." Whom God hath joined together, let not man put asunder. There is a joy that has no peace in it. There is a peace that is dull and dead and joyless. But the mark of the followers of the Lord is the mystical marriage union of the two. It is joy *and* peace in believing.

And how eminently fitted is the Gospel message to sustain this fine reaction on experience. The Gospel is good news; it is the most joyful news that ever broke upon the ear of man. Sweet is the message of returning spring after the cold and dreariness of winter. Sweet is the message of the morning light after a night of restlessness or pain. But a thousand times sweeter, a thousand times more wonderful, is the message which has been ours since we were children and which will be ours when the last shadows fall. Do we believe it? That is the vital question. Do we hold to it through the shadows and the buffetings? Do we swing it like a lamp which God has lit over the darkest mile our feet have got to tread? Then, like joy and peace in working and in loving (with which we are all perfectly familiar), we shall experience with all the saints joy and peace in believing.

The God of Hope

Now the God of hope fill you with all joy and peace in believing, that ye may abound in hope, through the power of the Holy Ghost—Rom. 15:13.

In the Hebrew language, as scholars know, there are several different words for rain. From which we gather that in Hebrew life rain was something of very great importance. It is the same, though in the realm of spirit, with the names of God in the letters of St. Paul. The variety of divine names there betrays the deepest heart of the apostle. Think, for instance, of the names one lights on in this fifteenth chapter of the Romans, all of them occurring incidentally. He is the God of patience and of consolation (v. 5). I trust my readers have all found Him that. He is the God of peace (v. 33), keeping in perfect peace every one whose mind is stayed on Him. He is the God of hope (v. 13), touching with radiant hopefulness everything that He has made, from the mustard seed to the children of mankind.

Think, for instance, how beautifully evident is the hopefulness of God in nature. Our Lord was very keenly alive to that. There is much in nature one cannot understand, and no loving communion will interpret it. There is a seeming waste and cruelty in nature that often lies heavy on the heart. But just as everything is beautiful in nature that the hand of man had never tampered with, so what a glorious hopefulness she breathes! Every seed, cast into the soil, is big with hopefulness of coming harvest. Every sparrow, in the winter ivy, is hopeful of the nest and of the younglings. Every streamlet, rising in the hills and brawling over the granite in the valley, is hopeful of its union with the sea. Winter comes with iciness and misery, but in the heart of winter is the hope of spring. Spring comes tripping across the meadow, but in the heart of spring there is the hope of summer. Summer comes garlanded with beauty, but in the heart of summer is the hope of autumn when sower and reaper shall rejoice together. But a woman in travail is not a hopeless woman. Her heart is "speaking softly of a hope." The very word *natura* is the witness of language to that hopeful travail—it means something going to be born. If, then, this beautiful world of nature is the garment of God by which we see Him, if His Kingdom be in the mustard seed, and not a sparrow can fall without His knowledge, how evident it is that He in whom we trust, who has never left Himself without a witness, is *the God of hope*.

Again, how evident is this attribute in the inspired word of the New Testament. The New Testament, as Dr. Denney used to say, is the most hopeful book in the whole world. I believe that God is everywhere revealed—in every flower in the crannied wall. But I do not believe that He is everywhere *equally* revealed anymore than I believe it of myself. There are things I do that show my character far more fully than certain other things—and God has made me in His image. I see Him in the sparrow and the mustard seed; I see Him in the lilies of the field; but I see more of Him, far more of Him, in the inspired word of the New Testament. And the fine thing to remember is just this, that the New Testament is not a hopeless book. Hope surges in it. Its note is that of victory. There steals on the ear in it the distant triumph song. It closes with the Book of Revelation where the Lamb is upon the throne. And if *this* be the expression of God's being far more fully than anything in nature, how sure we may be that He is *the God of Hope*.

And then, lastly, we turn to our Lord and Savior. Is not He the most magnificent of optimists? Hope burned in Him (as Lord Morley said of Cromwell) when it had gone out in everybody else. There is an optimism based on ignorance: not such was the good hope of Christ. With an eye that sin had never dulled, He looked in the face all that was dark and terrible. There is an optimism based on moral laxity: not such was the good hope of Christ. He hated sin, although he loved the sinner. Knowing the worst, hating what was evil, treated by men in the most shameful way, Christ was gloriously and sublimely hopeful till death was swallowed up in victory; hopeful for the weakest of us, hopeful for the very worst, hopeful for the future of the world. Now call to mind the word He spake: *"He that hath seen me, hath seen the Father."* He that hath seen into that heart of hopefulness hath seen into the heart of the Eternal. Once a man has won that vision though there are many problems that may vex him still, he never can doubt again, through all his years, the amazing hopefulness of God.

The Limits of Liberty

All things are lawful unto me, but all things are not expedient—1 Cor. 6:12.

It has been said by someone, I forget by whom, that a *Christian has no rights, he has only duties.* That is a very striking statement, and seems to sound the note of the heroic. Now in a loose and popular way, there may be some justification for that statement. It may have served its purpose as a word of warning to men who were always insisting on their rights. But for all that it should never have been spoken whatever purposes it may have served, for it is *utterly antagonistic to the spirit of the Gospel of our Lord.* If there is one thing Paul insists on more than another, it is *the rights of the believer in Christ Jesus.* He argues with a passionate intensity for the liberties of every Christian. Never is his style so animated, never so bold and luminous his thought, as when he fights the battle for his converts of their liberties in Jesus Christ. He knew that everything depended upon it, that the very life of the church depended on it. On it depended whether the church of Christ was to stand out or to be lost in Judaism. And so, sometimes by appeal to the Old Testament and always on the broad ground of grace, he appeals to his hearers to stand fast in the liberty wherewith Christ had made them free.

But then, following hard on this insistence and in some measure just because of it, we soon come to detect in the apostle the presence and pressure of another thought. Just as you have right through the Old Testament tremendous insistence on the awfulness of God, and then when God has been safeguarded so, we have the revelation of Christ that God is love. So in Paul you have first the splendid doctrine of the inalienable liberties of every Christian, and then the limitation of these liberties. So far from it being the case that a Christian has no rights, there is no man with rights so incontestable. They are to be cherished at whatever cost and in the teeth of angriest opposition. But then, having insisted upon that with all the emphasis of inspiration, Paul, with his wonderful knowledge of the heart, flashes light on the dangers of that liberty. All things are lawful to me, but all are not expedient. *A Christian is one who is willing to forego. He uses his liberties as not abusing them; he recognizes limits in their exercise.* And it is on these limits of our Christian liberty—limits, mark you, always self-imposed—that I wish to speak. Such limits, as I understand my Testament, are determined by one or other of three interests.

There is a passage in one of the Epistles which says, "Touch not; taste not; handle not." I know no passage in the Scripture that is oftener misunderstood than that one. It has been quoted as inspired direction to those who were yielding to temptation. It has been used as the motto of abstinence societies, as though it embodied apostolic counsel. Whereas as a matter of fact, if you read the passage carefully, you will find that the very opposite is true: these are the words of Paul's antagonists, and against their view of life he is in arms. *The earth is the Lord's, and the fullness thereof*—that is the ringing note of the apostle. There is nothing in it common or unclean: everything is to be received with thanksgiving. But then, having uttered that grand truth which we must never forfeit for any popular clamor, Paul proceeds to limit it in exercise by the consideration of his immortal well-being. *All things are lawful to me, says the apostle, but I will not be brought under the power of any. I will not let anything usurp dominion over this temple of the Holy Ghost.* In other words, this brave and thoughtful man who insisted so passionately on his rights in Christ deliberately limited these rights in the interest of his individual safety. I know few sentences in literature more touching than the closing sentence of the ninth chapter here. "I keep under my body . . . ," says the apostle, "lest . . . I myself should be a castaway." I keep under my body in our version, but the word in the original is far more graphic. It is a word borrowed from the prize ring: it means, *I beat my body black and blue.* Now whatever Paul was, he was no ascetic and certainly he never preached asceticism. I can imagine the scorn he would have poured on the wild asceticism of the Middle

Ages. Yet here, lest he should be a castaway, lest he should be rejected at the end, deliberately and in sternest fashion, he limited his great liberty in Christ. Think of it—this great apostle haunted with fears of being cast away: never quite sure of himself—never quite certain that he might not be tripped some day and overthrown! It seems incredible and yet to Paul it was so far from being incredible that he crushed his body down in terror of it. "Stand fast, therefore," he says to the Galatians, "in the liberty with which Christ hath made us free." Cherish as a principle that is inestimable the fullness of your liberties in Christ. But then remember that you are only human and weak and very liable to fall, and use your liberty as not abusing it.

Now as that was the apostle's practice, so it ought to be the practice of all Christians. It is along these lines that in Christ Jesus we ought to seek to regulate our lives. *There are many who would exalt into a principle what may be only a salutary safeguard.* There are many on the other hand who in the name of liberty pave their way to misery and ruin. But he who is wise—he who is taught of God—will be careful to avoid these *two extremes,* for neither of them has the mind of Christ. *On the one hand, he will assert his liberty. He will say all things are lawful unto me.* He will give no place in the charter of his rights to the touch not and the taste not and the handle not. But then recalling the awful possibility that in his voyage he should be cast away, *he will impose upon himself stern limitations.* He will remember how the best have fallen and fallen tragically in unexpected ways: he will remember that life is full of peril and that for the surest foot the ground is slippery; and so in the interests of individual safety—and we cannot afford to trifle with our safety—he will say all things are lawful unto me, but all things are not expedient.

And may I say in passing that such action is in full accord with the teaching of our Lord. I say it because there are so many nowadays who want to distinguish between Paul and Jesus. Now it is true that *through the life of Christ there breathes the spirit of most glorious freedom.* Think of His teaching on the Sabbath for example; think of Him at the marriage feast at Cana. There is a geniality, if I may put it so—a human breadth in His teaching and example which has no better witness than just this, that it made every Pharisee indignant. All that is gloriously true, yet remember that this is also true. Never was there a teacher sent from God who could be so stern and severe as Jesus Christ. It was not the ardent

146

and impetuous Paul—*it was the gentle and genial Savior who said,* "If thy right hand offend thee, cut it off, if thy right eye offend thee, pluck it out." Is there anything radically bad in the right hand? It is the organ that I stretch out in prayer. Is there anything radically evil in the eye? God has made it, and what He made is good. And yet according to the word of Jesus, the hour may come when *for a man's own safety it were wise to forfeit the gladness of the eye and cut away the glory of the hand. Mark you, if thy right hand offend thee—there is no talk of anybody else.* It is in the interests of a man's own life that he must use this drastic limitation. And so you see Paul is but echoing what he had learned from his Redeemer when he says, in the interests of personal safety, all things are lawful but all are not expedient.

The classical instance of this Christian attitude is found in this first Epistle to the Corinthians. It is so interesting and so significant that you will bear with me if I give it in detail. The apostle pictures a Corinthian Christian invited to dinner by a friend. That friend is a heathen man and in comparatively humble circumstances. Now in the food that was set upon the table it was almost certain there would be temple meat: meat, that is, of beasts that had been sacrificed and then sold to the market by the priests. And the difficulty for the Christian guest was this, was he at liberty to eat that meat? If it had been offered to idols in the temple, would not eating it mean fellowship with idols? It was about that difficulty that they wrote to Paul, and his answer is supremely noble. Go to your dinner, he says, and ask no questions. Eat what is set before you and be thankful. If you start worrying about things like *that,* you will do conscience irreparable mischief. *The earth is the Lord's, and the fullness thereof.*

But now suppose that next to that Christian brother there is sitting another and a weaker Christian. He is struggling to be true to Christ, but the pull of the old life is terrible. And he turns to his stronger brother by his side, and he says to him anxiously, "That is temple meat." The question was (and it was a daily question) what was the stronger brother to do then? If he partook, his neighbor might partake, and that might be opening the gate to ruin. He would go home beset by the dark sense that he was again in fellowship with devils. But, on the other hand, if he did *not* partake out of consideration for that weaker conscience, what became of his liberty in Christ? So they wrote to Paul about that also, and I think you know how he replied. As a Christian man, he said, you are duty-bound to consider the weakness of your brother. Knit into fellowship by Jesus Christ, called to the hearing of each other's burdens, God forbid that you should use your liberty to offend one of these little ones. Mark you, there is no word of personal safety now. The stronger brother was perfectly secure. For him an idol was nothing in the world, and he could eat and drink with a good conscience. The only question was, how would his action affect the tempted and weak Christian by his side, and Paul says *that* is to be determinative. It might be very annoying to be hampered so. One might regard his neighbor as a nuisance. It was hard that a man should not enjoy himself because he had a weakling looking on. And it is then that Paul, in that great way of his, lifts up the matter into such an atmosphere that the man who is tempted to chafe at his restrictions bows his head in shame. Have you forgotten, says the apostle, that for that weak brother Jesus died? Have you forgotten that Christ endured for him the agony and the anguish of the Cross? Compared with *that,* how infinitely little is any sacrifice that you are called to make in the restriction of your Christian liberty.

And so we are taught this second lesson about the limits of our Christian rights. We are bound to limit them not only for our own sakes; we are bound to limit them for our brother's sake. No man liveth to himself, and no man dieth to himself. If we believe in the Fatherhood of God, then we believe in the brotherhood of man. And only he has the mind of Christ to whom that thought of brotherhood is regulative, not only in the exercise of power but also in the exercise of liberty. There are many things in life that are quite lawful and on whose lawfulness we must insist. There are things that you and I could practice safely, and be all the happier for our practice of them. But if to our brother they be fraught with peril and if they make it harder for him to do what is right, then for our brother's sake, if we are Christians, we are called to the limitation of our liberty. Mark you, there is no room in Christianity for the over-scrupulous and worrying conscience. We are in Christ, and the Son hath made us free, and we are never to lose the gladness of that freedom. All that the Scripture insists upon is this, that we are to use it in the bonds of love and never to hesitate to limit it if so doing we can help a brother. You say that is hard? I grant you it is hard. The Gospel admits that it is hard. It may be irritating when we want to *live* to have to consider the weak brother so. And then, flashing upon us in its glory, there comes the thought that Christ has died for him—and after that we do not find it hard. Once realize the sacrifice of Christ and all our little denials are as nothing. He gave His life up for that weaker brother, and shall not we give up our liberty? It is thus that we come to have fellowship with Him and to know Him better as we take our journey, for *fellowship grows not alone but by what we get: it grows also by what we yield.*

In the ninth chapter of this epistle we have a great instance of that motive. Paul has been arguing with overwhelming power for the right of the preachers of the Word to receive payment. He appeals to Scripture—he argues by analogy—he urges the great plea of common sense. He gives a demonstration irrefutable of the right of Gospel preachers to be paid. And then with one of those swift turns of his which help us to know him and to love him, he says, but I—I have not used this right lest I should hinder the Gospel of Christ. There is an instance also in the life of Jesus which will help you to understand my meaning. It is when He was asked to pay the temple tax. It is only Matthew who narrates that incident, and it is natural that he should tell it for Matthew had been a tax-gatherer himself once and would be interested in taxes all his life. Well, when Jesus heard of the demand, you remember what he said to Peter? What thinkest thou, Simon, of whom do the kings of the earth take custom or tribute—of their own children or strangers? Peter said unto him, Of strangers; and Jesus answered, Then are the children free. What He meant was that He was free, for the temple was His Father's house. He could have claimed exemption as a right. It was part of the liberty of sonship. But then had He insisted on His rights, is it not easy to see what would have happened? Jesus saw in an instant what would happen. He had proclaimed the sanctity of law: now men would say He was a law-breaker. He had urged obedience to Moses' representatives: now He would be openly defying them. And so, not with His eye upon His own but with His eye on the unbelieving world, the tax was paid lest they should be offended. In other words, Christ limited His liberty in the supreme interests of the Gospel. Deliberately did He forego His rights when to assert them might have been a stumbling block. He was come to seek and save the lost, and though the lost might hate Him and revile Him, He would do nothing howsoever lawful that might make them harder to be won.

As it was with Jesus, so must it be with you and me. If we are members of the body of Christ then we have a duty to the world. It is not part of a believer's calling to consult the *opinion* of the world. A man may sometimes bear the greatest resemblance to his Lord when his action is laughed at by the worldly wise. All we are taught is that *in our use of freedom we must remember those who are without, and how, by what we allow ourselves in Christ, they are like to be affected towards the Gospel.* If the kind of life that we are living makes it less easy to believe in Christ; if our behavior whether at work or play is silently hardening anybody's heart, then, though everything we do is justified and well within the boundaries of our liberties, in the eyes of Jesus there is something wrong. All things are lawful, but all are not expedient, sometimes in the interests of our safety. All things are lawful, but all are not expedient, sometimes in the interests of our brother. All things are lawful, but all are not expedient, because around us there is a Christless world and men with their poor blind eyes are judging Christ by what they see in His professing people.

The Grace of Happy-Heartedness

I would have you without carefulness—1 Cor. 7:32.
Cast thy burden upon the Lord—Ps. 55:22.

There are few graces which the world admires so much as the grace of a cheerful heart. There is a certain perennial attraction in men and women who bear their burdens well. When we see a face all lined with care it often touches the chord of pity in us. We are moved to compassion when it flashes on us what a story is engraven there. But the face that really helps us on our journey is seldom the face of battle and of agony; it is the face which has its sunshine still. None of us is enamored by a frown. All of us are attracted by a smile. We recognize by an unerring instinct that in happy-heartedness there is a kind of victory. And so we love it as we love the sunshine or the song of the birds upon the summer morning. It takes its place with these good gifts of God.

Children are possessors of this sunny attribute. That is one reason why the presence of children is such a perpetual solace and so refreshing. Children are far from being little angels as every father and every mother knows. They can be cruel and intensely selfish and amazingly and unblushingly untruthful. Yet when the worst is said of them that can be said, there yet remains in them this touch of heaven which is a greater blessing to the world than all the modern methods of communication. They cry, and then in the passing of an hour the heart that was inconsolable is healed. They scowl (and they are not pretty when they scowl), but so far as I know them they never bear any malice. They bully in the most shocking fashion, when you and I happen to be absent, but if they bully they almost never brood. "I would have you without carefulness"—that is how the great apostle puts it. He was one of these men whose interests were too vast to allow him time for watching little people. But Christ, whose interests were far vaster, somehow or other always had time for that, and so He puts it, *not* "I would have you without carefulness," but "except ye become as little children."

Of course we must distinguish happy-heartedness from that poor counterfeit we call frivolity. A child may be absolutely irresponsible, but a child is never frivolous. No one is so swiftly touched to wonder. No one is so deeply moved with awe. When our children laugh at what to us is sacred, it simply means that they do not understand. The things that are wonderful and great in their eyes are not at all what we consider so, and note, you never find them mocking at what is wonderful and great to *them*. Now that is the very hallmark of frivolity. It recognizes what is great and jests at it. It is not an intellectual inability; it is much more truly a moral inability. Some of the most frivolous people I have known had plenty of brains and were as sharp as needles; it was their heart and not their brain which was contemptible. The great instance of frivolity in Scripture is that of the men who refused the invitation. They were by no means intellectual fools, these men. They could do a bit of work and do it admirably. But when this moment came they all made light of it—they took it as a joke though it was kingly—they lost the opportunity of their lives because of their old habit of belittling. Different by all the world from that is the sweet genius of happy-heartedness. It is as swift to recognize the best as is frivolity to have a laugh at it. Indeed so far as my experience goes, frivolous people are commonly unhappy and are very often trying to forget something which is akin to tragedy.

Now we are all apt to think that such a happy disposition is just temperamental. We are apt to think it is just born with people, and of course in a measure that is true. There are those with a perfect genius for the sunshine, and those with a perfect genius for the shadow. There are those who will carry a burden in a happy way without the slightest aid from any faith, and you, who wrestle in prayer about the thing, are bowed with it to the very ground. And not only is it temperamental. We might go further and say that it is racial. Broadly speaking, as we survey the world, we find it to be a national characteristic. For the Irish have it and the Scots have not; and the southern peoples and not the northern peoples; and the Kaffir boy out in South Africa will go singing and laughing over his work all day while his Dutch master, for all his Bible reading, will have a face as long as his prayers.

But there is one thing in the Bible I have often noticed. I wonder if it has occurred to you? It is how often it classes with virtues to be won what we have reckoned to be gifts of nature. The Bible is always true to the great facts. It never diminishes nor distorts anything. It recognizes in the most liberal way the infinite divergencies of nature. And yet I am often struck by how often it takes these natural endowments and says to you of what you do *not* have—"that is a virtue to be won." Think of courage—do not we regard that as a gift? Don't we know that certain men are born courageous? Do you think every boy could say what Nelson said: "Fear, mother—what is fear? I never saw it"? And yet this courage, which with perfect justice we are in the way of regarding as temperamental, is viewed in Scripture as something to be won. Take joy. Are we the masters of our joy? Is not the capacity for joy inherent? Are there not those who gravitate to joy as there are others who gravitate to gloom? And yet our Savior says to His disciples, "These things have I spoken to you, that in me ye might have joy." And the fruit of the spirit is love and joy and peace.

Well now, as it is with these, so I take it as with happy-heartedness. In the eyes of God and in the light of Scripture it is a shining virtue to be won. It may be easier for some than others just because of the nature God has given. But remember we do not win our best when we have won our most congenial virtues. A happy disposition is possible for all—that is what I want to urge tonight—and the unfailing secret of it lies in the casting of the burden on the Lord. It does not matter what the burden be. Burdens are just as various as blessings. They may be secret, or they may be public. They may be real, or they may be imaginary. But once a man has learned this deepest lesson that God is with him and will see him through, I say to the weariest and most desponding soul that happy-heartedness is in his grasp. Many of the heaviest burdens men can bear have to be borne where eyes can never pierce. Many of the heaviest burdens men can bear fall on them through the relationships of life. It matters not. There can be no exceptions in the magnificent impartiality of God. *Cast thy burden on the Lord.*

Now I want you to notice—it is very important—the words in which our text is couched. It is "cast thy burden *on the Lord*"; it is not "cast thy burden anywhere." I think there is nothing poorer or more cowardly than just the desire to be rid of burdens. It is always the mark of meanness in a character and the sorry witness of a contracting soul. For life grows richer by what we have to bear, and sympathies grow tenderer and broader, and the world expands into a richer place through things which we once thought would make us poorer. They say that the Indian by putting his ear to the ground can hear far off the galloping of horses. Erect, there is not a sound upon the breeze. Prone on the earth, he hears the distant trampling. And I dare say there are some here tonight who lived and moved upon a silent prairie until somehow they were bowed into the dust. The Bible never urges any man recklessly to cast his cares away. As soon would it urge the captain of a ship to cast out his ballast when he was clear of port. Knowing the preciousness of what is heavy, it bids us summon to our aid the power of God, and it is *that* which makes all the difference in the world. Now we know we are in the hands of One who providently caters to the sparrow. Now we know that on the line of duty we shall have strength for all that must be done. Now we can laugh with the children in the thick of it, and have our sunshine even in December, for God is with us and His name is wonderful and underneath are the everlasting arms.

In closing I have one thing more to say—one thing I never think of without shame. It is how much easier this secret is for us than it ever could have been for David. "Cast thy burden on the Lord," he wrote—and of course he had first done it for himself. Now tell me, what was that Lord to David—that Lord into whose keeping he committed everything? He was the King eternal and invisible, and clouds and darkness were around His throne, and men looked to the left hand and He was not there, and to the right and they could not find Him. Was not the faith of these old Jews magnificent? Could you have trusted in such a God as that? Could you have believed that the infinite Creator would open His arms and take your burden in? It might have been easy for a Greek to do it for he believed in the divinity of man, but how a Jew rose to a faith like that is to me as wonderful as any miracle.

But do you see how everything is changed now? We have *Christ* and that makes all the difference. For do you remember how, when Christ was here, men came and cast their burdens upon Him? Everyone did it, and did it as by instinct—it did not matter what the burden was—and "he that hath seen me hath seen the Father." Run through the gamut of our human burdens, and tell me if there were any that they failed to bring. They brought their sicknesses and they brought their fears. They brought their children and they brought themselves. And the strange thing is that though Christ was angry sometimes, and His eyes flashed in righteous indignation, not in a single instance do you find Him angry because anyone cast a burden upon Him.

My brother and sister, if your faith is to be real, shall I tell you what you must always do? You must always carry into your thought of God what you have learned and seen of Jesus Christ. "He that hath seen me hath seen the Father:" He is the express image of His person. You must carry up into your thought of God all the revelation of His Son. And I tell you that when you once do that the Fatherhood of God becomes so wonderful that even you, with your weak and trembling faith, are able to cast your burden upon Him. It took a hero to achieve it once. The weakest woman can achieve it now. It was once the act of a sublime enthusiasm. It is now within the reach of everyone of you. So sure are we in Christ of God's deep sympathy and of His care for us and of His love, that there is not a man or woman here who may not know the strength of happy-heartedness. Therefore I charge you in the name of Christ that you are not to let that burden weigh you down. I charge you to remember that you sin if you live in gloom and miserable wretchedness. Never frivolous, but always reverent—happy-hearted just because *He* knows—I know no better way in this strange world of glorifying the Father and the Son.

The Wonder of That Night

The same night in which he was betrayed—1 Cor. 11:23.

Attention has been directed in these days of ours to what is called the method of suggestion. The power of suggestion. The power of suggestion to influence thought and conduct is one of the great themes of educational science. We are taught that beneath our consciousness there is a whole world within each of us that lies asleep, and that it depends on the suggestive touch whether it will awaken to evil or to good. Now there can be little question that in throwing in this clause, Paul is acting on the method of suggestion. He is not just stating an historic fact nor indicating a bare point of time. He is conveying to the Corinthian church by the suggestion of the betrayal-night a veiled and delicate rebuke.

Recall the circumstances of that church at Corinth. It was in a sad and pitiable state. It was rent with such unseemly factions that any one but Paul would have despaired of it. A church is always in the most deadly peril when its divisions are felt at the Lord's Table. It is bad enough when they interfere with service; it is far worse when they invade the ordinance. Yet at Corinth that was what had happened, and brotherly love had vanished from the ordinance and pride and selfishness and disregard of decency had reared their heads at the communion table. It was to such a church that Paul was writing when he said, *"On that night in which he was betrayed."* Let them but think of that, in all the pathos of it, and it would shame them into a better spirit. How could any of them be proud again, or drunken or scornful of the poor, when they remembered that their feast was instituted in the infinite

156

sorrow of betrayal-night. In other words, Paul flung this clause in to quicken and intensify right feeling. It was not an item of information merely; it was a call to worthier communicating.

One of the great features of the Last Supper was the prayer of thanksgiving which Jesus offered. It had its place, no less than the breaking of the bread, in the revelation which Paul had had from Christ. What was included in that thanksgiving is one of the things which God has hidden from us. We know from the Gospels that the bread and wine were blessed, but no one imagines that *that* was all. Clearly, there was such an outpouring of the heart, such adoration of the Heavenly Father, that none of the little band in that upper room ever forgot it to his dying day. John carried the thought of it to Ephesus. Peter recurred to it in distant Babylon. It had moved them to a depth of awe and wonder that was vivid to their last hour of ministry. Whenever they met to break the bread again on distant shores and after the lapse of years, swift as an arrow-flight their hearts went back to the wonderful thanksgiving of Jesus.

So powerfully has that been impressed upon the church that thanksgiving has always distinguished the Lord's Table. In every fellowship and throughout all the ages one great mark of the Communion Service is gratitude. One of the oldest names for the feast is eucharist, and eucharist is the Greek for thanksgiving. One of the oldest traditions of the Table is that the poor should be remembered at it. And all this thankfulness expressed in name and offertory is not only the witness of our debt to God, it is the witness also of the depth of feeling that was stirred by the thanksgiving of Jesus. It is that which is written out in after ages. It is that which is testified to in every ordinance. Every time we meet to break the bread, we touch on the wonder of the upper room. We touch on the awe that filled the little company, as with the filling of the Holy Ghost, when they listened with rapt hearts and straining ears to the thanksgiving of their Master and their Lord.

Now what was it that made that thanksgiving so wonderful? Well, that is a question we cannot fully answer. It may be that even if you and I had been there we could not have explained why we were moved so. But this is certain, that as the days went on and the disciples looked back upon it all, the thanksgiving grew doubly wonderful to them because of the hour in which it had been spoken. On that night in which he was being betrayed—it was on *that* night our Lord broke into thanks. Think of it, in such an hour as that, no room for anything but an adoring gratitude! No wonder Peter never could forget it—no wonder John never could forget it—they never could forget that joy in God in the tense agony of the betrayal-night. Had Christ been looking forward to triumph the next day they might more easily have comprehended it. Had He been ringed about with perfect loyalty—they could have understood it then. But on that night on which He was betrayed—that *then*, in such an hour, Christ should adore, was something that grew and deepened in its mystery the more they brooded on it in the years.

There is nothing more notable in the memorial supper than the perfect confidence of Jesus in the future. No trace of doubt can be detected in Him—no slightest misgiving seems to have crossed His heart—as He looked away from His own little company down through the ages that were yet to be. Like all great moments in our earthly life, the Lord's Supper has a twofold reference. It reaches back into by gone days; it stretches forward to the untrodden future. And one of the singular things about our Lord which has attracted the eyes of every age is that at the Table, looking forward, He was possessed with a quiet and perfect confidence. "This do in remembrance of me,"—then He was to be loyally and lovingly remembered. "Ye do show the Lord's death until he come,"—then His memory was to last while the world lasted. In loving hearts right through the ages, on and on till the last trumpet sounded, Christ never doubted that His Name would live in warm and powerful memorial. Had He looked with quiet confidence across the *past*, it would not have arrested us so much. For all the past had been leading up to Him, and He had perfectly fulfilled the will of God. But that with equal confidence, unsullied and serene, He should have anticipated all coming time is something that has always stirred the church.

Of course it is possible to minimize this thought as it is possible to belittle everything about Christ. We are told that He was thinking only of His own here, and that His coming was expected in a year or two. There was no vision of the coming centuries—no thought of you and me on that evening—it was a word spoken to the disciples only till in a dozen years or so their Lord should come again. Of course there is much to be said for that view, or thinking men would never have advanced it. But deeper than any arguments in favor of it is its injustice to the *spirit* of the scene. And once we have grasped the spirit of the scene and turn to the life of Christ for confirmation of it, we see that it is something more than sentiment which finds the centuries in the heart of Jesus here. We learn from some of His most familiar parables how slowly and gradually the kingdom was to come. It could no more be hurried on than one could hasten the growing of the mustard seed. We learn, too, that Jesus had an eye which ranged away beyond the bounds of Israel: "Go ye into all the world and preach the gospel to every creature." It is that far-ranging and large spirit which you must carry into the upper room. An hour of high intensity like this was certain to be an hour of vision. If ever Christ saw imperially and magnificently, and we know from other sources that He did, would it not be on the eve before that day which was to close His earthly ministry by death? I believe, then, that in the upper room Jesus had an eye for all the ages. I believe that He was looking down the centuries to the table which is spread for you and me. And the singular thing is that with a range like that over the illimitable fields of time, Christ should have shown such quiet and perfect confidence.

It is that wonder which is deepened as we recall the season when it was exhibited. Do we not feel afresh the marvel of such confidence *on that night in which He was betrayed?* *Now* it was evident beyond dispute what was moving in the heart of Judas. Now at last came leaping to the surface the treachery that had been brooded on in secret. And if this was the issue of the years of fellowship–this unutterable malice of today– was it likely there would be a bright tomorrow? Christ had spared no pains on His betrayer. He had lavished His love upon him constantly. He had done everything to woo and win him, and every effort He had made was baffled. And it was *then,* in such a bitter hour, when He well might have lost His faith in human loyalty, that He looked forward with confidence unquenched to the loyal remembrance of the ages. Christ knew in the quiet of that evening what was involved in the treachery of Judas. Already He saw the shadow of the cross and heard the evil voices crying "Crucify him." Yet with so much to drive Him to despair–so much to suggest to Him that He had failed–with a heart as calm as any summer sea He looked away to the loyalty of time. "This do in remembrance of me: ye do show the Lord's death till he come." Think of it, this grand unfaltering confidence amid the despairing horrors of that night! It would have been wonderful at any time, but surely we feel afresh the wonder of it when we remember that it was exhibited on the night in which He was betrayed.

The Lord's Table is a feast of love, and yet the word *love* was never spoken at it. It is the picture of a love that is commended to us not so much in words as in deeds. In the early church they used to have a love-feast, and the love-feast was at first associated with the communion. But gradually and with growing insight the love-feast fell into disuse. Men came to feel that they did not need a love-feast to express the love that was in Christ; it was exhibited in all its height and depth in the simple ritual of the Last Supper. Here in the quiet of the upper chamber was given the pledge of a love that was unquenchable. Here there was gathered into one swift moment the yearning and the tenderness of years. Here did there flash out as in a flame of glory the love which had been striving through the past and which tomorrow, on the cross of anguish, was to be consummated and crowned in sacrifice.

Now do you not feel the wonder of that love afresh as you recall when it was pledged and sealed? That sealing would have been wonderful at any time, but on such a night as that it passeth knowledge. Had it been some Pharisee who was betraying him, we should not have marveled at it so. But it was no Pharisee—no enemy—it was His own familiar friend in whom He trusted. Yet in the very hour of His betrayal when any other heart might have grown bitter, Christ deliberately seized his opportunity to show forth and to seal His dying love. Mazzini, that great-heart of Italy, tells us something of his sad experience. He tells us how bitter he grew—how sick of soul—when the men who had followed him fell away from him. But on that night when all forsook Him there is not one trace of hardening in Christ; on the contrary, it was that hour He chose to institute the memorial of His love. Is not this the wonder of Christ's love, that right through that betrayal it survived? And the question is, have not we too betrayed Him since we last gathered at the Communion Table? God knows we have, yet shall we eat and drink because of a love that has survived *our* past—that has forgiven everything in mercy, and in mercy will not let us go.

Forewarned, Forearmed

We are not ignorant of his devices—2 Cor. 2:11.

This is a chapter of autobiography. It is one of the glimpses we get into the great human heart that everywhere throbs in these epistles. Some men's doctrine is so divorced from their life and their experience that the two seem separate spheres not to be thought of at the same moment. But it is never so with a really sincere man: and it is never so with Paul. What he believed was so bound up inextricably with what he was that he can pass from doctrine to his own history, and from his history back again to doctrine, and it all seems quiet natural. O why is life so separated, part from part! Why are there these great gulfs between our Sunday and our Monday, our brain and heart, our doctrine and our practice! All Paul's theology is useless—God may condemn us by it—unless the tides of it sweep into every creek and inlet of this so broken and mysterious shore.

Well, in this chapter of autobiography our text occurs. "We are not ignorant of his devices." Do you observe that gracious *we?* Only God's perfect gentleman would have written that. As a matter of fact, these men of Corinth were ignorant of the devices of the devil. Had they but known them, he never could have spread such havoc in the church as these two letters reveal. An uninspired man, blind to the possibilities in others, would have said *I.* But Paul wrote in the Holy Ghost and had the outlook and the hope and the magnificent prospects of the Holy Ghost for every man within him. And in the power of that, he elevates these Corinthians to his own level—some day they shall be there—and he says *we.* It is the way of Paul. It is the way of Christ. It is the way of love: expecting great things from the most ignorant man; and by the very sunshine of the expectation, starting the growth of them.

Now I want in a simple way to expound on some of these devices. "Knowledge is power," said Lord Bacon: and to know some of the subtleties of that malevolent power that fights against us is so far to be forearmed. Paul does not tell us what the devices were. But probably the devices of today are very much the same as in Paul's time. For underneath all changing years and the growing complexities of life, this heart keeps wonderfully constant; and the arts that take it and that snare it *now*, took it and snared and slew it eighteen hundred years ago. We are not ignorant of his devices—what, then, are some of these?

There is a tendency in all language to do that. Whether it springs from a very natural desire to hide the uglier sides of human life or whether it is the survival of some old pagan feeling that tried to propitiate the gods of nature by fair words, we cannot tell. But every language has been rich in what grammarians call euphemisms—those nice and delicate words that cover some offensive truth. When Prince George of Greece went over to Crete to become governor, there had been fierce rioting and bloodshed between the Muslims and Christians. And when he arrived and was received with great enthusiasm, the correspondent of the *Times* gave a very curious description of the scene. "The long rows of ruined houses, beneath which in some cases, the fire is still smoldering," he wrote, "are almost concealed by festoons and banners." It was an attempt to decorate and hide the tragedies. And language is always doing that. No man has ever loved to call the seamier side of things by its right name or to look the darker facts of life straight in the face. And from the first, language has been busy in fashioning its own festoons and banners to hide these ugly things. It is this tendency of human speech that is caught up and wrested by the devil into an engine and instrument of ill. If, in the natural shuddering at death, I shrink from saying, "My mother is dead," and say instead, "She is gone," there is no harm in that. But if by any trick of speech I veil the filthiness of sin, or if I cannot see how odious evil is because I have dubbed it with some pleasant name, I have been ignorant of his devices. Who called the world of self and pleasure the happy world? Who named the business man whose transactions border on the shady the smart man? Who said that the adulterer who is breaking his wife's heart had his little weakness? Who smiled and said the profligate was only fast? Or called the sowing of a harvest of misery for children's children the sowing of wild oats? O cease that speech! Call vile things by their vile names, and be not ignorant of his devices.

Our characters are complex products, and in every one of us strong elements and weak are strangely blended. The strongest Achilles has his defenseless heel. And the worst of us is not altogether bad, the weakest of us not altogether weak. There is something that still rings true; there is some chord that will still make some music in us. Thou hast a worst side, and generally men take thee on thy worst side. But thou hast a best side, and God takes thee on that. And Satan, transforming himself into an angel of light, assails on that side too.

The Bible has many instances of that. Who above all patriarchs and prophets was noted for his meekness? Was it not Moses? Yet it was Moses who broke the tables in a passion and failed in the grace that most distinguished him. Whom do we call the father of the faithful? Is it not Abraham? Yet the worst sin in Abraham's life sprang out of want of faith. And patient Job sinned through impatience: and the brave Peter fell through cowardice. And gentle and most tolerant St. John, in that one hour when he would have the fire on the Samaritan villagers, was like to be the most intolerant of all. And did not Christ know this? Christ's loftiest passion was for the kingdoms of the world that He might bring them into obedience to God. And it was there that the Prince of Darkness struck at him: "All these things will I give thee if thou wilt fall down and worship me."

O friend, remember that. Where thou art strongest, watch! Where thou art best and bravest, be on thy guard! The choicest gifts that God has dowered you with may be your snare, and all that is best in you may be your ruin. The victim of intemperance might have been a happy man today but for the kindly heart and splendid fellowship that made him the darling of the social company. It was the best in him that gave a standing-ground for Satan. All that was best in him has proved his curse.

It is one mark of practical genius to choose the right instruments to do its work. A born administrator is a man who not only works hard himself, but has the skill of choosing the right men to be his assistants.

That is always a mark of practical capacity. And a true general shows his genius to command by the way in which he uses each branch of the service—cavalry, artillery, and infantry—for its proper work. Every administrator must make use of agents; and he displays the greatest genius for administration who picks his agents with the greatest skill.

What a magnificent administrative genius that power must be that plots our ruin if we judge it by a test like that. Could you conceive a finer choice of instruments than Satan makes when he is seeking to overthrow a human soul? Out of a hundred gates into your hearts and mine, he passes by those that are barred and chooses one that will open at a touch. His is the plan and his the whole device. But he gets other hands and other hearts to do the work; and the whole history of the tempted world, and the whole story of your tempted heart, tells the consummate genius of the choice.

Think of our Lord's experience. First, in the wilderness Satan tempted Him. He came himself that time: he sent no messenger and used no agent. It was a personal conflict between the Prince of Darkness and the Prince of Life. But the next time the baffled tempter fell back upon this old device. Next time he does not come in person: he comes incarnated in Simon Peter. What, was it not a master-stroke of genius to reach at the heart of Jesus through the loyal heart of that disciple? And when Jesus turns and detects Satan's voice in Peter's tongue and cries, "Get thee behind me, Satan, thou savorest not the things of God," He was not ignorant of his devices.

And do you think that artifice is disused today? Has Satan's brain grown blunted in these latter times? It is not the men who hate us and it is not the men and women we despise who tempt us most. It is those we trust and those who love us best who often prove hell's aptest messengers. If we but hated those who tempt us, life would become a very easy thing. It is because we love and reverence them so that for a thousand men and women life is hard. Come, tempter, in thine own cursed shape, and any coward shall beat thee off. But come through the loving heart of Simon Peter, and look through the loving eyes of Simon Peter, and speak through the loving lips of Simon Peter—and only Christ can make us strong to say, "Get thee behind me, Satan."

To sham defeat is a well-known trick in warfare. Nothing will sooner disorganize a regiment than to see the enemy routed on the field.

While the fight rages, a man is nerved and strung for he is carrying his life in his hand and knows it. But with the victory there comes reaction, and men grow careless; and there are battles where the enemy has shammed defeat just to inspire that careless spirit. O sirs, we are not ignorant of his devices! *This* old device of sham defeat—have you not seen it? You fought like a man with your besetting sin and mastered it. God keep you watchful. God keep you on your guard. One careless hour and the routed sin is at the gates again, and the whole battle has to be fought anew. We thought the sin was dead, and it was only sleeping. We thought that we had slain that habit, and it is stealing over us again. We thought we had defeated Satan, and Satan only shammed defeat. Keep the loins girded and the lamps burning and the hand upon the sword until the end. Our unseen foe is a consummate strategist. Many a soul has been lost because it won—won in the first encounter, then said all's well and laid its arms aside—till the old sin crept us again and sprang and the last state was worse than the first.

We are always prone to put the accent there. It is very hard to grasp the true splendor of the present. Today seems insignificant; tomorrow shall be the real day for us. God never speaks that way. God's Bible never speaks that way. It tells us that the present is divine, and lays the whole emphasis upon today: "Now is the accepted time." And the Holy Ghost is saying, Today.

And this is the arch-device of the arch-tempter. In every life, for every start and every noble deed, God says, Today. In every life for every start and every noble deed, the devil says, Tomorrow. Is it conversion? Today, says God: Tomorrow, whispers Satan. Is it the breaking with that sin? Tomorrow. Is it the starting on a higher level? Tomorrow. Tomorrow, tomorrow, always tomorrow!—till by tomorrow's road we are at Never—and the chance is gone, and the dream has vanished, and the hope is dead. O friends, young men and women, be not ignorant of that device. It will never be easier to come to Christ than now. It will never be easier to make the start than now. God says, Today, tonight! And God who says it is here to give the power that can save now, and can cleanse now, and can send you home now with old things passed away and all things new in Jesus Christ.

The Inescapable Elements of Life

Approving ourselves . . . in necessities—2 Cor. 6:4.

When the apostle speaks about necessities he does not think of necessary things. That is not the sense of the original. There *are* things, the opposite of luxuries, without which we could not live at all. Such are food and drink, and the air of heaven to breathe, and the refreshing ministry of sleep. But "necessities," in the idiom of the Greek, does not connote such necessary things; it means *experiences from which is no escape*. It is in such experiences Paul wants to be approved—to show himself a gallant Christian gentleman. He is determined to reveal his faith and joy in the inescapable elements of life. And so, brooding upon the text, one comes to ask the question, what are those things no one can escape from, in the strange and intricate complex of experience?

One thinks first of *certain bitter things* that reach men in the realm of mind or body. There are sufferings which pass away; there are others out of which is no escape. If a man falls ill of diphtheria or fever, he recovers, in the good providence of God. If he meets with an accident and breaks his arm, that fracture may be perfectly united. But there are other things, in the range of human ills, from which there is no prospect of escape in the long vista of the coming years. There is blindness, lameness, deafness, or congenital deformity of body. There are brains that never can be brilliant and faces that never can be beautiful. There are thorns in the flesh, messengers of Satan, hindering influence and power and service that are going to be present to the end. It is in things like these that Paul is quite determined to show himself an ap-

166

proved minister of God—brave and bright, faithful to his task, free from the slightest trace of jaundiced bitterness. And to do *that* is a far higher thing than to come untarnished from temporary trial. It is to "come smiling from the world's great snare, uncaught."

Then one's thoughts go winging to temptation, for temptation is one of the "necessities" of life. Separate from each other in a thousand ways, we are all united in temptation. A man may escape the gnawing tooth of poverty or the anguish and the languor of disease. He may escape imprisonments and stripes and the "slings and arrows of outrageous fortune." But no man, be he wise or simple, rich as Croesus or poor as Bartimaeus, ever escapes the onset of temptation. Temptation is a most obsequious servant. It follows a man everywhere—into the church, into the sheltered study, into the sweetest and tenderest relationships. Men fly to the desert to escape temptation only to find that it is there before them, insistent, as in the crowded haunts of men. *That* is the reason why our Lord was tempted. A Christ untempted is no Christ for me. He might be the Son of God in all His fullness, but He never for me could be the Son of Man. It is in such "necessities," or, in our Western idiom, such inescapable elements of life that the apostle yearns in Christ to play the man. Is there any finer victory than that? To resist the devil when he leaps or creeps on us clad in the most alluring of disguises; to do it not once, but steadily and doggedly, for when the devil comes he always comes again—*that* is a far higher thing than to pass untouched from temporary trial. It is to stand (as Browning says) pedestalled in triumph.

Another of the "necessities" of life is what our Savior calls the cross. Just as in every lot there is a crook, so in every life there is a cross. You remember how our Lord declared this—"If *any man* will come after me, let him take up his cross"—*not* certain men in strange peculiar circumstances, but *any man*, right to the end of time. From which we gather that in the eyes of Christ the cross was universal in experience, one of the things that nobody escapes. The cross is anything very hard to carry—anything that takes liberty from living—anything that robs the foot of fleetness or silences the music of the heart. And men may be brave and hide the cross away and wreathe it with flowers so that none suspects it, but, says Jesus, it is always there. There are only two things men can do with crosses—they can take them up or they can kick against them. They can merge them in God's plan of life for them, or they can stumble over them towards the glen of weeping. And what could be finer, in the whole range of life, than just to determine as the apostle did to be divinely approved in the cross? To take the cross up every morning and to do it happily for Jesus' sake—never to quarrel with God for its intrusion—never to lose heart nor faith nor love—that fine handling of one of life's "necessities" is indispensable to following Christ and is, through Him, in the compass of us all.

One last "necessity" remains: it is the grim necessity of death. For sooner or later death comes to every man; from the grip of death nobody escapes. Men used to ponder deeply upon death. Philosophy was the preparation for it. Books were written that dealt with holy dying. Preachers preached "as dying men to dying men." *Now* that has passed—men's thoughts are turned to life—they have abandoned the contemplation of the grave; and yet from death nobody escapes. Death is the last and grimmest of "necessities." "The paths of glory lead but to the grave." Death, like temptation and the cross, is an inescapable element of life. And then the apostle says: "In that last hour, when my eyes close on the familiar faces, God grant me grace to show myself approved." I go to be with Christ which is far better. O death, where is thy sting? The Lord God is merciful and gracious blotting out our transgressions like a cloud. With such a hope, with such a Father-God, with such a Savior on the other shore, the very weakest need not fear to die.

A Plea for Simplicity

The simplicity that is in Christ—2 Cor. 11:3.

There are some words that have a tragic history. To the hearing ear and to the understanding heart they whisper strange secrets about human progress. If we could follow them through all their changing meanings we should be reading the story of mankind. Nor, indeed, when we think of it, is this to be wondered at. For language is the echo of the soul. And whenever the soul of man has struggled heavenward I shall hear its echo high among the hills. The man who thoroughly knew the English tongue could almost sit down and write an English history. It is because we now rise and now fall that words become ennobled or debased.

Now one of the words that has a pitiful history is that word simple. It has wandered far from the simplicity of Christ. It has so changed its meaning and lost its early character that we are almost ashamed to use it in any other than a derogatory manner. Once, to be simple meant to be free from guile. Simplicity was the opposite of duplicity. But in the struggle with the world's sharp wits, the guileless man has generally fared so badly that the simple man has become the simpleton. I warrant you there was a world of holy meaning in the word innocent when Adam and Eve first felt the taint of sin. Yet now we look at the idiot, and we pity him, and we say, "He is an innocent." So once to be simple meant to be a Nathanael. And now it almost means to be a fool.

And yet, if we have ever studied history at all, we must have been struck with a certain sweet simplicity about the characters of the very greatest men. There is something of the child about the greatest; a certain freshness, a kind of sweet unconsciousness; a happy taking of themselves on trust; a sort of play-element throughout the drama. And all the time, powerfully, perhaps silently, they were swaying and steering this poor tossed world. Did you never feel that simplicity in Martin Luther? And did it never arrest you in George Washington? And did you never mark it in the great Duke of Wellington? One of the finest odes Tennyson ever wrote was his ode upon the death of that great duke. And I do not believe in all the noble verse of it, it rises to anything loftier than this:—

> Foremost captain of his time,
> Rich in saving common-sense,
> And, as the greatest only are,
> In his simplicity sublime.

The greatest souls, then, have been truly simple. It is that simple element that has charmed the world. And I cannot think of any better witness to the abiding charm of true simplicity than the way in which vice has always tried to imitate it. Make up your mind clearly on this point: that sin is never simple, it is subtle. No matter how we interpret the story of Eden, the insinuating serpent is still sin. All sin is subtle, intricate, involved; leading a man into an infinite maze. It can give a hundred reasons for its counsel, when a good conscience is content with one. Do you remember how the great poet of Germany in his immortal tragedy of *Faust*—do you remember how he pictures Mephistopheles as the master of a consummate subtlety? He is always changing, that evil incarnation. He is always compliant: he is never the same. To Margaret he is one thing, and to Faust another. He is exquisitely accommodating everywhere—until we feel afresh how subtle sin is, what an utter stranger to genuine simplicity! And when sin shams that it is very simple—and it is very fond of that device—we learn how attractive simplicity must be. It is a well-known practice of the hypocrite to make believe he is unusually candid. One of the last arts of an abandoned woman is to act like an innocent young girl again. It is the unwilling tribute of the bad to that simplicity of soul that charms the world, but which is lost when the eye ceases to be single and when the conscience ceases to be true.

Now the most casual student of the life of Jesus must have noted the simplicity of Christ . In a sense far deeper than any other captain, our Lord is in His simplicity sublime. His name shall be called Wonderful, it is quite true. He was the Counselor, the everlasting King. But He was holy, harmless, undefiled; and a little child shall lead them, said the prophet.

Think of His mode of life: was it not simple? It puts our artificial lives to shame. There is a music in it, not like the music of the orchestra, but like the music of the brook under the trees. He loved John and Peter, not the Pharisee; and He drew to the children, not to the scribe; and it was all so natural and simple, that the blind Jews said, this is not the Christ. Had He come greatly with the sound of a trumpet, they would have hailed Him and cried, Behold! Messiah cometh. But they missed the divinity of what was simple, and He came unto His own and they received Him not.

Think of His teaching: was not that simple too? It puts our sermons and our books to shame. There is a false simplicity that springs from lack of thought—and there is a spurious and forced simplicity that I have heard some ministers adopt when they began, with a smile, to preach to the children—and how the children hate it! But true simplicity is the first-born child of earnestness and of a deep and certain knowledge of the theme, and it was that, irradiated with divine compassion, which inspired the simplicity of Christ the teacher. Some cynic once said a very bitter thing about the style of Gibbon the historian. He said that the style of Gibbon was a style in which it was impossible to tell the truth. With the deepest reverence for our ascended Lord, I should venture to say just the opposite of Him—the style of Jesus the Teacher was a style in which it was impossible to tell a lie. It was so clear, so pure, so exquisitely truthful. It was so urgent in its invitation. It was so sharp and straight in its rebuke. It rang so true to their own village accent, and was so fragrant with the sweet scent of their own hills, that men did not realize in that simplicity the wisdom and power of the Eternal God.

But the simplicity of Christ comes to its crown in the feast of the Lord's Supper. There is no gorgeous rite or showy ceremonial. There is nothing of that many-colored pageantry that had once been needful to attract the world. A cup of wine and a piece of broken bread—these are the seals and symbols of the Gospel. And I never feel the simplicity of God and of God's great plan for rescuing the world—I never feel it so powerfully and so freshly as when I sit at the communion table. There are great mysteries in our redemption. There are deep things that even the angels cannot fathom. But in the center is a fact so simple that its best ritual is bread and wine.

Indeed that very simplicity, I take it, is part of the offense of the cross. For such a complicated curse as self we should dearly love a complicated cure. We are like Naaman, the leprous captain of Assyria, who came to Israel to be cured of leprosy. And Naaman was mightily vexed and indignant when he was told to wash in Jordan seven times. I recall how M'Crie in his great *Life of Knox* mentions among the things that hindered the progress of the Reformation, the great simplicity of the pure Gospel. There was something fascinating to the youthful mind in the intricate subtleties of medieval logic. There was a certain appeal for them in that vast rambling structure, that had been built by the schoolmen and called theology. And when the evangel came with its glad news of pardon, and out of the mists and chaos of the ages stepped Jesus with the dew of His youth still on His brow, it was all so simple that they took offense. O friend, don't you take offense! Remember that ours is a universal Gospel. It has been preached by many a graveside. It has been sung in the villages of India. It has been spoken beside the Tigris and Euphrates. It has cheered the sick, it has comforted the dying, it has done that and a thousand times more, and you do not want an intricate Gospel to do that. I have a Savior who looked on life as life; and never thought of it as some quiet academy. I have a Gospel that in its great simplicity is level with the strain of life and death. It is worth preaching. It is worth believing. An intricate faith in such a world is self-condemned. The cross is, as the greatest only are, in its simplicity sublime.

I want you all then to feel again, still more I want you all to practice, the true simplicity that is in Jesus Christ. And what we need is a little more faith in God, a little more independence of the world, a little more trust in an indwelling Holy Ghost and the separate guidance He is giving to each. One of the foremost of our living critics says a beautiful thing about the songs of Shakespeare—the songs that we find scattered through his plays. He says that the songs of Shakespeare are the only perfectly simple songs in English, and they are that because of Shakespeare's faith. Other men halted, hesitated, and were afraid. They said, *"That* will look foolish, and what will men think of *this?"* until the touch of simplicity was gone. But Shakespeare, thinking of no man, sang like a bird; trusted his genius, and was very simple. And so I want you to trust your God. And if we hold to it quietly, without fret, that it is always better to be good than bad, that it is always better to be pure than impure, that duty is duty, that conscience is supreme, that God is living, that Jesus died for us; then, in spite of all the genius of Shakespeare, our song, our life-lilt, our music of the soul, may come to be just as simple as was his.

The Apostolic Paradox

As unknown, and yet well known—2 Cor. 6:9.

It will at once occur to you how true this was of the apostles. There is not one of that first band of missionaries who were sent out to evangelize the world of whom we might not say in the words of our text, that they were unknown and yet well-known. There are no names in Christendom today more honored than the names of these evangelists. Wherever the Gospel of Jesus Christ is preached and wherever the Word of God is read and loved, the names of Peter and James and John and Thomas are familiar in our ears as household words—yet how little we know of any one of them! We have a few glimpses of them in their work; we hear them speaking a few words of arguments, or it may be we have a brief writing from their pen. But what their childhood was and who their friends were; how they looked or what befell them in old age—all this, and much more, is shrouded in darkness. Of all the disciples, then, it is singularly true, that they are unknown and yet well-known.

Nor does this hold only of the disciples. It is equally clear in the case of our Lord Himself. If our lot had been cast in Galilee while Jesus lived, there would have been few days in which we should not have spoken about Him. Men were intensely curious about Jesus, and every scrap of information was treasured. He was the daily topic of the marketplace; when women gathered at the well they spoke about Him; the dullest peasant in the remotest village had been startled to attention by His miracles—Jesus of Nazareth was indeed well-known. Yet after all how little they understood Him! In what obscurity He lived and wrought! Some thought He was Elias; others that He was Jeremiah; and not a few said "He is beside Himself." And outside of Palestine was the wide and noisy world with its senates and its markets and its armies, and into its voices of business and of pleasure there had never come one whisper of the Savior. You see how true it was, then, even of Christ, that He was unknown and yet well-known.

But if the words were true of the disciples and of Christ, they are not without truth for you and me. If we are striving to live the Christian life, this will also be one mark of our endeavor. I wish then to handle that rich theme, and to show how the Gospel carried out in life will make a man unknown and yet well-known.

First, then, *"unknown"*—I shall suggest to you some of the reasons that make the Christian life an unknown life.

Well, to begin with, Christianity lays its chief stress upon qualities that do not impress the imagination of the world. There is nothing to startle and nothing to arrest in the kind of disposition which it inculcates. The spirit that is enforced in the beatitudes is not the spirit which the world applauds. What are the qualities that men admire? What is it that draws the attention of the crowd? Is it not brilliant gifts, ingenuity, physical dexterity, or audacity? I need not remind you that you look in vain for these in the program of the Galilean. "And He opened His mouth and taught them saying, Blessed are the poor in spirit, for theirs is the kingdom of heaven. Blessed are they that mourn; blessed are the meek; blessed are the merciful; blessed are the peacemakers." It is not a moral attitude such as that which makes a man the idol of the street. *Our Lord deliberately laid His emphasis on the undramatic qualities of life.* With a true insight into what was noblest and a true scorn for what was merely show, He caught the mighty and hurled them from their seat and exalted those of low degree. Instead of pride, Jesus proclaimed humility; instead of revenge of injuries, long-suffering; endurance was to supplant retaliation, and tender mercy the old and passionate hatreds. And it is the crowning of these unobtrusive virtues and the recognition of these voiceless things that make the Christian as a man unknown.

The distinctive exercises of the Christian are exercises which he never can reveal. Among all the differences between the pagan faiths and the faith which is our treasure and our glory, none is more marked and more notable than the change from an outward to an inward worship. It is almost impossible for us to realize how wholly external the old religions were. The idea that a man might move among his fellows, carrying all his religion in his heart, would have been laughed to scorn in pagan Rome. It was under the shadow of consecrated temples, or where the altar stood ready for the oxen, or within the sacred circle of the augur, or in the brilliant procession through the streets, it was in such scenes that the religious life of paganism found its peculiar and distinctive exercises. It knew not the secret of the closed door nor of the head anointed during fasting.

I need hardly stay to tell you how Jesus Christ has come and changed all that. The distinctive exercises of the Christian life are not procession and sacrifice and augury. The distinctive worship of the Christian life is worship which we never can reveal. Could you conceive of anyone in earnest making a parade of secret prayer? Are there not hours of fellowship with heaven which would be tarnished if we talked of them? Do we ever speak of the minute denials or of those strengthenings of the will in little things which every honest Christian practices? All that is most distinctive in the Christian—his prayer, his battle, his joy, his cross-bearing—takes place in the mystical room with the closed door. And it is this—the silence and the secret—that makes the Christian as a man unknown.

Again, the distinctive service of the Christian life is not a service that attracts attention.

When a man embarks on a political career, he knows that the reward of eminence is fame. Just in proportion to his genius or eloquence will the eyes of a waiting nation turn towards him. When a man adopts a military career, he hopes for some action that may bring him glory. He dreams of doing some gallant deed and waking to find that he is famous. In the life of politics then, as in the life of war, a certain fame is quite inevitable, and he who wins the laurel in the senate or shows conspicuous courage in the field is certain to attract attention.

But the distinctive service of the Christian life is not a service that attracts attention. There is no glitter and no glamour in it. There is none of the pomp and circumstance of war. It is a quiet and lowly service; it is a work of faith and a labor of love; like the Lord who inspires it, it will not strive nor cry, nor lift up its voice in the streets. It climbs the dark stair and enters the wretched home where the poor wife, perhaps, is lying on a sickbed hoping against hope and praying to God that her husband will not come reeling home tonight, and there it ministers with unwearied patience and with a love that will not let go. It gathers the children into the mission school, prays over them and visits them at home, and in spite of discouragement it perseveres for it hears the Savior saying "Feed my lambs." It visits the fatherless and widows in affliction, it sings in the hospitals, it stands at the prison gates. It comes like a glimpse of sunshine to the poorhouse; it takes the fallen by the hand and calls her sister. All that is going on in this great city. Yet when you open your paper you never read of that. You read of pantomimes and of concerts and of the fiscal question and of the discussions in the House of Commons. *The truest service of the Christian life is never a service that attracts attention.* The kingdom cometh not with observation. The seed was growing while the farmer slept. It is this lowly and unnoticed service, done for the sake of Him who died for us, that makes the Christian as a man unknown.

But I have yet to mention the deepest of all reasons, and I shall give it to you in the apostle's words. "For ye are dead," says Paul in a great passage, "and your life is hid with Christ in God." Mysterious words—deep beyond our searching; yet boundless in encouragement and hope! For they tell us that if we be Christ's indeed, our true life cannot be seen of men; it is hidden with Jesus Christ in God's pavilion till the day comes when it shall be revealed. When on a frosty night you look up at the Northern star, you have never said of it "unknown and yet well known?" There is not a sailor in our hemisphere but knows it. It is the first star which we point out to our children. There are countless stars whose name we never learn, but the Northern star is well-known to all. But are there mountains in it and are there valleys? Are there lakes and seas or are there living creatures? "Ah," says the sailor when I ask him that, "I don't mean that I know it in *that* sense." Unknown and yet well-known, you see, and unknown because hung aloft in heaven; and ye are dead and your life is hid in heaven with One who is the bright and morning star. If, then, you are truly following Christ never be anxious to explain yourself; do not be eager to be understood and never grow impatient to be recognized. Take up thy cross; study to be quiet; redeem the time; follow the gleam bravely. Remember that with all the saints you are to walk heavenward as a man unknown.

But in spite of the obscurity of the Christian life, it is true that the Christian is well-known.

First, he is well-known when he little thinks of it. I have often been struck in preaching throughout Scotland with one feature of our church's life. I do not think I was ever in a parish where there was not one elder who stood out from all his brethren as a man of wisdom and of the spirit and of prayer. Those of you who were trained in country homes, perhaps more especially in country manses, will, I am sure, corroborate what I say. The elder may have lived in the humblest circumstances and been utterly unknown to the great world beyond, but everyone trusted him and everyone revered him and knew that he was a man of God. No one had ever seen him at secret prayer, yet no one ever doubted that he prayed. He never whispered what his right hand was doing, yet somehow all the village had the news. He moved about happy to be unknown and yet never dreaming how well-known he was. There is a deep sense in which that holds true of all loyal followers of Christ. Their life is telling where they may never think and their influence is far wider than they dream. The world is full of eager and watchful eyes, and there is not a man so poor but he has his audience. Someone is always helped or always hindered by the kind of life we lead from day to day. Back to thy duty then; take up thy cross. Resume thy service with all its disappointment. There are hearts that are thanking God for thee today–thou are unknown, and yet well-known.

Again, the Christian is well-known in heaven. In that great world where God the Father is and where there is one like to the Son of Man; in that eternal home where the angels are and where they watch with profoundest interest this earthly drama, there is nothing of more absorbing interest than the struggle and the service of the saint. Many of our estimates are overturned in heaven. There are strange reversals of magnitude in glory. Things that seem mighty here are trifles there, and the world's least is sometimes heaven's greatest. We often read of deafening applause, and it may be that the applause *is* deafening in the little area of some city hall. But the same applause given in the Highlands would hardly waken an echo in the valley and not a sound of it would reach the ear of him who was standing on the mountaintop. So, much of the noisy cheering of the world has died away before it reaches glory, and yet all heaven was watching Jesus Christ who would not strive nor cry nor lift up His voice in the streets. It is the trials and triumphs of the spirit that are of vital interest to the heavenly hosts. It is the cry and the yearning of the soul which echo in the heart of the Redeemer. There is not a prayer that we utter but He hears it. There is not a temptation we master but He sees it. We cannot do the smallest deed of kindness but like a dove it flies back to the ark. Unknown—yes, the Christian is always that, and yet I think he is well-known in heaven.

Then, lastly, the Christian may be unknown now, but he shall be well-known in the last judgment.

If there be any truth in the Gospel which we preach, the day is coming when the books will be opened and the small and great shall be summoned before God. You will be there and I shall be there; we shall be face to face with Almighty God at last. And swift as a flash of thought all that we were and did shall leap into light before ten million eyes. I forbear to dwell upon the awful misery of the man or woman whose life has been a lie. Faced by that God who is a consuming fire, and still more, faced by the love of Christ, what words in the whole range of human speech could tell the horror of that last unmasking? God grant that it be not thus with you and me! But what words shall ever tell the joy of the last judgment if we have really been trusting Christ and fighting heavenward! "Lord," we shall say, "was it I who prayed these prayers, was it I who gave that cup of water to the little one? I had quite forgotten it. It had passed with time." But the Lord shall answer, "Child, I never forget." "Lord," we shall say, "was it I who won that soul in the days when I labored in Sunday School? I thought my work was a failure with the boy." So all that we ever strove to be and do, our secret hope and cry and struggle and victory—all shall be written out and meet us again when we stand before the judgment seat of God. And then we shall understand what our text means, "As unknown, and yet well-known."

The Tyranny of Type

There are diversities of operations—1 Cor. 12:6.

There is a constant tendency in social life to reduce men to a common level. Society is not only an organ of expression; it is an organ also of repression. Men who have spent their days in lonely places are often of unusual character. They are rugged and intensely individual; they look on the universe with their own eyes. But when they move into a crowded city where a thousand interests are interwoven, immediately a social pressure begins to work which silently brings about uniformity. Conformity, says Emerson in a great essay, is the virtue most in demand in society. Society has its standard, whether low or high, and by that standard it measures everybody. Hence is it that in social life there is increasingly felt the tyranny of type. Hence is it that in advanced societies it is not easy for a man to be himself.

Now if that is true of social life, it is true also of religious life. One might almost take the words of Emerson and say, "The virtue most in demand in *religion* is conformity." In its origin, regarding it historically, there is nothing so individualistic as religion. It is born in a universe that is untenanted, save for the individual and his God. But gradually this solitary yearning finds itself echoed in the heart of multitudes, and then religion broadens into fellowship. It is no longer a solitary life: it has now risen into a social life. It has its wide and interlacing interests—its complex and multifarious relationships. And so just as in secular society, though with far greater havoc here than there, you have in religion an increasing tendency to reduce every thing to common levels. It is the constant danger of the church to have room only for one particular type. She is tempted increasingly to look askance on everything that does not conform to that. And it is when we are likely to be overridden by what I call the tyranny of type that we ought to remember the infinite divergencies which are indicated in our text. There is one God who worketh all in all. That is the bond of union and of unity. At the back of everything, as an unfailing reservoir, is the plenitude of His power and His grace. But as from our earthly reservoirs there will flow water to serve a thousand purposes, so with the manifesting of the grace of God. To change the figure, sunshine is but one, yet how diverse are its operations. It touches the hedgerows, and they are green again. It falls on the waters, and the vapors rise. it lights on the sleeping lilies of the field, and they awake and clothe themselves with scarlet so that even Solomon in all his glory was not arrayed like one of these. Therefore if God works so in nature, shall He not work as variously in grace? It is a temptation we must guard against, that of imposing our standards on the infinite. And on that temptation and some correctives to it, as we see it in certain spheres of our religion, I should like to elaborate.

In some of our old theological treatises we find what is called the *ordo salutis*. That is to say, everything is handled in a certain definite order of salvation. There are distinct and peculiar experiences following each other in well-defined succession, and it is expected that every child of God will show these in his discipleship. In regard to conversion, this passion for conformity is best witnessed in revival times. It was so in Wesley's day, and it was so in Moody's, and it was so in the late Welsh revival. Men were hardly considered to have come to Christ—they were not soundly converted, as the expression is—unless they could bear personal testimony to a certain definite experience. That experience began in misery, through the convicting power of the Holy Ghost. Then it passed into agonizing prayer, and then in an instant into light and liberty. And always there was the lurking feeling that if a man knew nothing of these depths and heights, it was questionable if he was savingly united to Christ Jesus. That feeling, in our quieter times, is perhaps less prevalent than in revival times. Yet even now when we speak of coming to Christ or when we use that fine old word "conversion," is there not a tendency to exclude everything except one recognized experience?

Now against that craving for conformity I want to put you on your guard. It is not by one road that men come to Christ. There are as many roads as there are hearts. The wind bloweth where it listeth, and thou canst not tell whence it cometh, or whither it goeth. And so, says the Lord Jesus Christ, is everyone that is born of the spirit: there is the freedom of the breeze in the new birth. It took the earthquake to convert the Philippian jailer, but it took no earthquake to open Lydia's heart. It took the glare of light to convert Paul, but there was no such light for the Ethiopian eunuch. The one was dazzled and heard a voice from heaven and was smitten to the earth and blinded—and the other was quietly reading in his chariot. There are people who insist that every Christian must have a dated and definite conversion. There are others, and they are poor psychologists, who have no faith in sudden conversion. But who are *thou* to limit the Almighty, either on this hand or on the other? The wind bloweth where it listeth, saith the Lord. We all know the hour of Paul's conversion—can you give me the hour of Timothy's conversion? From a child he had known the Holy Scriptures and had been cradled in the love of Christ. For him the tide was not like that of Solway, rushing inland faster than the horseman: for him it was like our estuary tide, moving in sweet silence to the flood. There are men who have to starve in a far country before they awaken to a Father's love. There are others who awaken to that love who have never left the shelter of the home. There are men who have to be crushed into the dust by the convicting power of the Holy Ghost. There are others who are gently wooed and won. There is one God who worketh all in all. Beware of putting limits upon Him. Give Him His freedom when He stoops from heaven to get into living touch with living men. On one man He will flash like lightning. On another like the sun He will arise. There are diversities of operations.

That thought is very beautifully hinted at in one of the visions of the Revelation. John saw a city—it was the heavenly city—and it had not one gate, but twelve. On the east three gates, and on the north three gates, and on the south three gates, and on the west three gates—it was John's commentary on his Master's word, "Come unto me, and I will give you rest." He had leaned upon that Master's bosom and known the infinite riches in that little room, and now brooding upon all that, he saw these avenues. On the east three gates—then men shall come to Him with the gladness of the sunrise on their brow. On the north three gates—then men shall come to Him out of a bitter and a barren wind. On the west three gates—then men, whose hopes have sunk like the sun into the sea shall seek the city. On the south three gates—then from a lovely land they will reach One who is altogether lovely. If you are traveling by the great north road, do not think that yours is the one road. If you have a friend upon the eastern highway, do not imagine that you must go with him. What I mean is, the one important thing is to find Christ; it is not which route you take to come to Him.

There is a word that Paul is fond of using in the opening of his letters to the churches. He addresses his converts by the name of saints—"unto the *saints* which are in Ephesus." Now mark you, Paul was not writing to a few people only. He was writing to everyone who was in Christ. He was not selecting a few outstanding Christians when he wrote "unto the saints which are in Ephesus." He was thinking of the master and the slave—of the mother—of the soldier in the guardroom, and what varieties of character were there it does not take much genius to discover. Unto the saints which were in Ephesus—and one of them would be a strong stern man, and one would be a shy and shrinking girl, and one would be a blundering agitator interfering with everybody's business, and one would be a dreamer of sweet dreams. Unto the saints which are in Ephesus—the point is that *all* of them were saints. There was room in the word, in its grand Pauline usage, for every variety of man in Christ. And you have but to think what it means now as you catch it falling from the lips to recognize how it has been contracted. A saint? We all know what that connotes. Perhaps we have known a saint—she was our mother—gentle and unworldly, and there was the light of heaven on her face. My sister, I know she was a saint; but where the spirit of the Lord is there is liberty, and I want to ask you what right you have to narrow to that type the grand old term. Cromwell, in that grim way of his, called his choicest regiment—*the saints*. They were not childlike: they were grizzled veterans whose ears were ringing with the clash of steel. Saints? It sounds absurd to call them saints; and yet, mind you, Cromwell had the right for he knew that for the battered soldier there was sainthood as well as for the sweet and gentle soul. I want to see room made within the church for every type and variety of character.

I want to see the man of action there, and the thinker and the scholar and the laborer. And I want each to feel that in the eyes of Christ there is no favored or peculiar type, for there are diversities of operations.

Of course there is a certain general likeness between all who are in Jesus Christ. If we walk in the light, says the apostle, then have we fellowship one with the other. Just as men engaged in perilous callings are molded broadly into a common likeness such as the miner who has his peculiar stamp and the fisherman his unmistakable bearing, so in the perilous calling of the Christian there are powers as of the mighty deep at work which silently impress a common likeness. A true Christian, whatever be his temperament, will always differ from a true Mohammedan. An ardent Buddhist could never be mistaken for an ardent follower of Jesus Christ. But the wonderful thing about that common life, in which all share who are in Jesus, is that it comes not to repress but to intensify the individuality.

Let me point out in passing how clearly this is shown in the case of the first disciples of our Lord. What you see in them all as they companied with Christ is the intensifying of their personality. One might have thought that a fellowship like Christ's would have had a certain repressing influence. It was so overpowering, that fellowship, it was so penetrative and commanding. But the strange thing is that so far from doing that, somehow it touched the strings of personality, and every man of them became himself when he became a follower of Jesus. Peter never grew like John. John was never the replica of Peter. Thomas—you would have known him anywhere, he was so gloomy and so doubting and so loyal. Each of them was empowered to become—not what his neighbor nor what his brother was—but what he was *himself* in God's eyes, according to the pattern in the mount.

Lastly, and in a word or two, let us think of Christian service.

One of the most familiar scenes in Scripture is the fight of David and Goliath. To me the choicest moment of that scene is when David was getting ready for the fight. I see Saul lending him his armor, and it was a very honoring bestowal. I see David, restless and uneasy, handling the great sword as if he feared it. And then I see him laying all aside and crying out, "I cannot go in these," and fingering his well-loved sling again. For *Saul* there was but one way of fighting. He had never dreamed of any other way. There was only one tradition in his chivalry, and every fighter must conform to that. But David, fresh from the uplands and the morning and the whispering of God among the hills, must have liberty to fight in his own way. The one was all for immemorial custom. The other was determined to be free. The one said, "It has been always so," and the other, "I cannot go in these." And remember that it was not Saul who was *in the line of God's election*, but that young stripling from the Bethlehem pasturage who in his service dared to be himself.

Now in our thought of Christian service, we need to be reminded of that scene. We must guard against narrowing our thought of service into half a dozen recognized activities. When Christ was on earth, the twelve disciples served Him, and it was a noble and a glorious service. But have you exhausted the catalogue of services when you have named their preaching and their teaching? The woman who washed His feet was also serving, and Martha when she made the supper ready, and the mother who caught up her little child and brought it to Him that it might be blessed. "I cannot go with these, I have not proved them. I cannot use the helmet and the shield." Who wants you to? There are hands which can wield no sword but which can carry a cup of water beautifully. There is something thou canst do in thine own way—something for which the church is waiting. *Do that*, and do it with thine heart, and perchance thou shalt do more than thou hast dreamed.

Free Grace

And he said unto me, My grace is sufficient for thee.—2 Cor. 12:9.

What the thorn was of which the apostle speaks is a question we never can answer. A hundred explanations have been given, yet certainty has never been obtained. Each age has its own interpretation, each commentator has his chosen theory, and we are still as far away from exact knowledge as ever. We may learn a little, it is true, from the language in which the apostle tells us about it. He tells us his trouble was a thorn. It was not like a cut of sword or a gash of a saber; it was something to all appearance insignificant, but how it festered! It was not in the spirit, it was in the flesh; it was a bodily and not a mental torment. Thus far Paul himself is witness; but beyond that we go at our own risk. Paul was not at all the kind of man to dwell with evident relish on his ailments. Paul was a gentleman and hid all that, kept a happy face to the wide world, and only when the cause of God demanded it, when he might help to glorify the Lord, did he touch in the most delicate fashion on the things that were given him to suffer.

But if we cannot tell what the apostle's thorn was, we can at least discover what it did for him. It was as rich in blessing for his soul as the sweetest promise of his Lord. In the first place, it helped to keep him humble when in peril of spiritual pride; in the second place, it drove him to his knees, brought him as a suppliant to the throne; and thirdly, it gave him a new experience of the sustaining of the grace of God, "My grace is sufficient for thee."

Now, what is grace? Is it the same as love? Yes, at the heart of it, it is the same as love. When you get deep enough down to the heart of it, love and grace are indistinguishable. The difference is that love can travel anywhere, upwards, or on the levels of equality, but grace can only travel downwards. A king can always be gracious to his subjects; a subject can never be gracious to his king. He may love his king and be intensely loyal, but he can never be gracious to his king; for grace is love able to condescend to men of low estate, leaning down with royalty of pity to the lowly and wretched and lost. That is why we call it sovereign grace; it is a peculiar prerogative of sovereignty. That is why we talk of free grace. That is why, when we think of the grace of God, our thoughts go out immediately to Christ, for it is in Christ and Christ alone we learn the love of God to sinful men.

So far, then, for the setting of the words. And now I want to speak of certain seasons when you and I, as Christian people, find this text upon our hearts. True, we need its message every hour, for we are not under the law but under grace; but for the grace of God in Jesus Christ there is no hope, even for a day; and yet to us as to the apostle here, seasons come of quite peculiar need when, like a cry of cheer across the storm, we hear, "My grace is sufficient for thee." On one or two of these seasons let me briefly touch.

This word is full of joy when we awaken to a sense of our own sin. It is, we notice, one of the features of our age that it is shallow in its sense of sin. It does not feel the burden of its sin in the profound way our fathers did. Partly owing to that lack of quiet which is so notable in recent years, partly owing to the attention which is now directed to the social gospel, believers are not so deep in their own hearts as were the Christians of an older school. Now, that may be true or that may not be true, but this, I think, has never been gainsaid: sooner or later if one believes in Christ, he is wakened to a sight of his own sin. It may be given him at his first approach to Christ, be the cause that leads him to the Savior; or, being brought to Christ in gentler ways, it may visit him further on his journey. Sometimes he is awakened in the heart by contact with a pure and holy life; sometimes it is by the preaching of the Word or by the singing of a simple hymn. Sometimes it is in the seasons of the night when a man is alone with his own conscience; sometimes it is by reading the Bible; or it is born of great sorrow falling, not upon us, but on another; there is something in the suffering of our loved ones that makes us feel mysteriously guilty. It is in these ways, as in a hundred others, that the Spirit of God convicts us of our sin. We get a swift glimpse of what we are—see what we are for ourselves. Now there is no talk of reformation, we want something more radical than that; and for the first time we cry despairingly, "Lord, be merciful to me a sinner." Is it not in such an hour that our text reveals the richness of its meaning? It is then we awaken to the Godhead of Christ: "My grace is sufficient for thee." Deeper than our deepest sinfulness is the grace of God in Jesus Christ; able to forgive and to redeem is the love that was revealed on Calvary. Suppose that in the whole of history there had never been anyone so vile as you, yet even to you this very moment is offered abundant and everlasting pardon. It was sufficient for David in his lust, so terribly aggravated by his birth and station; it was sufficient for Peter when he denied his Lord who was going to shed His blood for him. The penitent thief found it enough for him. It was enough for him who had the seven devils. There is nothing that grace will not attempt, and there is nothing that grace cannot achieve. When we are awakened to a sense of sin the only word to rest upon is this, "My grace is sufficient for thee."

Once more this word is full of comfort in the seasons when we are called upon to suffer. It is a condition of our present life that no one ever is exempt from suffering. That is a stated part of the agreement on which we get our leasehold of the world. To one suffering is of his body, to another it may come in mind. One it may reach in his material fortunes, another through a brother or a son. In one case it may be swift and sharp, vanishing like a summer tempest, while in another it may be long and slow and linger through the obscurity of years. There are many to whom God denies success, but to none He denies to suffer. Sooner or later, stealing from the shadow, it lays its piercing hand upon our hearts. Had it been otherwise the heart of man would never have been a man of sorrows to suffer as He suffered who is our ideal.

Now when we are called to suffer there is nothing more beautiful than quiet fortitude; to take it bravely and quietly and patiently is one of the noblest victories of life. There are few sights more morally inspiring than that of someone who has a cross to carry; someone of whom we know, perhaps, that every day must be a day of pain, yet we never hear a murmur from him, he is always bright. He is so busy thinking about others that he never seems to think about himself. I have known people such as that; I do thank God that I have known them! There is no sermon so moving in its eloquence as the unuttered sermon of the cheerful sufferer. Among all the thought that God has given to make that victory possible to us, there is none more powerful than this, "My grace is sufficient for thee."

A friend of mine not long ago was visiting one of the hospitals in London. She was greatly touched by the look of happy peace on the face of one of the patients in a ward. A little while afterwards she asked a nurse who was the greatest sufferer in that ward, and the nurse, to her intense surprise, indicated the man she had first noticed. Going up to him, she spoke to him and told him what the nurse had said, and how she admired his courage when night and day in such pain. "Ah, miss" he said, "it is not courage; it is that," and he pointed to his bed-head, and there was a colored text with *this* scripture upon it. It was that which upheld him in the night; it was that which sustained him in the day. It was the love of God in Jesus Christ making itself perfect in his weakness.

Then there is the hour when we are assaulted by temptation. Like suffering, temptation is universal, and like suffering, it is infinitely varied. Probably in all the human family no two are ever tempted quite alike. It is true that temptations may be broadly classified, clustered, as it were, around common centers. There is one class that assails the flesh, another that makes it onset on the mind; yet every temptation is so adapted to the person tempted that perhaps in all the ages that have gone on one was ever tempted just like me. To me there is no argument so strong as this for the existence of a devil. There is such subtlety in our temptations that it is hard to conceive of it without a brain. We are tempted with incomparable cunning; temptation comes to us all so subtlety and so sure that nothing can explain it but intelligence. Temptation is never obtrusive, but it is always there. It is beside us in the crowded street; it has no objection to the lonely moor; it follows us to the office and home; it dogs our footsteps when we go to church; it insists in sharing in our hours of leisure, and kneels beside us when we go to pray. At one and twenty we are sorely tempted, and say, "By-and-by it will be better; wait till twenty years have passed away, temptation will no longer assail us." But forty comes and we are tempted still; not now as in the passion of our youth, but with a power that is far more deadly because it is so hardening to the heart. There is not a relationship so sweet and sacred but temptation chooses it for its assault; there is not an act of sacrifice so pure, but temptation meets us in the doing of it. It never despairs of us until we die. So tempted as we are, is there any hope for us at all against that shameless and malevolent intelligence? Yes, we are here to proclaim that there is hope in unremitting watchfulness, there is hope in every breath of prayer. "Satan trembles when he sees the weakest saint upon his knees"; but above all there is hope in this: when we are tempted and are on the point of falling, we can lift up our hearts to Christ and hear Him say "My grace is sufficient for thee." Was He not tempted in all points like as we are, and yet was He not victorious? Did He not conquer sin, lead it captive, and lay it vanquished at His feet forever? And now you are His and He is yours; that victory which he had won is yours. It is at your disposal every hour. Say to yourself when you are next tempted, "He is able to keep me from falling. He that is with me is mightier than they that are against me." Better still, say nothing, but just listen as He rises up beside His Father's throne and calls to you, His tempted children, "My grace is sufficient for thee."

Again, shall we not need this word when life is ending, when we come to die? There is no pillow for a dying head except the grace of God in Jesus Christ. When I was a young minister in Thurso I was called into the country one beautiful summer day to the bedside of an elder who was dying. He was a godly man, a grave and reverent saint, a man whose only study was the Bible; summer and winter he was never absent from his familiar corner in the sanctuary. And now he was dying, and, as sometimes happens even with the choicest of the ripest saints, he was dying in such a fear of death as I have never witnessed since that hour. Outside the open window was the field with a shimmer of summer heat upon it; far away there was the long roll of the heavy waves upon the shore; here in the cottage was a human soul that walked reverently and in the fear of God, overmastered by the fear of death. Well, I was a young man then, very ignorant, very unversed in the deep things of the soul, and I tried to comfort him by speaking of the past—what an excellent elder he had been; and I shall never forget the look he gave me, or how he covered his face as if in shame, nor how he cried, "Not that, sir, not that! There is no comfort for me there." It was then I realized for the first time that the only pillow to die on is free grace. It was then I felt how all we have done is powerless to uphold us in the valley of death, for all our righteousness are as filthy rags and bring no ease upon a dying bed.

This is our only stay: "My grace is sufficient for thee."

Galatians through Hebrews

The Offense of the Cross

Then is the offense of the cross ceased—Gal. 5:11.

One thing which marks the ministry of Paul is how he lovingly yearned over the Jews. With a quenchless and intense desire, he prayed that they might be brought into the fold. Never did mother so long for the saving of her son as Paul longed for the saving of his countrymen. He was willing to suffer anything or everything, if only his people Israel might be won.

It is when we remember that deep longing that we realize what the cross meant for Paul. For the great stumbling block of faith to the Jews—the offense that made the Gospel of Christ smell rank to them—was, as our text indicates, the cross. Take that away, and it would be a thousand times more easy to win the Jews to the acceptance of the Lord. Say nothing about that, just slur it over, and you would take half the difficulty out of the way of Israel. Yet in spite of his yearning to see Israel saved, that was the one theme which Paul would not ignore. God forbid, he says, that I should glory save in the cross of Jesus Christ my Lord. There is a great lesson there for Christian teachers and for all who are trying to advance Christ's kingdom. The more earnest and eager they are to have men saved, the more willing are they to go to all lengths to meet them. And that is right, for we must be all things to all men—to the Jews as a Jew, to the Romans as a Roman; but remember there are a few great facts we cannot yield, though they run counter to the whole spirit of the age. It were better to empty a church and preach the cross than to fill it by keeping silence like a coward. It were better to fail as Paul failed with the Jews than to succeed by being a traitor to the cross. Religion can never be a pleasant entertainment. When the offense of the cross ceases, it is lost.

Now I want to make it a little plainer to you why the cross was an offense to the Jews and to put things in such a way that you may see at once that the same causes are operative still.

First then, the cross was offensive to the Jews just because it blighted all their hopes. It shattered every dream they ever dreamed, every ideal that ever glimmered on them. No telegram of news full of disaster, plunging a man into unlooked-for poverty—no sudden death of one to whom the heart clings, laying a man's life in ruins at his feet—not these more certainly shatter a man's hopes than did the cross the vision of the Jews. They had prayed for and had dreamed of their Messiah, and He was to come in power as a conqueror. "Prepare ye the way of the Lord, make his paths straight"—you can almost hear the tramp of victorious feet. That was the light which burned in the Jewish darkness; that was the song which made music in their hearts. Then in the place of that triumph, there comes Calvary. In place of the Christ victorious, Christ crucified. And was this the Messiah who was to trample Rome, pierced in hands and feet by Roman nails? To the Jews a stumbling block: you cannot wonder at it when every hope they had formed was contradicted. Yet in spite of it all Paul preached Christ crucified, and that was the offense of the cross.

Now I venture to say that that offense of Calvary is just as powerful now as it was then. If I know anything about the ideals men cherish now and about the hopes that are regnant in ten thousand hearts, they are as antagonistic to the cross as was the Jewish ideal of Messiah. Written across Calvary is sacrifice; written across this age of ours is pleasure. On the lips of Christ are the stern words, I must die. On the lips of this age of ours, I must enjoy. And it is when I think of the passion to be rich and the judgment of everything by money standards; of the feverish desire at all costs to be happy, of the frivolity, of the worship of success; it is when I think of that and then contrast it with the "pale and solemn scene" upon that hill that I know that the offense of Calvary is not ceased. Unto the Jews a stumbling block—unto far more than the Jews: unto a pleasure-loving world and a dead church. Therefore say nothing about it; let it be; make everything interesting, pleasant, easy. Then is the offense of the cross ceased—and with it the power of the Gospel.

Second, the cross was an offense to the Jews because it swept away much that they took pride in. If there was any meaning in Calvary at all, some of their most cherished things were valueless. The Jews were preeminently a religious people, and this is always one peril of religious people. It is to take the things that lead to God and let the heart grow centered upon them. There was the ceremonial law for instance, with its scrupulous abhorrence of defilements. No one who has not studied the whole matter can ever know what that meant to the Jew. And there were the sacrifices smoking upon their altars, and the feasts and festivals and journeys to Jerusalem. And there was the temple, that magnificent building, sign of their hope and symbol of their unity. At least let this be said of that old people, that if they were proud, they were proud of worthy things. It is better to be proud of law and temple than to be proud of battleship and millionaire. Yet all that pride, religious though it was—that pride, deep-rooted as the people's life—all that was swept away like autumn leaves if there was any meaning in the cross. No more would the eyes of men turn to Jerusalem, no more would sacrifices fill the altars, no more was there room for ceremonial law if the Son of God had died upon the tree. And it was this crushing into the very dust of all that was dearest to the Jewish heart that was so bitter an offense of Calvary.

And today has that offense of the cross ceased? Has that stumbling block been removed out of the way? I say that this is still the offense of Calvary, that it cuts at the root of so much that we are proud of. Here is a woman who strives to do her duty. God bless her, she does it very bravely. Here is a student proud of his high gifts. God prosper him that he may use them well. But over against reliance upon duty and all attempts of the reason to give peace, there hangs the crucified Redeemer saying, "No man cometh unto the Father but by me." Here is the offense of the cross in cultured ages. It is that a man must come with empty hands. He must come as one who knows his utter need of the pardoning mercy of Almighty God; and in an age like ours that leans upon its heritage and is proud of its magnificent achievement, that call to unconditional surrender is the offense of evangelical religion. We are all tempted to despise what we get freely. We like a little toil and sweat and travail. We measure the value of most things not by their own worth, but by all that it has cost us to procure them. And Calvary costs us nothing though it cost God everything; the love and the life of it are freely offered; and to a commercial age and a commercial city there is something suspicious and offensive there. Ah sirs, if I preached salvation by good works what an appreciative audience I could have. How it would appeal to many an eager heart! But I trample that temptation under foot, not that I love you less but that I love Christ more, and I pray that where the gospel is proclaimed, the offense of the cross of Christ may never cease. I do not believe that if you scratch a man you will find underneath his skin a Christian. I do not believe that if you do your best, all is well for time and for eternity. But I do believe—

> Not the labors of my hands
> Can fulfill Thy law's demands;
> Could my zeal no respite know,
> Could my tears forever flow,
> All for sin could not atone:
> Thou must save, and Thou alone.

Third, the cross was an offense to the Jews because it obliterated national distinctions. It leveled at one blow those social barriers that were of such untold worth in Jewish eyes. It was supremely important that the Jews should stand apart; through their isolation God had educated them. They had had the bitter-sweet privilege of being lonely, and being lonely they had been ennobled. Unto them were committed the oracles of God; they were a chosen nation, a peculiar people. The covenants were theirs, theirs were the promises, the knowledge of the one true God was theirs; until at last, almost inevitably, there rose in the Jewish mind a certain separateness and a certain contempt, continually deepening, for all the other nations of mankind. They had no envy of the art of Greece. They were not awed by the majesty of Rome. Grecians and Romans, Persians and Assyrians—powerful, cultured, victorious—were but Gentiles. There is something almost sublime in the contempt with which that little nation viewed the world. Then came the cross and leveled all distinctions; it burst through all barriers of nationality. There was neither Jew nor Gentile, Greek nor barbarian, but Christ was all and in all. Let some wild savage from the farthest west come to the cross of Christ pleading for mercy, and he had nothing less to do and nothing more than the proudest Jew who was a child of Abraham. One feels in an instant the insult of it all, how it left the Jew defenseless in the wild. All he had clung to was gone; his vineyard-wall was shattered: he must live or die now in the windswept world. And this tremendous leveling of distinctions—this striking out Jew and writing in humanity—this, to the proud, reserved, and lonely people, was no small part of the offense of Calvary.

Now I would not have you imagine for a moment that Christ disregards all personal distinctions. If I sent you away harboring the thought that all who come to Christ get the same treatment, I should have done Him an unutterable wrong. In everything He did Christ was original because He was fresh from God into the world, but in no sphere was He so strikingly original as in the way in which He handled those who came to Him. So was it when He was on the earth; so is it now when He is hid with God. There is always some touch, some word, some discipline, that tells of an individual understanding. But in spite of all that and recognizing that, I say that this is the "scandal" of the cross, that there every distinction is obliterated, and men must be saved as lost or not at all. You remember the lady from a gentle home who went to hear the preaching of George Whitefield? And she listened in disgust to a great sermon and then, like Naaman, went away in a rage. "For it is perfectly intolerable," she said, "that ladies like me should be spoken to just like a creature from the streets." Quite so: it is perfectly intolerable—and that is the stumbling block of Calvary. Are you who may be cultured to your fingertips to be classed with the savage who cannot read or write? It would be very pleasant to say No—but then were the offense of the cross ceased. A friend of mine who is a busy doctor in a thriving village not ten miles from Glasgow was called in the other day to see a patient who, as was plain at the first glance, was dying. And the doctor, a good Christian, said, "Friend, the best service I can do you is to ask, Have you made your peace with God?" Whereon the man, raising his wasted arm and piercing the questioner with awe-filled eyes, said, "Doctor, is it as bad as that?" I want to say it is always as bad as that. I want to say it to the brightest heart here. You do need pardon and peace with God in you. Say, "Thou, O Christ, art all I want." And then, just as the wilderness will blossom, so will the offense of the cross become its glory.

Acceptance in the Beloved

To the praise of the glory of his grace through which he hath made us accepted in the beloved—Eph. 1:6.

It ought to be noted carefully by all who ponder the interior life that acceptance is something different from forgiveness. One might be forgiven and not accepted. If a man wrought me some deadly injury, by the grace of heaven I might forgive that man; yet I might warn him that he must keep his distance and never cross the threshold of my home. So conceivably might God forgive the guilty sinners of mankind and yet forbid them entrance to His dwelling-place. At the pleading of the woman of Tekoah, David forgave Absalom. Yet for two years that forgiven child never looked upon his father's face (2 Sam. 14:28). The palace gates were barred for him; he had no access to the royal chambers; he was forgiven, but he was not accepted. Acceptance is reconstituted fellowship. It is liberty of access to the palace. It is an authoritative welcoming to the home and heart of God. And though always this implies forgiveness, the two are not identical whether in the affairs of earth or heaven.

It ought again to be noted that acceptance does not necessarily follow on forgiveness. It is not an inevitable consequence; it is an added miracle of grace. When the prodigal took his homeward way he had a deep conviction that he would be forgiven. But he had no assurance that he would be accepted and so have the run of the old home. Forgiven, he would have been well content to be as the lowest of the hired servants and lodge with the other servants in the shed. The father forgave him when he ran to meet him. There was fatherly forgiveness in

200

the kiss. But what amazed the prodigal and broke his heart was the welcome which followed on forgiveness. The ring on his finger, the robe upon his back, the filial liberty in the old home, these were the acceptance of the prodigal. He might have been forgiven without these. These were not of the essence of his pardon. These were the signs and tokens of a love that could never do enough for the forgiven. That is why the apostle tells us here that the amazing experience of acceptance is "to the praise of the glory of His grace." Acceptance is not a necessary corollary. It is not an implication of remission. It is an implication that we are in the hands of One who in His love can never do enough. He might pardon us and make us hired servants; but love can never be content with that. It crowns forgiveness in the welcome home.

Again we are told (and the words are haunting words) that this acceptance is in the Beloved. One can fittingly illustrate that thought from what one has seen in human life. A well-beloved, perhaps an only son, announces that he is going to be married. His mother who has been praying about that waits eagerly to see his choice. And sometimes seeing, she is disappointed, and her mother's heart is very sore within her for the girl "is not like her son at all." Then frequently follows something very beautiful. I have seen it a score of times with admiration. That foolish, giddy, ill-adapted girl gets a most tender welcome to the home. She is treated with an infinite consideration; she is borne with, her faults are overlooked not for her own sake, but for that of the dear boy who has chosen her to be his bride. She is accepted *in the beloved:* for his sake she gets that tender welcome. She is cherished and treated as a daughter and made one of the family because *he* is dear. And something like that is in the writer's mind when he finds the secret of divine acceptance not in us, but in the well-beloved Son. Pardon does not instantly make holy, and without holiness how shall we see God? We are worse adapted for that heavenly fellowship than the most foolish maiden is for marriage. But if the Son hath chosen the Church to be His bride, and if the mother-heart be a sacrament of God, then in the Well-beloved there is welcome. For His sake we have the run of home. We are adopted into the family of heaven. We are loaded with unfailing kindness. We are always taken at our best. With the heavenly Father as with the earthly mother there is welcome for the chosen of the Son. We are accepted *in the Beloved.*

I should like to close upon another thought—we are accepted in Him that we may serve. Very often in that word acceptance there is the suggestion of expected service. When a candidate for office is accepted, that acceptance is the road to usefulness. When an editor accepts a manuscript, that means that the manuscript is going to be used. And when God not only pardons but accepts, it implies that He is set on using us "to the praise of the glory of His grace." Just as election is not a selfish privilege but heaven's method of broadcasting its blessings, so acceptance (election's other side) is heaven's prelude to spiritual fruitfulness. For the slave knoweth not what his lord doeth and his best obedience is mechanical, but he who has the run of home is free. We are accepted not for an hour or two; we are accepted that we may abide. And abiding, as our Lord has taught us, is the secret of all fruitfulness. Accepted service is not brilliant service—brilliance is very often fruitless—it is the service of those who never cease to wonder that they are *accepted in the Beloved*.

The Evangelical Grace of Tenderheartedness

Be ye kind one to another, tenderhearted—Eph. 4:32.

The first thing to impress me as I read these words is the change which had been wrought in the apostle. There had been a day, not so far away, when you would scarce have expected such a word from Paul. When Paul first appears on the scene, he seems the incarnation of hardheartedness. He is a Pharisee, cruel and intolerant, delighting in sacrifice and not in mercy. He holds the clothes of the murderers of Stephen, intensely interested in that ghastly spectacle, and he makes havoc of the Church of Christ. Is it not remarkable that such a man should become the advocate of tenderness? No softening of the years could have wrought that. It is a tribute to the power of Christ. For if it was Christ in Paul that made him great and inspired him to be the evangelist of nations, it was also Christ who made him tenderhearted. There are men who are constitutionally tender, but I do not think that Paul was of that kind. He had to fight his way out of the stony ground into the green pastures of this grace. And when we remember how Paul had lived at Ephesus and how he had labored night and day with tears, we feel what an urgency his word would have, "Be ye kind one to another, tenderhearted."

There *is* a tenderness—and it is very common—which is the antithesis of strength. There is no justice in it, no morality, no love of the good, no hatred of the bad. It is the overflowing of an easy nature that often works irreparable wrong just because it has not strength enough to take a firm stand for what is right. It is weak. Not such is the tenderheartedness of Paul. It knows the cleavage between light and darkness. It knows that it may be cruel to be kind and that sometimes it may be kindest to seem cruel. But it also knows how lonely people are; how sad the heart may be for all the laughter; how heavily the burden of the cross may weigh, although the face is always brave and bright. Be ye kind one to another, tenderhearted. You can never tell what that other soul is bearing. The men and women you are inclined to envy—if you knew all, you might not envy them. And it is this—this instinct for the deeps, this surmise of what is hidden in the shadow—it is this that gives to tenderheartedness its power and its place in Christian brotherhood.

1. Custom—There are several causes working in the world which make it a hard thing to keep the tender heart. One of the commonest of all is custom. Do you remember, in the parable of the sower, what happened to the seed by the wayside? It fell on the pathway that led across the field, and the birds of the air came and picked it up. It was not stony ground on which it fell; it was not foul with thistles and with thorns; it was good ground, but it was beaten hard by the passing of innumerable feet. Little children had gone that way to school; grave and reverend men had gone to the synagogue. And the feet of happy lovers had been there, and the weary step of the farmer going home, until at last, under that ceaseless traffic, the surface had become impenetrable, and the strip that might have been golden with a harvest was just the happy hunting ground of birds. Are we not all exposed to such a hardening with the constant traffic of our days? Ah friends, what open hearts we had when heaven lay about us in our infancy! But now we are dulled down a little; we are less sensitive, less eager, less receptive; and one inevitable peril of all that is the peril of ceasing to be tenderhearted.

2. The struggle to live—Another enemy of this same grace is the fierce struggle which many have to live. Men say it is difficult to be true today; it is equally difficult to be tender. You could hardly expect a soldier on the field to be a perfect pattern of gentleness. At home he might be that—with his own children—scarcely amid the rigors of the war. And in that city battle of today which we disguise with the name of competition, a man must be in deadly peril of losing the genius of the tender heart. In simpler communities it was not so. Life was easier in simpler communities. And time was longer, and men had more leisure, and the sense of brotherhood was not quite lost. But in the city with its stress and strain, with its pressure at every point, and with its crowd, life may have the joy of growing keen, but it has also the risk of growing cruel. It is not often that the successful man is what you would call the tenderhearted man. The battle has been too terrible for that: there has been too much crushing underfoot; and always when a man tramples upon others, he tramples in that hour on his own heart. Now I want you to remember that when Paul wrote to Ephesus, he wrote to a city like Glasgow or like Liverpool. He was not addressing a handful of quiet villagers. He was writing to a commercial metropolis. And that, I take it, just means this, that Paul was alive to the dangers of the city and knew how supremely difficult it was there to keep the secret of the tender heart.

3. Sin—But the greatest enemy of tenderheartedness is the old sad fact of sin. Sin is the mightiest antisocial power that ever alighted with curse upon the world. Sin blights all that is fairest in the character; sin coarsens everything that is most delicate; sin in the long run softens nothing; it hardens everything it touches. You would think from the popular novels of today that sin is something which transfigures life. Young men and women, don't you believe it; that is the most tragic of fallacies. Sin at the heart of it is always vile. Deck it in any garments that you please, sin leaves us narrower, impoverishes life, always ends in hardening of the heart. There is an old legend of the goblin horseman whose steed might be heard galloping at midnight. And the legend was that where the hoofs alighted, the grass would nevermore be green again. I think that is a parable of sin when a man gives it the rein within his heart; "it hardens all within, and petrifies the feeling." Sin hardens a man's heart towards his wife. It hardens a man's heart towards his children. It hardens him to the touch of human need and to the call which the world makes upon his sympathy. And that is why the grace of tenderheartedness is so conspicuously a Christian virtue— because it betrays that conquest over sin which has been won for us in Jesus Christ.

Think for a moment of the case of David to illustrate what I have been saying. By nature David was a gallant soul, and he was as tender-hearted as heroic. When a shepherd, he had faced a lion; when sent to the army, he had faced Goliath. No one could question the magnificent courage of one who had these fine actions to his credit. And yet this David, when he lit on Saul asleep alone in a cave and at his mercy: this David, who had matched himself with giants, was too tenderhearted to destroy him. One blow, and he was monarch of a kingdom. One blow, and a crown was on his brow. And there was not a Jewish warrior in his train but would have said "It is the will of God." But David could not do it—it was impossible, and David was never greater than just then, when at the back of all his bravery he showed the chivalry of the tender heart. But then there came the day when David sinned, and I shall draw a veil over his sin. But who is this plotting against Uriah and making him drunk and sending him out to die? Ah friends, this is that very David who had once been so chivalrous and gentle but who now, in the grip of a dark passion, has forfeited his tenderness of heart. I thank God he got it back again when he cried in penitence to heaven. "Create in me a clean heart," he cried, "O God, and renew a right spirit within me." But I thank God too that the story is all here to warn us against the hardening of sin, to teach us how all that is fairest in the best may blighted by the power of its curse.

I know no virtue that is more often disguised than the virtue of which I am speaking. It is not one of the qualities of which men are proud as they are proud of courage or endurance. On the contrary, they are a little ashamed should one suspect them of being tenderhearted. And so very often they hide it out of sight and wrap it up in the most strange disguises and assume a manner that is so far from gentle that it takes a little while to guess the truth. It is not always those of gentle manners who really possess the gentlest hearts. Some of the tenderest men I ever knew have had a rough, even a boisterous, exterior. They were like Mr. Boythorn in *Bleak House* who was always for hanging somebody or other and all the time was feeding the canary that nestled without a tremor in his hand. I am not sure that had you seen our Lord, you would have fathomed His tenderness at once. Had you seen Him when face to face with Pharisees, I may say without a doubt that you would not. It was one of those secrets that was revealed to children, for children have far quicker eyes than we, and they detect, as by a kind of genius, the gentleness that is hidden in the heart. The French have a proverb which says this—there is nothing so tender as the austere man. Like other proverbs, that has its exceptions, for there are austere men who are not tender. But at least let it teach us not to be rash in judgment, not to sum up at once against our brother. There are men who seem to have a face of brass, and all the time they have a heart of gold.

This, too, is one of the works of memory. God has given our memories that calling. It is one of the great works of memory to keep a man tenderhearted in the struggle. I always remember that story of John Newton with whom Christ dealt in such a signal way. As a young man he was desperately wild as if God had given him over to work iniquity. And yet in the wildest of it all, he tells us, he could never forget the soft hand of his mother. Although he was a thousand miles away, he felt that soft caress upon his head. "I will arise and go unto my Father"—was not that the memory of home? "And the Lord turned and looked on Peter"—do you not think the past was in that look? Peter was hardening his heart that night; he was a reckless and a desperate man; and the Lord looked, and all the past revived, and then like summer tempest came his tears. Do we not all have hours like that when the past revives to make us tenderhearted? That is one of the offices of memory where the heart is in daily peril of hardening. And it may be that is the deepest reason why men so often grow tenderer with age. Once they were living in the fierce light of hope; now in the softer light of memory.

But the great secret of the tender heart lies in the fellowship of Jesus Christ. It is a continual wonder about Jesus that He was so strong and yet so tenderhearted. No authority could make Him fearful; no array of power could ever daunt Him, and yet a bruised reed he would not break, and smoking flax He would not quench. He was no tender because He knew so little. He was tender because He knew so much. All that was hidden from duller eyes He saw—all that men had to bear and battle through. Their helplessness, their crying in the night, their inarticulate appeal to heaven—all this was ever audible to Jesus and kept His heart as tender as a child's. And He never lost this tenderheartedness even in the darkness of the cross. Men scorned Him, and they spat on Him, and crucified Him, yet "Father forgive them, for they know not what they do." And what I say is that when that mind of Christ is given by the Spirit to you and me, then whatever happens, however we are treated, we shall be kind one to another, tenderhearted.

The Uplift of the Body

He is the Savior of the body—Eph. 5:23.

Students of the New Testament have often remarked how much mention is made of the body. Our text is only one of many passages which arrests us with this unusual emphasis. Of all the books in the world's literature, there is none which insists upon the soul so urgently; yet there is no book in the world's literature which has done so much to dignify the body. One of the errors of popular evangelism is that it thinks of nothing but the soul. That too was one of the errors of monasticism, and indeed ultimately proved its overthrow. It was false to the noble proportions of the Bible and tried to spurn what Scripture never spurns, and in the long run had to pay for that by being swept into oblivion. It is extraordinary how many people want to be a little wiser than the Bible. It is extraordinary how many people want to be a little more spiritual than Christ. They take the part and treat it as the whole; they are blind to everything except the spirit; they never seem to have caught the flash of glory that the Bible has cast upon the body. "We ourselves groan within ourselves, waiting for . . . the redemption of our body" (Rom. 8:23). "Know ye not that your body is the temple of the Holy Ghost who is in you?" (1 Cor. 6:19). "I beseech you, therefore, brethren, by the mercies of God, that ye present your bodies a living sacrifice, holy, acceptable unto God" (Rom. 12:1). Such words, and they might be multiplied by ten, are not at all impertinent intrusions. They are wrought into the web of Scripture, and they are part and parcel of its message; until at last, by such recurrent whispers and by a hundred other hints and shadowings, we come to see that the Word of God in Christ is the true charter of the human body.

Now I question if we always realize the importance of this Gospel emphasis. For we have never known the outlook of the heathen, nor have we been "suckled in a pagan creed." To know what Christianity has done for women, we should need to have lived before Jesus Christ was born; and we should need to have lived before Jesus Christ was born to know what it has accomplished for the body. It is true that among the ancient Greeks, whose worship was just the worship of the beautiful, the charm of physical beauty was appreciated as perhaps it has never been appreciated since. But a nation, like an individual, may be exquisitely sensitive to beauty, and yet may wallow, as I fear the Greeks wallowed, in horrible and disgusting sin. To the pagan the body was a slave, and no one could care less how to treat a slave. To the pagan the body was a curse, for evil had its seat and center in the flesh. Or at the best the body was a clog, a sorry prison for an immortal spirit, a scaffolding that would be knocked in pieces when the palace-courts within were perfected. You cannot wonder that with attitudes like these, the pagan world was sunk in immorality. You cannot wonder at what we read in Romans when you remember what the Romans held. And what I say is that you must remember it—you must remember the depth and the disgrace—if you would understand what Christ has done in rescuing the body from dishonor. No longer can we treat the body as an alien. We have learned that it is a friend and not an enemy. It is no prison house with grated windows; it is a temple where the Spirit dwells. And such is the honor that has fallen upon it that even the bodies of our dead are precious and are clothed in new garments and laid in a quiet grave with a certain gentle reverence and respect. It was one of the first effects of Christianity that it put a stop to the burning of the dead. Men felt that it was a kind of sacrilege to burn a temple of the Holy Ghost. And that alone, which everywhere and always accompanied the preaching of the Gospel, will show you what a change had been effected in the popular concept of the body. Now this is the question which I want to ask, How did the Gospel of Jesus work that change? How did it lift the body from the mire and crown it with glory and with honor? What are the new facts, or what are the doctrines, which have given to the body such high dignity that we may say of Christ unhesitatingly, He is the Savior of the *body?*

The first is the great fact of the Incarnation. It is the coming of the Son of God in human form. The Son of God dwelt in a human body, and that has clothed it forever with nobility. If human flesh and sin were indistinguishable, do you think the Word would have become flesh? Had the flesh been ineradicably vile, would the Son of God have worn it as a garment? Wherever sin may have its source and spring, it is not in the human body, else when Christ took a body to Himself, He would have taken to be His comrade what was vile. So long as you think of God as far away, so long it is possible to degrade the body. For the spirit is willing but the flesh is weak, and every sense may be a road to ruin. But if the Son of God has tabernacled here—if perfect purity and love have dwelt here—if the immortal King has stooped to earth and taken to Himself the seed of Abraham, then the body never can be despised again. It was that fact which altered the world's standpoint and cast a glory on the human frame. The body had been the instrument of sin; now it was made the instrument of Christ. Through human lips the voice of God had spoken. Through human eyes the pity of God had looked. The love of God had wrought through human hands and gone its errands upon human feet.

We may throw a certain light upon that change by remembering what has happened in other dwellings. If someone whom we reverence has been born there, the place is never ordinary to us again. There is a house in Stratford built of common brick, not differing outwardly from other houses, yet in that home the poet Shakespeare lived, and to it thousands of pilgrims turn their feet. There is a cottage in Ayrshire, just an old clay building, low-roofed, confined and damp, yet in the fullness of the time Burns was born there, and it is not a mean place to Scotland now. It is the genius who adorns the house. It is the saint who glorifies the dwelling. Wherever the home has been of one we love, there forever is a hallowed spot. And when we think of all we owe to Christ, when He became poor for our enriching, it helps us to realize a little better how His coming has glorified the body. He took upon Himself the seed of Abraham. Can you dishonor the seed of Abraham now? He passed through the doorway of this little cottage. And will you spit upon the cottage wall? The flesh is vile, said the old pagan thinker—the flesh is the great enemy of the spirit. And John, looking that old world in the face, said, "The Word was made flesh, and dwelt among us" (John 1:14).

The second factor in this change of view was the compassionate care of Jesus for the body. And I sometimes think we scarcely realize what is meant by the healing miracles of Christ. We study the separate miracles apart till we almost forget the import of the whole. We treat them as isolated incidents or as witnesses of Christ's divinity. But the miracles are really more than that. They are a revelation rather than an argument. They are not added to confirm the mission, but are themselves a vital part of it. They teach us that this despised body is part of the manhood which the Lord redeems. They teach us that the love of God for man is love for the body as well as for the soul. They teach us that there is no part nor organ, nor any faculty nor sense nor limb, but has a share in that redeeming work which brought our Savior from the throne to Calvary. Do you remember how Christ refused to interfere when one wanted Him to interpose about his property? "Master, speak to my brother, that he divide the inheritance with me"—and Jesus refused to speak a word. But tell me, did He ever refuse to interfere when the blind eyes looked up to Him for sight?—or when the foot was lame or when the arm was helpless or when the tongue was sealed within the lips? Always remember that the love of Christ encompasses every organ we possess. It is the love of God touching the human frame that it might never be bestial anymore. We have a beautiful hymn which we are fond of singing. It is "Jesus, lover of my soul." But I want someone to write me another hymn, beginning "Jesus, lover of the body."

I think, too, that when we remember this, we see more clearly why miracles have ceased. I dare say to some of you it has seemed strange sometimes that there are no such miracles today. Have you not longed for a miracle of healing when someone whom you loved was very ill? Have you not thought how all the world would sing if that cold face would only smile again? And if Christ is the same today in love and power as when He moved along the ways of Galilee, why, you wonder, should it not be so? Still in the world are eyes that cannot see and lips that crave for utterance in vain. Still in the world are little suffering children and loved ones whose brows are drawn in anguish. And Christ—where is His hand of healing, and where is His touch that brought the strength again, and where is His voice that spoke and men were cured and the light of life came thrilling to the dead? Now will you just remember what was the deep purpose of these miracles? Will you remember that they were wrought to teach us that the body is the temple of the Holy Ghost? And if that lesson has been learned by Christendom so that Paul could say "He is the Savior of the body" (Eph. 5:23), then the work of the healing miracles is done. Nay, I beg of you, say not it is done. Its spirit is moving in a thousand channels. It has founded the hospital and built the infirmary, and inspired the science and the skill of Christian medicine. It has passed into the life of every doctor who is walking worthy of his high vocation. It has possessed the heart of every true nurse. The lesson of the miracles was mastered, and the great Teacher laid aside the lesson-book. But when a lesson has been learned—what then? Does it not mean that we are fit for greater things? So "greater works than these shall he do" (John 14:12) said the Lord—greater things even than a miracle; and in the sympathy and skill and care of Christendom that promise has been abundantly fulfilled.

Then the third factor in that change of view was the doctrine of the resurrection of the body.

One of the greatest thinkers of the ancient world, in what is perhaps his choicest dialogue, has given us in his own matchless way some of the reasons why men should welcome death. He felts that the fear of death was an unworthy fear, and he tried to combat it by quiet argument, and one of his strongest arguments is this, that at death we are done forever with the body. We shall never more be clogged and troubled by it. It will never hamper the bright soul again. Death is the bird escaping from its cage. Death is the prisoner breaking from his cell. The kindliest attribute of death, for Plato, was not just that a man would be at rest then. It was that a man after his weary battle would be done forever with a body.

Brethren, who name the Name of Christ with me, do you always remember that that is *not* our faith? We believe in the Holy Ghost and in the Catholic church and in the resurrection of the body. That is one thing which Jesus never doubted. That is one mystery He never questioned. And now it has passed from the consciousness of Christ into the consciousness of all His people. If there is any meaning in His empty grave and if our bodies are a living sacrifice, then in the future, body, soul, and spirit, we shall be forever with the Lord. It was that mystery, touching a thousand hearts, which set a halo of glory on the body. It was the thrill of resurrection-doctrine, and the open secret of the empty grave. It was the certainty that the glad day was coming when the body of our humiliation would be changed and would be fashioned by the power of God into the likeness of the body of Christ's glory.

And so I ask you, as I close, to think again of sins against the body. In the light of all I have been trying to say, I ask you to set aside these sins you know so well. No one could think that much harm was done if the scaffolding around some temple were defaced; and when the Roman sinned against his body, it was only the scaffolding he seemed to touch. But the Gospel has banished forever that conception, for in the light of Christ the temple is the body, and hence the heinousness of all such sins for every man who calls himself a Christian. If the body after all were but a cage, it might not be very wrong to be a sensualist. If the body after all were but a prison, the guilt of drunkenness might not be great. But if the body was the home of Jesus—if it is the temple of the Holy Ghost—if Christ has come to ransom and redeem it—if it is to be raised incorruptible and glorious—then drunkenness and un-cleanness and excess, and every defiance of the laws of health, are sins not easily to be forgiven. Young men, keep yourselves pure. Young women, be scrupulously modest. You can train your body to be the best of comrades. You can train it to be the deadliest of enemies. What multitudes there are in this great Babylon who have presented their bodies to the devil! I call you to present yours to God, a living sacrifice, holy and acceptable.

The Shield of Faith

Withal taking up the shield of faith—Eph. 6:16 (R.V.)

The armor of the ancients was of two different kinds, and both kinds were absolutely necessary. It was partly armor for attack and partly armor for protection. Now very generally, in the New Testament, faith is one of the weapons of attack (1 John 5:4). We see that magnificently illustrated in the pageant of the eleventh of Hebrews. But *here,* and it may be only here, Paul looks on faith in quite another light, for he sets it among the armor of protection. Faith is not here the power that leads to victory; it is the power that protects us in battle. It keeps us unembittered and serene amid the mysteries and buffetings of life. To believe that love is on the throne and that through everything there runs a loving purpose, is in the deepest of all senses to be shielded.

How effectual that shielding is, is shown by the apostle's choice of words. And exquisite and unfailing niceness of selection is the real meaning of verbal inspiration. There are two words in the Greek tongue for shield; the one is common and the other rare. The one connotes a little shield or target; the other a frame that covered the whole man. And it is notable that only here—nowhere else, I mean, in the New Testament—is the latter word employed. Faith is not a partial protection; it casts its defense over the whole of life. It is a means of safety for the intellect, as surely as for the passions of the heart. It guards the feet when they are prone to wander, and the hands when they are growing weary, and the eyes when they are drawn to what is wrong. The shield of faith is an all-embracing shelter. It is coextensive with our being. Faith in God through our Lord Jesus Christ is nothing less than a universal safeguard. All was choicely shown to the Ephesians by the word which the apostle used when he bade them take up the shield of faith.

But if faith be a protecting shield, what then of the apostle's own experience? So far from being defended from life's ills, he knew them all in an abounding measure. He was not protected from cold or heat or hunger, nor from shipwreck, nor from the hand of robbers (2 Cor. 11). He was not protected from bodily infirmity, for he suffered from his lacerating thorn (2 Cor. 12). Everything that makes life bitter was mingled in the cup of the apostle, and yet he dares to speak of faith's protection. I think there are many who have still to learn that faith was never intended for exemption. Faith is not given to guard the life *from* anything; it is given to guard the life *in* everything. It empowers one to bear, and to bear cheerfully, what otherwise would break the heart and darken the loving ordering of God. To pass through the very worst that life can bring, undismayed in soul, and unembittered; to tread the darkest mile and sing in it; never to lose heart, or hope, or love; that is what faith achieved for the apostle and can achieve for everyone of us, and *that* is the shielding power of faith. So was it with our blessed Lord. When He came here, He was offered no exemption. He was a man of sorrows, and He suffered, and He was tempted in all points like as we are. Yet to the end, in a faith that never faltered, He was loving, tranquil, and forgiving and under the cross spoke about His peace.

One should notice, too, that this protecting faith is one that we require to make our own. In the apostle's words, we have *to take it up*, in the same way as we take up our cross. There is a faith that is part and parcel of our being. It is ours without any conscious effort. We believe quite naturally when the sower sows his seed that there will be a harvest in the autumn. But to believe, when life is stern and sorrowful, that God is with us and loves us as a Father, that is not natural to sinful man. We have to take it up, in the apostle's words. We have to summon up the resources of the soul. We have to use our will in a deliberate effort, if such a faith is to be part of life. And it is just there that the Lord Jesus makes all the difference to us in our weakness, for God commendeth His love to us in this, that while we were yet sinners Christ died for us.

The Tactfulness of Love

And this I pray, that your love may abound . . . in all judgment—Phil. 1:9.

The word that is here used for judgment is a very interesting word. It occurs nowhere else in the New Testament. Its primary signification was perception by any of the senses, but gradually it got specialized into perception by the sense of touch. And so, rising into higher spheres (for words have their own moral history), it came to mean what we describe as tact. Tact is the same word as *touch*. Tact is the kind of way in which we touch things, but not in a material sense like wood or stone. It is the unseen substance of which life is made with its sensibilities and shrinkings, its strange and instantaneous reactions. Such contacts we are forced to make in every period of life. Our years are spent in ceaseless interaction with the lives of other people. And whenever we learn to touch these other lives delicately and understandingly, then we possess the charming grace of tact.

Now it is notable that Paul connects this grace with the growth and deepening of love. When love abounds, it inevitably blossoms into all kinds of delicate perception. These Philippians to whom he wrote seem, happily, to have been ignorant of heresy. But they were very ready to misunderstand each other; there was a good deal of social bitterness in Philippi. The grace they lacked, sometimes without ever meaning it, was that interior delicacy which would not hurt or irritate another. There are many people who mean well yet are always rubbing others the wrong way. Often they are quite unconscious of it and never dream of the hurt that they are causing. And one can gather from this letter that in Philippi, for all its orthodoxy, there was a good deal of that social unpleasantness. Paul was perfectly aware of that. He had his hand on the pulse of all his churches. He saw how it spoiled the joy and peace and harmony that ought to reign and rule among the saints. And the notable thing is he does not waste his time in exhorting his children to a greater tactfulness—he prays that they may have a greater love. He goes right down to the heart of things. He fixes his attention on the center. Let love have a controlling place, and the touch will become infinitely delicate. What to avoid, what *not* to say or do, that is not a secret of the intellect; it is always a secret of the heart.

This tactfulness of love is apparent in many different spheres. Watch a botanist handling a flower—you can tell that he loves it by the way he touches it. Look at a mother with her little baby—her very touch reveals the mother-heart. I can often tell if a young fellow loves books, not by the clever way in which he speaks of them, but by the way in which he handles them. Let a rough, coarse man once love a woman, and it is amazing how tactful he becomes. He begins to divine, by the genius of the heart, the delicate attentions she is longing for. For there are little acts of courtesy and grace that mean far more than any gold or silver to such as may be sensitively inclined. It is always a sure mark that love is dying when tact takes to itself wings and flies away. When the delicate perceptions disappear, it is a token that the heart is hardening. And that is the tragedy of many lives, not the blighting touch of infidelity, but the roughened touch (so rough that it may hurt) which betrays the decadence of love.

In its roots as well as in its fruits, true tact differs from diplomacy. I would venture to say that tact is always spurious when it is not rooted in the soil of love. There is a kind of tact that springs from fear, though no one ever may suspect its origin. It shuns offense, not for the sake of love, but because offending might prove perilous. The eye may be fixed, not on the other person, but on one's own quietness or prosperity, either of which may be endangered by the rough or ill-considered touch. True tact is different from that. It owns no kinship with cowardice at all. It is one of the finest flowerings of love; it is the exquisite perception of the heart. That is why Christian tact so far surpasses anything the world had ever known in any of the religions of antiquity. The gospel has done tremendous service in the education of the heart. Giving it at last a worthy motive, it has released the hidden capacities of loving. And so doing, it has poured a wealth of meaning into the gracious tactfulness of love.

Nowhere do we find this tactfulness of love so perfectly revealed as in our Lord. The infinite delicacy of His touch is the measure of His loving heart. When the leper cried for healing, we read that the Lord touched him; it was not alone His hand that touched him, it was a yearning and redeeming love. That lonely, isolated soul got far more than the cleansing of his leprosy: he got the glad assurance of a Friend. Christ had an exquisite way of understanding people, of handling them with unexampled delicacy, of avoiding what might vex or irritate. And all this sprang not from a quick intellect, priding itself on knowing human nature, but from the depth and wonder of His love. That was where Paul learned his lesson. That taught him what to pray for. It was no use praying for a finer tact unless first there was a fuller love. First the roots, and then the fruits. First the deepening, and then the delicacy. First the dew of heaven on the heart—and tactfulness blossoms as the rose.

The Subjugation of Our Higher Longings

Having a desire to depart, and to be with Christ; which is far better. Nevertheless to abide in the flesh is more needful for you—Phil. 1:23, 24.

One cannot wonder that the Apostle Paul had a desire to depart and to be with Christ. He longed for the consummation of his fellowship. Whatever difficulty there may be in reconciling Paul's views of the beyond, there can be no question that central to them all was the thought of personal fellowship with Christ. And in the Roman prison with its inactivities and its long hours for quiet meditation, that longing grew imperious and dominant. Death had no terrors for him. It was the swift passage to a full communion. It would unveil for him the well-beloved face of the Savior to whom he owed his life. He was not "half in love with an easy death," but he was passionately in love with Him into whose presence death would usher him. This was the deepest longing of his soul—to be with Christ which was far better. His highest ambition was to win that intimacy which would be uninterrupted and complete. He longed for the hour when, through the gate of death, he would pass into the presence of that Lord who had so marvelously rescued and redeemed him.

But on that great loving heart of his, Paul bore forever the burden of his converts. He was their one spiritual father, and he loved them as a father loves his children. There comes a time in the life of growing children when they emerge from the control of fatherhood. Trained and disciplined, they stand on their own feet now and fight their own battles with the world. But Paul's children were only infants yet in constant need of guidance and advice which nobody but he could ever give them. Thus it was that, through his highest longing, there broke the tender urgings of apostleship. Sweet would it be to see his blessed Lord—but what would all his little children do? Bereft of him and of his loving counsel, in a crooked and perverse generation, would they ever come to maturity of faith? To Paul that consideration was determinative. It laid a masterful hand on his desires. His yearning love for the souls which God had given him must be regulative of his deepest life. And so, in the interests of his own who leaned on him and needed him so utterly, this great heart rose to the lofty heroism of subduing the highest longing of his soul.

Now very often in the Christian life there comes a difficult issue such as that. The struggle is not waged around our worst; it emerges on the levels of our best. That there are lower longings the Christian must subdue is one of the primary findings of discipleship. This is in no sense *self*-repression, for sin is not of the essence of the self. Often the hardest moral problem meets us, not when called to subjugate the lower, but when summoned to subjugate the higher. Just as the sorest decisions that may face us are not always between right and wrong but are sometimes, in this intricate life of ours, between the competing claims of right and right; so not infrequently the hardest thing in life is not the conquering of our lower longings, but the quiet and lovely renouncing of our higher. Beautiful things we have set our heart upon, dreams we have long cherished, spiritual ambitions that have been our intimates since first we passed from darkness into light—to let these go, quietly to yield them up when the finger of God points us to another road, that is one of life's most lofty heroisms. So was it with the apostle in his prison. His whole soul longed to be with Christ. That (for the Greek is stronger than the English) was a very great deal better. And then in his fatherly yearning for his converts who leaned so hard on him and loved him so, he subjugated the longing to depart.

This higher spiritual renunciation may come to men in very different guises. It is various as the complexity of life. It may present itself to the young woman longing to give herself to Christian work, yet with little motherless children in the home entirely dependent on her care. It may face the young fellow in business whose fondest ambition is to be a minister, but whose business is the one support of a frail mother or an invalid sister. Many a young disciple has longed with all her heart to serve on the foreign mission field, and then the unmistakable pointing of God's finger has indicated another road for her. And perhaps no struggle she ever had with sin was so bitter as the sweet acceptance of a lowlier and more homely lot. It is hard to part sometimes with lower cravings; it is often ever harder to part with higher ones—to lay our spiritual ambitions down at the call of simple duty or of love. And it is always a great thing to remember that the saints of God have shared in that experience and been perfectly familiar with its bitterness. Here was Paul, a prisoner in Rome. His great desire was to be with Christ. The deep, passionate longing of his soul was to get home, that he might see his Savior. And nothing is finer in that noble heart of his than the subjugation of that higher longing for the sake of those who loved him and who needed him.

The Form of a Servant

He took upon him the form of a servant—Phil. 2:7.

On one occasion our Lord announced "I am among you as one who serveth." That was the summation of His ministry. The word for *serveth* which St. John gives us is a word of very large and liberal meaning. It includes services of every kind, however high or exalted they may be. But when St. Paul says of that same Lord that He took on Him the form of a servant, *that* is an entirely different word. It is the common term for slave, or, as we might put it, for a domestic servant. There was nothing of lofty ministry about it; it was colored with contemptuous suggestion. Paul was thinking of his home in Tarsus where, unregarded and unthanked, the slaves were busy in menial occupations. No one knew better than the great apostle that life in its last analysis is service. The Grecian stateman and the Roman general were the servants of commonwealth or empire. But what awed Paul when he thought of Christ was *not* that He was found in such a category. It was that He humbled Himself to the likeness of a slave. There is a service which is highly honorable. It is compatible with great position. I have a postcard I once got from Mr. Gladstone, and it is signed "Your obedient servant." But the slave's service was of another order, quite apart from honorable ministries, and in *that* lay the wonder of the Lord. The slave legally had no possessions, and *He* had not where to lay His head. No freeman acknowledged a slave in public places, and from *Him* men hid, as it were, their faces. The slave was universally despised, and his master could maltreat him as he pleased. And *He* was despised of men and, being maltreated, opened not His mouth.

This aspect of the Lord's obedience constitutes the wonder of His childhood. It explains as it illuminates the strange silence of the Gospel story. There are apocryphal gospel of the infancy that credit the little Boy with various miracles. He strikes a comrade who instantly falls dead; He makes clay sparrows and they fly away. But the real wonder of the childhood does not lie in miracles like these, but in *this*, that even in His boyhood He took on Him the form of a servant. Did Mary never ask Him in the morning to go and fetch the water from the well? Did she never say, "Child, I'm very tired today, will you run to the village shop and take a message?" And the beautiful way in which He did such biddings was a far more wonderful thing to seeing eyes than any reported miracles on sparrows. He, the eternal Son of God, running little errands for His mother; He, who might have grasped equality with God, lighting the cottage fire and fetching water—*that* was the astounding thing to Paul, as it was to all of the evangelists, as is so clear from their majestic silence.

Or, again, we think of these long years when He was the carpenter of Nazareth. And once again legend has been busy seeking to give content to these years. Strange stories soon grew current of amazing things that had happened in that workshop. Beams had been miraculously lengthened, and plows, in a moment, miraculously made. But to all this, in the inspired evangelists, there is not even a reference in passing. For *them* the abiding wonder lay elsewhere. Do any of my readers keep a shop? Don't *they* know how hard it is to serve their customers? Aren't some of these customers very hard to please and often irritating and unreasonable? And one may be certain if it is so in Britain where at least the atmosphere is Christian, it would be worse in uneducated Nazareth. The carpenter was at the beck and call of everybody. There was no pleasing some of the folk in Nazareth. It was a thankless and often humiliating service, that of a carpenter in a provincial village. And to Paul the wonder of these years was not the miraculous lengthening of beams. It was the stooping to a drudgery like that. In the beginning was the Word, and the Word was with God, and the Word was God. Christ was the brightness of His Father's glory, and the express image of His person. And then Paul thought of the carpenter's shop at Nazareth with its exacting uneducated customers and wrote, *He took on Him the form of a servant.*

In the public ministry, again, there is one incident which illuminates our text. It is an hour the world will not willingly let die. In the East it was one of the duties of the slave to wash the feet of the arriving traveler. For men wore only sandals then and the highways (save in rain) were very dusty. And Peter at any rate never could forget how once, and very near the end, the Master had done that office of the slave. Would he not be certain to tell that to Paul when they talked together, as we know from the Acts they did? Would not Peter enact it and draw back his feet to show Paul what had actually happened? Perhaps it was *then* there flashed into Paul's mind the magnificent daring of our text coupling the Lord of heaven with a menial slave. Jesus, knowing that He was come from God and went to God, girded Himself and washed the disciples' feet. He did it *not* forgetting His divinity. He did it because He knew He was divine. Brooding on which, Paul took his pen and wrote, "Who being in the form of God, *took on him the form of a servant.*"

Living Dangerously

Epaphroditus, my brother and companion in labor, and fellow soldier . . . for the work of Christ he was nigh unto death, not regarding his life [Greek : gambling with his life]—Phil. 2:25, 30.

All we know of Epaphroditus is told us in this letter. He is one of those brave souls who leap into the light in connection with the imprisonment of Paul. It has been thought that he might be identified with the Epaphras of the Colossian epistle. But even if the names be one, such identification is improbable. It is scarcely thinkable that the pastor of Colossae should be so associated with a church in Europe as to be made its delegate to Paul. It is as a delegate we hear of him. For that perilous office he had volunteered. He had undertaken to convey to Paul the offerings of the Philippian Church. And of the risks involved in such a journey and in visiting a suspect and a prisoner, we have sundry hints in the apostle's words. No compulsion had driven Epaphroditus. He had taken all the hazards cheerfully. The strain of it all had told on him so terribly that he was brought down to the gates of death. And the point to note is how the great apostle "grappled him to his soul with hoops of steel," and spoke of him in terms of loftiest eulogy.

It is a very interesting word which Paul uses when he says that Epaphroditus "did not regard" his life. It is a word from the language of the gambler. In the long hours of his imprisonment, Paul had narrowly watched his Roman guards. He had heard them talking about boxing matches; he had been a spectator when they played at dice. And as he saw them gambling with their money and taking risks in a reckless way, his thoughts went winging to Epaphroditus. That was the kind of thing

226

which he had done. He had deliberately gambled with his life. For Christ's sake and for the Church's sake he had flung caution to the winds of heaven. And that loving and self-forgetting recklessness so stirred the gallant heart of the apostle that Epaphroditus is immortalized. Had he played for safety he would have stayed at home. He would have pled the urgencies of work at Philippi. Probably his health was none too good, and he had doctor's orders against going. But Epaphroditus took the risks—lived dangerously—gambled with his life—and so lives within the Word of God forever.

One understands how the great heart of Paul clave so closely to Epaphroditus. The spirit of that inconspicuous delegate was the spirit which burned in his own breast. Like all great missionaries, Paul did not dwell on dangers. He only spoke of them when he was forced to. In his tremendous eagerness to spread the Gospel, he almost forgot the risks that he was running. But if ever a man gambled with his life, lived dangerously, and took the hazard, it was the great apostle to the Gentiles. He, too, might have played for safety. He might have advanced a score of reasons for it. That lacerating and gnawing thorn, for instance, would not *that* justify the nicest caution? But Paul forgot his caution and took risks that well might have appalled the strongest heart in the ardor of his love for the Lord Jesus. The love of Christ constrained him. He lived dangerously for the Lord. The motto of Paul was never "Safety first"; from the beginning to the end it was "Christ first." That was why he found a kindred spirit in this obscure delegate from Philippi who would have nothing to do with self-regarding caution, but for love's sake gambled with his life.

This lofty disregard of self is inherent in all Christian service. A certain joy in living dangerously is one of the first-fruits of the Spirit. In the upper chamber, before Pentecost, the disciples were very careful of their lives. The doors were shut for fear of the Jews. They trembled at every step upon the stair. But when the Holy Spirit came on them in power, there was a kind of reckless gaiety about them which made men think that they were filled with wine. The doors were no longer barred now. They did not jump at every mounting footstep. That mighty rushing wind which swept the chamber somehow had swept their caution right away. They were ready to take any risks now, in the spiritual baptism of Pentecost, and like this delegate, they gambled with their lives.

Later on we read of two of them that "men took knowledge of them that they had been with Jesus." And what was it that carried this conviction? It was the defiant boldness of the two. Heedless of safety, imperiling their liberty, they proclaimed the resurrection of the Lord—and men took knowledge of them that they had been with Jesus. The strange thing is that one of the two was Peter—and immediately we remember the denial. Peter had played for safety then. To save his skin he had almost lost his soul. Now, in the power of Pentecost, that same Peter was sublimely reckless. He was living dangerously for his Lord. All great servants have had that spiritual mark. St. Francis had it when he had kissed the leper. Luther had it when he *would* go to Worms though devils were thick as the tiles upon the house-tops. And nobody, however quiet his sphere, is ever thoroughly equipped for service unless, like Epaphroditus and the rest of them, he is prepared to gamble with his life. I have heard of ministers who were afraid to visit where there was fever or diphtheria or smallpox. I have even known of them being dissuaded from it by loving members of their congregations. Doubtless Epaphroditus was besought so by those who prized his ministry at Philippi; but *he that saveth his life shall lose it.*

This holds also of the life of intellect as certainly as of the life of action. To live by faith is always to live dangerously. My old professor, Lord Kelvin, once said in class a very striking thing. He said that there came a point in all his great discoveries when he had to take a leap in the dark. And nobody who is afraid of such a leap from the solid ground of what is demonstrated will know the exhilaration of believing. To commit ourselves unreservedly to Christ is just the biggest venture in the world. And the wonderful thing is that when, with a certain daring, we take Lord Kelvin's leap into the dark, we discover it is not dark at all, but life abundant, and liberty, and peace.

The Power of the Resurrection

That I may know . . . the power of his resurrection—Phil. 3:10.

Of the fact of the resurrection, Paul had not a shadow of a doubt. It was one of his indubitable certainties. He himself had had a revelation of the Lord which had altered the whole tenor of his life. He had known and conversed with those who saw Him in the days that followed upon Easter morning. Whatever might be doubtful to his intellect or might remain a matter of conjecture, his life, both of experience and thought, was based upon the fact that Christ was risen. But the power of a fact is to be distinguished from the fact itself. The power is the influence it exercises in its various relationships to life. And so the power of the resurrection is not the power that raised Christ from the dead, but the increasing pressure upon life of the stupendous fact that Christ is risen. To penetrate more fully into this, to grasp it in its infinite significance, that was the ambition of St. Paul as he made his lonely way among the mysteries. Like some bright star the fact was always shining. It was unalterable and unsetting. His passion was to know the power of the fact.

One thinks, for instance, of its evidencing power. The resurrection was the seal of heaven. In it the stupendous claims of Jesus were guaranteed and ratified of God. The dark hours when He lay buried were to the disciples hours of anguish. They could not reconcile that last indignity with the magnificence of His spiritual program. It must have seemed to them, and seemed to everybody, as if all that they had shared in was a dream now quenched forever by the grave. The fact of death extinguished all their hopes. It invalidated every claim of Jesus. It brought down into a hopeless ruin the building they had thought to be of God. And the first great power of the resurrection, its primary influence upon thought and life, was the power to scatter the agonizing doubts that filled the breasts of those who trusted Him. It gave beauty for ashes and the oil of joy for mourning. It guaranteed the Messiahship of Jesus. It flooded with the authority of heaven the vocation of their blessed Lord. That was why, in the earliest Christian preaching, there was such impassioned and unswerving emphasis on the resurrection of the Savior. It was not an isolated fact. Isolated facts are quite inoperative. It was a fact fraught with a tremendous influence on the whole concept of the Lord. Every word He spoke and every claim He made was charged with new and heavenly significance under the power of the resurrection.

Or one thinks again of its sustaining power amid the tasks and burdens of mortality. It gave to men, wherever they might wander, the near presence of a living Friend. The soul thirsts for a living God, and the heart thirsts for a living friend—for one who knows and understands and loves in the intimacy of a present fellowship. And the power of the resurrection is that it answers that steady yearning of the heart in a way no memories can ever do. It gives us a Friend who is alive, closer than breathing, nearer than hands or feet. It confronts our lives not with the storied past, but with One who lives and loves us to the uttermost. And the best of all is that this living Friend has sounded all the depths of human life and has "come smiling from the world's great snare uncaught." What the law could never do for Paul was done victoriously by the risen Savior. In fellowship with Him he triumphed, and when he was weak then he was strong. His one passion was to know more fully the resources of that living Friend. *That* was the power of His resurrection.

Or one thinks of its exalting power which was never absent from the apostle's thought. The spiritual power of the resurrection is its steady upward pull upon the life. When one is climbing in our Scottish highlands, there are often places perilous to negotiate. In such places it is a mighty succor when someone above reaches down a helping hand. And the mystical thought that Christ was gripping him from the upper security of heavenly places turned the apostle into a daring climber on the steeps that lead to God. Christ was above him—He was risen. He was stooping down to lift the climber up. Paul felt the urge of the true mountaineer which lies in seeking the things which are above. But for him there was the splendid certainty that he was not going to perish for before him and above him there was Christ. In union with Him there was an upward pull. Paul turned his back upon the lower things. Just because Christ was risen and above him, he must gain in Christ the heights of holy living. Had you asked the apostle, I think he would have answered that *that* was the dominant thought within his breast when he wrote of *the power of His resurrection.*

The Discipline of Thought

Think on these things—Phil. 4:8.

When we speak of unseen things, we commonly refer to things that are eternal. We associate the unseen with the world beyond the veil where the angels of God, innumerable, are around the throne. Now it is true that that is an unseen world though the time is coming when our eyes shall see it, but we must never forget that far nearer to us than that there is another world which also is unseen. We live in a day of very strange discoveries and look on many things that were once invisible. By means of our telescope we see very distant stars, and we can watch the beating of our hearts. But the world of thought, of feeling, of passion and of desire—that world still baffles the finest powers of vision; as surely as there is an unseen heaven above us, there is an unseen universe within. What a mysterious and strange thing is life—a burning point, and around it what a shadow! How utterly must a man fail who walks by sight and who will not recognize the all-embracing mystery! Deep calleth unto deep wherever man is—the invisible deep within to the unseen depths beyond. It is one distinguishing feature of the Gospel that it never makes light of these great and awful things.

Let us turn to the world within, our thoughts. For I believe that most of us give far too little heed to what I might call the discipline of thought. "If there be any virtue, or any praise, think on these things." First, I shall speak on the vital need there is of governing our thoughts. Next, on how the Gospel helps men to this government.

First, then, on the government of our thoughts—and at the outset I would recognize the difficulty of it. I question if there is a harder task in all the world than that of bringing our thoughts into subjection to our will. It is very difficult to regulate our actions, yet there is a social pressure on our actions. It is supremely difficult to order our speech aright, yet speech is restrained and checked by countless barriers. Every time we act and every time we speak we come into direct contact with society, and prudence and self-love and reputation and business interests admonish us instantly to walk with caution. But thought is free—at least we think it is. It is transacted in a world where none can observe it. The law cannot reach us for unclean imaginations. Think how we will of a man, he cannot charge us with libel. All the prudential safeguards which God has set on speech, and all the deterrent motives which surround our deeds, are lacking when we enter the silent halls of thought. It is that—perhaps above all other things—which makes the management of thought so difficult. It is the secrecy—the absence of restraint—the imagined freedom of the world within. And yet there are one or two considerations I can bring before you that will show you how, in the whole circle of self-mastery, there is nothing more vital than the mastery of thought.

Think, for example, how much of our happiness—our common happiness—depends on thought. We begin by imagining it depends on outward things, but we all grow to be wiser by and by. "There's nothing either good or bad," says Shakespeare, "but thinking makes it so." Now of course that is only half a truth. There are things that in themselves are forever good, and there are other things that eternally and everywhere are bad—never be juggled out of these moral certainties. But in between these everlasting fixities there lies a whole world of life and of experience, and what it shall mean for us—how we shall regard it—depends almost entirely upon thought. Our happiness does not depend on what we view. Our happiness depends on our point of view. There are men who can think themselves any day into a paradise, and others who think themselves into a fever. Have we not known or met or read of men and women who seemed to have everything this world could give, yet only to look at their faces or their portraits was to read the story of frustration and discontent? But St. Francis of Assisi, the sweetest of all saints, sitting down to dine by the roadside on a few crusts of bread, was so exquisitely and radiantly happy that he could not find words enough for thankfulness. That then is an integral part of happiness—the discipline and the government of our thoughts. Basically, it is not things themselves, it is our thoughts about them, that constitute the gentle art of being happy.

Again I want you to consider this—how much of our unconscious influence lies in our thoughts. Not only by what we do and what we say, but by the kind of thoughts we are cherishing in secret, do we impress ourselves upon our neighbors and help or hinder the little world we move in. That very suggestive and spiritual writer, Mr. Maeterlinck, puts the matter in his own poetic way. He says, "Though you assume the face of a saint, a hero or a martyr, the eye of the passing child will not greet you with the same unapproachable smile, if there lurk within you an evil thought." Now probably there is a little exaggeration there; one thought, flashing and then expelled, may not reveal itself. The totality of saintly character is too great to be overborne by the intrusion of one shadow of the devil. But it is certain that by the thoughts we harbor and let ourselves dwell upon and cherish in the dark, we touch and turn and influence our world when we never dream that we are doing it. There is nothing hidden that shall not be revealed—what a depth there is in that one word of Jesus! He is not merely thinking of God's judgment bar tomorrow. He is thinking of the undetected revelation of today. Christ recognized that the kind of thing we brood on, the kind of thought we allow ourselves to think, though it never utter itself in actual words, or clothe itself in the flesh and blood of deeds, encompasses and affects the life of others like a poisonous vapor or like a breath of spring. Your secret is not such a secret as you think. Why are men drawn to you? Why are men repelled by you? Why is it that sometimes we instinctively shrink from people in the very first hour that we meet them? It is because the heart—more powerful than any x-ray—deciphers for itself the secret story, brushes past speech and deed into the hidden place and apprehends the existence that is there. To think base thoughts is a sin against our neighbor as surely as it is a sin against ourselves. To be unclean even in imagination is to make it harder for others to be good. In the interests of our influence then, no less than of our happiness, you see the need of governing our thoughts.

There is only one other consideration that I would mention, and that is the power of thought in our temptations. In the government of thought—in the power to bring thought to heel—lies one of our greatest moral safeguards against sin. You have all read the words of Thomas A. Kempis in that immortal book, "The Imitation of Christ." They occur in his thirteenth chapter, *Of Resisting Temptation*. How does sin reach us? That is his question—and this is his never-to-be-forgotten answer to it: "For first here cometh to the mind a bare thought of evil, then a strong imagination thereof, afterwards delight and evil motion, then consent." First, a bare thought—that is the beginning, and it is then that the government of thought means heaven or hell. For if a man has disciplined himself to crush that thought—which may come to the purest and holiest mind—still better, if he has acquired the power to change the current and to turn his thought instantly into other and nobler channels, temptation is baffled at its very start and the man stands upon his feet victorious. A man will never regulate his passions who has never learned to regulate his thoughts. If we cannot master our besetting thoughts, we shall never master our besetting sins. I think you see, then, that in the interests of morality no less than in the interests of our happiness and influence, it is supremely necessary that we all give heed to the great subject of thought—discipline.

So now in the second place, I wish to ask how the Gospel helps us to that. I wish to ask why a Christian above all other men has powers available for governing his thought. To some of you the mastery of thought may seem impossible—it is never viewed as impossible in Scripture, and the secret of that Gospel-power lies in the three great words—light, love, life.

Think first of light as a power for thought-mastery. We all know how light affects our thoughts. In twilight or darkness what sad thoughts come thronging, which the glory of sunlight instantly dispels. I have a dear friend who is a terrible sufferer and who rarely has any quiet sleep after three in the morning, and the worst of wakening then, he tells me, is that that is just the time when everything seems melancholy, cheerless, hopeless. We need the light if we are to see things truly. We need the light if we are to think aright. And the glory of Christ is that by His life and death He has shed a light where before there was only darkness. What had the old and beautiful religion of the Greeks to say when a man was confronted by sorrow or disease? It was dumb, it turned away its head in silence; it had no light to shed upon the mystery—till men, having no light to think by, lost all thought-control and wandered into a labyrinth of evil. But the sufferings of Christ have shed a light on suffering. The death of Christ has shed a light on death. Faced by the worst now and called to bear the cross, we can think bravely and luminously of it all. The light of Christ, for the man who lives in it, is an untold help in the government of thought.

Then think of love—Is it not one mark of love that our thoughts always follow in its train? A love that never thought about the loved one would be the most heartless and hopeless of all mockeries. A man who is deeply in love with a good woman thinks of her every hour of the day, and there is no such certain sign of love's decay as the dying out of gentle and sweet thoughtfulness. That sign a woman instantly detects—it is the unuttered tragedy of countless lives—and the sorrow of it springs from the intuition that thought is under the mastery of love. Do you see then how the Gospel helps us to thought-control? At the very center of its message it puts love. It shows us a Savior who lived and died for us and who stretches out His pierced hands towards us. It speaks of Gethsemane and Calvary and at its burning heart reveals a love that passes the love of women. "Simon son of Jonas, lovest thou me?"—that will determine the current and trend of thought. That master-passion is the power of God for bringing every thought into captivity. If the love of a woman can control and purge our thoughts, how much more the love of Jesus Christ!

Then think of life—are not our thoughts affected by the largeness and abundance of our lives? When life is poor and feeble, base thoughts scent us out as the vultures of the desert scent out the dying traveler. Half of the vile or bitter thoughts we think are the children of our lusterless and unprofitable days. Expand the horizon—get a new breath of life—and they take to themselves wings and fly away. Now what did Christ say about His coming? I am come that they might have life, and have it more abundantly. Life is expanded and filled with undreamed-of fullness when we live in the glad fellowship of Jesus. And that great tide of life, like the tide of the sea that covers up the mudbanks, is the greatest power in the moral world for submerging every base and bitter thought. Do you know anything of that light—

that love—that life? What a great deal we miss in ignoring Jesus Christ! The king's daughter is all beautiful *within*—just because her king is her Redeemer.

How to Control Your Thoughts

"Those things . . . do"–Phil. 4:9.

We are all familiar with the difference that is made by the thoughts that arise within our hearts. Often they cast a shadow on our universe. A man may waken in the morning singing and address himself cheerfully to duty, and then, suddenly, some unbidden thought may creep or flash into his mind—and in a moment the heavens become cloudy and the music of the morning vanishes and there is fret and bitterness within.

Things have not altered in the least. Everything is as it was an hour ago. The burden of the day has not grown heavier, nor has anybody ceased to love us. Yet all the world seems different, and the brightness has vanished from the sky under the tyranny of intruding thoughts.

No one can achieve serenity who does not practice the control of thought. You cannot build a lovely house out of dirty or discolored bricks. The power of our thoughts is so tremendous over health and happiness and character that to master them is moral victory.

This mastery of our thoughts is difficult, but then everything beautiful is difficult. The kind of person I have no patience with is the person who wants everything made easy. When an artist paints a lovely picture, he does that by a process of selection. Certain features of the landscape he rejects; other aspects he welcomes and embraces. And if to do that even the man of genius has to scorn delights and live laborious days, how can we hope without the sternest discipline to paint beautiful pictures in the mind?

So is it with the musician when he plays for us some lovely piece of music. Years of training are behind the melody that seems to come rippling from his fingers. And if he has to practice through hard hours to produce such melody without, how can we hope, without an equal effort, to create a like melody within?

There are two moral tasks that seem to me supremely difficult and yet supremely necessary. One is the redemption of our time; the other is the mastery of our thoughts. Probably most of us, right on to the end are haunted by a sense of failure in these matters. But the great thing is to keep on struggling.

We see, too, how difficult this task is when we compare it with mastery of speech. If it be hard to set a watch upon our lips, it is harder to set a watch upon our thoughts. All speech has social reactions, and social prudence is a great deterrent. If you speak your mind, you may lose your position, possibly you may lose your friend. But thought is hidden—it is shrouded—it moves in dark and impenetrable places; it has no apparent social reactions. A man may be thinking bitter thoughts of you, yet meet you with a smile upon his face. A typist may inwardly despise her boss, yet outwardly be a model of obedience. It is this secrecy, this surrounding darkness, that has led men to say that thought is free, and that makes the mastery of thought so difficult.

Now, the fine thing in the New Testament is this, that while it never calls that easy which is difficult, it yet proclaims that the mastery of thought is within the power of everybody. Think, for instance, of the Beatitude "Blessed are the pure in heart." Whenever our Lord says that anything is blessed, He wants us to understand that it is possible. Yet no man can have purity of heart, as distinguished from purity of conduct, who is not able to grapple with his thoughts. Again by our thoughts we shall be judged—that is always implied in the New Testament. Christ came and is going to come again, "that the thoughts of many hearts may be revealed."

But I refuse to believe that men are to be judged by anything that lies beyond their power—to credit *that* would make the judge immoral. Then does not the great apostle say, "If there be any virtue, . . . think on these things?" It would be mockery to command us to think if the controlling of our thoughts were quite beyond us. It may be difficult, as fine things always are, but the clear voice of the Word of God proclaims that it is within the capacity of all.

If, then, someone were to ask me how is a man to practice this great discipline, remembering the experience of the saints, I think I should answer in some such way as this: You must summon up the resources of your will. You must resist beginnings. You must remember the most hideous of sins is to debauch the mind.

You must fill your being so full of higher interests that when the devil comes and clamors for admission, he will find there is not a chair for him to sit on. Above all, you must endeavor daily to walk in a closer fellowship with Christ. It is always easier to have lovely thoughts when walking with the Altogether Lovely One.

The Virtue of Forbearance

Forbearing one another—Col. 3:13.

If a man is to live with any joy and fullness and to find what a noble abode this world may prove, there are three virtues which he must steadily pursue. The first is faith in God, for without faith existence will always be a tangled skein; the second is courage, for every life has its hills and we face them poorly if our heart is faint; and the third is forbearance—forbearing one another. It is on forbearance then that I desire to dwell, and I propose to gather up what I wish to say in this way. First, I shall touch on some of the evils of the unforbearing spirit. Second, I shall indicate the character of true forbearance. Then I shall suggest some thoughts to make us more forbearing.

First, then, some of the evils of the unforbearing spirit; and one of the first of them to arrest me is that it *makes life a constant disappointment.* I have often wondered that there is no trace of disappointment in the life of our Lord Jesus Christ. You may call Him a despised man if you will, but you could never call Him a disappointed man. He came to His own and His own received Him not; they laughed Him to scorn and then they crucified Him; yet when He entered the glory and saw His Father's face, do you think He said, "Father, it has been a tragic disappointment"? For all its sorrow, life was not that to Christ: it was full and fresh and dew-touched to the close, and one of the sources of that unfailing freshness was our Savior's knowledge of the secret of forbearance. Jesus expected great things from humanity. Jesus never expected the impossible. I like to think that He who made the heavens was ready when the hour came to make allowances. Depend upon it that if we expect the impossible, we are doomed to the disappointment which is worse than death. There is only one highway to the world's true comradeship—it is the road of forbearing one another.

Another evil of the unforbearing spirit is this, that *it presses hardest on life's tenderest relationships.* It becomes powerful for evil in that very region where ties are most delicate and life most sweet. There are some worms that are content to gnaw green leaves and to spend their lives on the branches of the tree. But there are others that are never satisfied with leaves, they must eat their way into the red heart of the rose. That is the curse of the unforbearing spirit—it gnaws at the very heart of the rose of life. It is comparatively easy to be forbearing with those whom we rarely meet and whom we hardly know. We are all tolerant of those who lightly touch us. But it is with those whom we meet and among whom we mingle daily, who share the same home with us, who live with us and love us—it is with those that it is often hardest to forbear, and it is on those that the sorrow of unforbearance falls. There are ministers who can speak well of every congregation except the one which they have been called to serve. There are husbands who are gentle to everybody's faults with the exception of the faults of their own wives. And it is just because unforbearance has a greater scope in proportion as life's ties grow tenderer and dearer, that the Gospel of love insists so urgently on the duty of forbearing one another.

But there is another evil of the unforbearing temper—*it reacts with certainty upon the man himself.* For with what judgment we judge we shall be judged, and with what measure we mete it shall be measured unto us. If we are intolerant, we become intolerable. If we never make allowances for anybody, God knows the scant allowance that we get. Just think of the Pharisees a moment. Their crowning vice was that they were unforbearing. There was not a little that was good in many Pharisees, but they were harsh and censorious and exacting—need I remind you of the vials of stern judgment that were poured on the Pharisees by Jesus Christ? Let that suffice for the evils of unforbearance. It makes life one constant disappointment. It presses hardest on life's tenderest ties. It reacts inevitable on the man himself.

In the second place I wish to indicate the character of true forbearance, and it is urgently important that we should pay heed to this. For the devil has got his counterfeit of every grace, and a counterfeit grace is sometimes worse than sin.

The first thing that I would say about it is that true forbearance begins in a man's thought. It is a good thing to be forbearing in our acts, a great thing to be so in our speech, yet I question if we have begun to practice rightly this preeminently Christian virtue till we are habitually forbearing in our thought. "Master," said the disciples, "shall we call down fire on these villages? They would not receive us: shall we clear them away like Sodom?" And it was not quite for their words that Christ rebuked them—yet know not what spirit ye are of. Ah, if our bitter and unforbearing words flashed into utterance without any thought, they would not wound so nor would they leave these scars that the kindnesses of weeks cannot efface. It is because they so often betray the unforbearing thoughts that have been harbored in secret and cherished in the dark that the bite of them is like a serpent's fang. We talk of a hasty word, but a hasty word might mean little if it were only the out-flash of a hasty thought. What a hasty word often implies is this: that in secret we have been putting the worst construction upon things; then comes the moment of temper when the tongue is loosened, and we never meant to utter what we thought, but it escapes us—only a hasty word—yet the bitter thoughts of a fortnight may be in it. True forbearance begins in a man's thought.

Again, true forbearance is independent of our moods. It does not vary with our varying temper. It is a mock forbearance that comes and goes with every variation in the day. There are times when it is very easy to be forbearing. When things have gone well with us, when we are feeling strong, or when some great happiness has touched our hearts—it is not difficult to be forbearing then. When we are in a good humor with ourselves, we can be in a good humor with everybody. But true forbearance is not a passing gleam nor is it the child of a happy mood or temper; it does not depend on the state of man's health or on whether or not he has had a good day at business. It is a virtue to be loyally practiced for Christ's sake whatever our mood or disappointment be. I should not have wondered much if Christ had been forbearing when He rode in triumph into Jerusalem. Amid the cries of Hosanna and the strewing of the palm branches it might have been easy to have congenial views. But when His face was marred more than any man's, when they were looking on Him whom they had pierced, when the nails were torture and when the cross was agony, was it not supremely hard to be forbearing then? Yet it was then that the Redeemer prayed, "Father, forgive them, for they know not what they do." Forbearance must not vanish when we suffer.

There is one other mark on which I would insist and it is this, that true forbearance helps to better things. It is like the sunshine which brings the summer nearer; it is part of that gentleness which makes men great. There is a certain lenient indulgence that is the very antipodes of this great virtue. There is a soft and easy way of smiling at all sin that may send a man to the devil double-speed. Such leniency is the leniency of Antichrist. Christian forbearance never makes light of sin; it never oils the wheels of Satan's chariot; it can be stern, it whets its glittering sword; if a man is a scoundrel it can tell him so. But it never despairs, never passes final judgments, see possibilities, touches the chord of brotherhood until a man feels that someone believes in him, and sometimes it is heaven to feel that. One day they dragged a poor women before Christ, and the Jews would have stoned her, for she was taken in sin. But Jesus said, "Neither do I condemn thee; go, and sin no more," and I am certain she never so sinned again. Peter was saved by the forbearance of Christ Jesus—"and the Lord turned, and looked upon Peter." Thomas was saved by the forbearance of Christ Jesus—"reach hither thine hand, thou doubter, let Me not scold thee." The forbearance of Christ was a great moral power, and all Christian forbearance must share the same prerogative.

Then lastly let me suggest some thoughts that may help to make us more forbearing.

First think how little we know of one another. We know far too little to be censorious or harsh. One secret of the perfect gentleness of Christ is His perfect knowledge of everyone He met. I suppose that most of us have known some man whom for years, perhaps, we used to judge unkindly. We never like him and our thoughts of him were bitter. Then one day we learned the story of his life, and we found that long ago when the heavens were blue above him, there had fallen on his life some crushing blow; and we say "If we had only known that story, we should never have judged the man as we have done." It is well to remember how ignorant we are when we are tempted to be unforbearing. There may have been something in the upbringing that would explain a score of things if we but knew it. There may have been elements that made the temptation awful, yet how we jested and sneered when someone fell! Forbearing one another—because of life's complexity; because we cannot see, because we do not know; because only God can tell the million threads that are woven into the tapestry of being. Our very dearest are such strangers to us that it is always wisest to forbear.

Next think how greatly we ourselves need forbearance. Even if we do not give it, we all want it. I suppose we all irritate and alienate other people a thousand times more often than we ever dream of. If other people are doing so to us, it is but reasonable to think we are doing so to them. Never a sun sets but a man feels how easily he might have been misjudged that day. Never a morning breaks but a man knows that he will make demands on the forbearance of the world. If we need forbearance, then let us give forbearance. If we need to be kindly judged, let us judge so. Let us forbear one another because of our own great need.

Lastly think how God has forborne us. The forbearance of God is a perpetual wonder. He has been willing that men should taunt Him with being idle, and He has been willing that men should say He did not care rather than that He should seem an unforbearing God. Is there no secret passage in your life which being trumpeted abroad would have almost ruined you? God in His mercy has never blown that trumpet blast, and His long-suffering has been your salvation. Then we are such poor scholars in His school; we are so backward and so soon turned aside; we make so little progress in His teaching and are so keen about everything save Him—surely there is no forbearance in the world like the forbearance of our heavenly Father. It is a great example: shall we not copy it? Days will be golden and silenced birds will sing when we revive the grace of forbearing one another.

The Perfecting Power of Love

Above all these things put on love, which is the bond of perfectness—Col. 3:14.

We are accustomed to think of Paul as a dogmatic writer, never so happy as when immersed in argument, but we must not forget with what affecting tenderness he has written of the grace of love. Great intellectual strength like that of Paul is often intolerant of tender feeling. Moving along the lines of demonstration, it disdains the heart as a true source of knowledge; but from that temptation Paul is entirely free for while he is the very prince of reasoners, he insists with every increasing emphasis on the power and the primacy of love. It is not John, it is Paul who tells us that love is the fulfilling of the law. It is Paul who writes that wonderful hymn of love which we find in the thirteenth chapter of Corinthians. So here it is Paul who, after a noble passage describing our death and life in Jesus Christ, bids us put on the bond of charity.

Now a word or two will explain to us the figure which the apostle uses to convey his meaning: "Above all these things put on love, which is the bond of perfectness." The picture in the apostle's mind is that of one who is putting on his raiment. He sees a man throwing around his body the loose and flowing garments of antiquity. And then it occurs to him that these loose garments, no matter how fine or beautiful they be, can never be worn with comfort or grace unless they are clasped together with a girdle. Without that girdle drawing all together, they hamper and hinder a man at every turn. It is the perfect bond of robe and tunic, the final touch that makes them serviceable. And so, says Paul, is it with love; it is the girdle of every other grace; it is the final touch that beautifies the whole and makes every garment of the spirit perfect. Under the figure, then, there lies one thought—it is the thought of the perfecting of love. Love is the girdle binding all together and giving to everything its proper beauty. On that, then, I want to dwell a little; on love, not in its inherent qualities but in its singular and in-communicable power of perfecting everything that clothes our being.

How true this is of spiritual gifts we learn from the first epistle to the Corinthians. That church at Corinth was very rich in gifts; so rich, that there was trouble over them. One had the gift of prophecy and one of prayer; one had the gift of tongues and one of healing; and every man in the ardor of the spirit was claiming for his own gift a proud preeminence until at last the danger grew so great and the scandal of bickering so soul-destroying that the Corinthian Christians wrote to Paul begging him for his advice and guidance. What was the counsel which the apostle gave? First, he said, covet earnestly the *best* gifts. Remember, he means, that though all gifts are of God, yet all are not equal in spiritual value. But then immediately he turns from that as though it were too hard for these Corinthians, and he says "and yet I show you a more excellent way"—and that more excellent way is love. It is thus that Paul introduces that great chapter in which He glorifies the powers of love. There will be no more trouble about spiritual gifts if love is the girdle which includes them all. Without love, the graces of the spirit will irritate like flowing garments in the gale. Love is the perfect bond which makes them serviceable, keeping each in its peculiar place.

Not only is this true of spiritual gifts; it is true of artistic and intellectual gifts. Over them all a man must put on love, for love is the final touch that perfects them. Take for example the happy gift of song which God has bestowed so freely on His children. We have all listened, I take it, to some singers who have set us wondering at their perfect art. Artistically there was not a flaw to find; there was consummate mastery and perfect execution, and yet the song somehow failed to move us or to strike a responsive chord within our breast. The gift was there—that no one would deny—and it had been trained with splendid perseverance, but there was one thing lacking to complete it and that was the perfecting impress of the heart. You can arrest and dazzle without love, but without love you cannot charm or win. You cannot open these ivory and golden gates that lead to the secret places of the soul.

Hence a poor gift, if there be love behind it, will set the eye glistening with tears while the most brilliant gift, if it be loveless, will leave us wondering and leave us cold. I have heard preachers whose intellectual gifts were such that any man might covet them. Yet they never moved me to abhor the wrong or kindled me to joy in what was fair. But I have heard others whose gifts were not remarkable but who were on fire with love to God and man, and there was a power about their simplest word that made a man ashamed of his poor life. My brother and sister, whatever be your gift, over that gift put on the belt of love. Covet earnestly the best gifts, but covet love to beautify them all. Study is noble, and discipline is good, and perseverance is a heroic virtue; but in all the range of gifts there is not one that does not call for love to perfect it.

If one were asked to explain what life is, it might be difficult to give an answer. Perhaps we get nearest to life's deepest meaning when we interpret it in terms of service. All life is service. We all must serve to live. Obedience is the first condition of all progress. Hence Christ, the consummation of humanity, was among men as one who serveth.

Now I think that when we look at service, we can distinguish three ascending stages in it. In the first place, and on the lowest stage, we discover the service of necessity. There are many things which we are forced to do and which we would never dream of doing were we free. They meet us in the performance of our work perhaps, and we would gladly shirk them if we could. But we cannot shirk them if we wish to live; they are part of the terms on which we have our being; they are the very condition of existence and not to render them would be suicide. Such service to which we are compelled is the poorest and the lowest form of service. True, it is dignified when it is bravely borne and carried through in an unmurmuring way. But the very fact that it is forced upon us and would be at once rejected were we free, invests it with a certain meanness and robs it of liberty and of delight.

The next stage is the service of duty—all that we do because it is our duty. It is the service we render not because we must. It is the service we give because we ought. It, too, may be uncongenial service—not at all what we should have chosen for ourselves, and we may think it hard that we should have been summoned to bear such burdens or carry through such tasks. But conscience tells us it is the path for us, and so we pray to God to strengthen us and then, with whatever manhood we possess, we go quietly forward on the path of duty. There is always something noble in that service, yet it is hardly the highest kind of service. There is a lack of joy in it—a lack of music—there is not the gladsomeness as of a happy child. Something is wanting to make the service perfect, to make it a thing of beauty and a joy forever, and what it lacks to crown it with delight is the final touch of love. It is love that makes every service perfect. It is love that turns the task into delight. Love never asks how little can I do. Love always asks how much. And that is why in all the range of service there is no service like that inspired by love, whether the love of a mother for her children or that of Jesus Christ for all mankind.

I might illustrate this ascending scale of service by an imagined case from our old customs. Think, then, of some young man a hundred years ago drafted into the service of the navy. Caught by the draft and torn away from home, how intolerable that service must have seemed! For a time, it would be the bitterest of drudgery performed with many a muttering and curse. There was no escape—it had to be performed—the lash and the irons followed disobedience; that, in the harshest and extremest sense, was the service of necessity. But can we not imagine that young man rousing himself into a worthier mood? At the call of danger he would forget his bondage and think of the peril of his native land. And patriotic feelings would arise and his duty to his country would awake, and now his service would be a nobler thing because it was the service of his duty. But now suppose that a young man like that had sailed in the same vessel with Lord Nelson and had learned to love Nelson with that devoted love which filled the breast of every man who sailed with him. How different would his service now become! How gladly would he toil and fight and die! The thought of duty would be absorbed in love, and love would make his service perfect.

Once more, I want you to observe that love is needed for the perfecting of relationships.

If you were to ask me what it is that makes life rich, I should answer that chiefly it is life's relationships. It is in the ties which link it to the lives of others that life enlarges to its greatest measure. Just think how poor your life would be today if the cords were cut which bind you to your friends. Son, father, sister, brother, friend and comrade—what would life be without such words as these? For no man liveth to him-self—when he attempts it he is no longer living. It is in its wide and various relationships that life is ennobled and enriched.

Now when you come to think of it, you find there are three great enemies of a sweet relationship. The first is selfishness, the second pride, and the third destroyer of life's ties is fear. No man or woman who is selfish can ever know the joy of a deep relationship. If you are selfish you cannot *be* a friend. If you are selfish you cannot *have* a friend. For we never tell our secrets to the selfish nor open our hearts to them in confidence nor lean upon them with that confiding hope that calls for, and is always sure of, sympathy. Then in pride is a strange power of isolation. We say of the man who is proud that he is cold. No one is warmed by him in this chill world. No warmth of other lives dispels his iciness. The proud man is the solitary man and so always is the man who is afraid, whether it be the savage in the forest or the fearful sultan upon an Eastern throne. Where there is selfishness, then, or pride or fear, you never can have the fullness of relationship. Something is lacking in every human tie so long as these are mighty in the heart. And it takes a power that can conquer these and whose empire means the killing out of these if the relationships that make our lives are to come slowly to a perfect growth.

It takes a power that can conquer these—you know as well as I do what that power is. Nothing but love, possessing all the heart, is able to dispossess these enemies. Love is the sworn enemy of selfishness, for it sets a crown upon the other. Love is the sworn enemy of pride, for love is ever warm and humble. And as for fear, there is no fear in love, but perfect love casteth out fear, for fear hath torment. It is thus that love is imperatively needed for the perfecting of every human tie. Like a girdle you must clasp it on, if you would wear the garment of relationship. It and it only is the bond of perfectness between one life and every other life. Without it we may eat and drink and sleep. But with it in our daily life, we live.

So love is needed for the perfecting of gifts, for the perfecting of service and relationship. Now in closing and in a word or two, it is needed for the perfecting of religion.

It is a matter of infinite debate where precisely religion begins. Is it in fear of the darkness, in dread of the unknown; is it in some dim feeling of dependence? Brethren, we may have our own thoughts on that matter as a fascinating question of psychology, but wherever religion begins in the heart of man, it can never be perfect till it reaches love. If no relationship of earth is perfect till love has entered with its benediction, how can a man's relationship to God be perfect, if love is wanting there? For true religion is not a thing of doctrine nor of eager and intellectual speculation: it is the tie that binds the life on earth to the infinite and eternal life beyond the veil. I grant you that the distance is so vast there that you cannot gauge it by any earthly tie. I do not like that form of pious speech that is too familiar and has no place for awe. Yet the fact remains that every earthly tie is but a shadow of our tie with God, and if these cannot be perfect without love, no more, you may be sure of it, can that. Only when a man can lift his eyes and say with a cry of victory, "God loves me"; only when he believes though all be dark that the God who reigneth is a God of love; only then does his religion become a real, a very present help in time of trouble, a well of water in the burning desert, a cooling shadow in a weary land.

It is just that and nothing else which makes ours the perfect religion. For the perfecting of religion love is needed, and that love has been revealed in Christ. God commendeth His own love to us in that while we were yet sinners Christ died for us. God so loved the world that He gave His only begotten Son, that whosoever believeth in Him should not perish. When we have gazed upon the face of Christ, there are a thousand things we still may doubt; but there is one thing we can never doubt again, and that is the love of God. Love is the perfect bond between man and man. Love is the perfect bond between man and God. How shall we win it where everything is dark and a thousand divine providences so baffling? Blessed Savior, we turn our hearts to Thee. We gaze upon Thy pierced hands and feet. He that hath seen Thee hath seen the Father. We rest at last upon the love of God.

The Thankful Spirit

Be ye thankful—Col. 3:15.

The people to whom this was addressed were mostly people in very humble circumstances. Many of them would have been slaves. Their lot at the best was not a pleasant lot. Their privileges were as few as their enjoyments. And always in a heathen city to be a Christian aggravated everything. Yet the singular thing is that when the apostle wrote them, in such letters as this to the Colossians, he never seems to have offered them his sympathy. When death enters any of our homes, the mourners receive many kind letters. I have often wondered what fashion of a letter the apostle would have written in such circumstances. That it would have been exquisitely gracious we may take for granted from all we know of him, but unquestionably its leading theme would have been praise. The truest sympathy sometimes is not pity. The truest sympathy sometimes is encouragement. The hand that helps is the hand that points the way to new fidelity and service. And so the apostle never hesitates, even when writing to Colossian slaves, to urge them to the grace of thankfulness.

In doing so he of course was calling them to what he himself practiced so magnificently. Perhaps there never was a more thankful heart than the heart of the Apostle Paul. Would you know, asks William Law the mystic, would you know who is the greatest saint? It is not the man who prays most or who does most. It is the man who is most thankful. And certainly, tried by such a test, you might search the annals of the Christian church and not discover a greater saint than Paul. You have but to think of him in the prison of Philippi singing praises there to

God at midnight to see how he had practiced what he preached when he urged the Colossians to thankfulness.

And so I should like to dwell a little upon that most important Christian duty, and I begin by saying that true thankfulness is probably harder and rarer than we think. All of us abhor ingratitude. We speak of it in the severest terms. I have heard people, Christian people, say they could forgive anything except ingratitude. And yet as life goes on, we often find that the sins which are hardest to forgive are the sins which are easiest to commit. On one occasion our Savior healed ten lepers. He healed them all and healed them equally. Yet of the ten, only one came back and showed himself a grateful man. And we might question without any cynicism whether among all of us who name the Name of Christ today, even one in ten is truly grateful. Doubtless all these ten, while cursed as lepers, had thought that it would be heaven to be healed. They had pictured it and dreamed of it, and in their dreams had worshiped their deliverer. But among all the hours that come to us to test us and to reveal our hearts, there are few hours more penetrative than the hour in which we get all that we want. The thing we coveted was one thing. When we get it it is another thing. It was so easily given. It cost so little. And, after all, did we not deserve it? Indeed, when we look around upon our fellows and see how many have got far more than we, is there any cause for gratitude at all? No doubt such thoughts were in the lepers' hearts. No doubt they were in the Colossians' hearts. And he must be strangely ignorant of his own heart who has never been conscious of that quiet revulsion. And that is why, over and over again as if calling us to what is rare and difficult, the Gospel exhorts you and me to be thankful.

Of course, in times of special mercy, thankfulness is an instinctive feeling. There are hours when it is natural to weep and hours when it is natural to cry "Thank God." When a child is rescued from a burning house, when a man is rescued from a watery grave, when the crisis is past and the light of life comes back as in a fever or from the surgeon's knife, then in a rush of feeling from the depths pure and fervent gratitude is born. And God, who may have been long ignored, is recognized again in that glad moment as He who woundeth and yet His hands make whole. Christian friend, all such hours are good: but in any life such hours come very seldom. And it is not the rare hours that show the man: it is the common hours of common years. It takes far more than one exciting moment to tell you that anyone is really brave. And it takes far more than any tragic moment to tell you that anyone is really thankful. To be thankful in the sense of Scripture is to be thankful every ordinary day. It is to bear our routine burdens cheerfully, to meet our common sorrows without murmuring. It is so to feel the hand of God in everything, so to acknowledge the ordering of His love that for us there is nothing common or unclean. He who is rarely clean is not a clean man, and he who is rarely thankful is not a thankful man. The very joy and power of this great grace lie in the fact that it is universal. And that was what mightily impressed the world when the Christian Gospel began to spread abroad; it was the wonderful gladness of it all.

Thankfulness, when you come to think of it, really depends upon our view of God. As is our God, so is our gratitude. If all that happens to us comes by chance, then of course no man can be grateful. Gratitude is not a duty then, for there is no one to be grateful to. Nor can gratitude ever be a duty if God be only a cold and distant Spirit who takes no personal interest in men. Given a heaven like that, at his best two duties alone are in the power of man. The one is fortitude to face the worst, and the other is resignation in the worst. And that is why in the old pagan world the noblest gospel that was known was that of fortitude and resignation. Then came the Gospel of the Lord Jesus Christ, and resignation was swallowed up in thankfulness. And it was not because their lot was different: it was really because their God was different. They had been awakened through their Lord and Savior to a God whose name and character was Love, Love that stooped from heaven to the cross. Given such love, such individual love, life becomes a different thing at once. There is a loving purpose in its darkest hours; a loving watchfulness in all its ordering. And the moment that anyone awakes to that and with all his heart and soul believes in that, then gratitude is born. That is why Paul says in another passage, "In everything give thanks." Not in some things of quite peculiar gladness, but in everything give thanks. For in everything there is the love of God; love is ordering and arranging everything and willeth not that any man should perish.

The spirit of universal thankfulness was very conspicuous in Jesus Christ. You do not think of Jesus as resigned: you think of Jesus as rejoicing. There are three occasions in the life of Christ when you find Him giving thanks to God. Three times over, from the depths within, His thankfulness welled over into speech. And one has only to study these thanksgivings and all that is implied in them to realize the thankfulness of Jesus. Once He gave thanks for common things when He broke the loaves upon the mountainside. Once He gave thanks for ordinary people in that God had revealed His secret unto babes. And once in the darkest hour of His life on that night on which He was betrayed, He broke forth into such glorious thanksgiving as none who heard it ever could forget. Think of it: on that night on which He was betrayed when all He had toiled for seemed to be in vain, when the cross was waiting Him and all its agony, and the spitting and the mocking and the grave. Yet on that night we find our Savior thankful and pouring out His gratitude in prayer. My brother and sister, it is that great example that lies at the back of a command like this. We are to walk even as Jesus walked. We are to be thankful as He was. Not for the glad things only but for the shadowed things, not for the great things only but for the common things, and why? Just because God is love and in love is ordering all, and all things are working together for our good.

This grace of thankfulness diligently cultivated is one of the secrets of true happiness. It is not the happy people who are thankful. It is the thankful people who are happy. Happiness does not depend on what we have, else those who have the most would be the happiest. As a matter of fact, how often do we find that those who have the most are not the happiest? Happiness does not depend on what we have: it rather depends upon our point of view, and he who has won the thankful point of view is always on the highway of gladness. The flower that to the farmer is a weed may to the botanist be treasure trove. The rain that is so vexing to the child is just what the angler has been looking for. And so in life there are a thousand things that have an equal power to vex us or to bless us, according to our different point of view. No one who murmurs is ever really happy, and no one who worries is ever really happy. They have forgotten God and let Him out, and to leave Him out is to leave out the music. And it is only when, through Christ our Savior, we come to see His loving hand in everything that we win the thankful, grateful heart without which nobody ever can be glad.

Ungrateful people are never happy people. They are always querulous and discontented. The more we are thankful for our everyday mercies, the more does life become a joyful thing. And that is why Christian life is always joyful, because everything the years may bring to us, Christ makes it possible for all who trust Him to cultivate the thankful spirit. The tiniest gift from somebody we love is of more value than many a costly offering. We take it gratefully just because love is there, and, taking it gratefully, it makes us happy. And so when we learn, as every man can learn, that God is love and that in Him we live, there is a worth in things we never saw before. The way to be glad is to be grateful, and the way to be grateful is to trust in God, to trust in Him as Jesus trusted Him on that night in which He was betrayed. Thus grows the assurance that there is no mistake, that He is watching, guiding, guarding, blessing us, which, when a man has learned, he ceases murmuring and finds that being thankful he is glad.

But not only is thankfulness the spring of joy, it is also the source of dedicated service. And that is why the service of the Christian is perhaps the finest service in the world. We have all heard of the slave who after years of slavery was purchased by a stranger and set free, and how he fell at his liberator's feet and offered him all his service for the future. And we do not need to read how that new service, offered freely from a grateful heart, was richer than all the service of the past. Once he had toiled because he had to toil, and now he toiled because he loved to toil. Once he had done his work in daily fear, and now he did it all in daily gratitude. And that swift change of motive in his heart, from the haunting terror of the lash to love, made all the difference in what he did. It made all the difference to him, and it makes all the difference to us. Service is changed down to its very depths when we realize that we have been redeemed. And when we realize that we have been redeemed, not with gold but with the blood of Christ, what can we say each morning that we awaken but "Thanks be unto God for his unspeakable gift." My brother and sister, be ye thankful. It may be a secret you have never learned. Think of all you owe to God in Christ, you who are less than the least of all His saints. So shall there come new peace into your life, a happiness to which you are a stranger, a passion to do a little ere the night fall for Him who loved you and gave Himself for you.

In the Name

And whatever ye do in word or deed, do all in the name of the Lord Jesus,
giving thanks to God and the Father by him—Col. 3:17.

To the original readers of this letter this text would have a deep significance, and it would have that because to them there was so much that was mysterious in a name. With us there is little meaning in a name. It is a handy badge of recognition. What's in a name? That which we call a rose by any other name would smell as sweet. But with the eastern it was very different. It was no chance that called a rose a rose. There was a deep, a mystical connection between the name and the thing signified. That applied to every name, but was particularly true of names of persons. It was no accident that of two disciples, the one should be called John, the other Peter. Men felt that the hand of God was in the matter moving those concerned to make the choice and in that choice embodying or foreshadowing the glory or the weakness of the character. No name was arbitrary to an oriental. No name was ever given haphazardly. As the years passed and character was formed, it was discovered that the name was prophecy. Something happened which confirmed the choice and showed the infinite wisdom which had guided it and deepened within the hearts of men the reverence for the mystery of names.

Now it is in the light of that that we must read and understand our text. Whatsoever ye do, says Paul, do all in the name of the Lord Jesus. That does not mean that ere we begin to work, we should invoke the name of the Lord Jesus. Many of us, I trust, do that, but that is not what Paul is teaching here. True is it, true beyond all words, that everything is sanctified by prayer, yet that is not the doctrine of our text. When an ambassador at some foreign court utters his message in the name of Britain, that means that behind his message is the authority and power of Britain. He is not speaking as a private person. He is not himself the source of what he says. He is the channel for the will of Britain, and all the power of the empire is behind him. That is the apostle's meaning when he bids us labor in the name of Jesus. He wants us to realize that behind us is the power of the Lord Jesus Christ. He wants us to feel in everything we do, however great it be or however small, that we are but channels for the will of heaven. It is one character of the God of love that He is ever striving to express Himself. In Him is life, and life is never satisfied saving in outflow and in utterance. And so I take it that in every sunset and in every bird that sings upon the tree, you have a partial utterance of God. They cannot tell that they are voicing Him. They do not know the life that is behind them. But you and I, fashioned in His image, have been endowed with faculty to know it. And I would to God I could impress upon you what an enormous difference it makes just to realize that it is so. To feel that I am a channel, not a fountain, to feel that God needs me to express Himself, to feel that through my toil, however lowly, the will of heaven is working to its goal, it is that which ennobles life, sheds a sanctity on all its drudgery, helps it even in its dreariest, to be in heavenly places with Christ Jesus.

And that I take it is the most important question with which we are ever faced about our work. I feel it more deeply every year I live. Many are busy working with the brain, and many are busy working with the hand. And some are teachers, others doctors or lawyers, and some spend their days in the market. And some are occupied in lowly work and others in the control of vast concerns. Here is a woman whose appointed sphere is in the home among her growing children. There is a man whose business interests extend through half the countries of the world. Well now, the question I want to ask is this—in what light do you regard your work? Under what aspect do you think of it? On the answer to that question far more depends than you might every dream of and there are only two answers which are possible. The one is that you yourself are the source and origin of all you do. It is your brain that has achieved success. It is your hand that has procured your welfare. The other is that you are not a source, but only the channel of a greater power which from an infinite fountain in the heavens is flowing out through you upon the world. Give the one answer, and you stand alone. You are fighting for your own hand in loneliness. But give the other and believe the other, and behind that toil of yours is God. It is He who is working through that brain of yours. It is He who is toiling through that hand of yours. It is He who is moving out into that expression through every honest task you ever tried. That is the spirit of our text. Do everything in the name of the Lord Jesus. Just stop a moment and try to realize that you are the instrument of God in Christ. There is not a thing you do then whether in shop or home or office, but will begin to flash with a new meaning and seem as if it were worthier to be done.

Now there is one objection to this view of service which may be and often has been urged. It is that if we are but channels, then our activity is likely to suffer. If it is Jesus who is working through us, would it not be best to be still and let Him work? If through us the will of God is moving, is it not our duty to be passive? So men have speculated upon this and thought that human activities would slacken if once it were brought home to men and women that they were but channels of the will of Christ.

Well now, there is a passage in the Acts that may help to throw some light on that. It is the memorable passage of the healing of the lame man at the gate Beautiful. Peter and John were going up to pray, and doubtless they were thinking about Christ. And then the cripple cried to them for money, and somehow it brought Jesus very near them. For they remembered how He used to look and how a great compassion would possess Him when such a cry came ringing in His ear. It was then that Peter felt through his own soul the moving of the power of Jesus Christ. And he cried out with a loud voice, "In the name of Jesus of Nazareth, rise and walk." And the point to note is that just then when Peter was most a channel for his Lord, so far from being listless or inactive, he was intensely and tremendously alive. It was not his power. It was that of Jesus. It was not he who was working, it was Christ. Yet look at his eyes burning upon the cripple. Look at his hands outstretched to lift him up. The whole impression is of a man alive, quick to the finest fiber of his being, and quick simply because he knew that he was working in the name of Jesus.

As it was with Peter, so is it with everyone who makes this great discovery. When once we feel that God is using us, then every activity is quickened. Is the branch less active in the vine because it is abiding in the vine? Does it begin to say, I need not toil because my life is flowing from the stock? Why, brethren, it is that very fact, that inflow from a source beyond itself, that stirs it into life abundant. Let it be separated from the parent stem and every leaf upon the branch will wither and every tendril will lose its power to twine and every grape will dry and die. But let it live in union with that stock, drawing upon a power beyond itself, and every part of it is energized. Every leaf of the branch is busy now, a little kingdom of organized activities. Every grape, like the old temple, is being built without the sound of tools. And all this, mark you, this unwearied toil as if a thousand unseen hands were occupied, begins and has it being in the fact that the branch is not a fountain but a channel. So is it, I say, with every man when he first thrills to think that God is using him. It does not weaken him. It strengthens him. It makes him not less industrious, but more. Everything that we do is better done, more purely, more intensely, and more patiently, when it is done in the name of the Lord Jesus.

Now, when we grasp that thought and apply it to our duties, two results are almost always found. Of these two the first is this, a certain calmness and peace of the heart.

Readers of the Gospel story have often noted the perfect peace of Christ. It breathes upon us as a breath from heaven in every page of the evangelists. Never was a life so full as Christ's. Never was one so busy or so broken. Well He knew what overpressure meant and all the vexatiousness of interruption. And yet the calmest sea of summer evening when not a ripple is playing on its surface does not convey to us such peace unutterable as does the life of the Lord Jesus. Now, if you want the secret of that peace, I think you have to turn to John to find it. It is in that Gospel that you see most clearly how Jesus looked upon His work. And the great fact that shines upon these pages is just the fact that Jesus was a channel, a channel deep beyond all human fathoming, for the conveyance of the Father's will. No words of mine could exaggerate that thought. It is written large throughout the whole Gospel. Moment by moment, Jesus Christ is doing that which His Father has given Him to do. And the great peace that clothed Him like a garment and kept Him tranquil under intense pressure was just His certainty that this was so. All might forsake Him, but He was not alone. All might gainsay Him, but it mattered not. Christ was no fatalist who buoyed Himself with the dark sophism of the inevitable. He walked abroad in perfect filial freedom, grasping constantly His Father's hand, and He was always tranquil in His work because His work was given Him by God.

Now, brethren, as it was with Christ, so in a measure is it with us all. To feel that God in Christ is working through us is one of the surest secrets of tranquility. Men have often noted the great calm that is one of the most common virtues of the fatalist. He will face death after the manner of heroes; he will suffer in quietness where we would cry aloud; he will display the magnificence of patience just because his heaven is dark with fate. Now no man who believes in Christ can ever seek the refuge of the fatalist. Where the Spirit of the Lord is there is liberty. He is the Son, and He hath made us free. But what I say is that that quiet heart, touched with a happiness he never knew, is yours and mine more than the fatalist's when once we grasp the doctrine of our text. Think of yourself as the one worker, and ah, how soon the burden overwhelms you. How quickly do things get in disarray, how often are you on the margin of despondency. But think of yourself as God would have you think, as but the channel for the will divine, and into every day there will come peace. You cannot be spoiled by your successes now, for it is not you who are triumphing but God. You cannot be shattered by your failures now, for God has His own purposes in failure. Through you the will of heaven is being done. Through you the infinite is finding utterance. Once let a man or woman wake to that and peace shall flow upon him like a river.

It is thus, too, let me say in passing, that the bitterness of competition dies away. I have more faith in this text for that than in all the propaganda of the socialist. Here for example are two ministers whose churches are not far from one another. Or here again there are two Sunday school classes whose teachers are from the same church. Well now, if these ministers or teachers think of all they are doing as their own, I say there is almost certain to be bitterness. All success that may attend the one will stir a pang of envy in the other. There may be all the semblances of brotherhood, but never the true brotherhood of hearts. There is but one way to make sure of that—to make us comrades while we are still competitors—and that is to feel that at the back of all both bear the name of Jesus Christ. Then shall we strive our hardest for our own, but never shall we begrudge another's striving. The very power that is using him is flowing to its accomplishment in us. So are we summoned from our isolation and called in service to the truest unity, a unity that is a living thing because of the diversity it holds. I have spoken of ministers and Sunday school teachers, but remember these are only examples. Lawyers and doctors, artists, men of trade, remember that the same applies to you. I want you to feel today about your rival of whom so often you have had bitter thoughts that God is moving to express Himself through him as surely as through you. That will not make him any less your rival. God has no purpose to abolish rivalry. When He does that, the rose will cease to charm and the iris to change upon the burnish dove. But now from the breast of rivalry has vanished that gnawing bitterness which made it hell. We are the thousand channels of the one, and of every channel He has need.

There are times, I take it, in all callings, when men feel bitterly the sense of pettiness. To some it becomes almost intolerable that they should be living such a petty existence. They know the stirring of a larger life; they hear the whispering of undeveloped powers; they feel that they were meant for great things and could achieve them if the way were open. Yet every morning they must return to duty, to undistinguished and often sordid duty, and it is very far from easy in that duty to keep alive the nobility of work. We, the minister of Jesus Christ, through your liberality are set apart. You have said to us, You go apart, my brother, and traffic with heaven while we are in the market. Then come to us upon the Lord's day and give us some of the riches of your argosy, for we are soiled in battling with the world. Would you not think, sir, that a toil like that would be illumined with a constant dignity? Alas, how far is that from being the truth. How much have we to do that seems unworthy. And what I say is that if even on us there steals too often the sense of degradation, how much more constantly must it intrude on you. You feel that you were meant for better things. Sometimes that buying and selling grows contemptible. You feel as Grotius felt, who on his deathbed said, "I have spent my life laboriously doing nothing." What is the use of it all—this daily routine, this buying and selling for a little money, this drudgery that we lay down tonight only to resume tomorrow morning?

The Gospel understands that as it understands our complex nature. And the relief it offers against that is found in the thought of our great text. True to the heavenly wisdom which inspires it, it never loses its feeling of proportion. It does not mock you by assuring you that every service is of equal glory. But it relieves you from the sense of pettiness, inevitably, perfectly, immediately, the moment you deeply feel that what you do is done in the name of the Lord Jesus. The smallest token is a lovely thing when there is a heart that loves behind it. A single word may be a cheering thing when behind it is a heart of trust. So when behind our labor there is Christ, when we are the instruments of Christ, then the sorriest drudgery of earth begins to wear a crown upon its head. Once you feel that everything you do is God seeking to express Himself, once realize that you are but a conduit for the outflowing of the will divine, and as the dustiest hedge will flash and sparkle under the glistening dew of the May morning, so will the lowliest labor be ennobled. It is not you who are working now. It is Jesus who is working through you. It is His will that is being done on earth in every labor that you set your hand to. And this, remember, is as true when you are cleaning dishes or selling at a counter as when you are teaching in the Sunday school or preaching the riches of His grace.

For we must never forget, to put it in the language of the poet, that God fulfills Himself in many ways. Those of us who have sailed upon the Rhine know what a mighty stream it is as it flows proudly through the heart of Europe. It sweeps along in its channel, powerful in its silence and its swiftness. And many a vineyard ripens on its shores and many a castle looks down upon its waters. But when it comes at last into that region which is to join its waters to the sea, there the single channel becomes fifty. And some of them are great and noble streams, and some of them are tiny rivulets. And some of them wash the walls of busy cities, and some go wandering in lonely places. Yet every channel, be it great or little, be it the haunt of commerce or of dream, is carrying the one river to the sea. Say not that the tiny rivulet is different from the flood where steamers ply. Both are flowing because behind them both is the one mighty volume of the Rhine. And so behind your life and mine, however different these lives may be, is the one river of the will of God. It is His will that is finding its fulfillment wherever a mother is working in her home. It is His will that is finding its fulfillment in the honest labor of the shop and office. And the great secret that redeems our toil and robs it of its depressing pettiness is just to realize that that is so.

One of the few men of genius I have known was Professor Lord Kelvin. Well, I shall tell you one thing that always impressed me about Lord Kelvin; it was the number of people he kept busy. Some were busy working out his problems, some in superintending his experiments, many in making his innovative machines, and others I suppose in cleaning them. But what impressed me was how many men, from the apprentice to the finest engineer, were all required to carry out completely the workings of that single brain. Now, brethren, uplift your thoughts from men and fix them upon the genius of God. Think of the infinite life there is in God; think of the infinite thought which that implies. Then tell me how many thousand workers will be required upon this earth of ours if in its height and depth that will of God is to be carried out into expression. I want you to feel that there is room for you. I want you to feel that there is need of you. I want you to feel that through your lowly task, the Infinite is pressing to its utterance. And I say this, that when that breaks upon you with all the thrill of a new discovery, the sorriest drudgery a man is chained to ceases to be sorry from that hour.

To the Half-Hearted

Whatsoever ye do, do it heartily, as to the Lord—Col. 3:23.

I want you to note how our text is introduced; it has a very sugges-tive and illuminative context. "Servants, obey in all things your masters according to the flesh," that is verse twenty-two; and then, "Whatso-ever ye do, do it heartily, as to the Lord," that is verse twenty-three. Now the servants of whom Paul speaks in verse twenty-two are not do-mestic servants in our sense. They were slaves, bought for a little money; the property and the chattels of their master. Yet even to slaves who got no wages and who had no rights, clear and imperious comes the command of God, "Whatsoever ye do, do it heartily."

Now I think that is very suggestive for today. I can hardly talk to a mas-ter-painter or a master-baker, but I hear complaints about the degeneracy of labor. Men are not faithful, they have to be watched like children; the loyal service of an older day is dead. So say the masters; and on the other hand the men say that had they a more direct interest in their work and a more immediate concern in its prosperity, they would throw themselves into it with doubled zeal. Now all that may be true. But the point is that if the Bible holds and if this text be really the Word of God, nothing on earth, not even the worst relationships of capital and labor, can ever excuse half-hearted work. Your hours are long?—so were those of the Colossian slaves. Your pay is poor?—the Colossian slave had none. Your mistress is tyrannical and mean?—but the Colossian mistress lashed her servants. Yet whatsoever ye do, ye slaves, cries Paul, do it all heartily as to the Lord.

I want you to note, too, that this text was never better illustrated than in the life of the man who was inspired to pen it. There was an enthusiasm and a concentration about Paul which have won the admiration of men of all time. "One thing I do, forgetting the things that are behind, I press towards the mark," says the apostle; and whatsoever he did, he did it heartily as unto the Lord who loved him so. It is so easy to preach and never intend to practice. It is so hard to practice first and then to preach. It gives a wonderful power to our text and charges its mandate with redoubled urgency when we remember who the writer was. Men have brought many charges against Paul, but I do not think his bitterest enemy has ever charged him with half-heartedness. There is a glow and fervor in the man that marks in an instant the divine enthusiast. Others might waver, Paul battled to his goal. Others might yield, Paul was invincible. And had you seen him working at his tentmaking in the late night when the city was asleep, you would have found him plying the tentmaker's needle and singing, I doubt not, as in the prison at Philippi, with the very heartiness and zeal that filled his preaching of Christ crucified.

It is then of this whole-heartedness, of this fine concentration or enthusiasm, that I want to speak. And I should like to say by way of caution, that true enthusiasm is not a noisy thing. Whenever we think of an enthusiastic crowd, we think of uproar, tumult, wild excitement. And I grant you that in the life of congregated thousands, touched into unity by some great emotion, there seems to be some call for loud expression. But just as there is a sorrow that lies too deep for tears, there is an enthusiasm far too deep for words; and the intense purpose of the whole-hearted man is never noisy. When the children of Israel, defeated by the Philistines, sent for the ark of God into the camp, do you remember how, when the ark appeared they shouted till the earth rang and rent? Yet in spite of the effervescence of emotion, they were defeated and the ark of God was captured. But Jesus, in the enthusiasm of His kingly heart, set His face steadfastly to go to Jerusalem; and yet He would not strive nor cry nor lift up His voice in the streets. The noisiest are generally shallow. There is a certain silence, as of an under current, whenever a man is working heartily.

> Prune thou thy words, thy thoughts control
> That o'er thee swell and throng;
> They shall condense within thy soul
> And change to purpose strong.

Whole-heartedness, then, is never a noisy virtue; and I have thought it right to dwell on that that we may be on our guard against its counterfeits. But if it is not noisy, this at least is true of it: it is the basic condition of the best success. The chairman of the Congregational Union of Scotland, in an address he delivered some time ago at Glasgow, told us that a friend had met him lately and said to him, "I suppose you have heard that Mr. So-and-so has failed?" The chairman had not heart it. "Well he has," said his friend, "and little wonder, for he starved his business. He did not even put *himself* into it." He did not put himself into the work; he did not do it heartily as to the Lord. And could we trace the history of failure—that long, sad story of the world— I think we should find that for everyone who went to the wall through want of intellect, there were a score who reached that pass through want of heart. To concentrate as all the apostles did, to have the resolute enthusiasm of Jesus, *that* spirit has something congenial to success in it; and I use success in its best and noblest senses, some of which the world might call defeat.

But the virtue of whole-heartedness is more than that. It is one of the conditions of the truest happiness. There comes a certain joy as of the morning, a certain zest and buoyancy of spirit, when whatsoever we do is done heartily as to the Lord. When we are half-hearted, the hours have leaden feet. We become fretful, easily provoked; the very grasshopper becomes a burden. But when, subduing feeling, we turn with our whole energy of soul to grapple with our duty or with our cross, it is wonderful how under the long shadows we hear unexpectedly a sound of music. To be half-hearted is to be half-happy. It is to live in a lack-luster kind of way. And so it is to live in an unChristlike way, it is to know little of the joy of Jesus. Do you not think the joy of Jesus Christ was linked, far down, with His whole-hearted service? He never could have spoken of His joy but for His unswerving fidelity to God. And when at last upon the cross there rang out the loud, glad cry, "It is finished," there was joy in it because the stupendous work of saving men had been carried through to its triumph and its crown.

And there can be little question that the more heartily we do our humble duty, the more we feel we are doing it for God. It is one of the secrets for bringing heaven near us, for feeling the Infinite with us and within us, to be whole-hearted in the present task. Thinkers have often noted this strange fact: great enthusiasms tend to become religious. Let a man be mastered by any great idea and sooner or later he will find the shadow of God on it. But that is true not of great enthusiasms alone; it holds of whole-heartedness in every sphere. When Luther said, "Laborare est orare"—to labor is to pray—you may be sure that that great soul did not mean that work could ever take the place of prayer. He knew too well the value of devotion and the blessed uplifting of the quiet hour with God ever to think that toil could take its place. But just as in earnest prayer the heavens are opened to us and we are led into the presence and glory of the King, so in our earnest and whole-hearted toil, clouds scatter, the mists of feelings and passions are dispelled, and we are led into a peace and strength and sweet detachment without which no man shall see the Lord. It is in that sense that to labor is to pray. To be whole-hearted is to be facing heavenward. And the great loss of all half-hearted men and women is this, that above the dust and the stress and strain of life, above the fret and weariness of things, they catch no glimpse of the eternal purpose, nor of the love, nor of the joy of God.

Indeed, if that old saying "like to like" be true, the men who are half-hearted must be blind. For if there is one demonstrable fact I think it is this: we are the creatures of a whole-hearted God. When I remember the thoroughness of the Creator's workmanship; when I think of the consummate genius and care that He has lavished on the tiniest weed; when I recall the age-long discipline that was preparing the world for Jesus Christ; I feel that the heart of God is in His work. And I feel, too, that if my heart is not in mine, I must be out of touch with the Creator. The gods of savages are generally lazy because the savages themselves are lazy, and they have spiritual sense enough to know that there cannot be communion without kinship. But our God is the infinite Creator; the master-builder, the thorough and perfect workman. And I don't know how a half-hearted servant can have any kinship with a whole-hearted Lord. O brother, whatsoever ye do, do it heartily, that you may come into line with the eternal. It is the pity of all half-hearted men that they are out of harmony with God.

One other word on our text and I am finished. I want you to note how the writer lays his hand on the real secret of all great enthusiasm.

He centers his appeal upon a person. Had Paul been writing in some quiet academy, the text, I dare say, might have read like this, "Whatsoever ye do, do it heartily, for that is the road to nobility of character"; or "Whatsoever ye do, do it heartily, for that is the secret of success." But Paul did not write in any quiet academy. Paul wrote for the masses. Paul wrote for the whole world. And he knew that nothing abstract, nothing cold, would ever inspire the enthusiasm of thousands. A cause must be concentrated in some powerful name; it must live in the flesh and blood of personality if the hearts of the multitudes are ever to be stirred and the lives of the many are ever to be won. So Paul, with the true instinct of universal genius, gathered all abstract arguments for zeal into the living argument of Jesus. And whatsoever ye do, do it heartily, as what? *as to the Lord.*

And so by the roundabout road of this address, you see I have brought you back to the feet of Christ, and wherever we may start from, I trust always to leave you there. I believe that the secret of all worthwhile living lies in the company of Jesus Christ. And for making us earnest, thorough, quietly resolute, no matter what fickleness or cowardice we start with, there is really nothing like fellowship with Him. Do you want to be truer? Get a little closer. Are you ashamed of your half-heartedness? Get nearer. Then back to your work again, alone yet not alone: for the time flies and eternity is near, and you shall pass this way but once.

Folk Who Are a Comfort to Us.

These . . . have been a comfort unto me—Col. 4:11.

The word comfort in our text is a very interesting word. This is the only place where it occurs in the books of the New Testament. It is quite another word the Lord uses when He speaks of the Holy Ghost, the Comforter. When He says, "I will not leave you comfortless," that, too, is an entirely different word. The term which is used here, and here alone in the whole range of the New Testament, is our English word *paregoric*. Now paregoric, in Greek just as in English, is one of accepted terms of medicine. Paregoric is a doctor's word. And one likes to think that the Apostle Paul in his employment of such a word as this betrays, it may be quite unconsciously, the influence of the beloved physician Luke. I suppose that every real friendship has an influence upon the words we use. When we admire anybody very much, we often find their words upon our lips. And Paul, who like so many other people had an intense admiration for his doctor, would naturally use the words of Luke.

And certainly he could not have used a more appropriate or delightful word. Are you aware what paregoric means? I consulted my English dictionary to see how paregoric was defined, and I found that paregoric was a medicine that mitigates or alleviates pain. And what could be more delightful than the thought that there are men and women who are just like that—they mitigate or alleviate our pain. Pain is one of the conditions of our being. Pain is something nobody escapes. All life is rich in pain, as the throat of the bird in the spring is rich in song—the pain of striving, the pain of being baffled, the pain of loneliness and incompleteness, the pain of being misunderstood. There are people who augment that pain, sometimes without meaning it. How often is the pain of life increased by those unfortunate people who mean well. But who has not numbered in his list of friends somebody whose Christlike ministry has been to alleviate the pain of life? Such were the apostle's paregoric. Such are the paregoric of us all; often humble people, not in the least distinguished and not at all conspicuous for intellect; yet somehow, in the wear and tear of life and amid its crosses and its sorrows, mitigating and alleviating pain.

Often those who alleviate life's pain, who are paregoric in the apostle's sense, are the members of our family circle, the dear ones who dwell with us at home. There was a time in Principal Rainy's life when he was the most hated man in Scotland. Scarcely a week passed in which the newspapers had not some venomous attack upon him. And all the time, neither in face nor temper did Rainy show one trace of irritation, but carried himself with a beautiful serenity. One day Dr. Whyte met him and said, "Rainy, I cannot understand you. How do you manage to keep serene like this, exposed to all these venomous attacks?" And Rainy answered without an instant's pause: "Whyte, *I'm very happy at home.*" The wounds were deep, but there were hands at home that were always pouring balm into the wounds; gentle kindly ministries at home that mitigated and alleviated pain. And how many there are in every rank of life who find their courage to endure in secret sweet comforting like that. In the perfect trust of little children, in their innocence and blessed ignorance, in the love of someone who is dear, who understands yet is always bright and hopeful, how many men have plucked up heart again, found the bitter pain of life alleviated, been strengthened for their battle with the world.

Again, think of the comfort that we get from any friend who really understands us. Such appreciative and understanding souls—are these not the apostle's paregoric? Our Lord knew that. Never was man misunderstood as He. Misunderstood when He spoke or would not speak—misunderstood in every deed He wrought—misunderstood upon the cross. Think of the exquisite pain of it for that sensitive and sinless heart—fresh from the understanding of high heaven, that constant misunderstanding of mankind. And then there came an hour when Simon Peter inspired by the Holy Ghost cried, "Thou art the Christ, the Son of the living God." It thrilled our blessed Master to the depths. Life was different. He was understood. How instantly did it alleviate and mitigate the bitter pain He had to bear. And whenever in this difficult life of ours God sends us somebody who understands, is it not always paregoric to the soul? To have somebody whom we can trust—who, we are sure, will never misinterpret—who never judges us except in love—who appreciates and understands—what earthly comfort in all the range of comfort can for one moment be compared with that?

There is one thing more I want to say and that, too, was in the apostle's mind. Remember you can be a comfort to another though you never know anything about it. Just as the finest influence we exercise is often that of which we are unconscious, so the greatest comfort that we bring is often the comfort we know nothing of—not our preaching nor our words of cheer, but the way in which we bear ourselves in life when the burden is heavy and the sky is black. "No man liveth to himself." Let men and women behave gallantly and behave so because they trust in God when life is difficult, when things go wrong, when health is failing, when the grave is opened; and though they may never hear a whisper of it, there are others who are thanking God for them. Every sorrow borne in simple faith is helping other men to bear their sorrows. Every burden victoriously carried is helping men and women to be braver. Every cross, anxiety, foreboding, shining with the serenity of trust, comes like light to those who sit in darkness. People say sometimes, "I would give anything to comfort so and so." Dear friend, if you walk in light and love, you *are* a comfort when you never know it. And other people, writing their epistle (though it will never be equal to Colossians), will put your name in to your intense surprise and say, *"You* were a comfort unto me."

The Ambition of Quietness

We beseech you . . . that ye study to be quiet, and to do your own business—
1 Thess. 4:1, 11.

The church at Thessalonica to which Paul wrote the letter was in an unsettled and distracted state. The Gospel had come to it in such reality that it was tempted to be untrue to duty. We have all known how a city is excited when tidings are brought to it of some great victory. The streets are thronged; the schoolboys get a holiday; men find it hard to persist in the day's duty. It was with somewhat of the same intensity of impress, with its consequent unsettlement and stir, that the news of the risen Christ came to this city. Bosomed in that news, too, was the assurance that the Christ who had risen was soon to come again. However Paul's views may have changed in later years, when he wrote this letter that was his firm belief. And you may be sure that what Paul believed he taught so that (as you may see on every page here) the Thessalonians were filled with a great joy that in a little while Christ would come again. It was that which made them so troubled when one died, for they feared he had missed the glory of Christ's coming. It was that which made it very hard to labor, for who could tell but that Christ might come that day. And as with most excitement there is a certain restlessness and an unloosing of the tongue in noisy speech, so among the Christians of this early church there would doubtless be some lack of self-restraint. It was to combat that almost inevitable state of mind that Paul gave the counsels of our verse. He was not speaking to philosophic students. He was speaking to handicraftsmen, many of them weavers. And he said, "Make it your ambition to be quiet, and to do your own work as we commanded you, that you may walk honorably towards them who are without."

Now the truth which unites the clauses of our text is that quietness is needed for true work. Study to be quiet and to do your business; you will never do the one without the other. In a measure that is true of outward quiet, at least when we reach the higher kinds of labor. The thinker, the student, the poet, cannot work when they are tortured by perpetual din. Every man who is earnest about the highest work makes it his ambition to be quiet. Is he an artist? he seeks a quiet studio. Is he a thinker? He seeks a quiet study. The best of the Waverley novels were all written in the dewy stillness of the early morning before the locust-bands that swarmed to Abbotsford put quietness out of the question for Sir Walter. Of course there is a certain type of man that is largely impervious to outward tumult. Mr. Gladstone could read and write in Downing Street in total oblivion of the marching of the Horse Guards. But that does not mean that he did not require quietude; it means that he could command an inward quietude and that he was master of such concentration as most of us have only in rare moments. It is the duty of every man who does the higher work to make it his ambition to be quiet. If he is called to his task by the clear will of God, he must strive for the right conditions for his task. And to me it is wonderful how in this age of din when the uproar of life is so all-penetrating—how work that is fine and delicate and beautiful manages to get itself fulfilled at all.

But the words of our text have a far deeper meaning than can ever be exhausted by quietness of circumstances. They tell us that the best work is never possible unless there be a quietness of the heart. When a man is inwardly racked and torn and restless, you can very often tell it on his face. But if it only told on his face it would be little; the pity is that it tells upon his work. No matter how humble a man's task may be, no matter how ordinary and uninteresting, he cannot set himself to do it faithfully without imprinting his very being on it; and if within the man there is no peace but a surging of turmoil or unrest, that inward tumult will tell on all his toil and subtly influence everything he does. It is one of the legends of our Savior's childhood that in Joseph's workshop He was a perfect worker. If He made a plow, it was a faultless plow. If He made a toy, there was not a flaw in it. It is only a legend, and yet like every legend, it leans for its secret of beauty on a truth, and the truth is that here was perfect peace, and perfect peace produced the perfect work. Study to be quiet and to do thy business. Make it thine ambition to have a heart at peace. Without that there is no perfecting of fellowship, and without it no perfecting of toil.

Think for example of the disquiet of despondency; does not that tangle all that we put our hand to? Let a man be plunged into profound despondency and every blow of his hammer is affected. There comes to all of us, in spite of resolve and prayer, hours when the zest and charm of things depart; hours when there is no edge on any feeling and when all the expanse is desolate and parched; hours when a man is unutterably wretched and when a woman will weep for one kind word. It may be that there is sin deep down in that, or it may be that the frame is overtaxed; or that melancholy mood may come, we know not how, in the very season when we looked for gladness; but coming with its profound unsettlement, it steals the joy from everything we do and spreads itself like some benumbing poison through the living tissue of our work. The slightest task weighs heavily upon us and difficulties are magnified a thousandfold; things that yesterday we could have faced with ease seem to be insurmountable today; but it is not things which have changed, it is ourselves; we are grown nervous in a deep disquiet. We cannot throw ourselves upon our task with joy, for we have lost our peace of heart.

The same is true of the unrest of the passions; work becomes drudgery in their disquiet. Let a man be secretly tossed by any passion and how irksome grows the routine of ordinary days! It is hard to bend the head over one's books when the voices of the sweet world begin to call. It is hard to serve in warehouse or shop when the heart is torn and tortured with anxiety. It is hard to take up the tasks of life again and to be courteous and whole-hearted and unselfish when the waves of a recent and overwhelming sorrow are breaking and beating still upon the shore. Luther used to say about his preaching that he never could preach except when he was angry. Perhaps there are some of us who would be better preachers were we a little more angry now and then. But the anger that kindles a man's powers is rare, and the anger that degrades or darkens them is common. The angry man is generally wrong, and when a man is wrong his work is never right. The best school work is never done in the tumultuous days before vacation. The best work of a clerk is never done in the whirling season when he is in love. Why, when a domestic servant grows forgetful and handles things in an absent-minded way, does her kind mistress smile and say, "Mary must be in love"? I protest against exciting books and plays. I protest against exciting games and dances. And I protest against them because their net result is to make life not easier but harder. For nine-tenths of an honest life is toil, and toil demands a certain noble quietude, a settlement of spirit which is hard to keep and perilously easy to destroy. It is no chance that this exciting age should be an age of much disgraceful workmanship. I hear on every hand today bitter complaints of the rarity of true and faithful service. And I say no wonder when the ambition of the day is at every cost to be excited. The day of faithful work will come again, but only when men study to be quiet.

Again, the need of inward quiet for toil is seen in the working of an uneasy conscience. Are we not tempted to think of a guilty conscience as something a little apart from daily life; something which has to do with a great God and is therefore remote from the business of the hour? I want you to learn there is not a thing you do, not a task or duty you can set your hand to, which is not adversely and evilly affected, if at the back of all there is an unquiet conscience. You may be a student working at your classes or a servant busied in the sunless kitchen; you may have to control a mighty business or in that business you may be the humblest clerk; but whatever your work is, a conscience void of peace will tell upon and influence that work and interpenetrate it all so surely that to its finest fiber it will feel your guilt. We smile a little today at the great text, "Be sure your sin will find you out." We have grown so liberal and so enlightened that we can jest at twilight superstitions. But if one thing is certain, it is that that text is true and that every sin we have cherished finds us out, and finds us out not by the trump of God, but by the resistless evolving of its consequence. Some find us out long after in our bodies. Some find us in the bosom of our pleasant homes. Some lie asleep till we are near our victory, and then they waken and snatch away the laurel. But always, in the temper of our work, in the tone and strength of it and in its joy and quality, there is more than the impact of our brain and hand, there is also the impact of our conscience. Conscience makes cowards of us all, and if a man is a coward his work is sure to show it. There must be peace within, and the joy that comes from peace, if the smallest task is to be well done. And that is why the Gospel of Christ Jesus which through the precious blood brings peace of conscience, has given the world a new ideal of work and enriched the humblest worker with new joy. Study to be quiet, then, and do your business. Make it your ambition to have the rest of Christ. A heart tumultuous and burning and restless is a sorry comrade for the leaden days. But a heart at peace, and passions in subjection, and a conscience void of offense towards God and man, will send a man whole-heartedly to duty and help to make that duty a delight.

The Moral Conditions of Belief

*. . . a good conscience; which some having put away (thrust from them—R.V.)
concerning faith have made shipwreck—1 Tim. 1:19.*

We must try to understand what the apostle means when he speaks
of putting away a good conscience. He means what in the idiom of
today we describe as tampering with conscience. The good conscience
of our text does not just signify an approving conscience. It signifies a
conscience that is working well, just as we might speak of a good clock.
And as a man can tamper with his clock, so can he subtly tamper with
his conscience until at last it ceases to be good. Let conscience work in
liberty, and it registers unalterable certainties. It takes such things as
truth and love and purity and stamps them with the signature of God.
And whenever anybody begins to doubt and question these abiding
and instinctive certainties, he is thrusting from him a good conscience.
Men do that often under the stress of passion. They make the worse
appear the better reason. They are eager to get the approval of their
conscience for actions that are dubious or immoral. And conscience
is such a delicate adjustment that for long periods they can achieve
this, though I question if they can ever do it permanently. Such action
implies a certain violence, and the word Paul uses carries that suggestion. It is the word that is used of the Egyptian when he pushed away
the interfering Moses (Acts 7:27). A little violent handling of one's conscience like a little violent handling of one's clock, and we silence the
chiming of God's hours.

Now we know that when anyone does this, he invariably makes shipwreck of his life. But Paul tells us that if anyone does this, he invariably

278

makes shipwreck of his faith. Our Christian faith is a faith that God is love, and that in His love He gave us the Lord Jesus. It is a faith that we all are precious to the Father and are being guided to a perfect life. And this inspiring and sustaining faith, says Paul, does not strike its roots into a brilliant intellect; it strikes them into the soil of a good conscience. Tamper with conscience and God becomes unreal. Circumvent it, and the invisible grows dim. Wrest and manipulate its instant verdicts, and love and honor disappear from heaven. A man may have faith in all the Christian verities though his intellectual processes be childish; but he never can have faith in them once he begins to juggle with his conscience. To put it in more modern language, the conditions of all living faith are moral. They lie not in intellectual apprehension, but in honesty of intention and of heart. All which is fitted to be of infinite comfort to those who grope in intellectual darkness and are troubled because they cannot understand. Nobody makes shipwreck of his faith because he is powerless to understand. No ship that has set sail for heaven ever founders because the brain is dull. Shipwreck comes when the inward voice of conscience, challenging to truth and love and purity, is disowned in the interests of sin.

That this, too, was the teaching of our Lord is seen in His most exquisite beatitude. Blessed are the pure in heart, He said, for they shall see God. Now, to see God is not to set our eyes on Him. It is to have a living faith that He exists. It is to believe, what Christ Himself believed, that He is a loving and redeeming Father. It is to believe that just because He loves us He is guiding us with perfect understanding and carrying out His purpose in the world. A faith like that alters the whole of life and makes the sun shine in the darkest day. A faith like that is better than a fortune. It inspires serenity and courage. And the one condition of that faith, according to the teaching of our Lord, is not intellectual but moral. To be pure of heart is not to be perfect, else were there no hope for any man. It is to be sincere and single-eyed. It is to refuse to juggle with our conscience. It is to hold to it through every temptation that the imperious voice of conscience must be heeded, and that love and truth and purity and loyalty are demanded at whatsoever cost. Live like that, says Jesus, and you will never live long in a godless universe. Do your duty, as conscience tells you to and God will surely bless in your life. The strange thing is that with Jesus, as with

Paul, there is no word of intellectual processes. The conditions of belief are moral.

So are we led to this great truth for all who are really eager to believe. The way to faith is not the way of intellect. It is rather the simple way of duty. Far better than puzzling our brains is to do the next thing that is demanded. It may be hard to know what we should believe: it is seldom hard to know what we should do. And in doing that, at the command of conscience, with a single eye and a pure heart, we find ourselves, perhaps when we never dreamed of it, on the avenue that leads to God. We come to feel that truth is on the throne, or conscience never could demand truth. We come to feel that love is in the heavens, because at every hazard we must love. And as truth and love and purity and honor are but idle words without a person, duty brings us to the feet of God. To be pure-hearted is the way to see. To do His will the way to know. To listen to conscience and never seek to juggle with it is to touch the reality of all its values. He who does that, although the winds be contrary, will never suffer shipwreck in the deeps, but will come at last to his desired haven.

Christ and the Hope of Immortality

Our Savior Jesus Christ . . . hath brought . . . immortality to light through the gospel—2 Tim. 1:10.

There are two ways in which Christ has worked in His long task of the regeneration of mankind. He has brought among us from heaven what is new, and He has consecrated what was old. There is a widespread tendency in theological thought to belittle the originality of Jesus, just as once there was the opposite tendency to ignore Jesus' relation to the past. But both extremes are not only false to Scripture, but they are also false to Christian experience which always blends the new and old together. If any man be in Christ, he is a new creation. There are ten thousand times ten thousand lives that can testify to that. There is something original and fresh and new in every truly regenerate experience. And yet the grace that has inwrought the new takes into its bosom all the old, and uses it for the service of the kingdom. Old tendernesses begin to live again. Old hopes lift up their faces to the morning. Chords that were broken begin again to vibrate with a music that whispers of the long ago. So in Christian experience as in the Scripture, there is ever the mingling of the new and the old; new power and, through the inflow of that power, old hopes and yearnings and longings realized.

And among these yearnings of mankind, one of the deepest is that for immortality. Christ did not bring it here, He found it here, deep in the shadowy places of the soul. We have read of instances in which a great musician has heard a beautiful voice out in the street. It was that of

281

some poor girl singing for bread in the shadow of the London twilight. And recognizing the beauty of the voice, the master has had it trained at his own cost till it became a thing of joy to multitudes. In some such way, out in the crowded thoroughfares, our Master heard the voice of immortality. And He recognized the range and beauty of it, undisciplined and uncultured as it was. And so this Easter, the question which I want to ask is this, How did Christ train that singer of the street? In other words, what difference has Christ made to the yearning of the heart for immortality? What is the contribution of our Lord to the belief in a life beyond the grave? I think, laying aside what is debatable, we may sum it up in these three propositions. First, Christ has confirmed the hope of immortality. Second, Christ has enriched the thought of immortality. Third, Christ has enhanced the power of immortality.

Now I do not think, friends, that I speak unguardedly when I call the hope of immortality a universal hope. We come upon it in the remotest ages and find it among the most barbarous peoples. It was this faith that built the pyramids. It was this that reared the mighty Etrurian tombs. It was this that led men to embalm their dead and to lavish art and treasure on embalming. It was this that placed the food within the coffin and the piece of money in the corpse's hand, which slaughtered the horses of the departed warrior and burned the widow on her husband's pyre. It was this that made Socrates despise his poison as something that could not touch his real self. It was this that drew Plato to his loftiest argument in words that thrill and throb unto this hour. From the lowest depths of damp and sunless forests to the heights of intellectual and spiritual genius, men have cherished the hope of immortality. The strange thing is that that undying hope has never, out of Christ, become a certainty. It is an instinct of all untutored hearts, and yet an instinct that never has been verified. And this is the first great service of the Lord to that universal hope of immortality, that He has turned it, for all who trust in Him, into a full and glorious assurance.

If, then, you ask me how He accomplished that, I reply that the answer is twofold. He has done it first by the doctrine He has given us of the relationship of God and man. Christ's proof of immortality is not our instinct; Christ's proof of immortality is God. If we are His children and if He truly loves us, it is incredible to Christ that we should cease to be. Once realize the Fatherhood of God, and Jesus was never weary of proclaiming it, and on the bosom of that Father-hood there nestles the immortality of man. There is no proof that I am an immortal being merely because God is my creator. He is the creator of these myriad creatures that dance and die upon a summer's evening. But if God be my Father and if He really loves me with the splendor and passion of a father's love, then I am His and He is mine *forever*. Here, for instance, is an earthly father standing beside the deathbed of his child. And he bows his head over a breaking heart, and he strives to say, "Thy will be done." But had he the power to baffle death and to drive him across the threshold of the home, with what a will would he exercise that power. My brother and sister, God *always* has that power, and if He loves as an earthly father loves, death will never rob Him of His child. It is thus that Christ has confirmed our human yearning. He has rooted it in the Fatherhood of God. He has taught us that at our worst we are so dear to God that nothing shall ever separate us from Him. Christ's proof of immortality is not an argument built on the disproportions of humanity. His proof is a love that will not let us go.

But Christ has not only confirmed it by His teaching. He has also confirmed it by His life. The life of Jesus, for the seeing eye, is the crowning argument for immortality. One of my acquaintances in Glasgow is a German gentleman who has been resident in Scotland thirty years. Well, when I spend an evening in his company, his fatherland grows very real to me. One of my old friends who was at college with me is now an honored missionary in Africa, and there is nothing more living for me than Africa after an hour or two with Donald Fraser. Now that was the kind of impression Jesus made. He irresistibly suggested heaven. He lives so near the frontiers of eternity that the glory of it smote Him on the face. And men awoke to feel that all their yearning for a life that was larger than the life of time was answered in the life of Jesus Christ. He satisfied the longing of the heart. He was the confirmation of its surmise. He carried in Himself, for all who knew Him, the overwhelming proof of a beyond. And it is this, sealed in the resurrection, that has touched the flickering hope of all the world and turned it into the certainty of Christendom.

Now I hesitate to make broad and sweeping statements when I am so conscious of imperfect knowledge, but there is one broad statement

I can make, I think, without any fear of contradiction. It is that in the ancient, as in the savage world, immortality has always been a dreary prospect. It has never thrilled with any sense of joy, but rather with a sense of desolation. It has never been thought of as a life enriched, but always as a life impoverished; never as a life to be desired, but rather as a lot to be endured. There are one or two passages in the Old Testament that rise magnificently into a clearer air: "In thy presence is fullness of joy"; "I know that my redeemer liveth." But these are the utterances of glorious souls who saw like Abraham the day of Christ, and the usual outlook is different from that. The future is a shadowy realm of silence. It is a lonely, desolate existence. There is no vision of God in Sheol nor any voice of praise nor any human warmth or cheerfulness. And you cannot wonder, when you remember that, how the saintliest Jew shrunk from it with horror and cried in agony when death approached, "Deliver me from going down to the pit."

My brother, I need hardly say to you how radically Christ has altered that. If He has deepened the shadows for all who are impenitent, He has banished them for all who are His own. Just as God, when He takes some sluggish creature and enriches it with new wealth of being, gives it a new capacity for joy, but also a new capacity for pain; so Christ, taking the thought of immortality, left it no longer dull and rudimentary but capable of all the blessedness of heaven and all the anguish and bitterness of hell. Enrich the great idea of patriotism, and you shall have blood in it as well as triumph. Enrich the great idea of home, and you shall have anguish there as well as love. Enrich the great idea of immortality, and you shall have joy and glory in its compass and also, by a law inevitable, the possibility of awful woe. Now that is exactly what Jesus Christ has done. He has heightened and deepened immortality. He has made it far more glorious than before. He has made it far more dreadful than before. He has filled it for the finally impenitent with an agony of remorse that is appalling, and He has filled it for every childlike heart with a bliss that is beyond compare. Eternity can never be colorless again for anyone who has heard the word of Jesus. Either it is unutterable loss, or else it is unutterable gain. And that is what I mean when I suggest that Christ has enriched the thought of immortality as He has enriched the thought of motherhood and home.

Now, of course, all hopes must have a certain power. Men are always molded by their hopes. The kind of thing you long for in the shadow always affects and influences character. But it is unique, and has often been observed, that among all the hopes which men have cherished, few have been so powerless out of Christ as the universal hope of immortality. As if a child at play should find a diamond and look on it merely as a curious pebble and only understand its priceless value when one passed by who had the eye to see, so in the garden of the heart men found eternity and never understood the riches of it till Someone came along whose hands were pierced. The most that the future had ever done for men was to fill them with a vague and haunting fear. It had never inspired them, never come with comfort, never upheld them when the way was weary. And what I say is that Jesus took that yearning, lying unused in every human soul, and turned it into one of the mightiest powers that has ever been brought to bear upon humanity.

Think, for example, of how the Christian faith has brought immortality to bear on work. It has given an impulse to all honest toil that has practically changed the face of Christendom. If all our striving is to cease at death—if every effort is to be ended there, well might we ask, when effort costs so much, whether all our effort were worthwhile. But if all we have striven to do, and all we have failed to do, is to be perfected in the eternal morning, then in the dreariest hour or task we pluck up heart again. Our toil is not a task of three score years. Our toil is a task that has eternal issues. Every capacity that we have fought our way to, we shall carry over into the beyond. So in the thick of it there steals upon our ear the music of the distant triumph-song, and we thank God and take courage by the way. Divorce our duty from our immortality, and duty becomes incredibly hard. It is when a man can say, I am *forever,* that he can say with a glad heart, I *ought.* And that is why duty has blossomed like the rose, since Jesus lived, and died, and rose again, because He has touched it with the hand of the forever.

Think, lastly, how our Christian faith has brought immortality to bear on sorrow. It has given beauty for ashes, the oil of joy for mourning, the garment of praise for the spirit of heaviness. You young people, who have not drunk of sorrow yet, will think I am using exaggerated language. To you it is Glasgow which is intensely real and the beyond which is the pageant of a dream. But there is someone sitting beside you here tonight who has laid her treasure in a little grave, and for her it is Glasgow that is the place of shadows, and the one intense reality is heaven. The one thing love refuses to believe is the foolish doctrine of annihilation. Love wants the loved one not for twenty years. Love wants the loved one forever and forever. And now comes Christ to every breaking heart, and says, "Let not your heart be troubled. In my Father's house are many mansions: I go to prepare a place for you." What is all your philosophy to that, splendid though be the triumphs of philosophy? Do you think your philosophy will climb those attic stairs and give its comforts to that lonely widow living there? Yet that is what Christ is doing every day in the lonely attic room and in the crowded Babylon, to Queen Alexandra mourning for her brother and to the father mourning for his child. And we do not sorrow as those who have no hope. We are begotten into a lively hope. "In my Father's house are many mansions. If it were not so I would have told you." Death is no journey into the obscure night where the wild beasts are crying in the dark. It is the passing for all who are in Christ into a larger and a brighter room.

The Tragedy of Renounced Service

Demas, . . . my fellowlaborer—Philemon 24
Demas—Col. 4:14.
Demas hath forsaken me, having loved this present world—2 Tim. 4:10.

The disloyalty of Demas has had a strange grip upon the minds of men. It has appealed to the imagination. The fact that we know nothing of him save in these three texts, his presence in the little company that moves in and out of Paul's imprisonment—these glimpses have arrested men and drawn their thoughts to Demas as to someone mysterious and elusive. Then conjecture has been rife as to the ways in which he loved this present world. Was it lucre that tempted him, as Bunyan thought, or just the pressure of the lower standards? On such things we cannot dogmatize, for the apostle does not give us details; he did not expatiate on things that hurt him. All the same, it seems to me that we do know a little about Demas. These three references, put in their right order, surely betray something of the man—not, of course, of how the world allured him, for that must rest forever hidden, but of the gradual declension of his life. The chronology of the Epistles is not certain, but on many points there is a large agreement. Philemon was written earlier than Colossians and Second Timothy a great deal later. May we not trace, then, in this triple reference something of the soul-history of Demas that ended in such pitiable fashion?

In the first reference Demas is described as one of the apostle's fellow-workers. He was one of that company of eager toilers to whom we owe the spreading of the faith. From the fact that he went away to Thessalonica, we might infer that he was a Thessalonian. Backsliders

287

are like dying exiles, they begin craving for the familiar places. Demas, then, would be one of the early fruits of the apostle's visit to that European city, and the fruit, for long, was sweet to the taste. Demas was not content to confess Christ. He must serve and be a fellow-worker. He must do something for the Lord who saved him and for the apostle whom he loved so well. And it seems to me that so long as he was serving he found himself raised above the world: so long as he was serving he was safe. Men talk of the joy and liberty of service, and there are multitudes who have known the truth of that. But there are many who have never realized the spiritual strengthening of service. Christian service is like other work in that it helps to keep our besetting sins at bay, and in drearier hours saves us from ourselves. So was it, I believe, with Demas. He was kept as long as he was serving. He was master of all his timidities and cravings in the years when he was laboring with Paul. The earliest reference to Demas, full of affection and of gratitude, is "Demas, my fellow-worker."

Then the years pass and he is named again—but this time he is not a fellow-worker. All that we hear in the letter to Colossae is the one word Demas. He is still the companion of the great apostle; but he is not the fellow-laborer now. He seems to have grown weary in the service; perhaps he was disappointed in the fruits of it. He had been dreaming that he would change the world with the magnificent message of the Christ, and Rome was pretty much where he had found it. So far he had not swerved in his personal loyalty to Paul. He loved him. He owed his life to him. There was nothing he enjoyed more than to listen to him. But he did not love to preach now as he used to do nor to go out and brave the ridicule of crowds nor to give himself to the training of the young. Had you told Demas that the day was coming when he would desert his spiritual father, he would have indignantly repudiated the calumny. Yet anyone who knows the human heart knows that he was on the highway to apostasy from the hour that he ceased to be a fellow-laborer. No man can cease to serve without good reason and yet maintain unimpaired the older loyalties. When the spirit of willing service goes, all the enthusiasms begin to die. Prayer is stinted, criticism enters, churchgoing becomes very intermittent, and slowly the whole character is changed. Paul, with his fine delicacy, does not hint at this. He does not exclude Demas from the greetings. But he is perfectly conscious of the change and of the possibilities involved in it. Once (and he wrote it with a grateful heart) it was Demas, my fellow-worker. Now it is simply Demas.

And then the years go by, the bitter dragging years, and once again we have the name of Demas. And with a great ache in his heart, Paul has to write, "Demas hath forsaken me." It was not in the least a sudden thing. Paul had long foreseen that it was coming. The vessel had been straining at its moorings, and the cable had been gradually fraying. Idle, not serving as he used to do, no longer forgetting everything in labor, Demas was unequal to the strain. It all began when Demas ceased to serve and, ceasing to serve, also ceased to pray. All he had given up began to claim him then. The old life became intensely vivid. And the tragedy is that, going back to it, it never could content his heart again after the glory that had come—and gone. Paul was not only sorry for himself. He was a thousand times sorrier for Demas. He knew the disappointment and unrest that awaited him in the old familiar scenes. I think the tear of an infinite regret would blot the parchment as he wrote, "Demas hath forsaken me, having loved this present world."

The Selective Power of Personality

Unto the pure all things are pure—Titus 1:15.

It would be an interesting but a melancholy study to consider the texts of Scripture which have been misapplied. It would not only illuminate many a heresy; it would lead also to the secret springs of conduct. Some misapplications we should group together as arising from the imperfections of our version. Others we should find taking their rise in the sinful bias of the will. Others rather owe their origin to the proverbial character of certain words of Scripture and to the constant tendency of men to use proverbs in a mistaken way. It takes more wit to use a proverb wisely than it took originally to coin that proverb. It is far easier to strike out an apothegm than in some complex moment to apply it. Hence is it that certain words of Scripture, our present text being one of them, are in real danger of misapplication.

Have we not all heard these words misapplied? The commonest misuse of them is when something offensive has been spoken, something coarse or allusively indecent, and someone with a hot heart has protested against the evil remark. Immediately, sometimes with a smile or more often with the suspicion of a sneer, he is told that unto the pure all things are pure. The devil can cite Scripture for his purpose, and such a citation is the devil's handiwork. Our text does not mean that good and evil have their being in our thoughts about them. There are things that are everywhere and always right, and there are things that are everywhere and always wrong, and there is little hope for any man who has learned to tamper with these immutables. A deadly fever is not less infectious because I am fortified against it by some antidote.

It is still deadly, in its inherent virulence, though I may be immune against its ravages. Even though every mind were as pure as the unsullied snow upon the Alps, there would still be things that were indecent. In a bare and literal sense, it is not true that unto the pure all things are pure. Unto the pure, till the last trumpet sounds, there will be words and actions that are horrible. It is that conviction which inspires the home and gives stability to nations, and when it is lost in a degenerate charity, the day of moral decadence has come.

What then is the true meaning of our text? Well, it is something of this kind. It is the inspired if proverbial expression of the selective power of personality. Everything with which we come in contact carries a large diversity of meaning. There is nothing we meet with in our daily walk but is capable of different interpretations. And how we shall interpret all that wealth and what we shall see in it as it steals by, all that is really determined by what we are. By all the influences that played on us in childhood and all the activities of our maturer years, by every battle we have quietly fought and every burden we have bravely borne, by the unhindered trend of leisure thought, by temptation, friendship, religion, you and I, whether for weal or woe, have forged out our personality. It is the only thing that we possess really, yet it is something more than a possession. It is by that, and that alone, that we interpret everything around us. All the wonder of the sky and sea, all the experience of light and shadow, all the countless activities of life, are accepted and interpreted by that. It is not in the light of the wisdom of the ages that you and I read the drama on life's stage. For few men have ever learned that wisdom; and those who have, have learned it all too late. It is in the light of all we have made of ourselves in quiet years and immemorial days when we prayed God to give us strength to stand or yielded to the importunity of sin. By that we see—by that we read—by that we interpret God and man and everything. That is the key which unlocks every door opening on to the riches of the universe. And that, I take it, was in the apostle's mind when, brooding deeply upon this life of ours, he said, moved by the Holy Ghost, unto the pure all things are pure.

Now let us carry that thought into one or two spheres, and first let us think of nature. One of the noblest odes in literature is the ode of Coleridge written at sunrise at Chamounix. The poet is gazing upwards at the Alps, and he hears a mighty song of praise to God. The torrent praises Him; the eagle praises Him; the forest of pine and the snowy summit praise Him. There is no discord in that mighty chorus—"earth with her thousand voices praises God." But now there comes reeling on to that same scene some poor drunkard with his sodden brain. And the same torrents are sounding in his ears, and the same peaks are white against the heaven. But for him, ruined by his vice and fashioned by his past into a beast, neither in cataract nor snow nor forest is there heard one syllable of heaven. Both look on the same mystic dawn moving on tiptoe where man hath never trod; both hear the rush and swirl of the one river that hurries from the everlasting snow. And to one it is the echo of that song which was sung in the high heaven when Christ was born; to the other it is the echo of despair. In other words, faced by this wondrous world, you and I always get just what we bring. We see its power and glory *through* the eye, but never do we see them *with* the eye. We see them with all that we have made ourselves—with every coveting and every conquering—with every virtue that has been wrestled for and every passion that has been brought to heel. That is why places which speak to one of peace, speak to another of sinful opportunity. That is why sky and sea to one are paradise and to another are but air and water. That is why, in apostolic thought, unto the pure all things are pure.

The same thought also applies to language just as truly as it applies to nature. Through all the range of it, language is colored by the abiding mystery of what we are. It might well seem to the casual observer that there were few things more fixed and definite than words. The fact that there are such books as dictionaries argues for the stability of words. And yet those words, which we are always using and which seem fixed and rigid as the hills—there is scarce one of them but is affected subtly by this tremendous fact of personality. In every term we use there is some shade of meaning which has never quite been caught by other men. There is some suggestion that is all our own, whether it be a high suggestion or an evil one. And the point is that all that verbal coloring, which gives to our words an individuality, springs from the kind of life we have experienced and the character we have been forging in the dark. It is in that sense I understand our Lord when He says that by our words we shall be judged. If we are but drawing on a common stock, I can find in our words no principle of judgment. But if on the common language that we use we cast the shadow of our deepest self, then in our words, when all the books are opened, there will be more of revelation than we dream. It is a truth of widest application that the style is the man. It is true of Shakespeare and of Browning, but it is also true of you and me. We take the words the dictionary gives us, and then we so mold them by our secret self that the day is coming, if Christ is to be credited, when by our words we shall be judged. To put it otherwise, all mastery of language is at the heart of it a moral business. It is not merely an artistic victory; it is a moral and spiritual victory. He who has conquered words and made them serve him so that they throng to him in power and beauty has conquered things more powerful than words in the secret battle-places of the soul. Behind the glory of the words of Ruskin lies the moral enthusiasm of Ruskin. There is the pressure of a dauntless courage in the superb carelessness of Walter Scott. And who does not feel, in reading Stevenson, the presence of these very qualities which made that life of his, with all its suffering, such a quietly heroic thing. Unto the pure all things are pure. It is the inward self that shapes the instrument. It casts its shadow whether for weal or woe on the universal heritage of speech. And that is why—let me again repeat it—when the day of reckoning is come, we are told by One who ought to know that by our words we shall be judged.

Now if that be largely true of all speech, it is especially true of the great words we use. It is true, for instance, in a very solemn way of the greatest of all words, God. In the Shorter Catechism, when we were children we learned the answer to the question, "What is God?" Some of us can repeat that answer still, and it would be hard to match in its sublimity. Yet it is not the light of any catechism that has lit up for us the name of God; it is the light of the life we have experienced since we were cradled at our mother's knee. I knew a little girl in an orphanage who would never sing a hymn with Father in it. Her father had been a drunken ruffian, and in her wretched home he used to beat her. And she had taken all that childish sorrow and had carried it up into the gates of heaven so that for her there was a cry of terror in the sweetest and tenderest name of God. It is thus that that great name is molded for us. It is colored by the hand of memory. It comes to us impoverished or enriched by all that home has been and all that church has been. That is why God to one means everything; that is why to another it means nothing. That is why to one it is a name of terror and to another of infinite encouragement. No definition of the wisest catechism shall ever tell what God is to the soul. It is the soul itself which answers that.

Passing from language, I would note again that the same thought applies to human life. In the selective power of personality is the secret of our estimate of conduct. It is one of the commands of the New Covenant—"Judge not, that ye be not judged." That is a warning which we all need against censorious or hasty judgments. But you must remember that Christ never meant by these words to disapprove of the faculty of judgment; as a matter of fact we are so constituted that each of us is judging all the time. Every action, whether small or great, is summoned imperiously to our judgment-bar. Swiftly, instinctively, unhesitatingly, we pronounce sentence on it there. We do it every day a hundred times, and do it we must if we are to be men, for it is that faculty of moral judgment which separates us from the beasts that perish. Now there are certain acts so clearly good that the worst of men cannot but admire them; and there are other acts so clearly bad that they are universally condemned. But in between these two extremes lies a whole world of effort and accomplishment, and how we shall judge all that when it confronts us, depends on the deep fact of what we are. There is nothing that reaches us but has its contact with the life which is lying hidden in the soul. It touches secret forms of hope and passion which we thought were dead but which were only sleeping. And it is all that hope and all that passion and all the complex whole that we call self which passes sentence on the acts of men as they rise up for judgment in the gate. In other words, when we are judging others we are passing silent judgment on ourselves. Things will be mean to us if we are mean. Things will be great to us if we be great. By all we have struggled for with many a failure, by every ideal we have lost or won, by hidden lust, by secret sham, do we interpret the drama of mankind. Give me a man who has lived for ten years purely, and he shall find purity on every hand. Give me a man whose life has been a mockery, and all the world shall be a mockery to him. In every sneer, in every commendation, in every word of praise or word of blame, we are but registering what we have made of life since our feet were on the uplands of the dawn.

There came a poor woman once, with hair disheveled, and she anointed the feet of Christ with ointment. Do you remember how diversely that act was viewed by the guests who were reclining at the table? To One of them it was a deed of love that was to be told wherever the Gospel should be preached; to another it was the wild extravagance of an impulsive and abandoned woman. Both looked on the same vase of alabaster; both watched the moving of the same white fingers; but the one who looked upon the deed was Judas, and the other was the Son of God. And in their looks, swift as a swallow's flight—different from each other as night from day—there is a glimpse into that awful gulf which parted the betrayer from his Lord. Unto the pure all things are pure. We see by all that we have become. If we have lived disloyally like Judas, then shall we look upon a sorry spectacle. But if it has been "the utmost for the highest," as it was with Him whom we adore, then may we also catch the gleam of splendor in the ointment lavished on the feet.

In closing I ask you to observe that we have here the secret of social influence. It is a well-known fact that just to see the best has a strange power of calling out the best. Arnold of Rugby believed so in his boys that they grew ashamed to tell a lie to him. Men have a curious and subtle way of answering to our expectations of them so that oftentimes they will act honorably because they are assured we think they are honorable. To see the finest, in a world like this, is a sure way of evoking what is fine. It was in such a confidence that Jesus worked in His mighty task of bringing in the kingdom. If then we have power by what we see and if what we see depends on what we are, I say that the most urgent of all social duties is the duty of a man to his own soul. I have no faith in any social service that springs from careless and unworthy character. There cannot be any vision in such service, and without vision service is in vain. We need a heart that scorns what is contemptible and clings tenaciously to the highest if men and women are to feel the touch that helps them to be better than themselves. Unto the pure all things are pure. We see the best, and help to make it so. Every victory we win alone is aiding our brother to be a better man. Don't say you can do nothing for your fellows; you can do more for your fellows than many a noisy demagogue by being patient, loyal, true, and pure in the life which no human eye can see.

Christ and the Fear of Death

And deliver them who through fear of death were all their lifetime subject to
bondage—Heb. 2:15.

There are two feelings which the thought of death has always kindled in the human breast, and the first of them is curiosity. Always in the presence of that veil through which sooner or later we all pass, men have been moved to ask with bated breath, What is it which that veil conceals? It is as if the most diaphanous of curtains were hung between our eyes and the great secret, making men the more wistful to interpret it. It has been said by a well-known Scottish essayist that this would account for the crowd at executions. You know how the people used to flock by the thousands when a criminal was to die upon the gallows. And Alexander Smith throws out this thought that it was not just savagery which brought them there. It was the unappeasable curiosity which death forever stirs in human hearts.

But if the thought of death moves our curiosity, there is another feeling which is always linked with it. Death is not alone the source of wonder. Death has ever been the source of fear. How universal that feeling is we see from this, that we share it with all animate creation. Wherever there is life in any form there is an instinct which recoils from death. When the butterfly evades the chasing schoolboy—when the stag turns at bay against the dogs—we have the rudiments of that which in a loftier sphere may grow to be a bondage and a tyranny. The fear of death is not a religious thing, although religion has infinitely deepened it. It is old as existence, wide as the whole world, lofty and deep as the whole social fabric. It touches the savage in the heart of

Africa as every reader of Dr. Livingstone knows, and it hides under the mantle of the prince as well as under the jacket of the prodigal. How keenly it was felt in the old world every reader of pagan literature has seen. The aim and object of the old philosophy was largely to crush it out of human life. In the great and gloomy poem of Lucretius, in many a page of Cicero, above all in the treatises of Plutarch and of Seneca, we learn what a mighty thing the fear of death was with the men and women of the Roman Empire.

Of course I do not mean that the fear of death is always active and present and insistent. To say that would be an exaggeration and would be untrue to the plain facts of life. When a man is in the enjoyment of good health, he very rarely thinks of death at all. When the world goes well with him and he is happy, he has the trick of forgetting he is mortal. He digs his graves within the garden walls and covers them with a wealth of summer flowers so that the eye scarce notices the mound when the birds are singing in the trees. We know, too, how a passion or enthusiasm will master the fear of death within the heart. A soldier in the last rush will never think of it though comrades are dropping on every side of him. And a timid mother, for her little child's sake, or a woman for the sake of one she loves, will face the deadliest peril without trembling. For multitudes the fear of death is dormant else life would be unbearable and wretched. But though it is dormant, it is always there ready to be revived in the last day. In times of shipwreck—in hours of sudden panic—when we are ill and told we may not live, then shudderingly as from uncharted deeps, there steals on men this universal terror. Remember there is nothing cowardly in that. A man may be afraid and be a hero. There are times when to feel no terror is not courage. It is but the hallmark of insensibility. It is not what a man feels that makes the difference. It is how he handles and controls what he feels. It is the spirit in which he holds himself in the hour when the heart is overwhelmed.

Nor can we be altogether blind to the purposes which God meant this fear to serve. Like everything universal in the heart, it has its duty in the plans of heaven. You remember the cry wrung from the heart of Keats in his exquisite music to the nightingale. "Full many a time," he sings, "I have been half in love with easeful death." And it may be that some who read these pages have been at times so weary of it all that they too have been in love with easy death. It may have been utter tiredness that caused it. It may have been something deeper than all weariness. Who knows but that some may even have dreamt of suicide? Brethren, it is from all such thoughts and from all the passion to be done with life that we are rescued and redeemed and guarded by the terror which God has hung around the grave. Work may be hard, but death is harder still. Duty may be stern, but death is sterner. Dark and gloomy may be the unknown morrow, but it is not so dark and gloomy as the grave. Who might not break through the hedge and make for liberty were the hedge easy to be pushed aside? But God has hedged us about with many a thorn—and we turn to our little pasturage again. When Adam and Eve had been expelled from Eden, they must have longed intensely to return. It was so beautiful and the world so desolate; it was so fertile and the world so hard. But always when they clasped repentant hands and stole in the twilight to the gate of Paradise, there rose the awful form with flaming sword. Sleepless and vigilant he stood at watch. His was a dreadful and terrible presence. No human heart could face that living fire which stood in guardianship of what was lost. And that was why God had placed His angel there, that they might be driven back to the harsh furrow and till the soil and rise into nobility while the sweat was dropping from the brow. So are we driven back to life again by the terror which stands sentinel on death. So are we driven to our daily cross, however unsupportable it seems. And bearing it, at first because we must, it comes to blossom with the passing days until we discover that on this side of the grave there is more of paradise than we had dreamed. Christ then does not deliver us from the deep instinct of self-preservation. That is implanted in the heart by God. It is given for the safeguarding of His gift. It is only when that fear becomes a bondage and when that instinct grows into a tyranny that Christ steps in and breaks the chains that bind us and sets our trembling feet in a large room. The question is, then, how did He do that? How has Christ liberated us from this bondage? I shall answer that by trying to distinguish three elements which are inherent in that fear.

In the first place, our fear of death is in a measure but a fear of dying. It is not the fact of death which terrifies; it is all that we associate with the fact. We may have seen a deathbed scene of agony; it is a memory which we shall never lose. We may have read a story of torment in the closing hours. And it is not what death leads to or removes, but rather that dark accompanying prospect which lies hidden within a thousand hearts as an element of the terror of the grave. I think I need hardly stop to prove to you that this is an unreasonable fear. If there are deathbeds which are terrible, are there not others which are quiet as sleep? But blessed be God, Christ does not only comfort us when we are terrified with just alarms: He comforts us when we are foolish children. Clothed with mortality, He says to us, "Take therefore no thought for the morrow." Dreading the pain that one day may arrive, He says, "Sufficient unto the day is its own evil." He never prayed, "Give us a sight of death, and help us to contemplate it every hour we live." He prayed, "Give us this day our daily bread." Christ will not have us stop the song today because of the possible suffering tomorrow. If we have grace to live by when we need it, we shall have grace to die by when we need it. And so He sets His face against that element and says to us, "Let not your heart be troubled." "My grace shall be sufficient for thee, and my strength made perfect in thy weakness."

Secondly, much of our fear of death springs from the thought that death is the end of everything. It is always pitiful to say farewell, and there is no farewell like that of death. You remember how Charles Lamb uttered that feeling with the wistful tenderness which makes us love him. He did not want to leave this kindly world nor his dear haunts nor the familiar faces. And deep within us, though we may not acknowledge it, there is that factor in the fear of death—the passionate clinging of the human heart to the only life which it has known. We have grown familiar with it over the years. It has been a glad thing to have our work to do, and human love and friendship have been sweet. And then comes death and takes all that away from us and says it never shall be ours again, and we brood on it and are lonely and afraid. Thanks be to God, that factor in the fear has been destroyed by Jesus Christ. For He has died, and He is risen again, and He is the firstfruits of them that sleep. And if the grave for Him was not an end, but only an incident in life eternal, then we may rest assured that in His love there is no such sadness as the broken melody. All we have striven to be we shall attain. All we have striven to do we shall achieve. All we have loved shall meet us once again with eyes that are transfigured in the dawn. Every purpose that was baffled here and every love that never was fulfilled, all that, and all our labor glorified, shall still be ours when shadows flee away. This life is but the prelude to the piece. This life is the introduction to the book. It is not *finis* we should write at death. It is not *finis*, it is *initium*. And that is how Jesus Christ has met this element and mastered it in His victorious way and made it possible for breaking hearts to bear the voiceless sorrow of farewell.

Thirdly, much of the fear of death springs from the certainty of coming judgment. Say what you will, you know as well as I do that there is a day of judgment still to come. Conscience tells it, if conscience is not dead. The very thought of a just God demands it. Unless there be a judgment still to come, life is the most tragic of mockeries. And every voice of antiquity proclaims it, and every savage tribe within the forest; and with a certainty that never wavered it was proclaimed by the Lord Jesus Christ. Well may you and I fear death, if "after death, the judgment." Seen to our depths with every secret known, we are all to stand before Almighty God. Kings will be there, and peasants will be there, and you and I who are not kings nor peasants. And the rich and the poor will meet together there, for the Lord is the maker of them all. It is that thought which makes death so terrible. It is that which deepens the horror of the tomb. Dwell on that coming day beyond the grave, and what a prospect of terror it is! And it is then that Jesus Christ appears and drives these terrors to the winds of heaven and says to the vilest sinner, "Son of man, stand upon thy feet." He that believeth *hath* everlasting life. He gives us our acquittal here and now. He tells us that for every man who trusts Him there is now therefore no condemnation. And He tells us that because He died for us and because He bore our sins upon the tree and because He loves us with a love so mighty, neither life nor death can tear us from it. That is the faith to live by and to die by: "I will both lay me down in peace and sleep." That is the faith which makes us more than conquerors over the ugliest record of our past. O death, where is thy sting? O grave, where is thy victory? Thanks be to God, who giveth us the victory through our Lord Jesus Christ.

The Temptations of Calvary

In all points tempted like as we are—Heb. 4:15.

That our Lord's temptations were intensely real is the accepted faith of Christendom. He was tempted in all points like as we are. Unless He was really and cruelly tempted and knew the full meaning of resistance, He can never, in any helpful way, be the brother of tempted men and women. And if He be not Brother then He is not Savior, for a Savior, whatever else he be, must be vitally identified with man. Our Lord's sinlessness was not endowment. It was rather an unparalleled achievement. It was not a gift bestowed on Him by heaven. It was a moral and spiritual victory. It was wrought out, moment after moment, by a will sustained in perfect poise with God, instantly and unswervingly obedient. Now always, where the heart is, there is the sorest onset of temptation. Temptation has always its eye upon the citadel, though it may seem to be leveled at the outworks. And that is why, right through the Gospel story, the bitterest temptations of our Lord are to be found converging on the cross. How, then, was our Lord tempted in regard to the great experience of Calvary? To what suggestions, winging from the darkness, had He to offer victorious resistance? Let us reverently give our thought to that.

We see Him first, and we see Him often, tempted to avoid the cross. That sore temptation never left Him. At the very outset of His ministry, such was the suggestion of the devil. It runs like some dark thread of hell through all the encounters of the wilderness. Let Him with all His brilliant gifts ally Himself with worldly policies and what need would there be of the bloody way of Calvary? It smote Him again after

301

many days and this time through the lips of Simon Peter. Was not our Lord recalling the scene out in the wilderness when He said, "Get thee behind me, *Satan*" (Matt. 16:23)? And near the end when the Greeks came craving an interview with Christ, was that not the old temptation back again? Why, in that thrilling hour, did our Lord say "Now is my soul *troubled*" (John 12:27)? Why did He not rejoice in spirit when the "other sheep" were coming to His feet? Surely it was because these Greeks were envoys offering an open door to the big world without the imminent agonies of Calvary. It is notable that in the Gospel of St. John there is no mention whatever of Gethsemane. To St. John that offer of the Grecian world was the spiritual equivalent of Gethsemane. It was the temptation to achieve the kingship on which His kingly heart was set by some way other than the cross. He was tempted to avoid the cross, to shun it, to take some other road. Have we not all been tempted just like that? And does it not bring the Master very near us in a brotherhood intensely real to remember that He was victorious just there?

Once again our Savior was tempted to hasten on the cross. He was tempted to antedate the hour of God. We read, for instance, that when the sisters sent for Him, He abode two days still in the same place where He was (John 11:6). For One who was the Good Physician that was an extraordinary thing to do. If we summoned our doctor to a dear one and if for two days he never came, we should find it very hard to call him good. Was He waiting to augment the miracle? But then Lazarus was already dead (11:39). We He waiting to test the sisters' faith? But is that how Jesus deals with loving friends? He was waiting because He saw so clearly that the raising of Lazarus would seal His doom (11:53), and He dreaded to antedate the hour of God. Human love was calling Him to Bethany. Affection for His friends was calling Him. Going, He signed His death-warrant—but was it His Father's will that He should die yet? And so, though drawn by the cords of love to go, He waited in quiet fellowship with Heaven until the will of God was perfectly revealed. How often had He said "Mine hour is not yet come." With what profound conviction did He know that God had His appointed hour for Calvary. Might not these drawings of love be but the devil's stratagem to interfere with the ordered times of heaven?—and He abode two days still in the same place where He was. Once more does not that bring Him very near us? Have we not all been tempted to hurry on God's hour? There are few things more difficult in life, sometimes, than just to wait patiently for God. And *He* was tempted in all points like as we are.

Lastly our Lord was tempted to come down from the cross. "Let him now come down from the cross, and we will believe him" (Matt. 27:42). When these voices broke upon His ear, were they not fraught with terrible temptation? Think of the agony He was enduring in His so sensitive and sinless frame. Think how the very passion of His heart was that these men and women should believe in Him. And as these cries rang upon His ear did they not carry with them the suggestion that in one instant He might escape His torture, and doing it win the allegiance of His own? Tempted in every prospect of the cross, our Lord was tempted on the cross itself. By one swift action might He not end His agony and win the great ambition of His life? And the wonderful thing is that on the cross as in the desert at the opening of His ministry, He steeled Himself against these tempting voices. They said "Come down, and we will believe in you." We believe, because He did not come down. To us the glory is in His hanging there till He cried in a loud voice "It is finished." And when we are tempted, as we so often are, to release ourselves when "crucified with Christ," what a comfort that we can quietly say, "He was tempted in all points like as we are."

The Sinlessness of Christ

In all points tempted like as we are, yet without sin—Heb. 4:15.

It might seem at first as if the sinlessness of Jesus were a matter far away from human need. It is as if we discussed the color of the stars or the density of water in the depth of ocean. Why should we trouble ourselves, it may be asked, over an abstract question such as this? Were it not better, in a reverent faith, to leave these mysteries alone? It is enough for me (a man might say) that Jesus of the Gospel story was the friend of publicans and sinners and went about doing good. The one fatal objection to that attitude is that to a thoughtful mind it never can be permanent. Steadily, whatever point we start from, we are forced into the presence of this problem. And especially is that true of all of us who believe in a Gospel of redemption and who cannot conceive of a message of good news which has not redemption at its heart. The keystone of our faith is this, that Jesus the Lord suffered for our sins. But if Christ was sinful, as you and I are sinful, then not for our sins, but for His own, He died. So all the efficacy of that atoning death, with all the preaching of Christ crucified, rests ultimately on the sinlessness of Jesus. It is not, then, an unimportant theme. It is one of the most important of all themes. It lifts the cross out of the realm of tragedy into the clear air of willing sacrifice. Only if Jesus Christ was sinless can we be certain of what is all-important—that in a free action of redeeming love He died for our sins according to the Scriptures.

Now when you study the New Testament writings—I mean the writings outside the four Gospels—one thing that becomes plain is this, that they all record the sinlessness of Jesus. However the writers differ in their outlook—and each of them has his unique outlook—however they may diverge from one another in their concept of the work of Jesus, yet there is one point on which they all agree, and that is in conceiving Christ as sinless. John had lain upon the Master's bosom, and he writes, "In Him there was no sin." Peter had known Him in the closest intimacy, and he writes, "He died, the righteous for the unrighteous." Paul writes, "He who knew no sin was made sin for us." And the writer of Hebrews in our text says, "He was tempted in all points like as we are, yet without sin." These are but a few texts out of many which indicate a perfect unanimity. Each writer may use the fact in his own way, but all of them insist upon the fact. And what we have to ask is this, How was that profound impression generated so that not one writer of the New Testament doubts for a moment the sinlessness of Christ?

Let me say in passing that it helps us to conceive how powerful this impression really was when we recall the nature of the earliest heresies. When men today have doubts about the Lord, it is the divinity that is the point of difficulty. You and I may doubt if He was God, but we never for an instant doubt that He was man. Yet the singular thing is that in the earliest heresies the point of difficulty was the opposite. Men did not doubt if Jesus was divine then, but they doubted if He was really human. Now it seems to me that no mere moral grandeur will ever quite explain these earliest heresies. One is not less a man, but more a man, if he is morally and spiritually wonderful. That strange belief uttered in early heresies, that Christ was not human as you and I are human, can only rest on the profound impression that He stood apart from all in being sinless. The nearer then to the historic Christ, the more intense the belief that He was sinless. The closer that men stand to Him, the more profound does the impression grow. And so we must go back to the record of the Gospel story and try to discover how that impression was created.

In the first place I should like to make clear that it was certainly not created by insistence. Christ never insisted on His sinlessness—never took pains to prove that He was sinless. There are some things on which our Lord insisted with a self-assertion that is most magnificent. I am the truth, He said—I am the life. No man cometh to the Father but by Me. Yet though no one who ever taught mankind has made such stupendous claims as Jesus Christ, you never find Him saying, "I am sinless." On the contrary, one might almost say that He deliberately veiled that fact. So did He live in fellowship with outcasts that they called Him the friend of publicans and sinners. And once when a lawyer, with the gloss of a compliment, came to Him and said, "Good Master," Christ checked him instantly—"Why callest thou me good? there is none good but one, that is, God." Clearly then, for reasons we can only guess at, Christ did not passionately insist upon His sinlessness. However the impression was created, He never declared it so.

How then was the impression generated? Well, the first answer is that those men who companied with Jesus did not recollect one deed of sin. When the years of ministry were closed, they would recall it all in tender memory. They would summon to the sessions of sweet thought the days they had spent together in the villages. And as they did so and as they talked together of the time when it was bliss to be alive, silently it would be borne in upon them that they had never seen one trace of sin in Jesus. They had been with Him in His temptations, and they had seen Him in the widest range of circumstances. They had known Him in hunger and in weariness; they had watched Him in rapture and in agony. And yet as they looked back upon it all in the penetrative light of memory, they could not recollect one single incident which suggested to them the thought that Christ had sinned. Thus it was that the deep impression was created. It was a judgment based upon the memory of the wonderful years they had spent with Jesus. Could they have recalled one single instance in which the conduct of Jesus had been flawed, then neither in Peter nor in John would we have found the sinlessness of Christ.

Now all that is absolutely true, yet it is far from being all the truth. It is quite impossible to build a Christian doctrine on any negative basis such as that. Granted that they had never known Christ to sin, is that any adequate proof that He was sinless? Had they been watching Him with unwearied eyes from the moment of His birth to the cross? On the contrary, they had only known Him for three brief years out of the three-and-thirty, and of these three years there was many a day when they were never in His company at all. What of the long years of village childhood? What of the crucial time of ripening manhood? What of the still and happy days in Bethany when Martha and Mary were the only company? There was no Peter to be observant there nor was there any John to watch and to remember; there was only the love of women so adoring that the universal voice has called it blind. Had any of the disciples detected sin in Jesus, we should never have had the faith that He was sinless. But to call Him sinless because they saw no sin is something that no reasonable man can do. For immediately on doing it, there arises before him all the unchronicled and unrecorded years when Christ was hidden from the eyes of watchers in shadows that were as enwrapping as the grave.

The true foundation of the doctrine lies deeper than any absence of the act. It was not thus, at least not thus alone, that the profound impression was created. What impressed men in Jesus Christ was not merely the absence of any act of sin, but rather the absence of any consciousness of sin. It was that never once did he make a confession. It was that never once did He betray penitence. It was that never once upon His lips was there whisper of remorse or of regret. The nearer a man lives to God, the more intensely active is his conscience. He becomes sensitive to shades of guilt that are imperceptible to common men. Yet Christ, who lived in a fellowship with God that is admittedly unique and uncommunicable, never betrays so much as by a word the faintest trace of consciousness of sin. As Simon Peter grew in spirituality, he cried, "Depart from me, O Lord, for I am a sinful man." As Paul advanced in the deep things of heaven, he came to know he was the chief of sinners. But Jesus, who through all His earthly years was walking in perfect union with His Father, never once whispered, "Father, I have sinned." We see Him in those high and holy seasons when He was looking back upon His past. We overhear Him in His hours of prayer; we see Him in the agonies of death. Yet in such seasons when purest and holiest souls feel above everything their need of mercy, the pure and holy soul of Jesus Christ was absolutely unconscious of that need. We have had very many shining saints in Christendom, and they have differed vastly from each other. But there is one point in which they are all alike, whatever their century or their communion. And it is this, that as they have wrestled heavenward and grown in grace and fellowship with God, out of the depths has come the fervent cry, "God be merciful to me a sinner." It is not your worldly man who utters that. It is not your nominal and easy Christian. As life in God becomes more real and deep, steadily the sense of sin is deepened. And the one thing you will note in the experience of Jesus Christ is that with a life in God unparalleled, He never had any consciousness of sin. And He was always talking about sin, remember. It was a theme which was ever on His lips. He poured the vials of His withering anger upon the man who thought that he was righteous. Looking abroad upon the world of men He saw no hope for them except in penitence—"I will arise and go unto my father, and say unto him, Father, *I have sinned.*" Now it was that fact, as I understand the Gospels, which created the profound impression of Christ's sinlessness. It was that He had eyes to see sin everywhere—yet had no eyes to see it in Himself. It was that other men when they are called to die cry out into the dark, "Father, forgive me"; but that the Master when He came to die said, "Father, forgive them"—not forgive Me. There is not a trace in Christ of any healed scar. There is not a trace of regret or of remorse. In all the history of the Redeemer there is no word of penitence nor any sign of shame. And all this, with a heart so sensitive and with a life so flooded and absorbed with God, can only mean that Jesus Christ was sinless.

No one can study the prayers of Jesus Christ without discovering what he owes to the Old Testament. Christ fed and nourished His piety on the sublime words of psalmist and of prophet. And though His soul was steeped in prophecy and the language of it rose to His lips in prayer, there is one point at which He stops, saying, as it were, "Thus far and no further." It was with the Scripture that He met the tempter. It was with the Scripture that He assailed His adversaries. It was of the Scripture that His heart was full as He hung in His last hours upon the cross. Yet never once, though claiming as His own that wonderful heritage of faith and prayer—*never once* does He personally use the cry of prophet or psalmist for forgiveness. Isaiah had cried, "Woe is me, for I am a man of unclean lips." David had cried out of a broken heart, "Against Thee, Thee only, have I sinned." Yet Christ, who was so steeped in these old writings that their language rose to His lips as if by instinct, never uses—never repeats—these penitential and brokenhearted prayers. Now all that we ever find in Holy Scripture is the transcript of our deepest life. We can only use its language with sincerity when it has some link with our experience. All that answers to us as if it were our own comes to our lips when we draw near to God; all else, though it speaks as with the tongue of angels, can never rise to heaven in our prayers. Why is it then that Jesus Christ is silent with such a treasury ever at His hand? Why does He use the psalmist's adoration, yet never in one word the psalmist's penitence? The only answer of which I can think is that in all the experience of Jesus there was nothing which answered to that heavenward cry in which psalmist and prophet prayed for pardon. Had He felt in Himself the slightest need, He would have used the penitential language. For there is nothing like it in the world, it is so poignant and sincere. Yet Christ who used all else never used that—never took up a single word of it though from a child in the sweet home of Nazareth He had been fed on the word of Holy Scripture.

There is one other aspect of the matter that I can hardly avoid saying a word upon. It is that if Christ be sinless, then what becomes of His temptations? Now let me say, and say with all my heart, that I hold the temptations of Jesus to have been intensely real. He is no brother to me unless in all reality He was tempted as the Son of man. And the point is, how could He be tempted so—truly intensely and terribly tempted—if He was indeed a sinless Savior? I shall not profess to give a perfect answer for I am not here to give little answers to great questions. But I am here to suggest to you such thoughts as I may have brooded on in quiet hours. And I think that there are two considerations which throw light upon the difficulty, and these two I would put as follows.

The first is that the bitterest temptations are not always dependent upon sin. They spring from the conflict, not between right and wrong, but from the conflict between right and right. If a man, for instance, is tempted to become drunk, then of course within his heart there must be evil. And if all temptations were of that complexion, then Christ our Savior could never have been tempted. But I submit that in this life of ours there are other temptations more bitter than that which if a man has experienced and resisted, he has sounded all the depths of moral trial. Here, for instance, is a student who has come out of a humble home. And he is brilliant and successful in all he does, and the way is opening for a fine career. And then one day there comes to him the news that his father is smitten with some dread paralysis and that the little family business will be ruined unless the son comes home, and comes at once. On the one hand is his duty to his mother and to the little children still under her care. On the other hand is his duty to himself and to the gifts of intellect which God hath given him. And what I say is that in these rival voices calling each of them as with the voice of heaven, there are all the elements of a moral conflict beside which that of the drunkard is a sham. For you have not exhausted moral conflict when you have told of the conflict between good and evil. Subtler than that, and sometimes far more terrible, is the conflict between good and good—the duty that we owe ourselves faced by the duty that we owe our brother; the duty that we owe our wife and children faced by the duty that we owe to heaven. What I mean is that if all human progress were merely a progress from bad to good, then in Christ who was entirely good, there could have been no progress through antagonism. But if within the circle of the good many of our fiercest battles must be fought, then it is easy to see why a sinless Savior might be tempted as we are. Yes, and if sinless, might it not be the case that He felt temptation more terribly than we? For there are calls that are deadened for everyone of us just because our hearts are dulled through sin. Had we been less dulled, with what intense appeal certain claims might have come home to us, and so would the temptation have been so much more the awful.

And the last thought that I would leave with you is that the sinlessness of Christ was not a gift to Him, but rather I should call it an attainment. "Why callest thou me good?" He said; "there is none good but one, that is, God." Christ never claimed and never had on earth an absolute and unconditioned goodness. His was the goodness that was always perfect because through every condition it was tested and never failed, even in hours of agony, in a perfect and filial response. The God who dwells in heaven cannot be tempted. He lives in absolute and unconditioned goodness. He dwells in heaven where there is no temptation above the smoke and stir of this dim planet. But Christ was human to the very depths and knew all the play of emotion and impulse, and felt every influence that breathed upon Him, crying to Peter, "Get thee behind me, Satan." From moment to moment He had to choose His course. From moment to moment He had to trust His Father. From moment to moment He had to resist, even though it was a mother who appealed. And we call Him sinless not as God is sinless, who cannot be tempted nor touched in the high heaven, but as one who never failed and never faltered in the fulfillment of His Father's will. To you and me the heavenly Father speaks as He spoke to the well-beloved Son. And you and I hearing Him misinterpret Him, and at the end of the day are sorry and ashamed. Christ caught the faintest syllable of heaven. Christ interpreted it all without a flaw. Christ bowed to it joyfully and without a murmur even when the will of God was Calvary. That is the sinlessness of Jesus Christ—not an unethical gift, but an achievement. It was wrought out from stage to stage in perfect obedience to the heavenly Father. And so I think there falls an added glory on the deep mystery of Jesus' sinlessness when we remember that right to the very end He was tempted in all points like as we are.

The Interceding Savior

He is able also to save them to the uttermost . . . seeing he ever liveth to make intercession for them—Heb. 7:25.

There are times in life when it is very helpful to know that somebody is praying for us. It strengthens us when we are prone to faint. When some difficult duty lies ahead, when we have to undergo an operation or when death has taken away a loved one and we are overwhelmed with loneliness, the certainty that friends are praying for us is a mighty succor to our trembling hearts and often ministers quietness and confidence. I have often heard missionaries say that what sustained them was their assurance of the prayers at home. During the war many of our boys used to speak of the difference this made. It reinforced their hearts and kept them strong to know that folks at home were praying for them. Indeed, I have found that many who never pray are eager to have the prayers of others when facing a crisis in their lives.

Now our text tells us that somebody is praying for us, and the somebody is our risen Savior. That is the only meaning which our text can have, and with all its mystery we thankfully accept it. We light on the same truth again in the song of triumph in the eighth chapter of Romans. John, too, in his old age, dwelt on the consolation of that thought (1 John 2:1). And if we only let it sink into our hearts, we find it the good news of God. Others may forget us in their prayers; there is One in heaven who never does forget. Others may fail us when their lamp burns low; He ever liveth. We are engirdled by the prayers of One who loves us and has the ear of God and therefore is able to save unto the uttermost.

Nor was this ministry begun in heaven; it was carried over from the days on earth. Our Lord on earth was an interceding Savior. One remembers His words to Simon Peter recorded in the Gospel of St. Luke: "Simon, Satan hath desired to have thee, but I have prayed for thee that thy faith fail not." And if our Lord so prayed when He was here, why should it be thought a thing incredible that He would continue that ministry in heaven? Does not Satan desire to have us just as he desired to have Simon? And often when our foot has well-nigh slipped, have we not escaped out of the fowler's snare? And why should we be charged with being mystical because we adoringly ascribe our rescue to the intercession of the risen Lord? Did He not say, "I will pray the Father, and He shall give you another Comforter"? Have we never experienced with an inward certainty that in the hour of need that Comforter has come? All fresh enduements of the Holy Spirit, whether for service or for suffering, are intimations of a praying Savior.

Again, we remember another intercession, "Father, forgive them; they know not what they do." And if He prayed that prayer when on the cross, we may be perfectly certain that forgiveness followed. Did not He say beside the grave of Lazarus, "I know that thou hearest me *always*"? How little any of us know what we are doing! How often we say, "If I had only known!" Hence springs remorse and agony of conscience and thoughts which reproach us in the silent night. In such seasons, may we not lift our hearts to Him who ever lives to intercede and hear Him praying for our human ignorance as once He prayed upon the cross? So much of our sin is not deliberate. Evil is wrought by want of thought. We are such ignorant and foolish beings that we can rarely follow our actions to their issues. But He is praying for us just as He prayed on Calvary, and He is able to save unto the uttermost because He ever liveth to make intercession for us.

And then one thinks what this implies, for prayer is never an isolated thing. Whenever anybody prays for you, it means that he bears you on his heart. When a mother prays for her boy who is a prodigal, that is a token that she loves him still. When a sister prays for a brother who is careless, that means that he is very dear to her. If our Lord is praying for us in His ascension, that tells us He has not forgotten us but is eager to help us in our need. Prayers that do not lead to action are mockeries. True prayer issues in endeavor. Unless we are willing to help the man we pray for, our prayers are nothing else than empty breath. Thus do we find assurance of His help when the way is dark and the heart is very sore, in the good news with which the Gospel rings, that He ever liveth to make intercession for us.

Through the Eternal Spirit

Christ, . . . through the eternal Spirit offered himself without spot to God—
Heb. 9:14.

It is not likely, from the turn of the expression, that the writer is thinking of the Holy Spirit, and probably we shall get nearest to his meaning if we recall his outlook upon life. For him there were two worlds, one the visible world that lies around us with its fields and its oceans and its cities, with its splendors of the Jewish Temple; and then beyond that another world, invisible yet not necessarily distant, free from the relativities of space and time. To most of us the world we see is real, and the world we cannot see is but a shadow. To this writer the visible is shadow, and the unseen is the intense reality. Everything here that is bright and good and beautiful, even the ark, the altar and the Temple, are but copies of the realities beyond. John tells us he was in the isle that is called Patmos, and then he adds, "I was in the spirit." There were two environments for him, and there are two environments for everybody. And the worth of life rests on the possibility of piercing through the visible environment into the realities beyond. To the author of Hebrews, that is what Jesus did for the common man and woman in the street. He lifted their lives out of the shadow-world into what this writer calls the world to come. And by the world to come he does not mean a world that is to come when life is over, but is to come, by the saving grace of God, into the midst of our shadow-life today.

Now when the writer thinks of the death of Christ, that eternal world was always in his view. All other sacrifices were in the shadow-world; this is the region of reality. When a lamb was offered upon a

315

Jewish altar, that offered lamb was, as it were, a sacrament. It was a visible sign of something deeper. It was a hint of an invisible reality. But when Christ died, into this shadow-world there broke the great reality at last—the world to come came upon the cross. In this world are many different spirits. There are various spirits of selfishness and hate. In the eternal world one spirit reigns forever—it is the spirit of self-forgetful love. And in the animating and triumphant spirit of the world that is ignorant of space and time our blessed Savior gave up His life on Calvary. All that inspires reality—all that constitutes its very heart, all that differentiates the world to come from the shadow-world of time and sense leapt into the light and shone into the eyes of lowly men when Christ offered Himself upon the cross.

But even so we scarcely reach the depths of that most beautiful expression. For to the Oriental (however it be with us) the word spirit was never an abstraction Shining through the letters he saw God; it brought him into touch with the Divine; it was in God that there lay that innermost reality which we describe as the spirit of eternity. Now think again of the sacrifice of Christ. In every other religion that we know of it is man who gives the sacrifice. He goes to his herd and takes his bulls or goats, and in expiation he offers them to God. But the glory of our Christian faith is this, that there is not man who gives the sacrifice. The giver of the offering is God. God so loved the world that He gave. Yes, dying upon the cross for us, Christ showed the reigning spirit of reality. But dying, He did even more than that—He showed that spirit in the heart of God. It was not to change that heart but to reveal it; not to gain but to display its love that our Lord died upon the tree. Through the eternal spirit, through that spirit which reigns where things are real, through that spirit which from all eternity has had its source and dwelling in the heart of God, our Lord offered Himself upon the cross.

Then blended with that, though it seem strange to us, is the thought of the freedom in which our Savior died. That great thought is never far away from the heart of this inspired writer. When we say that ours is a religion of the spirit, we do not only mean that it is spiritual. We mean that it moves in the region of the spirit, free from the chafing fetters of compulsion. And always, to New Testament writers, spirit conveys that atmosphere of liberty as of the wind that bloweth where it listeth. Now once again think of the death of Christ. Was it inevitable and compelled. Was our blessed Lord in the grip of cruel hands? Was He held in the resistless power of Rome? No, says our writer, and he says it passionately, returning again and again to the great thought, our Lord died in real and spiritual freedom. The cross was not repression. It was final, full, deliberate expression. It was not endured in the spirit of a slave—it was welcomed in the spirit of a Son. It was not borne in any grim necessity, but in the perfect freedom of a sonship that found its joy in doing the Father's will. Picture the struggling and resisting beast dragged to the sacrifice of Jewish altars. Through compulsion it was haled to death. The cords of bondage were upon its horns. But Christ offered Himself through the eternal spirit—the free glad spirit of an eternal sonship—and that made all the difference in the world.

The Anguish of the Light

But call to remembrance the former days, in which, after ye were illuminated, ye endured a great fight of afflictions—Heb. 10:32.

This is a very remarkable conclusion to a verse that suggests the blessings of the light: it is one of those suggestive anticlimaxes that are so familiar to students of the Scriptures. No blessing is nobler than illumination. It tells of the benediction of the light. It speaks of a life that has arisen from darkness and moved into the glorious shining of the sun. And yet, when we expect to hear of summer's gladness and to catch the sound of music in the blue heaven, we hear of battle with its blood and misery and the cry and agony of wounded men. After illumination a great joy? We should have looked for some conclusion such as that. After illumination a great sense of liberty and a peace that the world cannot take away? Scripture does not deny these blessed consequences, but in its splendid fidelity to all experience it says that after illumination may come battle.

Think first then of the illumination of the intellect and of all that follows on the light of knowledge. That is not always liberty and power: sometimes a conflict which is very terrible ensues. When Eve in the virgin paradise of God ate of the tree of the knowledge of good and evil, her eyes were opened and she was illuminated with the light that never was on sea or land; and yet that light did not bring peace to Eve, neither gladness nor any rest of heart, but only the sorrow of a weary struggle. The more we know, the more we want to know. The more we know, the more we cannot know. And doubts are born and speculations rise and much that once seemed certain grows unstable until at last, wearied and perplexed, not through the power of darkness but of light, a man begins to realize how grim is the struggle that succeeds illumination.

Nor is that consequence less notable in the lesser field of personal experience. There are those who can recall the struggle that followed the clear shining of the light. Take for instance *a young man,* a student, who has been trained in a pious home. There he accepted without serious questioning the faith of his father and mother. Their character commended it to him—he saw it lived and therefore felt it true—and in a faith that never had been shaken, he joined in worship and bowed his knee in prayer. There are many who never lose that childhood's faith. They grow as the lily and spread their roots as Lebanon. It is no necessary witness of superiority that a man should have come to his own by way of agony. But often, with all that light of knowledge which the years bring to most of us today, there falls a different story to be written. Illumination comes by what we read; it flashes upon us in our college lectures. And the world is different and God and man are different from all that we cherished in our childhood's days. And then begins that time of stress and strain, so bitter and yet so infinitely blessed, through which a man must fight his way alone to faith and peace and character and God. There is a strife that is nobler than repose. There is a battle more blessed than quiescence. There is a stress and strain which comes when God arises and cries to a young heart "Let there be light." All which, so modern that it seems but yesterday, is yet so old that Scripture understands it, hinting not vaguely in our text of the struggle that succeeds illumination.

Think next of the illumination of the heart. The illumination of the heart is love. Just as the light of the intellect is truth, so the light of every heart is love. Without love the heart is always dark, and *with love the heart is always light. The commonest dwelling becomes a palace with it, and there is sunshine for the dreariest day.* And all the wealth and joy of fame and whirl of fashion can never irradiate this heart of ours like love. He who dwelleth in love dwelleth in God, and he who dwelleth in God is in the light. The luster of the heart is always there, but it is unlighted until love comes in. And now call to remembrance the former days in which, after ye were illuminated, ye endured a great fight of afflictions. Many years ago some of you mothers here gathered your firstborn child into your arms, and there was such gladness in those eyes of yours that every neighbor saw your life illuminated. And now as you look back upon it all and think of all that has come and gone since then, you know the sorrows that have followed love. What sleepless nights—what hours of weary watching—what seasons of agony when death was near! What struggle to do that which was hard to do when wills were rebellious and lips untruthful. All this has followed the illumination that came when the love of motherhood was born, and all this is the anguish of the light. Let a man love his work, and in that light he shall be led to many a weary wrestling. Let a man love his land, and in that light he shall take up burdens that are not easily borne. Let a man love his risen and living Savior, and in that light his life shall be a battlefield as he wrestles darkness. Love has its triumphs, but it has its tortures. Love has its paradise and it has its purgatory. Love has its mountains of transfiguration, and its olive gardens where the sweat is blood. Love is the secret of the sweetest song that ever was uttered by human lips, and love is the secret of the keenest suffering that ever pierced the heart.

Then observe how true this is of the illumination of the will. For our will like our intellect has its great hours when in the light of heaven we see light. It may be we had been groping in the darkness not seeing clearly what our duty was. And choice was difficult, so much depended on it: there was so much to win, so much to lose. And then it may be in one radiant hour never to be forgotten through the years, we heard as it were a voice behind us saying, "This is the way: walk ye in it." Very probably we had prayed about it, for it is in such seasons that men learn to pray. We cried, "It is not in man that walketh to direct his steps: Lord, lead me, for I know not which way is best." And then, perhaps by some word from friendly lips or by some providence or disappointment, clear as the sun shining in the heavens we saw what for us must be the path of duty. Such hours of high and resolute decision are among the greatest hours of human life. There is not a power or faculty we have that is not illuminated by the glory of them. And yet the struggle and torment that preceded them when we were stumbling and groping towards a decision may not be half so terrible and searching as the struggle and the strain that follow after. Never are things renounced so sweet to man as in the season when they are renounced. Never is the alternative so winning as in the hour when it has been rejected.

Never do things given up appeal to us so sweetly and so subtly and so secretly as in the season when we have turned our back upon them and set our faces bravely toward the dawn. The most difficult task in life is not to win; the most difficult task is to keep what we have won: never to falter from the verdict of our high and radiant hours when the shadows deepen, never to go back on our decisions, never to listen again to any voices which in our worthiest and purest moments we knew to be the voices of the enemy. That is the reason why all great decisions ought to be reinforced by prayer. There is no weapon on earth like prayer for helping us to keep what we have won. For prayer unites us to the living Christ, touches the vilest of us with the touch of heaven, and brings to our aid that power of perfect living which was witnessed long ago in Galilee. Tasks in hours of insight willed must be through days of gloom fulfilled, but in the gloomiest day a man may lift his heart up and draw for his need out of the grace of Jesus.

And in closing I want you to take our text in regard to the illumination of the conscience. Do you remember when *conscience* was illuminated was a great fight of afflictions you endured? That may have happened many years ago when you were young and ardent and impressionable, and yet so unsearchable are the ways of God that perhaps it is happening to some of you now, after many prayerless, careless, and hardening years. You recall how David after a great sin hardened his heart and justified himself. And then by the word of Nathan the prophet there flashed on his conscience the light of a holy God. Whereupon that mighty soul, after he was illuminated, broke out into that penitential agony which has come ringing down the ages and shall ring on forever: "Create within me a clean heart, O God, and renew a right spirit within me. Purge me with hyssop, and I shall be clean; wash me, and I shall be whiter than snow." That is not the crying of despair nor of the soul that has forfeited the everlasting mercy: it is the eternal crying of the human conscience that has been irradiated by the light of God. My brother and sister, if God has so come to you, He will never leave you nor forsake you. He has a purpose of peace towards your soul that has been destined from the bosom of eternity. He has begun His saving work in you which only awaits the fullness of response to result in the blessedness of power and in the rest and liberty of heaven.

Patience

Ye have need of patience—Heb. 10:36.

There are some virtues which are exclusive virtues and are only demanded in peculiar circumstances. They have at the best a partial application. In certain emergencies they are obligatory or in certain social relationships; but that virtue of which we speak now can never be included among these. The child needs patience when he goes to school, for without it he will never learn. They boy needs patience on the football field, for without it he will never play. The mother needs it among her growing children: the father amid the anxieties of business: he who is in work needs it every day, and he who is out of work needs it even more.

There are certain natures, it is true, more liable than others to impatience, and sometimes the finest natures are so tempted. There is a note of impulse and of eagerness in certain natures which are full of charm; a nimbleness of apprehension, a sudden flashing as of a swallow's wing; and often it is natures such as these which do so much to beautify society that are most sorely tempted to impatience. It is the fairest of our Highland lakes which are most liable to sudden storm. In a tamer country they would escape the squall; we could depend on them more in duller levels. But the very grandeur of the hills around them tosses them swiftly into wild commotion, and so is it with certain men and women. We think of Moses, meekest of God's servants, shattering the tables of the law. We think of Peter in impulsive loyalty cutting off the ear of the priest's servant. And we seem to see the Highland lake again with its silent hills forever reaching heavenward and its hollows which are the caverns of the wind.

It is well also to remember constantly that there is a noble and an ignoble patience. Of this, as of all the other virtues, the devil always has
his counterfeit. If we seek for the perfect pattern of patience, instinctively we turn to our Redeemer; yet of one thing Christ was utterly impatient, and that one thing was evil. Those fierce denunciations of the
Pharisees, that groaning beside the grave of Lazarus, are all in the picture of the patient Christ. It is the duty of no one to be patient when
evil can be checked or wrong be righted. All our liberties were won for
us by heroic impatience of the wrong. There are times when patience is
the badge of weakness and ruthlessly betrays the faithless heart; there
are times when impatience is divine. Had Robert the Bruce been patient under tyranny, where would our liberty have been today? Had
Knox been patient and borne the yoke in meekness, where would have
been the Church of Christ in Scotland? And had we been patient in
this present hour when the dearest human rights are being imperiled,
when nations are being trampled underfoot, when the bond of honor
is a scrap of paper, Christ would have said to us, "I never knew you; depart from me, ye cursed of my Father." So long as evil is avoidable,
every follower of Christ must be impatient with it. It may be criminal
to be a martyr when it is possible to be a soldier. No man is worthy to
be a Christian citizen or to have a place within the Christian commonwealth who cannot be splendidly impatient sometimes with
tyranny and cruelty and evil. My Christian friend, that is ignoble patience—shall I tell you what noble patience is? Noble patience is the
cheerful bearing of what is inevitable and unavoidable. It is in the chastisements sent to you from God; it is in the sufferings which you have
to bear; it is in the trials upon the line of duty, that "ye have need of
patience." Ignoble patience is the child of cowardice. It is afraid "to
lose with God." It is the fruitful mother of injustice, the perpetuator
of social abuses. Noble patience welcomes what is sent, believes that
behind everything is God, issues in a quiet which is victory. Matthew
Arnold in one of his choicest poems calls patience "the neighbor of
despair." But the patience of the Lord Jesus Christ is never the neighbor of despair. It is the neighbor of high and quenchless hope, of confidence that the best is yet to be, of trust in the providence which
counts the stars and providently caters to the sparrow.

Always, too, we should remember that patience is something different from endurance. It is possible to endure and not be patient. Endurance is a very noble virtue; nothing great was ever done without it. There is a world of meaning in our Scottish proverb, *He that tholes, o'er comes*. But patience in the fullness of its import is ethically finer than endurance: it is endurance with sunshine on its brow. Patience is endurance which is willing. It is endurance with gladness in its mien. It is the endurance which recognizes God and the infinite wisdom of His ordering. It is the endurance which is only possible when one is sure that love is at the helm and that all things work together for his good. A man may endure with curses in his heart. But patience has no curses in its heart. "Let not your heart be troubled, neither let it be afraid." Patience is endurance in Christ's company, and it takes the cross up with a ready mind, for it leans upon the perfect love of God.

Patience is needed in peculiar measure for all development of human character. "In your patience possess ye your souls"—your *selves*. Every man, that is, has a true self hidden amid the ruins of his nature. And as a mother from a burning homestead saves her child, so man must win his life. And the only way to do it is the long way, the long and tedious and patient way—in your patience ye shall win your souls. Just as there are no shortcuts to heaven, so are there no shortcuts to character. If it takes long to grow a mustard seed, it will take longer still to grow a man. And therefore we have need of patience when we are tempted to what is swift and flashy; tempted to forget that of all lengthy ways there are none so lengthy as the ways of God. "All these things will I give thee, if thou wilt fall down and worship me." It was the great temptation of Christ as He looked out upon His opening ministry. And then He chose the long and lowly way by the garden of Gethsemane and Calvary, and so came to His kingdom and His crown.

Once again, do we not need patience in regard to the plans and purposes of God? "The mills of God grind slowly." Beautiful is the patience of a nurse ministering to some restless invalid; beautiful the patience of a mother among her children who are never still; but in a world like this where night is loath to flee and the crimson morning is so slow in coming, it calls for a patience not less real than that if man is to believe in God. Think of the state of things today. Every hospital is full of wounded men; every city thronged with homeless fugitives; every field

324

in Northern France today has been opened for the burial of the slain. And all this after the faith of centuries and the mystic communion of the Holy Supper and the praise unceasing from a million tongues to "Jesus, lover of my soul." My Christian hearer, that is hard to bear, and it is harder still to understand. It is as though He who sitteth in the heavens were making merry with the toil of ages. And what I say is that in this present hour, more than in any hour that we have lived—we have need of patience. Patience to believe that with the Lord a thousand years are as one day; to believe that He maketh the wrath of man to praise Him, and the remainder of His wrath He shall restrain; to believe that He is King of kings, that in His hand there is the heart of princes, that He seeth the end from the beginning. It is not enough, remember, to endure. About our endurance there is no debate. As Britons with a lineage of heroes we shall carry through the task we have begun. But we are more than Britons, we are Christians; we have made our peace with God through Jesus Christ, and as Christians we have need of patience. Endurance says, "I will carry this thing through." Patience says, "God reigneth." Endurance says, "Lord, increase my courage." Patience says, "Lord, increase my faith." Endurance says, "Give me the iron will that I may never falter in my calling": but patience, "Open mine eyes that I may see." That is why at such a time as this there is supreme need of spiritual patience. It is not that the issue may be victory; endurance might be adequate for that. It is that through all gathering of storm clouds which hang so dark around the throne in heaven, we may walk quietly as men who have a God.

In closing may I ask you to observe how the Gospel always has been the friend of patience? It has been so mainly in two ways, and the former is by making love supreme. What is it, tell me, that makes the mother patient amid the worries of her little family? What was it that made Jacob patient when for seven years he served for Rachel? Duty can touch the heart to stern endurance, to scorn delights and live laborious days; but for the finest patience you need love. And now I turn to the old Gospel story, and what do I find in the very center there? I find a love sealed in the cross of Christ, a love victorious which will not let us go. It is that love, in its infinite benediction falling with power on our fretting hearts, which helps us to the patience that we need.

And then, the other secret? The other is the hope of immortality. For a thousand worries Christ has given patience by bringing immortality to light. There is a splendid saying of St. Augustine's which everyone of us should take to heart. "God is patient," says St. Augustine, "because He is eternal." With all eternity to work His works in, how could the Almighty worry or chafe; and Christ has brought immortality to light. We are no longer the creatures of a day. We do not cease our service at the grave. All we have striven to do and striven to be shall be carried over into the great forever. There is something very quieting in that; something which sheds a gleam on every failure; something which helps us wonderfully in those seasons when above everything we have need of patience.

The Tent and the City

By faith he [Abraham] sojourned in the land of promise, as in a strange country, dwelling in tabernacles with Isaac and Jacob, the heirs with him of the same promise: for he looked for a city which hath foundations—Heb. 11:9,10.

In this great chapter, the roll call of the heroes, Abraham occupies a very honorable place. His life was so preeminently one of faith in God that in this muster of the faithful that was inevitable. There have been men who in some great hour of life or death have risen to a sublime heroism of trust. There have been others whose faith has been most notable in the quiet tenor of uneventful days. But the faith of Abraham did not fail nor falter when he was commanded to sacrifice his son; it rarely deserted him in the days which had no history as he rose and toiled and slumbered in his tent; and it is this inclusiveness—this reach from the least to the greatest—which makes the faith of Abraham unique. Never forget that the faith which we profess should dominate us as Abraham was dominated. That man is not to be reckoned a religious man whose religion is seen only in a few shining hours. Like the glow of health which spreads through a man's whole being, it must show itself in every deed and every day. The temple may manifest it, but so must the tent.

Abraham, then, was a dweller in a tent: that fact had made a deep impression on the writer, and immediately he tells us the secret of that tent-life—he looked for a city whose builder and maker is God. The tent and the city, then: that is my theme. What thought does that sharp antithesis suggest? I shall group what I wish to say under these heads. First it is the tent which makes the city precious. Second, it is the city which explains the tent.

327

First, then, it is the tent which makes the city precious. We see at a glance that it was so with Abraham. It was the very insecurity of that tent-life, the isolation of it and its thousand perils, that made the dream of a city so infinitely sweet. Had Abraham spent all his days within strong walls he would never have known the power of that ideal. Mingling with other men in crowded thoroughfares and sharing in the security of numbers, life would have been too rich, too full, too safe, to leave any place or power for this vision. But life in the tent left room and verge enough. What could be frailer than that covering of skin which shook and flapped at every wandering breeze? How it strained when the blast from the hills swept down on it! How the lashing rain in the dark night would soak it! It is in such surroundings, perilous, lonely, comfortless, that men begin to dream about a city. That is the meaning of God's treatment of Abraham. That is why God housed him in a tent. It was not to harden him nor yet to crush his pride; it was to waken him to the worth of the ideal. It took the tent so fragile and unstable, so lightly rooted, so easily overswept, to make God's promise and prospect of a city a very precious thing to Abraham.

I cannot help but think that as God dealt with Abraham, so does He deal in providence with us all. There is a flood of light poured on life's darker aspects for me when I remember the city and the tent. After all, the important thing is not what we live in; the supremely important thing is what we look for. It is not my actual achievement which is vital; it is the purpose, the aim, the direction of my life. If life is to be redeemed from sense and time and brought under the powers that are eternal, the eyes must be opened somehow to God's city. "And how shall I open them?" says the Almighty. How shall I make the unseen city precious? The answer to that lies in the tent of Abraham—so insecure, so perilous and so frail. From which I learn that much of life's harder discipline, and many a dark hour that men are called to, is given to humanity by Abraham's God that hearts may begin to hunger for the city.

For example think of sickness in that light. Is it not often the tent that makes the city precious? A man must be finely endowed and finely strung if perfect health does not dull his vision a little. When morning by morning through unbroken years a man has no pain, no sufferings, no frailty—it is strange if there are not some stars across the sky to which the perpetual sunshine does not blind him. But sooner or later to most men there comes sickness; they are sent out like Abraham into the lonely tent. They waken at night to feel their insecurity: another blast and the tent may be in ruins. And who does not know when such hours have come and gone how the eyes have been opened to a thousand things? Springtime is sweeter and the joys of each day; there is not a bird in the tree that does not sing with richer music. Home is more precious, and the play of children, and the love we leaned on far too little once. There is not a promise of God that does not have new meaning; there is not a prayer that is not somehow more real. We did not want that tent-life of the sickroom: we did not choose it; it seemed an interruption. We thought it hard that in the midst of activity should come "the blind fury with the abhorred shears." But for us as for Abraham, it was purposed after all; and somehow the tent has made the city precious.

In the same light also we may look on death. For we must never forget that death is more than a tragedy. It is shrouded in unutterable loss, yet in the midst of the loss God has implanted gain. There is nothing in the world so cruel as death, nothing so pitiless or so remorseless. It fills the heart with a loneliness far deeper than that of the solitary tent of Abraham. Yet how many homes have been purified by death! How many hearts that once were utterly worldly have been taught to think of heaven through bereavement! There are some things that are never seen so clearly as when they are seen through the sad veil of tears. Death has made tender every human tie; death has made possible the sweetest memories; like the darkened glass through which we can look at the sun, the shadow of death has given us the power of vision. It is impossible to say how self-centered we had been, how selfish, how blind to the unseen and eternal, had the world never known the mystery of death. It is the tent, then, which has made the city precious. It is the frailty, the insecurity, the loneliness that have turned men's hearts to the abiding things. Like Abraham we are led out to a strange land with only a few frail cords to hold our dwellings until the city of God, deep-founded and eternal, never to be shaken and never overthrown, becomes infinitely attractive to the heart.

Nor can I leave this subject without pointing out to you how it bears evangelically upon the fact of sin. Many a man is brought to see his need of Christ by the same experience as was vouchsafed to Abraham. God has a hundred ways of making Christ Jesus precious. The avenues to the feet of the Savior are innumerable. There is nothing more dangerous than to teach that in coming to Christ all men must have the same uniform experience. Often it is to all that is best in us that Christ appeals; it is on our highest and best side that Christ approaches: we look for a Savior and we recognize Him because we are hungering and thirsting after righteousness. But often—remember—it is the very opposite; it is not our best but our worst that makes the Savior precious. God leads us to Christ not by our brightest hopes, but by deepening in our hearts the sense of sin. Never did David so feel his need of God as when he cried, "Against Thee, Thee only, have I sinned." Convicted of his guilt and conscious of his wickedness, God in that hour became most precious. And so in us when the old satisfaction goes, when we feel our unworthiness and when we cry "Unclean, unclean"—in that very moment are we ready to see Christ as infinitely fairer than we ever dreamed. We are made lonely that we may need His fellowship. We are shown our helplessness that we may see His power. We are taught by the Spirit of God how worthless is our righteousness that our eyes may be opened to the righteousness of Christ. Like Abraham, we are made to dwell in tents—ragged, unsightly, insecure, and lonely—but it is the tent which makes the city precious.

But I pass on now, and in the second place: it is the city which explains the tent. We could never have understood the life of Abraham, never have rightly appreciated his behavior, if the Bible had not told us the hope that was in his heart—he looked for a city whose builder and maker is God. Abraham was a very wealthy man and there was nothing to prevent him building a home in Canaan. Had he raised a palace for himself there and had he fortified it, it would have seemed a perfectly natural thing to do. He had been bred in the country of Chaldaea where walls were might and castles were magnificent; towers, fortresses, buttresses, castellations—on such things had he feasted his boyish eyes. Doubtless he hoped as many a boy has done for the day when he should build a castle for himself. But the day comes when he is free to do it, and yet never one stone is laid upon another. He is rich and powerful, let him build his fortress now. But he doesn't give it a thought; he dwells in tents. And you will never understand that tent, never know why Abraham chose it, until you are told the secret of his heart. Others might dwell in tents because they were lazy. Other might dwell in tents because they were misers. Others might dwell in tents because they were restless and had the spirit of wandering in their blood. But the conduct of Abraham is not to be explained so: it is his vision which interprets it. You learn the secret of the tent when you remember that he looked for a city whose builder and maker is God.

Now doesn't this suggest to us a caution when we are tempted to be rash in judgment? I am amazed at the rash and foolish way in which we pass judgments on each other. Of our brother's hidden life we know so little, of the ideals that are haunting him we are so ignorant—yet we look at the tent he lives in and we judge him by it as if we could read the meaning of the thing. But you may depend upon it that you will never know a man until you know the hopes which animate him. You may think that the tent proclaims the man a sluggard, but in the sight of God it may seal him as a saint. And it is because we are ignorant of the secret of our brother and of all that is stirring and calling in his heart that so often we judge him falsely.

Here for example is a young man with what we call a strong artistic temperament. And nothing will satisfy him but to be an artist; by night and by day he dreams of little else. Everyone tries to dissuade him from that calling: it is painted to him in the blackest colors; he is warned of the disappointment he will meet with; but it is all useless, he will not give it up. Then come long years of hardship—perhaps starvation—and men smile at him and say, "What a fool he was! If he had only become a partner in his father's business, how very comfortable he might have been!" But the heaven-born artist is looking for a city, he is haunted by the vision of ideal beauty: the world is a palace to him, it is full of joy, he can see all the stars from the door of his poor tent. Men pity him and count up what he has forfeited, but he is a thousand times richer than the men who pity him. They cannot understand why he is radiant, for it takes the city to explain the tent.

Or here is a young woman who instead of living idly, resolves to be of some service while she can. She has been eating her heart out with having nothing to do, but now she has been awakened by the grace of God. Once the puzzle was how to kill time; now the problem is how to expand it. There is so much to do, so many lives to help, so many services of all kinds to render. Deliberately she forsakes much that was sweet, dwelling in tabernacles with the heirs of the same promise. She is often weary visiting the poor for life is a sterner thing than she had dreamed. And her old friends, perhaps her own sisters and brothers, cannot understand this change at all. But her eyes have been opened—that is the reason—she is looking for a city that hath foundations now. She has felt the constraining power of the love of Christ. That has become her secret and her song. It is the Spirit of Jesus, welcomed to her heart, which interprets the lowly service of the life. It takes the city to explain the tent.

Brethren and sisters, it makes all the difference in the world what you and I are looking for. It is by what our hearts are set on and by what our thoughts are given to that the tent we dwell in is glorified or cursed. In the roomiest mansion a man may still be miserable if there is nothing but that dwelling in his heart. In the poorest tent a man may still be happy if he looks for a city where is the love of God. I earnestly entreat of you to look to God, to fix your gaze on the Lord Jesus Christ, to lift up your hearts to Him continually, to say, "O Lamb of God, I come." That was the secret of the peace of Abraham. That will make any tent become a temple. We can do much, bear more, and be amazingly happy when our life is hid with Christ in God.

The Cloud of Witnesses

Wherefore seeing we also are compassed about with so great a cloud of witnesses, . . . let us run with patience the race that is set before us, looking unto Jesus—Heb. 12:1, 2.

While the word witness in the New Testament generally has the sense of testifier, there can be little question that in this striking figure it bears the common meaning of spectator. The writer is thinking of a Roman racecourse on some day of national festivity. There is the runner straining every nerve. There is the emperor within his purple curtains. And around the course, tier above tier, till the uppermost figures are as a haze of cloud, is the vast multitude who are looking on. Every eye is fixed upon the runners. When the race is in progress every breath is held. There is an intentness we can scarce conceive today, for then the issues might be life or death. Thus though witness in other parts of Scripture generally signifies a testifier, there can be little doubt that here it means spectator. We must beware of forcing Scripture words into one unalterable meaning. Words are plastic things; they are responsive; they alter with the urgencies of thought. Our Lord would take some great and simple word, like bread or life or water, and in the compass of a sentence would pass from one meaning to another.

So I take it that the writer means there are innumerable spectators of our human life. As we toil and struggle a thousand eyes are on us as eager as any at a Roman racecourse. These witnesses are not angelic beings. The writer here is not thinking of the angels. They are not the denizens of earth still with us in the fellowship of home. The key to the interpretation of these witnesses is found in the preceding chapter where we hear the roll call of the faithful. They are great saints, like Abraham and Noah, the spirits of just men made perfect, the child you lost in the first bloom of innocence, the dear boy who laid down his life in the war, the father who feared God, the mother or sister who was a saint, all watching us with the absorbed attention of the spectators on a Roman racecourse. He calls them a cloud because of their vast number. We still speak of a cloud of flying things. He calls them so because a cloud is far above resting on the bosom of the sky. And he says, "Children, when tempted to give up in the great race and to be overcome by some besetting sin, take a quiet moment and remember that you are encompassed by a great cloud of witnesses."

Now this thought when we let it play its part is rich in very real encouragement. Think how it reanimates our hopes. Professor Henry Drummond used to tell us of a student sitting for his examination. Every once in a while out of his pocket he took something and gazed at it a moment. The examiner, naturally suspicious, stole up to see what he was looking at and found it was the portrait of the girl he hoped to marry. It inspired him just to see her face. It heartened him to feel that she was watching. He worked better when he thought that he was working under the loving gaze of those dear eyes. And to know that eyes like that are watching us from the other side, within the veil, is one of the secret encouragements of life. If you have to undergo an operation, no one so inspires you as the man who has been through it. If you have to make your dwelling in a deadly climate, it is the man who has lived there who makes you hopeful. "Why," he says, "I lived there for years, and look at me"—the picture of good health—and so he reanimates your hopes. Now I remember that our writer's witnesses are not angelic nor celestial beings. They have lived our life and fought our battles and known our suffering and temptation. And if now they rejoice in the light and love of God, liberated from sin and pain forever, what a new hope stirs within the heart! There steals on the ear the distant triumphant song. We are watched by those who have arrived—the saints of old, the children we have lost, the dear ones who have gone before. We are like swimmers battling in an angry sea when suddenly we hear voices on the shore, and, hearing them, we pluck up heart again.

Nor can we reasonably doubt that we are helped by the prayers of that great cloud of witnesses. Let us return to the figure for a moment.

If in the tiers of the old amphitheater there was seated the wife or mother of the runner, would she not pray to all the gods she knew that her beloved might carry off the crown? And if our loved ones lean from the galleries of heaven while we are running the race of life and death, is it not conceivable they are praying also? If the child every night at bedtime here prayed for its father and its mother, if the wife every quiet morning here prayed for her husband and her children, I cannot conceive that in a better world where being is not altered but expanded, these beautiful activities should cease. The souls under the altar cry for vengeance. Is the cry for vengeance the only prayer in heaven? Are there not golden bowls there full of odors which are the prayers of the saints? I think we shall never know how much we owe when we are weary, suffering, tempted, overwhelmed, to the prayers offered within the veil by those we have loved long since and lost awhile. We are encompassed by a cloud of witnesses. They watch us, they love us, and they pray for us. Wherefore let us run with patience the race that is set before us. And when we remember that we owe all this to Him who brought life and immortality to light, let us run looking unto Jesus, who is the author and finisher of faith.

On Weights

Let us lay aside every weight, and the sin which doth so easily beset us . . . looking unto Jesus—Heb. 12:1, 2.

When the writer speaks of the sin which doth beset us, he is not referring to one particular sin. The thought that one sin may be especially perilous is not present in his mind at all. He is thinking of all sin, of sin in its largest compass, and he says of all sin that it easily besets us which probably means that, like a binding garment, it clings to us and hinders us from running. Notice that he does not say, "Let us lay aside our weights, *even* the sins that so easily beset us." He puts an "and" between the words to indicate that the one obstruction may differ from the other. All sins are weights, but all weights are not sins; and both alike have to be laid aside.

A moment's thought ought to make plain to us this great distinction between weights and sins; it is one that vitally concerns our progress. There are some things that everywhere are right, and there are other things that everywhere are wrong. No matter who does them or why they may be done, their relation to the law of God is fixed. They do not take their moral tone from circumstances nor are they relative to a man's place or powers. There are things that are everywhere and always right, and there are things that are everywhere and always wrong. Now could we take every detail of human conduct and place it in one or other of these categories, life would present a very simple problem; but the complexity of life consists in the fact that there are acts innumerable which cannot be so classified. There are a thousand things that no man dare call wrong, for they show none of the charac-

336

ters of sin; on the contrary, they may be precious gifts which in other circumstances might be rich in blessing; but if they hinder you when you struggle for the best and burden you so that you run unworthily, then they are weights and must be laid aside.

That this is also the teaching of our Lord is evident from some of His memorable sayings: "If thy right hand offend thee, cut if off"; "If thy right eye offend thee, pluck it out." Is there anything sinful in the hand and eye? Are they not instruments and avenues of blessing? Of all the gifts that man has had from heaven, there are few that can be matched with hand or eye. In the right hand has waved the sword of freedom. In the right hand has been grasped the pen of genius. By the right hand is wrought that common toil that sets a hundred temptations at defiance—yet "if thy right hand offend thee, cut it off; if thy right eye offend thee, pluck it out." Do not misinterpret that deep word of Jesus. He spoke as a poet speaks, who through the concrete has visions of abstract and universal truth. He meant that even the choicest of our blessings may be so twisted and turned into a snare that a man may have to say, "This is a weight for me," and with swiftness of farewell, lay it aside.

Of course we shall remember that there are certain weights which are a help and not a hindrance to our progress. They impart a certain momentum to the character and carry a man through obstacles victoriously. There are men who by nature are lightweights with little chance of prospering in this hard world, and God has to steady them with burdens sometimes if they are to run with patience the race that is set before them. I would not like to travel in a train if I were told that it was light as matchwood. I should not like to put to sea in an ocean liner if I were informed there was no ballast in her. When there are curves to be taken or storms to be encountered, when the way is beset with obstacles or perils, you need a certain weight to ensure safety, and you need a certain weight to give you speed. I have no doubt that this is the explanation of many of the weights that we must carry. They steady and ballast us; they give us our momentum as we drive ahead through the tempestuous sea. Life might be lighter and brighter if we lacked them; but, after all, there are better things than gaiety. It is a real weight to a young man, sometimes, that he has to support an aged relative. There is much that he craves for which he can never get so long as that burden at home is on his shoulders. But has not that burden made a man of him—made him strenuous and serious and earnest? He might have run his race with brilliance otherwise, but he runs it with patience now, and that is better. There are few weights like the weight at a father's heart when his little and well-beloved child falls sick. It is with him when he wakens in the morning, and it hangs about him heavily all day. But how often does it touch his heart with tenderness and call in his roving and unworthy passion, making him vow to be a better father, and bringing him back to the secrecy of prayer. There are weights that are helps then, and not be cast aside. They are of God's appointing and must be carried bravely. There are burdens which we know in our conscience to be hindrances; but there are others which in the eyes of God are blessed.

Nor is this a matter in which one who is wise will ever dare to pass judgment on another. We can tell as the days go by what are weights to us; we can never tell what are weights to other men. The thing that vexes us at every turn and causes us wearily to sigh for freedom, may to another man be a good gift of God that sends him singing and happy on his journey. If you were to clothe a modern army officer in the chain-armor of a medieval knight, it would be almost insupportable to him and would prove itself an intolerable weight. But the knight himself, "pricking o'er the plain" or dashing into combat with the Saracen was safe and strong when girded with that mail. There are few who could handle the sword of Sir William Wallace; it is so massive and of such a weight, yet in the hand of Wallace it used to flash like lightning—to him it was not a burden but a joy. Never, then, judge others in such matters and never permit others to judge you. In things indifferent it is a sign of weakness to be quickly influenced by the report of others. The personal test which one should boldly use when he is doubtful of any act or habit is to ask himself, "Is this a help or hindrance in the patient running of the race." If he can honestly say it is a help, then probably it would be cowardice to reject it. There are times when it is the duty of a Christian to insist bravely upon his Christian liberty. But if his conscience tells him that it is a hindrance, then let him dismiss it though it should take the sunshine from the morning and silence all the singing of the birds.

Sometimes, too, these things that we call weights are of the most insignificant and trifling kind. They are like the weights beside a chemist's scales, so tiny as hardly to be visible. I wonder what a thorn would weigh? There would be a good many thousands to the pound. Caught in the fleece of a sheep upon the hills, it would not hinder it from freest movement. But plunged in the flesh of a great saint like Paul, it hampers and retards at every turn till even the thorn for Paul becomes a weight and drives him in entreaty to the throne. I think there are few things sadder in the world than the trifling nature of much that hinders men. There are thousands who are within an ace of running well, with one thing only between them and freedom. And that if often such a little thing—such a trifle, such an insignificancy—that the pity is that a man should be so near, and yet, from the triumph of it all, so far.

> Oh the little more, and how much it is!
> And the little less, and what worlds away!
> —Browning, *By the Fire-side,* 39

If men were ruined only by great sins there would be a tragic splendor in existence. No one can study a tragedy of Shakespeare without being purified at heart. But men are not only ruined by great sins; they are also beaten in the race by little weights, and it is just the relative lightness of the weight that is the pity of a thousand lives. If that should describe your case, my brother, I plead with you to lay aside that weight. It may be hard; indeed it is often harder to lay aside the little than the great one. Others may smile at you not grasping what it means; they say, "What does it matter, it is such a trifle?" But in the sight of heaven and at the bar of conscience, you know it is keeping you from running well.

But someone will say to me, "That is good advice, but I have had as good advice before. It is not advice I want, but it is power to do it, for I have tried a dozen times and failed." Well, I believe you—I have had that experience; but never since I saw what this text meant. "Lay aside every weight, *looking unto Jesus*"—there is the open secret of success. Depend upon it, if you look at the weight only, you will never have the heart to lay it down. It will never seem to you so fixed and firm as in the hour you are determined to reject it. And once rejected, all that you had against it will be so overborne in wild desire that with greedy hands you will draw it back again to find it doubly sweet because forsworn. That is the certain path towards darkness and tears, for every such failure leaves the conscience poorer. The saddest hour is not when a man is beaten; it is when he says, "O God, this is impossible"; but there is no such hour, even for the weakest, if he will only act as this text bids him, and "lay aside, looking unto Jesus." Keep your gaze fixed on Jesus Christ the crucified. Direct every power of your heart towards Him. Believe in His nearness, His love, His mighty power—He carried the weight of the world's guilt triumphantly. It is wonderful, if one will but do that, how the weight that seemed to be soldered will grow movable so that a man may cast it from him and waken the next morning—free!

And now I have just one other word to say. It is about these weights which we cannot lay aside. It is about these things which really may be hindrances and which yet we dare not or cannot put away. It may be perhaps some bodily defect. It may be some relationship at home. It may be the result of folly long ago; and today it hangs about us like a weight, and we know we shall never lose it till the grave. Such things we cannot or dare not lay aside. What then? Must they always and to the end be weights? Ah, whether a thing shall be a weight or not depends enormously on how we carry it. Suppose you take a truck-load of steel plates and empty these steel plates into the sea. They sink immediately. They are far too heavy a weight to be borne by the yielding and never-resting ocean. But fashion a thousand such plates into a vessel; hammer and rivet them into a ship of steel; and the ocean will bear them as she would an almond-branch and never feel that weight upon her bosom. It is not the thing itself that is the weight; far more often it is the way we carry it. If we be selfish and loveless and out of touch with God, the very grasshopper may be a burden. But if we believe; if we have hope and charity; if we trust in the love of God and look to Jesus; these weights which we cannot lay aside will become light just because carried well.

James through Revelation

The Discipline of Uncertainty

Ye know not what shall be on the morrow—James 4:14.

This, you say, is nothing original and I grant you at once it is not unusual. But the singular thing about the Bible is that it is never afraid to announce what is taken for granted. There are writers who would sooner commit crime than have it said that they were uttering ordinary thoughts. They are so desperately eager for originality that to say what is taken for granted seems the worst of sins. But the Bible, the most original of books, the most original book in the whole world, is never in the very least afraid to lend all its authority to the obvious. The fact is that as we get older, we come to love these trite observations more. Voicing the deepest of immemorial years, they express our emotions as nothing else can do. We all begin by loving what is clever; that is generally a sign of immaturity. And then comes life and love and suffering, and we see what the great adages mean.

Well now, taking this trite adage, I want to ask, what do you think would happen if we knew? If we knew what tomorrow would bring forth, what do you think the net result would be? God might easily have made us so. There is nothing incredible in that. Now just suppose that we had such a sense as could infallibly penetrate tomorrow, what do you think the result would be? Do you think life would be easier or more difficult? Would it be a richer thing or poorer? What do you think? Well, the judgment of all who have dwelt upon the thought is that that knowledge, so far from being a gain, would be to everyone of us a loss. And I want to show you what things we should lose if God withdrew that curtain of obscurity. I want to show you that

343

the gain of knowledge would never compensate the loss of power. And I want to show it just that we may learn how merciful God is in His denials, in what He refuses as well as what He gives.

At intervals, right down through the Christian centuries, men have believed that the end of the world was coming. On such a day in such a definite year, the trumpet was to sound, and the end come. And the singular thing is that in every case, from the day of Paul to that of Halley's comet, such a conviction of a certain future has proved itself a curse and not a blessing. Never has it shown the slightest power to make men better or to make them purer. Never has it touched the best within them. Always has it touched the worst within them. It has unlocked the secret wells of cowardice that I suppose lie deep in every heart and degraded men to the level of the beast. If I had my way with fortune-tellers, I would have them banished out of every city. I am amazed that honorable newspapers would dare to publish their predictions. Of course they are charlatans, these fortune-tellers, but the point is that if they were genuine, the knowledge they offer us is just the knowledge that always has proved morally disastrous. Do not smile at the old Bible, my young friend, because it makes it criminal to consult a witch. The Bible is still a little wiser than you are. It knows, and nineteen hundred years have added their witness that it is the truth, it knows that could we know tomorrow, life would practically be unlivable.

Well now, supposing that we knew, what is the kind of thing that we should lose. First I name the element of surprise. I question if we realize how deeply our debt is to the unexpected. I question if any man could live his life if it were robbed of power to surprise him. You know how much of the charm of any character lies in the sweet surprises of its outflow. You know how much of the charm of any road lies in the turn and unexpected view. And if our life in all its dreary days lay open to our gaze, the loss of interest would be incredible. Sometimes you have been asked or have asked another, "Would you like to live your life again?" And the answer to that is almost always, "No, I should not like to live my life again." And yet, my brother, I doubt that you would say that yours has been an unhappy life. The happiness has been far greater than the misery. Deep down, within that answer of negation, there is this thought that I am trying to voice. There is the thought that life was bearable when every tomorrow had its cloudy curtain. But to repeat it with the daily certainty of what the next day would usher in would be a task beyond our powers. Every sorrow would be doubly bitter because of the shrinking of a thousand yesterdays. Every joy would have its plumage tarnished because we had handled it before its summer. So would we weary in our brightest June and tremble when the storm was on the sea and be less glad and brave than we are now under God's great kindness of surprise. Shall I tell you why it is that childhood is generally happier than age. It isn't merely that the life is fuller, though that of course has got its part to play. It is that in childhood everything is strange—every window opens on the infinite—every day that breaks, even in rain, is big with a whole world of possibility. In middle ages we are past the unexpected. We have almost lost the power to be surprised. That is why many a man in middle age is haunted by a lack of interest in things. Now just suppose that all life were like that— that it could never surprise us any more—to me at least it would become unbearable.

The next thing that we should lose would be the spirit of vigorous alertness. And of that we have a kind of parable in what we see in the dumb animals. Suppose, for instance, that you catch a bird and take it into the safety of your home. And every day you tend it and feed it until at length it learns that food is certain. Do you know what happens, although you might not guess it? Do you know what every naturalist knows? Every instinct of that little captive is silently but surely being dulled. Once it was wild and everything was dark. The bird was at its best when things were dark. Once it didn't know where its breakfast was when it awoke at dawn and was hungry. But now it knows—you are its little providence, and you have taught it what will come. And it is very sweet to have that certainty, but something better than sweetness is departing.

And that is what would happen to you and me could we see the content of tomorrow. It might be sweet, but what man cares for that if something better than sweetness were to go. I do not want a satisfying life. I want a life responsive and alert. I want to be quick to see and to hear and to seize upon the will of God. And what I say is, that this fine alertness, which is the mark of progress and of victory, would be more difficult a thousand times were we always certain of tomorrow.

Many of you here have been to London. Well, what happened when you went to London? Didn't you cover more ground in one day than many a Londoner does in half a year? He knows it all, every street of it, every park of it and every palace. You are alert because it is unknown. Or to put it another way, here is a man who has to sail for India in six months. He is home on furlough—he has six months to rest—and he gets so fat that you would hardly know him. But here is another man, a soldier, who any hour may get his call to active duty, and I tell you that is the man who is alert. No wandering very far from where his home is. No laying long plans for a fine summer. He knows that sooner or later he must go, perhaps tonight. That man may lose a little as anyone does when he chooses to live the soldier's life. But he is always fit and always ready, and it is the uncertainty that makes him so. So is it with the uncertainty of death. So with the uncertainty of trial. And it is just the darkness of it all, the feeling that we don't know what may come, that helps us to be watchful every day.

The next loss that I would mention is that of the tenderness of love. Do you wonder how that would go if we could see tomorrow? Well, in a word or two let me explain it. There is a fern known to every botanist which goes by the name of the sea-spleenwort. It is a very beautiful fern, dark green, burnished as if the angels had been busy with it, and you only find it where the breakers are and in the dark shadows of the caves. Take it out into the glare of the sun and gradually its beauty will depart. It has too passionate a hold on life to die. It will still flourish on the garden rockery. But never will you see it at its finest, save where the shadow is, the bare rock, and the murmur or wild music of the sea.

Now is there nothing in love akin to that—nothing in the affections of the heart? They become beautiful and doubly tender under the haunting shadow of uncertainty. I do not say that we should cease to love if we knew certainly all that was to be. Love is too deep for that, too vital, too intertangled with the roots of being. But I do say that wherever there is love, there is a wistful tenderness in love that nothing but uncertainty could give. Wherever a mother is praying for her children, wherever a father is working for his children, wherever husband and wife are knit together in the heavenly sacrament of wedded hearts, there the darkness that enwraps tomorrow is like the minor chord in a great melody that speaks in joy of a suggested sorrow and brightens sorrow with encircling joy. If we knew everything, love would be too hard. If we knew everything, love would be too easy. If we knew everything, we should be brokenhearted. If we knew everything, we should be unconcerned. And so our Maker in His perfect wisdom has made us a little lower than the angels, and even the angels cannot love as we do. If you knew your child would die next January, wouldn't it be very hard for you to discipline him? Wouldn't you be tempted every hour to say, "It doesn't matter, let him have his way." And so that child of yours would miss the discipline that he should carry over to eternity, and perhaps his endless future would be different because you knew the secret of tomorrow. It is far better that we do not know. It is better in the interest of love. It makes us stronger not to know the worst. It makes us tenderer not to know the best.

And then, finally, would there not be a loss of trust in God? I do not think that any one can doubt that. Here is a soldier, let us say, on the eve of some desperate engagement. The man has long forgotten his mother's God, but old memories are coming back tonight. Perhaps he is praying although no one knows it, praying as he has not prayed since childhood, and the man is praying in the darkness because he knows not what a day may bring. Here is a patient, and tomorrow morning she has to undergo an operation. It is a very serious operation—very critical, and she knows it. And why is she lifting up her heart to heaven, and why are friends remembering her in prayer? Why? Because all the skill of all the schools cannot tell her what a day may bring. Tell that soldier that he will be safe and would his knees be bent in prayer tonight? Tell that patient that all is well with her and would her heart be clinging to that text? Ah, sirs, there may be many things which make it hard for us to trust in God, but the shrouded tomorrow makes it easier. Therefore I thank God for it tonight. It is a part of the ladder to the throne. Now we know in part and see in part, and perhaps the part is greater than the whole. The day is coming in the light of God when yesterdays and tomorrows should have fled. Meantime life is richer and not poorer because we know not what a day may bring.

The Living Hope

Blessed be the God and Father of our Lord Jesus Christ, who, according to his abundant mercy, hath begotten us again unto a lively hope by the resurrection of Jesus Christ from the dead—1 Pet. 1:3.

One of the glorious things in our religion is the preeminence it gives to hope. There is a radiant hopefulness in Christianity that is discoverable in no other faith. When the Gospel was first preached, the hopes of men were practically dead. As one of the old satirists expresses it, the world had the death-rattle in its throat. And then came the message of the Gospel, and everywhere, like the blossoming of spring, hope began to blossom in the world. As Peter puts it here, men were begotten into hope. The first effect of being born again was the awakening of hope within the heart. Like little children opening their eyes on the face of a mother bending over them, men, reborn, looked on the face of hope. Life was no longer dull and dreary and desperate. Hope touched the bitterest experiences. The song of hope sounded through the night and could not be silenced even by the grave. It is difficult for us to realize the tremendous difference that Gospel hope made in a world whose highest reach was Stoicism.

Now the interesting thing is that here St. Peter calls that hope a living hope. And in that word *living* there is a wealth of importance that all our thinking never can exhaust. It implies that other hopes are dying. They grow dim and fade away and vanish. They buoy us up and lure us on, and, having accomplished that, they disappear. But though that contrast was in Peter's mind, and in the mind of every reader of his letter, there was something far more positive than that. A living hope is a hope that answers life. It is a hope that is commensurate with life. It moves triumphant through every sphere of life in which the regenerate man may find himself. Let life bring with it what it will in the whole range of possible experience, and the shining of the living hope is there. It is always easy to be hopeful when we see the glory of a new dawn. There are times when men are as naturally hopeful as birds are naturally musical. But to be hopeful when things are dead against us and life is cruel and not a star is shining, *that* is the victory which overcomes the world. A hope like that is never natural. It is something into which we are begotten. It lives in the harshest experience of life. It moves and has its being in Gethsemane. Thus it is called a living hope because it interpenetrates the whole of life and brightens even the darkness of the grave. Such was the hope of Jesus. It shone through every chamber of His being. It was radiant in the agonies of Calvary not less than among the lilies of the field. It was a hope commensurate with life in its whole expanse of suffering and sorrow—and into that living hope we are begotten.

Then this living hope, St. Peter tells us, is based on the certainty of future blessedness, and here we must be careful to distinguish. Very commonly, in the New Testament, heaven is set as the object of our hope. It is for that sweet country that the heart is longing; it is the hope of God's elect as the hymn says. But sometimes as in our present passage, heaven is not the object of our hope, but the great certainty from which there springs the new-born spirit of hopefulness in life. Tell me that death ends everything and that my strivings are never to be crowned, and I may still toil and suffer on, "with head bloody but unbowed." But tell me that a fuller life is coming when the broken arc will grow into the circle, and hope sings its music in my heart. The sea shore is a dull and dreary place when over it is nothing but the mist. But when the vault of the sunlit heaven over-arches it, the barren sand becomes a thing of beauty. And only when the mist goes and the blue of heaven is radiant over life, does glory lie on the path of our pilgrimage. Every true believer hopes for heaven. He also hopes just because of heaven. He is begotten into a living hopefulness because some day there is to be a crowning. He does not struggle on despairingly as if everything were to be cast into the void. He is the child and heir of immortality.

And then St. Peter tells us that we win that hope by the rising of Jesus from the dead. We are begotten into a living hope by the resurrection of the Lord. Note that the resurrection does not *give* that hope, for it lies latent in the human breast. In every human heart, when we decipher it, are intimations of immortality. The thoughts that wander through eternity and the shadows that fall upon our hours of triumph and the things on board of us "not wanted for the voyage," and the "forever" graven on the heart of love, all these are stirrings, as of a babe unborn, in the secret places of our being—all these are hints that heaven is our home. The resurrection is not a bestowal. The resurrection is a confirmation. It makes our latent hope a living hope. It brings the struggling embryo to birth. All our human yearnings are authenticated by the tremendous fact of resurrection. We are begotten into a living hope by the rising of Jesus from the dead.

Doing Things Happily

Having your conversation honest among the Gentiles—1 Pet. 2:12.

That word *conversation,* as we all know, has a different meaning on our lips from that which it bears in Holy Scripture. Words are like men and have their history, and sometimes the history leads upward and sometimes it moves down to lower things. Conversation on *our* lips just means talk; in the Bible it means the life behind the talk; the general course and tenor of the life, the way that a man has of doing things. Then the word *honest,* while including honesty, has suggestions that honesty does not convey. It is not the Greek equivalent for honest; it is the Greek word for beautiful. And so an old Scottish saint and scholar who was always discovering charming things in Scripture used to say that what this text means is, *Do things bonnily* or in our vernacular, it is not enough just to do things if you are seeking to commend the Lord. You may do the right things in the wrong way. You may do them in a way that causes pain. The mark of the follower of the Lord Jesus is that whatever he has to do in life, like his Lord, he tries to do it attractively.

That our Lord expected this of His disciples is seen clearly in the Gospel story. For instance, think of what He said of fasting. When hypocrites fast, said the Lord, they do it in an ugly way. Not only do they obtrude their sadness, they make a practice of disfiguring their faces. And the word for disfigure in the Greek is a very interesting word; it means to dim the luster so that the beauty vanishes away. A fasting hypocrite was not a pleasant sight, and he did not want to be a pleasant sight. He wanted men to know that he was fasting, and he conveyed the information by his ugliness just as hypocrites to this hour try to show they are "fasting from the world" by deliberate rejection of the beautiful. Now Jesus, for all His geniality, knew the moral necessity for fasting. He knew that for natures such as ours occasional fasting is imperative. His aim was not to discourage fasting; He took it for granted that His own would fast; His aim, here and everywhere, was to discourage ugly ways of doing it. When thou fastest, He says, anoint thy head, give thyself the oil of joy for mourning. Wash off the disfigurement of sadness so that nobody would dream that you were fasting. In other words, what the Lord says is this, "Child, with the seven devils in you, fast; but see to it that you always do it pleasantly." The same thing applies to prayer. The same thing applies to alms-giving. How much almsgiving is robbed of grace because of the ugly fashion of its exercise? No right thing is perfect in the Lord's eye however unassailable its rightness, unless it is also beautifully done.

This is what profoundly impressed men in the life and walk of our Lord Himself. "We beheld his glory," says the great apostle, *full of grace and truth.*" Now grace, whatever else it may be, is charm. It may be more; it never can be less. Grace is something exquisitely beautiful whether on the lips or in the life. And what moved men who had companied with Jesus, and what filled them with adoring wonder, was that always and in every circumstance they had found Him full of grace and truth. There is a kind of truth that is not charming. It is harsh, uninviting, and repellent. It may be the very opposite of falsehood and yet the very antithesis of love. But the truth in Jesus was a charming thing; it had all the attractiveness of beauty; and men, remembering it, said, "We beheld his glory, full of grace and truth." All the truth He uttered, He uttered beautifully. Men wondered at the words of grace upon His lips. All the truth He did, He did beautifully. He *was* the truth—yet "altogether lovely." And so Peter, writing to these early Christians, says, "Friends, do you want to exhibit Christ among the pagans? Then whatever you do, be sure you *do it beautifully.*"

One might illustrate that from every stage of Christ's life. Just think for a moment of the foot-washing. It is John who tells us of the foot-washing; it is Luke who interprets its significance. Luke tells us that on the way up to the capital the disciples had been quarreling about precedence. They had been arguing their respective claims to greatness, and doing it with heat. Could you have wondered if their Master, angry, had scorched and shriveled them with *truth?* But you see He was full of *grace* and truth. He took a towel. He girded Himself. He poured the water into the basin. Probably without one word, He stooped down and began to wash their feet. And when there flashed on them the truth about themselves, and with it the truth about their Lord, did they not feel He was altogether lovely? He might have healed the leper with a word—instead of that He touched him. When He brought Jairus' daughter back from death, He commanded that something be given her to eat. What a beautiful touch; and Peter saw it, and seeing it never could forget it; and so he writes, "Do you want to show forth Christ among the pagans? See to it, then, that you always *do thing beautifully.*"

That, then, we must always set before us if we really want to commend our blessed Savior. The right things are not wholly right in *His* eyes—unless they are also beautifully done. It is a great thing to give alms. It is a great thing to take one's cross up daily. It is a great thing to be a faithful wife or husband. It is a great thing to help a brother. But "what do ye more than others?" Well, there is one thing more that you can do. For the Lord's sake you can always *do things beautifully.*

The Cross and Sin

Who his own self bare our sins in his own body on the tree—1 Pet. 2:24.

The cross, though it be a single fact, is a fact with large diversity of meaning. Its significance is inexhaustible. Calvary is the uttermost of service; it is the commendation of the love of God; it is the compendium of self-sacrifice. But we must never forget that right through the New Testament, whatever its other implications may be, it stands in vital relationship to sin. No one will ever understand the cross who does not set it as the Bible sets it in immediate relationship to human sin. The question we have to ask then is this: What does the cross tell us about sin? What do we learn about the fact of sin when we set it in the light of Calvary?

The first thing which the cross tells us is that sin is something tremendously important. God did not just utter warning against sin; He gave His only begotten Son to die for it. There are many things we are willing to be taxed for, but we should never dream of letting our sons die for them. But some years ago when war broke out, we were willing to give our sons to die for liberty. Fathers gave their sons to die for liberty because liberty is so tremendously important—and God gave His Son to die for sin. It is important in His eyes for many reasons, perhaps most of all because He loves His children. Anything is important in *our* eyes that keeps our own dear children from the best. And the one thing that keeps *His* children from the best and tricks them and robs them of their heritage is the dark fact that we call sin. It disables and enfeebles them. It saps their character and wrecks their homes. It lies at the back of every tragedy that we read of in our daily newspapers. *We* may not "bother about sin," but God bothers intensely about sin—and He bothers most because His children are precious to Him.

Again, the cross tells us that sin is neither hopeless nor incurable. Into a hopeless and despairing world came the thrilling hopefulness of Calvary. When a surgeon is called in to see a patient, his conduct is determined by his hope. If there is hope that the patient can be saved the surgeon proceeds to operate. But if the case is absolutely hopeless and if the seal of death is on the patient, no surgeon worthy of the name will lift a finger. He acts because he hopes. He intervenes because he hopes. If there is not a single ray of hope, he holds his hand and he does nothing. And the very fact that God has intervened and given His Son to die for us on Calvary tells us that sin is not incurable. From the first hour that the cross was preached, that thrilling hope entered the human heart. Despair, which held the old world in its grip, went flying away in the wind. If the heavenly Surgeon had seen fit to operate, then sin was not incurable; there was healing and all the joy of life for the vilest sinner of mankind.

The other thing which the cross tells us is that if sin is to be grappled with, God must come right into it. I illustrate that from what my eyes have seen among the sick and blind in the jungles of heathendom. If these poor sufferers are to be saved, there *must* be intervention from a higher realm with its science and its knowledge of the Christian art of healing. It is not enough to send them drugs or medicine. Someone from a higher sphere must come among them carrying in his heart and head and hand the science and the skill of the learned. I have been helped to understand the incarnation by living with doctors in the heart of Africa. If sickness *there* is ever to be grappled with, some one of great ability must come into its midst. And if sin is ever to be grappled with, God must come into its midst. And this we adoringly believe that He has done when in the person of His beloved Son He lived our life and died for sin on Calvary.

And if anyone asks how that can save us, let us think of the penitent thief a moment. That thief is a living picture of us all. There he hung suffering condemnation for his undisciplined and lawless life. And then he turned his eyes and saw Jesus of whose beautiful life he had heard a hundred times (Luke 23:41). There *He* hung sharing the condemnation, bearing it in His body on the tree, and it was *that* which broke the criminal's heart and has broken the hearts of sinners ever since. Jesus did not stand beneath the cross and speak to him sweet and comfortable words. Jesus cried in the freedom of His will, "Hang Me on that cross beside My brother." And there they hung Him and pierced His hands and feet, those hands and feet that had always moved in loveliness—and the dying thief saw it and was saved. God grappled with sin on Calvary by bearing it; by sharing in its condemnation; by taking its agony into His own heart; by letting Himself be pierced by all its arrows. No wonder that the great apostle facing a decadent and rotting world cried "God forbid that I should glory save in the cross of our Lord Jesus Christ."

Keeping in Love With Life

For he that will love life (lit., he that wisheth to love life), and see good days, let him refrain his tongue from evil, and his lips that they speak no guile; Let him eschew evil, and do good; let him seek peace, and ensue it. For the eyes of the Lord are over the righteous, and his ears are open unto their prayers—
1 Pet. 3:10–12.
What man is he that desireth life, and loveth many days, that he may see good?
Keep thy tongue from evil—Ps. 34:12, 13.

These words of Peter are not original; they are a quotation from the Book of Psalms. The interesting thing to note is how Peter gives a new turn to the old thought. The psalmist asks, Do you desire life; do you want to live for many years? Peter asks, Do you wish to love life, to find it sweet and delightful to the end? In other words, the psalmist teaches us how to live if we want to reach old age, while Peter teaches us how we ought to live if we want through everything to find life lovable.

At the back of Peter's mind there lies the thought that in youth we are all in love with life. That is an experience, not a problem. To the child life is always sweet in spite of the childish bitterness of tears. To the young man or woman life is thrilling in its morning freshness of sensation. Of course, that very freshness and intensity has its reaction in the realm of suffering and darkens all the stars it sets shining. Still, speaking generally, we are all in love with life at one-and-twenty. We do not need to be taught to make life exquisite. It is fashioned so by Him who commands the morning. The difficult thing is to keep in love with life through all the experience of the years, through the sorrows and trials of the after days and the disappointments which are the lot of everybody.

It is notable that in Peter's answer there is not a word about poverty or hardship. That is one of the silences of Scripture which are as eloquent as any speech. Desperate poverty may make a man rebellious; it may rouse him against the social order; it may fill him with passionate anger at the flaunting of luxury and wealth. But that very anger is a token that poverty has not lost its love for life, for we are never angry about things that are indifferent. Poverty, strange though it may seem, does not throw men out of love with life. Far more often it is the idle rich who have lost the tang of living. I have scarcely ever known a working person for whom life was not sweet. But I have known scores of rich and idle people who were dead sick of everything.

Nor is it less important to observe that Peter says nothing of suffering or cross-bearing. There is not a hint that we must shun the cross if we want to keep in love with life. One might think that constant suffering would create a loathing against life, or that a hidden cross, borne daily, would transform life into a thing unlovable. As a matter of fact, witnessed by experience, it does nothing of the kind. Suffering is a challenge; it calls out what is bravest in us; it makes us set our teeth and hold on tighter, determined never to be beaten. And who does not know how many a woman's life grows richer and more Christlike by some daily hidden cross she has to bear? Peter never dreams of saying that we must shun the cross to keep in love with life. *That* would make it impossible for most of us.

Now just here we face the splendid fact that our Lord was in love with life right to the end. To Him it was a glorious thing, and He came to give it more abundantly. Every element was in His cup that might seem to make life unendurable. There was hardship, poverty, misunderstanding; there was infinite and unutterable loneliness. Yet at the end, and in agony, He cried, "Father, if it be possible let this cup pass from me," (Luke 22:42) and "this cup" was not life, but *death*. Buddha said, Life is an evil thing; let us be done with it, and win Nirvana. Christ said, Life is a glorious thing: believe on Me and have eternal life. And yet His life knew all the depths of suffering and was tempted in all points like as ours is and was passed in a loneliness we cannot fathom.

And just here we come to Peter's answer, for do you not see what Peter's answer is? He says, If you want to keep in love with life, then live as the blessed Master did. Keep thy lips from speaking guile—there was no guile upon His lips. Eschew evil and do good—He went about continually doing good. Seek peace and ensue it, and He is the Prince of peace forever in a divided and alienated world. For Him life was not possessions. It was character; it was service; it was love. And do you want to keep in love with it? Then you must follow in His steps. Put first things first. Give primacy to character. Serve your brother. Walk in love—and you will keep in love with life to the end.

And then remember life was sweet to Jesus because He lived it under the eye of God. He felt, as nobody else has ever felt, the continual presence of the Father. There was no God for Buddha. There is no God for any pessimist. For Jesus, God was Father: He was Friend; He shared in every heart-beat of His child. And does not Peter say, If you want to keep in love with life as Jesus did, right on to the end, then never forget that the eyes of the Lord are on you, and His ears are open to your prayers. When over life there is an arch like that, when underneath are the everlasting arms, when there is a heavenly hand to guide and a heavenly breast on which to lean, then, bring life what it may, a man is able to keep in love with it till the day break and the shadows flee away.

What to Do With Our Cares

Casting all your care upon him; for he careth for you. Be sober, be vigilant—
1 Pet. 5:7, 8.

The cares of which the apostle speaks were those associated with persecution. He was writing to those who might, at any moment, be exposed to the fury of the populace. A great deal of pagan trade was intimately bound up with idolatry. Wherever the Gospel came and took a grip, it began to interfere with trade. And for that, as for many other reasons, Christians were never safe. Their life was one of continuous anxiety. Such anxieties are gone now where the populace is nominally Christian. But care remains, haunting the human heart and robbing life of the gladness of the sunshine. And so to us, in a land that is called Christian as well as to those sojourners in paganism, comes the message of the great apostle. The question, then, for all of us is this: How does a man cast his care on God? That I should answer by asking another question: How does a man cast his care on anybody? Our Lord was very fond of that procedure, arguing from the lesser to the greater, and reaching heavenly things through things of earth.

In human life, then, we cast our cares on anybody when we confidently rely on him. We can illustrate that by the captain of a ship. When a wild storm falls upon a vessel, the passengers are naturally anxious. Children cry; women begin to tremble; men look grave and often become silent. And then they see the captain on the bridge relaxed, smiling as he talks to his officer, and they remember he never lost a ship and is reputed the finest captain in the service. The moment they see that their anxieties begin to vanish. Trusting the captain when the storm is raging, they find that they have cast their cares on him. And whenever anyone trusts God and quietly puts his confidence in God, he awakens to the same discovery. "Thou wilt keep him in perfect peace whose mind is stayed on Thee," and then the prophet adds, "because he trusteth in Thee." Trust is the great antidote to care. It is by simple, quiet, unswerving confidence that we cast our cares on anybody, and just so do we cast our cares on God.

Once again we cast our cares on anybody when we go to him and talk things over frankly. That is one of the benefits of friendship. The chief office of friendship, says Lord Bacon, is the ease and discharge of the swellings of the heart. And then he adds that the man who has no friend is a cannibal of his own heart. That is to say, he eats his heart out because he has no one to whom he can resort to speak of the anxieties that gnaw him. People often approach me for advice, and frequently go away without it. And yet they thank me when they go away and say that everything looks different now. You see, what has helped them isn't my advice; it is just that they have talked the matter over with one who feels for them and is a friend. Friendship is like a lancet; it opens the abscesses which are very painful. And as it is with a true friend on earth, so is it with our truest Friend in heaven. When we go to Him and tell Him all, opening our hearts to Him in quiet communion, how wonderfully do we discover that we have really cast our cares on Him! Be careful for nothing, says St. Paul, but in everything let your requests be made known unto God. And then what happens? Are your requests granted? The wise apostle says nothing about that. But he *does* say, and it is always true, that the peace of God which passeth understanding shall keep your hearts and minds through Jesus Christ.

Once again we cast our cares on anybody when we do our duty by him faithfully. I think of the public servants of Glasgow Corporation. The dustmen who pass my windows in the morning have their cares just like other men. They are married and have to feed and clothe their wives and children. And yet so long as they do their duty faithfully, they have no need to worry about that. They cast their cares upon the Corporation. Is not that precisely what our Savior meant when He was speaking about care and worry? "Seek ye first the kingdom of God . . . and all these things shall be added unto you." Put God first, be loyal to Him daily, live for the happy service of the kingdom, and will God do less than the Glasgow Corporation? If any man is living for self, he has no warrant to cast his care on God. But if he lives for service and not self, he can lean his weight upon the word of Jesus. There is a deeper meaning than we think of in that word of our Lord beside the well, "My *meat* is to do the will of him that sent me."

And then when our cares are cast on God, what kind of life does God expect of us? It is here that Peter displays a heavenly wisdom, for he says, "Be sober and be watchful." It is a perilous thing to have a load of cares. It is fraught with manifold temptation. It may make a husband very cross and irritable as many a wife knows. But never forget that to be free from cares may be as perilous as to be burdened with them, and that's why Peter adds, "Be sober and be watchful." I have known people suddenly freed from care by some large legacy of fortune—and that freedom has sometimes been their ruin. God does not make His children carefree in order that He may make them careless. Surely better a thousand cares than that. He makes them carefree that with undivided heart they may give themselves to the service of their brother and to the glory of His blessed name.

Inspiration Not of Private Interpretation

No prophecy of the Scripture is of any private interpretation—2 Pet. 1:20.

There are some texts with the words of which we have been familiar since our childhood, and yet we may never have seriously asked ourselves what is their true meaning. Their cadence lingers with us through the years enriched with recollections of the sanctuary, associated in sweet and tender ways with worship at the family altar, and yet it may be that all the time we have been misinterpreting the Word of God or reading into it a sense that was not there. Now this text which I have chosen is one, I think, that is often so misread. The words have a most familiar sound, but have we ever really thought what they imply?

Observe that prophecy is a very large term. You must not confuse it with the word prediction. As the priest was one who spoke *to* God, so was the prophet one who spoke *for* God. And so the word prophecy, in such a place as this, is practically equivalent to our Scripture which is the revelation of God through man to us.

Well then, our text is sometimes held to mean that you and I must not interpret Scripture privately: that is, we must not take the Word of God and wrest it to our peculiar circumstances. That that is a common mishandling of Scripture everyone of us knows. When men are in doubt about some action, they often seize on a text to quiet their conscience. And it is this taking of the Word of God at large and using it for our own private interest that Peter is supposed to be speaking of here. Now that is a warning which is always timely and never antiquated nor out of place. It is possible now as nineteen hundred years ago to wrest the Scripture to our own destruction. Yet the whole tenor of the passage shows us that it was not *that* which was in the mind of Peter when he wrote, "No prophecy is of private interpretation."

Again, these words have been taken to mean that we must not isolate the separate words of Scripture. We must not divorce them from the general sense and give them a private meaning of their own. The word heresy, as many of you know, means such a picking and selecting. A heretic was a man who, out of the whole broad truth, chose out for himself this portion or that portion. And all the evils which have followed heresy have sprung from the false and often passionate emphasis which was laid on the part and not the whole. Now that also is an important truth for we must never isolate the words of Scripture. We must never take this text or that and interpret it out of connection with the whole. Yet once again, studying our passage and looking to the general bearing of it, I think it is clear that *that* was not Peter's thought when he spoke about private interpretation.

What, then, did the apostle mean? Well, it is clear that he meant something of this nature. The interpretation he speaks of is not yours or mine—the interpretation he speaks of is the prophet's. The writers of Holy Scripture were not annalists; the writers of Holy Scripture were interpreters. Before them passed, as in some vision, the doings of God in providence and grace. And the prophet's work was to interpret these and to show their meaning and convey their message so that men might be built up in their faith. Now what Peter teaches is that that interpretation was not in any sense the prophet's own. He looked at things and saw meaning in them, but it was not his own meaning that he saw. It was not natural insight that conducted him nor any genius to discern what mattered—all *that* would have been a private rendering, and a private rendering is not the Scripture. No prophecy is a prophet's own interpreting. It is not given by the will of man. It is the interpretation of events by something different from human genius. It is the interpretation of events by the inspiration of the Holy Ghost dwelling in men and using every faculty for the glory of God and the blessing of mankind.

364

This view of Scripture is common both to the Old and New Testaments. I should never dream of building up the doctrine if it had no other warrant than this text. I need not dwell on the Old Testament for the fact is too patent there to be disputed. "And the word of the Lord *came* to Joel;" that is the attitude of all the prophets. But it may be that you have never noticed how the New Testament adopts that attitude in regard to the testimony of the apostles to Jesus and to His death and resurrection. Does it not seem a very simple thing to bear testimony to certain facts of history? Could not an honest man with a fair mind have borne witness to the crucifixion? And yet the apostles, who from first to last were witnesses and nothing else than witnesses, are regarded as only fit for that by the indwelling of the Holy Ghost. The Spirit of truth who proceedeth from the Father—it is He who is to witness, said our Lord. And we are witnesses of these things, cries Peter in the Acts, *and so also is the Holy Ghost.* In other words, these men who wrote the Scriptures interpreted the facts, not privately, but through the Spirit given from the Father, which was something other than their own genius.

Now this view of Scripture inspiration, which I can't see how any can dispute, sets it apart at once *in kind* from inspiration of every other sort.

Think, first, of the inspiration of the historian. Now a true historian is not an annalist. He is something more than a mere chronicler. It is for him to show the connection of events and to estimate their importance by what they bring forth. If he does that feebly and confusedly, then we say he is a poor historian. If he does it in a large and illuminative way, we say he has a genius for history. Yet even when there is a genius for history, logical power, and a grasp of facts, all that we expect in the historian is his personal interpretation of the past. That is why Robertson will treat a period in a manner wholly different from Hume. That is why Lecky, handling the same facts, will give them a different complexion from Macaulay. They are inspired, if you care to call them so, using the word in a loose and general way, yet at their best and wisest all they give us is their private interpretation of the past.

Or think of the inspiration of the dramatist as we have it for instance in the plays of Shakespeare. We would say that Shakespeare is inspired, and that in a broad sense is true. Well now, suppose you take the play of *Macbeth*. You say that that is an inspired play, and I ask you what you mean by that? Well, there is only one thing you can mean if your words have any significance at all. You mean that Shakespeare took the few pages of some chronicle, and he touched them with life, covered them with beauty, and filled them with passion and reality, and this he did with his *own* imagination, with all the teeming wealth of his *own* brain, with all the warmth and passion inextinguishable of his own private and peculiar heart. *Macbeth* and *Hamlet* came by the will of man. They are the triumph of individual genius. Their power is contained in the fact that they *are* the rendering of one personality. Were they less private in their interpretation, they would never move us as they so profoundly do. They do not live because the facts are facts. They live because Shakespeare is Shakespeare.

Now in contrast, there stands the inspiration of the Scripture. Unlike all history and every drama, no prophecy is of private interpretation. When a poet is most genuinely inspired, then is he most genuinely himself. When Wordsworth is at his finest and his purest, then is he most emphatically Wordsworth. But what you are taught about Holy Scripture is that it came not by the will of man, by holy men of God spoke as they were moved by the Holy Ghost. Isaiah did not look at events and study them and say, Now this is my interpretation of them. John did not look at the cross and at the grave and say, This is how it all appears to me. But they looked at everything under that light of God which is only kindled by the Holy Spirit, and looking so, they saw, and seeing wrote. Understand that I do not suggest they were passive: to say that would be to misinterpret everything. Probably their powers were never so alive as when they were writing a Gospel or epistle. All I say is, and all that Scripture says is, that what you have in the Bible is not genius; it is something different from and something more divine than a private interpretation of events.

If there were ever writers of vigorous and independent personality, I think you may be sure that these writers were the men who have given us the New Testament. If there were ever men who would have looked at facts in diverse or antagonistic ways, John and Paul and Peter were such men. In other words, had the Scripture which they wrote been their own personal interpretation, then almost certainly you would have found between them difference that were irreconcilable. And the very fact that these are never found when they are handling the deep things of God is a witness to an inspiration different in kind from that of genius. There is the freest play of personality—the writers are penmen and not pens—and at the back of every chapter which they wrote is a rich and individual experience. Yet such is the deep and underlying unity in all that is essential to salvation that the more we study, the more we are convinced that the Scripture came not by the will of man. No prophecy is a private rendering. Had it been so we should have had many Bibles. We should have had a Bible of John where everything was love perhaps, and a Bible of Paul where everything was righteousness. And the very fact that the Testament is *one*, when men so different were the writers of it, speaks of more than individual genius in all its interpretation of events.

Now if this is the Scriptural view of inspiration, then we may proceed to ask another question. We may ask, Are there any features in the Scripture which help to corroborate this view? No prophecy is a private rendering. The Scripture came not by the will of man. Are there any features in the Word of God which would incline us to accept that as the truth? In other words, do we find in Holy Scripture what it is almost incredible that we should find had the writers been consulting their own will? When a man is following his own inclination, there are certain things which he avoids. There are aspects of things which from certain standpoints may be highly and naturally uncongenial. And if you find these very aspects dwelt on and expanded and enforced, then you may reasonably conclude that something else is active besides the writer's individual will. Now that is exactly what one finds in Scripture, and finds it increasingly so the more one's knowledge grows. There is a certain curious want of correspondence between the message and the men who uttered it. And I shall close by touching upon that in one or two of its most salient features that we may see how evident it is that Scripture came not by the will of man.

First, then, I note how often prophetic doctrine contradicts the bias of the will. If there is one thing clear in the prophets it is this, that the truths they uttered were often uncongenial. Now men have spoken uncongenial truths sometimes under a compelling sense of duty. When every interest urged them to be silent, their conscience has compelled them to speak out. But you can never explain that old prophetic fire by saying that it was duty which impassioned it, for duty seemed to point the other way. The call of duty is the call of loyalty. The call of duty is the call of home. The call of duty is the call of patriotism when the enemy is marching on the gate. And yet how often these old prophetic heroes lifted their voices up in the name of God, and contradicted every such call. Humanly speaking, they dared to be disloyal. Humanly speaking, they betrayed their country. Humanly speaking, they advocated courses that to the wisest seemed to lead to ruin. And if time has showed that they were *not* disloyal but the truest patriots in Israel, that only means that in their word of prophecy they were moved by a wisdom higher than their own. They crushed into the dust their private prejudices. They shattered by their speech their private hopes. They flung to the winds, when they lifted up their voice, their private interests and advantages. And what I say is that if the word of prophecy had come to us solely by the will of man, the Bible would have a different tale to tell. No prophecy is of private interpretation. No one would dream it was, who knows the prophets. It is not thus even the bravest speaks when he is speaking at the call of conscience. This is the speaking of men who in their darkness were under the moving of some mighty power, who sat enthroned above the dust of things and saw the end from the beginning.

The same compulsion, as of some higher power, is seen in the portrayal of great Scripture characters. You have characters set up as an ideal, and then mysteriously that ideal is marred. The Jew had essentially a concrete mind. He loved to see all excellences embodied. At the heart of him was a hero-worshiper mightily influenced by old example. And that is one reason why in the Old Testament so much place is given to biography in the lives of Abraham, Moses, and David. Now remember that a Jewish writer never hesitated to idealize his hero. If he thought it was good for edification, he would unhesitatingly paint a character without a flaw. And yet the strange thing is that in the Word of God these grand ideals which are to inspire the world are dashed with weakness and tarnished with iniquity and broken sometimes by the most shameful fall. There was one hero who was the friend of God—what a glorious theme for any Jewish writer! There was another after God's own heart—can you not picture how he would be described? Yet the one—Abraham—descended to mean trickery, and the other—David—fell to the very depths, and all this has been written down for us in the stern pages of the Word of God. My brethren, if the Scripture had come by the will of man, you would never have had anything like that; if prophecy had been a private rendering, you would have had lives like those of the medieval saints. And the very fact that you have falls like these in characters which were meant to lead the world is a witness to another will than ours. When He, the Spirit of Truth, is come, said Jesus, He will lead you into all truth. It was that spirit which came upon the prophets and led them into the darkest truth unwillingly. In no other way can I explain these tragic pages by writers who knew nothing of historic method and who would never have hesitated to idealize the past for the glory of their people Israel.

And then, lastly, we trace the same compulsion in the self revelation of the writers. We trace it in David in the fifty-first Psalm for instance, and we have it manifestly in the apostles. I want you to remember that these apostolic writers were men of like passions with ourselves. They were actuated by the same desires and they knew the pressure of our common hopes. They knew, as every man must know, the desire to stand well with those who heard of them and to hand on to the future some worthy memorial of themselves. Now the point is that being men like that, they never hesitated to reveal themselves. They wrote of their weaknesses and of their sins in the very record that told the love of Christ. They concealed nothing for the sake of fame, sheltered nothing for the sake of honor, cast no veil on an unworthy hour even in the sacred cause of friendship. Could not Peter have instructed Mark to cover up the tale of his denial? Might not John, being the friend of Peter have dwelt a little less upon his fall? But the Scripture came not by the will of man nor is any prophecy a private rendering, and there it all stands written to this hour. There is no hurling of contempt at Judas—a chapter like *that* would have been very natural. There is no golden and enhaloed picture of the men who had left everything for Jesus. John knew not what spirit Christ was of. Peter denied Him with a fisher's curses. Judas in a profound and awful silence goes to his own place—and that is all. That is not the moving of the will; that is the moving of the Holy Ghost. *That* is the kind of thing which Scripture indicates when it says of itself it is inspired. If there is one thing growing ever clearer as knowledge widens and the ages pass, it is that Scripture came not by the will of man.

The Slowness of God

One day is with the Lord as a thousand years, and a thousand years as one day—2 Pet. 3:8.

It is not difficult to understand the mood of those whom the apostle is addressing. He is addressing men who were perplexed by the seeming inactivity of God. When they first entered on their Christian calling, they had been thrilled by certain glorious promises. Christ was to come again, and to come quickly, and they were to share in the triumph of His coming. But now the months had lengthened into years, and life went on unbroken and unchanged, and they looked heavenward and looked in vain for the epiphany of Jesus and His saints. It was to such men that Peter wrote—to men who were disheartened and discouraged. They were ready to cry as Jeremiah cried, "O Lord, thou hast deceived me, and I was deceived." And the task of Peter was to comfort them and to show them the meaning of that apparent slackness and to teach them that there was a purpose big with mercy in that perplexing slowness of the Lord. It was Augustine who said this of God: God is patient because He is eternal. He takes His time because all time is His. There are a thousand years within His day. And that is a lesson we will dwell on now.

Think of the sphere of revelation. Does not that mark of slowness meet us there? The one thing God has never done, is to be in a hurry to reveal Himself. Suppose you were to ask a child this question, How do you think that God will speak to men? Would not the answer be of sudden voices pealing from the silence of the sky? Well as a matter of fact God *has* spoken to men, for that is just what we mean by revelation,

371

but His speaking has been as different from that as a strain of music from the din of thunder. Not suddenly, in one stupendous moment, has God declared the riches of His grace. That would have been cruelty and not kindness, for men would have been blinded by the glare. It has been here a little, there a little; one syllable today and one tomorrow, until at last these broken syllables blended in the Incarnate Word. By everything they tried and all they suffered, men were taught a little more of God; by the voice of conscience which they could not stifle, by the vision of ideals they could not crush; by all the whisperings of the world without, by all the yearnings of the heart within; by the song of psalmist, the oracle of prophet, the blood of the sacrifice upon the altar. I think of that first promise made in Eden that the seed of the woman should bruise the serpent's head. How long, O Lord! Why tarry the wheels of thy chariot? When shall this promised deliverer appear? And we know what ages had to pass away and what eager faces had to be lifted heavenward ere in the fullness of the time there came the Savior. When He came, a day was as a thousand years—in that one day was blessing for millenniums. But *till* He came it was the opposite, a thousand years with God were as a day. And men arose and played their part and died, and generation succeeded generation, and all the time, slowly yet unceasingly, God was making ready for Christ Jesus.

And note that this mark of God is very conspicuous in the life of Jesus. With such a mighty task to do and only three short years to do it in, I do not think that we could have been surprised had we caught the accent of haste in Jesus' life. But the one thing you never come upon there is haste. There is always urgency, but there is never hurry. You get the impression as you follow Christ that with Him a thousand years are as one day. Think of the third temptation in the desert when the devil took Him up into the mountain. "All these kingdoms will I give thee," he said, "if thou wilt fall down and worship me." But the way of the devil was the immediate way, reckless of means so that the end was gained; and the way of Jesus was the long, long way, which He is mystically treading still. All the kingdoms will I give thee *now*— the devil is always conjuring with *now*. For one brief moment Jesus Christ was tempted to get at His triumph by the shortest road. But He put it from Him and chose the long slow way that led Him through the garden to the cross, and has led Him through the ages to His victories in a thousand earnest and consecrated servants. There is more than the touch of the hero about that. There is the touch of the divine. God is patient because He is eternal and that is the patience of Jesus. His love was mighty, yet His approach was slow. One day was a thousand years with Christ, and yet a thousand years were as a day.

The slowness of God, again, is often manifest in regard to the great matter of our duty. Not all in a moment, but rather step by step, does God reveal the pathway of our duty. Think, for example, of the case of Paul when he was on his missionary journey. First he wished to go southward to Galatia, and the Spirit of God forbade him to go there. Then his heart turned northward to Bithynia: would it not be a joy to preach the Gospel there? But once again his will was crossed, and the Spirit of God suffered him not. We understand now why that was so: he was being led to the great hour at Troas. He was traveling to the man of Macedonia and to the summons from the shore of Europe. But the point to note is that Paul did not know that; nor could he tell why doors were being shut: he could only leave it in the hand of God who seeth the end from the beginning. How easy it would have been for God to let Paul know why he was being baffled. But it was not thus that heaven dealt with Paul, and it is not so that heaven deals with us. God leads us forward one step at a time, giving us light and strength for that one step, and only as we take it and are strong does He reveal the pathway of our duty.

Sometimes God is very swift in penalty; at other times, inexorably slow. There are sins which instantly condemn a man and make him a social outcast in a day. They cannot be hidden, and, being spread abroad, they shatter the character and blight the home. But if there are sins that go before to judgment, I think there are far more that follow after, and such sins may track a man for years before at long last they track him down. I have never heard that this word has been canceled: "Be sure your sin will find you out." You think that because five years are gone, or ten, it is all right; your sin is dead and buried. But with God a thousand years are as a day. He tarries, but he has not forgotten. Seek ye the Lord while He may be found; call ye upon Him while he is near.

I turn now for a moment or two to some of the spiritual bearings of this slowness, and in the first place, I detect in it what I would call an element of knowledge. It is impossible for one to learn the nature of something that flashes by and then is gone. A man is dazzled by it, and he wonders about it, but of its real nature he is still in ignorance. And so should we be ignorant of God, save as a being of tremendous power, if He flashed upon us and vanished from our sight. You cannot hurry if you are teaching children, especially if they are a little stupid. You must linger and spell the word again and again and be at infinite pains to make things clear. And what are we but little, stupid children spelling our way across God's lessonbook, and needing to have it syllable by syllable if we are ever to make it into sense. Why, think of the children of Israel in the desert. It took them forty years to get to Canaan. And could not God by one almighty act have carried them there in a single hour? Of course He could, for He is God Almighty—He could have brought them there in a moment; but ah, what a vast deal they would have lost, but for the slowness of their leadership. It was that which taught them how merciful God was. It was that which taught them that He cared for them. It was that which gave them the manna in their need. It was that which brought the water from the rock. They learned all that just because God was slow and led them by a way that was circuitous and brought them home, not by a hasty march, but by the discipline of forty years. It may be just the same with you, my friend. The long way may be the kindest way. It would be very sweet to get at once all that you crave for in your heart of hearts. But then if you got it you would miss the best—all that God is and wants to be to you—and I think a fuller earth is bought too dear, when it is purchased by an emptier heaven.

Also in the slowness of God I can detect an element of testing. It does not only show us what God is, it helps to show us what we are ourselves. It is true that sudden trial may do that. A single moment may reveal the deeps. There are men who have never known all that was in them till they were suddenly faced by swift temptation. But perhaps the truest test is not the sudden—a man may be worse or better than himself then—the truest test of what we really are lies not in the sudden but the slow. Judge Simon Peter by his one denial, and you place him far down the line of saints. Many a man might have been loyal then who had not a tenth part of Peter's faith. I want a longer estimate than that; one that takes measurement of usual years, one that has watched the character unfold under the slower discipline of God. A fiery trial may be a bitter thing; a long-continued trial may be a bitterer. To see no end to it, no gleam of blue, *that* is a harder thing than any paroxysm. There is no sorrow that is so hard to bear as the sorrow that is gnawing every morning. There is no work that is so hard to do as the work that never blossoms into fruit. "Thou shalt remember all the way the Lord hath led thee, to prove thee, and know what was in thy heart." Not only to know *God* was Israel led so; God led them that they might know *themselves.* So you and I are led by devious roads where we are often alone and often weary until at last, thank God, we know ourselves and know our utter need of Jesus Christ.

And then in closing, in God's slowness is there not often an element of tenderness? "I have yet many things to say unto you, but you cannot bear them now." You would never dream of telling a little child the story of the disappointments of the world. That would be cruel; it would blight those hopes that set the heart to music in the morning. So God is slow to break upon our vision, and He covers up tomorrow in a cloud and withholds an answer to our prayers, because He knows that we could never bear it. We think He loves us when He speaks to us. He loves us just as much when He is silent. The love of God is never slow to bless but, it is often very slow to speak. So we go forward rescued from despair just because God refuses to be hasty, saved by His slowness from tomorrow's trial until tomorrow's sun is in the east.

The Necessity of Acknowledging Sin

If we say we have not sinned, we make him a liar–1 John 1:10.

This text is just a little difficult to understand, and the difficulty is of a peculiar kind because it is not quite so easy to see what is the connection between the conclusion and the premises. "If we say that we have not sinned," that is premise; and "we make God a liar," that is the conclusion. There are some texts in Scripture a little difficult to understand because the phraseology is difficult, and there are some texts hard to understand because they seem to contradict our highest moral sense; but this is one of those numerous texts where it is a little hard to see the connection between the conclusion and the premises. If John had said, for instance, "If we say we have not sinned, we are fools," or "If we say we have not sinned, we know nothing whatever about ourselves," you would have understood that at once. But John says, "If we say we have not sinned, we make God–not ourselves–a liar," and to the thoughtful mind there is just a little difficulty in gathering the connection.

But before we face that difficulty there is one question I have got to ask and answer, and that is, How is it that people say, "We have not sinned"? It is not just saying it with our lips; but I want to ask in what peculiar ways do common people like you and me say in their hearts, "We have not sinned"? Well, of course, everybody does it in the first place who conceives that he is perfect, but that is such an extraordinary state of mind and so uncommonly rare that I do not imagine I need touch on it except for a moment. In the course of my long pastoral experience, meeting with all types of men and women, I do not remember a single sane person who ever thought he was perfect. I remember one poor man, but then he was insane, and he also thought that he was Christ. Remember, perfection is your ideal and mine—"Be ye perfect as your Father in heaven is perfect"; and I have never put any limits to what the Spirit of God can do for any man who constantly yields himself up to it. I have never put any limits, no matter what a man's past is, no matter how hard his heart is, no matter what his circumstances are, to what the Spirit of God can do for anybody who opens his heart to Him every morning; but at the same time this is the universal Christian experience. The more you yield yourself, the more you hitch your wagon to that star, the more you wrestle on toward heaven against storm and wind and tide—the more you feel and know you are a sinner. Paul began by saying about himself that he was less than the least of saints. When he got to know Christ a great deal better he called himself "the chief of sinners." Therefore I do not think one need say anything about that, for who is the fool who for one moment conceives that he is perfect. If there is, may God have mercy, not upon your soul, may God have mercy on your mind. But then a far more common way than that is for people to deny that what they have done is sin; that is to say, to make excuses for themselves that they would never dream of making for anybody else. Of course, I am not talking about you, I am talking about myself as well, for there is no man or woman, no matter how God's grace has gripped him, who is not always prone to make excuses for his own conduct that he would never dream of making for anybody else.

For instance, sometimes you read of a man stealing money. Well now, if his neighbor did it, of course he would be a thief, but the man is so earnest he is going to pay, but he wanted time, that in him it is not sin; or perhaps he gets such a starvation wage that he says he is just taking what he has a right to, and then he says, "I have not sinned." Many of you are tempted to tell lies just because the truth would cause such pain or discomfort to somebody you love, and you say you have not sinned because you have done it out of human kindness. You would never admit that in anybody else. Of course today, when people on every hand are breaking the seventh commandment, dashing in pieces the covenant of honor and purity, of course they all say that it is love; love is such a beautiful thing it justifies anything, does it not? Or perhaps they say it is necessity, and necessity knows no law. In a thousand ways like that today people are juggling with their conscience, and just saying, Whatever be the case with others, of course I have not sinned. Perhaps equally common among people who are led by the cold light of intellect rather than by the flaming light of passion, is the thought that sin does not exist; it is only a dream of fussy theologians, there is no such thing. What is sin? Now sin, if it is anything, of course, is a transgression of the law of God; sin is the free act of a free man. Sin is something for which you—nobody else—are responsible; therefore if you are liable, the punishment, that is the guilt, is a reality, and always with guilt there comes fear. Now when anybody takes up a view of life that just denies the reality of these things, robs them of what is essential in their meaning, don't you see he says, "I have not sinned"? If sin is a necessity, a necessary negative if you have got to get a positive, if sin is only imperfection, not a fall down but a fall up, letting the ape and tiger die, only a necessary stage in evolution, if everything is determined by heredity, well, of course, you say you have not sinned; whatever you have done, that does not exist. These things seem very modern, but they were all present, mark you, with John at Ephesus, and John says, "If any man says he has not sinned, he makes God a liar." Now don't you see what it means? You know if I called a man a liar, what I imply is that that man has been speaking, and probably speaking to me, and when you call God a liar you imply that God has been speaking to you. And John's point is that whenever and in whatsoever way God speaks, the basis of His speech is the fact of sin. In every voice God uses he talks on the understanding, implied or asserted, that sin is a reality, and therefore our duty is to try and examine the various voices of God and see whether that is true or not.

For instance, for I never like to leave this out, I suppose most of us would say that God talked to them in nature. In this beautiful world, I hope you have all got enough of a receiving set within you to hear God talk to you in nature. Of course, without that we never would have any science. If I can take up a book and read it and understand it, it means that behind that book there is a mind kindred to my own. And if science can read the book of nature—that is exactly what it does, we dwell not in a chaos but in a cosmos—if science can read the book of nature, then there is a mind behind it cognate and kindred to our own. I wonder why it is, if you were out in a great storm in peril of shipwreck, you would immediately feel you were a sinner. I wonder why it is when you walk over the moors of Arran every bird and every beast flies from you in dread; the game birds and the rabbits and the deer fly from you in dread. Is not something wrong? Has not some harmony been broken? Do you think God ever intended that? Now I do not say anything about the pain you feel when you are confronted with perfect beauty. I do not say anything of the song of birds that, as Burns says, "Ye'll brak my heart"; but what I do say is, even in the dim voices of nature God does not only say, "Child, am not I beautiful?" but God says, "Child, you have broken something, you are a sinner."

Then does not God talk to you in conscience? Don't you believe that in the still small voice of conscience God is talking to you? I beg of you never to give up that faith. If your conscience is not dead, and it is dead in some people, seared with a hot iron, what does it say to you? Does it say, "Child, your temptation was too strong for you, therefore you are not guilty"? Does it say, "Child, these are dreadful circumstances you live in, therefore you are not guilty"? Does it say, "Child, it is all heredity, and the blame rests on your grandfather"? It says, "Child, you are guilty." It says to you, "Whatever your temptation or heredity, *you* are guilty; nobody else." And if you say you have not sinned, that you could not help it, that things were too strong for you, that you were in the hands of a determined fate, don't you see you make God a liar whenever He talks to you in conscience?

Then I hope everybody agrees with me that God speaks to us in the Old Testament. Well now, if you do, that whole utterance is based upon the reality of sin and nothing else, except God Himself willing to forgive it. Take the story of the fall: what is at the back of it? That sin is real, that guilt is real, that the fare that follows guilt is real, and that is the very meaning. Then you have the sacrifices of smoke at the Jewish altars, the forty years' wandering in the wilderness, the seventy years' exile in Babylon, and the anguish of the Psalmist, and you have the trumpet cry of the Prophet that he is the Lord God who forgiveth sin. Then you say sin is not a reality; it does not exist; it is only a negative. You make God a liar in the whole utterance of the Old Testament. Don't you see?

Then far above the Old Testament, we have the New Testament, and I who know a little about Plato and Dante and Shakespeare never hesitate a moment to call the New Testament the most wonderful book in the world. Written by men of strong individuality, each of them with his own angle and his own outlook, each with his own aspect of the Lord, and yet all of them banded together as with a band of steel in this one conviction, that man needs redemption and that God in His mercy is willing to give it now. You get so tired of books whose only parrot-cry is, Educate, educate, educate; books that tell you that give time to our human race and it will evolve into a kind of superman. The New Testament comes to you and me and says, "Child, first of all there is a barrier between you and God, and that barrier has got to be taken out of the way." In other words, you do not want to be reformed, you need to be born again and then you can start educating and evolving. The whole New Testament is based on this, that you and I are guilty sinful creatures, and if you come along and say, "We have not sinned," you are making God a liar as He speaks to us in the New Testament.

And then, of course, the whole argument comes to its height in this: God in His infinite mercy has talked and spoken to you and me in our blessed Lord and Savior Jesus Christ. "In the beginning was the Word, and the Word was with God, and the word (the expression of the thought—the Oratio against the Ratio) became flesh and dwelt among us." "His name shall be called Jesus." Why? Because He is a beautiful teacher, because He is our example, because He is a great social leader? "His name thou shalt call Jesus: for He shall save His people from their sins." There were things that our blessed Lord made very light of, things that He did not care a straw for, and sometimes they mean everything to us; but there was one thing our Lord never made light of; rather He deepened it, intensified it all the time, and that was the fact of human sin. It was that which brought Him here; it was that which sent Him among the publicans and sinners; it was that that nailed Him to the cross. And if you venture to say, "I have not sinned;" "It was not sin at all;" "Sin does not exist;" don't you make Him just a liar when he talks to us in the Lord Jesus Christ? I beg of you not to do it. Life is far too serious for that. To wrap yourself up in excuses is to be naked before the great white throne. It is far better just to say however

380

humbling it is, "God be merciful to me, a sinner." "Seek ye the Lord while He may be found, call ye upon Him while He is near. Let the wicked forsake his way and the unrighteous man his thought, and let him return unto the Lord, and He will have mercy upon him, and to our God, for He will abundantly pardon."

The Crowning Vision

We shall see him as he is—1 John 3:2.

Whether we shall see *God* as He is, is a question that has been often agitated in the schools. No man hath seen God at any time. That we shall know Him with a knowledge intimate and satisfying is the Scriptural hope which we all cherish. God doth so interpenetrate all heaven that to be in heaven is to be in God. But whether we shall see Him face to face, and have an immediate vision of His being, is a question on which men have reverently differed. Even the seraphim around the throne veil their faces with their wings before Him. These mighty creatures, the bodyguard of heaven, cannot brook the glory of Jehovah. And so it has been reverently questioned whether it will ever be possible for man to see a glory which they cannot bear.

But if God, in His essential being, may be forever shrouded from our human gaze, it is not so with the Lord Jesus Christ. If there is one thing clear upon the page of Scripture, it is that when the believer wakes in glory he shall behold his Savior face to face. Now we see through a glass darkly; we are like men beholding in a mirror. We walk by faith, or we strive to walk by faith, and faith is the evidence of things not seen. But when earth retires and we awake in heaven, faith shall be perfected in sight: and then we shall see Him as He is. Eye hath not seen and ear hath never heard the things that God hath prepared for them that love Him. That is the faith in which the saints have lived, and it is in such a faith that they have died. And of all the things that God hath so prepared there shall be nothing half so wonderful or satisfying as the immediate vision of our Savior.

I should like to note that these words of John are to be taken in their deepest sense. We shall see Him *as He is.* Our first thought would be to take these words as a vivid contrast to what our Savior *was.* Now we see Him as He was; then we shall see Him as He is. But the thought of the apostle goes far deeper than any difference between past and present: we are to see Him as He really is. John knew, as all the apostles knew, that his exalted Lord was always one. That He is the same yesterday and forever is the consistent testimony of the apostles. And what John means is that now we see Him dimly, whether in Galilee or on the throne, but then we shall see Him as He is. In our very clearest moments here we see Christ but dimly and imperfectly. All we have ever seen and known of Him is, as it were, "the outskirts of His ways." And the wonder of the sight of heaven is this, that with eyes made perfect by the love of God, for the first time we shall see Him as he is. It is often a very thrilling moment when we first see people as they really are. We thought we knew them, and then some hour arrives when heights and depths in them flash out upon us. And then we feel that we have never known them, never understood their real character, never fathomed their depths of personality. In some such way, when we awake in heaven, we shall feel that we have never known the Savior. Now we know in part and see in part; then shall we know even as we are known. At last, when we are purged and purified, and when the love of God has given us eyes to see, we shall see Him as He is.

It is this immediate vision of the Lord which will crown the blessedness of heaven. The joy of heaven is the beatific vision. That heaven is a very real place in the unvarying teaching of the Bible. "I go to prepare a place for you," says Christ ; and "in my Father's house are many mansions." But a mansion may be very beautiful and adorned with every treasure wealth can purchase, and yet the heart may be very lonely there. There is nothing more desolate than a beautiful home when somebody who was its light is gone. All that art can minister and wealth supply seems but a mockery in such an hour. And so the very magnificence of heaven would only make it a more lonely place if the presence of our Savior were not there. As with homes, so is it too with countries, and heaven is often spoken of as a country. The most beautiful scenery God ever made can never satisfy the human heart. And heaven shall be far more beautiful than earth, for it is reality and earth the shadow, and yet a man might be unhappy in it. That is why Paul, whenever he thinks of heaven, immediately passes to the thought of Christ. He knew all about the sea of glass, but he never dwells on that. He never says, when life is hard and difficult, "I have a desire to depart and go to heaven"; he says, "I have a desire to depart, and be *with Christ.*"

That we shall see Him there as He is we may regard as certain, when we remember that there we shall see Him *at home.* I think you must always see a man at home if you want to see him as he really is. Of course, there are some homes of which that is not true. There are homes where a person is not his real self. That is especially true of sensitive children in homes where there is more ridicule than sympathy. And the untold evil of such homes is this, that they make the child shrink into himself, which is the very thing God meant no child to do. It has not been my lot to meet with many hypocrites, but I have watched them closely whenever I have met them; and my experience is that very often hypocrisy can be traced back to the home. When a child is repressed instead of being encouraged, when it is afraid to open its lips lest it be jeered at, then it grows reticent and loses all self-confidence, and hypocrisy becomes perilously easy.

But while that is true and very sadly true, it only emphasizes what I have been saying, that where there is love and sympathy at home, it is there that a man is seen just as he is. He may be a better man, or he may be a worse man, than he is in the judgment of the world. He may be far more generous, amiable, patient; or, on the other hand, he may be less so. But the point is that in the freedom of the home, where there is love and fellowship and sympathy, a man is recognized in his true nature. I have been honored by the friendship of good men whose name is fragrant in city and in market, men whom the bitterest rival never dared to associate with a dishonorable thing, and yet there were depths in them of patient love and heights of idealism quietly realized that could never be known to anyone on earth save to those who had the friendship of their home.

And there "we shall see him as he is"; in heaven we shall see Him in His home. We shall no longer see Him among those who scorn Him; we shall see Him among the multitudes who love Him. Foxes have holes and the birds of the air have nests, but the Son of Man hath not where to lay His head. He had only one place here to lay His head, and that was on the cross. And if here, despised and rejected, He was so wonderful and full of grace—what will He be at home! Here He could not turn without men judging Him. Here He was always being misinterpreted. Here, when He wanted to do a deed of love, they laughed Him to scorn. And if in spite of all that human treatment, He was so gloriously and infinitely gracious here, what will He be in the liberty of home? There will be nobody to insult him there. There will be none to hinder Him, because of unbelief. Love will surround Him, and nothing else than love, in the multitude whom He has ransomed. And who can tell what depths will be disclosed then in Him who was so exquisitely gracious when He could not move a finger without cavil.

Then, once again, we shall see Him as He is because *we shall be no longer children*. "Beloved, now are we the children of God; but it doth not yet appear what we shall be." In our version it is translated sons of God, but in the revised version you will find it *children*. That is a small change, but a very important one, and what it means is this. It means that the word for sons (which Paul was so fond of) is a different word from the one which John here uses, and it is different because the thought is different. When Paul speaks of the sons of God, he thinks of the liberties of sonship. But when John speaks of the children of God, he thinks of the weakness and ignorance of childhood. And so John says, "Beloved, we are children now—ignorant and inexperienced children—but the day is coming when we shall not be children, and then we shall see Him as He is." Many of you can appreciate that out of your own experience. When you were a child, you had a loving father, and even as a child you knew he loved you. But it was not till you grew to manhood or womanhood, perhaps when your father was sleeping in his grave, that you ever really understood his character. As a child you used to see him writing, or going out on visitation. Or perhaps some evenings he would be very quiet, and your mother would watch him with an anxious face. But what it all might mean you did not know then, because you were children at the time. My friend, you know it all today. You know how honored and loved your father was. You are no longer children, and so now you see what as a child you had no eyes to see. And beloved, now are God's children, and it hath not yet been manifested what we shall be, but we know that when it shall be manifested, we shall see Him *as He is.* Every believer shall be a son in heaven, but no believer will be a child in heaven. The love of God will draw us into manhood, fresh from the releasing of the grave; and in that manhood we shall begin to see what here as children we have no eyes to see, the wonder of the love of Jesus Christ. Words will come back to us we heard in childhood and which we never understood in childhood. Things that seemed cruel and hard to us in childhood will dawn upon our memories again. And being no longer children but grown men, under the quickening of the love of God, we shall understand at last what it all meant. "When I was a child, I spake as a child, I understood as a child, I thought as a child. But when I became a man, I put away childish things." And so in heaven, being no longer children, we shall put away our childish ignorance, and at last shall see Him as He is.

The third ground of our assurance that we shall see Him so, lies in the fact that then *we shall be like Him.* "We know that when he shall appear we shall be like him," and being like Him, "shall see him as he is." Unless you have some affinity with people, you never see them as they really are. You must have the music of poetry within you if you are really to understand a poet. Personality is wonderfully sensitive—not consciously but by its very nature—and never reveals itself in any fullness save under the sunshine of affinity. You may have known a man for years, yet never known him, just because you are radically different from him. And then some one comes along who understands him by some divine affinity of nature. And in a week or two that kindred soul begins to see what you have never seen; he is like him and sees him as he is. That is especially the case with children. They have an unerring instinct for those who understand them. You must have the childlike heart to see the child. You must have the Christlike heart to see the Savior. And it is just because at last we shall be like Him in the fullness of our glorified humanity, that in heaven we shall see Him as He is.

The Omniscience of Love

For if our heart condemn us, God is greater than our heart, and knoweth all things—1 John 3:20.

There are some texts of Scripture, and this is one of them, which are very generally misinterpreted. This does not speak of a condemning God, but of a God whose name and character we love. As commonly and perhaps naturally understood, the whole verse has to do with condemnation. We rise from the condemnation of ourselves to the far severer scrutiny of God. If our own imperfect consciences condemn us, how much more awful must the condemnation be of One who is greater than our heart and knoweth all things. Now if the verse stood in any other context, that would be quite a reasonable rendering. We know that the heavens are not clean before Him, and that He chargeth even his angels with folly. But let any one meditate upon the context here and note what the apostle has in view, and he will see that such rendering is impossible. The apostle is not writing to condemn. The apostle is writing to encourage. He wants to give the believer, in his despondent hours, something that will encourage and assure him. And so he says, if our own hearts condemn us, there is still one thing that we can do; we can fall back on the omniscience of Love. There are hours when our hearts condemn us *not*, says John, and then we have confidence towards God. We do not doubt Him then—we know we are His children—we have a childlike liberty in prayer. But when the sky is darkened and we lose assurance, when we hear nothing but self-accusing voices, then the only way to peace is to remember that the God of love is greater than our hearts. He knoweth all the way that we have traveled. He remembereth what we have quite forgotten. He is the light, and dwelleth in the light, above the spiritual darkness which engirdles us. In those condemning hours when we see nothing except our own exceeding great unworthiness, our Father sees the end from the beginning. That is unquestionably the apostle's meaning, and that unquestionably was the apostle's comfort. From an accusing conscience and a condemning heart, he casts us over on an omniscient God. And the unfaltering teaching of this letter is just that that omniscient God is *love*, who, knowing everything, will pardon everything, in the infinite sacrifice of Christ.

It has been thought by many, and I believe with truth, that there is a beautiful reminiscence here—a reminiscence of that scene beside the Sea of Galilee. "Simon, son of Jonas, lovest thou me?" "Yea, Lord, *thou knowest* that I love thee." Three times over Simon had denied; three times over was the question put. Who can doubt that on that summer morning, faced by the Lord whom he had treated so, Simon Peter had a condemning heart. Only a week before the Lord had looked on him, and he had gone out into the night and wept. He had promised to play the hero in the crisis, and he had proved the veriest of cowards. And now, with all these memories of betrayal crying out to condemn him in his heart—"Simon, son of Jonas, lovest thou me?" What was there that Simon could appeal to? His word? His word had broken like a straw. His past—when only a few days before he had been false and recreant to the Master? But Peter cast himself in his despair upon the perfect knowledge of his Lord—"Lord, *thou knowest all things,* thou knowest that I love thee." John was present when these words were uttered, and words like these can never be forgotten. They haunt the memory and deepen in significance and live again when the hour of teaching comes. And I for one believe that that sweet hour was vividly present to the mind of John when he gave the Church the comfort of our text. When our heart condemns us we are like Simon Peter, and like Peter we have nothing to plead. But when our heart condemns us, we can still turn to God who is greater than our hearts and knoweth all things—knoweth what no one else could ever know, judging us by our failures and betrayals, that we still love Him, and still desire His presence, and still want to follow and to serve.

Sometimes these self-condemning seasons come when a man has fallen into shameful sin. He has been walking unguardedly and prayerlessly, when lo, his feet are in the miry clay. Perhaps the most deadly sins in a believer's life are sins for which his heart does *not* condemn him; sins so habitual and so customary that conscience long ago has ceased to warn. But there are other sins in a believer's life so false to all that he has struggled for, that to commit them is to be self-condemned. In such a season the whole world is darkened. We cast our moral shadow on the universe. In such an hour our hope in Christ is dimmed, and all that we have striven for seems vanity. In such an hour when our heart condemns us, our only refuge from despair is this that God is greater than our heart and knoweth all things. He knoweth all the past and all the future, knoweth that we were meant for better things. He knoweth that in the bosom of the prodigal there is still to be found the memory of home. He knoweth that the precious blood of Christ is able to cleanse the very vilest stain, and that though our sins be as scarlet they shall be white as snow. All that, when our heart condemns us, we forget. All *that* the God of love never forgets. He knows how weak we are—how we are tempted—He knows our frame and remembers we are dust. Things which are blotted out when we have sinned, the faith and prayer and toil of long ago—He knows, and knowing will be merciful, and being merciful will lead us home.

Another season of self-condemnation is the silent season of the night. When the eyes are sleepless and the brain is busy, a very common visitant is fearfulness. There is a vivid picture in the Son of Solomon of the terrors which beset an eastern king. Threescore mighty men stand around his tent because of fear in the night. But one does not need to be an eastern king, haunted by visions of poison or dagger, to know the fear that lurketh in the darkness. Dim and shadowy and ill-defined anxieties are the worst of all anxieties to bear. Troubles wholly known are bearable; it is when half-known that they sap the heart. And such are the forms that visit us by night when the eye is sleepless and the brain is busy, oppressive shadows, spectral and illusive. In the light of day we see things as they are. We see things in their just proportions then. And perhaps the essential quality of courage is just to see things in their true proportions. But in the nighttime there are no proportions; everything is confused and undefined; we lie at the mercy of vague and spectral terrors. Sometimes that fear in the night regards our health; sometimes our future or our children. Sometimes it overwhelms us in the silence with an utter hopeless sense of our unworthiness. And it is in such seasons, when our heart condemns us, that from the verdict of our heart we should appeal to Him who is greater than our heart and knoweth all things. It is the duty of every believer to abstain from judging in an hour of gloom. The verdict of a desponding hour is the most worthless verdict in the world. Only He who dwells within the light can see things as they are and as they shall be, and He is greater than our heart and knoweth all things: knoweth all that tomorrow shall bring forth, knoweth all that we shall need tomorrow; knoweth our children and how we pray for them, and how they were dedicated to Him in infancy. And He who is thus omniscient is Love, and willeth not that any man should perish. He is the Lord God merciful and gracious.

Another self-accusing hour in life is the hour when opportunity is over; the hour which is always striking for humanity when the home is empty and the grave is full. Such a season, like all life's greatest seasons, is compact of very diverse feelings. There is the sorrow of parting in it; there is loneliness; there is a strange unreality about familiar things. But always, in such seasons of bereavement, there is the arrowy feeling of remorse for what was never done or done unkindly before the pitcher was broken at the fountain. It is *not* when love has been shallow that it hurts. It is when love has been real that it hurts. It is when the service of love has never faltered that love feels, when all is over, its unworthiness. It is the mother who has loved her children, and laid her life down daily for her children, who feels, when the flowers are fresh upon the grave, what a far better mother she might have been. There is a remorse which is as black as hell and has no refuge in Almighty God. It is the remorse of cruelty—of base neglect—of shameful desecration of life's sanctities. And yet I question if that satanic misery, falling as it does on hardened hearts, is half so keen or arrowy or exquisite as the remorse of love. The hour of sorrow is an hour of darkness, and in darkness we do not see things as they are. Out of a million words that we have spoken, one word—perhaps a bitter one—remains. Out of a thousand days of quiet happiness which leave no living memorial in sorrow, one day abides in which the tongue was bitter or in which the deed was unthinking or unkind. Beloved, when our hearts condemn us so, there is just one thing that we can do. When our hearts condemn us, we can turn to God who is greater than our hearts and knoweth all things. We can appeal to Him. He knows it all. He has been watching through the forgotten years. And there we can leave our cause in quiet confidence till the day break and the shadows flee away.

In closing, let me point out to you that there is another self-accusing hour in life. It is the hour of spiritual privilege, like that of the holy season of the Lord's Supper. Will you recall that scene upon the Sea of Galilee when the nets were filled till they began to break? Will you recall how Simon Peter cried, "Depart from me, O Lord, for I am a sinful man"? Faced by the wonderful goodness of the Lord to him; treated with a love that was magnificent, Peter was conscience-stricken and ashamed. I do not know how you may feel, my friend, when people are wonderfully good to you; but I can at least answer for what *I* feel—I feel unworthy and undeserving wretch. And if the wonderful goodness of our fellowmen to us gives us often the self-condemning heart, how much more the goodness of the Lord! That is why, at the table of the Master, conscience so often wakes within the breast. "Here, O my Lord, I see thee face to face," and seeing thee face to face my heart condemns me. Beloved, if thine heart condemn thee, make thine appeal to the eternal Father, for He is greater than thine heart and knoweth all things. He knoweth that thou art not satisfied. He knoweth that thou art hungering and thirsting. He knoweth that thou art poor and needy, and that other refuge hast thou none. *Sursum corda.* Up with thine heart to Him. Cast thyself on His omniscient love. The eternal God is thy refuge, and underneath are the everlasting arms.

Have You Tried the Way of Love?

He that dwelleth in God, and God in him—1 John 4:16.

In a thoughtful book I came across a striking suggestion about Jesus. It is that the question He is always asking is, "Have you tried the way of love?" His teaching was infinitely varied and exquisitely adapted to the moment. He couched it in a hundred forms according to the demand of the occasion. But the question He was always asking, and which He is always asking still, is, Have you tried the way of love? There is nothing radically new in this, for love is native to the human heart. In the dimmest past and in the darkest spot some spark of love is found. The glory of Jesus is that He brought love to light as He brought immortality to light and proclaimed its application everywhere. The worth and wonder of love was not a new thing in the world when Jesus came. It is embedded in every great literature and freely recognized in the Old Testament. What Jesus did was to exalt it into a compelling and universal motive applicable to the whole of life. Others had bidden us to love our friends; Jesus made us love our enemies. His followers are not to love selected souls; they are to *walk* in love. With difficult people, with all who irritate us, with those we can scarcely think of without bitterness, Jesus always confronts us with the question, *Have you tried the way of love?*

It is there He so transcends the older Covenant which He came not to destroy but to fulfill. For the question of the Old Testament is this, Have you tried the way of *justice?* There is a great deal of love in the Old Testament, but love is not yet in the middle heaven of noonday. The moral glory of the older Covenant is not its passionate insistence upon love, but its passionate insistence upon justice. Instead of wild and unrestrained revenge, it enforced an equal retribution. If a man lost an eye he might demand an eye; if a tooth, he might demand a tooth. Right through the law of Moses and the prophets, and on to the Baptist's preaching in the wilderness, there is one long cry for social justice. Then came Jesus, and the cry for justice was transcended in the cry for love. He says to the man embittered by his blinding, Have *you* tried the way of love? And He means that by the way of love something more is gained than retribution, for the enemy is turned into a friend. For conquering enemies and settling problems, Jesus believed in love alone. Love to Him was the universal solvent of the injuries and injustices of life. We may smile at that and call it idle dreaming—"Behold, this dreamer cometh." But for the Lord it was "the only way."

It is notable that Jesus never defines love just as He never seeks to define faith. These monosyllables reach the heart of things, and in the heart lies their interpretation. But no one can read the sayings of our Lord, nor recall His training in the home of Nazareth, without recognizing that His thought of love was colored by the relationships of home. To Him nothing was more heavenly than the love which He had found in family circles with its understanding and forbearance, its quiet self-forgetfulness and sacrifice. Like golden threads there runs through all His teaching tender memories of the humble home at Nazareth where love reigned, illuminating poverty and triumphing over every household jar. That was what love meant for Jesus. He wanted to universalize the home. Get that spirit to reign in the broad world, and the wilderness would blossom as the rose. In the quick, instinctive sympathy of home, in its patience and understanding and self-sacrifice, there lay the key for the sweetening and transfiguring of every relationship of life. To try the way of love, for Jesus, meant to try everywhere the way of home. In the family it had been gloriously successful—why not in other relationships as well? The pity was men were afraid to try it, as they are mostly afraid up to this present hour—as if justice could ever suffer where love reigns.

But if love was colored by the hues of home, our Lord's insistence was not based on that. He called on men to try the way of love because He knew it was the way of God. He found that as he wandered in the fields—did not the rain fall on the evil and the good? Did God withhold

His sunshine from the sinner on the strict and narrow plea of retribution? He found that in *Himself,* sent in the very lavishness of love, for God so loved the world. For Jesus, love was not an attribute of God; it was the depth and center of His being. God was not fatherly; He *was* a Father, loving His children as a father does. His perfection was not a rigid justice, but an infinitely loving heart—and we are to be perfect even as He is. That was why Jesus was so daring, though all the world might reckon Him a dreamer. To Him the way of love was God's way, and God's way is the only way. Undeterred by the mockeries of men and resolute in "the foolishness of God," He confronts our broken world today, still asking, *"Have you tried the way of love?"*

Love Perfects Service

Keep yourselves in the love of God, looking for the mercy of our Lord Jesus Christ unto eternal life—Jude 21.

Think of some young man a hundred years ago drafted into the service of the navy. Caught by the press-gang and torn away from home, how intolerable that service must have seemed! For a time, it would be the bitterest drudgery performed with many a muttering and curse. There was no escape—it had to be performed—the lash and the irons followed disobedience; that, in the harshest and extremest sense, was the service of necessity. But can we not imagine that young man rousing himself into a worthier mood? At the call of danger he would forget his bondage and think of the peril of his native land. And patriotic feelings would arise and duty to his country would awake, and now his service would be a nobler thing because it was the service of duty. Then suppose that a young man like that had sailed in the same vessel with Lord Nelson and had learned to love Nelson with that devoted love which filled the breast of every man who sailed with him. How different would his service now become! How gladly would he toil and fight and die! The thought of duty would be absorbed in love, and love would make his service perfect.

Contrasted Environments

I was in the isle that is called Patmos . . . I was in the Spirit—Rev. 1:9, 10.

The two brief texts which I have chosen suggest the two environments of life, and do so in a very vivid way. For John, the one environment was Patmos, a rugged and inhospitable island where the sound of the breakers was never far away and everything was desolate and dreary. But along with that there was another, unseen and yet intensely vivid, for John says, I was in the Spirit. He was moving in a spiritual world, living in heavenly places with Christ Jesus. He was engirdled by the love of heaven and by all the promises of God. And there is one very delightful little touch that reveals to the discerning heart which was the real environment for John. He does not tell us that he was in Patmos. He says he was in the isle that is *called* Patmos. He had heard that name upon the lips of others, and he took it upon their authority. But, he adds, I was in the Spirit. He needed no one's authority for that. In this environment he was at home.

It is instructive to contrast these two environments which have their parallels in every life. We note, for instance, that one of them was visible and the other unseen by any human eye. When John awakened in the morning, we can picture the scene that broke upon his vision— the stern hills, the debris of the mines, the waves washing on the barren shore. It was a desolate and dreary prospect, made more so by the sea, for no Jew ever loved the sea. Had *that* been all, what a profound depression would have settled down on the apostle's heart! But the beautiful thing is that the moment he awoke he was conscious of another environment than that. And the question for all of us is this, are we alive to that unseen engirdling when we waken to the duties of the day? There are many people who feel a deep depression when the routine morning breaks on them again. They have to drag themselves out: they see nothing before them but drudgery. But what a profound difference it makes when, with the returning of the daylight, we waken to the spiritual environment! Still we are in Patmos. It is by the will of heaven that we are there. I pray not, says the Lord, that Thou wouldst take them out of the world. But the dreariest Patmos becomes bearable when the life is hid with Christ in God. I was in Patmos. . . . I was in the Spirit.

Again, I note that the one environment was not of the apostle's choosing; the other depended on himself. If John had had the ordering of his ways, he certainly never would have chosen Patmos. He was an old man now—his years were ebbing out—he had reached the period when rest is sweet. He was quietly happy in his home at Ephesus, and there he had the society of Christians. Then suddenly the mighty arm of Rome had gripped him and carried him to exile—and he was in the isle that is called Patmos. A greater power than he had sent him there; it was not the place of his desire. There was no resisting that iron arm of Rome—to it the individual was as nothing. And then in Patmos, his forced dwelling place, John moved freely into another world, for he kept himself within the love of God. He was imprisoned and yet he was at liberty, for where the Spirit of the Lord is, there is liberty. In the bitter bondage of his exile, the Son had made him free. The sharp contrast between life's compulsion and the heart that triumphs in the midst of it, is all in these two little sentences, "I was in Patmos. . . . I was in the Spirit."

For as it was with John, so is it with every one of us: there is an element of necessity in life. We do not choose the country of our birth, nor our parents, nor the homes where we are cradled. We do not choose the schools where we are educated, nor perhaps the particular places where we dwell. But *how* we live there, in what atmosphere, environed by what unseen presences, all that is within the compass of our will. In Patmos we may be in the Spirit, and the fruit of the Spirit is love and joy and peace. We can have liberty and rest in Patmos, though we be set there by grim necessity. How many dream that life would be far richer if they only had the wings of a dove to flee away! But—"I was in Patmos . . . I was in the Spirit."

397

I note in closing that in these two environments there was the contrast of loneliness and company. Amid the desperate and hardened criminals incarcerated on this island, John was more lonely than had he been alone. In the one environment he was a solitary: in the other he had a vision of the Lord. He was in living touch with an ascended Savior. He had a Friend who understood. And that made all the difference to him as it makes all the difference to us amid the enforced loneliness of life. Even Patmos became bearable for John when he realized that Christ was there. He would move among these desperadoes as a man who has a satisfying secret. They were in Patmos, and they hated it. There was no other environment for them. Is there another environment for *you?*

The Note of the Heroic

His eyes were as a flame of fire—Rev. 1:14.

It is notable that in this vision of the ascended Savior, the eyes should have been as it were a flame of fire. That is hardly the characteristic we should have expected after hearing of hair that was as white as snow. The snow-white hair suggests to us venerable age; it hints at the passing of unnumbered years with the inevitable quenching of the fire of youth; but when we should look for eyes that were very gentle or that were filled with the wise tenderness of age, we find that His eyes were as a flame of fire. Now that contrast at once suggests to me this thought. In Christ there is not only a beauty as of silvered age; there is also a fire and a heroism as of youth.

And it is on that note of the heroic I ask you, as we begin to think upon the matter, to bear in mind one very simple distinction. It is that the thoughts that cluster around the *heroic* are not exactly those which the word *hero* suggests. A hero is just the embodiment of our ideal. He is the man who represents to us all that we dream of, whom we can clothe in every virtue and grace we consider fine. There is nothing fixed or defined, then, in the meaning of hero; its importance is relative to the qualities we admire. The hero of an unscrupulous man of business is often a man who is only more unscrupulous. The heroine of the woman of the world is sometimes only a more worldly woman. In a hero there may be absolutely nothing heroic; if we are degraded, so shall our ideals be. But heroism is always lofty and disinterested; it is courage touched into self-forgetfulness; it is enthusiasm with the crown of sacrifice upon its brow; it is the genius of the heart defying

399

prudence. A hero may have very evil eyes; but wherever the true heroic is, there the eyes are as a flame of fire.

Now as civilization advances and grows more complex, there is one kind of heroism that is less and less demanded. It is the heroism that may be described as physical and has for its basis what we call animal courage. In a rough and lawless and unsettled time, it might benefit a man very little to be gentle. The man who would live must have a ready sword and wield it valiantly, sometimes, for wife and children. Such times, then, in a nation's history—as we have had long periods like that in Scotland—are times that call out and develop physical heroism. It is always an early epoch in a country that is known by the name of its heroic age. But as civilization advances, life takes other aspects. The relations of man to man become more intricate. The sword that once was carried in the belt is handed over to be wielded by the law; life becomes ordered, settled, and secure. There is consummate need to be intelligent and tactful; there is less need now than once for physical heroism. We are never awakened mornings now to hear that the Highland marauders are "out" and are marching on the city. And that implies that as civilization grows and communication increases and law becomes supreme—and may I add as anesthetics are discovered that remove the necessity of facing up to pain—the accent is shifted from merely *physical* heroism and is inevitably placed on other virtues.

But as the need of physical heroism declines, the need of spiritual heroism steadily grows. The very causes that have lessened the value of the one have helped to heighten the value of the other. We are in no danger now from Highland marauders: the dangers that menace us are far more subtle. They spring from that lowering of moral standards that is unavoidable in our complex society. It is not easy to be oneself now, we are so interlocked with one another. We have lost a little liberty, with all our gains, and are molded more into a common pattern. The pressure of public opinion is tremendous, and public opinion makes for an average type. It is, therefore, more difficult now to be honestly true to oneself. It takes a little more heroism than it did once. We are more tempted to conform to common standards, to barter our birthright of individuality, to be what a hundred interests would have us be, rather than the men God meant that we should be. And so the need of spiritual heroism grows as the need of physical heroism lessens. The hair of

His head was white as snow, we read—that does not even suggest a young society. When time has mellowed the spirit of a people, when age has tempered the passion of its youth, when the riot of its blood is somewhat cooled, and it is venerable, stately, and august, it is *then* (if Jesus Christ be living) that there will be eyes that are like a flame of fire.

Now we cannot turn to the earthly life of Jesus without being struck with one marvelous union there. I refer to the union of what was beautiful and gracious with all that was in the truest sense heroic. We know that a bruised reed He would not break. We cannot fathom the depths of His compassion. There was never a patience like His patience with the twelve; there was never a pity like His pity of the sinner. He was gentle, charitable, courteous, kind, a perfect pattern of moral beauty. But the wonder of that beauty is magnified a hundredfold when we remember the heroism with which it went hand in hand. If to be true to one's mission and to stand alone, if to be faithful and joyful and quiet and undaunted, if to challenge all the powers of hell to combat, if to march forward without a falter to a cross—if that be heroism in its noblest meaning, then Jesus of Nazareth must have been heroic. Tenderness is great and heroism is sublime. In Christ there was tenderness infinite and heroism matchless. The eyes that wept beside the grave of Lazarus were eyes that were like a flame of fire.

In some degree, then, as we grow like unto Christ, that union of qualities will be found in us. It is a distinctive mark of that new character that has been built up through the powers of the Gospel that there is ample room in it for all that is gracious and, at the same time, for all that is heroic. There were two great schools of philosophy in Rome in the age preceding the entrance of the Gospel there. The one was Stoicism and the other Epicureanism, and each had its own ideal of human character. The aim of the Stoic was to foster heroism; he crushed out the affections ruthlessly. The aim of the Epicurean was not heroism; it was just to fashion amiable gentlemen. But the *needs* of the human heart broke down the first, for pity and love demanded recognition. And the *grandeur* of the human heart broke down the second, for there is that within each of us that craves for self-sacrifice. What the world needed was a type of character that could embrace and glorify the two ideals, and I humbly submit that the Gospel gave us that. There is a place in it for pity, and there is room for love; there is dew and sunshine for the tenderest affections that nestle in the shadow of the heart; but there is room for the heroic too. We have a cross to carry; we have a witness to bear. We have a life to live; we have a death to die. We are following a hope that is sublime, and we don't fare well without a little heroism. We shall be poor disciples of a compassionate Lord unless we have eyes that can soften into pity. But we shall be poor soldiers in the mystical warfare unless these eyes are as a flame of fire.

It is notable, too, that as the spiritual life of Christendom has deepened, as it has grown richer with the passing of the ages, it has brought with it a deeper and truer concept of what spiritual heroism really is. There is a well-known poem by Tennyson under the title of St. Simeon Stylites. It is a gruesome description of one of these pillar-saints whom people venerated in the Middle Ages. St. Simeon spends his years on the top of a high pillar; he is scorched by the sun and is swept by the storms of winter. He grows blind and deaf; he is racked with intolerable fevers and chills. He is praying night and morning for heaven's pardon. And round the base of the pillar people are ever thronging to do reverence to this ascetic saint. Now that is an extreme case, I grant you willingly; and it is almost repulsive, even in Tennyson's hands. But the fact remains that, in the Middle Ages, it was such lives that were the types of moral heroism. Even St. Francis, the gentlest of all mystics, was desperately cruel to himself. It was very noble—I think we all feel that. It was very noble; but it was mistaken. And we should thank God that we are living in a time when the heroism of self-suppression is disowned to make room for the nobler heroism of service. It is not on the tops of pillars that we look for saints now. It is not in cell or monastery that we search for heroism. The Christian doctor who labors among the leprosy patients, the Christian student who will hold fast to truth though a score of voices denounce him as a fool, the Christian worker who goes down into the slums and toils there for the poor and the fallen for whom Jesus died, the gentle Christian girl who volunteers for mission work in the jungles—it is these that are *our* types of the heroic. The heroism of the hermit is gone. We have drunk more fully of Christ Jesus now. We have seen more deeply into these wonderful eyes which John says were like a flame of fire.

But I must close, and I do so with two remarks. The first is that there is always danger for a church when the note of the heroic passes from its life. It is very pleasant to be very comfortable and to talk about one's good-natured congregation. But the eyes of the vision were not good-natured eyes; they were eyes that burned as with a flame of fire. It was heroism that made Christ's church in Scotland. And it was heroism that saved Christ's church in Scotland. It was secession, and deposition, and disruption, in the times that are well described as moderate. And when that uncalculating enthusiasm passes and leaves us comfortable and statistical and unmoveable, let us beware lest a voice say to us also, "I know thy works, that thou art neither cold nor hot."

And the second is: I appeal to the young men on the ground of the heroism of Christ Jesus. Mr. FitzGerald, the translator of *Omar Khayy'am,* in an exquisite little piece he calls "Euphranor," has some suggestive words on chivalry. He says that the charm of chivalry was just its note of heroism; and if it appealed—as it certainly did appeal—to the bravest and noblest and most gallant men, it was just because it put the accent there. May I not do the same with Jesus Christ? I think it is a true appeal to opening manhood. Never forget the heroism of Jesus, nor the heroic in the Christian calling. The time will come when you will need Christ's tenderness. You will want a gentle Lord, and you will find Him. But today it is a call to the heroic that appeals, and I thank God I can hear that call in Christ. Go! mother, bowed with a mother's sorrow—go to the graveside where Jesus wept. But eager, gallant, generous heart of youth—why should I lead *you* to that scene of tears? You crave a heroic captain for the battle, and the eyes of Christ are as a flame of fire.

His Eyes

His eyes were as a flame of fire—Rev. 1:14.

When John was an old man he had a vision of the ascended Lord.
One thing that instantly struck him in that vision was that His eyes
were as a flame of fire. And one likes to think that in that touch there
is some sweet and haunting recollection of eyes which he never could
forget. Sir Walter Scott tells us that the eyes of Burns were the noblest
he ever saw in human head. Anyone who ever saw the eyes of Mr.
Gladstone will carry some thought of their splendor to the end. And
John could never forget the eyes of Christ, the depth of them, and how
they glowed and burned: His eyes were as a flame of fire. Of this there
is singular corroboration in the words of the father of the epileptic boy.
"Master," he cried, "look upon my son, for he is my only child." The
Roman centurion wanted Christ to speak, but all that this father craved
for was a look—what a tribute to the power of Christ's looks! It might
be profitable to meditate a moment on some of the recorded looks of
Christ.

There is, for instance, the look of detection. You have that in the
story of the poor, ill woman who pushed through the crowd and
touched His garment's tassel and immediately found that her flow of
blood was staunched. Perceiving that virtue had gone out of Him, the
Master asked, "Who touched me?" The disciples ridiculed that question in the thronging and surging of the crowd. And immediately, we
read, our Lord looked around to see who had done this thing—and the
woman came trembling to His feet. In that look she felt that she was
seen. Under that gaze she knew that she was known. She was singled

out from all that surging multitude by the penetrating eyes of Jesus. This poor woman felt that instantly, and I believe that everybody feels it who comes into personal contact with the Lord. We have all known people who suggest that look. They seem to see right into us and search us. There is often something strangely disconcerting in the steady gaze of an innocent little child. And when we remember that our Lord was sinless and uncoarsened by any touch of evil, we begin to appreciate why it was that His eyes were as a flame of fire. It was along such avenues that men were led towards the divinity of Jesus. Had they not read in the psalms, "There is not a word in my tongue but lo! O Lord, Thou knowest it altogether"? And then—they met with Jesus, and the Psalm came floating back into their memories, for immediately they felt that they were known.

Then, again, there is the look of anger in the story of the man who had the withered hand. We read that our Lord looked round on them with anger, being grieved at the hardness of their hearts. *Our* anger is so often sinful that we hesitate to think of Christ as angry. When a husband is angry with his wife he is generally repentant towards nightfall. But the anger of Christ is a pure and holy thing; it is the other side of His burning love for souls, and whenever anyone despises souls His eyes are as a flame of fire. I do not think you ever find Christ angry at the hideous treatment He Himself received. Smitten, you never hear Him crying, "God shall smite thee, thou whited wall." All this He bore in patience and in beauty, as a heavy part of the cross He had to carry— His anger flamed and burned at other's wrongs. Sometimes the deepest anger is the anger that does not say one word. Sometimes in a look is a rebuke more poignant than in the bitterest speech. I don't think anyone ever would forget the look of anger in the eyes of Christ that day. God grant that it never light on us.

And then there is the look of disappointment. We have that in the fall of Simon Peter when the Lord turned and looked on Peter, and Peter went out into the night and wept. There was more than disappointment in that look. There was the tender memory of happier days. There was the love that gripped him in his weakness, and held him, and would not let him go. But it seems to me that what broke the heart of Peter and drove him out into the night to weep was the look of utter disappointment. We speak of the ascended Christ and sing our praise to the triumphant Christ. But do we ever think in quiet, reflective moments on the disappointed Christ? Is there anyone who reads this column on whom the Lord is looking, as He looked on Peter, with a look of utter disappointment? He expected such splendid things of you. He remembers the love of your espousals. He recalls the day of your conversion. He sees you as you bowed in dedication. And now, are you worldly, sensual, dishonest? Have you a name to live and yet are dead? And the Lord turned and looked on Peter, and Peter went out into the night and wept.

And then there is the look of trust, of quiet and perfect confidence in God. For that we turn to the stupendous miracle of the feeding of the hungry thousands. First, our Lord made everyone sit down; then into His hands He took the loaves and fishes. And *then*—what did He do then?—did He break the bread and give it to the multitude? Not so; He *looked up* and blessed and broke, and no one ever would forget that scene—the crowd, the solitude, the greenness of the grass; and, in the hush, the Savior looking up. One look around to see that all were seated. One look downward to the sorry loaves. Then, in the great quietness, one look upward, to draw for His need on God's unfailing reservoirs. Do *you* meet things like that? Do *you* know the power of that upward look? One look upward, and our Lord was ready for everything that mighty hour demanded.

Reverence

And when I saw him, I fell at his feet as dead—Rev. 1:17.

John was a prisoner in the isle of Patmos when he had this revelation of Jesus Christ. He had been banished thither because he was a Christian; and if the early legends can be trusted, he was condemned to the hard slavery of the Patmos mines. But sweet are the uses of adversity. There are some things we cannot learn in Babylon that become plain to us in sea-girt Patmos. There are some sights we are blind to in the markets: our eyes are only opened in the mines. It was not at home that Jacob had his Bethel: it was in the hills, a wanderer and alone. It was not at Pharaoh's court that Moses saw Jehovah in the burning bush: it was when flying from Pharaoh in the desert. It was not in peaceful days that Stephen saw heaven opened and Jesus standing at the right hand of God: it was in the hour of martyrdom. And this vision of Jesus, the alpha and omega, the first and last, whose head and hairs were white as snow and whose eyes were as a flame of fire,—this vision came to John, an exile in the mines. "It is adversity," says Bacon in his priceless essays, "which carrieth the greater benediction, and the clearer revelation of God's favor."

Now there are many lessons in this story. An old and fragrant commentary that I opened on the chapter rises into a height of eloquence, lost in this day and age, over these eyes that were like a flame of fire. But I want to center on one point only. I want to take this falling-down of John as a true instance of a truly reverent spirit. John saw, John worshiped, John adored. And we are living in a world that's full of God, and we have something better than a vision; we have the word of prophecy. And do we stand or fall upon our faces, and are we reverent or are we not? that is the question.

I do not think that the most cheerful optimist would dare to assert this was a reverent age. Of course we shall always have some reverent souls in every congregation, but reverence is not a note of modern life: still worse, it is not a desire. There was a time when to be thought reverent was an honorable thing. Now, to be thought reverent is to be old-fashioned. Men want to be smart and clever and successful, and somehow reverence does not agree well with these. We are all busy: few of us are reverent. Yet without reverence life is a shallow thing, and true nobility of character is impossible; and without reverence we shall be strangers to the end to all that is best and worthiest in our faith.

Can we explain the comparative absence of this grace? I think we can. It springs from certain features of our modern life, and the first of these is the wear and hurry of it. It is no chance that the most reverent hour in Moses' life was in the desert. It is no accident that John fell down as dead, not in the streets of Babylon, but in the isle of Patmos. It was no whim, though it seems whimsical to us, that a prophet of reverence whom we lost a week ago should have denounced our crowded city life. It is not easy for an overdriven man to keep a reverent heart. It is very hard to feel perpetual reverence when life for thousands is a perpetual rush. When I travel fast enough by train, castles and towns and woods and battlefields flash for an instant and are gone, and the great things are but little for the speed. So in the rush of life, worrying, leisureless, the great things of the soul and of the universe are dwarfed, and it is hard to be a reverent man. There is a certain leisure needed for the cultivation of a truly reverent spirit, a certain inward quietness, a certain detachment from the present day. But do note that leisure is a thing of heart and not of hours. Some of our hardest workers, who never enter a church door, it may be, are far more reverent, and being more reverent are better men, than many a church-goer who never felt the awe of things and never fell down at His feet as dead.

The lack of reverence too, I cannot doubt, is partly due to the spirit of inquiry of today. God knows that if to be reverent meant to be ignorant, some of us, in the eagerness to know, would say farewell to reverence forever. But is not the keenest teacher sometimes as reverent and humble as a little child? We had three great professors in my day at Glasgow, men known in every academy in Europe—the one for Greek, the other for medicine, the third for natural philosophy—and only to hear them was to be reminded of Sir Isaac Newton who felt like a little child picking some pebbles from the shore and casting them into the infinite ocean of the truth. Still, for all that, it is the truth that an inquisitive age is rarely reverent. And of all inquisitive and critical times, I fancy we have fallen on the worst. We are all eager: few of us are reverent. We are never afraid to criticize, but we have almost forgotten to adore. We can discuss these seven golden candlesticks, and trace the sources of the vision in Daniel, and smile at the strange mixing of the metaphors; but "when I saw Him," says John, "I fell at His feet as dead."

But this present lack of reverence has another source: it is the dying-out from heart and conscience of the fear of God. "Ah, Rogers," said Dr. Dale of Birmingham to his old friend,—"ah, Rogers, no one fears God now." And there can be little question that in the largest sense Dale was right. Man's views of God have changed in the past century. It was the Sovereignty of God that was the watchword once. It is the Fatherhood of God that is the watchword now. And no man can quarrel with that change of emphasis, when we remember how it has flashed new light upon the love of God and kindled into meaning many a page and parable. But things are not right if we can only love God more by reverencing Him less. And who can doubt that something of the majesty, and something of the grandeur, and something of the awesome fear of God is gone in this reiterated insistence on His Fatherhood? I sometimes think God had a special purpose in giving us the Old Testament in our Bible. With all its difficulties, I feel it was preserved to counteract a natural tendency of man. For God in the Gospel comes so very near us, and the love of God shown in the love of Jesus is so brotherlike, that only to realize it is to run the danger of forgetting reverence and growing very familiar with God. And it takes all the Psalms and all the prophets, with their magnificent Gospel of a Sovereign God, to make us fall down at His feet as dead. O living Spirit, open our eyes and give us back again something of the fear of God! For we shall never love or serve Thee well till we have learned to reverence Thee more!

Now what is reverence? It has been variously defined, but perhaps the old definition is the best. It is the practical recognition of true greatness. It is my attitude of heart and mind when I am confronted by the truly worthy and the truly great. It does not matter of what kind the greatness is: it may be the greatness of my brother's character, it may be the greatness of this mysterious world, or it may be the greatness of Almighty God; but the moment I see it, feel it, and recognize my place, I am a reverent man.

And that is the condemnation of the irreverent man. He may be clever, but he is always shallow. He may be smart, but he is blind. To live in a universe like this and to find nothing to reverence is to condemn, not the world, but myself. Irreverent men are often amusing, and are always selfish. For not to see and feel what is sublime, and not to be touched by what is truly great, is a true token of a selfish heart. The other side of reverence is humility. The other side of irreverence is pride. It is the course of the irreverent heart that underneath all lightness and all jest it is a stranger to the humility of Jesus.

Now where does individual irreverence begin? I think that generally it begins at home. When I have ceased to reverence myself, it is the hardest thing in the whole world to reverence my brother and to reverence God. If I am mean, I shall read meanness in my neighbor's heart. If I am selfish, I shall find selfishness in the most Christlike thing my neighbor ever did. We all get as we give. If there is nothing great in you, no hope, no ideal, you pay the penalty by finding the world mean. If there is any glimmering of greatness in you and any passion for righteousness and God, it is wonderful what a grand world this becomes, and what new worth we find in other men, and what a majesty we see in God.

Now there are two things in the life of Jesus that arrest me. And the first of these is His reverence for God. Jesus knew God as God was never known on earth before. God was His Father in far deeper senses than He is yours or mine. His intimacy with His Father was complete. He was at home with God. Yet nothing can match the perfect reverence of Christ towards this Father He knew and loved so well. I can always speak of Jesus' fellowship with God. It is a misuse of language to speak of Jesus' familiarity with God. There is an awe and reverence in all the recorded communication of Jesus with His Father that is as wonderful as His perfect trust.

But still more arresting than the reverence of Jesus for His God is the reverence that Jesus had for man. Sometimes you reverence a man because you do not know him well; you get to know him better, and your reverence dies. Christ knew men thoroughly. Christ knew men through and through,—their thoughts, their hopes, their fears, their weaknesses, their struggles, and their passions. Christ saw each sin more deadly and each vice more horrible than the most tender conscience in its most tender hour had ever dreamed of. If you had seen what Christ had seen, you would have spurned your brother. If you had known what Jesus knew, you would have spat on him. The wonder is Christ reverenced him still, still thought it worth His while to teach him, still thought man great enough to live for, still thought man great enough to die for. There never was a reverence so loving, there never was a love so sweetly reverent, as the love of Jesus Christ for you and me, fallen men, yet still in our ruin not without tokens of a heavenly greatness and of the God who made us in His image!

So as I think on reverence, and link it with the supreme reverence of Jesus, I learn three lessons that may guide *us* to a more reverent life.

And first, if we are ever to grow reverent again, we must know more. The reverence of ignorance is gone. Half-knowledge is irreverent: a fuller knowledge will make us reverent again. Jesus was reverent because His knowledge was perfect: we are irreverent because our knowledge is shallow. When we know *man*, far off, as Jesus knew him, we shall find something to reverence in our most ordinary brother. When we know *God* as Jesus knew Him, we shall adore. And is that knowledge possible to me? Thank God, through daily fellowship with Christ, I may follow on to know the Lord.

And then, if we are ever to grow reverent again, we must trust more. If John had never trusted Christ, he never would have seen the vision and never would have fallen at Jesus' feet as dead. I cannot reverence a *man* whom I distrust, I cannot reverence a *God*. It wants deep faith to make me reverent. It wants a perfect faith like Jesus had to make me perfectly reverent like Him. I never can be noble without reverence. I never can be reverent without faith.

And if we are ever to grow reverent again, we must love more. There never was a time when so much was spoken and written about Christian love. If we loved more and said less about it, we might revive our dying reverence. Oh, how much of our so-called love to Jesus is spurned by an infinite God because the feeling of reverence is not in it.

411

It is so easy to talk of leaning on Jesus' bosom. It is so easy to forget that he who leaned on Jesus' bosom fell down at Jesus' feet as dead. I plead for more love, not to increase, but to remove that light familiarity that blots our Christian service. For love reveals, love sees, love breaks the bars, love reads the secrets both of man and God. And when I have seen my brother's secret story, and when I have seen into the deep things of God, I never can be irreverent again.

White Raiment

He that overcometh, the same shall be clothed in white raiment—Rev. 3:5.

The color white, which is so often mentioned in the Bible and always with an element of symbolism, is emblematical of purity. It is the symbol of purity in every language; the outward sign of it in every ritual. When I was in the country a few weeks ago, the grip of winter was still upon the land. But there was one bank, rising from the road, that was covered with innumerable snowdrops. And one could not look at them, so quietly beautiful, braving the bitterness of icy mornings, without recalling this text in Revelation: "He that overcometh shall be clothed in white." It was that thought which made the psalmist cry, "Wash me, and I shall be whiter than the snow." It was that which clothed the priest in his white robes when he stood to minister in holy things. It was that which filled the heart of the apostle when he looked heavenward and saw a throne, and the throne was white because of Him who sat on it, for He is infinitely and forever holy.

Now I dare say there are some who feel a sense of shame when they hear that. If white is the sign and sacrament of purity—God pity them, they shall never wear it. Is there no young man here who has been living foolishly since he awoke to the liberty of manhood? Is there no young woman who is very different from what she was a dozen years ago? "Character," said Mr. Moody once, "character is what a man is in the dark," and if we knew what you were in the dark, would there be any hope of white apparel? I answer most emphatically, yes. That is the Gospel I am here to preach. It is not to the heart of childlike innocence that the white raiment of our text is promised. It is to everyone who overcomes; who rises from his past and is ashamed; who cries, from the very margin of despair, "Create within me a clean heart, O God."

Then once again, I want you to observe that white was the color which indicated victory. It was so not only in the Bible, but also in the literature of Greece and Rome. Today, we do not so regard it. It is not significant of triumph now. The white flag is the symbol of submission, and the white feather is the badge of cowardice. But in the ancient world of Jew and pagan there was no such sinister suggestion in it: it was not the color of the coward then; white was the color of the conqueror. There is a legend in the myths of Greece which illustrates this in a pathetic manner. It relates to Theseus, son of Aegeus, who was so mighty in succoring the weak. And it tells how Theseus, before he sailed to Crete to do battle with a horrid monster there, made an agreement with his aged father. If he was slain, his vessel would come home under the dark sails she always carried. But if he slew the beast and was victorious, his sails were to be white on his return. And Theseus slew the beast and was victorious, but quite forgot his promise to this father, who, seeing no sail of white upon the ship, flung himself over the steep cliff and perished. That is a legend from the myths of Hellas; may I take one now from the traditions of Rome? Well, there is one in Vergil which occurs to me and which, I take it, every schoolboy knows. For when Aeneas, in his flight from Troy, came with his comrades to the coast of Italy, the first objects seen upon the shore were four white horses in the pasture. They were horses and so they spoke of war, but they were white and so they spoke of victory. And that was a happy omen for the voyagers and was accepted as a sign from heaven. So in Greece and Rome as in Judea, there was nothing in white suggestive of submission; but there was something which suggested victory and whispered the exultancy of triumph.

Do you see then another facet of our text—he that overcometh shall be clothed in white? It means that the battles which are won in secret shall some day be the vesture which we wear. Our hardest conflicts are not fought in public; our hardest conflicts are on a hidden field. There is no one to rejoice when we are conquerors; no one to hear the tidings of defeat. And yet these hidden conflicts of the heart, which we imagine to be so unobserved, get themselves written out upon the character and clothe us at the last as in a garment. There is really no such thing as secret sin. Sin is always making for the surface. Thy speech betrayeth thee—thy look is tell-tale—if not today it will be by and by. And at the last no victory is secret, though it be won in solitude and silence. There is not a point in the whole range of character but some day shall reveal its influence. That is one swift suggestion of our text—he that overcometh shall be clothed in white. It tells that the hidden issue of today which it is well to cherish when we are alone with our besetting sins. Out of our hidden triumphs God is weaving the robe that is to clothe us by and by.

Observe, also, that white is the color which expresses joy. It does so because it is the color of light, and there is something cheerful in the light. We do not speak about the *day* of sorrow; we speak and sing about the *night* of sorrow. "The night is dark, and I am far from home," is the utterance of one in heaviness. But light is cheerful and it heartens us and it summons forth the music of the birds, and so there has always been the thought of joy in the radiance which is the badge of day. White is not the color of the mourner. White is the color of the happy bride. It is the sacrament of what is glad; the symbol and interpreter of joy.

And so our text hints at this other truth—a truth which we can never take to heart too much. It tells us, in the symbol of apocalypse, that overcoming is the road to joy. It is not by doing just what we want to do—it is not by yielding to every gust of passion—it is not thus that life becomes a glad thing with a sound of music in its desert-mile. It is by taking up the cross in patience; it is by holding fast to lowly duty; it is by trampling on the wild beast within until he learns who is the master there. If to be happy is your one ambition, you may be certain you will not be happy. The young fellow who is bent on a good time finds out at forty what a fool he was. It is not thus that happiness is won; it is by traveling on a harder road where there are marks of blood upon the soil and the shadow of a cross upon the hill. Why was the joy of Christ so rich and full? Was it not partly because He overcame? He was tempted in all points like as we are, yet He never swerved from His appointed way. And so with us, however we may be tempted, there is always joy in mastering temptation. To yield to it is always to be miserable. To conquer it is always to be glad. He that overcometh will be clothed in white. He will grow happier every year he lives. And life will be richer and the world more wonderful because he is fighting bravely in the silence. For the last result of sin is always sadness and the disappointment of an empty heart and a pilgrimage across a loveless country where all the water-wells are dried up.

Once again I want you to remember that white is the clothing of heavenly service. It is the garb which all the angels wear, and the angels are the ministers of God. Has not our Master taught us thus to pray, "Thy will be done on earth as it is done in heaven"? The type and pattern of perfect service is the unceasing ministry of angels. And always, when they are busied in that ministry and speeding on the errands of their King, we read of the angels that they are clothed in white. Do you remember what the women saw within the tomb on resurrection morning? They looked for Jesus and He was not there, but the tomb was not empty though their Lord had risen. For, sitting on the stone there was a man, and the women hurried back to the eleven to tell them that they had seen a vision of the angels. And he was clothed, not in the garb of woe, but in radiant clothing of white, for in the sepulcher, as before the throne, he was busied in the service of his King. That thought was very familiar to the Jew. He always associated white with angels. Flying abroad upon the wings of help, the angels were always garbed in white. And so the color came to speak of service, of instant and unquestioning obedience, of readiness to do the will of God though the path of ministry was to a grave.

Do you not see, then, another fine suggestion in "he that overcometh shall be clothed in white"? It means that if we do not overcome, we cannot hope to have the robe of service. It is not only on our own account that God is calling us to self-subdual. If we are to serve with any power and blessing, one of the first essentials is self-conquest. For all our influence upon other lives is rooted in the silent depths of what we are and takes its character of weal or woe from the victory or from the failure there. Think, for example, of the home. Have we not all known angels in the home? We think of the mother of our childhood, perhaps,—so patient, so gentle, and so loving. But what we never saw when we were children was the self-denial which lay behind the service, the quiet mastery of mood and temper which came with benediction to the home. He that overcometh shall be clothed in white. Self must be mastered or we shall never serve. We must learn to do things when we feel least like it. We must crush down that rising irritation. And that is what made Christ the perfect servant—that He had been so perfectly victorious and had a heart which was the joyous home of wisdom and serenity and prayer.

Then, in closing, we must not forget that white is symbolical of Christ Himself. Think for example of the Transfiguration. Moses was there and Elijah was there, yet we do not call it an hour of heavenly conference. We call it what it is called in Scripture, the hour of the Transfiguration. And that just means that the wonder of the hour was the transfiguring of Jesus Christ when His garments shone with such a whiteness as no fuller on earth could whiten them. What was the color of Christ's dress we don't know. When He was mocked, they decked Him in purple. But the garb of the glorified Christ is not purple. It is a dazzling and lustrous white. And he that overcometh shall be clothed in white. He shall be like Him, for he shall see Him as He is. He shall have washed away forevermore all that would separate him from his Lord.

He Knocks

Behold, I stand at the door, and knock—Rev. 3:20.

We are all familiar with the picture by a well-known artist which portrays Christ standing at the door. It is one of the few pictures on a text of Scripture which has caught the imagination of the people. We see the door hanging on rusty hinges and covered with the trailing growth of years. And we see Christ, clad in His kingly robes, out in the dew and darkness of the night. And in the one hand He bears a lighted lamp whose rays are penetrating through the chinks and crevices, and with the other He is knocking at the door. You know the title the artist gave that picture. He did not call it "Christ knocking at the door." He called it—and there is spiritual genius in the title—"I am the light of the world." For him the wonder of it all was that the light which is life and blessedness and victory should be so near the door of every heart.

And after all, when you come to think of it, that is the most wonderful thing about this text. It is not the knocking at the closed door; it is the overwhelming thought of Him who knocks. Were it some emperor whose word is law to millions, it would be sufficiently awful and impressive. Were it some angel as he who came to Abraham, it would be a very memorable visitor. But when a man goes apart into some silent place and dwells upon the fact that knocking at his heart is **CHRIST**, I tell you it thrills him to the very depths. Not Jesus, who walked amid the fields of Galilee. He is no longer walking amid the fields of Galilee. He is no longer rejected and despised, homeless, with no shelter for His head. He is the risen Christ, exalted to the heavens, invested with all the authority of glory and yet, behold He stands at the door and knocks. At the door of your heart, my brother and my sister. You know what passions and what sins are knocking there, clamorous rabble—Christ is standing, the living, glorious Christ, and in infinite mercy He is knocking too.

And that just means, stripped of its metaphor, that Christ is not far away from any man. Wherever on earth there is a beating heart, there is a yearning Savior. The best is never far away from men. That is one of the joys of this strange life. God has not hidden what is true and beautiful in inaccessible and distant places. Sunshine and summer and the little children, and duty and chivalry and faith and love, are nearer than breathing and closer than hands and feet. The highest and holiest are never inaccessible. And so do not think of it as a thing incredible that Christ should be very near to you. He is not hidden in the light of heaven beyond the shining of the farthest star. Life is mysterious, and God is wonderful, and the infinite is round about us everywhere, and Christ is not far away from any man. But, Lord, I am a bad man—Behold I stand at the door and knock. But, Lord, Thou knowest that secret sin of mine, and what a wretched, hollow life I have been living. Yes, my brother, He understands all that, and for all that He shed His blood for thee, and now He is standing knocking at thy door. Thy door—thy life—thine everlasting being. He wants to save it into life and victory.

And in what way does Christ knock? I answer, in a hundred different ways. He has a knock that is very imperious sometimes, and sometimes one that is infinitely gentle. He knocks in all the mercies you enjoy, in health and strength and happiness and home. He knocks in the tender memories of childhood of a father's character and a mother's love. He knocks in the thought of all that has been done for you, and of the love that has girdled you from infancy, and of the mercy that has never yet forsaken you from the hour of your birth until today. Sometimes He knocks in the strange sense of loneliness that steals upon the heart on busiest days. Sometimes He knocks in all that deep unrest that craves it knows not what, and never finds it. Sometimes He knocks in bitter disappointments and in bitter regrets over the might have been and in love baffled till the heart is breaking. He is knocking when a man has sinned and hates his sin and loathes himself as vile. He is knocking in the despairing sense that our vices and habits are mightier than we. He is knocking in every business in the hopeless tangle we have made of things, in the sickness that lays us prostrate for a season. He is knocking in the gift of little children, in the worries and trials and gladnesses of home. He is knocking when two lives are joined together. He is knocking when two lives are separated—in the last parting when the grave is dug, and the heart is empty and the coffin full. Lo! I am with you always, even to the end of the world; always at the door and always knocking. And that is our hope—that Christ is not far away, but that He is here in infinite grace to save. For when He ceases knocking we are lost.

Indeed, I have often thought in quiet moments that that is the truest interpretation of all life. When I think of all that life has meant for me, it seems like someone knocking all the time. You remember that famous moment in *Macbeth* when the murderers hear the knocking at the door. And you recall how De Quincey in his so subtle essay has shown us the dramatic significance of that—how into a room reeking of blood and murder, self-absorbed, oblivious of environment, the knocking came, and with it in a flash the thought of the great world that lay beyond. Shakespeare did not summon any calling voices. He was too consummate a master to do that. Your inferior dramatist who knew not life would have given you shouting and the trampling of men's feet. But Shakespeare gives a knocking at the door—some hand, unknown, knocking—that is all, and the murderers, who had forgotten everything, waken to realize the world again. My brother and sister, if we were left alone we should be always in danger of forgetting everything—we should forget, if left alone, that God hates sin, that death is coming, and that heaven is real. And so, as I look back over my life, it seems to me there has never been a providence that has not been meant by God to be interpreted like that knocking at the door in Shakespeare. In every triumph someone has been knocking; in every failure someone has been knocking—in every hour of pain and call of duty and baffled effort and yearning for the beautiful. Until at last there grows upon a man the sense that life is deep and rich and wonderful; a little chamber red with blood and sin, but round it a spiritual unseen environment. Infinite love is pressing in upon us; infinite grace that can save unto the uttermost; infinite power that can redeem the weakest and cleanse him and set him on his feet. And to all that, out of the selfishness which is our birthmark and our heritage, we are awakened by the knocking of the Christ.

To come back to that picture of which I spoke in starting, I remember somewhere reading a story about it, and the story was that when the picture was finished a friend came into the studio to inspect it. And he looked at it and admired its exquisite grace and saw at once its spiritual significance. And then he turned to the artist and said to him, "It is very beautiful, but there is one mistake. You have forgotten to put a handle on the door." And the story told how Holman Hunt explained to his visitor that that was no mistake. Had there been any handle on the *outside*, he told him, Christ would have turned it and would have entered in. But this was a door that had no handle there—a door that could only be opened from the *inside*. If any man will open to Me, I will come in to him and sup with him.

And that just means, stripped of its imagery, that to the knocking of Jesus Christ each one must individually respond. We must open our hearts to the living, present Christ, and say, "Come in, thou blessed of the Lord." No man has a more profound faith than I have in the absolute sovereignty of Almighty God. I should not be a Scotsman if I disbelieved it, and I should be untrue to all that God has shown me. And yet so intricate are earth and heaven, and so respectful of His children's liberty is God, that till a man lift up his voice and cries "I will," Jesus Christ will never cross the door sill. That is just where so many are making a mistake. They are always waiting for something irresistible. They are waiting for the moment when some power divine will shatter the door and enter in, in spite of them. My brother, I want to tell you quite plainly, that hour will never come. "If any man will open the door"—it is the one condition of all blessing. You must respond. You must open wide your being. You must say to the living Lord and Christ "Come in." And the wonder of the Christian Gospel is just this, that all you have striven and struggled for and failed in becomes a thrilling power and possibility the moment with all your heart you have invited Christ in. That was the message that rang through a dying world and made it hope again and live again. It is no scheme of social reform. We could have that and more without a Christ. It is peace with God and victory for you. The sunshine is a very marvelous creation, but it will never open any blinds for you. *You* must open them—a very simple thing—and all the mystery of the light will flood the room. And so with Christ—more glorious than sunshine—Christ the living, reigning, mighty Lord—if any man will open, I will come in.

The Rainbow and the Throne

And immediately I was in the spirit: and, behold, a throne was set in heaven . . . and there was a rainbow round about the throne, in sight like unto an emerald—Rev. 4:2, 3.

This vision, like all the visions of the Apocalypse, is given for the most practical of purposes. It is not the dreaming of an idle seer. It is a message of comfort for bad times. You know the kind of scenery one meets with in the latter portion of this book. There are pictures of famine and of bloody war, pictures of sickness and of death upon his horse. Here, then, before the unveiling of these horrors we have the eternal background of it all. "And I looked," says John, "and lo, a door in heaven; and I saw a throne, and Him that sat thereon." God's in His heaven, all's right with the world—that was the meaning and purpose of the vision. Let famine come and fearful persecution; let the Christians be scattered like leaves before the wind—there was a throne with a rainbow round about it; and in the heavens a Lamb as it had been slain.

Now I would like to dwell for a little while on the rainbow around the throne like to an emerald. Do you see any mystical meanings in that rainbow? I shall tell you what it suggests to me.

In the first place it speaks to me of this, that the permanent is encircled by the fleeting.

Whenever a Jew thought of the throne of God, he pictured one that was unchangeable. "Thy throne, O God, is an everlasting throne," was the common cry of psalmist and of prophet. Other thrones might pass into oblivion, other kingdoms flourish and decay. There was not a

423

monarchy on any side of Israel that had not risen and had fallen, like a star. But the throne of God, set in the high heaven where a thousand years are as a day, *that* throne from all eternity had been, and to all eternity it would remain. Such was the throne which the apostle saw, and round about it he beheld a rainbow. It was engirdled with a thing of beauty which shines for a moment, and in shining vanishes. The permanent was encircled by the transient. The eternal was set within the momentary.

The same thing also is observable as God reveals Himself in human life. God has His purpose for every heart which trusts Him, nor will He lightly let that purpose go. We are not driftwood upon the swollen stream. We are not dust that swirls upon the highway. I believe that for each of us there is a path along which the almighty hand is guiding. Through childhood with its careless happiness, through youth with its storm and manhood with its burden, everyone is being surely led by Him who sees the end from the beginning. And I looked, and lo, a throne in heaven—and "the kingdom of heaven is within you." And round about the throne there was a rainbow—symbol of the transient and the fleeting. And so it is that you and I are led amid a thousand evanescent things, under the arch of lights that flash upon us, and have hardly flashed ere they have disappeared. It is commonplace to speak of fleeting joys—and our troubles are often as fleeting as our joys. And then what moods we have; what moments of triumph; what bitterness of tears! And often they visit us just when we least expect them, and we cannot explain them as they come and go; and yet, through every mood and every feeling, the will of God is working to its goal.

Another truth which is suggested here is that power is perfected in mercy. The rainbow has been symbolical of mercy ever since the days of Noah and the flood. God made a covenant with Noah, you remember, that there should never be such a flood again. Never again, so long as earth endured, was there to fall such desolating judgment. And in token of that, God pointed to the bow, painted in all its beauty on the storm cloud,—that rainbow was to be forever the sign and sacrament that He was merciful. Do you see another meaning of that bow, then, which John discerned around the throne of God? What is a throne? It is a place of power; the seat of empire, the symbol of dominion. So around the infinite power of the Almighty, like a thing of joy and beauty, is His mercy. Round His omnipotence, in perfect orb, is the enclosing circlet of His grace. It is not enough that in heaven is a throne. God might be powerful, and yet might crush me. It is not enough to see a rainbow there. God might be merciful, and yet be weak. There must be both, the rainbow and the throne, the one within the circuit of the other, if power is to reveal itself in love, and love to be victorious in power.

We see that union very evidently in the life of our Lord Jesus Christ. One of the deepest impressions of that life is the impression of unfathomed power. There are men who give us the impression of weakness. We cannot explain it perhaps, but so it is. But there are other men, who, when we meet with them, at once suggest to us the thought of power. And you will never understand the life of Christ, nor the bitterness of hate which He evoked, until you remember that always, in His company, men felt that they were face to face with power. Think of His power over the world of nature—He spake, and the storm became a calm. Think of His power over disease and death—"and Lazarus came forth, bound in his graveclothes." Think of His power, more wonderful than either, over the guiltiest of human hearts—"Thy sins, which are many, are forgiven thee." And I looked, and lo, I saw a throne—wherever Jesus was, there was a throne. But was that all, and was there nothing else, and was it power unchecked and uncontrolled? Ah, sirs, you know as well as I do, that around the living throne there was a rainbow—a mercy deeper, richer, more divine, than Noah had ever deciphered on the cloud.

The same thing is also true of human character. It takes both elements to make it perfect. When human character is at its highest, its symbol is the rainbow around the throne. All of us admire the strong man—the man who can mold others to his will. There is something in titanic strength that makes an irresistible appeal. Yet what a scourge that power may become, and what infinite wreckage it may spread—all that needs no enforcement for a world which has known the evil genius of Napoleon. Mercy without power may be a sham; but power without mercy is a curse. It is not a throne which is the ideal of manhood; it is a throne encircled by the bow. It is power stooping to the lowliest service; it is strength that has the courage to be tender; it is might that can be very merciful, with the mercy of the Lord Jesus Christ.

I sometimes think, too, that this heavenly vision is just a type of what our homes should be. In the ideal home there will be kingship, and yet around the kingship will be beauty. There are many homes today which have no throne. There is no government; there is no subjection. The thought of fatherhood has been so weakened that it has lost its attribute of kingship. The children are the real masters of the home; by their inexperience everything is regulated. And I looked, and lo, a door into the home—and within it, no vestige of a throne. Then in other homes there is no rainbow. There is no beauty; there is not any tenderness. There is no play of color on the cloud; no shining when the rain is on the sea. And the merriment of the children is repressed, and the father does not understand his child; and the child, whose heart is yearning for a father, has no one to appeal to but a king. Surely, if home is to be heaven, we want a vision like that of the apostle. We want a throne in token of authority, for without that, home is but a chaos. But if little lives are to be glad and beautiful, and if there is to be radiance on the cloud, we also want the rainbow around the throne.

There is just one other lesson I would touch on—the heavenly setting of mystery is hope.

As the apostle gazed upon the throne, there was one thing that struck him to the heart. "Out of the throne came voices, thunderings and lightnings." Whose these voices were, he could not tell. What they were uttering, he did not know. Terrible messages pealed upon his ear, couched in some language he had never learned. And with these voices was the roll of thunder; and through it all, the flashing of the lightning; and John was awed, for in the throne of God he was face to face with unutterable mystery. Then he lifted his eyes, and lo, a rainbow, and yet it was different from earthly rainbows. It was not radiant with the seven colors that John had counted on the shore of Patmos. It was like an emerald—what color is an emerald? It was like an emerald; it was *green*. Around the throne, with its red flame of judgment, there was a rainbow, and the bow was green. Does that color suggest anything to you? To me it brings the message of spring time. You never hear a poet talk of *dead* green; but you often hear one talk of *living* green. It is the color of the tender grass and of the opening buds upon the trees. It is the color of rest for weary eyes and hope for weary hearts.

Brethren, is not that the message which has been given us in Jesus Christ? When you see God, mysteries do not vanish. When you see God, mysteries only deepen. There is the mystery of nature, red in tooth and claw; so full of cruelty, so full of waste. There is the mystery of pain, falling upon the innocent and bowing them through intolerable years. There is the mystery of early death with its blighted hope and with its shattered promise. There is the unutterable mystery of sin. Out of the throne came thunderings and voices. Out of the throne voices issue still. And we cannot interpret them—they are too hard for us, and we bow the head and say it is all dark. Nay, friend, not altogether dark, for around the throne of God there is a bow, and all the rest of the green fields is in it, and all the hope of a morning in the spring. Have we not Christ? Has He not lived our life? Had He not taught us that the worst and vilest sinner is good enough to live for and to die for? Has he not conquered death?—does He not live today?—is not the government upon His shoulder? A man can never be hopeless in the night who once for all has cast his anchor there. Have you done that? Are you a Christian? Have you cried, "Lord, I believe, help thou mine unbelief?" Why then, my brother, you are in the spirit, and for you a door is opened into heaven. And though for you mystery will not vanish and much that was dark before will still be dark, yet round and round all that is unfathomable, there is the encircling radiance of hope.

The Feeding of the Lamb

The Lamb which is in the midst of the throne shall feed them—Rev. 7:17.

The first words which John ever heard of Jesus were words that described Him as a Lamb. When John was a disciple of the Baptist's, drinking in inspiration from that stern teacher, he had heard these words fall from the Baptist's lips, "Behold the Lamb of God which taketh away the sin of the world." The apostle was a young man then, aflame with eager hope, and the words of the Baptist sank deep into his heart—so deep that through all his after years he loved to think of Jesus as the Lamb. What experiences John had had and what a vast deal he had suffered when he came to write this book of Revelation! Life and the world were different to him now from what they had been in the desert with the Baptist. Yet in Revelation some twenty seven times John repeats the sweet expression "Lamb of God"—the first words he had ever heard of Christ. How blessed is a life when from its first stage to its last there runs through it one regulating thought! What concentration it bestows on character! What vividness it gives to the perceptions! There are men who are everything by turns and nothing long—unstable as water, they shall not excel. New ideas seize on them powerfully today, and other ideas as powerfully tomorrow. But men like John, grasping some great truth early, hold to it through storm and sunshine, through Babylon and Patmos, till it expands and breaks into a thousand meanings and becomes a thing of beauty and a joy for ever.

Various thoughts are at once suggested to me by the beautiful and musical message of our text and the first is that Christ in heaven today is the very Christ who walked by the banks of Jordan. "Behold the

Lamb of God," said the Baptist there; and "in the midst of the throne, a Lamb as it had been slain." In the opening chapter of this book of Revelation there is a strange and wonderful vision of the Lord: His head and His hairs were white as snow, and His eyes were as fire, and His feet were like fine brass as if they burned in a furnace. There is deep meaning in every line of that description, but perhaps the first thought to arise in us when we read it is that this is not the Jesus whom we knew in Galilee. It is august and terrible—a vision of light and splendor—and John when he saw it fell at His feet as dead, but it is not like Him who agonized in Gethsemane and whose tears fell beside the grave of Lazarus. But *here* it is the Lamb in the midst of the throne, as in the desert it had been the Lamb of God. Here, in the glory, it is the Lamb slain, as in Isaiah it had been a lamb led to the slaughter. And we feel at once that not all the height of heaven, nor all the inconceivable grandeurs of God's throne, have changed the nature or the love of Him who was pointed to beside the Jordan.

I think we all need to be assured of that, for we are very prone to disbelieve it. Somehow, we think, our Savior in the glory must be different from what He was long ago. We know that He is no longer rejected and despised, and we know that the body of His humiliation has been glorified, until insensibly we transfer these changes from His outward nature to His heart as though death and resurrection had altered that. So we conceive Christ as far away from us, separated from the beating of the human heart; glorious, yet not so full of tender brotherhood as in the days of Capernaum and Bethany. That error is combated by the vision of the Lamb in heaven. Purity, gentleness, and sacrifice are there. The wrath of the Lamb grows terrible just as we remember that that wrath is love rejected and despised. And in the Last Judgment when the Lamb shall be our judge it will not be the majesty of God that will overwhelm us; it will be that we are face to face, at last, with the love and with the sacrifice of Christ.

Another thought which our text suggests is this, that we shall need Christ in heaven as much as we do here. The Lamb which is in the midst of the throne shall feed them—even in heaven there shall be no feeding without Christ. I ask you to note how carefully in these verses John distinguishes between Jesus and His Father. Who shall feed the redeemed? The Lamb in the midst of the throne. Who shall wipe away their tears? Not the Lamb, but God. Now I cannot dwell here on the reasons—the deep reasons—why the consoling of heaven is named as the Father's work; what I ask you to note is that the satisfaction of glory is not a thing of course, that comes inevitably—it is entirely dependent on Christ Jesus. The Lamb which is in the throne shall feed them. On the Lamb depends the satisfaction of eternity. Heaven might be heaven, and God might still be there in His eternal splendor; but even in heaven the redeemed would starve, save for the Lamb in the midst of the throne.

We all know in some measure how great and how constant is our need of Christ on earth. There are moments—often moments of distress and darkness—when every true follower can truly say, "Thou, O Christ, art all I want." In the soberest senses it is the Lamb who feeds us *here*—it is on Him we are dependent for everything that nourishes us—without His love and His sacrifice and His revelation of God, there would be no spiritual pasturage on earth. But do we not sometimes think that death will change all that? Are we not prone to imagine that in the world beyond, the need of being nourished by Christ Jesus will be less? Have we not some dim idea that heaven is like a garden—so fair, so fragrant, and so beautiful in itself, that only to open our eyes there will be rest, and only to wander in its sunshine will be peace? However such an idea may arise within us, remember that it is not the concept of the Bible. The Lamb which is in the throne shall feed them; the need of Christ in heaven is supreme. Every tie that binds us to Him here is strengthened there; all feelings of dependence are infinitely deepened. All that we owe to Him on earth is but a tithe of what we shall owe to Him when we awake.

It is suggested, too, by the words of the original that this feeding shall be a perpetual process. Not once nor for a day shall the Lamb feed the flock; He shall feed them continually and forever. As John looked back on his discipleship in Galilee, one feature of it impressed him very powerfully. It was that the Lamb of God, whom the Baptist had directed him to follow, had taught him everything gradually and slowly. One truth today, one miracle tomorrow, and always and only as the disciples could bear it; little by little, with perfect adaptation, had the Lamb led them into ever deeper knowledge. That was one mark of the feeding of the Lamb, and every year that he lived, John grew more grateful for it. He saw the patience and the gentle constancy with which he had been led into all truth.

And now in Patmos John lifts his eyes to heaven, and there are they who came out of great tribulation; and the Lamb is there—a Lamb as it had been slain—and the Lamb which is in the midst of the throne shall feed them. What did that mean to John? What did it recall to him? It spoke to him of quiet perseverance. There was progress and ever-growing reception of the truth in heaven for John, and there was all that, because the Lamb was there.

Have you incorporated that thought into your view of glory? It is bound up with the true thought of Christ. Just because He is the same yesterday and forever, there will be gradual unfoldings of joy through all eternity. It is true we shall hunger no more, and we shall thirst no more. We shall be satisfied when we awake. Yet John had been satisfied in his first hour with Jesus, but what great and lofty truths had he still to learn! Not all at once shall the mysteries be solved and every truth we have longed to know be taught us. Not all at once shall the full and glorious secret be flashed in its splendor on our awakened eyes. Through all eternity we shall go on to serve. Through all eternity we shall go on to learn. The love of God will expand and deepen endlessly so that every fresh hour will have its sweet surprise. Not God in the first person, but the Lamb—the gradual and patient teacher of the Twelve—the Lamb which is in the midst of the throne shall feed them.

Lastly, and most significant of all, will you note the position in which the Lamb is standing. Be sure it is no chance that the saints are fed in glory by a Lamb who stands, where?—in the midst of the throne. Not in the confines of heaven, not on its distant borders, does the Lamb stand who shall pasture the redeemed. In the very center and seat of power He has His place: He is the Lamb in the midst of the throne. There are few grander pictures in the Bible than John's conception of the heavenly kingdom. It is like one of those drawings by Dore' of the Paradise of Dante in which there is circle within circle of wheeling angels. That is the kind of vision which John had of glory, as if from its utmost and dim verge it were filled with ranks and choirs; and as the circles drew nearer and nearer to the center, they were composed of nobler and more glorious beings. In the very center of that mighty confluence was a throne—it was the throne of the immortal and eternal

God. And in the very center of the throne, standing in front of it, there was a Lamb. And not any angel from distant rank or choir, not even the flaming cherubim or glowing seraphim—not these, but the Lamb in the midst of the throne shall feed them. That means that the redeemed shall be fed not only gently, but by One who stands in the place of sovereign power. None can gainsay Him there; none can withstand Him; none can contest His access to green pastures. The Lamb who feeds them is in the midst of the throne—the scepter of universal power is His now.

In this present world of shadows and of sorrow, have we not often longed for an authoritative voice? Are there not mysteries on every hand that press upon us with a terrible insistence on our hearts? And men try to explain these things to us, and such men may be taught of God, yet the noblest explanation leaves a ring of cloud so vast that we can only bow the head and say, Now we know in part and see in part. It is true that God does not leave us in the darkness—His word is a light unto our feet. When we trust Him there is always light for the next step, and it is the next step that is the road to glory. Still, there remains much doubt and much uncertainty, baffling us and sometimes overwhelming us, and these always will remain till one who knows us thoroughly speaks to us from the very center of authority. That is the meaning of the Lamb in the midst of the throne. Before the mountains were created or the hills were formed, that throne was there. From it the worlds were created; from it the nations were fashioned; from it has gone forth the plan of every life. Every shadow was foreseen there, every tear and every grave—and from the midst of *that* throne the Lamb shall feed them. Does not that illuminate the joy that cometh in the morning? Does it not assure us that we shall be satisfied?

How Science Helps Religion

And the earth helped the woman—Rev. 12:16.

One hears a great deal from many different quarters of the conflict of science and religion. It might be well if we heard a little more of the various ways in which science has helped faith. Of this help in the realm of *applied* science one scarcely needs to speak. It was science which built those mighty Roman highways which, at the Advent, carried the Gospel everywhere. And how railways and steamships and cars and planes have been the servants of missionary work is a familiar fact in all Christendom. To the scientific concept of the printing press the debt of the Gospel is incalculable. It has scattered the tidings of the Savior to the remotest corners of the world. And if our missionaries can live and labor now in regions that were once the white man's grave, we owe it to the activities of science. Such facts are familiar to us all, and there is little need to dwell on them. In the evangelization of the world, applied science has been a powerful helper. But there are other and perhaps deeper ways, more vital than such applications in which, in the language of St. John, the earth has helped the woman.

To begin with, modern science has taught us that it is our duty to look facts in the face, never to come to them with preconceptions, never to shut our eyes to anything. In that respect, I venture to suggest that our blessed Lord had a scientific mind. He never came to things with preconceptions; He never shut His eyes to anything. He saw the vultures gathering by the carcass as well as the chickens gathering to their mother. He saw the tiny sparrow falling dead as well as the sparrow happy in its nesting. No man can have the mind of Christ who has not the courage to have the eyes of Christ. *He* rejected the traditions of men and saw things for Himself. And is not *that* the method of all modern science by which it has found the wonder of the world—to reject the traditions of the fathers and see things for itself? Science has done that with nature, and doing it has won her victories. The world has proved itself a thousand times more marvelous than the traditions of the fathers ever dreamed. Jesus did that with men and women, with the Magdalene, with Peter, with Zaccheus, and in a deep sense, we are *saved by being seen.*

That thought of method may be pushed a little further, and I do so in the words of Huxley. "It seems to me," said Huxley, "that science teaches in the clearest manner the truth embedded in the Christian thought of entire surrender to the will of God. Sit down before the fact as a little child (the very word is Christ's), be prepared to give up every preconceived notion, follow humbly wherever and to whatever end nature leads, or you shall learn nothing. I have only begun to learn content and peace of mind since I have resolved at all risks to do this." Now tell me, what is the essence of religion, I mean on the side of the response of man? Is it not summed up in this single word, entire surrender to the Lord Jesus Christ? As evangelical preachers constantly proclaim, it is *not* enough merely to admire Him. It is *not* enough, gazing on His beauty, to call Him the Altogether Lovely. You must trust Him, become a little child, yield yourself to Him in full surrender, if peace and power and liberty and knowledge are ever to possess the soul. Now when the preacher proclaims that, there are those who say, "I don't believe it. I'm captain of my soul and master of my fate. I am free. I am going to stand upon my feet." Then comes the scientist (our supposed enemy) and says, "Friend, you're in the wrong, the preacher's right. The only way to peace and power and knowledge is the childlike way of full surrender." So the earth helps the woman. So science corroborates our faith. The scientist finds that he is more than conqueror, in precisely the same way as the believer. And yet men talk, till one is sick of it, of the conflict between science and religion.

Lastly, science helps religion by the new majesty that it has given to faith. That may seem a daring thing to say: let me explain my meaning. A Christian is a man who lives by faith—as a simple matter of fact we all do that. You cannot mail a letter without faith; without faith you cannot board a train. But a Christian is a man who takes that faith which runs like a thread of gold through all our life and centers it on the Lord Jesus Christ for time and for eternity. Now there are not a few who hold that science is the enemy of faith; that the more you expand the realm of exact knowledge, the more you contract the realm of faith. Whereas the truth is, the more that knowledge grows in a universe which thrills with the Divine, the more does faith become imperative and wonderful. Things do *not* grow less mysterious, they grow more mysterious as knowledge widens. To Peter Bell the primrose is a weed: to Tennyson the wallcress is a microcosm. The faith of a Lord Kelvin (as I who was his student know) is a thousand times larger and more wonderful than the faith of the untutored savage. When I think of the presuppositions on which the chemist builds, of the postulates demanded by the physicist, of the invisibilities that science reaches when she resolves matter into energy, I feel that science is founded upon faith as truly as the life of the believer. So my hope is that in coming days science and religion will be at peace again. Like righteousness and peace in the old psalm, the dawn is breaking when they will kiss each other. Then with blended voices, they will lift their common praise to Him, Whose we are, and Whom we serve.

The Problem of Pain

Neither shall there be any more pain—Rev. 21:4.

The problem of pain, I think, is in its full intensity a modern problem. There is today a sensitiveness to pain which in past ages was unknown. When you go back three or four centuries, you read of the most excruciating tortures. And you say how cruel must men have been in those days when they would actually use those frightful instruments. Well, of course there was much cruelty about it, but remember there was also a certain callousness—an absence of that quivering sensibility which makes us shrink from suffering today. Still more conspicuously was this the case in the ancient world of Greece and Rome. It was a cruel and a callous world. It was not alive to the mystery of pain. Even the Book of Job, which deals with suffering, is not perplexed about the fact of suffering. It is the question why the *righteous* suffer that forms the burden of the Book of Job. The problem, then, has become insistent in these latter days. Is it possible, do you think, to find the reasons that may have led to this emergence? Why, in other words, are we today more sensitive to pain than men were once? Why do we dwell on it more and feel its pressure more than men seem to have done in the old world? Let me suggest to you three reasons that may help to account for that new sensibility.

In the first place, the keener sensitiveness to pain springs partly from our new power of escaping it. The fact that we can so often cheat it now has had the effect of calling attention to it. So long as anything is quite inevitable, we grimly and silently accept it. *Death* is inevitable—no man can escape it—and you and I seldom dwell on death. But just suppose that some man were to come and tell us a secret for escaping death—and wouldn't the fact of death leap into prominence? So is it with the fact of pain. Men thought that pain was inevitable once. There it was, and one had just to bear it, and that was the end of the whole matter. But now, thanks to the discoveries of science and to the wonderful appliances of Christian medicine, we look on pain in quite a different light. A doctor will actually come to you and say, "It is your duty *not* to suffer." I had a first-rate doctor who once said to me, "You have no right to suffer pain like that." And it is just this sense that pain is not inevitable, but may be escaped from and avoided somehow, that has helped to call attention to its problem.

A second reason for the pressure of the problem is to be found in the new sense of the solidarity of life. We feel our common suffering now with all creation in a way that was undreamed of once. Men, of course, have always recognized that there was a common suffering between them and the dumb animals. But in bygone times it was not of *that* they thought; it was rather of the chasm between man and beast. Now, however, it is not on the chasm that thought is centered, it is on the wonderful closeness of the ties that link all living things into a unity. Now the moment you have built that bridge, there comes galloping over it the form of pain. For pain is universal in the world; wherever there is life, there is suffering. And it is the new sense which we have gained of the suffering throughout the animate creation that has given the matter a new prominence. You know how John Stuart Mill has dwelt on that. You know how Huxley has dwelt on that. They have taken the pain of bird and beast and fish and flung it in the very face of God. And what I say is that that new concept of the groaning and travailing of all creation helps to explain the pressure of the problem.

But there is another reason, it seems to me. It is not scientific; it is theological. It is the discovery we have made in these last days of the full humanity of Jesus. Can you detect the bearings of that upon the question? Let me try in a sentence to explain it to you. Well, so long as the faith was viewed as a body of doctrine, so long there was little room in it for pain. It was with *sin* it dealt. It was on sin it centered. It was through sin it reached the love of God. But the moment that out of the mist of ages there stepped the figure of the man Christ Jesus, in that moment there flashed upon the world the recognition of the fact of pain. Here was the Christ, the very Son of God, and He was infinitely sensitive to pain. It was His passion to cure it when He met with it. For Him it was a terrible reality. And I suggest that it is the human Christ who has become so real to us today who has made real to a thousand hearts the problem of our human suffering. Men are not deeply interested perhaps in dogma now, but they are deeply interested in Christ Jesus. They want to look at the world through Jesus' eyes in a way that was never thought of in past ages. And I think that when you get that standpoint, immediately, as in the days of Galilee, you are confronted not alone with sin, but also with the terrible spectacle of pain.

Now to show you the place that pain has in our being, there are one or two facts I want to bring before you. And the first is that our capacity for pain is greater than our capacity for joy. You experience, for instance, a great joy. Does that prolong its sway through the long months? Do you not know how it exhausts itself and dies, as Shakespeare says, in its own too much? But now you experience great pain, and I never heard that *that* must necessarily exhaust itself—it may continue with a man for years. That means that our capacity for pain is deeper than our capacity for joy. And I mention that to show you how our nature, when you come to understand it in the depths, is in unison with the message of the cross.

Another fact which we shall pick up as we pass is that pain is at the root of life and growth. It is not through its pleasures but through its pains that the world is carried to the higher levels. You remember how Burns wrote about our pleasures?

> But pleasures are like poppies spread,
> You seize the flow'r, its bloom is shed

That is not only true of men; it is true also of the progress of the world. It is through suffering that we are born, and it is through suffering that we are fed. It is through agony that we have won our poetry; it is through blood that we have reached our freedom. It is through pain—pain infinite, unutterable, the pain which was endured by Christ on Calvary—that you and I are ransomed and redeemed. Now that is a fact, explain it how you will, and we are here to deal with facts. I do not deny that pain may be a curse—remember that it also is a power.

We owe our laws to it, and all our institutions of health and welfare. We owe to it our salvation. We owe to it the fact that we are here and able to look the problem in the face.

And then the third fact I note is this, and to me it is of the deepest significance. It is the tendency which men have always had to think of pain as acceptable to God. We talk today of the duty of happiness till people are almost tired of hearing of it. Now not for a single moment would I question that it *is* our duty to be happy. But how significant and singular it is that in every country and in every age men should have looked on suffering and pain as something that was acceptable to God. You have it in the Roman knight who, to appease the gods, leaped into the chasm. You have it in the Indian fakir who sits for years in an attitude of misery. You have it in the pilgrim to the shrine; in the hermit and in the lonely anchorite; in every saint who ever scourged himself; in every savage who has made his offering. Whatever else that means (and it means much else), it hints at something mysterious in pain. Men feel instinctively that in the bearing of it there is some hope of fellowship with heaven. You may despise the hermit, and you may flout the saint when the weals are red upon his back, but an instinct which is universal is something you do well not to despise

That leads me to touch just for a moment upon the purifying power of pain, for that is more closely akin than we might think to the feeling that it pleases God. Now I am far from saying that pain *always* purifies. We have all known cases where it has not done so. We have known men who were hardened and embittered by the cup of suffering they had to drink. But on the other hand, who is there who has not known some life that was transfigured, not by the glad radiance of its joy, but by its bearing of the cross of pain? How many shallow people has pain deepened! How many hardening hearts has it made tender! How man has it checked, and checked effectively, when they were running head-long to their ruin! How many has it weaned from showy things, giving a vision of true riches, and steadying them into a sweet sobriety as if something of the unseen were in their sight! Pain may warn us of the approach of evil. It is the alarm bell which nature rings. Pain may be used in the strong hand of God as a punishment of the sin we have committed. But never forget that far above such ministries, pain, when it is willingly accepted, is one of the choicest instruments of purifying that is wielded by the love of heaven. Fight against it and it shatters you. All the tools of God have double edges. Rebel against it as a thing of cruelty, and all the light of life may be destroyed. But take it up, absorb it in the life, weave it into the fabric of the being, and God shall bring the blossom from the thorn

And that thought, as it seems to me, may throw some light on the sufferings of the innocent. One of the hardest questions in the world is why the innocent should have to suffer so. There is no perfect answer to that question, nor ever shall be on this side the grave. But is there not at least a partial answer in what I have been trying to say? If pain were a curse and nothing but a curse, well might we doubt the justice on the throne; but if pain is a ladder to a better life, then light falls on the sufferings of the innocent. It is not the anger of heaven that is smiting them; it may be the love of heaven that is blessing them. There are always tears and blood upon the steps that lead men heavenward to where the angels are. Mark you, not by the fraction of an ounce does that lighten the guilt of him who causes suffering. It only shows us how the love of God can take the curse and turn it to a blessing.

So I am led lastly to consider this, What has the Gospel done to help us to bear pain? I shall touch on two things which it has done.

In the first place it has quieted those questionings which are often sorer than the pain itself. It has helped us to believe that God is love, in the teeth of all the suffering in the world. Have you ever noticed about Jesus Christ that He was never *perplexed* by the great fact of pain? Death troubled Him, for He groaned in spirit and was troubled when He stood before the grave of Lazarus. But though the fact of death troubled His soul, there is no trace that the dark fact of pain did so—and yet was there ever one on earth so sensitive to pain as Jesus Christ? Here was a man who saw pain at its bitterest, yet not for an instant did He doubt His Father. Here was a man who had to suffer terribly, and yet through all His sufferings God loved Him—it is these facts which, for the believing soul, silence the obstinate questionings forever. We may not see why we should have to suffer. We may not see why our loved ones have to suffer. Now we know in part and see in part; we are but children crying in the night. But we see Jesus, and that sufficeth us. We see how He trusted. We know how He was loved. And knowing that, we may doubt many things, but we never can doubt the love of God again.

And in the second place, it has helped us here by giving us the hope of immortality. It has set our pain in quite a new environment—the environment of an eternal hope. I wonder if you have ever thought of the place and power of hope in human suffering? Hope is might in all we have to do; but it is mighty also in all we have to bear. When once you get the glow of a great hope right in the heart of what you have to suffer, I tell you that that suffering is transfigured. Two people may have to endure an equal agony—taken abstractly, the pains are much alike,—but the one sufferer may be a hopeless man, and the other a woman with the hope of imminent motherhood: and who shall tell the difference there is in the bearing of everything that must be borne through the presence or the absence of such hope? It is just there that Jesus Christ steps in. He has brought immortality to light. Our light affliction which if but for a moment worketh for us an exceeding weight of glory. Out of Christ we thought it was unending. We thought we never should have strength to bear it. But now, against the background of the glory, our light affliction is *but for a moment.*

Service in Heaven

His servants shall serve him—Rev. 22:3.

Of the life of the glorified in heaven Scripture does not tell us very much. And not a little of what is *does* tell is poetically and imaginatively described. There is, for instance, the familiar figure of the harp in the hands of the redeemed. It is easy to make a joke of that and so to turn beatitude to ridicule. But what Scripture is trying to convey is that in heaven utterance shall be music, and therefore self-expression shall be perfect. Music can say what speech can never say. It is more subtle and delicate than speech. It voices the deeper yearnings of the soul in ways that words are powerless to do. And if the utterance of heaven is to be music, then self-expression will be perfect there, and the loneliness of personality will be gone. Here we are all lonely. We long to express ourselves and cannot. There are a thousand things in every heart which it is quite impossible to utter. And the mystical meaning of the harp in heaven is not only that praise will echo there, but that at last we shall be no more lonely, but be in perfect accord with each other.

But if not a little is poetic imagery, there are glimpses that must be literally taken. And all such glimpses are radiant with comfort for the sojourner amid the shadows here. We read that in heaven there shall be no temple, for worship and being will be coextensive. We are told that there are many mansions, for individuality will be preserved. We are assured there will be a place prepared, just as *here* there was a place prepared when the cradle was ready and the little garments and the nurture of the mother's breast. We do not need to translate these into prose like the harp under the fingers of the glorified. If there is poetry in such expressions, it is the poetry which is the stuff of heaven. And so the words which form our text yield their comfort when they are taken literally—His servant shall serve Him.

Perhaps the first suggestion of the words is that in heaven there will be continuity. The ruling passion of the life on earth will be the ruling passion of the life beyond. A true believer is a man who serves. He does not live for self; he lives for others. He follows One who left His high estate that He might take on Him the form of a servant. And Scripture assures us that our service here, transferred in an instant by the grave, is to be carried on in the land beyond the river. With powers quickened by their earthly exercise, with zeal made warmer by rebuffs, with wisdom gained through many a mistake as we sought gropingly to help some brother, we shall enter heaven to discover that the reward of service is a greater service, and that crowning is really continuance. For such service there will be ample room if heaven is the sphere of endless progress.

But if there be the thought of continuity, along with it there is the thought of contrast. As if *at last,* when the mists have rolled away, His servants shall serve Him. Here our finest service is imperfect; at the best we are unprofitable servants; self mingles with everything we do; unworthy motives touch and tarnish everything. But *there* where self is swallowed up in love and everything that defileth is excluded, in reality and in spirit and in truth, His servants shall serve Him. Think of some of the things that mar our service here. There is, for instance, the frailty of the body. How tender was that word of Jesus in Gethsemane. "The spirit is willing, but the flesh is weak." Are there not many who read this little article who would give worlds to be in a greater service, but are debarred by frailty of body? There are the limitations of our ignorance, for here we know so little of each other. We long to help and do our very best, perhaps only to find that we have hurt. And then there is the shortness of our time, and the interruptions of sickness and of night, and the undeviating pressure of the hours. All this the Bible knows. It knows our frame and remembers we are dust. It knows our longings for a truer service than any we have been able to achieve. And then, when heart and flesh are failing and we lament the little we have done, it opens the lattice of heaven for an instant and says, "His servants shall serve him." *There* there shall be no more night. There the

443

limits of time shall all have vanished. There we shall never misinterpret anybody, for we shall know even as we are known. With motives undefiled, with knowledge perfected, with the tireless zest of the eternal morning, *at last* His servants shall serve Him.

The Beatific Vision

And they shall see his face—Rev. 22:4

It should be noted that this beatitude of glory immediately follows on another. It immediately follows on the promise that His servants shall serve Him. We might draw the two into a unity by the suggestion that the glorified continually serve, and serving, continually see. There is a deep sense in which we see through serving. Service is one of heaven's eye-salves. A mother sees more in her child than anybody else does, in the loving patient service of her motherhood. It is when a man serves nature with an entire devotion, such as the naturalist or geologist or astronomer, that he begins to see in her things more wonderful than men had dreamed. The best way to see Christ here is to serve Him. If any man will *do,* then shall he *know.* To take one's cross up and to help is the open secret of fellowship with Jesus. And the apostle hints that in the life of glory our service, which shall be perfected at last, is going to issue in unclouded vision. The glorified shall serve and they shall see. They shall see just because they serve. Their vision shall be purified because in heaven their service shall be perfect. Is it not often the frailty of our bodies or the presence of other motives in our service that dims for us *here* the vision of the Lord?

Or, again, if we find in seeing all that is implied in contemplation, is it not a beautiful thought that in the life of heaven service and seeing shall be one? Amid the shadows of this lower world, activity stands apart from contemplation. The world is like that blessed home in Bethany where were active Martha and contemplative Mary. It is hard, in multifarious duties, to keep that child-like purity of heart without which no man shall see God. There are those who have so many meetings that they almost forget to meet with Him. How few, immersed in an untiring labor, keep the secret of an unruffled calm. And then John tells us that in the brighter world His servants shall serve Him, and yet in the very thickest of the service they shall see His face. Action will not be divorced from contemplation. The one will never make the other harder. Toiling Martha will never be grudging Mary, whose eyes are homes of silent prayer. The glorified, in utter self-abandonment, will give themselves to the services of God, yet never for one instant will they lose the beatific vision of His face.

And another implication is that in heaven there is perfect satisfaction. What a thrilling satisfaction to the heart just to see the face of somebody we love! We cherish their photograph when they are absent, and in quiet moments we gaze upon the photograph. They write us letter, and how we long for them. At other times they communicate by phone. But when the door opens and we see the loved one's face, what an exquisite and thrilling satisfaction—and so, says Scripture, shall it be in heaven. Here we have His photograph. Here we have His love-letters. Here, often, do we catch His messages in the silence and secrecy of conscience. But *there* we shall see Him as He is, face to face, without a cloud between, and we shall be satisfied when we awake.

The Reign of the Saints

And they shall reign forever and ever—Rev. 22:5.

I venture to say that with this expression there creeps in a touch of unreality. It is difficult to associate thrones with the immortal life of our beloved dead. We can readily picture them as serving, for they loved to serve when they were here. Nor, remembering how they searched for it, is it hard to believe that they see His face. But to conceive of them as reigning and having crowns and sitting upon thrones introduces a note of unreality. For many of them that would not be heaven. It would be the last thing they would desire. For they were modest folk, given to self-effacement, haunting the shadowy avenues of life. And if individuality persists, they will carry over into another world those lowly graces that made us love them here. We can always think of an Augustine as reigning. But the saints we knew and loved were seldom Augustines. They were gentle souls, shrinking from publicity, perfectly happy in the lowest place. It is hard to see how natures such as that could ever be quite at home in heaven, if in heaven their calling were to reign. But the Scripture cannot be broken. It is revelation, not conjecture. If there is anything in it that offends the heart, we may be certain the error lies with us. So I believe that the difficulty here and the jarring note that grates upon the sensitive lie in our wrong ideas of reigning.

That there is something wrong in these popular ideas is demonstrated by one forgotten fact. It is that the saints do not *begin* to reign when they pass into the other world. If kingship were confined to heaven, the nature of it would lie beyond our understanding. It would be one of those things that eye had never seen, which God hath prepared for them who love Him. But kingship is *not* confined to heaven, according to the concept of the Scriptures. It is a present possession of the saints. We do not read that Christ will make us kings. We read that He *hath made* us kings (Rev. 1:5). Loosed from our sins in His own blood, we begin to reign in the moment of redemption. And the reign in glory, which troubles meek souls, is not something different from that, but *that* enlarged and expanded to its fullness. This harmonizes with the general mind of Scripture in the glimpses it affords of immortality. It pictures it as a completion rather than as a contradiction. It takes such human things as love and service and tells us that in the land beyond the river such beautiful graces are going to be perfected. In what sense, then, do the saints reign *here?* How is the humblest child of God a king? There is no throne here, nor any visible crown, nor any of the insignia of regality. If we can grasp the kingship of believers amid all the infirmities of time, we have the key to understand the mystery of their reign forever and forever.

And it is just here that a word of Christ's casts a flash of light upon our difficulty. "The kings of the Gentiles," He says "exercise lordship, *but* it shall not be so with you." Are not all our common thoughts of kingship taken from the royalty of such monarchs? Does not their state and insignia of it fill our minds when we meditate on reigning? And Jesus tells us that this whole concept, gathered from the facts of earthly lordship, is alien now and alien forever from the lordship and dominion of His own. He that would be greatest must be least. The monarch is the servant. Kingship is not irresponsible authority: it is love that gives itself in glad abandonment. It is love that goes to the uttermost in service just as He went to the uttermost in service and so reigns forever from the cross. It is thus a Christian mother reigns amid the restless rebellions of her children. It is thus that many a lowly toiler reigns over the hearts and lives of everyone around him. It is thus the Salvation Army lassie queens it over the rough and reckless slum though she carry no scepter in her hand and her only crown be the familiar bonnet. The kingship of believers *here* has nothing whatever to do with pagan lordship. At the command of the Lord Jesus we must banish such concepts from our mind. The only kinship of the saints on earth is that of the glad abandonment of love in an unceasing and undefeated service.

Now it seems to me that all our trouble vanishes when we carry that thought into the other world. If *this* be reigning, then in the life of heaven our dear ones will be perfectly at home. We would not have them other than we knew them when they were with us here amid the shadows. The thought of heaven would be too dearly purchased if it robbed us of their lowly, quiet gentleness. But if the sway they won over our hearts on earth, perfected, be their eternal reigning, then they can still reign and be the same. Reigning will not alter them. It will not render them irrecognizable. It will not touch that lowly loving service which made them so inexpressibly dear. It will only expand it into fullest kingliness, setting a crown of gold upon its head. They shall reign forever and forever.

The Root and the Star

I am the root and the offspring of David, and the bright and morning star—
Rev. 22:16.

Nothing is more notable in Jesus than the union of apparent contradictories. Qualities of the most diverse characters are brought into a perfect harmony in Him. When we set out to copy any brother, we are wrested from our true development. For other lives, even at their finest, are fragmentary and incomplete. But nobody who aims at following Christ can ever be false to his true self, for the character of Christ is universal. He combines the most opposing temperaments and reconciles diversities of being. Everything that all are meant to be, our blessed Savior actually was. That is the truth which lies in the assertion, so often fiercely combated, that our Lord was not a man but *man.* Speaking evangelically, it is only the redeemed who are *in Christ.* Not till we are born again are we in His as the branch is in the vine. Yet in the matter of ideal character, in all its infinite diversity, there is a mystical sense in which our Savior embraces the whole human race. Nobody becomes anybody else when he aims at imitating Jesus. He grows near to his highest self when he becomes more like his Lord. For all the partial ideals of life which give to it an infinite variety blend into a perfect unity in the perfect character of Jesus.

Now, something of that reconcilement is seen in the imagery of our text. Between a root and a star there is a world of difference, and yet Jesus tells us He is both. He takes objects from two different worlds, and in both of them He finds Himself. He selects things that seem to have no unity, and He compares Himself with both of them. He brings together in a single sentence objects that are utterly unlike, and yet He sees in each of them something that is an image of His being. Take these figures separately and they are rich in spiritual significance. Take them together and they are big with hope for all the diversities of character. Men who are as different from each other as a root is different from a star may find all that they seek for in the Savior.

One notes, for instance, how this twofold figure combines the local and the universal. A root is embedded in a single spot; a star rains its influence on the world. If a root is to grow it needs a certain soil, for there and there alone it finds its nutriment. To that environment must come the searcher if he wants to get his hand upon the root. But in the crowded city and the lonely glen and far away on the solitudes of ocean a man may lift his eyes towards the heavens and be comforted by the shining of a star. The root is grounded in one place; the star sheds its light on every place. The root is fixed in a definite locality; the star is the joy of all localities. And then one thinks of Jesus, born in Bethlehem and growing up in Nazareth and yet today the light of the world. Go to Africa, and there you find Him. Travel to India, and He is there. Multitudes who have never been to Bethlehem have experienced the power of His name. Rooted deep in the rich soil of Palestine, the image of a root is not enough. On sinful men a million miles from Palestine He has shone as the bright and morning star.

Another aspect of this twofold figure is the union of the hidden and the evident. A root is something concealed from observation; a star is conspicuous in its shining. There are roots which lie very near the surface, and there are others which run very deep. But one mark of every root is this, that it shuns the light and moves into the darkness. And just there, between root and star, what a world of difference there is, for a star is something that is seen. Nobody in the brightest day can see a root. It lives and moves concealed from human eyes. But in the darkest night the stars are shining in the wonder of the heavens. And does not one feel at once that it takes both, infinitely diverse though they be, to picture for us the mystery of Jesus? The kingdom cometh not with observation, yet Jesus could not be hid. The mighty world knew not when He came, and yet He is the light of every man. He lives in the secret of the heart and in our hidden being has His dwelling, and yet in the outward and habitual life He reveals the shining of His presence.

And then lastly in this twofold figure we have united the earthly and the heavenly. For a root is one of the children of the earth, and a star one of the glories of the sky. You find the root where common feet are treading, where lovers walk and little children play. You find the star beyond all human reaching in the infinite heights of heaven that are above us. And then we think of Him, whom we discover on our Emmaus roads, while He shines on us from the altitude of glory. One cannot explain these things nor understand them. They are mysteries beyond our fathoming. How can one be here, where the green grass is, and yet radiant in a world beyond our reach? And then we remember how these contradictions were reconciled in the consciousness of Him, who called Himself a root, and then—a star.

Meditations on the Psalms

The Privilege of Worship

As for me, I will come into thy house in the multitude of thy mercy—Ps. 5:7.

David was a man of many privileges bestowed on him in the goodness of his Lord. He had the privilege of the poetic heart and the privilege also of a royal estate. But in this text he singles out a privilege we may all share with him. It is the privilege of public worship. "As for me," he says, "I will go into thy house." The very thought of it was a delight to him. It made a secret music in his heart when the hour of public worship was approaching. For him the recurring summons to the sanctuary was not a call to be grudgingly obeyed. It was the happiest summons of the week.

This is perhaps the more remarkable in the light of the personality of David. His was one of those poetic natures for which the world is all aflame with God. We read in Revelation that in the other world there is no temple. *There* there is no need of any sanctuary, for the whole expanse of heaven is a sanctuary. And there are natures in this present world so quick to see and feel that God is everywhere, that the whole universe for them is aglow with His presence. For them the great Creator is not far away. He is very near and He is always speaking. It is His voice that is calling in the sea and in the wind that bloweth where it listeth. The tiniest weed, the day-spring and the evening, the stars and the bird on the branch are but the manifold and changing shadows of that infinite perfection which is God. It is with such thoughts that the poet walks the world. It was with such thoughts that David walked the world. For him in every field there was an altar and a sacrifice in every breath of evening. And the wonderful thing is that with a heart like that, that saw God everywhere and worshiped Him, there should have been this overwhelming sense of the privilege of sanctuary worship. "Let others do what they like," is what he means, "as for me, I will go into thy house." There was something there that nothing else could give him, neither the lonely mountain nor the sea. And so at once, as reasonable men, we find ourselves confronted by this question—what was there in the worship of God's house that made it thus indispensable to David?

Well, in the first place, in the house of God there was for David the sense of human fellowship. In the deepest yearnings of his heart, he felt in the sanctuary that he was not alone. It is a lonely thing to be a king, and David the psalmist was a king. He lived in a certain solitary grandeur which is ever the penalty of royal estate. And then for him there was another loneliness that pierces deeper than that of regal state—it was the loneliness of the poetic heart. To be a monarch is to be a solitary, and to be a poet is to be a solitary. The one is separated by his rank from men, and the other by his inspiration. And it is when one recalls that David was not only a monarch but a poet too that one begins to understand his loneliness. He craved for fellowship, as we all do, and for him it was very difficult to find. He had to deny himself those pleasant intimacies that are so heartening to the common man.

My brother, out of a loneliness like that can't you gather the exquisite delight with which the poet-king would turn his steps to the communion of the house of God? There he was no longer solitary. There he was a subject, not a king. There he was a brother among brothers under the shadow of a Father-God. And every sacrifice upon the altar and every word of penitence and praise told of a fellowship that lay far deeper than everything that can sunder human lives.

Deeper than everything which separates is the need of pardon for the sinner. Deeper than every individual craving is the craving for fellowship with God. No wonder, then, that David loved the sanctuary. No wonder that with eager feet he sought it. No wonder that the hour of public prayer was the most cherished season of his week. Seeking that fellowship which every soul demands, no matter how richly gifted it may be, he said: "As for me, I will come into thy house."

Brethren, as with David, so with us, that is the privilege of public worship. In all the deepest regions of our being, it is the assurance of a real fellowship. In the market-place, men meet and mingle on the basis of a common interest in business. In the home, lives are united by all the tender ties of human love. But in the sanctuary, the ground of fellowship is the common need of our immortal spirit which knows its weakness and its need of pardon and cannot be satisfied with less than God.

When Christian was in the Valley of the Shadow, you remember, he heard the voice of Faithful on ahead. And it cheered him and comforted his heart to know that there was another in the Valley. And that is one thing the sanctuary does for us in a way that nothing else can ever do as we fight our battles, fall and rise again, and wrestle heavenward against storm and tide. It tells us there are others in the Valley. It gives us the happy certainty of comradeship. In common prayer we voice a common need, and in common praise a common aspiration. And within the house of God we come to feel that we are not alone, and to feel *that* is like a strain of music. Without that fellowship we should despair, for the pathway is infinitely hard. Without that fellowship, knowing our instability, we might falter and fall by the wayside. And then there falls on us the benediction of worship and we are wakened to the sense of brotherhood. Others have known the things that we have known, the failures and the struggles and the yearnings. Others as vile as we have been redeemed and became more than conquerors in Christ. Others, too, have been tempted to despair and have thought of the heavens as brass and yet have known that to depart from God was the avenue to death. My brother, it is such things that we learn in public worship in the house of God. No lonely meadow, no still and shady woods, no lonely mountainside can teach us that. And therefore from all the ministries of nature will the true seeker turn to the house of God, saying with the poet-king of Israel, "As for me, I shall come into thy house."

In the second place, within the house of God there was for David the message of the past. There was memorial of all that God had been in His unfailing shepherding of Israel. In the life of David, as in the lives of all of us, there were seasons when he was hard pressed—seasons when the sky was dark and lowering and all the sunshine seemed to have departed. And who does not know how in such times as these the light of the countenance of God is quenched as though He had quite forgotten to be gracious. Such tragic hours were in the lot of David. There seemed for him to be no justice anywhere. Slander was rife and treachery was busy; hatred was malignant and victorious. And in such hours as these it seemed to David, who was a man of like passions with ourselves, as if the covenant of heaven were broken and his movements unseen by his God. What David needed in such hours as these was a larger message than his life could give him. He needed a reassurance of his God drawn from the wonderful story of the past. And Israel's faith was that sweet reassurance to be found. There in the house of God stood the ark that had been borne through all the wanderings of the wilderness. There was the mercy-seat where God had dwelt under the sheltering wings of golden cherubim. There was the pot of manna from the desert that had fed the hungry in their hour of need. There was the rod of Aaron that had budded. "As for me, I will come into thy house." David went to revive his courage by the past. When times were tragic, when faith was hard to keep, he went to learn the ways of God again. And so, refreshed and strengthened with that view of all that the living God had been to Israel, courage returned and dying hope revived, and David was made equal to his day. No man knew better than that poet-king the healing and help of the ministry of nature. But in hours like these when faith was tested, it was not to meadow or mountain that he turned; it was to the sanctuary, to the house of God, to the shrine and witness of an unfailing covenant—"As for me, I will come into thy house."

And so it is with you and me as we turn our steps on the Lord's day to the sanctuary. We come to gain for our uncertain hearts the large, grand assurance of the past. As we listen there to the reading of those Scriptures that have been the stay of countless generations, as we lift our voices in those ancient hymns that were sung by thousands who are now in glory, are we not lifted above our cloudy present, where the divine purpose is so hard to see, into a region that is full of God? We have no ark, no golden cherubim, no budding rod, no gathered manna. But we have something that is far more eloquent of what the Lord has been throughout the ages. We have the broken bread and we have the wine in the memorial Supper of our Savior which unites us with every faithful heart that ever trusted in His grace. All that is given us in the sanctuary, and given us nowhere else than in the sanctuary—that sight and sense of all that God has been in the large and roomy spaces of the ages. And so we are kept from the blackness of despair and from thinking that God has forgotten to be gracious when, in our separate and individual lives, we look for Him and our eyes are dim. Blessed be God for the ministry of nature and for all the peace and healing of His hand. Blessed be God for the heather on the hill and the music of the stream in the valley. But when the way is dark and faith is difficult and prayer seems empty, we need another ministry than that. We need the testimony of the ages then. We need the ministry of the long past. We need to know that God has kept His promises from generation unto generation. And such is the testimony that like a flowing tide is borne in upon our darkened souls when with the poet of Israel we say, "As for me, I will come into thy house."

Third and last, within the house of God there was for David the blessed sense of mercy. "As for me, I will come into thy house in the multitude of thy mercy." Will you observe it is mercy—in the singular. It is not mercies—in the plural. The mercy of God is not many different things; the singer knew that mercy is all one. And yet to him that attribute of mercy was of such various and changing feature that the only way in which he could describe it was to compare it to a multitude. In a great crowd there is one common life. It is one life that animates the whole. Yet in a crowd, how that common life expresses itself in a thousand different ways. And so for David there were a thousand tokens that the Lord God was merciful and gracious, and yet he knew that the mercy was all one.

Ah, how utterly David *needed* mercy. Without mercy there was no hope for him. He, the poet and king of Israel—what a guilty sinner he had been! My brother and sister, it was in search of mercy, mercy to pardon his sin unto the uttermost, that he cried out of a broken heart, "As for me, I will come into thy house." He had searched for mercy in creation and it had baffled him to find it there. He had looked to the stars for it and to the firmament, only to learn the littleness of man. And then in agony, and with that sense of guilt which was wrought by the Holy Spirit on his heart, he had turned to the house of God and found it there. Mercy—it was the message of the ark, for above the ark there was the mercy-seat. Mercy—it was the message of the manna, for it had been given to a rebellious people. And every sacrifice upon the altar, and every offering accepted there, spoke of the Lord God merciful and gracious. That was what David needed above everything, and that was what only the sanctuary gave him. No forest depth, no everlasting mountains, gave him the peace of reconciliation. And that was why David with his poet's heart, alive to all the music of the universe, turned to the sanctuary and cried, "As for me, I will come into thy house."

My friend, as with David so with us: of all our needs, our deepest need is mercy—mercy to pardon, mercy to receive, mercy while we live and when we die. Without a mercy infinite and boundless, there is no hope for any mortal man. Without a mercy glorious and free, there is nothing but a fearful looking for of judgment. And I do not know of anywhere within this universe where there sounds out the silver bell of mercy save in that ministry of reconciliation which is the message of the house of God. I turn to nature and I don't find it. I search for it in vain among the hills. I hear it not in the song of any brook nor in the organ-music of the sea. But the moment I enter into the house of God, clear as a trumpet, soft as the breath of evening, I hear of a mercy that is high as heaven and deeper far than the abyss of sin. Though your sins be as scarlet, they shall be white as snow; though they be red like crimson, they shall be as wool. Christ hath died, the just for the unjust. He is able to save unto the uttermost. My brother and sister, whatever else we need, that is the deepest need of every one of us, for without that mercy none of us can live, and without it none of us can die in peace. Cherish, then, all that is bright and beautiful in the world around you and in the sky above you. Walk with an open ear, as David did, for every accent of the great Creator. And then like David, poet-king and sinner, feeling your need of the everlasting mercy, say to your soul afresh this Lord's day, "As for me, I will come into thy house."

The Gentleness of God

Thy gentleness hath made me great.—Ps. 18:35

It will be generally agreed that David was one of the great men of the race. In his trust and courage and leadership and genius he stands among the heroes of humanity. Now David had had a strange and varied life. He had been hunted like a partridge on the hills. He had suffered disloyalty at home and sorrowed in the death of Absalom. But *now*, as he looked back upon it all, what stood out in transcendent clearness was the unfailing gentleness of God—*not* the infliction of any heavenly punishment, though sometimes punishment had been severe; *not* the divine apportioning of sorrow, though he had drunk of very bitter sorrow. What shone out like a star in heaven, irradiating the darkness of his night, was the amazing gentleness of God. David could say with a full heart, "Thy gentleness hath made me great."

With a like sincerity can we not say it also? When we survey our course and recollect our mercies and recall the divine handling of our childishness, the confession of David is our own.

We feel the wonder of the gentleness of God when we remember it is conjoined with power. When infinite power lies at the back of it, gentleness is always very moving. There is a gentleness which springs from weakness. Cowardice lies hidden at its roots. It comes from the disinclination to offend and from the desire to be in good standing with everybody. But the marvel of the gentleness of God is that it is not the signature of an interior weakness, but rests upon the bosom of Omnipotence. In a woman we all look for gentleness; it is one of the lustrous diadems of womanhood. In a professional military man we scarcely expect it; it is not the denizen of tented fields. And the Lord is "a might man of war," subduing, irresistible, almighty, and yet He comes to Israel as the dew. The elder spoke to John of the lion of the tribe of Judah. But when John looked to see the lion, in the midst of the throne there was a *lamb*. Power was tenderness—the lion was the lamb—Omnipotence would not break the bruised reed. It is the wonder of the gentleness of God.

Again, the gentleness of God is strangely moving when we remember it is conjoined with purity. There is a kind of gentleness, common among men, which springs from an easy, tolerant, good nature. To be gentle with sin is quite an easy matter if sin is a light thing in our eyes. It is easy to pardon a child who tells a lie, if lying is in our regard, but venial. And when we are tempted to think of God like that, as if heaven were rich in tolerant good nature, then is the time to consider the cross. Whatever else we learn at Calvary, we learn there God's estimate of sin. In that dark hour of agony the judgment of heaven upon sin is promulgated. And when *that* steeps into our being, so that we measure things by the measurements of Calvary, we are awed by the gentleness of God.

Then to all this must be added the fact of our human provocation. For, like the children of Israel in the wilderness, we are continually provoking God. Every mother knows how hard it is to be always gentle with a provoking child—how likely she is to lose her temper with it and how she longs to shake it or to slap it. But no child is ever so provoking to the tender heart of a good mother as you and I must always be to God. When we sin, when we fail to trust Him, when we grow bitter, when we become despondent, how ceaselessly provoking *that* must be to the infinitely loving heart in heaven. Yet David could say, as you and I can say, looking back over the winding trail of years, "Thy gentleness hath made me great." Nothing is more provoking to a parent than when a child refuses to take medicine, screaming and fighting against it desperately, though the cup be entirely for its good. The question is, *How do you take your medicine?* Do you grow faithless, hard, rebellious, broken-hearted? How provoking must that be to our Father. Yes, think on God's power and on His purity, and add to that our human provocation, if you want to feel the glory of His gentleness.

It always seems to me that tenderness and gentleness implies that we are sick. In our Father's sight we are all ailing children. We have all noticed how when one is sick everyone around grows strangely gentle. There is an exquisite gentleness, as many of us know, in the touch of a true nurse. Even rough, rude men grow very gentle, as is seen so often in war, when they are handling a wounded comrade. When he was well they tormented him; they played their jokes on him and coined his nickname; but when wounded, stricken, bleeding, shattered, they showed themselves as gentle as a woman. And I often think that the gentleness of God, could we track it to its mysterious deeps, is akin to that of soldier and of nurse. We are a sin-sick race. We all have leprosy. We are full of "wounds and bruises and putrefying sores." They that are whole have no need of a physician, but they that are *sick*. Love in magnificence may suit the angels. But in the world's great battlefield and hospital, Love binds on the cross and walks in gentleness. "Thy gentleness hath made me great."

What exactly may be meant by greatness is a question that we need not linger to discuss. It is enough that the writer of this verse was conscious that he had been lifted to that eminence. That he had been in extreme distress is clear from the earlier verses of this chapter. His heart had fainted—his efforts had been in vain—his hopes had flickered and sunk into their ashes. And then mysteriously, but very certainly, he had been carried upward to light and power and liberty, and now he is looking back over it all. That it was God who had so raised him up was, of course, as clear to him as noonday. He had sent up his cry to heaven in the dark, and to that cry His greatness was the answer. But what impressed him as he surveyed it all was not the infinite power of the Almighty; it was rather the amazing and unceasing gentleness wherewith that infinite power had been displayed. "Thy gentleness hath made me great," he cried. That was the outstanding and arresting feature. Tracing the way by which he had been led, he saw conspicuous a gentle ministry of God.

Let me say in passing that that wonderful concept is really peculiar to the Bible. I know no deity in any sacred book that exhibits such an attribute as that. Of course, when one believes in many gods, it is always possible that one of them is gentle. When the whole world is thought to be tenanted with spirits, some of them doubtless will be gentle spirits. But that is a very different thing indeed from saying that the One Lord of heaven and earth has that in His heart which we can dimly picture under the human attribute of gentleness. No prophets save the prophets of Israel ever conceived the gentleness of God. To no other poets save these Jewish poets was the thought of heavenly gentleness revealed. And so when we delight in this great theme, we are dwelling on something eminently biblical, something that makes us, with all our Christian liberty, a debtor unto this hour to the Jewish prophets for bringing this to our attention.

Now if we wish to grasp the wonder of God's gentleness, there are one or two things we ought to do. We ought, for instance, always to lay it against the background of the divine omnipotence. You know quite well that the greater the power, the more arresting the gentleness becomes. As might advances and energy increases, so always the more notable is gentleness. It is far more impressive in the general of armies than in some retired and ineffectual dreamer. The mightier the power a commands, the more compelling is his trait of gentleness. If he is ruler of a million subjects, a touch of tenderness is thrilling. And it is when we think of the infinite might of God, who is King of kings and Lord of lords, that we realize the wonder of our text. It is He who calleth out the stars by number and maketh the pillars of the heaven to shake. And when He worketh, no man can stay His hand, nor say to Him, What doest Thou? And it is this Ruler, infinite in power, before whom the princes of the earth are vanity, who is exquisitely and forever gentle.

Again, to feel the wonder of God's gentleness, we must set it against the background of God's righteousness. It is when we hear the seraphs crying "Holy" that we thrill to the thought of the gentleness of God. There is a kind of gentleness—we are all familiar with it—that springs from an easy and uncaring tolerance. It is the happy good nature of those characters to whom both right and wrong are nebulous. Never inspired by any love of goodness and never touched by any hate of evil, it is not difficult to walk the world with a certain smiling tolerance of everybody.

Now there have been nations whose gods were of that kind. Their gentleness was the index of their weakness. Living immoral lives in their Olympus, why should they worry about man's immortality? But

I need hardly take time to point out to you that the one radical thing about the Jewish God—one unchanging feature of His being—was that He was infinitely and forever holy. He was of purer eyes than to behold iniquity. "The soul that sinneth," said the prophet, "it shall die." And He visits the sins of the fathers on the children, even unto the third and fourth generation. All this was graven on the Jewish heart and inwrought into Jewish history; yet the psalmist could sing in his great hour, "They gentleness hath made me great." I beg of you, therefore, never to imagine that the gentleness of God is only an easy tolerance. Whatever it is, it certainly is not *that*, as life sooner or later shows to every man. Whatever it is, it leans against the background of a righteousness that burns as doth a fire, and I say that helps us to feel the wonder of it.

The same jewel upon the bosom of omnipotence flashes out as we survey the Bible. The Bible is really one long record of the amazing gentleness of God. Other features of the divine character may be more immediately impressive there. And reading hastily, one might easily miss the revelation of a gentle God. Yet so might one, walking beside the sea, where hammers were ringing in the village workshop, easily miss the underlying music of the waves ceaselessly breaking on the shore. But the waves are breaking although the hammers drown them, and the gentleness of God is always there. It is there—not very far away—at the heart of all the holiness and sovereignty; it is there where the fire of His anger waxes hot and His judgments are abroad upon the earth, and men are crying, "It is a fearful thing to fall into the hands of the living God."

Take, for instance, that opening Scripture of Adam and of his sin and exile. Whatever else it means, it means unquestionably that God is angry with disobedient man. And yet at the back of it what an unequaled tenderness, as of a father pitying his children and loving them with a love that never burns so bright as in the bitter hour of necessary punishment. Losing his innocence, in the love of God Adam found his calling and his crown. He fell to rise into a world of toil, and through his toil to realize his powers. So looking backward through that bitter discipline, unparadised but not unshepherded, he too could surely say with David, "Thy gentleness hath made me great."

Or think again of the story of the Exodus, that true foundation of the Jewish race. It took one night to take Israel out of Egypt but forty years to take Egypt out of Israel. And while that night, when the first-born were slain, was dark and terrible with the mighty power of God, what are those forty years of desert wandering but the witness of the gentleness of heaven? Leaving Egypt a company of slaves, they had to win the spirit of the free. Leaving it shiftless, they had to win reliance; leaving it cowardly, they had to learn to conquer; leaving it degraded, as slaves are always degraded, they were to reach to greatness by and by, and looking back on it all what could they say but this, "Thy gentleness hath made me great." Never forget that in its age-long story the Bible reveals the gentleness of God. Hinted at in every flower that blossoms, it is evidently declared in Holy Scripture. It is seen in Adam and in Abraham. It is seen in the wilderness journey of the Israelites. It is found in the choicest oracles of prophecy and in the sweetest music of the Psalms.

I think, too, that as life advances, we can all confirm that that is true. We all discover, as the psalmist did, how mighty has been the gentleness of heaven. In the ordinary sense of the word, you and I may not be considered great. We have neither been born great, nor have we come to greatness, nor has greatness been thrust upon us. And yet it may be that for you and me life is a nobler thing than it was long ago, and truth is more queenly, and duty more dignified, than in the past. We may not have won any striking moral victories, yet our life has leaned to the victorious side. We have not conquered yet all that we hoped to conquer, yet our will is serving us better through the years. There are still impurities that lift up their heads and still passions that have to be brought to heel, yet it may be that you and I are now nearer the sunrise than ten years ago.

If, then, that is the case with you, I urge you to look back on the way that you have come and think of all that life has meant for you. Think of the temptations that would have overcome you had not God in His gentleness taken them away. Think of the courage you got when things were dark; of the doors that opened when every way seemed barred. Think of the unworthy things that you have done which God in His infinite gentleness has hidden—of the love that inspired you and the hope that came to you when not far distant was the sound of breakers. You, too, if you are a man at all, can lift up your eyes and cry out, *God is just.* It may be you can do more than that and lifting up your voice say, *God is terrible.* But if you have eyes to see and a heart to understand, there is something more that you can say, for you can whisper, "To me, in pardoning, shielding mercy, God has been infinitely and divinely gentle." If every lily of the field lifting its head can say, "Thy gentleness hath made me great"; if every sparrow chirping on the eaves is only echoing that meadow music, then I do feel that you and I, who are of more value to God than many sparrows, owe more than we shall ever understand to the abounding gentleness of heaven.

Now it seems to me that this gentleness of God reveals certain precious things about Him. It reveals, for instance, and is rooted in His perfect understanding of His children. There is a saying with which you are familiar; it is that to know all is to forgive all. That is an apothegm, and like all apothegms, it is not commensurate with the whole truth. Yet as a simple matter of experience, so much of our harshness has its rise in ignorance that such a saying is sure of immortality—to know all is to forgive all. How often you and I, after some judgment, have said to ourselves, *If I had only known.* Something is told us that we knew nothing about, and instantly there is a revulsion in our hearts. And we retract the judgment that we passed, and we bitterly regret we were unfeeling, and we say we never would have spoken so, had we only known.

The more we know—I speak in a broad way—the more we know, the more gentle we become. The more we understand what human life is, the great the pity we feel. And I think it is just because our heavenly Father sees right down into our secret heart, that He is so greatly and pitifully gentle. For He knoweth our frame and remembereth we are dust, and He putteth all our tears into His bottle. And there is not a cross we carry and not a thought we think but He is acquainted with it altogether. And all we have inherited by birth, of power or weakness, of longing or of fear—I take it that all *that* is known to the God of Abraham, of Isaac, and of Jacob.

And then again God's gentleness reveals this to us—it reveals our abiding value in His sight. It tells us, as almost nothing else can tell us, that we, His children, are precious in His eyes. There are certain books upon my shelves at home with which I hardly bother to be gentle. I am not upset when I see them tossed about nor when they are handled in a rough way. But there are other books that I could never handle without a certain reverence and care, and I am gentle because they are of value to me. And the noteworthy thing is that these precious volumes are not always the volumes that are most beautifully bound. Some of them are little tattered creatures that a respectable servant longs to light the fire with. But every respectable servant of a booklover comes to learn this at least about his master, that his ways, like those of another Master, are mysterious and past finding out. For that little volume, tattered though it may be, may have memories that make it infinitely precious—memories of schooldays or of college days, memories of the author who was well known to him. It may be the first Shakespeare that he ever had, or the first Milton that he ever handled, and he shall handle it gently to the end, because to him it is a precious thing. So I take it God is gentle because you and I are precious in His sight. He is infinitely patient with the worst of us because He values the worst of us so dearly. And if you want to know how great that value is, then read this text again and again: "For God so loved the world that He gave His only-begotten Son, that whosoever believeth in Him should not perish."

Self-Ignorance

Who can understand his errors?—Ps. 19:12

It is the true desire of every earnest heart that preceding the Communion Service our thoughts should be turned inward in self-examination. Every astronomer worthy of the name is constantly careful to keep his lenses clean. But when he is on the verge of some great hour, then he cleanses them with double care. And so the Christian must always be watchful—must always be examining himself—but never more intensely so than at the time when he is looking for fresh discoveries of Christ. I want you, therefore, to follow me while I try to find why most of us are so ignorant of self. For of this you may be always sure, that the more we know what we really are, the better shall we know our need of Christ and of the glorious Gospel of His grace.

It is a full and busy life in which we share, and the hand of that life opens many doors, but not the door which leads into the heart. Moments are precious now and days are full. Interests are manifold and ever changing. There is not an attic window which does not open on the panorama of the mighty world. And just as the Indian, putting his ear to the ground, can hear far off the galloping of horses, so all the movement and music of humanity is morning by morning borne upon our ear. It was a saying of John Wesley that he had all the world for his parish. And there is not a farmer in the remotest village who could not say something of the same kind today.

Now none but a pessimist would ever doubt that in this full life are elements of value. It has developed man and enlarged his vision and helped to make him a little less parochial. It has turned the Gospel into a world-wide message in a way that was never possible before. All this is good and we are thankful for it. There is something in it which exalts the Savior. We are learning the kingship of Jesus Christ today in a manner that was undreamed of once. And yet with it all there is a certain loss—a loss of quietness and of introspection. We have an added knowledge of the world, and perhaps a lessened knowledge of ourselves. We know far more than our forefathers knew about Japan and India and Thailand. The question is, do we know any more about the spiritual kingdom that is *here*? And after all, no kingdom in the world can relay such mighty news as can the kingdom of man's own soul where heaven and hell are fighting for the throne. We have gained, and we have also lost. We have seen more widely, and are a little blinder. We know far more than our forefathers knew, and yet it may be we know a little less. It is far harder now than it was once to reap the harvest of the quiet eye by practicing, amid the stir of things, the quiet and kindly grace of recollection.

Another and deeper cause of our self-ignorance is the gradual and silent growth of sin. You are never startled by any noise of hammering when the chains of a bad habit are being forged. All of us are roused into attention when anything flashes suddenly upon us. It is one of the ministries of God's surprise that it arrests us when we are dull and heavy. But when a thing is gradual in its coming and steals upon us without the sound of a trumpet, it is always easy to be unobservant. If in a moment the sun shone out in splendor and midnight vanished and the sky were blue, how every eye would mark that miracle and see in it the hand of the divine! But like a true artist of Almighty God, the sun has a scorn for anything sensational, and never an infant is wakened from its cradle as, rising, the sun parts the curtains of the east.

Think of the way in which children grow. How silently they creep towards their heritage! It seems but yesterday since they were little infants and busied with the first stammerings of speech. And today they are fighting their battle with the world, and the mystery of life has touched them, and they are launched into the boundless deep—and still are children in their mother's eyes. We are all rocked to sleep by what is gradual. We let ourselves be tricked by what is silent. We miss the message of God times without number because He whispers in a still small voice.

And just as we are often dulled towards God, so are we dulled to our besetting sin for it has grown so gradually and strengthened with our strength and never startled us with any uproar. It is easy to see the sins of *other* people, because in a moment they are displayed to us. We see them not in the slowness of their growth, but in the sudden flash of their fulfillment. We see them as we see some neighbor's child whom for a year or two we have not set our eyes on, and then we say, "How the child has grown; I never would have recognized him!" That is how we can detect our neighbor's sin. That is how we fail to see our own. It has grown with us and lived in the same home and sat at the same table all the time—until today we are living such a life as God knows we never meant to live, and tampering with conscience and with purity as God knows we never dreamed to do. Had the thing leapt on us like a wild animal we should have aroused our manhood to resist it. But the most deadly evils do not *leap* on us. The most deadly evils *creep* on us. And it is that slow and silent growth of all that at last is mighty to confound which lulls men into the strange security which always is the associate of self-ignorance.

Another reason for self-ignorance is that you never know sin's power till you oppose it. It is as true of sin as of any other force that you must measure its power by resistance. It is not when you are walking *with* the wind that you can measure how strong the wind is blowing. It is when you turn into the teeth of it that you perceive the power of the blast. And you will never learn the power of sin, nor how sweet it is nor what a grip it has, till in the name of God you battle with it. That is what Paul means when, in Romans, he says "I had not known sin but by the law." It was when sin was checked by the commandment that it revealed the power which was in it. It was when God said "Thou shalt *not*," that sin began to struggle for its life; and the commandment came, says the apostle, and sin revived and I died. Try to lift up those chained arms of thine, and thou wilt find how heavy are the chains. Waken that sleeping devil in thy bosom, and thou wilt find it is a sleeping Hercules. It is thus that men are led to Jesus Christ and to feel their need of an Almighty arm and to cast themselves in great despair on Him who can save even to the uttermost.

Another cause of our self-ignorance lies in the interweaving of our best and worst. In deeper senses than the psalmist thought of, we are fearfully and wonderfully made.

I had the pleasure, some little time ago, of going over one of the cruisers of the Navy. There was a great deal that was good to see, and with consummate courtesy we were shown it all. But the feature which seemed to interest our guide most, and to which he called particular attention, was the watertight compartments of the ship. He pointed out the fittings of the doors. He showed us how ingeniously they set. When the doors were locked there was such nice exactitude that not a penknife could have been inserted. And all this meant that in the hour of battle, if the one cabin were flooded by a shot, the other compartments would be dry.

Now it is thus that men may build, but it is not thus that the Almighty builds. There is no door of steel which closes fast between the highest and the worst in us. If all that was bad in individual character stood by itself in perfect isolation, then we would feel the joy of what was good and the dark loathsomeness of what was evil. But human character is not constructed with separate departments for its good and evil. It is an intricate and inextricable tangle of what is beautiful and what is base.

"Then I beheld," says Bunyan in his dream, that "there was a way to hell from nigh the gate of heaven." I think that that is so with every man: his hell and heaven are never far apart. There is something of his weakness in his strength, and the beautiful and the ugly have strange kinships, and the good and the bad in him spring up together like the wheat and tares in Jesus' parable. Let the philosophers sift out our faculties. Let them distinguish the reason from the will. Let them treat on *this* page of the memory and on *that* page of the imagination. Our ordinary life makes merry with philosophers. And hope and faith and will, and height and depth, are interwoven in a waterlily—beautiful, yet rooted in the slime. How many a glimpse there is of heaven in passions whose appointed end is misery. And it is the interweaving of such opposites in the whole range of human life and conduct which leads so often and so easily to the peril and the evil of self-ignorance.

I shall mention but one more cause of our self-ignorance, and that is the low standard of our moral judgment. We manage to be contented with ourselves because of the poverty of our ideal. A sheep may look tolerably fair and clean against the greenness of the summer grass, but when the snow has fallen in virgin purity the sheep may be as a blot upon the hill. It is not the living creature that is different; it is the *background* that is different, and I want to ask you this straight question—*What is the background of life?* Is it the common standard of your class? Then you will never understand your errors. You are not worse than anybody else; you are as good as they are any day. But how that poor and shallow self-complacency is torn and tattered into a thousand shreds when the life which once accepted social values is set against the background of the Christ! Paul was proud of his moral standing once, for he could lift up his head with any Pharisee. But when Christ found him and made a man of him, the Pharisee became the chief of sinners. And it is always so when Christ comes in. We see the brightest and we see the worst. There is a heaven higher than our hope, and there is a hell deeper than we dreamed. Have you been awakened in any way like that? Are you profoundly dissatisfied with self? Have you had hours when you felt that in all the world there could be nobody quite so bad as you? Blessed be God for His convicting Spirit. It is better to feel *that* than to be satisfied. It is along that road, however dark, that the way lies for self-examination at the Communion Table.

Secret Faults

Cleanse thou me from secret faults.—Ps. 19:12

The secret faults of which the psalmist is speaking in this verse are the faults that are secret from even ourselves. They are the sins and failings in your life and mine of which we are unconscious. There are some faults we can keep secret from the world, and yet they are well known to those at home. The people we meet in the street may not suspect them, but our wives or mothers know them all too well. And there are other sins which a man may do in business so that his name smells rank among honorable dealers, yet the shadow of them may never touch his home nor the innocent faces of his adoring children. Such faults are secret beyond a certain circle. Love casts the mantle of her glorious silence around them. But it is not these of which the psalmist thinks when he cries, "Cleanse thou me from secret faults." He thinks of the faults and sins which in the sight of God we are committing, and yet we are ignorant of them and have never been awakened to them and are not conscious they are there at all.

Now that there are such faults in every one of us may be demonstrated along many lines. Think, for instance, how certain it becomes when we remember what we see in others. Is there anyone known to you, however good or beautiful, on whose faults or failings you could not put your finger? Is there any friend or lover or child or wife or minister whose weakness you have not long ago detected? They may not see it—it never obtrudes on them—they are quite unconscious that it is obvious to you. And so also as our neighbors move among us daily, and we see a hundred faults which they are blind to. Do not exempt yourself, I beg of you, from this general censure of humanity. You are bone of their bone, flesh of their flesh, born with their weakness, tempted with their sin. The very fact that all of us can see the mote that is in our brother's eye is proof that we have one in our own.

The certainty of such faults is proved again by our general ignorance of our own nature. There is not a man or woman whose life is not full of secret possibilities. Let the finger of love but touch a woman's heart, and you shall hardly know that woman by and by. Let motherhood come with all its infinite mystery, and she is enriched to the very heavens. Let a man be converted by the grace of God, as Paul was converted on the Damascus road, and life is expanded into undreamed-of fullness. We all surprise each other now and then, and now and then we all surprise ourselves—when love comes, or some great wave of emotion, or the sound of a trumpet and the call to battle. And if we believe in secret possibilities, on the basis of which Christ wrought from first to last, must we not also believe in secret sins? The fact is we should believe it instantly if it were not for the presence of self-love. Love thinketh no evil of the loved one, even when the loved one is oneself. And so in our secret virtues we believe, and in the hidden possibilities within us, but from our secret faults we turn away. That common attitude is intellectual cowardice. It is a man's first duty to face all the facts. To flatter other men is bad enough, but to flatter one's ownself is far more deadly. And therefore if you believe in hidden heights within you, I ask you also to believe in hidden depths and to cry as David cried, "Cleanse thou me from secret faults."

The exercise of a long-continued habit has a deadening power. There are sins which were not secret long ago, but habit and custom have made them secret now.

I well remember when I went to Dundee from the seclusion of my manse in Thurso, and how at first I found it hard to sleep at nights for the incessant noise of the railway and street. In Thurso, when night fell, the quiet was perfect. The countryside might have been wrapped in snow. There was no sound except the northern wind and sometimes the mystical calling of the sea. And then in the city there was the midnight traffic, and the jar and jolt and shrieking of the railway, and I would lie awake repeating, "Sleep no more, *Dundee* hath murdered sleep." All that lasted for a week or two, and then the clamorous voices became silent. And they died away and were no longer audible and never again disturbed the beatitude of rest. The noise was as loud as ever, and still the train rattled through the dark, but habit had made me oblivious to it all.

For good or for evil in this life of ours, habit is always busy doing that. Things that would wake us once and make us jump with fear are robbed of their power to disturb our slumber. And so the sins that long ago were open, and shocked us and made us blush to think of them, may have become with passing years our secret sins. You would have been very unhappy once, when day was over, if you had flung yourselves down upon a prayerless bed. And yet it may be that you do it *now* with never a thought that you are grieving God. You would have been miserable once and full of guilty shame had you been cruel, dishonest, or impure. And yet it may be that today you sin these sins without any inward unhappiness at all. My brother and sister, that is Satan's triumph—to take our open sins and make them secret: to take the faults that shamed us long ago and make us habituated and accustomed to them. When a man has ceased to be shamed and shocked by sin, when he does habitually what once he loathed and hated, let him beware for his immortal soul, for final impenitency crouches at the door. "Cleanse thou me, O Lord, from secret faults." They were not secret once in happy childhood. Then they distressed us and sent us out in misery, but they do not distress us for a moment now. So from the pressure of habit and of custom, touching us all into a certain hardness, we may be sure that we need to apply the psalmist's prayer to ourselves as well.

And may I say that among all our sins there are perhaps none more perilous than our secret sins. And they are perilous just because in them we have the preparation for our open falls. Our great sins are seldom momentary overthrows. They seldom reach us like bolts out of the blue. These dark and tragic falls that we all know are not isolated and independent things. They reach us by the hidden ways of darkness and out of the silent and interior life, so that on every hour of wreckage and disaster there is the pressure of our secret faults.

For every noble act you ever did, there was a conscious and an unconscious preparation. You were getting ready for it not only when you strove, you were getting ready when you never dreamed of it. By every virtue you clung to in the dark—by every beautiful thought you ever cherished—by the self-denials of each routine morning—you have been getting ready for your nobler hours. That is the road by which we reach our victories, and that is the road by which we reach our tragedies.

Our sudden overthrows, when character was forfeited, are never quite so sudden as we think. Through secret faults—through covetings unchecked—through lusts unbridled when they were still imaginations—a man goes out to his hours when peace is lost and the shame of the vanquished is written on his brow.

Professor Drummond, in his *Tropical Africa,* tells of the secret ravages of the white ants. He tells of their enormous powers of destruction and how insidiously and secretly they work. He tells how a man may be sitting in his hut, and may think of it as strong as on the day he built it, when suddenly he may discover that there is nothing around him but a shell. Silently the white ants have been at work eating out the heart of every beam: no one has seen them—no one has heard them toiling—no one has had any warning of their presence. And then in a moment comes the revelation when the very pillars of the house tremble, and the secret ravage is revealed.

"Cleanse thou me from secret faults—keep back thy servant from presumptuous sins." Answer that first prayer, our blessed Savior, and in it we shall have our answer to the second. For all those open shames of word and deed that we cannot remember without self-loathing are but the lurid flowering of that nightshade whose roots are in the secret of the heart.

In closing, I am eager to suggest to you that our secret sins have one peculiar benefit. Above all other sins which we commit, they lead us to feel our utter need of Christ. Let me make that plain by a simple illustration. If some beautiful garden that you love is only disfigured by a weed or two, it is quite within your power to pull those weeds out though they may be tough as crabgrass or as venomous as poison ivy. But if the soil is bad—filled through and through with seeds—tangled with root-stocks of pestilential things— then cleaning it out is quite another matter.

My brother and sister, when you come to think of it, that is like the garden of your heart. If all that needs to be rooted out are a few habits, then do it in God's name, for you have power to do it. But when you awake to the appalling certainty that down in your heart there is a world of sin, in that hour you realize your utter helplessness. Not what we know, but what we do not know, is the deepest cry of the human soul to Christ—that world unfathomed beneath the range of consciousness out of which spring adulteries and murders. You cannot reach that world which lies unseen, away deep down in your mysterious being, and yet unless it is reached and cleansed by somebody, you know there can never be victory for you. It is just there that Jesus Christ draws near. He is able to save *even to the uttermost*. He is able and willing this very day to work a radical cleansing within you.

Intimacy

The secret of the Lord is with them that fear him.—Ps. 25:14

When a man enjoys the friendship of the great, it is always considered an honorable thing. To have the confidence of famous people is a distinction of which everyone is proud. When people point to a man and say to you, "Do you see that man—he was the friend of Gladstone"; when we find ourselves in the company of one who enjoyed the intimacy of Carlyle, there is always a certain thrill in our hearts and a deepened interest in the happy person who enjoyed the freedom of familiar fellowship with those whose names are famous in the world. I noticed the other day in the newspapers the case of a lady who had died. What the facts were I do not recall, but I was impressed by one in particular. She had been the friend of Ruskin in her youth and had been honored with his close friendship, and every newspaper I got my hands on put that in large letters in the heading.

Now if that is so with great men, how much more will it be so with God! To be admitted to the confidence of God must be quite an incomparable honor. It is His hand that hath inspired the genius; it is His spirit that hath made the poet; it is He who hath quickened and kindled into greatness the mightiest upon the stage of history. And if it be honorable to be *their* confidant and move in the freedom of fellowship with them, how much more to be the confidant of God. That is the deep meaning of our text—"The secret of the Lord is with them that fear him." It is not the secret of His hidden counsel; it is the secret of His hidden heart. The psalmist tells us that there are certain people whom God delights to honor with His confidence and to whom He reveals Himself from day to day with a peculiar and delightful intimacy.

For those of us who believe on Jesus Christ as the perfect revelation of the Father, that selective freedom of God, if I may call it so, is abundantly confirmed and illustrated. There is no soul which Jesus will not save. There is no man whom Jesus does not love. There is no sheep crying in the wilderness whom the Shepherd will not leave His flock to rescue. Yet universal as His mercy is and stretching to the confines of humanity, Christ, like the Father whom He came to show, had His special and peculiar friendships. Out of the multitude who trusted Him, He chose twelve to be His special comrades. Out of the twelve He made a choice of three, and they were with Him when He was transfigured. And then out of the three He singled one who at the Supper lay upon His bosom and who has been known right down through the centuries as the disciple whom Jesus loved. Were there not fifty cottages where Jesus would have been an honored guest? Were there no sisters in Galilean villages to whom His coming would have been like heaven? And Jesus loved them all and blessed them all, yet was there one cottage that was doubly dear, and there was a brother and two sisters in it whom He loved in a special way. Broad is the love of Christ as the whole world—deep as our deepest need—it is high as our highest aspiration and as long as the enduring of eternity. Yet was the secret of the Lord with them that feared Him. He had His intimates and special confidants. There were certain men and certain women to whom He revealed the treasures of His heart.

Let me say in passing that this peculiar intimacy is always associated with the deepest reverence. Wherever we find it in the Christian centuries, one of its marks is an adoring awe. We have a proverb, known to all of you, that familiarity breeds contempt. We have another not less cynical, that no man is a hero to his servant. And the very fact that these proverbs live and move contemptuously through our common speech shows that they are not without foundation. Intimacy is not always a blessing. Sometimes it is sorely disappointing. There are men whose lives are like oil-paintings which look their finest from a little distance. But if that is so with men sometimes, never yet hath it been so with God. The closer the intimacy of a man with God, the deeper his adoration and his awe. Abraham was the friend of God, yet he was but dust and ashes in his own sight. Moses was drawn into His secret counsel, yet who was more devoutly reverent than Moses? John had looked into his Master's eyes, and lain at the Supper on his Master's bosom, "yet when I saw him," said that same disciple, "I fell at his feet as dead."

I well remember when I was first in Switzerland how we looked at the great Alps from afar off. And from that distance they were so sublime that one almost shrank from any nearer view. And yet when I spent a week embosomed by them with the glaciers reaching almost to the door, that vast sublimity was only deepened. They were not less wonderful when near at hand. They were a thousand times more wonderful and awful. There were voices whispering in these icy palaces which one had never heard from far away. And so when a man who sometimes was far off is brought nigh to God by the blood of Jesus Christ, he does not cease to reverence or adore. Always distrust the religion of a man who speaks to God as to a next-door neighbor. Always distrust that light familiarity with the Almighty Maker of the universe. To know Him best is to adore Him most. To have His secret is to worship Him. He who is closest to the throne is on his knees.

Nor can we justly quarrel with God because He exercises that selective freedom. It is the very thing which you and I are doing in the fulfillment of that life which is His gift. What is that life which you and I possess? What is it mystically, I mean, not chemically? The deepest truth of things is never chemical. The deepest truth of everything is mystical. And what is life, then, but the overflowing of the exhaustless fountain in the heavens? In Him was life, and the life was the light of men.

Now did you ever think how poor *our* life would be had we no freedom in our loves and friendships? Is it not just the genius of selection that makes one life richer than another? When everyone is kept at equal distance, life is a miserable and empty business. It lacks much of its music and charm. Don't we all have our chosen friends? Don't we have some who are our confidants? Don't we sometimes make the great discovery and in a moment recognize our own? We are like Jesus in that village street, caught in the rough pushing of the crowd, yet there was one touch unlike all others— *"Someone hath touched me."* Why is it that we are drawn to some people so unerringly and so effectually? And why to others, no matter how admirable, we never unbar the gateway of the heart? To me the meaning of it all is this, that life is interpenetrated with election, whether it be the life of man on earth, or the life of the Almighty in the heavens. Good unto *all* men is the Lord. He is the Lord God merciful and gracious. I believe in His great love to all the world which moved Him to send us His Son. Yet are there those whom He delights to know in all the freedom of a blessed intimacy. The secret of the Lord is with them that fear Him.

Now those confidants of God, if I may call them so, are never arbitrarily chosen. They are His friends because He wills it so, but they also become His friends by what they are. It is not always thus we make our friends. Our friendships are not always based on character. Often they take the line of least resistance, and sometimes they develop through a common jealousy or greed. But every friendship which is made with God is from the depths of character—the secret is with them *that fear Him*.

The note of the nightingale is never heard outside the borders of a certain area. You never hear it north of York. You never hear it west of the river Exe. You may take the eggs and have them hatched in Scotland and carry the fledglings to our Scottish woods, but never will the birds come north again to give us that wonderful music of the night. Outside a certain limit they are silent, and outside a certain limit God is silent. There are frontiers for the voice of heaven as there are for the voice of every singing bird. Only the frontiers are not geographical; they are moral and have to do with character. They are determined by what a man desires and by the deepest craving of his soul. The poorest peasant may know more of God than he who is a master of the sciences. The mystic cobbler may have such gleams of glory as put to shame the wisdom of the wise. For except we become as little children, we cannot even see the kingdom. Blessed are the pure in heart, for they shall *see* Him.

Put in another way that just means this, that we must wait on God if we would learn His secret. As the eyes of a servant wait upon her mistress, so, says the psalmist, must we wait on God. It is not by a hasty glance at an old masterpiece that you discern the wonder of the painting. When you confront a celebrated picture, the first feeling is often disappointment. It is only as you wait and watch and ponder, and quietly linger with revering gaze, that you detect its fullness and its depth and waken to the wonder of it all.

The farmers used to make merry with the poet Wordsworth when they saw him sitting hour by hour on some gray stone. Some of them thought he was an idle rascal, and more of them thought he was a little crazy. But Wordsworth was watching nature like a lover, and he was passive that he might catch her voice, and he waited on nature with such a splendid faithfulness that we are all his debtors to this hour.

A fickle man can never be a scholar, nor can he ever hope to be a saint. No secret that is rich is ever won without the reverence of assiduity. You must wait on Shakespeare and you must wait on science through a thousand struggling and laborious days if you are ever to read the mystic scroll they carry or wrest from it the message it conveys. No self-respecting man reveals his deepest to the chance visitor or to the casual comer. He keeps his best for those who love his company and who rejoice to be with him day by day. And so the secret of the Lord is kept—and kept forever—from the casual comer. The secret is with them that fear Him.

In closing I want you to remember that this secret is given for large issues. It is not bestowed for personal enjoyment so much as for the service of mankind. There are certain plants, like that exquisite child of the spring the woodsorrel, to which God has given two different kinds of flowers. The one is the white flower which we all love, but the other is hidden away beneath the leaves. It has no beauty that we should desire it, nor any petals which unfold in April, yet in that secret flower which you have never noticed there lies the beauty of another spring. So is it with the secret of the Lord, for it is not showy like a fair corolla, yet it gives to every life that knows it a certain gracious and beautiful fertility. The secret of the sun is in the *coal*, and it is that secret which makes the coal a blessing. It warms our dwellings and drives our engine wheels because the secret of the sun is there. And if for coal, so ugly and defiling, the secret of the sunshine can do *that*, who can tell what blessing may not radiate from him who has the secret of the Lord? It will not reveal to him tomorrow's story. It will not make him nastily infallible. He will be humble as a little child set in a world that is aflame with glory. But knowing God with such peculiar intimacy, for him tomorrow will be robbed of terror and in the weariest as in the roughest day there will be direction and repose.

Waiting Upon God

I wait on thee.—Psalm 25:21

In the great biblical thought of waiting upon God there are several interwoven strands of meaning, and it is well to try to distinguish some of these that we may better grasp the importance of the term.

The first meaning, nestling at the heart of it and never absent from the mind of any writer, is the concept of dependence. As the baby waits upon its mother for without its mother it will die; as the anguished patient waits upon the surgeon for in the skill of the surgeon is the hope of life, so when one is said to wait on God there is implied an entire dependence upon Him. There is a sense, in biblical phraseology, in which this waiting is a universal thing. "The eyes of all things living wait on thee." The bird that sings, the beast that hunts its prey— all of them are waiting upon God. But such an inescapable dependence does not bring the thought to its full blossoming. *That* demands a dependence which is conscious. It is when we realize, however dimly, that in Him we live and move and have our being, it is when we waken to the mysterious certainty that we all hang on God for every heartbeat—it is only then the word comes to its fullness in the deep usage of the Scriptures, and man is said to be waiting upon God.

Another strand of meaning in the word takes us into the region of obedience. *To wait on* is another term for service. The man who serves us when we sit down at the table and who is there just to supply our wants, we still distinguish by the name of *waiter.* When a prime minister waits upon the king, that is not an idle sauntering business. It is part of the service to which he has been called, a service which demands his highest energies. And so when a man is said to wait on God, it is not a negation of activity, for the thought of service runs right through the term. We wait on God whenever we help a brother and do it lovingly for Jesus' sake. We wait on God when we teach our little class or climb the stairs to cheer some lonely soul. The servant in the kitchen waits on God when for His sake she does her duty faithfully. The mistress in the living room waits on God when for His sake she is a lady to her servants. We are all apt to forget that and to narrow down these fine old Bible words. We are prone to limit the great thought of waiting to the single region of devotion. But the root idea of it is not devotion. The root idea is simple, quiet obedience. And what doth the Lord thy God require of thee but to obey?

Another of the interwoven strands is *love:* in true waiting that is invariably present. As love is the source of all the highest work, so is it the spring of all the finest waiting. Jacob waited for Rachel seven years, and the years were as a day or two to Jacob because of the great love he had for her. What makes the mother wait upon her child and rise from her pillow when she hears it cry? What makes her wait on it with tireless patience when it frets or tosses with fever? She may be only a frail and sickly woman, but she never wearies of waiting on her child, and the secret of it is a mother's love. Love beareth all things and endureth all things. Love can wait with a patience all her own. Love can achieve miracles of waiting, as many a young engaged couple knows. And that is why, if we are ever to wait nobly, in the teeth of all our natural impatience, we must be taught to love the Lord our God. It must have been very hard in the times of the older covenant for the common man to wait on God, for God seemed very far away then, and clouds and darkness were about His throne. But now, under the new covenant and by the revealing grace of the Redeemer, it is within the reach and compass of us all. If we hold to it that "God so loved the world," if we say believingly "Our Father," love to God, once so supremely difficult, is in the range of the ordinary heart. And, lovingly, we can wait as Jacob waited, and as the mother waits upon her child, with a service that knows no weariness at all.

There is only one other strand woven in the word and that is the strand of eager, tense expectancy. To wait on, in a hundred spheres of life, is eagerly and tensely to expect. You see that in the dumb creatures—

watch the dog waiting on his master. Is the master going to give him a bit of food? Is he going to throw that stick into the stream? You see that in any court of law when the accused waits on the verdict or the judge with an expectancy so tense that it is painful. Now apply that to the realm of prayer and how it illuminates the matter! To wait on God is not just to pray to God, for many pray and never expect an answer. To wait on God is to pray with tense expectancy that the prayer we offer will be answered, for He is the answerer of prayer. All prayer is not waiting upon God in the full and highest sense of the Old Testament. For a man may rise from his knees and forget the thing he prayed for and fail to keep on the lookout for an answer. Only when we pray and pray believingly, and climb the watchtower to see the answer coming, do we reach the fullness of that fine old term *waiting upon God*.

Beholding and Inquiring

One thing have I desired of the Lord, that will I seek after; that I may dwell in the house of the Lord all the days of my life, to behold the beauty of the Lord, and to inquire in his temple.—Ps. 27:4

In this verse, so full of riches, we have the spiritual ambition of the psalmist, and the notable thing is how his single purpose resolves itself into two parts. Just as the single seeds of many plants separate themselves out into two seed-leaves, and just as the sunshine, that most fruitful unity, breaks up, to put it roughly, into light and heat, so the spiritual ambition of the psalmist, of which he is speaking in this verse, reveals itself under two different aspects. One thing he desires of the Lord, and then that one thing shows itself as two things. He yearns to behold the beauty of the Lord and to inquire in His holy temple. And from this we gather that beholding and inquiring are but different aspects of one life, vitally interwoven with each other. They are not contrary nor contradictory like day and night or cold and heat. They are related elements in every life that is hungering and thirsting after God. All the experiences of the soul in its inward rest and never-ending searching may be summed up in beholding and inquiring.

One notes, first of all, how spiritual life runs down its roots into beholding. "We beheld his glory, full of grace and truth." "Behold the Lamb of God." There are three desires in the heart of every Christian; one is to run his course with honor. The second is to endure, without embittering, the bitterest that life can bring. The third and deepest of the three is this, to be always growing more like the Master in inward character and outward conduct.

Now tell me, what is the Gospel way towards the achievement of these deep desires? It is not speculation nor philosophy. It is a way within the reach of every man. To run with honor, to endure the worst, to be changed into the likeness of the Lord—all of them are based upon beholding. "Let us run with patience the race that is set before us, *looking* unto Jesus." "He endured as *seeing* him who is invisible." "We all with open face *beholding* as in a glass the glory of the Lord, are changed into the same image."

David was not a dreamer. He did not covet a temple-life of idleness. He wanted to run well and to endure and to be transformed into a glowing spirit. That was why, beset by sin, he cried with all the passion of his heart, "One thing have I desired—to behold."

The next suggestion of the words is this, that beholding is always followed by inquiring. We see that in every sphere of life and not only in the region of the spirit. Think, for instance, of the stars as they shone down on ancient man. For ages, in those dim and distant days, man must have been contented with beholding. But just because he was man, made in the image of God, he could not rest in any mere beholding. He began to wonder, and wondering *inquired*. What were these lamps glowing in the heavens? Who kindled them? Who kept them burning? Did they have influence on human life? Did they foretell the destinies of mortals? So man, confronted with the stars of heaven, first beheld the beauty of the Lord and then inquired in His holy temple.

Or, again, think of the world of nature that lies around us in its beauty. Touched with the finger of God, man has *beheld* that beauty in a way no beast has ever done. No dumb creature has any sense of beauty. Scenery makes no difference to it. The oxen, knee-deep in the pasturage, never lift their eyes up to the hills. One great difference between man and beast is this, that man, and man alone in this creation, has beheld the beauty of the Lord. The sunlight as it glances on the sea—the flowers that make beautiful the meadow—the haunting mystery of the deep forest—the lake, the lights and shadows of the glen—such things have touched the heart of man and moved him and thrilled him into song in a way no dumb creature ever knew. Just because man is man one thing is true of him—he beholds the beauty of the Lord. But just because man is man and not a beast, he never can rest content with mere beholding. There is something in him, the breath of his Creator, impelling him to ever-deepening wonder until at last in that wonder he *inquires.* "Hath the rain a father, or who hath begotten the drops of dew? Out of whose womb came the ice? and the hoary frost of heaven, who hath gendered it" (Job 38:28, 29)? So science is born, and all theology, and growing insight into the ways of God—because beholding is followed by inquiring.

There is one other relationship to mention, for without any question David knew it. The gladness of the spiritual life is that its deepest inquiries are answered by beholding. Let any man inquire after God, for instance, eager to know what kind of God He is, longing to be assured that He is Love so that He may be absolutely trusted—well, there are many ways that such a man may take in the hope of answering that deepest of all questions. He may examine the arguments for God, or he may read biography or history; he may turn to the reasonings of philosophy, or rely on the pronouncements of the Scripture. But, my dear reader, there is another way—it is what the Bible calls a new and living way: he can *behold* the beauty of our Lord. He can behold His love and carry it up to heaven and say, "That love of Jesus is the love of God." He can behold His care for every separate soul and lift that up to the heart upon the throne. He can behold His loyalty to His friends and His pardoning mercy for the guiltiest sinner, and then he can say, *"God is just like that."* Do that, and what a difference it makes. God is no longer cold and unconcerned. He is love. He actually cares. He will never do His children any harm. "We beheld His glory, full of grace and truth, the glory of the only-begotten of the Father." The agonized inquiries of the heart are answered—by beholding.

The Quality of Courage

Be of good courage, and he shall strengthen thine heart.—Ps. 27:14

There are three qualities, says Emerson in a familiar essay, which attract the wonder and reverence of mankind. The first is disinterestedness, the second is practical power, and the third is courage. Every mythology has its Hercules. Every history its Wallace or its Cid. There is nothing that men will not forgive to one who has exhibited conspicuous gallantry. Even the dumb animals are ranked by us according to their possession of this quality, the bravest being nature's aristocracy. There are people who make a joke of truth, but there are no people who make a joke of courage. The love of it, from Orient to Occident, is the touch of nature which makes the whole world kin. And that is why war will never cease to fascinate in spite of all proofs of its illogicality, because there is in war a matchless stage for the display of courage.

Nor can we wonder at this admiration when we remember the universal need of courage. There is no lot, no rank, no occupation, in which one of the first requirements is not fortitude.

When we are young we admire the showy virtues, and we put the emphasis upon the brilliant gifts. We are all enamored of what is glittering then, and we think that life is to grow great that way. But as the years roll on and life unfolds itself and we look on some who rise and some who fall, we come to revise our estimates a little. Then we discover that a certain doggedness is far more likely to succeed than brilliance. Then we discover that cleverness means much, but the courage which can persist means more. Then we discover what the master meant when at the close of the long years of toil, he said, Well done, *not* good and brilliant, but Well done, thou good and faithful servant.

Courage is needed by the mother in the home; it is needed by the young man in the office. Courage is needed for the hills of youth and for the dusty levels of our middle age. There is a courage peculiar to the pulpit, and another peculiar to the football field, and another peculiar to that darkened chamber where the head is throbbing and the lips are parched.

Let a man have all the talents without courage, and he will accomplish little in the world. Let a man have the one talent and a courageous heart, and no one can tell what things he may not do. Probably when the stories of our lives are written, our gifts will be found less diverse than we thought, and it will be seen that what set us each apart is the distinguishing quality of courage.

Courage is not an isolated virtue so much as the ground and basis of the virtues. It is like the tingling of health in a man's body which makes itself felt in every activity.

I cannot help but wonder at electric current. It drives an engine; it lights the house in the evening; it rings a bell. One single energy, and yet that single energy shows itself powerful in all these different forces, and so are the forces which God has given a man fed by the single energy of courage.

If could we get deep enough down among our vices, we would probably find they had a common source. Somewhere deep down in the unfathomed darkness there is one spark of hell that sets them all afire. So with our virtues and all that makes us men, there is one spirit that kindles and sustains them, and that enkindling energy is fortitude. For we never can be patient without courage and without courage we never can be pure. It calls for a little courage to be truthful, and it calls for a little courage to be kind. And sometimes it takes a great deal of courage just to say what we ought to say, and sometimes it takes more courage to say nothing.

My brother, in this strange life of ours, never forget that fortitude is victory. There is no final failure for the man who can say I am the master of my fate. Never to tremble at the looming shadow, never to shrink from the unwelcome duty, never to despair when things seem hopeless, is the one road to the music and the crown.

Do you know the commonest command in Scripture? The commonest command in Scripture is *Fear not*. Times without number in the Word of God it rings out upon us, Thou shalt not be afraid. For courage is at the roots of life, and it is the soil in which every virtue flourishes; it is no isolated or independent grace, but is the nursing mother of them all.

Now if this is so, it is at once apparent that the truest courage is an unobtrusive thing. There is nothing spectacular or scenical about it; it sounds no trumpet before it in the streets. I can agree there come moments in some lives when courage flashes into dramatic splendor. When the soldier kneels to save a wounded comrade—when the fireman risks his life to save a child—there is something in that which strangely moves the heart. That is the courage which thrills, and it is splendid, but the courage which thrills is rarely that which tells. No voices cheer it; no papers give its story; no medals reach it from any millionaire. It moves in the shadow of our dreary streets and dwells in the shelter of our humble homes and carries in a quiet and happy and victorious way the crosses which every morning brings. I suppose there was never anyone on earth quite so courageous as our Savior Jesus Christ. Yet give a pagan that life of His to read, and I do not think he would say, How brave He was! He would say, How loving He was—how infinitely patient—how radiantly peaceful in the teeth of calumny; yet love and patience and radiance and peace were but His matchless courage in disguise. The courage which tells is not the courage which clamors. The courage which tells is the courage which is quiet. It sounds no trumpet; does not strive nor cry; never lifts up its voice in any street. It does things when it feels least like them, anoints the head for every hour of fasting, comes to the cross in such a smiling manner that others scarce suspect the cross is there.

We see also along this line a thought that courage is different from insensibility. Courage is not the absence of fear; courage is the conquest of fear. One man, in some hour of peril, may feel that his heart is beating like a sledgehammer. Another, in an hour precisely similar, may scarcely be conscious of a quickened pulse. And yet the former may be the braver man if he does resolutely what the hour demands of him, for he has felt what the other never felt and feeling it, has brought it to subjection.

I often think of that fine old story of Henry IV, King of France. At the siege of Cahors, when he was young and in arms, his body began to tremble like an aspen. And he cried to his body so that all who were near him heard, "Vile carcass," he cried, "thou tremblest, but thou wouldst tremble worse if thou but knew where I am going to take thee in a moment." So saying, with a body trembling like an aspen, he flung himself into the thickest of the fight.

I have heard of two young men who had a cliff to scale, and one of them was very white around the cheeks. And the other looked at him and with a sneer said, "Why, I believe you are afraid."

"Yes," he replied, "I *am* afraid, and if you were half as afraid as I am, *you'd go home.*"

The fact is, that as you rise in being you rise in the nobility of courage. It is those who are capable of being most afraid who are capable of being most courageous. And that is why the courage of a woman is something loftier than that of any beast, for she has a heart that by the touch of God has been made sensitive to every shadow. You will never fathom the bravery of Christ unless you bear in mind that Christ was sinless. For sin is always coarsening and deadening—"it hardens all within and petrifies the feeling." And it is when we think that Jesus Christ was sinless, and being sinless was exquisitely sensitive, that we come to realize the matchless fortitude that carried Him without a falter to the cross.

I beg of you not for one moment to believe that because you feel afraid you are a coward. Moses and Paul and Jesus Christ Himself knew in its bitterness the shrinking of the flesh. Courage is not the absence of dismay; courage is the conquest of dismay. It is how a man deals and grapples with his trembling that makes the difference between strong and weak.

It is one of the happy things, too, in human life, that courage grows easier as life advances. If we are living well and doing our work faithfully, we grow more equal to our problem with the years. A child begins by fearing almost everything because it begins by knowing almost nothing. Every shadow may be a horrid specter and every dark room is full of ghosts. But the years pass and we enter many a shadow, and the abhorred specters are not there, and so our childish terrors pass away.

I knew an officer who in the thick of battle was reckoned among the bravest of the brave, and yet that man would blanch like any girl if he found himself in the presence of diphtheria. And I know scores of ministers within our city who would never think twice of visiting a diphtheria patient, and yet I am certain they would be ghastly spectacles within the fighting lines of Adrianople. The fact is that, far more than we imagine, courage is a result of habit. The soldier who trembled in his first battle will enter his twentieth without a thought.

And so God is kind to us as life advances, and the fiery ardors of our youth decay for with ripening knowledge some things become harder, but it does not become harder to be brave. The dash is gone. The youthful fire is gone. We are not heroic as at twenty-one. The old man cannot storm the heights of life with the reckless enthusiasm of the cadet. But he has seen such goodness of the Lord to him and had such sustainment in trial and difficulty, that he can lift up his heart and go forward gently where youth would despair in tragedy.

There are two open secrets of true courage to which I would call attention as I close, and one of them is self-forgetfulness. Just as the open secret of all happiness is never to think of happiness at all but to forget it and do our duty quietly and take the longer road that leads through Galilee, so the open secret of all courage is to forget there is such a thing as courage in the gladness and the glow of an ideal.

When David fought with the lion and the bear, he never thought of the lion and the bear. He only remembered that he was a shepherd, and that his duty was to guard the sheep. So doing his duty in brave forgetfulness, courage came to him like a bird upon the wing and sang its morning music in his heart.

When Captain John Brown, that fine American hero, was asked why others were conquered by his regiment, "Well," he replied, after a moment's thought, "I suppose it is because they lacked a cause." They had nothing to fight for that was worth a stroke, and having nothing to fight for or to die for, it followed "as the night the day" that they were ineffectual in battle.

The most timid creature will face tremendous odds when danger threatens its defenseless offspring. The Roman slave-girl will throw herself to martyrdom when she is animated by the faith of Christ. The woman, in her self-forgetful love for the infant that she has nursed at her bosom, will dare to starve and even dare to die. That is why love is such a nurse of courage, and that is where love is different from passion. For passion

is selfish and seeks its own delight and will ruin another if it is only grat-
ified. But love is unselfish and seeketh not her own and hopeth all things
and believeth all things, and like John Brown's regiment is always ready
because for the battle it never lacks a cause.

Desdemona, in a play of Shakespeare, is

> A maiden never bold
> Of spirit so still and quiet that her motion
> Blushed at herself,

yet standing at Othello's side, Desdemona confronts her father and her
world, and she confronts them because she loves Othello so.

Love for her fledgling makes the wild bird brave. Love for her baby
makes the mother brave. And now comes Christ, and by His life and
death writes that word *love* upon the gate of heaven. And so He has
made it possible for thousands, who otherwise would have faltered in
the shadow, to pluck up heart again and play the man and to be strong
and of good courage by the way.

The other secret of true courage is a strong and overmastering sense
of God. When you get deep enough, I think you always find that in
every life that has been brave. When Peter was separated from his Lord
for a while, then he denied Him with a fisherman's curses. With no
one near but the soldiers and the servants, he was as a reed shaken with
the wind.

But when the Lord came in and looked on Peter, Peter went out
into the night and wept; and so repentant, became a man again. When
I can go to my labors saying God is with me—when I can lie on my
sickbed saying God is here—when I can meet my difficulties saying,
This is God—when dying I can whisper He is mine—then in communion with that power and goodness I am no longer tossed and tem-
pest-driven, but in the storm and shadow I am strong. It is that
conviction Jesus Christ has brought to the weakest heart in the most
dreary street. Prophets and psalmists might believe it once, but the
poorest soul can believe it now.

To be in communion with God through Jesus Christ—to know that
He is ours and we are His—is the victory which overcomes the world.
Such courage is not based on fancied power. It is based on the absolute
and the eternal. It is not kindled by any glow of anger. It is kindled

and kept by the eternal spirit. So can the weakest dare to stand alone, and dare to live alone, and dare to die alone, saying *The best of all is, God is with us.*

Known in Adversities

Thou hast known my soul in adversities.—Ps. 31:7

One great comfort of assurance in this verse is that such knowledge is always very thorough. When someone has known us in adversities, then he has known us as we really are.

There is a sonnet by Blanco White, familiar to all the lovers of the beautiful, in which he develops the thought that but for the night, we should never know the stars. And so there is a very real sense in which we may say we never know a life till we have seen it in the darkness of adversity. When the sun is warm and all the leaves are green, you can scarcely see the cottage in the forest. But when the storm of winter sweeps the leaves away, then at last you see it as it is. It may be stronger than you ever thought, or it may be more battered and decayed, but always the winter shows it as it is.

Indeed, the revealing power of adversity strips the summer covering away. It shows us not in the setting of our circumstance, but as we are in naked reality. And therefore one who has known us in adversities, and been at our side in sorrow and calamity, knows us with an intimacy that probably nothing else can ever give. That is why the knowledge of a doctor is often more searching than that of any friend. That is why the knowledge of a wife often reaches to an unrivaled intimacy, for she has known her husband not only when all was well with him and when the sun was shining on his head, but when his heart was weary and his body sick and all his hopes seemed crumbled into dust.

It was a great comfort to the psalmist also that the Lord had pierced through every disguise. That is why he uses the word *soul*: "Thou hast known my soul in adversities." To the Hebrew, more simply than to us, that word "soul" just meant the real self. There was nothing theological about it. It was a common word in common use. And what the psalmist deeply felt was this: the knowledge of God had pierced through all disguises and known him in the secret of his being.

There are few things more beautiful in life than the way in which men and women hide their sorrows. On the street and in the shops there is a quiet heroism as great as any on the battlefield. You may meet a person in frequent conversation, yet all the time and unknown to you, some sorrow may be lying at his heart. How often a mother, when she is worn and ill, struggles bravely to hide it from her family. How often a husband, deep in business difficulties, struggles to keep it hidden from those at home. How often a minister, called from a scene of death which may mean for him the end of a friendship, has to go to a marriage and be happy there as if there were not a sorrow in the world. Talk of the disguises of hypocrisy! They are nothing to the disguises of the brave—those cheerful looks, that quiet and patient work, when the heart within is heavy as a stone. That Spartan youth who kept a smiling face while the fox was gnawing away at him has his fellows in every community.

But Thou hast known my soul in adversity. That was the joy and comfort of the psalmist. There was one eye that pierced through all concealment, and that was the eye of an all-pitying God. Others had known his outward behavior for in trials there are many eyes upon us. Others had heard his words and seen his actions and wondered at the courage in his bearing. But only God had read the secret story and seen how utterly desolate he was and known how often, in spite of all appearances, he had been plunged into profound despair.

There is a point where human knowledge ceases and beyond which human sympathy is powerless. It pierces deep if it is genuine, but there are depths to which it cannot pierce. And it was just there, in the region of his soul, that the psalmist felt that there was One who knew him and would never leave him nor forsake him. He felt it in the sustainment he received. He felt it in the strength that was bestowed upon him. He felt it in the peace that rested on him, a peace such as the world could never give. And so when the sun shone on him again, as sooner or later it does on all of us, he took his pen and wrote in gratitude, "Thou hast known my soul in adversities."

There was one other comfort for the psalmist at which our text hints unobscurely. He had been awakened through the knowledge that he speaks of to the infinite condescension of God's love.

A well-known German religious writer who has brought comfort to multitudes of mourners tells us how once he had a visit from a friend who was in great distress. This friend had once been a very wealthy man, and now he had fallen upon evil days, and that very morning one of his old companions had passed him without recognition on the street. Then Gotthold, for such was the writer's name, took him by the hand and, pointing upward, said, "Thou hast known my soul in adversities."

It is one of the sayings of the moralist that the world courts prosperity and shuns adversity. There are rats in every circle of society who all hasten to leave the sinking ship. But what the psalmist had awakened to was this: the eternal God, who was his refuge, had known him and acknowledged him and talked with him when his fortunes were at their very blackest. Nothing but love could explain the condescension. He had found in God a friend who was unfailing. "If I ascend into heaven thou art there; if I make my bed in hell thou art there." So was the world made ready for the Savior who, when other helpers fail and comforts flee, never deserts us, never is ashamed of us, never leaves us to face the worst alone.

The Reach of His Faithfulness

Thy faithfulness reacheth unto the clouds.—Ps. 36:5

The faithfulness of God is one of the strong truths of the Old Testament. It is one distinction of the Jewish faith, in contrast with the ancient pagan faiths. Pagan gods were not generally faithful whether in Babylon or Greece. They were immoral, careless of their promises regardless of their pledged word. And the wonderful thing about the Jewish faith was that the God of the Jews was always faithful both to His covenant and to His children.

Such a magnificent and upholding thought sprang not only from personal experience, it was interwoven with the fact that the Jewish religion was historical. The Jew could look backward over the tracts of time and discover there the faithfulness of God in a way the brief life might never show. As he recalled the story of the past, of Abraham traveling to the promised land, of the slaves in Egypt rescued from their slavery, of the desert pilgrimage of forty years, one thing that was stamped upon his heart, never to be erased by any finger, was that Jehovah was a faithful God.

That thought sustained the psalmist, and with him, all the saints of the old covenant. In the Old Testament the word "faith" is rare, but the word "faithfulness" occurs a score of times. And here the psalmist, in his poetic way, and like Jesus, drawing his images from nature, says, "Thy faithfulness reacheth *to the clouds.*"

One thinks, for instance, of the clouds of Scripture in such a passage as the Ascension story. When our Lord ascended to the Father, a cloud received Him from the disciples' sight (Acts 1:9). That was a

501

lonesome and desolating hour when the cloud wrapped around Him and He was gone. They had loved Him so and leaned upon Him so that I take it they were well-nigh broken-hearted. Then the days went on, and they discovered that the engulfing cloud was not the end of everything. It, too, was touched by the faithfulness of heaven. He had promised to be with them always, and He was faithful to that promise still. He had said, "I will manifest Myself to you," and that promised word was verified. The cloud had come and engulfed their Lord, and they thought the sweet companionship was over. But His faithfulness reached unto the clouds.

Again, one thinks of the clouds of history, for history has its dark and cloudy days. For instance, what a cloudy day that was when the Jews were carried off to Babylon. Exiled to a distant, heathen land, they thought that God had forgotten to be gracious. They said: "My way is hidden from the Lord, and my judgment is passed over from my God." It was not the hardship of exile that confounded them. It was that God seemed to have broken His covenant and had been found unfaithful to His promises. By the waters of Babylon they sat and wept. They hung their harps upon the willow trees. How could they sing of the faithfulness of God when He had let them go into captivity?

And yet the day was coming when the instructed heart would rise to another view of that captivity and say: "Thy faithfulness reacheth to the clouds." Memory became illuminative. Things lost grew doubly precious. Distance helped them to a clearer vision of what sin was and what God was. And then across that dark and cloudy day came the ringing of prophetic voices with the message of ransom and return (Is. 35). They were not forgotten. They were not rejected. Their way was not passed over by their God. Sunny days did not exhaust His faithfulness. It reached even to the clouds. And of how many a dark day of history (as when we revert in thought to the World Wars) can we set to our seal that this is true!

Again, one thinks how this great truth applies to the clouds that hang over our human lives. What multitudes can say, in an adoring gratitude, "Thy faithfulness hath reached unto the clouds"? Just as in every life are days of sunshine when the sky is blue and all the birds are singing, when every wind blows from where the Lord is and when we feel it is good to be alive, so in every life are shadowed days when the sun withdraws its shining for a season and the clouds return after the rain. It may be a time of trouble in the family or of great anxiety in business, the time when health is showing signs of failing or when the chair is empty and the grave is full. It may be the time when all that a man has lived for seems washed away like a castle in the sand. It may be the day of unexpected poverty.

How unlooked for often are the clouds of life. They gather swiftly like some tropical thunderstorm. We confidently expect a cloudless day, and before evening the sky is darkened. And yet what multitudes of folk as they look backward, with much experience in life, can take our text and in quiet adoring gratitude claim it as the truth of their experience. *You* thought (don't you remember thinking?) that God had quite forgotten to be gracious. Possibly you were tempted to deny Him or secretly to doubt His care for you. But now, looking back upon it all, you have another vision and another certainty, just as the experienced psalmist had. If there are any of those who read these lines for whom *this* is the dark and cloudy day, who are anxious and distressed, who say in the morning, "Would God that it were evening"—have faith. Do not despair. The hour is nearer than you think when you also will say with David, "Thy faithfulness reacheth *to the clouds.*"

The New Song

He hath put a new song in my mouth.—Ps. 40:3

When anybody sings it is an outward token of an inward happiness. Despondent people very seldom sing. When a man sings as he walks the country road it means that he has a heart of peace. When he sings while he is dressing in the morning, it means that he gladly accepts another day. And wherever Christianity has come, with its liberating and uplifting power, it has carried with it this note of singing gladness. The Stoic boasts, when life is harsh and cruel, that his head is "bloody but unbowed." Paul and Silas did far more than that; they sang praises in the jail at midnight. Their religion was an exhilarating business as all true religion ought to be. They had not only peace in believing; they had *joy*.

Now if you listen to anyone singing at his work you will catch the strain of an old familiar melody. Nobody dreams of practicing new songs when he is walking along a country road. Yet the psalmist, thinking of life's highways and of daily work and undistinguished mornings, says that God has put a *new* song in his mouth. You see, a song may be very old, and yet to *us* it may be very new. It may break on us with all the charm of novelty though it has come ringing down the ages. It may be like the coming of the spring which is always new and wonderful to us though every vanished year has had its spring. Generally, the new songs which God gives have come echoing down the corridors of time. Men sang them long ago in days that carry the memories of history. But when they come to *us*, and touch our hearts in fresh, vivid personal experience, they are as new as the wonder of the springtime.

One sees that very clearly with the Bible which is the grand sweet song of heaven for us. No mere critic can ever grasp the Bible any more than he can grasp the magnificence of Shakespeare. Now the Bible is a book for childhood. It has stories which enthrall the childish heart. There is the story of David and Goliath in it and of Daniel in the den of lions. And then comes life with all its changing years, with its lights and shadows and sufferings and joys, and what a new song the Bible is to us! The strange thing is it is an old, old song. It is "the song our mothers sang." It is the song that kindled the great heart of Knox and satisfied Sir Walter Scott on his deathbed. Yet when our heart is deepened and our eyes are opened by sin and suffering and loneliness and mercy, a new song is put into our mouth.

We see that this is how God deals with us when we think of the old sweet song of love. For all love is of God, and he that dwelleth in love dwelleth in Him. Every spring of love in earthly valleys flows from the heavenly fountain. Every spark of love in human breasts is a spark of the eternal fire. The love of home, of parentage and childhood, not less than "the way of a man with a maid," are but the ocean of eternal love creeping into the crannies of the shore. Now the song of love has gone echoing through the world since the first lovers gathered in the gloaming. Joseph knew to its depths the love of fatherhood. Yet when love indwells any human heart, its song is as new as the melody of spring, though since the dawn of time spring has sung its carol. Whenever a heart loves, God puts a new song into the mouth. No love song is a repetition, though the same things have been said a thousand times. And just because God has set His love on us, His old love songs are all new to us when first in the secret of our souls we hear them. God does not need to write new love songs. The old, old love song is the best. The heart is crying, "Tell me the old, old story." But the wonderful thing is that when we hear it, old though it is to *us*, it is so thrilling that a new song is put into our mouth.

I notice, lastly, that the newness of the song runs down to the mystery of individuality. The song is new just because we are new. We hear much today of mass production. It is because of mass production things are cheap. Had God made humanity by mass production, then human souls would have been cheap. But the very fact that we are individuals and that no two are alike in the whole world is a token that we were never made that way. No two faces are ever just the same; no two temptations ever quite alike; no two joys without their subtle difference; no two heart-breaks indistinguishable—it is this element of newness in the separate life of every man and woman that takes the old song and makes it new. The song was sung by David, but David and you were never standardized. It may be sung by multitudes in heaven, but your experience of mercy is your own. And so, when God in His redeeming love puts the old sweet song of grace upon your lips, the song is new—it is your very own—it seems as if no one else had ever sung it.

The Thirst for God

My soul thirsteth for God.—Ps. 42:2

When the psalmist wrote this he was a fugitive in hiding somewhere across Jordan. He had been driven out by rebellion from Jerusalem, which is the city of the living God. To you and me, rich in the truth of Christ, that would not make God seem far away. And doubtless the psalmist also had been taught that Jehovah was the God of the whole earth. Yet with an intensity of feeling which we of the New Covenant are strangers to, he associated Jehovah with locality. He felt that to be distant from the Holy City was somehow to be distant from his Deity. And so, in a great sense of loneliness and in a thirsty land where no waters were, he cried out, "My soul thirsteth for the living God."

But when a poet speaks out of a burning heart, he always speaks more wisely than he realizes. When the soul is true to its own prompting, it is true to generations yet unborn. In the exact sciences you say a thing, and it keeps forever the measure of its origin. But when an inspired poet says a thing, it endlessly transcends its origin. For science utters only what it knows, but poetry utters what it feels, and in the genuine utterance of feeling there is always the element of immortality. No one worries about the atoms of Lucretius, but the music of Lucretius is not dead. No one feeds upon the Schoolmen now, but thousands are feeding upon Dante. And the psalmist may have been utterly astray in his measurements of the sun and stars, but taught of God, he never was astray in the more wonderful universe of the soul. That is why we can take his words and strip them of all reference to locality, or there is not one of us, whatever his circumstances, who is not an exile beyond Jordan and thirsting for the living God.

Now it seems to me that such spiritual thirst involves the ultimate certainty of God. It is an assurance that is never antiquated, an argument that never fails. I thirst for water, and from a thousand hills I hear the music of the Highland streams. I thirst for happiness, and in the universe I find the sunshine and the love of children. *I thirst for God—* and to me it seems incredible that the universe should reverse its order now, providing liberally for every lesser craving but not for the sublimest of them all. I don't think, if such had been the case, that Christ would have said, "Seek, and ye shall find." For then we should have sought the lesser things and found them to our heart's content, but when we sought the greatest things of all, would have been hounded empty from the door.

That is why the psalmist also said, "The fool hath said in his heart there is no God." But there are men who have said that out of aching hearts and ruined homes. They have said it when love had proved itself a treachery. For sometimes the seeming cruelty of things, and the swift blows that shatter and make desolate, have blotted out even from devout hearts the vision of the Father for a little. God never calls these broken children fools. He knows our frame and remembers we are dust. He is slow to anger and of great compassion, and He will shine upon these shadowed lives again. But the fool hath said in his *heart* there is no God. He scorns the verdict of his deepest being. He believes his senses which are always tricking him. He doesn't have the courage to believe his soul. A man may say in his *mind* "There is no God," and God may forgive him and have mercy on him. But only a fool can say it in his *heart.*

This thirst for God is sometimes very feeble, though I question if it ever wholly dies. You may live with a man for months, perhaps for years, and never light on that craving of his heart. But far away in the ranches of the West there are rough men who were cradled in our Scottish glens, and you might live with them for months, perhaps years, and never learn that they remembered home. But some evening there will come a strain of music—some song or melody—and on that reckless company there falls a quietness and they cannot look into each other's eyes just then: and *then* it doesn't take a prophet to discover that the hunger for the homeland is not dead.

There are feelings that you can crush but cannot extirpate, and the thirst for the living God is one of these. You may blunt and deaden the faculty for God, but as long as the lamp burns, it is still there. It was that profound and unalterable faith which made our Lord so helpful for the most hardened sinners of mankind.

And then remember also that men may thirst for God and never know it. That eminent scientist Romanes tells us that for twenty-five years he never prayed. He was crowned with honor in a way that falls to few—and all the time there was something lacking. It was not the craving of a disciplined mind that feels every hour how much still remains to do; it was the craving of a hungry soul that never knew it was yearning after God. Then, in the embrace of love, they met, and meeting, there was peace. So it often is when souls are restless. They are craving for they know not what. And all the time, although they little dream of it, *that "know not what" is God.* For as Augustine told us long ago, God has made us for Himself, and we are restless till we find our rest in Him.

Hope Thou in God

Why art thou cast down, O my soul? . . . Hope thou in God.—Ps. 42:5

The psalmist here is not talking to an audience. He is talking to himself. "Why art thou cast down, O my soul? Hope thou in God." That is one of the habits of the saints, and it is always a highly profitable habit. It means that we look squarely in the face the things that are lurking in the shadows. And very generally when we do that, with the fears and despondencies that haunt us, things prove not so desperate as they seemed. We all know how in the dead of night the slightest noise is apt to startle us. Imagination riots in the darkness. But we smile when we switch on the light and find the footstep is only a creaking board and the knocking only the flapping of a blind.

So also with the soul, formless fears are always the worst fears. Nameless and undefined despondencies are often the most depressing of despondencies. And just to face them and drag them to the light and manfully charge them to declare themselves, is very often the springboard to new tranquility. Why art thou cast down, O my soul? Come, my soul, answer me that question! Stand there and be interrogated! Give thy reasons! Why art thou cast down? Very generally when one does that, things prove so much less hopeless than they seemed that the soul descries the glimmerings of morning.

Now many people, when they read these words, are apt to interpret them erroneously. They regard them as a call to trust; but that is scarcely the meaning of the words. When I trust a person, I do more than hope. When I hope, I do less than trust. To hope in God is therefore something different from a feeble and attenuated trust. It is to base every hope that burns within us on the profound recognition that God *is*. Base your hope, whatever your hope may be—and hopes are of a thousand different kinds—on the recognition that God reigns, and *that* God, the God of the whole Bible, a Father infinitely loving, has been revealed to us in the Lord Jesus. If that is false, if there is no such Being, our sweetest hopes are mockeries. We have nothing to build on but the sand. Our hopes may come to ruin at any moment. But if God is and we are sure of that, surer than we are of our hands or feet, then there is hope for us and for the world. Hope, my soul, because there is a God—that is what the psalmist really means. Hope, because *He* reigns. Hope, because *He* is on the throne. Hope, because He cares for you and loves you; because He cares for all the world and loves the world; because He so loved the world that He gave Jesus.

Now, let us apply that thought a little in relation to the future of our race. We have many gloomy prophets in the world today who think our race is hurrying to ruin. They study history and find no hope in history. They deny the reality of progress and have lost all hope in civilization. Education, men had hope in that. Civilization, they had hope in that. Increase of dialogue among the nations, men put their hope in that. And then the war came wrecking hopes just as it wrecked cathedrals, and all these rosy, radiant hopes were as houses built upon the sand. What a wise book the Bible is. How it rejects and refuses shallow hopes. It never says to us, "Hope thou in education." It says, "My soul, hope thou in God." Base thy hope on the fact that He is reigning and moving on in His eternal purposes to an end that shall be fair as a perfect day.

Consider the years that lie ahead, hidden in the shadows of the future. For some the prospect is very dark and frightening. Will your health hold out? So much depends on that for yourself and your wife and children. Will your powers hold out, or some day will they give? Will your loved ones all be spared to you? My dear friend, no hope that is worth anything rests upon contingencies like these. It rests upon the certainty of God. He reigns. He knows you and He loves you. In His eyes you are infinitely precious. If you ascend up into heaven, He is there; if you make your bed in hell, He is there. Would it not tarnish the glory of His name if for a single hour in all the future He were to leave you or forsake you? My soul, hope thou in God. Base your hope of the future upon God. Base it on nothing else and nothing less. Everything else and less is but contingency. Build on the sand, and though the sand is made of gold, when the storm comes everything may perish. But who is a rock like unto our Rock?

Lastly, think of the hope of immortality and of the joy and rest and liberty of heaven when life shall flower into full perfection and we shall meet our loved ones again. That hope is in every human heart, and the question is on what do you base it? Well, you may base it on the inward longing, or on the imperfection of our present being, or on the fact that there is so much on board that is not wanted for the voyage. But when the lights burn low and no argument can silence the questioning, "My soul, hope thou in God." Base your eternal hope on the life and love and promises of God. He is the God of Abraham, Isaac, and Jacob; He is not the God of the dead, but of the living. No mother would let death rob her of her child if her power were equal to her love, and with Him, love and power are alike infinite.

To the Disheartened

Why art thou cast down, O my soul?—Ps. 43:5

It is one source of the eternal freshness of the Psalms that they tell the story of a struggling soul. They open a window on to that battle-field with which no other battle can be compared—the moral struggle of the individual with himself. And it is well that that story should be told in poetry, for there is nothing like poetry for describing battles. There is a rich suggestiveness in poetry, a rush of emotion, an enthusiasm that catches and conveys the excitement of the field. The dullest war correspondent grows poetical, his words become colored, vivid, picturesque, when he narrates the actions in the war. It was right, then, that for this warfare of the soul we should have the strong music of the Psalms.

Now as we read that story of the psalmist's struggle, one of the first things to arrest us is the likeness of that battle to our own. Ages have fled, and everything is different since the shepherd-king poured out his heart in melody. And yet his failures and his hopes are so like ours, he might have been shepherding and reigning yesterday. We are so apt to think we fight alone. We are so prone to think there never was a life so weak, so ragged, so full of a dull gnawing, as ours. We are so ready to believe that we have suffered more than any heart that ever loved and lost. And then God opens up the heart of David, and we see its failures and we hear its cries, and the sense of loneliness at least is gone. He prayed as we have prayed. He fell as we have fallen. He rose and started again as we have done. He was disheartened, and so are we.

Speaking of disheartenment, there is one temperament that is peculiarly exposed to that temptation. It is that of the eager and sensitive and earnest soul. If you are never in earnest about anything, you may escape disheartening altogether. To be disheartened is a kind of price we pay for having a glimpse at the heavens now and then.

> The mark of rank in nature is capacity for
> pain;
> And the anguish of the singer makes the
> sweetness of the strain.

So the dull pain of being disheartened now and then is the other side of man's capacity for enthusiasm. Give me a flood-tide and I shall expect an ebb. Give me an earnest, daring, generous, loyal heart, and I shall know where to discover melancholy.

And one word I should like to say here—never pass judgments in your disheartened hours. It is part of the conduct of an honest soul never to take the verdict of its melancholy. The hours come when everything seems wrong. And all that we do and all that we are seem worthless. And by a strange and subtle trick of darkness, it is just then we begin to judge ourselves. Suspend all judgment when you are disheartened. Tear into fragments the verdict of your melancholy. Wait till the sunshine comes; wait till the light of the countenance of God comes, then judge—you cannot judge without the light. But in your darkness, stay yourself on God. Disheartenment is the wise man's time for striking out. It is only the fool's time for summing up.

No doubt there is a physical element in much disheartenment. There is a need of health; there is a lack of sunshine in the hills about it. When we are badly nourished and poorly clothed and live and sleep in a vitiated atmosphere, it is so very easy to lose heart. And all that inter-working of body and soul, with the reaction of a man's environment upon his life, should make us very charitable to our neighbor. If you knew everything, you would find more heroism in a smiling face sometimes than in the most gallant deed out in South Africa. Make every allowance for a disheartened neighbor. Be charitable. Be helpful and be kind. But in the name of the Christlike character you strive for, make no allowance, brother, for yourself. Allowance is merely the pet name for excuse. It speaks of that tender handling of ourselves which is so utterly foreign to a vigorous manhood. I must make no excuse. I must be at it when I feel least like it. It is so much better to live nobly than live long.

Now what are the common causes of disheartment? I think we can lay our hand on some, at any rate. And the first is the long and monotonous stretches of our life. "Variety's the very spice of life, and gives it all its flavor," sings the poet. And when there is no variety at all, no new horizon in the morning, but the same work and the same haunting worry, day in day out, we are all apt to grow disheartened. It is a dreary business walking in the country when the dusty road, without a turn or a bend, stretches ahead of you for miles. If there was only some dip and rise in the road, some unexpected scenery, some surprises, you would cover the distance and never think of it. It is the sameness that disheartens us. It is the dreary monotony of life's journey until we lose all spring and spontaneity, all freshness of feeling, all power to react; and we live and work mechanically, deadly.

Another cause is bitter disappointment. When we have made our plans, and suddenly they are shattered; when we have built our castles, and the gale come and brings them down in ruin at our feet; when the ties are wrenched and the loving heart is emptied, and in the bitterness of death the grave is full—we are all ready to be disheartened then. For where our treasure is, there shall our hearts be also; and when our treasure vanishes, our heart is gone.

The poet Wordsworth, whose calm, deep verse we should all keep reading in these hurrying days, tells us of the utter disheartening that fell on him after the French Revolution. He had hoped great things from that stormy time. He had hoped for the birth of brotherhood and freedom. He had thought that the race was going to shake its fetters off and proclaim the dignity of man at last. And when these dreams were blighted as they were, and instead of liberty and true equality there came the tumbrel and the guillotine and blood, "I lost," says Wordsworth,

> All feeling of conviction, and in fine
> Sick, wearied out with contrarieties,
> Yielded up moral questions in despair.

It was his terrible disappointment that disheartened him. Perhaps it is that, friend, that has disheartened you.

Another cause of the deepest disheartening is this: it is the apparent uselessness of all we do. It is the partial failure, it is the lack of progress, it is the fact that I strive and never seem to attain that lies at the root of spiritual despondency. "Ah, but a man's reach should exceed his grasp, or what's a heaven for?" says Andrea. And this very psalm from which we took our text, that thrills and wails with spiritual depression, begins with the cry of the soul after the Infinite "as the hart pants after the water-brooks." It is the other side of my glory, that disheartening. It is the witness of my kinship with infinitude. I am never satisfied: there is always another hilltop. I am never at rest: there is a better somewhere. And so I am disheartened—fool!—because I am something better than a beast and have been made to crave, to strive, to yearn, to hope—unsatisfied—till the day break and the shadows flee away.

Now I shall venture to give some advice against disheartenment (I have received help here from the sermons of Dean Paget), and the first is this: disheartenment can often be dispelled by action.

A friend who knew Robert Browning well has said of him that one of his priceless qualities was that he always made effort seem worthwhile. You came into his presence restless, wearied, with all the edge taken off moral effort by the doubts and criticisms of this troubled age, and you left him feeling that in spite of a thousand doubts, the humblest effort heavenward was worthwhile.

O, how I wish that every young man and woman could feel the same thing! For what we want is not more light. What we want is more quiet fortitude. It is to believe that effort is worthwhile. It is to hold it, though the world deny it, that man shall not live by bread alone. And though it is very easy to preach that, and we read it and sing it like a common thing, there is the power of God in it against moral collapse, and it carries the makings of moral heroism on its bosom.

And this is my second counsel to the disheartened. Remember, friend, what others have to suffer. Look around you and see the burden of your neighbor and mark the patience and sweetness of the man, until, in that great brotherhood of trial, you ask God to forgive your gloom and bitterness.

In the theater of the ancient Greeks—and the theater was religious, it was not vulgar then—they played great tragedies and brought the sorrows and passions of the noble on the state. And the men and women of Athens went to see them, and by the portrayal of these mightier sorrows, their own so shrank into an insignificance that they went home with something of new hope in them and the determination to be braver now. There are such tragedies today, my friend, and you cannot only witness, you can help. "When you are quite despondent," said Mr. Keble, "the best way is to go out and do something kind to somebody."

And lastly, in your hours of disheartenment, just ask if there was ever a man on earth who had such cause to be disheartened as our Lord. What griefs, what exquisite sorrows, and what agonies!—what seeming failure, what crushing disappointment! Yet on the very eve of Gethsemane and Calvary our wonderful Lord is talking of His joy. And when heart fails and faints, and I lose all will power, and my arm hangs helpless, and my soul seems dead, there is nothing like coming right to the feet of Jesus and crying with Peter, "Lord, save me or I perish." It is then that I take heart again to sing—

> The night is mother of the day,
>   The winter of the spring,
> And ever upon old decay
>   The greenest mosses cling.
> Behind the cloud the starlight lurks,
>   Through showers the sunbeams fall,
> For God who loveth all His works,
>   Hath left His hope with all.

The Joy of Jesus

God, thy God, hath anointed thee with the oil of gladness above thy fellows.—
Ps. 45:7

For all the sorrows that lay upon His heart and the heaviness of the cross He had to bear, there can be little question that Jesus impressed people as a very contented person. When He spoke about His joy nobody had to ask Him what He meant. It never seemed strange to those who knew Him best that He should talk to them about His gladness. They were so familiar with it in their daily conversation, even when everything was dark and menacing, that the mention of it never took them by surprise. His enemies described Him as a wine-bibber, and that does not suggest a gloomy person. He called Himself a bridegroom, and the ideal bridegroom is a radiant person. *We* want children to be men and women; *He* wanted men and women to be children, and children, whatever else they may be, are extraordinarily carefree little beings. How, then, shall we explain this gladness of the Man of Sorrows? How did He maintain, through darkest hours, this unworrying and radiant heart? It is profoundly helpful to meditate on that.

Supremely faithful to His high vocation, our Lord shone in the tranquil radiance of fidelity. One of the deepest attributes of duty is that the doing of it always leads to gladness. Wordsworth says of the man who does his duty that flowers laugh before him in their beds. To have a vocation and to hold to it, in spite of seductive and alluring voices, is the source of half the singing in the world. In the World War, in spite of all its sorrow, there was more singing than I ever heard before. Millions had something great to live for: something that was great enough to die for. And one of the sources of the joy of Jesus was that something great enough to live and die for had been given Him in the ordering of God. Voices called Him, as they call us all. Sometimes they bore the accents of a friend. He was urged to be careful and to guard Himself and to shun the agony of Calvary. But to all such voices He was deaf; He set His face steadfastly towards Jerusalem, and "flowers laughed before Him in their beds."

Another source of that joy of heart is to be found in the abundance of His life. We all know how when life is rich and full there comes to us a kind of inward radiance. Seasons arrive when life is at the ebb, and then "melancholy marks us for her own." But when the tide of life comes to the full again, immediately everything is different. The grasshopper has ceased to be a burden; everything is clothed in vivid coloring; in the dreariest period of bleak February we awaken in the morning singing. That is not only true of physical life; it is true of life in every sphere. It is "more life and fuller" if the jarring is to be changed into a song. How profoundly significant it is, then, that Jesus should be the enemy of death and should quietly affirm *I am the Life.*

All sin in its last results is impoverishing: of such impoverishing our Lord was ignorant. The life of God flowed through Him like a river, unchecked by any barrier of evil. Moment by moment drawing for His need out of the boundless life within His Father's heart, He had a joy the world could never give and could never take away.

The deepest root of all Christ's joy was that He never doubted God. And if ever a child had cause to doubt his father, I make bold to say that it was Jesus. Sent of God, He was a homeless wanderer: the Son of Man had not where to lay his head. Sent of God, men turned their backs on Him: He came to His own, and His own received Him not. Sent of God, He was ridiculed and mocked; He was beaten and insulted, and the nails were driven into His hands and feet. In such a life to trust was victory, and victory always is conjubilant. To live as He did, in a faith unfailing, is the victory that overcomes the world. *That* is why, right through the life of Jesus, there "steals on the ear the distant triumph song," sung not in celestial bliss but in the shame and agony of our mortality.

Why is a child such a unworried little creature? It is because he trusts his father and his mother. Why is the boat passenger untroubled in the tempest? It is because he absolutely trusts the captain. And the deepest root of the joy of Jesus was a trust in His Father which was perfect and which never faltered in the darkest hour. Why should you and I not live like that? The victories of Christ were won for *us*. A Christian does not so much win his victories as he appropriates the victories of Christ. Live as He did, trust as he did, keep the heart open to the inflowing tide, and in the dreariest days of February the time of the singing of the birds is come.

The River of God

There is a river, the streams whereof shall make glad the city of God.—Ps. 46:4

The Bible opens the history of man by showing him surrounded by a garden. It is in the midst of a garden he awakes, touched into life by the creating hand. There he learns his kingship in creation; there he discovers One whom he can love; there he walks in fellowship with God. We read, too, that through the garden ran a river. It flowed from Eden through the midst of paradise. On leaving Eden it parted into four, and its streams went out to fertilize the world. This, then, is the environment of man in the idyllic morning of his days—a garden of perfect beauty and delight made glad by the flowing of a river.

But as the history of man proceeds, of man in his relationship to God, the need arises of some other figure to illustrate the scenery of redemption. As long as man is unfallen, so long is a garden his true environment. There is no sin seeking to assail him, no hostile power bent upon his destruction. He can walk secure amid his garden groves and live without apprehension of assault.

But with the advent of sin, all is changed. There grows an antagonism between man and God. The Church of God separates from the world and lives engirdled by a deadly enemy. And just as this antagonism deepens, so does the thought of the garden become dim, and its place is taken in poetry and prophecy by the sterner concept of the city. For modern man the city is the home of commerce and its social life is the measure of its value. But in earlier times the value of the city lay mainly in the security it offered. And all who have seen a medieval city with its high walls and its defended ports will understand how in the day of trouble the city was the stronghold of the land. It was not to gardens that men fled for refuge when the trumpet rang its summons of alarm. They tilled their garden in the day of peace, but fled to the city in the day of danger.

And so as the conflict of the spirit deepened and life assumed the aspect of a war, the garden ceased to represent the Church, and the battlemented city took its place. That is why Scripture opens with a garden and closes its long story with a city. Slowly above the dust of spiritual battle there rose the outline of a city's wall, until at last, all that the psalmist hoped for and all that the prophet had declared in faith, was seen in vision by the seer in Patmos.

Now this identification of Church and city was greatly furthered among the Jews by one thing. It was greatly furthered for the Jews by the increasing importance of Jerusalem. So long as the Israelites were villagers and lived a pastoral or rural life, just so long their concept of a noble city was drawn from what they knew of foreign capitals. But as Jerusalem began to grow in numbers and to attract the attention of the world, then the associations of the city took a kindlier and more familiar tone. No Jew could picture a city of his God so long as the greatest cities were all heathen. There must be a capital of his own land to suggest and to inspire the figure. And so it was, as Jerusalem advanced and became the home of government and worship, that both prophet and psalmist with increasing confidence described the Church as the city of Jehovah. It was not just of Jerusalem they thought, though under all they thought about lay Jerusalem. Jerusalem was the sacrament and seal of the invisible city of their quest. Hence John in the closing page of Revelation, when he describes the city of his vision, says, "I saw the holy city, new Jerusalem."

Now between Jerusalem and other cities there was one point of sharp and striking contrast. Jerusalem stood almost alone in this. It had no river flowing by its walls. It was very beautiful for situation; and as a city compactly built together, it occupied a position of great strength, and its walls were a mighty safeguard round about it. Yet one thing it lacked to beautify its streets and to make it a safe shelter when besieged—and the one thing which it wanted was a river. Nineveh had the waters of the Tigris; through Babylon wound the streams of the Euphrates; the city of Thebes rose beside the Nile, and Rome was to win her glory by the Tiber.

Jerusalem alone possessed no river; no depth of water flowed beneath her walls; all she could boast of, beside her wells and springs, was an insignificant and intermittent stream. It is that which explains the psalmist's exclamation. A river!—the streams of it make glad the city. He sees Jerusalem, yet it is not Jerusalem, for in his vision there flows a river there. Once there had been a river in the garden when the garden was man's meeting-place with God, and now the garden has become the city, and behold there is a river in the city.

What then *is* this river which the psalmist sees in the city of Jehovah? There is no need for conjecture, for the psalmist himself tells us what it was: "God is in the midst of her," and he adds that it is the presence of God that is the gladdening river. It is Jehovah present with His Church that constitutes its gladness and refreshing.

I need hardly remind you how often in the Scripture God is compared with living waters. We read in Jeremiah, "They have forsaken me, the fountain of living waters, and hewed them out cisterns, broken cisterns, that can hold no water." Zechariah speaks of the fountain that shall be opened in Jerusalem for sin and for uncleanness. "And in the last day, the great day of the feast, Jesus stood and cried, saying, 'If any man thirst, let him come unto me, and drink.'" That, then, is the river in the city. It is the gladdening presence of Jehovah. It is God not distant in the heaven of heavens, but moving in the midst of our activities. For in that there is the secret of all strength, the hope of patient endurance to the end, and the gladness which is born of satisfaction of all that is deepest in the soul.

Let us remember, too, what John says of this river, that it proceeds out of the throne of God and of the Lamb. It is not without deep significance that John should have added these words—"of the Lamb." There is a presence of God throughout the whole creation, for all things have their being in Him. That river flows from the throne of the Creator. But the river in the city flows from the throne of the Lamb; its well-spring is in Jesus and Him crucified; it is in Christ once slain and now enthroned that the city of God has joy and satisfaction To His own city God reveals Himself, as He does not and cannot do unto the world. He comes to His own in the love of Jesus Christ, for he that hath seen Him hath seen the Father. And this is the river, not from the throne of God, but from the throne of God and of the Lamb, which flows and flows only through the city. This is that river which is full of water, and by the banks of which everything lives. This is the river which Ezekiel saw and which before long was deep enough to swim in. It is God, but it is God in Christ, the God of pardon and of full redemption. There is a river which makes glad the city, and it flows from the throne of God and of the Lamb.

But now, to carry out the thought a little, let us take some suggestions from the figure. And, first, the river in the city speaks of *joy*. Between the ancient and the modern city there is one contrast we might easily miss. We view a city as the home of pleasure, as the place where most enjoyment may be had; it is in a measure to escape from dullness and boredom that multitudes leave the country for the town. But for the Jew, the city in itself was not regarded as a place of gladness; there was always something of a shadow on its streets. As a matter of fact, it is in country life that the Bible finds its images of gladness. The city was but a sad necessity in a country which might be swept by war. And the gloomier the city was, the better; for the higher and more impregnable its walls, the greater was the safety it afforded to men who sought its shelter in the strife. Not of a city such as we know today would a Jew think when he read of the city of God. He would imagine one that was impregnable and could defy the siege of any foe. And so says the psalmist, "Lo, there is a river"—the city of God is girded with walls unshakable—yet through it flows the gladness of the hills and the joy of waters on which the sunshine plays. Safe is the man who dwells within these walls, for they are built by One whose workmanship is sure. His life is more than one of gloomy safety cut off from the liberty of plain and hill. At his very feet there flows a river, clear as crystal, making glad music, and he who stoops to drink of its clear stream is refreshed and made happy by its refreshment.

But aren't there many who are tempted yet to think of religion as a life of gloom? They may feel that it is safe to be religious, but that that safety is very dearly purchased. The city of God is but a gloomy place, and some day they shall enter its defenses; but today let them have the gladness of the mountains and the music of the broad and happy world. To all who may be tempted to think so comes the word of the psalmist— "Lo, there is a river!" Not only is the Christian life the guarded life, it is the life that is lived beside the stream of joy. For to know that God is with us in Christ Jesus and that He will never leave us nor forsake us, *that,* after all, is the unfailing secret of the happy and contented heart. Everything lives where this river flows. The tree of life is growing on its banks. To live with God is to redeem one's life from the worry and the rush that make it not worth living. The city of God is not a gloomy place, however it may look to those without; there is a river in its streets that makes it glad.

When you read the opening verses of this Psalm, you find yourself in a scene of wild confusion. The psalmist, in a few graphic words, pictures chaos in the world. The earth is reeling in the shock of earthquake; the mountains sink into the depths of the ocean; the waters of the sea rise up in fury and sweep with terrific force across the land. Everywhere there is uproar and confusion, an earth that is shaken to its very base, and men in terror and panic fear as if the end of all things was at hand. Then suddenly the psalmist calls a halt, and another vision breaks upon his gaze. A river, and it is flowing in sweet peace through a city that stands unshaken and unshakable. And nothing could be more striking or more beautiful than that swift passage from the roaring sea to the gentle gliding of that quiet river as it murmurs among the city streets. It is the psalmist's vision of the peace of all who have taken up their dwelling-place with God. This is a peace that the world can never give, for the world is in throes of earthquake and of storm. But it flows from the throne of God and of the Lamb; its source is a Savior crucified yet crowned; and it is the heritage of every man who believes in an enthroned Christ.

The life of the Christian should be like a river flowing through the streets of a great city. In the midst of all disturbance and dismay it ought to be like a picture of sweet peace. For he who has God beside him night and day and who continually stays his mind on God, amid all the disturbing tumult of his lot, has a heart at peace with itself.

We do not need to be told how a city's welfare depends upon its river. It is the Clyde that makes glad the city of Glasgow by bringing a livelihood to tens of thousands. There is hardly a dwelling on any street or terrace that is not influenced in some way by the river. Life may be hard enough for many citizens, but it would be harder and perhaps impossible if the sources of our river were to fail and its bed to become empty of its waters. On the Thames depends the prosperity of London, on the Clyde the prosperity of Glasgow; is it not equally true that on the river depends the prosperity of the city of God? For let the presence of God in Jesus Christ be withdrawn from the soul or from the church, and nothing can save that soul from being cast away or keep that church from the decay of death. No organization will avail if Christ is not present in its congregation. No wealth of learning, no beauty of ritual, is of the slightest use if that is lacking. Unless God is in the midst of her and His grace like a flowing river, the city of God can never hope to see the work of the Lord prospering in her hand. Brethren, for the sake of our own souls, and not less for the church which we belong to, let us covet more earnestly what is in our power, a life of unbroken fellowship with God. That is the victory that overcomes the world. That is the open secret of prosperity. That is the river from the throne of the Lamb that makes glad the city of our quest.

In closing let us note one other word. The psalmist does not merely speak about a river; he pictures the river branching into streams: "There is a river the *streams* whereof make glad." Now the word translated "streams" is rather "brooks." It is used everywhere of lesser rivulets, and it brings before us the thought of the great river with its waters carried along a hundred channels so that each garden-plot within the city has its own tiny, yet sufficient, stream. It is thus that the river makes glad the city of God, not merely by flowing in a mighty tide, but by coming into every separate plot in a channel peculiarly its own. And so the question for each of us is this, "Is God indeed mine—is He my own? Have I opened a way for Him into my garden—am I personally acquainted with His grace?"

It is not enough to live near the river and let it flow beside us in its beauty. God must be ours, and we must be His if we are to have the gladness of His presence.

The Ministry of Silence

Be still, and know that I am God.—Ps. 46:10

There are certain voices which we never hear except when everything is silent. They reach us as a revelation of the stillness. Sometimes on a summer afternoon one gets away from the city or the village and climbs up the grassy hillside till all the noise of human life is lost, and it is often then that there breaks upon the ear a certain indistinguishable murmur as of the moving of innumerable wings.

Travelers tell us that there are rivers flowing beneath the streets of the ancient city of Shechem. During the hours of the day you cannot hear them for the noise of the narrow streets and the bazaars. But when evening comes and the clamor dies away and the dew falls on the city, then quite audibly, in the hush of night, you may hear the music of the buried streams.

There are many voices like those hidden waters. You can only hear them when things are still. There are whisperings of conscience in the heart which take only a very little to drown. There are tidings from the eternal Spirit who is not far away from any one of us; tidings that will come and go unnoticed unless we have learned the grace of being still.

And yet the very element of stillness is one which is conspicuously lacking now. We have been taught the art of exercise, and we have lost the art of being still. A recent writer, in a brilliant essay on the music of today, tells us that we are living nowadays under "the dominion of din." And whether or not that is true of music, of which I am not qualified to speak, it is certainly true of ordinary life. Our forefathers may have had very imperfect ideals of Christian service. They may have tolerated social abuses which we would never tolerate today. But they had one element in their Christian life in more abundant measure than we have it, and that was the blessed element of silence. What peace there was in the old-fashioned Sabbath—what a reverent stillness in the house of God—what a quiet and peaceful solemnity in worship at the family altar! And if today we cannot but be conscious that something of that old spirit has departed, we know that something precious has been lost. It *is* gain to be immersed in service. It is a high ambition to be energetic. "Whatsoever thy hand findeth to do, do it with all thy might." And yet the Bible never says to us, "Be energetic, and know that I am God." It says, "Be still, and know that I am God."

Indeed, we are so in love with noise today that stillness is commonly looked upon as weakness. And it is well to remind ourselves occasionally that often the very opposite is true. When the rain beats against the window pane, we are awakened by its noise. But the snow falls so silently, that never an infant stirs within its cradle. And yet the snow may block up every road quite as effectually as a landslide and dislocate the traffic of a kingdom. Set a thousand digging shovels to work, and you produce a certain effect upon the soil. But when the frost comes with her silent fingers and lightly touches field and meadow with them, in a single night that silent frost will work more effectually than a thousand shovels.

God does not work in this strange world by hustling. God works in the world far more often by hush. In all the mightiest powers which surround us, there is a certain element of stillness. And if I did not find in Jesus Christ something of that divine inaudibility, I confess I should be tempted to despair. When Epictetus had had his arm broken by the savage cruelty of his master, he turned round without one trace of anger, and said to him quietly, "I told you so." And when a heathen satirist taunted the Christians, asking what nobler thing their Master did, one of them answered, "He kept silence." There is a silence that may speak of weakness. There is another silence that is full of power. It is the empty husk that rattles in the breeze. It is the brook and not the river that makes the noise. And it is good that we should remember that when we are tempted to associate quietness with weakness, as perhaps we are all tempted nowadays.

There is, of course, a certain kind of silence which is only the outward sign of self-absorption. It does not indicate that a man is hearing anything; it just means that he is withdrawn into himself. I have heard runners say that in long races they have been oblivious of every sound. There may have been a thousand voices cheering them on, and yet they seemed to run in a great silence. Perhaps all of us have had hours such as that—hours of suffering or of intense activity—when we felt ourselves alone in a deep solitude. That is the stillness of absorption. It is not the stillness to which our text refers. It is of another quietness that it speaks; the quietness which is the basis of communion. For there are times when we never speak so eloquently, and times when we never hear so finely, as when the tongue is silent and the lips are closed and the spirit is the one interpreter. A love that has no silence has no depth. "Methinks the lady doth protest too much." There are people whose love we instinctively distrust because they are always telling us about it. And perhaps it is simply because God is love, in all the glorious fullness of that word, that we have to be still if we would know Him.

Indeed, there is often no surer sign than silence that the heart has been reached and the depths been broken up. In their greatest hours men are seldom noisy. I have watched sometimes an audience at a concert—for to me the audience is more interesting than the music—and I have watched the listless attention which they gave to music that reached no farther than the ear. And then perhaps there was some perfect melody, some chord which had the insistence of a message, and it was as if a voice had cried out loud, "Be still, and know that I am God."

Charles Reade, in one of the best of his novels, tells a story of some Australian miners. He tells how they traveled through a long summer Sunday to hear the singing of a captive thrush. And they were reckless men familiar with riot, but when they heard it, there fell a hush upon them, for it brought back memories of childhood again and of England where they had been boys. In a greater fashion that is true of God. We do not clamber to Him by the steps of logic; we reach Him by the feelings of the heart. And it is just because, when the heart is moved profoundly, there falls upon it a silence and a stillness, that we are bidden in our text to be still and know that He is God.

Probably that is the reason, too, why great silences have a divine suggestion. Great silent spaces speak to us of God. I remember a year or two ago visiting the cathedral at Cologne. I suppose it is the most magnificent example of Gothic architecture in the world. And I recall vividly, as though it had happened yesterday, how, passing in from the crowded city streets, the thought of the presence of God was overwhelming. I knew He was present in the teeming city. I knew He was present in the crowded street. I knew that where the stir and traffic were, the infinite Spirit was not far away. And yet it is one thing to know, and it is quite another thing to feel; and in the calm and solemn quiet of the cathedral I felt that God was there. That is what spiritual men have always felt under the silence of the starry sky. That is why they have always thought of God when they lifted up their eyes unto the hills.

Our noisy, talkative life is like the surge breaking on the edge of the shore, and away beyond it is the silent ocean carrying the message of infinity. We lose our sense of God in a big city far more readily than lonely dwellers do. And we lay the blame of that upon a score of things—on the strain of business, on our abundant pleasures. Perhaps there is a deeper reason than all these; it is the loss of the ministry of silence: of the field and the meadow and the hill; of the solitudes which are quivering with God. Spare your compassion for the Highland dweller. The man may be far richer than you think. It may be he has kept what we have lost in the keen and eager zest of city life. It may be he has kept, in all his poverty, those intimations of a present God which are given where a great silence is, as of the lonely field or meadow.

I close by suggesting that this is the reason why God makes silences in every life; the silence of sleep, the silences of sorrow, and then the last great silence at the end. One of the hardest things in the world, as you all know, is to get little children to keep still. They are in a state of perpetual activity, restless, eager, questioning, alert. And just as a mother says to her child, "Be still," and hushes it to sleep that it may rest, so God does sooner or later with us all. What a quiet, still place the sickroom is! What a silence there is over a house of mourning! How the voices are hushed, and every footstep soft, when someone is lying within the coffin. Had we the choosing of our own affairs we should never have chosen such an hour as that; and yet how often it is rich in blessing. All the activities of eager years may not have taught us quite so much as that. There are things which we never learn when we are active. There are things which we only learn when we are passive. And so God comes, in His resistless way, which never ceases to be a way of love, and says, "Be still, and know that I am God." If that is so with the passive hours of life, may it not be so with the passive hour of death? What is death but the Almighty Father saying to our talking lips, "Be still"? And I for one believe that in that stillness we shall awaken to know that He is God, in such a love and power as will be heaven.

Sincerity

Thou desirest truth in the inward parts.—Ps. 51:6

There is a remarkable foreshadowing of the insight of Christ Jesus in these words. They ring with that depth which is so clear a note of Jesus' moral teaching. We have been inclined to think of the Old Testament as dealing with the outward sphere of action; we have been inclined to say that it was Jesus who first ran down the act into the heart. But we must not separate the Old and New by any hard and fast distinctions such as these. They intermingle, both in creed and character. If Abraham saw Christ's day and was glad, David saw Christ's day and was sad. He recognized God's passionate insistence that a man should be thoroughly sincere.

It is worth noting, too, that when David recognized this, he had a broken heart. David had sinned, and David was repentant; and a repentant man sees deeply. There are some hours in life when we are blind; hours when we see nothing and forget everything; and all our past, and all our honor and duty and God, and heaven and hell, fade and are blotted out. But when repentance comes, we see again. We see what we have done and what we are. We touch a sinfulness far deeper than our act. And that was David's case. On ordinary days he might have been content with ordinary sacrifices; but in an hour like this it was "Against thee, thee only, have I sinned," and "Behold, thou desirest truth in the inward parts."

This, then, is God's insistence on sincerity, and it is always a hard thing to be sincere. Life is so full of little insincerities that it is often the man who is seriously struggling to be true who feels most keenly how untrue he is. It is always a hard thing to be sincere. But there are times when it is harder than at other times. And it is especially hard today.

One reason it is so hard to be sincere is the fierce struggle for existence. There is a fierceness in modern competition that makes it very hard for a man to be a man. There are so many interests involved, so many whirling wheels within the wheels, that to be true to self is difficult. Men are not free as the shepherd on the hills is free. Men are combined and interlocked in the great mechanism of modern life until at last, to say what a man thinks and to be what a man is, is one of the quiet heroisms of honesty. Thank God, there are such heroisms!—as worthy of honor as any deed upon the battlefield. But when to be sincere spells heroism, we must not wonder if insincerity is common. Few men are heroes. For one soul that has a passion for sincerity, there are a hundred that have an overriding passion for success. And this, and the great gulf between Monday's warfare and Sunday's worship, and the compliances and the accommodations and the silences, have tinged our city life with insincerity.

I think, too, it is harder to be sincere because of the increasing pressure of public opinion. It seems there never was a time when the thought of so many was so quickly voiced and registered. For centuries the people had no voice. They lived and loved and had their griefs and died. But what their thought might be on the great themes mattered no more to their rulers than the thought of brutes. Then came the awakening of knowledge, the dawn of power, the rising of the people like a giant, the vote, the newspaper; until today the thought of the people has been caught and voiced, and public opinion is a dominant power. It is an untold blessing. But the voice of the people is not always the voice of God, and in the tremendous pressure of general opinion, it is harder for a man to be himself. It is a difficult thing to be an individual. I am so apt to be all warped and pressed out of the mental form that God has given me until my life becomes play acting and all the world a stage, and I don't have the courage to think, and I don't have the heart to feel, and I don't have the heroism to be myself. And losing my individuality, I cease to be sincere.

But perhaps the deepest cause of insincerity is that we are living in a time of transition. All times to some extent are that. There is never an age, however dull and dead, but the old like a river is watering its plains, and the new like a spring leaps up into the light. But there are some times when the transition is very sharp and clear, and we are living in such a time as that today. Old things are passing away. Old faiths are in the crucible again. Old truths have got to be recast and readjusted. There is not a doctrine, whether of heart or Bible, but earnest minds are trying to reset it in the growing knowledge of these latter days. In one pew a father and a son are sitting; and though the father may never dream of it, there is the space of centuries between the two. For the father, with all the loyalty of his heart, still clings to the great message of the past; and to the son the strain is to reconcile that message of his childhood with the wider horizon that he cannot yield.

That is the pain of a transition time. There can be little question that for many the only antidote for that pain is insincerity. It is impossible, it is utterly wrong, to cast away the past. It has meant too much to us and been too much to us for that. It is impossible, it is utterly wrong, to flout the new. It is the air we breathe. So springs the temptation to be insincere, to join in the worship that was formed and fashioned when faith was an enthusiasm, to sing the hymns that were the music of unclouded souls though the enthusiasm of our faith is gone and there are more clouds than sunshine in the sky.

Insincerity takes all dignity out of life, and makes this world a very low place. We think we can be insincere, and men will be tricked and never find it out. O brethren, God Almighty has His own awful ways of writing a man's insincerity upon the heavens and engraving it as with a pen of iron on the world. All reverence is impossible, all purity is stained, and all innocence rebukes me when I am insincere. If I am false and double, I cannot hear the laughter of my children but what it sends a pang of pain into my heart. Better be excitable, better be inconsistent, better be dead than insincere. Peter was excitable, brimful of inconsistencies; yet if ever a sincere heart beat, it was the heart of Peter—and Jesus was Christ to Peter and heaven was heaven. But Judas, I don't know what his other sins were, was insincere till he came to feel the very sincerity of Jesus was like an insult; and, insincere, he went to his own place.

Insincerity carries yet another curse. I hardly think that there is any sin that mars and distorts the character like this one. That master theologian Augustine gave us a phrase that has become historic. He spoke of splendid sins. And perhaps there are some sins that in some lights, though not the light of God, have certain elements of splendor in them. But all the insight and all the love of Augustine could never find an element of splendor in the man or woman who had ceased to be sincere. There is no sin that so eats the manhood out of us as insincerity. There is no sin that so robs character of its quiet and restfulness and strength, and leaves it restless, shifty, self-assertive, loud. The nation has often wondered at the sweet equanimity of our revered Queen. And it was Bright who said the Queen was the most truthful being he had ever met. It is the insincere man who exaggerates. It is the insincere who flatters. It is the insincere who plays the coward in the crisis. When I have won something of the sincerity of Christ, I shall know something of His strength and peace.

Surely no sin saps and undermines our influence as insincerity. Perhaps you think you have no influence. You feel yourself a very uninfluential person. Come, humblest woman reading this, it is not so! Most of us think far too much of our abilities and far too little of our influence. We are so interwoven in the web of life that we are making and molding each other every day. In ways mysterious, out of the depths of this mysterious self, we touch and turn each other. And perhaps the men who influence us most are the men who never tried to influence us at all.

Now the one bolt that falls out of the blue to shatter this unconscious influence of character is insincerity. I may be ignorant, and men may not despise me. I may be poor and still command respect. But ignorant or learned, rich or poor, once let men feel that I am insincere and all my influence for good, and all my influence for God, is gone. It's a sad hour when a son sees through his father. Sad for the father, twice sad for the son. And even if a minister has the eloquence of Paul, if his people distrust him, there will be no changed hearts. It is God's curse on insincerity. It is the separating, isolating power of that heart-sin. There is no more heart-lonely creature in the world than the man or woman who has grown insincere. And to be heart-lonely forever, that is hell.

First we must win a deeper reverence for ourselves. We must believe in individual possibilities. We must remember there are no nobodies with God. If I am only leaf tossed by the wind, if I am only a flake carried on the stream, if I am only a light that flashes and is gone, if it will be all the same a hundred years hence, it matters little whether I am sincere or not. I must not mock myself with any self-importance. But if I am a man called into being by an everlasting God, nurtured and bosomed in an eternal love, gifted with faculties that only eternity can ripen, and filled with a ceaseless craving for the truth, to be untrue to self is self-destruction. Therefore, when I am tempted to be insincere, I fall back first upon Bible doctrine. I see my weakness there. I see my fall. But I see there such hopes for *me*, such possibilities for me, that to be me—myself—becomes a new ambition. And to be myself is to be sincere.

Then we must gain a profound faith in God. There is no choice about it. We simply must. I defy any man to be consciously insincere who lives under these eyes that are a flame of fire. It is because God is distant, hidden in the clouds that are around His throne, that we dare be one man *within*, another man *without*. The old religious sculptors, says a writer, who came to their tasks with prayer and meditation on unearthly beauty, would never suffer any imperfect workmanship even though placed where man could never see it. And when one questioned them why the concealed parts of statues removed for human sight should be so exquisitely made, they answered that the eyes of the gods were there. "Why sayest thou, O Jacob, and speakest, O Israel, my way is hid from the Lord, and my going are passed over from my God?" It is a speech like Jacob's that makes insincerity so easy. It is the practice of God's presence which makes it hard.

And we must gain a closer fellowship with Christ. Of all the helps whereby I struggle onwards toward sincerity, there is none like daily fellowship with Him. If it ennobles me to live with noble souls, and makes me purer to have a pure woman for my friend, how will it shame me into a new sincerity to live with the sincerest heart that ever beat! There are some men with whom I could not gossip. There are some men in whose presence slander dies. There is one Man whose very company kills insincerity, and that is Christ. When I am near to Him, and He to me, I am proportionately true. When I have lost Him, banished Him, driven Him from His center and His throne, like a strong tide my insincerity creeps up again.

There is a sad lack of sincerity today, but let us not be blinded to the fact that sincerity is not the only virtue. I am not necessarily good, I am not necessarily right, I am not necessarily saved, because I am sincere. There is a call for new sincerity in every heart, yet that sincerity is but a stepping-stone. I may sincerely believe the earth is flat, and yet for all my sincerity the earth is round. I may sincerely consider my friend to be a hero, and yet in spite of that my friend may be a scamp. I may sincerely be convinced Christ never arose, yet Christ did arise and is at the right hand of God today. Sincerity without humility is the obstinacy out of which fools are made. The truly sincere man is always humble, feels like a child amid God's infinite mysteries and cries in his heart, "Light, light, more light"; till God in His own way leads him there. And the light is light indeed, and the light indeed is love. And neither height nor depth, nor life nor death, nor any other creature, shall separate him for the love of God, which is in Christ Jesus our Lord.

The Triumph of Trust

But I will trust in thee.—Ps. 55:23

The value of a word and the power that it has over our hearts depends largely upon the man who speaks it and on the circumstances of its utterance. When Paul said to the Philippians, "Rejoice in the Lord, and again I say rejoice," how inexpressibly these words are deepened by the circumstances of the Apostle—no longer young nor free, but a prisoner in a Roman cell with his life-work seemingly shattered at his feet. Living words have the quality of life. They are born and bear the fashion of their birth. They may be robbed of meaning, or may be filled with meaning, by the hour in which the spirit utters them. So it seems to me the only way to enter into the grandeur of our text is to learn the circumstances of the Psalm. What kind of man was this who said so confidently: "But I will trust in thee?" What were his circumstances? Was he happy? Was everything going very well with him? A study of the psalm will show us that.

First, note that he was a man unanswered. He knew the bitterness of heaven's silence. His opening cry in our deep psalm is this: "Hide not thyself from my supplication" (verse 1).

It is an easy thing to trust in God when swiftly and certainly our prayers are answered. There are some who read this column whose life is a compact of answered prayer. But when we pray and the face of God is hidden, and we are restless because heaven is silent—it is often difficult to trust Him then. Especially is that true of intercession when we have been praying for someone who is dear, that God would spare a life or kill a habit or bring the beloved prodigal home again. To continue trusting when we have prayed like that and the prayers have seemed to go whistling down the wind, is one of the hardest tasks in human life. The splendid thing is that the psalmist did it. He refused to regard silence as indifference. He knew that a thousand days are as one day to God and that sometimes love delays the chariot wheels. Heaven might be silent and the face of God averted and all the comfort of fellowship withdrawn, but "I will trust in thee."

Observe next, he was a man afraid. "The terrors of death are fallen upon me. Fearfulness and trembling are come upon me" (verses 4 and 5). Now if the writer of this psalm was David, he was one of the bravest souls who ever lived. As a shepherd lad, as an outlaw, as a king, he had given most conspicuous proofs of gallantry. Yet that gallant and courageous heart cries out: "The terrors of death are fallen upon me; fearfulness and trembling are come upon me."

Such hours come to the businessman when he has grappled with some big concern; to the lawyer on the eve of a very important case; to the mother, brooding in the quiet night on the responsibilities of her home and children; or to the pastor, praying for his flock. Suddenly our courage fails for reasons that are often quite inexplicable. Things are not different, duties are not different, but in a strange and mysterious fashion *we* are different. And men who faced the lion and the bear and were quick to answer the challenge of Goliath experience the fearfulness of David. All of us have fainting fits, even the strongest and the bravest; hours when the strong men bow themselves and when the keepers of the house do tremble. David had them in their full intensity, and the good thing is that when they fell on him, he lifted up his heart and cried, "But I will trust in thee."

Observe next, he was a man imprisoned. "O that I had wings like a dove! for then would I fly away and be at rest" (verse 6). Now this does not mean that he was in a dungeon. It is evident from the psalm that he was not. It means that he was weary of his lot; he was dead-sick of it; he loathed it. The meanness of things to that great heart had grown intolerable. He would have given worlds to fly away, but that was the one thing he could not do. In the providential ordering of heaven he was bound, as it were, by fetters to his place. And I believe there are few people anywhere, whatever their lot or calling, who have not known the longing to escape. To escape from the bondage of ourselves—what a craving we often feel for that! To get away—just to get right away—from the routine which meets us every morning, how overpowering at times is that desire! It was then that David rose to a better way. The wings of a dove would never give him rest. The thing he needed was to find his rest under the overshadowing wing of God—right there, just where he was, amid the burden and the cares of kingship, "I will trust in thee."

Observe lastly, he was a man deceived. Somebody he trusted had proven false, and it had almost broken David's heart (verses 12–14). A man his equal, his guide and his acquaintance to whom he used to turn for loving counsel; a man with whom, on quiet Sabbath mornings, he used to walk unto the house of God; a man whose friendship he had never doubted and on whose loyalty he would have staked his life had played the part of Iscariot to the psalmist. What a devastating revelation! What a tragic and desolating hour! How many people have lost their faith in God when they have lost it in a man or woman? Yet David, amid the ruins of that friendship, deserted by one he clung to as a brother, says, "But I will trust in thee."

Daily Defilements

Mine enemies would daily swallow me up.—Ps. 56:2

There are some enemies which only come to us at interludes. But you will note that it was different with the psalmist. It was not rarely and briefly that his enemies fell upon him to destroy him. What inspired his bitter cry was that everyday he lived he was in peril: "Mine enemies would daily swallow me up." He never woke with a heart that was at peace saying, "Thank God all is well today." At any moment he might hear the ringing of the battlecry. And it was that which almost broke his heart and drove him in a wild despair to God and robbed him of all power to be happy.

Now who the psalmist's chief enemy was we don't know, but if we don't know his, at least we know our own. The deadliest enemy we have to fight is sin. That is the power bent on our destruction which we must conquer somehow or be crushed. There are certain sins, like certain enemies, that give us times of rest between their onsets. There are certain temptations which, being foiled today, may not return until a year has passed. But there are others, like the psalmist's foes, whose peculiar characteristic is just this, that every morning when we wake up, we dread them, and everyday we live we have to battle with them.

I suppose there is no one reading this who cannot remember a day when he fell terribly. Have we not all had hours when we defied the right and broke down every barrier of conscience? My brother and sister, in whose heart such hours are living in all their bitterness, remember that there are other sins than these. When a soldier is out on a campaign, there may come a day when he is wounded. The bullet has found him and his rifle drops and he cries for water as they lift him, but remember that everyday that he marches, and many a day there is no thought of wounds, there is the gathering of dust upon his arms. Let that dust gather, and in a little while you would scarcely recognize him as a soldier. Let that dust gather, and in a week or two his very rifle will be a useless instrument.

And so with us too as we take up the spiritual warfare; there *may* come a day when we are badly wounded, but always and everyday there is the defilement of the march. There is the dust and soil of the everyday road. There are temptations that reach us not like a storm, but like the gentle falling of the rain.

Although seemingly minor and insignificant, these sins of everyday rob us of our present joy and peace. It is these which write lines upon the brow and bring the look of uneasiness into the eye. You may destroy the lute by breaking it in two, and there are homes and hearts ruined like that. But a little crack within the lute makes all the music mute, and so is it with our little sins.

Some fifty or more years ago there came into our country a new weed. It was a pondweed living in the water, and so it found its way to our canals, and it was a little and inconspicuous thing to which nobody except the botanists gave heed. Would you believe it, that in thirty years our canals were being choked by it? It blocked the channel, delayed the passing ships, threatened the very existence of the waterway. And it was far more difficult than ice to deal with for ice can be broken with sufficient pressure, but all the pressure in the world was powerless against this living and compliant tangle.

Brothers and sisters, you may be sure of this, that true peace demands an open channel, an unobstructed way to God if one is to walk with music in his heart. And I say that no tragic fall so blocks the channel between earth and heaven as do these daily little and unnoticed sins that grow and gather in the passing days.

It does not take a wound in the eye to make the eye a source of misery. Lodge only a grain of sand within its orb, and all the pleasure of vision vanishes. And so for multitudes who are not reprobate, who have been saved by Christ, there is no joy, no peace, no song, because of the intrusion of the little sins.

I know a meadow not five miles away where thirty years ago the trees were beautiful, and men would travel to see them in the summer for there were few elms like them by the Clyde. And now half of these elms are dead, and for the others summer is a mockery. And it wasn't a storm that did it: it was the daily pollution of our Babylon. They are still rooted in the finest soil, and you too may be rooted in Christ Jesus. No one would question that your deepest life is hid with Christ in God. But even so rooted, you may miss the joy of your salvation, and miss it because everyday you live you are subtly and insensibly defiled.

Such daily defilements have a peculiar power of fostering despair. They are like sickness in that point of view, and you know that sickness is a type of sin. Let a man be stricken with some sudden illness, and my experience is that he does not despair. Doctors will confirm this. It is not then that he loses hope or meditates on death. He summons all the strength that God has given him that he may battle the disease. Or if he is too weak for that, for disease in a day may make us weak as water, then he lies there, not in dull despair, but in a strange and acquiescent peace.

I shall tell you when it is that even the bravest is brought near the margin of despair. It is when everyday and all day there is the gnawing away of some hidden malady. It is when a man goes to work and mingles with his fellows in the street, and all the time, like a dull undertone, is conscious that there is something wrong. It is that which leads so often to despair. It is that which makes the thought of death familiar. It is that which is the secret, never guessed at, of many a startling and unexpected suicide. And I feel that in the realm of sin which is so strangely linked with that of sickness, there is something analogous to that. Did you ever know of anyone despairing after a terrible and tragic fall? I never read of any in the Scripture. I never saw any in my ministry. But ah, how many I have seen who come to despair of ever attaining the highest—they were so crushed, so humbled and disheartened by the defilement of their daily sins. It is our little sins and not our great sins which have such a terrible power to make us hopeless. For our great sins cast us upon Jesus, and there is always hope when we are there. But our little sins leave us with ourselves and seem to mock us when we seek the highest, and tempt us to think that what we hoped for once must always be impossible for us.

One thing at least is clear, and that is that we must never contemplate escape by flight. If God has given us our work to do, then we must continue with it in spite of all the soiling. There can be no escape from daily sin by flying from the path of daily duty. It is such dreams that builds monasteries, and many a monastery becomes like Sodom. You remember how Peter, on the mount of glory, wanted to build tabernacles there. He wanted to live forever in that solitude where all the voices of the world were hushed. And then the Savior led him down again, right into the jostling of the crowd, and Peter learned that life was not given for a hermitage.

What would you think of a man who left his home here and the business he made his living by all because amid our grimy streets his face and hands grew dirty everyday? Yet he who seeks to fly from his daily task because of the temptations which it carries and the defilement it inevitably brings is just as cowardly and absurd. Either you must conquer where you are, or you will not conquer anywhere. Flee from the devil, and he will resist you. Resist the devil, and he will flee from you.

Do you recall that hour when Christ washed His disciples' feet? Do you recall the word He said to Peter, "He that is washed needeth not save to wash his feet, but is clean every whit"? My brother and sister, in that great word of Christ's there lies the Master's answer to our question. There is His treatment of the daily stain. He that is washed—and Peter had been washed. He had been bathed in the spirit of his Lord. Once and for all, coming to Jesus Christ, his guilt had been washed away forever. And now says Jesus, "Let me wash thy feet; let me cleanse off the soil of the daily walk"; and what He said to Simon Peter then, He says to you and me. I do believe that when a man is saved, he is saved not for a time but for eternity. I do believe that when we look to Christ, in that very moment all our sin is pardoned. But everyday we need another cleansing for we have been traveling by dusty roads, and Christ is always stooping and ready to bestow His forgiveness. Do not rest at night till thou hast had it, brother. Summon the hours of the day before thee. Put forth thy feet and let Him wash them, for they are very dusty with the journey. So when thou wakest, thou shalt again be clean and ready for everything the day may bring, glad with the confidence of him who sang, "When I awake I am still with Thee."

Fear and Faith

What time I am afraid, I will trust in thee.—Ps. 56:3

Let us consider for a little while some of the springs of human fear, and then notice how many of our fears spring from the imagination. It has been said (and I think truly said) that life is ruled by the imagination. The things we picture and weave in glowing colors have a very powerful influence over conduct. Often that influence is stimulative, illumining the pathway to discovery; often it creates or liberates fear. People who are highly sensitive are far more apt to be fearful than their neighbors. There are a hundred fears that never touch the man of stolid, unimaginative nature. That is why for a certain type of person to be brave may be comparatively easy, and for another infinitely hard.

Now, the worst thing about this kind of fear is that reason is powerless to allay it. You might as soon allay a fire with good advice. Argument is cold. It cannot banish the specters of the soul. It has no brush that can obliterate the pictures of the imagination. But there is another way, more powerful than reason, to overcome imaginative fears, and that is the way of this inspired psalmist. Faith is the antidote to fear. It quiets fear as the mother quiets her child. The child still dreams, but the dreams are not reality. It is the mother's arms that are reality. So we, His children, dreaming in the darkness and sometimes very frightened by our dreams, find "underneath the everlasting arms."

Another very common source of fear is weakness or frailty of body. Everyone is familiar with that. When we are strong and well it is not difficult to keep our fears at bay. Fears, like microbes, do not love the sunshine. They need the darkness for their propagation. That is why, when the lights of life are dim, we readily become the prey of fearfulness. We can bear burdens without a thought when we are strong and vigorous and well; we can meet tasks with quiet hearts; we can bravely face difficulties—but these seem insurmountable when we are worn and often plunge us into the lowest pit. We must never forget how the state of the mind is affected by the condition of the body. Health is not alone the source of happiness. It is one of the perennial springs of hope. Many of our vague uncharted fears which haunt us and robs us of the sunshine are rooted in the frailty of our bodies.

Now I have no doubt that many of my readers are far from being physically perfect. The fact is, there are very few of us who could be described as physically perfect. And to all such, whatever their condition, I want to give these wonderful words of Scripture: "What time I am afraid, I will trust in thee." He knows our frame. He remembers we are dust. He made us and He understands us. He alone can perfectly appreciate the interactions of body and of mind. And when we trust Him in a childlike faith, nothing is more evident in life than the way in which He disappoints our fears. His grace is sufficient for us. Often when we are weak, then are we strong. Drawing from Him we find we have our fullness, given us daily as the manna was, until at last the "body of our humiliation" shall be fashioned like His glorious body, and then such fears will be laid to rest forever.

I close by naming one other source of fear, and that is the faculty of conscience. A guilty conscience is a fearing conscience—conscience makes cowards of us all. If we could get rid of conscience, what fears would go whistling down the wind! But God has so created us, that *that* is the one thing we cannot do. We may drug and dope it, we may silence it, we may sear it as with an iron, but, like the maiden, it is not dead but sleeping. It awakens in unexpected seasons, sometimes in the stillness of the night, or when our loved ones are removed in death, or when we see our sins bearing fruit in others; perhaps most often in our dying hours when the flaming colors of time no longer blind us and we draw near to the revelation of eternity. All the fears of our imagination, all the fears that spring from weakly bodies, all these, however haunting, are nothing to the fears of conscience. And the tremendous fact, never to be disputed by any theory of its evolution, is that *God* has put conscience in the breast.

But He who has put conscience in the breast has done something more wonderful than that. To minister relief to fearing conscience, He has put His Only-begotten on the tree. There, explain it as you will, is freedom from the hideous fears of conscience. There, explain it as you will, is release from the terrors of our guilt. One trustful look at the Lord Jesus Christ dying upon the cross of Calvary, and the fearfulness of conscience is no more. There is now therefore no more condemnation. Pardoned, we have joy and peace. God is *for* us on the cross, and if God be for us, who can be against us? Blessed Savior, who didst die for us and whose blood cleanseth from all sin, *What time I am afraid, I will trust in thee.*

The Rock That Is Higher Than I

Lead me to the rock that is higher than I.—Ps. 61:2

Whatever suggested the image of our text, the inward meaning of it is explicit. It is the long cry of the human heart for the forgiveness and comforting of God. There are times when the deepest craving of the soul is for something higher than itself. The self-reliance of our sunny hours is lost in a deep feeling of dependence. And that deep feeling of dependence, expressed in many relationships of life, is never satisfied nor perfected until it finds its rest in God. Now when the heart is over-whelmed (as was the psalmist's) there always falls a dimness on the eye. The rock of safety may be very near, but the mist hangs heavy, and we cannot see it. It is then the soul betakes itself to prayer and like the ship-wrecked sailor or the desert wanderer supplicates heavenly guidance to the refuge. There *is* a rock higher than our highest, but we all need to be led to it. No one can by searching find out God. And how we are led there by a most loving guidance, whether it be of providence or grace, is the question which arises from our text.

We see, for instance, how often men are led to the Rock by the bitter experience of failure. Man's extremity of need is heaven's opportunity of leadership. A pastor friend of mine was once traveling in a train. He was joined by a well-known merchant whose affairs were on the point of bankruptcy. And quite naturally, after a little talk, the merchant asked my friend if he would pray for him, and there in the carriage they knelt down and prayed. He was a strong, self-reliant man, that merchant. He was not given to asking help of anybody. But *now* the deepest craving of his heart was for something higher than himself on which to rest.

And much of what is difficult in life, and overwhelming to the point of heart-break, is but the kindly stratagem of heaven to lead us to the higher Rock. Those hours of heart-sinking familiar to us all, the feeling that we have spent our strength for nothing, the deep conviction which visits us in secret that all our righteousnesses are as filthy rags— such things, for ten thousand souls, have been the hidden leadership of heaven to the Rock that is higher than themselves. Deep is calling unto deep, the deep of misery to that of mercy. Out of the depths man is always crying. And though he often knows not what he cries for, God knows and answers through the dark by leading the overwhelmed soul to *Himself.*

Again, we note how often men are led thither by lowly devotion to the best. Loyal to the highest that they know, they are confronted by the higher Rock. If this universe is not a righteous universe and if love lies not at the heart of things, what use is there in striving to be righteous or in making love the passion of our lives? But the strange thing is that whenever a man is loyal to the best and worthiest he knows, he is never left with questions like that. He is led upward from his cherished loyalties to something loftier than his loyalties. It is a Rock, solid and impregnable; the Rock on which the universe is built. He passes upward from his values to the reality of what he values; he discovers he has aligned himself with God.

When men live for love and truth and mercy, God is always walking in their garden. They come to feel with deepening conviction that the things they strive for are not passing dreams, but answer to the realities of heaven. Do your duty, though it be very irksome, and do it because it *is* your duty; be tender-hearted, forgiving one another, no matter how you are tempted to be hard; and above you, over-arching you, the reality of what you strive for, you will discover God who is our Rock. "Inasmuch as ye have done it unto one of the least of these, ye have done it unto me." To be true to the highest that we know is to be led to the Rock that is still higher. "Madam," said Dr. Hood Wilson once to a lady lamenting she had lost the Lord, "go down and work in the slums and you will find Him."

But, above all, we are led to the Rock that is higher by the guiding hand of Christ—"no man cometh to the Father but by me." When we crave for the certainty that God is love, we may turn in vain to nature or to history. Nature and history have many voices, but they never cry, "I am the way." Only Christ proclaims Himself the way to One higher than our highest thought, because deeper than our deepest need. Thus, although the psalmist did not know it, he saw the day of Christ and he was glad. It was for Christ that he was yearning in that passionate out-cry of his spirit. It is He who takes us by the hand and leads us where philosophy can never lead us, to Love, to a Father on the throne, to "the rock that is higher than I."

Leaving It There

Leave it all quietly to God, my soul.—Ps. 62:1 (Moffatt)

There are times in life when it is a great help to have someone say to us, "Leave all that to me." Like a gentle wind it blows the clouds away. When one has a difficult schedule or has arrangements to make for a marriage or a funeral, to have someone who is competent and expert take over is often an untold relief. There is much in life that we must do ourselves, and no one can relieve us of certain duties. There are crosses each of us must carry and burdens nobody can take away. But how much more difficult life would be in times of anxiety or strain were there not someone standing by to say to us, "Leave all that to me." That is particularly the voice of fatherhood, which in reality is the secret of childhood's carefree spirit. A child does not worry about clothes or meals. Instinctively it leaves that to its father. And much of the joy of childhood springs from the trustful relationship to somebody who says, "Leave all that to me."

It is beautiful to notice how the psalmist had grasped that comforting energy of God. Baffled, betrayed, a prey to bitter anguish—"Leave it all quietly to God, my soul." And so for him, too, came interior peace, and the light of heaven began to shine again and the storm was changed to calm.

Now this command which the psalmist gave his soul is one of the secrets of the spiritual life. No passing of ages has made it less imperative. Think, for instance, of those ways of providence which it is impossible to understand, for in every life, however blessed and happy, there are things impossible to understand. And often these are strange and bitter and so difficult to reconcile with love that the bravest soul is near to unbelief. When prayers seem to go unanswered, when someone dear and young is taken away, when those who would not harm a living creature are bowed under intolerable pain, how hard it is to say that God is good, and saying it, believe it with a confidence which is pleasing in His eyes. We want to know. We want to understand. Sometimes, like Job, we expostulate with God. And so, expostulating, everything grows harder till we are brought to the margins of despair. How much wiser the attitude of David, plunged into the very sea of trouble—"Leave it all quietly to God, my soul."

We are not here just to understand. Now we know in part and see in part. We are here to glorify God by trusting Him even when we do not understand. And such trusting carries its own evidences in the rich inward peace it brings as if our life were in tune with the Eternal. "My meat is to do the will of him that sent me." His meat was neither to probe nor to expostulate. When the cup was bitter, when the cross was heaviest, when the lights were darkened in the Garden of Gethsemane— He left it all quietly to God.

Think of those intellectual problems which visit and perplex the human mind. There are times in life when these are very perplexing. Who that has ever thought at all has not had anxious thoughts about the doctrine of election? What, too, of the foreordering of God and of His sovereignty, universal and particular, if I am really a creature of free will? Such things, and a thousand things like these, puzzle and confound the human mind. And we are so made that we cannot avoid thinking of them with the mysterious facilities which God has given us. Yet I venture to say that something must be wrong if such great thoughts that have baffled all the centuries rob the believer of his joy and peace.

There are times when it is well to consider such things. A great problem may be an inspiration. The opposite of faith is never reason; the opposite of faith is sight. But there are other times when the highest part of wisdom is not to torment ourselves with things too high for us, but to give our souls the counsel of the psalmist— "Leave it all quietly to God, my soul." Someday we shall arrive and understand. We shall see His face and His name shall be on our foreheads—it shall be written out in the region of the brain. Meantime we have a life to live, a heart to cultivate, a service to perform. "What is that to thee—follow thou me."

Again, we are to remember the psalmist's counsel in the hours when we have done our best—and failed. The higher the service that we seek to render, the more are we haunted by the sense of failure. The man who has no goal doesn't fear failure. But in higher ministries, when soul is touching soul and we are working not in things, but lives, how haunting is the sense of failure. Every Sunday School teacher knows it well, every mother with her growing family, and every preacher of the Gospel. So little accomplished, so little difference made, so little fruit for the laborious toil, although the seed sown may have been steeped in prayer. Well then, are we to give up in discouragement? Are we to leave the battleline and be spectators because we hear no cheering sound of triumph? My dear reader, there is a better way, and it is just the old way of this gallant psalmist—"Leave it all quietly to God, my soul."

Often when we fail, we are succeeding. We are doing more than we have dreamed. We are helping with our rough, coarse hands because Another with a pierced hand is there. Do your best, and do it for His sake. Keep on doing it and don't resign. And as to fruitage and harvest and success—leave it all quietly to Him.

> When obstacles and trials seem
> Like prison walls to be,
> I do the little I can do
> And leave the rest to Thee.

Harvest Thanksgiving

The valley . . . are covered over with corn.—Ps. 65:13

One of the uses of the harvest festival is to awaken us to things we take for granted. We are always in danger of taking things for granted, especially in organized communities. The desert traveler can never take his water for granted, he has to shape his route to reach the wells. But in the city, where we have water supplied to every house, such a thing causes us no concern at all. That is especially true of daily bread. We just take it for granted. It has been bought at the baker's or the grocer's, and beyond that our vision seldom goes. And then comes the harvest festival, and beyond our city shops we see the golden mystery of harvest. We are awakened; we are shaken out of our ruts—and do you know what someone has said about these ruts? He has said that the rut only differs from the grave in that the latter is a little deeper. We are touched with the wonder of the commonplace—we feel the glory that invests the ordinary.

It is this, too, that makes it preeminently a Christian festival, for one of the beautiful things about our Lord was that He never took usual things for granted. The Pharisees were always doing that. They took the lilies of the field for granted. They took it for granted that if a woman was caught in sin, the God-appointed conduct was to stone her. And then came our Lord, with that dear heart of His, and He did not see just the glory of the rare thing; He saw the glory of the familiar thing—the sparrow and the mustard seed, and the woman who was a sinner on the streets.

It is very comforting to bear in mind that He never takes you for granted either. Other people are doing that continually: they have you classified and docketed in pigeon-holes. But to Him you are always wonderful though you are only a typist in an office and nobody would ever call you clever. Filled with the wonder and potential of the commonplace, *that* was the vision of the Savior, and it is to that that we are summoned by the recurrence of the harvest thanksgiving.

Another benefit of harvest festival is to impress on us our mutual dependence. It is a call to halt a moment and reflect how we are all bound together with one another. The priceless secret of cooperation is God's secret of survival. The individual needs everybody, and everybody needs the individual.

Now at every harvest festival, how vividly is that thought brought before us! It preaches, with a kind of silent eloquence, the interdependence of man. Those sheaves of corn that stand within the sanctuary—who plowed the fields for them? Who in the bleak morning sowed the seed, that sower and reaper might rejoice together? There are unknown plowmen and harvesters and millers and bakers whose names are never heard behind that loaf of bread on the table. Was that why the Master chose the bread to be the symbol of His dying love? He might have chosen one of the flowers which charmed Him and which He has bidden us to consider. But, choosing bread, He chose the staff of life, and that life wasn't one of isolation, but of a rich cooperating brotherhood. We are always in danger of forgetting that when we look at the bread on our table. And then the church comes with her harvest festival and says, "This do in remembrance," and we feel the interdependence of humanity and the fact that in back of everything the shops supply us with, stands the Creator, and on Him we utterly depend.

The Contradictions of Life

We went through fire and through water, but thou broughtest us out into a wealthy place.—Ps. 66:12

This psalm is the glad utterance of a soul that is looking back to the deliverance from Egypt. It is a song of praise for the great goodness of the Lord in bringing His people to the promised land. There had been times when that journey seemed a failure; times when the desert seemed so terrible that Israel began to cry again for Egypt. But God in His strange sovereignty of leadership was going to bring them on to Canaan yet. They had been brought through fire—the fiery sun in the wilderness of Sinai; the fiery serpents with the venomous bites. They had been through water. Had they not crossed the Red Sea and the Jordan dry shod? Now they looked back on it, and the great souls saw it had all been necessary. They had needed that baptism in the Red Sea; they had needed the chastening of the fiery serpents if God was to bring them into a wealthy place.

But when the poet speaks of fire and water, I think he means more than the material elements. The commonest word, for the true poet's heart, has wings that carry it away into the distances. There are suggestions, there are expansions in our ordinary vocabulary, for one who sees as every poet does. And the literal fire and the literal water for David flashed into types and symbols of far other things. Water! O God, were there no seas of sorrow, were there no floods of tears? Fire! And had no fiery trials befallen them out in the desert and down by Sinai? It was all that that was in the poet's heart; it was all that he saw again. In *that* sense, what a depth of meaning in the words: "We went through fire and water, but thou broughtest us out into a wealthy place."

Now there are many lessons in our verse. They are filled with the truth of the leadership of God, and we might spend many a profitable hour in thinking of that omnipotent Deliverer. But I want to take one simple thought to dwell upon. It is the apparent contradictions of our life. He speaks of fire and water: are they not very opposites? Fire mounts and water falls. And when we want to quench the fire, when the call rises to extinguish it, what do we use? Why, water. And "we went," said David, "through fire and water, but thou broughtest us out into a wealthy place." Life, then, has need of opposites. And life advances through its contradictions. If you are in line with the leadership of God, you come into your wealth by strange antagonisms. Now let us take that thought as a Scriptural lamp and swing it over some of the passages of life. There is a wonderful comfort and power in it for the right management of changing days. And think of life's common experiences first.

I take it that there is no one who has not known the music and the light of joy. It may have come like a bird upon the wing. It may have come more sternly when the fight was fought, when the hard duty was done. It may have leaped from one of these thousand wells that in the weariest heart, thanks be to God, are not quite silted up. And it made life so new, so rich, so filled with the possibilities of heaven that we were ready to pray when we were joyful and say that it was God who brought us here. And so it was, my friend, so it was. He creates light, and every good gift is from Him. And the pleasures of music, the song of birds, the laughter of children, the love of friends, these things and things like these, sources of happiness, crowned in the joy of Christ—these things are all from God.

And then come sorrow and suffering and loss, and gloom for the sunshine and weeping for the laughter. And the heart languishes and mourns like Lebanon for the great season of the cross has come. And all that we ever hoped is contradicted. And here is the exact opposite of all our joy. And if God was in *that*, how can He be in *this*, unless our Leader contradicts Himself?

But the strange thing about Jesus Christ is that He has saved us by being a Man of Sorrows, yet He was always speaking of His joy. And the strange thing about the Christian Gospel is that joy is its keynote, joy is its glad refrain; and yet it comes to me, to you, and whispers, My son, my daughter, take up thy cross and bear it. Did Jesus of Nazareth contradict Himself? Is the Gospel in opposition of the Gospel? Never, friend, not that: a house divided against itself is doomed. But it is through the strange antagonisms of the heart, and all the teaching of a diverse guidance, that we are brought at last to our wealthy place.

Remember, then, that even in daily life God means us to advance through contradictions. And when the brightness passes and the shadows come, when the song of the morning is changed into a cry, don't think that any unlooked-for storm has swept you from your charted course to heaven. It takes both lights and shadows to make a summer. There is December in the perfect year no less than June. The earth rolls on to harvest through night and day, through bitter cold and heat. And you and I need all that ever came to us if our field is to be golden by and by.

But passing from these common experiences of life, I note that we cannot open our New Testament without finding the same element of contradiction.

I think, for example, of the great words of Jesus, "Come unto me, and I will give you rest." And if there is one word that sums up the Gospel and carries all the Gospel blessings in its bosom, I don't know what it is other than that word "rest." Mr. Moody used to tell the story of a little girl who was very ill. And her mother sang to her all the familiar hymns and spoke to her of God and love, but the little daughter was restless and fretful still. And then her mother stooped down and without a word she took her child into her arms. And her child, with a look of unutterable peace, said, "Ah, mother, that's what I want."

Now, what is the very opposite of rest? The very opposite of rest is struggle. And what stands in flat contradiction to the thought of peace? It is the thought of war. And yet I cannot open my New Testament without finding that the follower of Christ is called to war. "Fight the good fight of faith," says the Apostle. "Put on the whole armor of God, that you may be a victor in the evil day. For we wrestle not against flesh and blood, but against principalities and powers." And how can this be? The Gospel of Christ is rest, and yet the note of struggle rings in it? And it is peace, perfect peace, to live with Christ, and yet the trumpet sounds the alarm of war? It is an opposition, a contradiction. The Bible seems in arms against itself. Here, you would say, is a divided house, and a divided house like that can never stand. But "we went through fire and water," says the psalmist, "and thou broughtest us out into a wealthy place!" And even fire and water are not farther separated from each other than the peace and war that helps us to our goal. I cannot explain these contradictions, but I *live* through them and they carry me on. For somehow I never have peace except I struggle, and I cannot struggle if I am not at peace.

There have been creeds that said, Why struggle, be at rest, but they have rejected the battle that the soul might be still. And there are creeds that have said, You have nothing to do with rest: strive on, fight on, for character, heaven, God. And both philosophies, for all the practical help they ever gave, have been only stillborn children. Christ comes: He opens His arms to these antagonisms. He takes the contradictory thought of peace and war into the very bosom of His Gospel; and there, in mysterious ways, they harmonize, and my life advances through these contradictions.

Now come a little deeper—into the realm of thought. There too, through fire, through water, through truths that seem opposed to one another, God brings His children to a wealthy place. There is one truth that is a little in abeyance nowadays: I mean the truth of the sovereignty of God. We dwell so lovingly upon God's fatherhood that we are almost in danger of forgetting His sovereignty. It comes like music from the hills to sing together, "God moves in a mysterious way His wonders to perform." Do you believe in a foreseeing God? Do you believe in a fore-ordaining God? Do you believe that the very hairs of your head are numbered, and that not a sparrow can be struck and fall without the prevision of the Infinite Mind? Then every event has been fore-calculated yonder, and every trifle is a pre-arrangement; and back of every word I ever spoke and every deed I ever tried to do, there moves the sovereign will of the Almighty.

Now tell me, in absolute opposition to that fore-ordering will—what stands? You answer in a moment—the free will of man. If I am free to exercise my will as I believe and not the helpless creature of necessity, what becomes of the pre-determining will of God? If there is one flat contradiction in the universe, I think, my friends, it is there. And am I to give up my moral freedom? Heaven guard me, never! And am I to cast the sovereignty of God to be swirled and scattered by the winds of heaven? No, God forbid, life would be a poor thing then. But I am to remember that I am going through fire and water in order that God may bring me to a wealthy place. I thought that joy and sorrow were contradictions, yet my life has been growing rich and deep through them. I thought that peace and war were contradictions, but I never could win my crown except for them. I thought the sovereignty of God and the free will of man were contradictions, yet it takes belief in both, even if unreconciled, to deepen, steady, and inspire my character. And someday, when the rolling mists have fled and the rosy-fingered dawn is on the hills, and in the dawn the King in His beauty comes, I shall find that things which to my finite and fragmentary mind seemed alien and utterly opposed to one another are blended into perfect accord in the infinite intelligence of God.

Watch the streets when the factories come out. Watch the children playing after school. There is movement, ceaseless activity, shouting voices; and you look at it and say, what life is there! It is life that is pulsing in these thousands of hearts. It is life that is moving in these thousands of feet. It is life that is echoing in these thousands of voices.

And then, on a quiet Sunday afternoon, you steal away to where the dead are lying. It may be there is someone of your own there, and a fresh flower lies upon the grave. And the eye is sealed and the voice is silenced, and the busy heart will never beat here again. And the gulf between joy and sorrow, between peace and war, is not so deep, so dark, as the great gulf between life and death. O death, thou last great enemy of life, what a measureless distance between thee and living! All other antagonisms are weak compared to this, the utter opposition of life and death.

But "we went through fire and water," says the psalmist, "but thou broughtest us out into a wealthy place." And no man ever wins his spiritual fortune but through the great antagonism of life and death. We are like seed corn with all life germinant here. But how are we to win our golden harvest? "Except a corn of wheat fall into the ground and *die.*" I live and die—to live. My life advances through that contradiction *now.* And in the great eternity, where the one light is God and where every wound is staunched and every tear is dried, I shall find that the burning fire of life was needed, and the waters of Jordan that quenched that fire were needed to bring me out into my wealthy place.

Summer and Winter

Thou hast made summer and winter.—Ps. 74:17

I suppose there are few who seriously doubt that the maker of summertime is God. There is something in every summer's glory that tells us of the touch of the divine, for here indeed we see the handiwork of God. But notice that in our text it says a great deal more than just that God hast made the summer. It says "Thou hast made the summer and the winter."

It was an old belief which is still held by multitudes that rival deities had been at work on nature. It was not the handiwork of one god; it was the handiwork of two gods. And all the sharp antagonisms of the universe and all the contrasts amid which we live were tokens of their mutual enmity. Had one made the glory of the day and the other the darkness of the night? Had one cheered us with the genial heart and the other cursed us with the bitter cold? It was one power that made the radiant morn, and another that made the deepening shadow. There were millions of people who believed that once, and there are millions who still believe it.

How different, how superbly different, is the spiritual vision of this singer of the Psalms! It was the God of Abraham who made the summer, and it was his God who made the winter, too. The very hand that decked the summer meadow and cast the mantle of green upon the forest touched that summer glory and it died. Thou hast made the summer *and* the winter. Thou hast clothed and thou hast stripped again. Thou has lengthened out the shining hours, and thou hast crushed them into a little space. Thou hast created the gentle breath of evening that falls on man with benediction, and thou the bitter and the piercing blast.

Now I want you to carry that great truth into regions which the eye has never seen. I want you to believe that one God has made the summer and winter of the heart. There are experiences which come to every man which are tingling with the touch of heaven. They are so radiant and so delightful that we never doubt the hand which gave them to us. It is good to be grateful for such recurring gladness, but more is needed for a life of victory. He who would conquer must have faith to say, "Thou hast made the summer *and* the winter." God is not only gracious when the sun shines, He is just as gracious when the wind is sharp. He gives the glory and He strips the glory, and on His vesture is the name of Love. He who can trace His hand when it is winter—who can still say He loves me and He knows—has won the secret of that abiding peace which the world cannot give and cannot take away.

What a summertime the patriarch Job enjoyed! How the sun shone on him for many days! There was no one like him in the land of Uz for health and wealth and happiness and peace. And then there fell on him the blast of winter, and he was desolate and deathly cold, and "The Lord hath given and the Lord hath taken away," said Job, "blessed be the name of the Lord."

Do you remember what his wife advised him? His wife advised him to curse God and die. Do you remember what his friends advised him? It was to confess that he had played the hypocrite. But Job was far too big a man for that. "Though he slay me yet will I trust him," he said. The faith in which he conquered was just this, "Thou hast made the summer *and* the winter."

And now another question arises: How does God make the summer? What is the unseen loom on which He weaves that garment of beauty which we see Him by? Don't consider me as being mystical when I reply that winter is the loom. It is a truth which science will corroborate that out of the winter He hath made the summer. When a child rises in the morning, what an exuberance of life there is! The eyes are bright and the feet swift to run and play; and all that life, so wonderful and glad, has been created in the womb of sleep.

We say that in winter everything is dead. That is what they said of Jairus' daughter. And then came Christ and looked at her and said,

"The maiden is not dead, but sleepeth." So we learn that in the dead of winter—and we never talk about the dead of summer—what we call death is but the child's sleep. Life has not vanished even though the eyes are closed. And then comes morning with all its joy and renewed life, all because of the quiet sleep of wintertime. There is no thrilling beauty of springtime without the chill of December. God needs the one if He would make the other. He fashions glory out of decay.

Consider that truth then and carry it to a higher sphere. It is as true of us as of the earth that winter holds the secret of the summer. Out of December, God will fashion June. Out of the cross, He fashions the crown. Out of the trial that was so hard to bear, He brings the beauty of the saintly character. "God be merciful to me a sinner"—that is the winter of our discontent, and yet when a man has cried that prayer of despair, he is preparing for his summer and his song.

There came to Glasgow, not so long ago, a pianist with an excellent reputation. I read the *Herald's* criticism of him, and there was one thing in it that I especially noted. The *Herald* said that he had been always brilliant—always been wonderful as an executant—but now there was a depth of feeling in him that had never been present in a suburb, I met a relative of the pianist. As we began to discuss him and the *Herald's* criticism of him, the relative said to me, "Did you notice that? And do you know what was the secret of the change? It was the death of his mother eighteen months ago." He was an only son, unmarried, and had been simply devoted to his mother. And then she died and he was left alone, and all the depths were broken up in him. And now he played as only he can play who knows what life and death are and what sorrow is—and out of the winter God had made his summer.

Perpetual sunshine may make men brilliant, perhaps, but never deep. They don't understand. They never know. They condescend, for they cannot sympathize, for much that is beautiful in men and women springs from the season when the tree is stripped. All that is fairest in the world rises from the darkness of the cross. My brother, that is also how He leads us, for to our hearts the world is but the shadow. He will never leave us nor forsake us.

There is only one answer that can be given to that question in the light of all that we have learned. Not just for their own sakes has He made them—not for their sublimity or beauty merely. Through night and day, through sunshine and through storm, God has His purpose which is never baffled. And that one purpose—how shall we describe it? Put in simple language it is this: It is the purpose of every living thing that after summer there should be the harvest. Of course, God has made purposes in every thing and every season. Undoubtedly when He made the summer beautiful, He meant it to give pleasure to His children. But there is one thing deeper than all others, and that is the mellowing of the harvest field. Nothing is beautiful in nature for its own sake. Beauty is a trust for other's sakes. Summer and winter look beyond themselves to the time when the flower shall wither and the fruit shall come. He that liveth to himself is dead. There is he that scattereth and yet increaseth. Our gifts—our summer sun and winter storm—these have an end to serve in other lives. We are not here simply to be happy. We are here to serve and be a blessing. And "Thou hast made our summer and our winter" that we may have the joy of harvesttime.

The Higher Purposes of Winter

Thou hast made . . . winter.—Ps. 74:17

It is always easy to believe that God has made the summertime. There is something in a perfect summer day that speaks to us of the divine. The beauty which is around us everywhere, the singing of the birds in every tree, the warmth of the pleasant summer sun, the amazing prodigality of life, these, as by filaments invisible, draw our hearts to the Giver of them all and make it easy to say, "Thou hast made the summer."

With winter it is different. It is not easy to see the love of God there. There is a great deal of suffering in winter both for the animal creation and for man. It may therefore aid the faith of some who may be tempted to doubt the love of God in winter if I suggest some of its spiritual accomplishments.

One of the higher offices of winter is to deepen our appreciation of the summer. We should be blind if summer were perpetual. Someone has said, and very truly said, that our dear ones are only ours when we have lost them. They have to pass away into the silent land before we know them for what they really are. And in like manner summer has to pass, leaving us in the grip of icy winter, before we fully appreciate the summer. It is not the man who lives in lovely Scotland who feels most deeply how lovely Scotland is. It is the exile on some distant shore, yearning for the mountains and the glens. It is not the man with abundant, unbroken health who feels most deeply the value of his health. *That* is realized when health is shattered.

In Caithness, where I lived four years, there is a great scarcity of trees. I never knew how much I loved the trees till I dwelt in a land where there are none. And we never know all that summer means to us, in its pageantry of life and beauty, till we lose it in the barrenness of winter. Lands that have no winter have no spring. They never know the thrilling of the spring when the primroses awake and the wild hyacinths, and the iris waves in the breeze. Thoughts like these, in January days, make it easier for faith to say, "*Thou* hast made the winter."

Another of the higher purposes of winter is the greater demands it makes upon the will. I should like to take a simple illustration. In summer it is comparatively easy to get out of bed at the appointed hour. For the earth is warm, and the birds are busy singing, and the light is streaming through the open windows. But in winter, to fling the covers off and get up when it is dark and perishingly cold, *that* is quite a different affair. That calls for a certain resolution. It makes instant demands upon the will.

Now broaden that thought to the compass of the day, and you reach a truth that cannot be denied. The countries where the will is most developed and where moral life is most vigorous and strong are the countries that have winter in their year. There "ain't no Ten Commandments east of Suez," says Kipling in a familiar line. The singular thing is that east of Suez there isn't any winter in the year. Rigorous winter days when life is difficult and when it takes some doing even to get up are God's tonic for His children's will. "O well for him whose will is strong. He suffers, but he does not suffer long." Let any young fellow have his will under control and he is on the highway to his victory. Summer is languid; winter makes us resolute. We have to do things when we don't feel like them. And Thou—the Giver of the Ten Commandments—*Thou* hast made the winter.

Another accomplishment of winter is to intensify the thought of home. In lands that bask in a perpetual sunshine, home-life is always at a minimum. I had a friend who for three years was prisoner in an internment camp in Germany. I asked him once when he felt most homesick, and I am not likely to forget his answer. He said that the only times when he felt homesick were when fog settled down upon the camp reminding him of winter fogs in Glasgow. In summer he was happy. It was good to be alive in summer. But when the fog came, he thought of lighted streets and saw his cozy and comfortable home. And always the thought of home is sweetest, and the home-life richest and most beautiful, in the dark, cold season of the winter. We talk in the same breath of hearth and home, and it is in winter that the hearth is glowing.

There is one poem about a humble home more beautiful than any other in our literature. It is a picture by the hand of genius of the joy and reverence of the hearth. But the "Cottar's Saturday Night" could never have been written in the tropics. It is the child of a land with winter in its year.

Now think of everything we owe to home. Think of what the nation owes to home. "From scenes like these auld Scotia's grandeur springs." Home is the basis of national morality. Is it not easier when one thinks of these things to say in the bitterest January day, "*Thou* hast made the winter"?

The last purpose of winter I shall mention is how it stirs our sluggish hearts to charity. With that we are all perfectly familiar. Did you ever watch a singer in the street in the warm and balmy days of summer? The passersby pay him little heed and rarely give him a coin even though he is singing all the charms of Annie Laurie. But in winter, when the air is biting, and when the snow is deep upon the ground, Annie Laurie brings him in a harvest. Folk are extraordinarily good to me in giving me donations for the poor. For one donation that I get in summertime, however, I get ten in the bitterness of winter. Winter unlocks the gates of charity. It unseals the hidden springs of pity. It moves us with compassion for the destitute, and so to be moved is a very Christlike thing. Such thoughts as these in stern and icy days, when we are tempted perhaps to doubt the love of God, make it easier to say with David, "*Thou* hast made the winter."

The Highway in the Sea

Thy way is in the sea.—Ps. 77:19

Doubtless when the psalmist penned our text, his first thought was the crossing of the Red Sea. He was seeking to revive his drooping heart by recalling the saving power of God in Israel's past. But the words of a true poet never end when we have found their literal significance. It is one mark of poetic inspiration that it is capable of indefinite expansion. It is not by narrowing down, it is by widening out, that we get to the real genius of a poet, and the writer of this psalm had the true gift. Thy way is in the sea—were there not glimpses in that of truths which the Exodus never could exhaust? So did the writer feel—so must we all feel—and it is on two of these suggestions that I wish to dwell.

There were two places above all others dreaded by the Jew. The one was the desert and the other was the sea. The desert—for it was the home of the wild beasts and the haunt of the robbers who plundered the Jewish villages, and it was across the desert that those armies came which besieged Jerusalem and pillaged it. And the sea—because it was full of storms and treachery in Jewish eyes; it was hungry, cruel, insatiable deep. It is very difficult for us who are an island nation to enter into that feeling of the Jew. The ocean is our defense and our great ally, and we have loved the sound of its waves since we were children. But to the Hebrew it was very different. For him there was no rapture in the lonely shore. He loved his fields and his vineyards and his markets, but the element he dreaded was the sea.

But now comes the voice of the great Jewish singer and says to the people, God's way is in the sea. In the very sphere and element they dread there is the path and purpose of divinity. They loved their gardens and the Lord was there. They loved their vineyards and the Lord was there. In places that were sweet and dear to them, there was the presence of the God of Israel. But nonetheless in the realm of what was terrible and in the regions which they shunned instinctively, there was the ordered path of the Almighty.

I think we should all do well to learn that lesson—God's way is in the very thing we dread. We are so apt to cry that God has forgotten us when the experience which we loathe arrives. We all love health, but we all dread disease. We love success, but we dread disappointment. We love the energy and glow of life, but we dread the silence of death and the cold grave—but the way of the Lord of heaven is in the sea. Believe that He is working out His purposes through what is dark as well as through what is bright. Believe that what is hardest to bear or understand is never disordered nor purposeless nor pathless. What is the object of thy greatest dread, O Hebrew? Is it the sea? "God's way is in the sea."

And second, the sea is the element of restlessness. That is a familiar thought in the Old Testament, receiving its noblest and most poetic expression in Psalm 107. It is not easy for us to realize how vividly this thought impressed the ancient world, for the most ignorant among us has been taught by science that nothing in the whole universe is at rest. The earth is flying with tremendous speed around the sun; and the solar system itself is hurrying somewhere; we hardly need to turn to the waves of the sea to get our parable of restless energy. It was very different with the Jew. For him, the earth was fixed under a fixed heaven. It was set fast by the ordering of God. And over against it, in the sharpest of all contrasts, rocked and surged the restless sea. The sea was the element of change, the home of restlessness. One day it was as calm as if it were asleep; the next it was tossed and rent in a storm. It was all that of which a Jew would think when the word came to him that God's way was in the sea.

Now, there is an unrest in our life that is the consequence and issue of our sin. It is as true today as when the prophet wrote it, that "there is no rest for the wicked, saith my God." Let a man deliberately choose the lower levels and yield up the reins to his baser nature, and his whole existence becomes one of the great discontent—there is nothing of God's way in that.

But there is a restlessness that is inspired; there is a discontent that is divine; there is a spirit within us that will not let us rest, and it is the very spirit of the wind-swept sea; and if there is one thing written clear in human history, it is that the way of God is there.

In one of Shakespeare's sonnets there is a memorable line, "With what I must enjoy, contented least." There can be little doubt, from the connection, that Shakespeare is referring to his plays. "With what I most enjoy, contented least"—then Shakespeare was not satisfied with Hamlet. There is a grand unrest there like the unrest of the ocean, and through the heart of it there runs the track of God. We are not here to be satisfied and indifferent. We shall be satisfied when we awake. We are here to strive and yearn and toil and pray for things that are too large for our three-score years. And in that distressing and yet divine unrest, there is the way and ordering of God. God's way is never in the stagnant pool; His way is ever in the restless sea. It is He who says to us, "This is not your rest." It is He who fills us with eternal hope. It is He who makes us rise after each failure to strive again for what we cannot reach. So we toil on and all we do is fragmentary, but we shall be satisfied in the eternal morning. He keeps us "climbing up the climbing wave" here, but in heaven there shall be no more sea.

The Secrecy of God

Thy way is in the sea, and thy path in the great waters, and thy footsteps are not known.—Ps. 77:19

Men tell us that there are few more impressive sights than that of a burial at sea. It is even more solemn and arresting than the last rites beside an earthly grave. There is the ceasing of the throbbing engines, the gathering of the hushed crowd upon the deck. There is the simple service, the lifting of the body, and then—the plunge into the deep. And it is this element of silent secrecy, this hiding in unfathomable depths, which thrills and solemnizes and subdues.

Something like that was in the poet's mind when he said of God, "Thy way is in the sea." Mingling with all his other thoughts was the thought that God has His unfathomable secrets. And it is upon that element of secrecy, so characteristic of the divine procedure, that I want to dwell.

The best gifts are always at our hand. The brightest are never far away. All things needed for the song and crown are in the region where our hearts are beating. And yet though they are here, they are not flaunting themselves. They are by our side, but they are never showy. There is no name inscribed upon their foreheads nor any blast of the trumpet on their lips.

Think, for example, of the gift of love. In the darkest spot on earth some love is found. I doubt if there is a man so brutal and so base that no one loves him and thrills at his approach. And yet how silent and how secret love is, hiding itself away from human eye and speaking in a momentary glance. Our poets liken love to a flower. It is red as the rose, white as the lily. Yet love is not a flower of the field; love is the treasure hidden in the field. And thousands cross the field and never see it nor do they dream of the treasure hidden there until at last, in the appointed hour, passes the traveler who understands.

It is always so with the love of man. It is always so with the love of God. God's love is here, and yet how secret and hidden it all is—how meaningless to the blinded—till Christ has come and shown His wounded side and led us to the glory of the cross.

The same thing also is true of the gift of life. Life is the one impenetrable secret. We have it and we thank God for it, and yet the wisest does not know what it is. It is not only of the heaven of heavens when looking up we say, "Thy footsteps are not known." It is not only where the sun is shining and where beyond the sun there are the angels. The deepest mysteries are not in heaven; the deepest mysteries are not in hell. The deepest mysteries are here where we are, and know not what we are. Life looks at us in every human glance. Life speaks to us in every human voice. Life speaks to us in every human voice. Life meets us riotously in the play of children. Life shines transfigured on the face of saints. And yet what is it, so near and yet so far; so strong and beautiful, and yet so frail; so evident that none can pass it by; so hidden that no human hand can reach it? It baffles science with all its mighty claims. It baffles philosophy with all its pondering. No thought can get at it. Yet it is here where you are sitting and where I am writing. God's footsteps are in the temple of my heart, and yet His footsteps are not known.

Not with the sound of a bell does God arrive when our feet are at the turning of the ways. Over the silent sea the boat approaches, but the oars are muffled and we don't hear it as it comes from the haven of the far away. Decked with the embroidery of common moments, the moments which are not common reach us. Wearing the aspect of our usual hours, our great hours of destiny arrive—and life shall never be the same again. We thought it was a common hand that touched us; we know now it was the hand of God. Ah, sirs, life would be easy if providential hours declared themselves; if they met us radiant and with an uplifted look, and cried, "I am one of thy great hours." But they never meet us in a guise like that—never betray their greatness by their bearing—we hear no sound of the approaching footsteps—thy footsteps are not known.

When Abraham rested by the door at Mamre, he saw three travelers drawing near to the tent. They were but wayfarers, thirsty and dusty, and he had no idea that they were angels. And it is always thus that the angel-hours come, wearing the garments of the undistinguished, treading on the dusty ways of life, worn with the everyday weariness of man. How many noisy hours have passed away, and left no impact upon our life. How many a little hour has been a seed, and it rooted deep and blossomed high as heaven. Yet was it borne upon the wind and so noiselessly and fell so lightly that we never noticed it; and its roots are deep today and its topmost branches in the sky.

You who are students of the Scripture know what a favorite thought the secrecy of God was with Jesus Christ. It is not in the whirlwind that the kingdom comes when it makes it lodgment in the heart. Christ will not strive nor cry nor lift up His voice in the streets—those steep streets that lead into the soul. The kingdom comes as if a man should sleep, and the seed should spring up he knows not how. The kingdom comes just as the leaven comes, and who is so watchful as to see it rise? When Christ was born at the inn in Bethlehem, choirs of angels were singing in the sky. And when Christ comes again there will be the sound of the trumpet and a light so bright that every eye shall see Him.

But when Christ comes into the human soul, He comes with voice so soft that none can hear it except the ear on which the message falls. Christ does not ride in uproar to the soul; Christ steals in quiet secretly. The kingdom cometh not with observation, and here the kingdom is the King. His knock is so clear that when He knocks, you hear it, but His knock is so soft that no one else can hear it. To everyone else it is an ordinary footstep, and to everyone else it is an ordinary hand. But to you there is a wound upon the hand and the print of the nails upon the feet. To you it is CHRIST, and He is yours forever in infinite and redeeming love.

Notable, too, is this element of secrecy in the life of Christ when He was here on earth. God hid Him under the garb of poverty and set Him amid the silence of the hills.

When a *man* has a message which he burns to make known, you know the passion that rises in his heart. You know how the beckoning hand of London calls him, and how he is restless till he has reached the capital.

But when *God* had a message, He despised the capital and passed it by and all the glories of it, and He sent His Son into a secret place where the wind was fresh upon the hills. There He was born, and men were in the inn jesting and drinking and knew not it was He. And kings were rioting and scholars pondering and armies marching with the imperial eagles. But not a whisper broke upon that riot nor hushed the play of the children in the streets nor fell on the legionaries with a sense of awe as at a greater captain than their own. Wrapped in the secrecy of distant Galilee, moving obscurely amid obscurer villages, shrinking when men would hail Him king, craving for Bethany in crowded streets—*that* was the signet on the hand of God; *that* was the seal of the divine procedure. The footsteps of Jesus of Nazareth were the footsteps of God, and yet His footsteps were not known.

So far, then, upon the spheres of evidence, and now a word or two upon the other aspect. Can we discern the spiritual uses of this great element in God's procedure? I shall tell you how it seems to me to bear upon our triumph or our failure.

In the first place the secrecy of God is meant to be a spur to drive us on. There are things which are better for us not to hear, and God has the gracious strength to keep a secret. How often have we said to someone, "Ah, how I wish you had never told me that!" We can never have the same thoughts again since that one word was whispered in our ear. And we put it away from us and it comes again, and it rises from the dead when we least wish it; and we are brought lower and we are ashamed, just because someone could not keep a secret. There are times when there is strength in speech. There are times when there is strength in silence. There are things that it was very sweet to tell, but life has been far harder since we told them. And that is why God is silent in His love and will not speak although our hearts are craving; and tomorrow we shall thank Him for the silence that seems to be almost cruelty tonight.

"My father," said Isaac, as they went up the hill, "Here is the wood, but where then is the lamb?" Poor child, so wistful and so happy, it would have been cruelty to have told him that. And so with us who are but wistful children, speech may be cruel and secrecy may be kind. When we reach the hilltop we shall see; and seeing we shall understand.

There is hope for the world and there is hope for men when we can say, "God's footsteps are not known." The footsteps of sin and vice are always known. There is nothing unobtrusive about them. They leave their print of filthiness and blood on every pavement and on every newspaper. And that is why a thousand men are pessimists, for these reeking footsteps are before them and they forget that God is also there—only *His* footsteps are not known.

Let some drunken husband kill his wife tonight, and you shall hear all about it in tomorrow's newspaper. And any scoundrel may have his doings published there so that any child can read about them. But thousands of homes were very happy yesterday and wives were singing and children were playing, but you shall read nothing in the papers about that. All that is of *God,* for love is of God; but then, you see, God's footsteps are not known. And no one buys the paper to read that, and it is not at all notorious or flaunting. And what I say is that you must remember that sin is riotous and God's way is in the still, small voice—or hope will go and hearts will be embittered and faith will die into the cold of death.

And then, in closing, the secrecy of God is surely meant by God to keep us faithful. It is the pattern for our everyday life. It is given to help us on our daily round.

Rarely are we summoned to great deeds. To many of us they never come at all. We are not beckoned along the shining road to anything that might arrest the attention of the world. We make our journey by a quiet way, with crosses that are commonplace and duties that are ordinary duties unlustered by any sparkle of glory.

There are blessings in a life like that, and there are hardships too. We miss the excitement and the music and the cheering. And it is on that level road when we are a little disheartened and discouraged that we should recall the secrecy of God.

When a man is famous, his footsteps are well known. He is not nearer God on that account. From the tiniest violet up to Jesus Christ, God moves in quiet and unobtrusive paths. And if it is thus He lavishes His beauty and makes His infinite sacrifice of love, we can be very near Him in our calling.

His way is in the sea, and so let mine be. Let me live and work where there is depth and freedom. His footsteps are not known—ah, happy God, who hast thus chosen to reveal Thyself! So would I move apart and live unknown and never seek the clamor and the show; for love is not there with gladness in its eyes, nor does the road to the kingdom lie that way.

Drink From the Depths

He . . . gave them drink as out of the great depths.—Ps. 78:15

The psalmist is here reviewing the providence of God that sustained
the children of Israel in the desert. That providence had made a deep impression on him, and he delights to dwell upon its wonders. There is a
sense, I believe, in which the poet is really the best of all historians. He
sees by the gift of a trained imagination into the hearts of men and the
character of movements. And though he may lack the minute and critical
knowledge that is in the keeping of laborious students, yet he often brings
us nearer to the truth than the man who discovers and refutes his errors.

One often feels that it is so with the psalmist, and especially when
he is dealing with the Exodus. For him the miracles that marked that
journey were not isolated and solitary splendors. They were rather the
discoveries of that power which is everywhere present and everywhere
upholding; only in other lives they dealt with small numbers of people
while here in the Exodus they are with large numbers.

Take for example the water from the rock of which the psalmist is
speaking in our text. The wonder that God gave them water as out of
the great depths comes to him in a flash. He sees the Israelites crowding
around the rock and saying in their hearts, "This cannot last long." He
sees them watching for the supply to fail as, of course, coming from a
rock, it must soon do. And then he sees their look of wild surprise when
it dawns on them that the stream is inexhaustible and is fed by channels
they know nothing of, from boundless and unfathomable reservoirs.

What the people crave for is a draught of water, and God in His
mercy gives them their desire. But He fills their cups, not from a little

cistern, but as from some illimitable ocean. And the psalmist knows that that is always true, for whenever the Almighty satisfies His creatures, He gives them to drink as out of the great depths.

Think, then, for a moment of the world of nature as it unfolds itself in all its beauty around us. There is not a bird or beast, there is not a tree or flower, but is ministered to in the way our text describes. I take the tiniest weed that roots among the stones—the flower in the crannied wall of which the poet speaks—and I ask, What does it need to live; what does it need that it may flower and fruit? The answer is that it needs a little warmth; it needs an occasional moistening with rain.

Now in a certain measure that is true, but you can never stop there in this mysterious universe. At the back of the warmth which it needs, there is the sun; and at the back of every raindrop, there is sky and ocean. And it takes the sun and sea and the white cloud of heaven to satisfy that tiniest weed among the stones, which may come to its delicate beauty only to be unregarded and perhaps crushed by a passing foot.

Try to explain the light that a rose needs, and you are carried into the depths of solar energy. Look at the raindrop on the hedge—has it not been drawn "out of the boundless deep"? And so there is not a rose in any garden nor a leaf that unfolds itself on any tree that is not ever whispering to the hearing ear, "He gave me drink as out of the great depths."

Again, think of our senses for a moment—think of our sight and hearing, for example. One of the plainest facts about our senses is the different way they translate what they receive.

To one man a rose is just a rose and no more. To another, in the smallest flower there are thoughts that often lie too deep for tears. And it is not the eye alone that differentiates, it is the life that is hidden deep behind the eye; He giveth them drink as out of the great depths.

Two men may listen to a piece of music, and one, as he listens, is profoundly stirred by it. There seems to pass before him, as he listens, visions of what is high and fair and beautiful. And he hears the calling of his brightest hopes and the cry of regret for all his wasted years and the stooping over him again of faces that he has loved long since and lost awhile. All this is kindled in some hearts by music—this burning of hope and haunting of regret; yet play that very piece before another, and it is sound and fury, signifying nothing.

Is not the ear of a dead person perfect? Is not every membrane and convolution there? Yet call to it or whisper to it passionately, and will it play its part and carry the news of love? Yesterday there would have been a smile of recognition; there is not a flicker of response today.

So at the back of every sense we have there is a depth that can never be fathomed. All that a man is, looks through his eyes. All that his soul is, listens through his ears. If the eye could speak or if the ear could speak, would they not echo the language of the text, "He gave us drink as out of the great depths?"

Again let us think for a moment of God's ways in providence—in the ordering and discipline of our lives. One of the lessons we learn as we grow older is that our discipline is not exceptional. When we are young our joys are all our own; we never dream that others could have known them. When we are young we take our little sorrows as if there were no such sorrows in the world. And much of the bitterness of childish trial lies in its terrible sense of isolation; in the feeling that in the whole wide world there is no one who has had to suffer just like us. It seems as if God has cut a special channel for us out of which no other life has ever drunk. In joy and grief, in sunshine and in shadow, we seem to move apart when we are children. But as life advances and our outlook broadens, and we learn the story of the lives around us, then we see that we are not alone but are being made to drink of the great depths.

It is not by exceptional providences that we live. It is not by exceptional joys we are enriched. It is not by anything rare or strange or singular that we are fashioned under the hand of God. It is by sorrows that are as old as man, by trials that a thousand hearts have felt, by joys that are common as the wind is common that breathes on the palace and on the poorest street. By these things do we live; by these we grow; by love and tears, by trials, by work, by death; by the things that link us all into a brotherhood, the things that are common to ten thousands hearts. And it is when we come to recognize that truth and to feel our comradeship within a common discipline, that we say, as the psalmist said of Israel, "He gave us drink as out of the great depths."

Now there is one thing that always arrests me in the Bible. It is that the Bible is such an ancient book, and yet is so intensely modern and practical. Think of the ages which have fled since it was written and how "heaven and earth have passed away" since then; think of our cities and of the life we live in them and of the stress and strain unknown in the quiet Bible times. To me it is wonderful, when I reflect upon it, that the Bible should be of any use at all now, and should not rather have moved into the quiet of libraries to be the joy of the unworldly scholar.

But if there is one thing certain it is this—the Bible meets the need of modern life. In spite of all criticism, as a practical guide there is no book to touch it. There is not a problem you are called to face and not a duty you are called to do; there is not a cross you are compelled to carry and not a burden you are forced to bear, but your strength for it all shall be as the strength of ten if you make a daily companion of your Bible. Now this is what you feel about the Bible, that it never offers a draught from shallow waters. You do not find there a set of petty maxims, but you find the everlasting love of God there. You do not find any shallow views of sin there, but a Lamb slain from the foundation of the world. And *that* is the secret of the Bible's permanence, when our little systems have had their day and ceased to be, then for sin and sorrow and life and death and duty, it gives us to drink as out of the great depths.

And think for a moment upon Jesus—of Jesus in relation to His words. If ever words were as water to a thirsty world, surely it was the words that Jesus spoke. How simple they were, and yet how deep! How tender and full of love, and yet how searching! They seemed to pierce into the very heart till a man felt that his secret thought was known.

Now there are men whose lives so contradict their words that when you know the men you cannot listen to them. And there are men who are so much less than their own words that when you come to know them you are disappointed. But what people felt about Jesus Christ was that when all was uttered, the half was never told, for at the back of all His words there was *Himself,* deeper unfathomably than His deepest speech. That is why the words of Christ will live even when heaven and earth have passed away. You can exhaust the cup or drain the goblet dry, but you cannot exhaust the spring fed from the deeps. And just because the words of Jesus Christ spring from the depths of that divine humanity, they will save and strengthen the obedient heart to the last recorded syllable of time.

The Witness of Locality

He let it fall in the midst of their camp.—Ps. 78:28

The writer of this noble psalm is meditating upon the past of Israel. He is recalling the wonders of the Exodus. He sings of how God fed the wanderers both with the manna and the quails. He gave them bread from heaven to eat and continued giving it in spite of all ingratitude.

But not only was the supply from God, there was another feature which impressed the poet, and it is this he writes of in our text. That bread might have been rained from heaven in places very difficult to reach. The quails might have fallen far away in regions almost inaccessible. And what impressed the poet was that God did not give His bounty in such a way—He let it fall in the midst of their camp. The gift was not far away from them. It did not call for any tiring journey. They had no long distances to travel to secure the necessities of life. God's gracious bounty, new to them every morning, fell just where they were—and the quick eye of the poet noticed that.

Then one thinks how true that is of other heavenly blessings than the manna. It is true, for instance, of the Bible—"The word is nigh thee, even in thy mouth." When we read a confession or a catechism, we feel that it is very far away. The truth it embodies is remote from the beating of the human heart. But the wonderful thing about the Bible is that it is not only the most divine of books. It is that, but it is also the most human. It comes right into these sinful lives of ours, portraying them and understanding them. There is the throb of the human heart in it as well as the throb of the great heart of God. Our joys and sorrows, our victories and failures, our hours of triumph and the shadows on them,

582

all these are mirrored on the pages of the Bible. It can never be treated just like other books. It is one great mark of inspiration that the Bible is not far away from life. He lets it fall in the midst of the camp.

And think how true this is of that unspeakable event, the Incarnation. In the fullness of the time God gave His Son. In palaces there is a certain isolation; they are remote from the common haunts of men. Even a cottage is a place withdrawn when within the cottage is a woman in travail. But not in a palace nor even in a cottage was our blessed Lord brought into our midst—He was born in the manger of an inn. Men were gathered there from every quarter. The world in miniature was there. Travelers had reached that inn by lonely roads, but it was not on lonely roads they found the Babe. They found Him amid a gathering of folks drawn from every section of society in the welcome afforded by an inn. The Child was born where there were human voices and all the stir and confusion of a crowd, where some were sleeping and others eating and many telling the adventures of the road. Where there was light and noise and the throb of human life, the Bread from heaven was bestowed at Bethlehem. He let it fall in the midst of the camp.

And this marked all the ministry of Jesus, distinguishing it from that of John the Baptist, for the Baptist was a solitary figure loving the lonely spaces of the desert. When men wanted to inquire of John, they had to go out and seek him in the wilderness. When they wanted to inquire of Jesus, they found Him on their trodden ways. He was a lover of the haunts of men, no stranger to their lowly cottages, sitting where the common people sat and perfectly familiar with the crowd. He gave them bread from heaven to eat, and it was given just as was the manna. He never reserved it for the monastic shelter nor for the quietness of the academy. He healed men and He taught men in the places where they lived and toiled, in the dull routine of daily living. In the fields, down by the seashore, in the narrow streets of unimportant hamlets, in the rooms of overcrowded cottages, in the thronged meeting-places of the cities, *there* He fed them with that wisdom which dwelt with God before ever the earth was (Proverbs 8:23)—He let it fall in the midst of the camp.

Equally does this apply to the rich provision of the Gospel now. We do not need to leave our place to gather it: it is given in the places where we are. The promises are not for imaginary circumstances; the promises are for here and now. The offered adequacy of the Holy Spirit is always available for us today. The fellowship of the Lord Jesus with all its cleansing and uplifting is not for the rare hours of mountain vision but for the common hours of ordinary life. Peace and joy are not for a few choice saints who move apart from the heavy cares of men. Serenity was never meant by heaven only for those who are withdrawn from things. The great distinction of the Gospel is that all its blessings are for common people immersed in the care and business of the hour. What struck this poet was that heaven's supply fell right among the places where people tabernacled. That is why God has poets in the Bible, because they see what others never notice. For *this* poet there was a wealth of meaning, which it has taken the ages to unfold, in the fact that when God gave bread from heaven. *He let it fall in the midst of their camp.*

Limiting God

They . . . limited the Holy One of Israel.—Ps. 78:41

Sometimes we fall into the sin of limiting God to the greater hours of our life. I take it that all of us are so tempted. When the Syrians were fighting Israel they found they were always beaten on the hills, from which they gathered that the God of Israel was a God of the hills and not of the valleys. And this exclusion of the will of God from the peaceful and lowly valley-land of life is not confined to Syrian mentality. Every life has its dramatic hours and knows the exhilaration of the heights. In such hours, "so nigh to God is man," we often are strangely conscious of His presence.

But to limit the Holy One of Israel to our rarer moments on the hills is to miss the wonder of His fellowship. He is as near us in the dreary day as in the day when all the birds are singing. He is as close to us in lowly duty as in the hours that are going to alter everything. He is present in the lilies of the field, according to the teaching of our Lord, as magnificently as in the earthquake or the storm. Do not confine God to the big things as if these alone lay upon His heart. Never reserve Him for the greater moments as if He had no feeling for the lesser ones. To do so is to fall into the sin which is recorded here against the ancient Jews. It is to limit the Holy One of Israel.

We are so ready to forget His sovereignty. It is true that often, when God has work to do, His choice of instruments at once commends itself. The man He chooses is exquisitely fitted for the peculiar task that is allotted him. But very often it is the other way—God's choice is mysterious and sovereign—the whole of history is one long commentary on the unlikely instruments of heaven. He wants a nation which shall bless the world, and He chooses a company of slaves in Egypt. He wants a messenger to carry doom to Eli, and He chooses Samuel, a little child. He wants a cradle for the beloved Son whose name is to be above every name, and He chooses a manger in the inn at Bethlehem.

I believe in an educated ministry. I trust we shall always have it in our land. It is one of the proudest boasts of Scotland that we have always had an educated ministry. But how often when we were priding ourselves upon our education, God in His sovereign fashion has come and put us all to shame by the preaching of uneducated men. You cannot limit the shining of the sun, and the Lord God is a sun. You cannot limit the breathing of the wind, and the Holy Ghost is like the wind. Men must watch when they want to keep their pulpits from the preaching of unordained servants lest they be limiting the Holy One of Israel.

Or again, aren't we often tempted to limit God in the matter of our prayers? We confine Him to one expected answer. What if our blessed Savior had done that? What if He had limited the Father? What if the only answer He would tolerate had been the passing of the bitter cup? Then he would never have had Calvary nor the blood that keeps the sinner from despair, nor the victorious power of His resurrection. I remember a chaplain saying to me in France that if the Germans won the war, he'd lose his faith. In the mercy of God, the Germans did not win. But there are few things more perilous in prayer than to make one's faith conditional, and *that* is what the Savior never did. He never said, "This cup must pass from me, or I shall cease to trust the love of heaven." He said, "Father, if it be possible . . . nevertheless thy will not mine be done." And always we must bear that in mind when we cry for anything upon our knees lest, even in our holiest moments, we limit the Holy One of Israel.

Lastly, are we not prone to limit God in regard to the compass of His power? We have many instances of that in Scripture. When, for instance, Jairus' daughter died, the servants went hurrying through the streets to Jairus. And when they found him, they cried, "Sir, she is dead. There is no use troubling Jesus any further."

What they meant was that as long as she was living there always was the hope that He might cure her. There was no such hope now that she was dead. They were limiting the power of Jesus. There were certain things that were beyond Him. And sometimes when we view society today, are we not subject to the same temptation? God keep us all, who are praying for revival and for the coming of His kingdom in the world, from limiting the Holy One of Israel.

God's Self-Limitation

God . . . delivered his strength into captivity.—Ps. 78:61

These words in their primary and historical reference refer to the taking captive of the Ark of God by the Philistines. What a terrific calamity that seemed to Israel! They thought that the glory of Israel had departed. To the whole world it looked as if God were overcome, as if some power had arisen that was really superior to God, or as if there was something in the world that would ultimately baffle and defeat His purposes. You can understand how, to a religious nation like the Jews, it was a tremendous and terrifying thought, as, of course, it ought to be to every man. And then this inspired writer came along being illuminated by the divine Spirit, and puts a different meaning on the whole thing—says that God designed it, says in his own poetic language that God, nobody else, *God* delivered His strength into captivity.

Don't you see in a moment how that thought would animate and inspire Israel? It was not enemies who had defeated God, it was God who had deliberately done it. God had not exercised His own omnipotence; He had self-limited Himself. And if we could only understand how God, not only with the Ark for that was typical, but right down the centuries, has voluntarily delivered His strength into captivity, I think it might confirm our faith.

Well now, let's consider the thought of God's sovereign will. The one jubilant note of the whole Bible is that God's will in itself is sovereign. "I formed the light and I created the darkness. I am God and there is none beside me." Anyone who imagines that there is any will in the universe that can ultimately thwart God is not making the Bible his rule of faith and life. Of course, that does not mean that God's will is arbitrary. God limits His rule of many things just because He is love. As Butler said in his own deep way, "God's being is a kind of law to His working." All God's workings must be love if He is love. But it does mean that God's will in itself is irresistible, that nothing can ever ultimately baffle it, that there is no rival in heaven or in hell who can ever stand against the will of God. Don't you see how that thought is bound up with the ringing note of triumph of the Bible? You have no assurance for the future of the world, but for the future of yourself, and yourself strangely corresponds to the greater progress of the world.

What a great comfort when a man can say, "This is the will of God, even our sanctification." Poor, weak sinners baffled everyday, it is God's will that ultimately we will be clothed in white. But if God's will can be thwarted, if there are powers abroad that limit His sovereignty, why, you and I in every effort may be just beating the air. Nothing may come of it. You know that makes life impossible, and therefore all the depths in your heart corroborate the jubilant assurance of the Bible. If it did not it would not be the Bible because the deepest mark of inspiration is within, and if the Bible did not correspond with all the voices from the depths of your heart, you might lay it aside as not being inspired. But when you come to the Lord Jesus, you find the Lord Jesus teaching you to pray, "Thy will be done."

Now if God's will is an irresistible will, and if it is always exercised as an irresistible will, why should you and I pray, "Thy will be done"? It will be done whether you pray or not; it will be done whether you help or not. It must be done if it is exercised as a sovereign will. Don't you see you are faced by this dilemma, though nobody likes the argument of a dilemma—either the will of God is not omnipotent (a thought that is intolerable to the human heart) or else for wise, holy purposes, when God is dealing with mankind, He does not totally exercise His sovereign will—He delivers His strength into captivity. And don't you see what His wise and holy purposes are?

My father used to spend his leisure in editing books, and I remember once, just when I was about to finish school, he was editing one of the cantos of *Childe Harold*. He had the introduction all shaped out and most of his notes were blocked, and he turned to me and said, "I am very busy. I want you to complete the editing of this book for me." You know, to this hour, I have never forgotten it. To this hour I remember the joy and pride I felt when I was called to be a fellow-worker with my father.

And if God's will for mankind were sovereign, if it just *had* to be, you could not be a fellow-worker with God. It would not make the least difference what you did, whether you prayed or worked or gave. God is so passionately eager that you and I, His children, should be raised up to the joy and honor of being fellow-workers with Him that He just does not exercise the sovereignty He might—He delivers His strength into captivity, limits Himself that His children may help Him. Surely that is a motive worthy of a father, and that is just the name that Jesus gives Him.

I don't want to be philosophical, but you might put it another way. You might think of the purpose. Well, now, if you are going to be a fellow-worker with a man, that man must have a purpose. If a man has a purpose for building a house, every mason, every bricklayer is a fellow-worker with him. If a shipbuilder has a purpose for building a ship, then the whole labor force can be fellow-workers with him. If a man has no purpose, you cannot be a fellow-worker with him. And it is just so with man and God.

But does it ever occur to you that to have a purpose is to limit yourself? The builder would not take months to build the house if he could do it like the palace of Aladdin, all in a moment. The shipbuilder would not spend years and millions if he could create a ship just in an hour. And don't you see, if God limits Himself, if God doesn't complete His purposes in a moment, if God doesn't say in the slums of Glasgow, "Let there be light," as He once said in chaos, it is because He is limiting Himself for a purpose. And only in a purpose can you and I, His children, ever be fellow-workers with Him. I don't have the least doubt that the sovereign will of God could convert Africa just as we worship here; I don't have the least doubt that He could change Ireland and make it in a moment the Island of the Saints, but He does not. Don't you see that if He did, you and I, His children, could never be His fellow-workers? I think if we could only grasp that thought, it might help to explain a good deal of the suffering in the world. It is the suffering of being sharers in a purpose.

Take, for instance, the great French general who commanded at Verdun. Well now, why did he struggle on there? Because he had the purpose of saving France. Not only he, but every man down to the foot soldier shared in his purpose of saving France. They knew perfectly well that if wounds, pain or death came, all was bound up in the purpose which they shared with their general. If God has a great purpose, and if the Lord says, "Thy will be done," we have got to share it; and if it is a purpose in which suffering is inevitable in such a world as this, doesn't it cast a good deal of light upon much of the suffering in the world?

I am quiet certain there is no Christian who, when he makes a choice, does not feel that that choice is a real choice, determined by himself. We all recognize that much of our battle is fixed for us by heredity, but there is not one of us who does not know in his heart that his fate is in his own hands. We are free creatures.

And don't you see why God made us like that? God's purpose was love; God wanted beings who could be in fellowship with Himself. It would be an awful thing to be a lonely God. God wanted beings who could share His purpose, think His thoughts after Him, enter into His will, pray to Him, be His children. And no one could do that unless he were free. God could easily have made us mechanical so that sin would have been impossible, so that everything we did would have been automatic. Do you think God could ever have shared His thoughts and purpose with beings like that? Don't you see, the moment He made us free, He delivered His strength into captivity? God has created something with which He cannot interfere. The one thing God can never do, for His gifts are without repentance, is to smash and shatter our freedom by the intrusion of omnipotence. God can do just what He does in Christ—He can woo, He can appeal, He can try to win, He can breathe His spirit on each one of us; but if we misuse our freedom, not even God will break in with His omnipotence to make it impossible.

And yet people say, Why does God allow sin? God does not allow sin. Why does God allow the slums of Glasgow? Why did God allow war? God never allows war. God, wanted beings to have fellowship with Him, made us free, and not even God, having made us free, will bring His omnipotence to stop us when our freewill misused gives us sin, misery, slums and war.

When God made us free, He delivered His strength into captivity, and in that sense it is in captivity still. Without our freedom what a poor, miserable thing life would be. I think all that is perhaps corroborated by a very deep feeling that God's children have that they can disappoint Him. If a child does something that is wrong, he disappoints his mother or his father, or a husband may disappoint his wife, and you and I can disappoint God. My dear brother, if our sin was predetermined from all eternity, we could not disappoint God, and there could be no joy in heaven over one sinner that repenteth.

Let us consider the thought for a moment in connection with Christ. Don't you see how it all comes to its climax, how God delivered His strength into captivity when He gave His only-begotten Son for you and me? He had done it before in regard to His sovereign will when He created free beings—He had done it because He was love. And then, in His own way, He did it to its utmost when He gave the Lord—He did it because He was love. "God so loved the world that He gave"—delivered Him to the captivity of the virgin's womb, delivered Him to the captivity of the body that had been prepared for Him so that the Lord emptied Himself and took on Him the form of a servant. Did you ever think how often the word "delivered" is used of the Lord Jesus Christ? "He was delivered to the high priest." "Pilate released Barabbas and delivered Jesus." "He was delivered by the counsel and foreknowledge of God." But most beautiful of all: "He was delivered for our offenses." Christ was the strength of God, and God delivered His strength into captivity. The marvelous and beautiful thing is just this, that by that deliverance you and I are saved.

Refusing to Go Back

So will not we go back from thee.—Ps. 80:18

To go back from God is to desert Him. It is to turn away the footsteps of our heart from Him. It is to doubt the vision we have had of Him in our more intense and illumined moments.

To determine that whatever comes, we shall not go back from God, is one of the open secrets of the saints. To cling to Him when life is difficult and we are tempted to question if He cares; to believe in Him with a simple childlike faith when clouds and darkness hide His throne—this is one of the triumphs of the spirit which makes the humblest life a thing of victory and brings it to the sunrise at the end.

When Mallory and Irvine were last seen climbing Everest, they were "going strong for the top." From that top, a thousand feet above them, nothing could turn them back. What a great victory it would be for all of us were we to say, like these heroic climbers, *So* we shall not go back from Thee.

We are tempted sometimes to go back from God by the apparent indifference of heaven. There are seasons of the soul when things unseen are touched with a strange sense of unreality. The lamp that burns upon my study table is as nothing to the radiance of the moon. But then the lamp is near me, and I read by it till I grow oblivious of the moon.

And so there are seasons when the things around us so grip us in their vividness that things eternal tend to grow unreal. At such times we do not renounce God, but we are often tempted to go back from Him. We grow oblivious to His peace and light and there passes a certain deadness over us as the winter, and we forfeit the joy of our salvation. Prayer becomes a chore; the Bible loses its fragrance and its dew. We are in the dark night of the soul and lying under spiritual desertion. But even *so* (observe the psalmist's word) the true heart will cry out of the darkness, "We will not go back from thee." To cling to God and His great love to us when things grow dim and shadowy and distant, to affirm God to our own souls in the hours when the unseen is as a dream is one of the tasks of all who claim the name of Christ. "So will not we go back from thee."

We are also tempted to this retrogression in hours when all the lights are burning low. None is so strong that he does not now and then have fainting spells. We lose heart, and a dull depression seizes on our spirits. We move on the flat margins of despair, and are all tempted to go back from God as the disciples were tempted to go back from Christ.

To be perfect as our heavenly Father is a standard that often seems impossible. Is it any use striving to be holy with these insurgent and rebellious hearts? Is not sainthood for rare and elect souls, and beyond the compass of our common clay? So are we tempted to take the lower road, thinking it more on the level of our powers, and we settle down into second best. That is the tragedy of many lives—they have settled down into the second best. They had visions once of the summit of Mount Everest; now they are content to dwell below it. But the real victory of this life of ours is *not* to gain the summit we have seen; it is to keep on climbing to the end. God's best in Christ is not for elect souls. It is for everyone who trusts Him. Things that are impossible with man are possible with God, and in spite of all our failures, *we shall not go back from Thee.*

The Glorious Lamp of Heaven

The Lord God is a sun.—Ps. 84:11

A week or two ago, when we were all looking with interest towards the eclipse of the moon, I took up again a fascinating volume which I doubt that many of you have read. The volume I refer to is the *Story of the Heavens* by Sir Robert Ball, and Sir Robert Ball is not only an astronomer who holds high and honorable rank among men of science, he is also a writer of pure and lucid English.

In reading that volume I was deeply impressed by all that Sir Robert had to tell about the moon, but I think that I was arrested still more powerfully by the strange and wonderful story of the sun. Time and again I found myself laying down the book overpowered by the thought that the Lord God is a sun. The kinship between that creation and its great Creator shone out from the pages in unexpected radiance. And so I have taken this poet's text and shall try, from one or two of the aspects thus suggested, to use it so as to illumine our thought of God.

First, I was struck by the results that flowed from the discovery of the right place of the sun. Astronomy is one of the oldest of the sciences and many very remarkable discoveries must have been made when the race was in its childhood. Especially in the East where the stars burn and glitter as with the intensity of some great moral purpose, students outwatched the lonely night in gazing and linked the stars with the destinies of men. But always, in the very center of their system, there was poised this earth on which we live. This was the focus, this was the midmost point, this was the pivot of the whole machine; and till the earth was displaced from her usurped centrality and cast into the outer circle of the system, progress was barred, true knowledge was impossible, and a thousand facts remained inexplicable.

I need hardly remind you that it was Copernicus who was the first to solve this problem of the center. It was he who proved that the sun and not the earth is the true center of our solar system. And how much we owe to that wonderful discovery—how many problems it has solved, how many truths suggested—all that could be most eloquently told by those who have given their lifetime to the science.

Now it seems to me that the progress of our life is not dissimilar to that progress of astronomy. We all begin in one way or another by making this earth on which we dwell the center. The first man is of the earth, earthy: "first, that which is natural," says the Apostle. Our hopes, our dreams, our joys and our ambitions cluster and circle around this present world. The strange thing is that while *this* remains the center, for us as for the astronomer much is dark. A thousand problems baffle our inquiry and a thousand questions are answered by a cry. What is the meaning of suffering or pain? Why are so many faces drawn in agony? Why are those who are too gentle to harm a living creature bowed down for years in intolerable anguish? These questions—and a score of problems as insistent—rise up to meet us and are unanswerable so long as this life, this earth, this present world remains the center of the moral system.

But the day comes—and it comes to every man—when he has his chance of being a Copernicus. He has his choice of making the great refusal or of making the greatest of all great discoveries, for the greatest discovery a man can make is that God is the center of the system.

"What is man's chief end?" asks our noble and strong old catechism—it is to glorify God and to enjoy Him forever. It is to realize that in the center does not stand the world, but the love and the wisdom and the will of the Almighty. And when once, through whatever pain and discipline, a man has discovered that fact about his universe, he is no longer crying in the night. He sees a meaning now where there was none before. He believes in the melody of minor chords. Problems are eased, dark facts can now be faced; there is light in the gloom and hope of a tearless morn—all this in some measure every man has known who has truly striven to make God the center.

The next fact that impressed me as I read was how beneficent is the power of the sun, and yet from what a vast distance it is exercised.

I doubt if the strongest language could exaggerate the indebtedness of the earth to the great luminary. We owe so much to it, and we are so dependent on it for every thought we think and every breath we draw, that no one can be much surprised at sun-worship. Without the sun our corn would never ripen, and we would have no harvest in our autumn fields. Without the sun there would be no dew at daybreak, no glory of clouds, never one shower of rain. Without the sun no breeze would ever visit us, no sail would ever be filled upon the sea. What lights our coal? The power of the sun. What drives our engines? The power of the sun. What alone makes physical life a possibility to the millions of the human race? There is a very literal sense in which it is true that in the sun we live and move and have our being. Yet the sun is an extraordinary distance from the earth—the sun is ninety-two million miles away. Can you conceive that distance? Can you grasp it? How many days do you think would be required to count it? Yet from *that* distance, vast beyond imagination, there acts and operates this great yet gentle power, mighty enough to make all the tropics burn, yet delicate enough to paint the tiniest weed.

Now I am sure that most of us here this evening have been oppressed at times by the thought of a distant God. Like Job, we have looked to the right hand and He was not there, and to the left, and have seen nothing of His form. Where is the heaven of heavens wherein God dwells? Where is the Holy of Holies where He has His throne? Is it not far away, in the clear and unsullied light, above the smoke and stir of this dim spot? Under the weight of thoughts like these, the distance of the Almighty Father chills us and we cannot pray with realizing power nor can we walk with realizing faith. Tempted and tried thus, let us recall our text: The Lord God is a shield—He is a sun. Wherever His throne may be, in distances illimitable, shall He be out-matched in power by His creation? If the orb of heaven can have his being ninety million miles away, and yet can fall with such power as to heat a continent, and with such exquisite nicety as to make the rosebud redden, why should it seem a thing incredible that the Creator who fashioned that glorious lamp should dwell immeasurably far apart, yet touch and turn and bless and save humanity? The isles are to Him a very little thing—the nations before Him are as nothing. Yet He knoweth the way that I take; He understands my thought; He will not quench the flax nor break the reed. Powerful yet very far away; thoughtful and tender though hidden in the distance; yes, David, we thank thee for that word, "The Lord God is a sun."

Once more I was greatly impressed by the thought that without the atmosphere, the sun could never bless us. Without the envelope of closely clinging air that encircles this globe like some diaphanous garment, the heat of the sun and all the light of it would fall quite ineffectually on the earth. When you climb a mountain you get nearer the sun; wouldn't you naturally think that it ought to get hotter there? As a matter of fact, it gets colder as we rise till we reach the peaks that are robed with perpetual snow. The reason is that we are piercing through that air which enwraps this little earth of ours. It is the atmosphere which mediates the sun, which catches and stores and distributes the heat. Were there no air, but only empty space, then the greenest valley would be like Mont Blanc, and the tropics would be ice-bound in a perpetual winter although the sun in itself were as fiery-hot as ever.

May I not use that mystery of nature to illuminate a kindred mystery of grace? It is one of the ways of God in all His workings to grant His blessings through an intermediary. You say that the sun is the source of heat and light; why then should anything be intruded between the earth and sun? I can only answer, So the Creator works—without that mediating element all is lost. You say that God is the source of love and blessing; why should anything intervene between God and man? I can only answer that it is the way of heaven to grant its richest blessing through a mediator. How often men and women have said to me, "I do not feel any need of Christ or Calvary. I believe in God, I reverence and worship God; but the sacrifice and the atonement just confuse me. I cannot make them real to my heart." But to me it seems that through every sphere of God's activity runs the great principle of mediation; and to me the presence of Christ is like the air, making available for my need the love of God. Remove the atmosphere and the sun will still shine in heaven. Take away Jesus and God will still be love. Banish the air, and the sun will not lose its heat. Banish the Christ, and God will not lose His power. But with the air gone, the glory of the sun will never fall so as to bless our little world; and with Jesus banished, the mercy and love of God cannot stream on our realms. Christ is the mediator of the better covenant. He stands—the vital breath—between God and us. Through Him the sunshine of heaven's love can reach us, and in the rays of that sunshine we are blessed.

Then lastly, when the sun is invisible we still see its reflected light; for we all know that the light which gilds the moon and gives a luster of brilliance to the planets is not the light of their own burning, but the light of the sun which to our eyes has set. Go out one of these evenings and look at the western sky where Venus is glowing in her unequaled splendor—then remember that but for the sunshine which has vanished for a few hours, there would be no such jewel in the darkness of night. I preached some time ago on that text of the Apostle, "What have ye that ye did not receive?"; but the evening star—had we ears to hear it— is preaching that text in the heavens every night.

Now in the spiritual world, aren't there also times when the sun seems to have set? There is such evil in the state and such quarreling in the church, that men are tempted to cry, There is no God. In such hours, urgent and paramount becomes the duty of personal faith. In such hours, Christian character is called for with an appeal that no other time can match. For the Lord God is a sun, and when He seems to sink out of the national or ecclesiastical horizon, then lives that still glow with His light amid the dark are the unanswerable argument for Him.

The Perils of Middle Age

The destruction that wasteth at noonday.—Ps. 91:6

In all literature, the life of man is pictured under the symbol of a day. There is something in the rising and setting of the sun that compares so closely to life's start and close that the correspondence has been universally perceived. We speak of the morning of infancy or childhood; we describe the older age as the afternoon of life; the declining years are the evening of our day; and the final efforts as the lingering gleams of sunset. It is in such language, drawn from the sphere of day, that we imaginatively describe the facts of life. This being so, you will at once perceive the meaning we may attach to noonday. The noonday of life is the time of middle age when the morning freshness of youth has passed away. And so the destruction which wasteth at the noonday, whatever its literal significance, may be referred to as the peculiar temptations of that period.

This long stretch that we call middle life is a period often overlooked. In a hundred special sermons to young men, you will scarcely find one which addresses the middle age. No doubt there is something to be said for that, for youth is the time of impression and choice, and the preacher feels that if he can influence youth, the trend of the later period is determined. But along with this wise reasoning goes another, which is as unwise as it is false and which is specially cogent with young ministers. It is the thought that after the storms of youth, middle age is like a quiet haven. It is the thought that youth is very perilous and middle age comparatively safe. I think that nothing could be farther from the truth than that and no outlook more pernicious. I am

600

convinced that of all moral perils, none are more deadly than the perils of the noonday. And could we only read the story of many Christians who in the sight of God have failed, I believe we would find that the sins of middle age have been more disastrous than the sins of youth.

Now one of the great features of middle age is that by that time a man has found his lifework. No longer does he wonder what the future may hold. No longer does he turn to the left and right wondering what path he should pursue. But whether by choice or by necessity, or by what men might call an accident, he has taken up once and for all his calling and settled down to the business of his life.

When one stands amid the Alps in early morning, it is often impossible to tell the mountain peaks from the clouds. For the rising sun, touching the clouds with glory, so fashions them into fantastic pinnacles that it would take a practiced eye to tell which is a cloud and which is a snowcapped summit. But when noonday comes, there is no longer any difficulty. The clouds have separated and disappeared, and clear and bold into the azure sky there rises up the summit of the Alps. So in our morning hour it is often hard to tell which is the cloud-capped tower and which is the hill. But as the day advances and the sun mounts to noonday, that problem of the morning disappears. For clear above us rises the one summit—clear before us stretches our lifework. For better or worse, we now have found our lifework, nor are we likely to change it till the end.

Now with this settlement into a single task there generally comes a certain happiness. We are freed from many disquieting doubts that troubled us when we stood on life's threshold. Unless a man's work is abhorrent—so uncongenial as to be utterly abhorrent—there is a quiet pleasure in those very limitations that are the noticeable marks of middle age. The river no longer swirls among the rocks nor is there now any glory of a dashing waterfall, but in the tranquility there is a placid beauty and the suggestion of abiding peace. Even more, there is an ingathering of strength—the strength that always comes from concentration. No longer does a man dissipate his power trying to open doors that have been barred; but knowing his work and limitations, he gives himself with his whole heart to his one task, and so is a stronger man in middle age than he was in the happy liberty of youth.

But just here arises the danger of that period—one form of the destruction that wasteth at noonday—and it lies in the narrowness of the one groove in which the lifework runs. The eager expectancy of youth is gone, and absorbed in the business on which his living hangs, a man narrows into a businessman. Strong because he is concentrated in his life's work, he may become weak in that very concentration. Quietly happy because he had found his groove, he may be further from God than in his wayward youth.

There is a question which we often use. We ask of such and such a man, "What is he?" And you know the answer which we expect to get—he is a teacher, a doctor, or an engineer. Now if the end for which a man was born was to be a doctor or an engineer, happy indeed would be that narrowness which is so clear a feature of the noonday. But when we remember what man is and yet shall be; when we think of Him in whose image man is made (which image it is the lifework to restore), what an irony it is and what a condemnation of the noonday that we should say of a man that he *is* a draftsman, or of another he *is* an engineer. Has the promise of the morning come to this? Are these the feet that are set in a large room (Psalm 31:8)? Have all the blessings of God been lavished on a man that he might become only a first-rate man of his business? No matter how successful he may be, if he is impoverished and narrowed by success, then in the sight of God he is in peril of the destruction that wasteth at noonday.

Faced, then, by that peril as we are, how may we reasonably hope to overcome it? One way is to have some consuming interest such as a hobby. It does not really matter what it is, if it is an avenue into a larger world. It tends to keep a person from being a mere machine and helps him through the perils of the noonday.

But there is something better than a hobby. It is the symmetry of the character of Jesus. It is the thought that there once moved on earth a Man who was perfect in the whole range of manhood. That is the value of fellowship with Christ in an age when specialism is inevitable. Christ touches every string upon the harp, for He vitalizes powers we would ignore. He came to give life, and to give it more abundantly, and so saves from the destruction of the noonday.

Another peril of the noonday is the decay and deadening of faith. There is no period in the whole course of life in which it is so hard to walk by faith.

In childhood, faith is an abiding habit. A child has a perfect genius for trusting. Dependent for everything upon the care of others, to lean on others is totally natural and a sheer necessity. And so in youth is found the lovely habit of trustful reliance upon another's love which makes the child, no matter what his faults, a type of the citizen in Jesus' kingdom.

Then in old age when the sun is setting, faith surely must become easier again. Standing so near the margin of this world, has a man no gleams and visions of the next? So soon to make that plunge into the darkness and to leave forever the "old familiar faces," how utterly and hopelessly hardened must a person be who has no thought except for the things he sees! I do not say that faith is ever easy. It is the greatest of ventures and of victories. It is the victory that overcomes the world, and not to be won without a weary battle.

But in middle age, as you will see at once, these helps and encouragements are missing. There is neither the stimulus of youth nor that of age to lead a man to trust in the unseen. We are self-dependent now and self-reliant; it is by the work of our own hands we live. Once we depended upon another's labor, but now our livelihood hangs on our own. Then, too, in the time of middle age there is generally a reasonable measure of good health. The days succeed each other at an even pace, and before us lies an unbroken stretch of road. Not yet do we discern the shades of evening nor feel on our cheek the chill wind of the twilight. We are far away from the brink of the beyond.

It is such facts as these that hint to us of the destruction that wasteth at noonday. No period is so prone to materialize the spirit or to blind a man to the range of the unseen. Then first relying on our personal effort and through that effort achieving some success; then awakening to the power of money and to all that money is able to procure; still unvisited by signs of dissolution and reasonably secure of many years yet to come, it is in middle age we run the tremendous peril of becoming worldly and materialized. Youth has its dangers, but they are those of passion and lack of control. But the sins of middle age, though not so patent, yet in the sight of God may be more deadly, for they lead to that encrustation of the spirit which the Bible calls the hardening of the heart.

Get a company of middle-aged men together and listen to their talk about their neighbors. Isn't it certain to come around to money—to their losses and successes and incomes? I do not imply that what they say is scandal, or even suggest it is uncharitable. I only say that they have materialized since the happy days when they were boys together. There is no time when it is harder to walk with God than in our middle age; no time when it is more difficult to keep alive the vision of the eternal and unseen. The sweet dependence of childhood has departed, and the heart has awaked to the power of the material, but the hand of death does not yet knock loudly. Brethren, who like myself have entered these mid-years, remember that Christ is praying that your faith does not fail. He knoweth the arrow that flieth in the morning; He knoweth the destruction that wasteth at noonday. May Christ deliver us from the hard and worldly heart. May He give us the hope that is cast within the veil. Not slothful in business, but toiling at it heartily may we endure as seeing Him who is invisible.

But not only is middle age the time when we are in peril of losing faith in God, it is also a time when we are in danger of losing faith in man. The two things indeed may be said to go together, the one making way for and drawing on the other, for between faith in man and faith in God there is a vital connection. In our days of childhood we believe in men with a romantic and splendid trust. We have not yet learned the motives that inspire them. It is from our father we take our ideas of manhood, and from our mother we take our ideas of womanhood. The father is always a hero to the child, and the mother is always worthy to be loved.

And then with middle age comes the awakening. We see how different men are from our imagination. The vision we had of them is rudely shattered, and with the shattering goes our faith. It may be that a young man goes to business under an employer who is a professing Christian. He may even be a pillar in the church in which the young man was baptized and trained. But in the business there are such shady tricks, such practices incompatible with honor, that in a year or two not all a father's pleading can prevail with his son to even take the Communion cup. It may be that a woman is deceived in love by someone of whom once she thought there was no better person in the world. It may be that a daughter comes to see that the mother whom she adored is but a worldly woman. Or it may be that, without sudden shock, we slowly discover the wheels within the wheels, the rottenness in much that is called business, the worship of power in much that is called the church. Very commonly it meets a man as youth expires and middle age begins. And it is this passage from the hopes of youth to the chilling experience of middle life that is so often attended by an eclipse of faith. Some men become utterly hard-hearted; others, tolerantly cynical. To some it is a positive relief to find the world no better than themselves. But to all it is a deadly peril—it is the destruction that wasteth at noonday.

There is only one help in that temptation—one help, yet it is all-sufficient. It is to remember that though He knew the worst, Christ never for an hour lost faith in man. Despised, deceived, rejected and betrayed, still in the eyes of Christ man is precious. His own forsook Him on the way to Calvary, and yet He loved His own unto the end. Great is our need of Christ in time of youth if we are to steer our ship amid the shoals. Great is our need of Christ when we are old if we hope to enter the eternal city. But not less great is our need of Jesus Christ in the dusty levels of our middle age if we are to be saved from that destroying angel—"the destruction that wasteth at noonday."

Self-Denial an Attitude of Worship

Bring an offering, and come into his courts.—Ps. 96:8

During worship there are certain demands made of every worshiper. There are certain elements which must be present if the worship is to be in spirit and in truth. There is, for instance, the attitude of thanksgiving for the goodness of God to us from day to day. There is the sense of spiritual need and the knowledge that none but God can meet that need. There is the sense of indebtedness to Christ who loved us and gave Himself for us, in whose death is our only hope and in whose Spirit is our only strength. All these attitudes must meet and mingle if our worship is to be really worship. Without them, a man may come to church and go away no better than he came.

But there is another attitude, not less important yet which is very frequently ignored, and that is the attitude of self-sacrifice. We all know that worship calls for praise, but we must remember it also calls for self-denial. There are many to whom worship is a joy; but it is more than a joy, it is a duty too. And it is a duty, when we conceive it rightly, of such a lofty and supersensual nature that to perform it rightly is impossible except in a certain measure of self-sacrifice and worship to God.

To begin with, that element of sacrifice is seen in the matter of the money offerings. "Bring an offering, and come into his courts." No Jew came to his worship empty-handed. To give of his means was part of his devotions. Of the thirteen boxes in the Temple treasury, four were for the free-will offerings of the people. And this fine spirit of ancient worship passed over into the worship of the Church and was enormously deepened and intensified by the new of the sacrifice of Christ. "Thanks be unto God for His unspeakable gift"—that was the mainspring of Christian liberality. It was the glowing thought of all that Christ had given which motivated the poorest to be givers too. And that so sanctified the Christian offertory that Paul could speak of the resurrection triumph, and then, as if unconscious of descent, add, "now as concerning the collection."

Now while all such offerings were acceptable to God and while all brought a blessing to the giver, yet from earliest times it was felt by spiritual men that the true offertory must touch on self-denial. You remember the abhorrence of King David against offering to God that which had cost him nothing. It is such touches amid all his failures that reveal the Godward genius of the king. And we have read of Jesus Christ and of His opinion of the widow's mite and of all the riches that He found in that because there was self-denial in her giving. It was a wonderful cry that broke from Zacchaeus' lips when he came face to face with Jesus Christ. "Lord," he cried, looking upon Jesus, "Lord, I give half my goods to feed the poor." He had always given in his Jewish way—he had never entered the Temple without giving—but now, under the gaze of Jesus, he felt that he could not give enough. Brethren, that is the mark of Christian giving. It reaches over into self-denial. I do not think we give in the spirit of Jesus until like Him we touch on self-denial, until His love constrains us to some sacrifice as it constrained Him to the sacrifice of all.

Let us then seriously ask ourselves—have we been giving to the point of sacrifice? Have we ever denied ourselves of anything that we might bring an offering and come into His courts? It is only thus that giving is a joy, only thus it brings us nearer Christ, only thus is it a means of grace as spiritual and as strengthening as prayer.

Gradually as men became more spiritual, the thought of self-denial deepened also. It was not enough, if one were to worship God, that he should bring an offering in his hand. Slowly it was borne in upon the Jew that the truest offering was in the heart. And it is very instructive in Scripture to watch the development of that idea—the gradual deepening of self-sacrifice as an element in acceptable worship.

Think in the first place of the case of David, a man who had been trained in ritual worship. You may be sure that from his earliest years he had never worshiped with that which cost him nothing. He had brought his offering, and he had paid for it, and he had denied himself that he might pay for it. The God whom he had found when he was shepherding was not a God to be worshiped cheaply. And then there came his kingship and his fall and the terrible havoc of his kingly character, and David found that all the blood of goats could not make him a true worshiper again. The sacrifices of God are a broken spirit—a broken and a contrite heart. Let him give his kingdom for an offering, and he would not be an acceptable worshiper. He must give himself—he must deny his lusts—he must lay aside his pride and be repentant, or all his worship would be mockery and the sanctuary a barren place for him. He knew from the first that worship meant denial. It was his thought of denial that was deepened. He found there was no blessing in the sanctuary unless his heart was penitent and humble. And that was a mighty truth for him to grasp, and it has enriched the worship of the ages and has passed into the newer covenant and into all the gatherings of its saints.

Now turn to David's great Son, and listen to the words of Christ Himself. He is speaking in the Sermon on the Mount about bringing the offering to the altar: "Therefore, if thou bring thy gift to the altar and there rememberest that thy brother hath anything against thee, leave there thy gift before the altar and go thy way. First be reconciled to thy brother and then come and offer thy gift." Now note that Jesus is talking about worship. His theme is not the patching up of quarrels. He is teaching us what attitudes are needed if we are to worship God in spirit and in truth. And not only does He insist on giving—He takes that, we may say, for granted—but He insists that at the back of every gift there should be the self-denial of the heart. It is far easier to give up a coin than it is to give up a quarrel. It is easier to lay down a generous offering than to lay down a long-continued grudge. And Jesus Christ insists that if worship is to be acceptable to God, the worshiper must lay aside his pride and humble himself as a little child. That is not easy—it never can be easy. That is far from natural to man. It is hard to do and bitter and opposed to natural inclination. And it calls for patience and interior sacrifice and prayerful, if secret, self-denial; and only thus, according to the Master, can one hope to be an acceptable worshiper.

Who, then, is sufficient for these things? That is just what I want to impress upon you, that worship is not easy; it is hard. It is not just a comfortable hour on Sunday with beautiful music and a fluent preacher; it is an attitude of heart and soul that is impossible without self-denial. I thank God that in the purest worship there is little demand upon the intellect. The humblest saint who cannot write a word may experience all the blessings of the service. But there *is* a demand upon the soul; there *is* a call to sacrifice and cross-bearing, for the road to church is like the road to heaven—it lies past the shadow of the cross.

Well, now, to come a little nearer home, consider our gathering at public worship. In the very coming to church week after week, there must be an element of self-denial. In country places it may be different, for in country places life is often lonely. And men, in response to their social instinct, are glad for the weekly gathering together in church. But in the city there is always company, and the difficulty is rather to get alone; and so there is not the social instinct to reinforce the call to public prayer. Were a man to abide just by his inclination, it is probable that he would seldom come to church. There was a time when he would have lost his good name by staying away; but that day is certainly not the present one. And he is tired when the week is over, and isn't the Sabbath a day of rest? And perhaps he is not feeling very well and the morning looks as if there might be rain. Not only so, but he tells you seriously that he gets more good at home than in church. That may be the flimsiest excuse, but it reveals that the natural inclination is not towards church. And making all allowance for habit or social pressure, the fact remains that self-denial is needed if one is to be in the sanctuary every Sunday. The point is that that very self-denial is good for man and pleasing to God. It is the best of all beginnings to the week just to crush a little our easy inclinations. To do on Sunday what is our Christian duty, and doing it, to bring our will into subjection, is a better beginning for a bright week than the finest sermon in the easy chair.

"Then Jesus as his custom was, went into the synagogue." Did you ever meditate upon these words? He was the Son, and heaven was His home, and yet as His custom was, He went to church. He never said "I do not need to go—I can have fellowship with God anywhere." He took up His cross and He denied Himself, and He has told us to follow in His steps.

In public worship we are not simply hearers; we are a fellowship of Christian people. You may go to a lecture just to hear the lecturer or to the theater just to see a play. It doesn't matter who is there beside you—they are nothing to you and you are nothing to them. Not one of them would do a hand's turn for you or seek to help you if you were in difficulty or visit you if you were sick. At the theater there is an audience, but not so in the church. In any sanctuary that is blessed by the presence of the Lord, it is a fellowship of men and women bound together by their common faith and loving one another in Christ Jesus.

Now, in every fellowship must not there be a certain element of sacrifice? Isn't it so in the home, if home is to be more than a mockery? In all fellowship there must be self-denial and a constant willingness to yield a little, and if that is so in the fellowship of home, it must also be so in the fellowship of worship. Just as a mother, worthy of the name, denies herself for her children—just as a husband will regard his wife in every choice he makes and every plan; so in the fellowship of public worship there must be mutual consideration, a constant willingness to forgo a little for the sake of others for whom Christ has died. The young have their rights, but they should not insist on them when they know it would vex and irritate the old. The old have their claims, but for the sake of the young, they will accept what may not appeal to them. And when a hymn is sung or the word is preached which seems to have no message for one worshiper, that worshiper will always bear in mind that for someone else that is the word in season. All that is of the essence of true worship and calls for a little sacrifice. A happy home is impossible without it, and so also a happy congregation. A tender regard for others by our side, with the denial that is involved in that, is an integral part of public worship.

The same truth is still more evident when we think of worship as our approach to God by the new and living way of Jesus Christ. Now it is true that we were made for God and that in Him we live and move and have our being. Yet such is the immersion in the world even of the most prayerful and most watchful that the approach to God with the whole heart demands a concentrated effort. Of course, we may come to church and be in church and never know the reality of worship. We may think our thoughts and dream our dreams and in spirit be a thousand miles away. But to quietly reject intruding thoughts and give ourselves to prayer and praise and reading is not always easy, and for some it is incredibly hard. If there were anything to rivet our attention, that would make all the difference in the world. In a theater we can forget ourselves, absorbed in the excitement of the play. But the church of the living God is not a theater, and in the day when it becomes theatrical, in that day its worship will be gone. If we want to wander, we can always wander. There is nothing here to rivet our attention. There are only a few hymns and a quiet prayer and the simple reading and expounding of Scripture. And it is for each one of us to make the needed effort and shut the gates and withdraw ourselves, and through that very effort comes the blessedness of the public worship of God in Jesus Christ. It is thus that worship becomes a heavenly feast—when we discipline our will to it. It is thus that worship becomes a means of grace in a hard-driven and hectic week. If it is to be a blessing, we must deny ourself and take up our cross; we must bring an offering of sacrifice and come into His courts.

Creation's Witness to the Youth of Jesus

Thou hast the dew of thy youth.—Ps. 110:3

By taking a bit of liberty with these poetic words, we shall apply them, without any prelude, to the person of the Lord Jesus Christ. Now, there are two expressions in our text to which we shall give attention, and the first of these is *youth:* "Thou hast the dew of thy youth."

They say that in heaven the saints are always young. No weariness of age can enter there. It is eternal morning around the throne of God. And if that is so, and I do not think it is a dream, it is because there is reflected the light of Jesus Christ on the face of every saint, and the light of Jesus is the light of youth. Christ is forever young. He is eternally the morning star. And that is the first thought our text suggests— the everlasting youth of Jesus.

But there is another keyword in our text, and that is *dew:* "Thou hast the dew of thy youth." And the thought of dew calls us back from the heavens and spreads before us this earth on which we dwell. There is no dew in heaven, for in heaven there is no night, no change of heat and cold, no need of the sun to lighten the day. It is this world which is the realm of dew. It is here that the miracle of dew is wrought, where every blade of grass on a summer morning sparkles and glances as if sprinkled with diamonds. To think of dew, then, is to think of nature. On the one hand we have the eternal youth of Christ, and for us who are Christians, Christ is the creator. On the other hand we have this great creation, the handiwork of this eternal youth. Let us combine the two. Let us try and discover the witness of creation to the perpetual youth of Jesus Christ.

First, then, we note that youth is the season of abounding energy. One characteristic mark of youth is physical energy. There is an eager strenuousness in developing life that is tamed or tempered by the advance of years. As life progresses, we rise to better things. There is a clearer vision and a steadier thought. But when the summits of middle life have been realized and the feet are traveling downwards on the slope, the tumultuous rush of bodily energy that made it once a joy to be alive is shrined with memories of the past. I do not mean that every young man is energetic. For sometimes some hereditary taint or perhaps sickness, and more often ill-regulated passions, rob opening manhood of its noble heritage. I only mean that in the plan of God and in the normal development of human life, youth is the season of abounding energy.

And our language witnesses to that. I have known old men whose hair was silvered and who had passed the threescore years and ten, who were still masters of an amazing energy. But not one says of them, "It is the energy of age"; rather we say, "Isn't it wonderful that even in age they should retain the energy of youth." So, all unconsciously, our common speech bears witness that youth and energy are linked together. And I cannot watch the romping of my child, who never walks if it is possible to gallop, but I learn again, in such a simple lesson, that abounding energy is a mark of youth.

Well, now, I pass from little things to great. I look abroad upon creation, and I am amazed at once by the tremendous energies with which this universe of ours is full. I watch the motion of the tides; I hear the roaring of the breakers; I mark the sweep of rivers; I am told of the resistless progress of the glacier. This solid earth is whirling around the sun, and the whole system, of which the sun is center, like a great bird is flying in space. And I cannot think of these resistless powers, and I cannot dwell on that tremendous speed, but I feel that the stamp of energy is on creation. Nor is that energy confined to what is great. It is just as wonderful in what is small. For the breeze will waft the tiniest seed and plant it in the fissure of a rock; and the seed will germinate, and the rock will crack and render asunder before the resistless energy of life.

Now as I see these energies of nature, I feel that the heart that fashioned it was young. There is no sign of the weariness of years. It is inspired with an abounding energy that tells me of a fresh and youthful mind. Although Christ lived from everlasting ages before the moment of creation came; the eternal morning was still upon His brow when He conceived and formed the world. There are the powers of youth in it. There are the energies of opening life. "Thou hast the dew of thy youth."

It is in youth, if ever, that the sky is golden. It is in youth the moss is velvet and the flowers are fragrant. It is in youth, if ever, that every dream is sweet and every sound is melody. As men grow older, life's highways become dustier. A grayer sky succeeds the golden morning. Thorns prick the hand and sometimes pierce the heart. And the world's voices, that seemed like music once, are strangely harsh and discordant now.

It is not that life grows poorer as it advances or ceases to be noble when the charm of its opening years has passed away. If we were sent here only to enjoy, the dying out of the romance of youth would be terrible. But God had far higher ends in view than that when we were so fearfully and wonderfully made. We are sent here to learn. We are sent here as boys are sent to school. Our threescore years and ten are God's grade school and college course. And it is not in the bright romance of youth that we learn the best and most abiding lessons. It is in the dogged doing of our duty, the quiet acceptance of our limitations, the patient carrying of our daily burden, and the stretching out to our brother of a helping hand. These, and not leisure, are life's true opportunities for culture. These are the roots of ethical nobility. And these, thank God, come faster with the hurrying years. Still, it is true that youth is the season of romance. In other words, life's time of light and brilliance comes not in age, but youth.

Well, now, I lift my eyes into the face of nature, and the splendor of light and the wealth of color there amaze me. If the heart that created had been weary with its years, and the creating hand had been outworn, I feel that the world would have been draped in monotone—and sea and earth and herb and cloud would have known no rich variety of color. But the whole of nature is flooded with light. And the colorings of the wide world are unsurpassable. And I cannot note the differing green on every forest tree, and I cannot examine the exquisite adornment of the tiniest flower, and I cannot watch the play of light and shade upon the sea, nor the magnificent splendors of the setting sun, but I am impressed that this is the romance of youth; that light and color is not the work of age, it is the outpouring of a youthful heart. It speaks of the perpetual youth of Jesus. "Thou hast the dew of thy youth."

To youth there is nothing impossible. When we are young, it seems easy to regenerate the world. We feel a healthy scorn for the small achievements of our ancestors. There is a splendid sweep in the designs of youth. As in the glowing heat the hardest metals are melted, so in the glow of youth the problems that have baffled ages are resolved. And the assurance and arrogance of youth which makes the wise man smile are but the tag-ends of these vast designs God loves to see in a young man's brains.

There are few lads, I suspect, who have not felt a quiet contempt for their father's abilities and their father's position. It seem a low thing to think of ending life as an unknown citizen. But as we grow we learn our limitations, and we match ourselves with stronger and subtler men, and a new respect is born in us for what others have done. We come to appreciate the honest work and character that have gone into the building of even humble homes. So vision and dreams vanish, and duty comes. We become thankful to get even a little done. But even that little we should never have accomplished but for the vast designs we had in youth. It needs the ideal, says the poet, to brush a hair's-breadth off the dust of the actual. I may miss the target by a thousand yards, but I shall shoot farther than if my range were fifty. In spite of the failure of the after-years, we shall thank God for the vast designs of youth.

Now we live in a world of vast design. Its *distances* are vast. There are stars so remote that their light set out to travel to us when Jacob lay asleep at Bethel, and it shall only reach our earth tonight. Its *times* are vast. For with creation, as with creation's God, a thousand years are as a single day. This vastness, then, of space and time that are in-wrought into the design of the creation are eloquent of youth. And as I dwell on that, I turn to Christ and say, "Thou hast the dew of thy youth."

I remember once preaching upon that text in Romans, "Experience worketh hope." A woman at the end came to me and said, "Ah, sir, that text may be in the Bible, but it is not true; for I have had a bad experience of life, and the little hope I ever had is gone."

And she was right, and the Bible was right too. For it is the experience of Christ that worketh hope, and not the experience of life. I was talking to one of our city's doctors this last week—and a doctor soon learns the secrets of a person's heart—and he told me that one of the hardest tasks for him was to keep up his hope in human nature. And how a Christless man could live for twenty or thirty years—I say live, not exist—and still be hopeful, I confess I almost fail to understand. Outside of Christ, experience tends to pessimism. It was so in the world when Jesus came. It is still so.

But youth is still incurably hopeful. There is an effervescent hopefulness in youth that is magnificent. And I must be blind indeed if in the world around me I have found no traces of that youthful spirit. In every spring there is the hope of summer. In every summer there is the hope of harvest. In every winter, when the fields are bleak and the cold gust goes whistling through the trees, there lies the hope that the flowers will spring again. And there is not a sparrow on the housetop and not a rabbit in the rocks that is not literally saved by hope. I catch the spirit of perpetual youth in that. It seems to me the world's reflection of the perpetual youth within the heart of Jesus. And I cry with David: "Thou hast the dew of thy youth."

So as we got out into the summer world, we shall take with us that thought of its Creator. And a thousand instances we cannot touch on here will show us the true handiwork of youth in nature. And when we worship in the temple not made with hands, and when we view the energy that reared the wondrous palace, the light and coloring that make it radiant, the vast design of its conception, the spirit of hope that breathes in all its lines, we shall rejoice in the eternal youth of Jesus. And we will remember that the Creator is our portion, and that He gives eternal life and eternal youth to us. For from the hour of the grave and through eternity we shall be young and bid defiance to weariness and death if we are living in the morning light of the eternal youth of Jesus Christ.

The Ignorance of the Expert

The stone which the builders refused is become the head stone of the corner. This is the Lord's doing; it is marvelous in our eyes.—Ps. 118:22, 23

Had it been others who had rejected this stone, there would be no reason for surprise. The man in the street can scarcely be expected to be an authority on stones. If my watch gets out of order, I would never dream of taking it to the shoemaker. If I did and he made a mess of it, I would have only myself to blame. I naturally take it to the watchmaker who has been studying watches since he was first apprenticed and who, in this particular business, is an expert.

The notable thing is that these builders who refused this stone were all experts. Stones were (if I might put it so) their bread. Daily they handled nothing else but stones. They were supposed to know everything about them. And yet these experts—these carefully trained specialists—had the witness of their folly facing them every time they passed the finished Temple. There, high up in the chief place of honor, was a stone they had condemned as useless. It was not hidden deep in the foundations. It was exalted so that every eye could see it. Someone had come along and had detected what none of the trained specialists had found—and the stone was now the headstone of the corner. Thus we see the important fact that specialists can be very blind occasionally. Experts, who give their nights and days to things, may sometimes miss the thing that matters most. All which, to dull, unlearned folk, is often so exceedingly astonishing that they can only say, "This is the Lord's doing; it is marvelous in our eyes."

That ignorance of the expert is one of the common facts of life. It's a common saying that the more one knows about a thing, the more he knows that he doesn't know. I think it is the Sadhu Sundar Singh who tells of an Indian friend of his who was an expert botanist. He could tell you all about the daffodil and give you an exact description of it. Yet when daffodils were brought to him as a gift once, he entirely failed to recognize them. He had never seen them growing in their beauty. That man was an accomplished botanist; he was an expert in his chosen science; he had mastered the orders and the genera and was an authority on habitats. Yet of the one thing that really matters in the daffodil springing up from our wintry soil, he was more ignorant than any English girl.

So men may know the planetary movements and never have felt the wonder of the stars. They may have mastered all the laws of rhythm, yet never been haunted by the spell of poetry. I am not disparaging the expert any more than I would the grammarian of Browning. Advancing knowledge always needs the specialist, and our indebtedness to him is boundless. I only wish to suggest that not infrequently the expert loses the forest in the trees, and somehow misses all that really matters.

I venture to think that, with peculiar force, this applies to the study of the Bible. Sometimes those who know most about the Bible know least of the living power of the Book. It would be impossible to put in words our debt to the exact study of the Bible. To multitudes it is a new book altogether as the result of a sane and sober criticism. Yet there are times when one profoundly feels how a man may be an expert in the Scriptures and yet miss the only things that really matter. One may discuss the problem of the Pentateuch, and do it with all the learning of the specialist; one may have mastered all that can be known of the relation of the Synoptic Gospels, and yet the Bible, the living word of God in its convicting and transforming power, may remain unto his heart as a sealed book. Sometimes there is an ignorance in experts far deeper than the ignorance of untrained people. They are like the Sadhu's Indian botanist who failed to recognize the daffodil. And all the time the poet and the child, ignorant of the elements of botany, may be enthralled and conquered by its loveliness.

There is something more needed by the Bible than any exactitude of knowledge. The Bible only yields its inmost secret when deep begins calling unto deep. That is why some poor unlettered woman may have a far truer grasp of what the Bible is than the specialist who is versed in all its problems. It has found her and made her glad. To her it is a word to rest on. It has proved itself a light unto her path and never fails her in any hour of need. And all this is so wonderful to her that like the psalmist, she can only say, "This is the Lord's doing; it is marvelous in our eyes."

We see the same fact with fullest clearness when we recall how Jesus was rejected. "He came unto His own," says John, "and His own received Him not." Now had the common folk alone rejected Him, we could scarcely have wondered at their doing so. For the common folk were looking for a king, and Jesus was not their idea of a king. The strange thing is that Jesus was rejected not by the common folk, but by the Pharisees—and the Pharisees were Messianic experts. They were specialists in the doctrine of Messiah. They were considered as knowing everything about Him. Night and day they had studied the Old Testament with a zeal that was little short of heroism. Yet when Messiah came they failed to recognize Him though they had given many a learned lecture on Him, just as the Sadhu's learned Indian friend failed to recognize the daffodil.

The stone was not rejected by the passers-by. The stone was rejected by the builders—by the experts, the specialists in stones, the men who were held to know everything about them. When our Lord selected that great saying and deliberately applied it to Himself (Mark 12:10), was He not sounding a warning down the ages that sometimes the experts may be wrong?

The Call of the Hills

I will lift up mine eyes unto the hills.—Ps. 121:1

It is generally held by those who are competent to judge that this Psalm dates from the period of the exile. It was written by one who was far away from Palestine, a prisoner in distant Babylonia. If that is so, it gives a new significance to the words of this text, for Babylonia was a level country, a land of vast and monotonous expanse. And it was out of the dreariness of such a land that the psalmist thought of the hills which he had once loved to look on and which were dyed with the memories of home.

When I lived at Oxford, a good many years ago, one of the tutors lay dying of cancer. It was a summer of perfect warmth and beauty and every meadow was a haunt of dreams. But the dying man was a native of Iceland, and amid all the glory of those days, the cry on his lips was to get back to Iceland just that he might see the snow again. That same feeling breathes in this verse: "I unto the hills will lift up mine eyes." The writer was an exile, far from home; he was in a land where everything was strange. What did it matter to him though Babylonia was fairer than the country of his birth? The hills of his homeland were calling him.

Yet we should do scant justice to the psalm if we thought there was nothing but homesickness in it. The deepest longing of the singer was not home. The deepest longing of his heart was God. It is difficult for us to realize that feeling, thanks to the teaching of the Lord Christ Jesus. We know that in Africa God would be as near us as here in Scotland. And though in a measure the Jew perceived that too, for he knew that the eyes of God go to and fro throughout the earth, yet nowhere did he stand so near to God as in the land of the Temple and the altar. It was for God, then, that this singer longed. It was towards God on which his heart was set. He was God-sick far more than homesick as he strained his weary eyes towards the west. And the strange thing is, that as he turned them so, looking and longing for the living God, what he saw was not any temple made by man—"I unto the *hills* will lift up mine eyes." Somehow, as his heart went out to God, there rose before him the vision of the hills. It was when his spirit was most deeply moved that he longed for the cathedral of the mountains. And I think you will find that that is always so, and that always, from the earliest date of time, it is to man as a religious being that the mountains have had a message and a call.

Mr. Ruskin, in his *Modern Painters,* has called attention to a suggestive fact. It is that the greatest painters of the Holy Family have always a hint of the mountains in the distance. You might have looked for a vineyard or a pleasant garden in the sunshine, but in the greatest painters that you find, it is "to the hills will I lift mine eyes." What they felt, with one of those intuitions which are the birthright and the seal of genius, was that for a secular subject a vineyard or a meadow might be a fitting background; but for the Holy Family and for the Child of God, and for the love of heaven incarnate in humanity, you want the mystery, the height, the depth, which call to the human spirit from the hills. It is not to man as a being with an intellect that the hills have spoken their unvarying message. It is to man as a being with a soul, with a cry in his heart for things that are above him. That is why Zeus in the old pagan days came down to speak to men upon Mount Ida. That is why the genius in painting Jesus Christ throws in its faint suggestion of the peaks.

Now it is not very difficult to see wherein this kinship exists. The intellect may be as a lowland scene; but the spirit of a man is always highland. We talk sometimes about a smiling landscape; at other times about a landscape of contentment. And you know the kind of scene these words convey with its quiet beauty and its wealth of rest. The cows are standing knee-deep in clover, and the brook has a murmurous and drowsy sound, and everything breathes the beatitude of peace. It is all tranquil, all beautiful, and the gentle love of God seems resting on it.

621

Yet tell me, in such a scene as that, do you detect the story of your life? If you do, either you are a saint or else the shallowest of living creatures. Most of us are so restless within that such a landscape never can portray it. Aren't there times when we are in the depths and feel as if we could never rise again; prayer seems useless and the heaven is brass and all we have ever striven for is vain? Please, God, we want to be rescued from that depth and start climbing up the hill again. The clouds will scatter and the clearer air will start us singing as we mount. These are our yearnings; these are our defeats; these are our hours of anguish and of glory; and we cannot speak of them but in the language which we have borrowed from the silent hills. Not in the loveliest village of the plain is there the transcript of the human spirit. It is too high, too deep, too full of tears ever to find its analog in that. Its sacrament is the region of the mountain with its wild loneliness and rugged liberty, with its depths where there is gloom and peril, with its peaks that rise into the realm of God.

Now it is very notable, that being so, that God should have led His people into Palestine. For when God has a work for nations to fulfill He is careful to set them in the right environment. You know what the great mission of the Jews was. You know the task which God entrusted to them. It was not to be leaders in intellect like Greece. It was not to be builders of an empire like Rome. The task of the Jew was to keep alive the thought of the divine, to stand in the midst of the polluted world as witnesses of the true and living God. Preeminently, the mission of the Jew was the religious and the spiritual mission; the soul was his science and his art. And the thing to note is, that in being called to that, they were delivered from a level land and brought into a country that had so many hills that they could not lift their eyes without beholding them. That was not a natural migration, for the trend of migrations is usually the other way. It was not a journey congenial to the Jews, for they dreaded the mountains then; they did not love them. But the hand of God was in it all, leading His people, whose mission was religion, into a land preeminently fitted to nourish and foster the religious life.

The Old Testament is the record of the soul and is written against a background of the hills. It is true that it does not open in the mountains, but in the luxuriance of a garden. Its opening scene is an idyllic picture in the bosom of an earthly paradise.

But when man has fallen and sounded the great deeps and begun to cry for the God whom he has lost, then we are driven from the garden scenery and brought amid the grandeur of the hills. It is on Ararat that the ark rests when the judgment of the waters has been stayed. It is to a mountaintop that Abraham is summoned to make his sacrifice of Isaac. And not on the plain where the Israelites are camped, but amid the cloudy splendor of Mount Sinai God reveals Himself and gives His law and enters into covenant with man.

Can you wonder that the exiled psalmist said, "I will lift up mine eyes until the hills"? They were dyed deep for him with sacred memory and rich with the precious heritage of years. Nor was it merely a heritage of home; it was a heritage of God and of the soul. Among the hills Israel had learned everything that made her mighty as a spiritual power.

By way of contrast, we might think a moment about what we call the bible of the Greeks. That is a name which we often give to Homer, and in a large measure it is justified. Now, as you know, one of the poems of Homer is a long account of the wanderings of Ulysses. Through many cities and many lands he goes. He is the very spirit of unrest incarnate. Yet very rarely in that noble poem do you read of the towering grandeur of the hills. You find exquisite paintings of many kinds of scenery, but scarcely a recognition of the heights. I do not know one scene in all the *Odyssey* where the mountains tower aloft as an environment. And the strange thing is that in the Old Testament there is hardly one scene of more than usual meaning that is not set within the circle of the hills. Ulysses is the spirit of unrest—but then it is not spiritual unrest. It is not the voyage of the human soul into the depths and heights of God. When you have that, you have a highland Bible—a Bible with Ararat, Moriah, Sinai—a Bible where you hear the mountain-call and lift up eager eyes unto the hills.

The same thing meets us still more forcibly in the life of our Lord and Savior Jesus Christ. Christ is not only the lover of the soul; He is also the lover of the hills. You could take the mountains out of the life of Socrates, and it would make little difference in that life. You could take the mountains out of the life of Shakespeare, and you would hardly alter it at all.

But did you ever think of what would happen if you took the mountains out of the life of Jesus? There would be no more Nazareth embosomed in the hills with its prospect to the south of storied places. There would be no temptation—no conquest of the devil—on the top of a mountain that was exceedingly high. There would not be any Sermon on the Mount. The Transfiguration would be gone forever. And all those hours of secret prayer alone among the hills would be missing. Strike out the hills, and the Mount of Olives goes with its wrestling through the blood-drops to the victory. Strike out the hills, and there is no more Calvary with its cross and His pierced hands and riven side. Strike out the hills, and the place of our Savior's ascension to His Father-God is missing. Did it ever occur to you how, when our Lord was risen, He said "I go before you into Galilee"? When His life was over and His victory won, where did He go?—back to the hills again. The crowd was to call Him in the coming ages, and He was to hear the calling of the crowd. But in that morning when He rose victorious, He went into the hills.

And now in closing let me dwell upon the genius of Christianity. It seems to me that if it is to be true to Christ, there must be the spirit of the mountains in it. We are always in danger of robbing our Christian faith of what is grand and rugged and mysterious. It is so gentle, so full of love, so exquisitely sweet and lovely. And the very presence of that quiet beauty in the Christian calling and the Christian character is apt sometimes to dim our eyes a little to the greatness and the grandeur of the Gospel. So consider more than the lilies of the field. Lift up your eyes unto the hills and remember how our Savior loved them, for in them there is a symbol of the message of the Gospel. We need a Gospel that shall be deep and high—deep as our sin, high as the throne of God. We need a Gospel that, far above all voices, will brood on us with unutterable peace. And it is just because in the Gospel of God's love we have that height and depth and everlasting strength, that we can lift up our eyes unto the hills and find we are not far away from Christ.

Forgiveness and the Cross

There is forgiveness with thee, that thou mayest be feared.—Ps. 130:4
In whom we have redemption through his blood, even the forgiveness of sins.—
Col. 1:14

There are millions of people for whom divine forgiveness is a great and thrilling fact. They could no more doubt it than they could doubt their being. Quite possibly they do not understand it, but one can enjoy things he doesn't understand. We daily use and enjoy a hundred things of whose nature we are ignorant. I light my room with electricity or revel in a glorious summer morning though I know practically nothing about electricity or the sun. And among these things stands out divine forgiveness as the greatest. For millions it is an experienced reality. It is the spring of joy, the source of liberty, the starting-point of victorious endeavor. Forgiven, the barriers are gone that raised themselves between the soul and God. Estrangement from their Creator has given place to sweet communion.

But the difficulty for many people is how forgiveness comes through the death of the Lord Jesus. Why can't a God of love forgive His children as the father of the prodigal forgave his son? When a wife forgives her husband, she doesn't need the intervention of another. She forgives him just because she loves him with a love that expects a brighter tomorrow. When a father forgives his erring child, it is a private and personal transaction where the intrusion of anyone else would be impertinence. Why, then, should our heavenly Father call for more than a repentant heart? Why should restoration to communion demand the agony and death of Jesus?

This difficulty is often aggravated by the glorious ringing note of the Old Testament: "There is forgiveness with thee that thou mayest be feared, and plenteous redemption that thou mayest be sought unto." Well, men say, that is enough for me, I needn't complicate matters by the cross; and they forget that the Old Testament is never final but rather God's avenue leading to the new. I give a child an apple, and tell him to eat it for it is good for him. It is only afterwards that the child learns why that apple should be healthful. A little boy puts coals on the fire, confident that they will warm the room. But why the coals should have their warming properties he only learns when he goes to school or college. That is heaven's universal ordering, first the fact and then the explanation. Life would be impossible to live if we could not use things till we understood them. And as God orders the whole of human life, so He does with Scripture, first proclaiming the eternal truth and then showing us the secret of it. The cross of the New Testament is not an intrusion on an old simplicity. The cross does not complicate forgiveness: it explains it and shows how it is possible. "There is forgiveness with thee," cries the psalmist; and the New Testament interprets that—Yes, there is forgiveness through the blood.

Surely it is evident that without the cross we could have no assurance of divine forgiveness. It is only in the life and death of Jesus that we can be perfectly sure of a forgiving God. God reveals Himself in nature. Could we be perfectly certain of forgiveness there? Even though nature carries glimpses of it, are these sufficient to assure the heart? Neither in nature nor in human history is there the luminous proof the sinner needs that there is forgiveness with God. That proof is given in Christ, and in Christ only. Only in the life and death of Christ can we be perfectly sure that God forgives. When we see Him dying on the cross for us in a redeeming love that traveled to the uttermost, God's forgiveness becomes certainty. A child in his earthly home needs no such argument. He is perfectly familiar with his father. He sees him every evening and has his kiss before he falls asleep. But the heavenly Father is different from that—clouds and darkness are about His throne— and so His children need for their assurance something that our children never do.

Again, we must not forget that earthly fatherhood can never exhaust the fullness of the Deity. In Him lies the fount of moral order without which life would be intolerable. A father at home who is a judge may freely forgive his child, but he cannot act like that on the bench. The morale of the State would go to pieces if the judge were to act just as the father does. He is to administer the law, and were every repentant prisoner forgiven, law would become a byword and a joke. That, as one of the Reformers put it, was a problem worthy of God—how to maintain and magnify the law, and yet freely forgive the transgressor; and God's answer is the cross of Christ. There we learn what heaven thinks of sin. There sin is seen in all its awfulness. There we behold the grandeur of the law in the very glance that tells us of forgiveness. The pardon of God is not the worthless pardon of an easy and tolerant good nature. He is just, *and* the justifier of all them that believe.

The Gifts of Sleep

He giveth his beloved (in) sleep.—Ps. 127:2

If we take the words of our text just as they stand, they are charged with deep and beautiful significance. They tell us what our own experience confirms, that sleep is the gift of God. The world has gifts which it gives to its favorite children. It loads them with wealth or honor or fame. But God deals otherwise with His beloved, for "He giveth to his beloved sleep."

It would, of course, be very wrong to say that sleeplessness is a mark of the divine displeasure. A man may be wrapt in the gracious peace of God, yet seek in vain the refreshment of sleep. Yet it is true that sleep, when it is given, is such a medicine for the weary and worn, that it can be nothing less than the gift of love. I think of Jesus in the storm-tossed boat, asleep on the pillow when everyone else was running around in wild alarm. I think of Peter fast asleep in prison when the coming morning was to bring his execution. I think of the tired worker when nightfall comes, and the sufferer who has been racked with pain through weary hours, and I learn how tenderly and deeply true it is that "He giveth his beloved sleep." Nor can anyone ever ignore that sweetest of all suggestions wherein the word is whispered over the sleep of death. A thousand memories of shadows and tears have clustered around that interpretation. It is when the fever breaks that one sleeps well, and when the struggle of life has ended and quiet peace has fallen, then love, through the mist of weeping, murmurs: "So he giveth his beloved sleep."

But though that is a comforting and blessed truth, it is not the true interpretation of the words. If you read the verse in relation to its context, you will see that that could hardly be the meaning. The psalmist is warning against overwork which degenerates into worry. He is picturing the man who overdrives himself until he has no rest and no peace. And all this pressure and nervous activity is not only a sin in the sight of God, it is also, says the psalmist, a mistake. It is vain for you to rise up early and to sit up late. You will never gain the choicest things that way. Let a man be nervous, overworked and tired, and he is sure to miss the worthiest and the best. God giveth to His beloved *in* sleep—when they are at rest like a child within its cradle, when they are free from that turbulence of wild desire in which the still small voice is quite inaudible.

Remember that the psalmist never dreamed of casting a slur on honest, manly labor. He knew too well the blessings that we gain, and the sins that we are saved from, by our work. What was borne in on his soul was that by overwork we lose more than we gain, for many of the richest gifts of heaven only approach us through the path of slumber. It is imperative that the soul should be held passive if we are to have the inflow of His grace. It is imperative that its uproar should be hushed if we are to hear the still, small voice. And it is that which the psalmist hints at here, when, in the intense language of a poet, he cries to men, "Your stress and strain are vanity; God giveth to His beloved in sleep."

There is a world of love encompassing an infant, yet how unconscious the baby is of it all! When our Savior was drawing near the cross, He said to His disciples, "I go to prepare a place for you," and they knew from that hour that when they awoke in glory, they would find that all was ready for their coming.

But not only in the land beyond the river is a place prepared for everyone God loves. When into this present life a child comes, hearts have been busy with preparation. Stooping over the little one is a mother's love and all the splendor of a mother's patience. Shielding it is a father's strength and eagerness to provide for all its needs. And it is clothed and fed with food convenient and rocked to sleep and sheltered from the storm. And should it become ill, the best skill in the city is not good enough for the tiny sufferer. What a wealth of love and care is here, yet what is more passive than that little infant! Have these small hands helped in the preparation? Has that little mind done any of the planning? Helpless it lies, and doomed to certain death, if life depended on its puny efforts. But "God giveth to his beloved in sleep"; He has prepared for His children, too.

If anywhere in life, it is in pleasure-seeking that it is vain to rise up early and to sit up late. Not when we are determined, come what may, to have a pleasant and a happy life does God bestow the music of the heart. He gives it when there is forgetfulness of self and the struggle to be true to what is highest though the path be through the valley of the shadow. The one sure way to miss the gift of happiness is to rise early looking for it and to sit up late waiting for it. To be bent at every cost on a good time is the sure harbinger of dreary days. It is when we have the courage to forget all that and to lift up our hearts to do the will of God that, like a swallow darting out from under the eaves, happiness falls upon us with glad surprise. Had Jesus lived just that He might be happy, He certainly would have escaped the cross. No one would have laughed Him to scorn in Jairus' house; no one would have pierced His hands and feet. But He came not to be ministered unto, but to minister and to give His life a ransom for many; and so you find Him talking of His joy. Brethren, remember that nine-tenths of our unhappiness is selfishness and is an insult cast in the face of God. But the way to be happy is not to seek happiness. It is to be awake to what is higher and asleep to self-satisfaction. And then, as time passes, comes the discovery that God giveth to His beloved in sleep.

The last gift of a kind God is heaven, and God giveth it to His beloved in sleep. We can never know how it would have been had man not sinned and fallen. Like Enoch, man would have walked with God till his never-halting footsteps brought him home. But death has passed upon all men for that all have sinned; yet "O death, where is thy victory?" God makes death's foul embrace His opportunity; He giveth to His beloved while they sleep. As one stands with sorrowing heart beside the dead and looks on him from whom the breath has flown, it is very strengthening and soothing to say, "God giveth sleep to his beloved." But isn't it better to lift our eyes to heaven and, thinking of its liberty and joy, say, "He giveth to his beloved in sleep."

The Searching of God

O Lord, thou hast searched me, and known me.—Ps. 139:1

We are prone to associate the searching work of God with events of a striking or memorable kind. It is in great calamities and overwhelming sorrow that we feel with particular vividness God's presence. When Job was in the enjoyment of prosperity, he was an eminently reverent man; but it was in the hour of his black and bitter midnight that he cried out, "The hand of God hath touched me." And that same spirit dwells in every breast so that God's searching comes to be associated with hours when life is shaken to its depths. Now the point to be noted is that in this psalm the writer is not thinking of such hours. There is no trace that he has suffered terribly or been plunged into irreparable loss. "Thou knowest my downsitting and my uprising"—my usual, ordinary, daily life—it was there that the psalmist recognized the searching; it was there that he awoke to see that he was known. And as the psalmist's, so our effort must be to try to discover how in our usual round, in the downsitting and uprising of our days, God searches us and shows us to ourselves.

In the first place, we are searched and known by the slow and steady passing of the years. There is a revealing power in the flight of time just because time is the minister of God. In heaven there will be no more time; there will be no more need of any searching ministry. There we shall know even as we are known, in the burning and shining of the light of God. But here, where the light of God is dimmed and broken, we are urged forward through the course of years, and the light of passing time achieves on earth what the light of the Presence will achieve in glory.

He is a wise father who knows his child, but he is a wiser child who knows himself. Untested by actual contact with the world, as children we dream our dreams in the sunshine of the morning. And then comes life with all its harsh reality and the changes of the years, and we turn around on the swift flight of time and say, "O Lord, thou hast searched me and known me." We may not have suffered anything profound; we may not have achieved anything splendid. Our life may have moved along in quiet routine, not outwardly different from the lives of thousands. Yet however dull and uneventful, God has so ordered the flight of time for us that we know far more about ourselves now than we knew in the dawn of our morning. Brought into touch with duty and fellowmen, we have begun to see our limitations. We know in a measure what we cannot do, and thank God, we know in a measure what we can do. And underneath it all we have discerned the side of our nature which leans towards heaven, and the other side on which there is the door that opens to the filthiness of hell. It doesn't take any terrible experience to learn our power and weaknesses. Each single day which makes up the passing years, slowly and inevitably shows it. So by the pressure of evolving time—and it is not we, but God, who so evolves it—for better or for worse we come to say "O Lord, thou hast searched me and hast known me."

Then also, God searches us by the responsibilities He lays upon us, for it is in our duties that the true self is searched and known. Think of those servants in the parable who got the talents. Could you have gauged their character before they got the talents? Were they not all respectable and honest and seemingly worthy of their master's confidence? But to one of the servants the master gave five talents, to another two, and to another one, and what distinguished and revealed each one was the use they made of that responsibility. They were not searched by what they had to suffer; the servants were searched by what they had to do. They were revealed by what their master gave and by the use they made of what they got.

And so, I take it, it is with all of us to whom God has given a task, a job, a talent—it is not only a gift to bless our neighbor; it is a gift to reveal us to ourselves. It is not always the greatest jobs that make the greatest demands on a man. It is sometimes harder to be second than first, and sometimes harder to be third than second. In the important jobs there is a certain glow, and generally a cloud of witnesses to cheer us on; but in the humbler jobs there is nothing of that. Great services reveal our possibilities; small services reveal our consecration, calling for patience and rigorous fidelity and the power that can endure through dreary days. So by the daily work we have to do and the task that is given us of God, we are tested in the whole range of manhood. There are no temptations more subtle or insistent than those that meet a man within his calling. There are no victories so quietly rewarding as those that are won within one's daily work.

God also has a way of searching us by lifting our eyes from the detail to the whole. He sets the detail in its true perspective, and seeing it thus, we come to see ourselves. You know how the writer of this psalm proceeds: "Thou knowest my downsitting and my uprising," he says. These are details, little particular actions, the unconsidered events of everyday. But the writer does not stop with these details—he passes on to the survey of his life: "Thou compassest my path and my lying down, and art acquainted with *all my ways.*"

You will remember that it was through details that Christ revealed the Samaritan woman to herself. She had been hiding her guilt from her own eyes by busying herself in the details of the day. And then came Jesus with His enlarged vision in which the days are all parts of the one life, and in the eyes of Christ she saw herself because she saw the details as a whole. "Come, see a man," she went and cried, "who told me all things that ever I did." Actually, it was an exaggeration, for Christ had not spoken to her very long. But when you get down to the spirit of the words, you never think of their exaggeration for they reveal the way that Jesus took in searching her and showing her to herself. He would not let her hide in the detail; He wanted her to have a vision of the whole. He wanted to show her what her life was like when looked at closely. And so this woman was searched and self-revealed through detail in its true perspective, and her conscience, which had long been slumbering, awoke.

I think that is often the way the Lord deals with you and me. We are all prone to be blinded by details so that we scarcely realize what we are doing. There are lines of behavior which we would never take, if we only realized all that they meant. There are habits and certain sins to which we would never yield if we only saw them in their vile completeness. But the present is so tyrannical and sweet and the action of the hour is so absorbing, that we cannot see the forest for the trees, nor see ahead the path that we are taking.

We often say when looking back upon our sufferings, "We wonder how we ever could have borne it." One secret of our bearing it was that we only suffered one moment at a time. And in looking back upon our foolish past, we sometimes say, "How could we have ever done it!"; and one secret of our doing it was that we only acted one moment at a time. When a man is dimly conscious that he is wrong, he has a strange ability to forget yesterday. When a man is hurrying to fulfill his passion, he shuts his ears to the call of tomorrow. And the work of God is to revive that yesterday and tear the curtain from the sad tomorrow and show a man his action of today set in the general story of his life. Sometimes He does it through sickness; sometimes in a quiet hour such as this. Sometimes He does it in a mysterious way by the immediate working of the Holy Ghost. But when He does it, then we know ourselves and see things as they are, and we are ashamed. Only then we can cry with David, "O Lord, thou hast searched me and known me."

We may never know ourselves until we see ourselves divested of all the trappings of self-love. It was thus, you remember, that He dealt with David when David had sinned so terribly. For all the depth and the grandeur of his character, David was strangely blind to his own guilt. But then came Nathan with his touching story of the man who had been robbed of his ewe lamb, and all that was best in David was afire at the abhorrent action of that robber.

Has God ever shown you your own heart like that, in drawing the curtain from some other heart? That, you know, is your story, your temptation, your sin in all its strength and sweetness. But ah, how very different it looks now when there is no self-love to plead for it and shield it, when there is no hand to weave excuses for it such as we make so quickly for ourselves. You thought that in yourself it was romance; but in another you see it as being disgraceful. You thought that in you it might be easily understood, yet in another it appears despicable. So in the mirror of another life God shows us what we do and what we are, and, seeing it, what can we do but cry, "O Lord, thou hast searched me and known me."

Someone may enter the circuit of our being, and the light they bring illuminates ourselves. We are all prone ordinarily to settle down into a dull routine. The vision of the highest fades away from us, and we go forward without any worthwhile ambition. Our feelings lose their freshness and zest, and we are no longer eager and strenuous as we once were. We become content with far lower levels of achievement now than would have contented us in earlier days. All this may come upon a man, and come so gradually, that he hardly notices all that he has lost. His spiritual life has grown so dull and dead that prayer is a mockery and joy is flown. Then we meet someone whom we have not seen for years, one who has wrestled heavenward against storm and tide—and in that moment we realize it all. Nothing is said to blame or rebuke us. The influence lies deeper than speech. Nothing is done to make us feel ashamed. We may be welcomed with the old warmth of friendship, but there is something in that nobler life suddenly brought into contact with our own that touches the conscience and shows us to ourselves and quickens us to a shame that is medicinal. It is often so when the friend is a human friend. It is always so when the friend is Jesus Christ. "Depart from me, O Lord, for I am a sinful man"—the very coming of Christ searches and sifts. But the joy is that if He comes to search, He also comes in all His love to save; and He will never leave us nor forsake us, till the need of searching is gone forever.

The Comfort of the Universal
Presence

*If I ascend up into heaven, thou art there: if I make my bed in hell, behold, thou
art there.—Ps. 139:8*

In the library of our university are certain old and interesting maps.
They have all the charms of a geography which knows no limit save
imagination. In modern atlases where there is ignorance, such ignorance
is wisely acknowledged. In older atlases, on the contrary, it is curiously
and cunningly concealed. And so in reading these dusty parchments
covering territories unexplored we are told that here are cannibals, or
satyrs and sundry other goblins.

All that has vanished from our maps today, but there is one thing
which is left to us still: it is that across the map, even to the remotest
boundary, we can write with full assurance *Here is God.* If I ascend to
heaven, thou art there; if I follow the beckoning of the rosy-fingered
morning, I am still in the keeping of the eternal Father. Do you and I
dwell on that as we should? Do we know the comfort of God's om-
nipresence?

There is nothing on earth, when we are being tempted, so arresting
as the sense of a presence. There are times of temptation when the wisest counsel is swept away from us like leaves before the gale; times when
everything we have resolved upon is broken like a thread of gossamer.
And how often in such times as these when counsel and resolve have
been cast aside, we have found restraining power in a presence. It may
be the actual proximity of someone or it may be only the presence in
the heart—the presence of someone who has passed on. But love is

mighty in resurrection power and eyes which we once loved are on us still, and only God in heaven could tell how many men have been helped by such memories.

There was a certain shopkeeper who had a portrait of Frederick Robertson, that great preacher, in his back shop. Whenever he was tempted to be dishonest, he went and looked for an instant at the photograph, and then the sorry thing he wanted to do became impossible. It was not Robertson's sermons which did that, searching and beautiful though they were. It was not the memory of those flaming words which scorched and shriveled what was bestial. What gripped that man and stayed his itching hand when he was tempted was the constraining power of a presence. That is often the power of little children. It is often the power of a good woman. We may not feel that someone is rebuking us; what we feel is that somebody is watching. Eyes are upon us, pure and tender, or eyes that we have not seen for many years; and God knows—*that thing*—we cannot do it.

Now as it is with the presence of our loved ones, it is so with the presence of our God. There is a mighty power to arrest us in the controlling thought that He is here.

There is an old story of a little girl who went to the attic to steal some apples stored there. On the wall hung the picture of some venerable and long-forgotten ancestor. And as she crept along the attic floor, the eyes of that old portrait seemed to follow her until in her childish fear she tore them out of the picture.

If one could only tear out eyes like that, sin would be infinitely sweet for multitudes. But there are eyes no human hand can reach; the eyes of memory and the eyes of God. And that, I take it, is what Scripture means in that text so often misinterpreted, "I will guide thee with mine eye."

Linnaeus, the great botanist, cherished an open heart for God in everything. Over his study door these words were written, *Numen adest, vivite innocui.* And what they mean is this: Live innocently; do not sully hand nor heart today: *numen adest*—deity is present.

Now let me ask you, have you tried to live, "as always in the great Taskmaster's eye"? Have you ever stopped in the jostling street and said to yourself, "God is now here"? Say it the next time you are worried, Martha. Say it when the waves are stormy, Peter. Say it, David, when on the roof at evening you catch that glimpse of beautiful Bathsheba.

Men who have tempers often excuse themselves—they cannot help it, they are built that way. But if you were in audience with King George, you could control that nasty temper perfectly. And the simple fact is that wherever you are, among the crowds or with your wife and children, you are always in the presence of the King. There is an arresting power in God's presence which few of us have ever really used. It is a great moment when we say with Hagar, "Thou God seest me." You who are very sorely tempted and know it is an hour of crisis, One who is infinite love and power and purity is right there with you, and He is watching.

Professor Henry Drummond used to tell us about a student at examination time. It was an examination of a decisive nature which would determine the young fellow's career. And every now and again he took something out of his pocket and gave it a glance, and then as quietly slipped it back again. The examiner had his suspicions aroused and stole up quietly for observation. And he saw—what do you think—scribbled notes? No, what he saw was not scribbled notes. It was a portrait of someone very dear and who would be dearer still for better or for worse through life's long battle—his lovely wife. It was not enough that he should know his subject well. He felt he needed something more than that. He felt he needed, just what we all need, the sustaining power of a loving presence.

And the One presence we can always have, through life and suffering and work and death, is that of Him who loves us to the uttermost. He is with us always and everywhere, when we awake and when we sleep. He is infinite love and perfect understanding and irresistible power that makes the devils tremble. And yet we fuss and worry and dread tomorrow but all in vain and as if everything had not been pledged to us in Christ. But, behold, everywhere Thou art there!

Still With Thee

When I awake, I am still with thee.—Ps. 139:18

A man whose religion is of a shallow kind is content with only an occasional acknowledgment of God. He has his stated seasons of approach to God and his rigid periods of worship. There are long stretches of time when, as the psalmist says, God is not in all his thoughts. He wages his warfare on the field of business in total forgetfulness of the divine—a mark of a religious life which is neither very deep nor very real. It never thrills in spiritual strength or joy.

Now in the book of Psalms, this is not so. The psalmist's recognition is continuous; always he sets the Lord before him. And it is this continual recognition and this unvarying practice of God's presence which kindles the psalmist when he is discouraged and brings the joy that cometh in the morning. When we go to sleep mastered by some thought, that thought is usually beside us when we awake. If it is trouble on which we closed our eyes, how swiftly in the morning it returns! And it was because the psalmist lived with God and went to sleep under the wings of God that he could take his pen and write in all sincerity, "When I awake, I am still with thee."

Our text is full of meaning when we think of waking up from our spiritual lethargy. There are times for most of us, in our spiritual life, when we are little better than asleep. Our prayers—how cold and formal they become; they are merely the semblance and mockery of prayer. And the Bible loses its freshness and its blessing does not leap to meet our needs when we come to it. There settles down a deadness on our spirits, and we go to church and listen to the preaching and might

639

as well be a thousand miles away. Who has not known such desert seasons, such days of lethargy? And to me the wonder of it all is that when the darkness passes and the dayspring comes, we are still able to lift our heads and say, "When I awake, I am still with thee." God has not forgotten to be gracious. We have been false to Him; not He to us. He has been longing to show His love again.

In all great sorrow there is something numbing, an insensibility like that of sleep. It is one of the triumphs of our modern medicine that it can apply opiates so powerfully. A prick of a needle and one forgets the agony of pain. But God has His opiates no less than man, and these are reserved for the hours when the physician fails, so that the mourner says, "I can't understand it—it is like a dream—I cannot realize it." There is mercy in that numbing of the spirit. The worst might be unbearable without it. When vividness of perception would be torture, God giveth to His beloved sleep. And it is when a man awakens for that sleep, slowly and heavily through dreary days—it is then that he can lift his heart to God and say, "When I awake, I am still with thee." The past may seem to be far away now, for there are days which do the work of years. But if the past is distant, God is near; nearer than He has ever been before. And the unseen is very real to us, and truths that once were on the dim horizon become the most tremendous of realities. And there are friends who cannot help us for we are moving in regions where they never traveled. But no man who believes in Jesus Christ can move in regions where God has never traveled, for down to the very bitterness of death, God in the Crucified has gone before. That is the joy of having God in Christ. You can never awaken to the bitter day and say, "Of *this*, the serene God knows nothing."

And then, in closing, doesn't our text also apply to the last awakening in eternity? "I shall be satisfied when I awake," and satisfied because I am with Thee.

I heard the other day of a young husband who had to go under the surgeon's knife. All went well, and as he awoke again, his first inquiry was for his wife and children. And he was satisfied when he awoke, not merely because of his life which he had regained, but because he was still with those who loved him so and who were all the world to him. That is the Christian doctrine of the future. That is the one clear point in all the mystery. I shall be satisfied when I awake, because when I waken, I am still with Thee—still with the God who was my shepherd here; still with the God who saved me and who blessed me; still with the God in whom I trusted amid the shadows and the doubts of time.

The greatest of all questions is just this, "Am I with God, and is God with me?" Do I trust Him and try to serve Him now? If not, when I awake—what then? But if I do and if I seek His face, then when I awake under the touch of death, this will be the glory of it all, that "I am *still* with Thee."

Showing It Before Him

I showed before him my trouble.—Ps. 142:2

What the trouble of the psalmist was it is impossible for us to say. It was so bitter in its onset that his spirit was overwhelmed within him.

In one of his sermons, Mr. Spurgeon touched on our ignorance of Paul's thorn in the flesh. He suggests that perhaps it is unspecified so that each of us may apply it to ourselves. And I think that the vagueness of the Bible is often of a deliberate intention in order that room may be left within its words for every variety of human need.

When Jesus said, "Let not your heart be troubled," He was not contemplating exemption for His own followers. He knew there would be troubles in their *lives;* what He enjoined was an untroubled *heart.* And one great help to an untroubled heart amid the thronging troubles of our lives is to be found in this practice of the psalmist. A brave man does not show his troubles before all the world. He tries to hide them and keep a smiling face in order that he might not be a discouragement to others. But to show before the Lord our troubles in the quiet moment when the door is shut is one of the secrets of serenity.

In one sense, one of the duties of friendship is just to lend an ear. It is an untold comfort when troubles are depressing us to have someone in whom we can confide. A brother is born for adversity, not just that he may lend a helping hand. A helping hand may be a blessed thing, but a helping heart is often better. To have somebody to whom we can open our hearts in the certainty of perfect understanding is one of the choicest gifts of human life. Visitors among the poor have experienced that. How often they bring comfort by just listening! Poor folk, toiling away bravely, discover an easing of their trouble when they can pour it all, if only for an hour, into a listening and appreciative ear. Now it was that easing which David found in God. He showed before Him his trouble. He did not brood on it in solitary bitterness; he quietly laid it before God. And though the trouble didn't disappear any more than the thorn of the Apostle, he gained a sweet serenity of spirit which made him capable of bearing anything.

And, indeed, that is the real victory of faith and of all who quietly wait on God. It may not banish all the trouble, but it always brings the power to bear it beautifully. There is a deep-rooted feeling in the heart that if we are God's, we ought to have exemption. Troubles that afflict the faithless soul ought to be averted from the faithful. But the age-long experience of God's children and all the sufferings of His beloved Son proclaim that this is not so. David was not protected from life's troubles, nor was Paul or our blessed Savior. David knew, in all its bitterness, what a thing of trouble our human life may be. His victory, and that of all the saints who have learned to show their trouble before God, was an inward peace that the world can never give and the darkest mile can never take away. God does not save His children *from* that dark mile. He saves His children *in* that dark mile. Whenever they show their trouble before Him, He shows His lovingkindness to them. He keeps them from an embittered heart; He puts beneath them the everlasting arm; He makes them more than conquerors in Christ.

One feels, too, that David, like Abraham, had seen the day of Christ. His personal trouble was of concern to God. One hears it said so often that in the Old Testament the nation was the unit, and one remembers right through the Old Testament the insistence on the majesty of God. Yet here is a troubled and persecuted soul who dares to think that the God of all the earth has a heart responsive to his very own trouble. He never dreamed it was a thing too petty for the concern of the infinite Jehovah. With a quiet confidence he showed it before Him who was the Maker of heaven and earth. And the wonderful thing is how this faith of David in the individual loving care of God was confirmed by great David's greater Son. Not a sparrow can fall without our Father. The very hairs of our head are numbered. If we, being evil, know how to give good gifts unto our children, how much more our Father? There would be no surprise in that precious teaching for one who could write in childlike trust, "I showed before him my trouble."

God Knows

When my spirit was overwhelmed within me, then thou knewest my path.—
Ps. 142:3

It is often a deep relief in trouble to have someone with whom the grief may be shared. There is a certain pride natural to us all which prompts us to hide what we may have to bear. There are trials, too, of such a peculiar character that we can never hope to find an understanding heart. Nevertheless, speaking in general terms, it is a mighty solace to be able in our dark and bitter hour to pour our story into another's ear. Now that comfort, you notice, was denied this psalmist. "No man careth for my soul," he said. Crushed as he was into the very depths, men passed him by in selfish disregard. There was no one to whom he could go for a word of cheer, no one who would be patient while he spoke, no one he could trust with the story of his sorrow.

It was in such an hour this singer did what is always wise in such hours. "I cried unto the Lord with my voice, with my voice unto the Lord did I make my supplications." Denied the privilege of human sympathy and with a heart that was likely to break for grief, "I poured out," he said, "my complaint before him; I showed before him my trouble." Now, that this was a step of profound wisdom is abundantly manifest by its results. God answers his prayer by breathing a new hope into the cheerless gloom of His petitioner until at last this brokenhearted suppliant is set so surely on the rock again that he cries, "The righteous shall compass me about, for thou shalt deal bountifully with me."

We have all seen, amid our Highland hills, a day that opened in utter desolation. There was the rolling mist, the drenching rain, the forlorn sighing of the cheerless wind. All nature seemed to brood in hopelessness as if she had forgotten to be glad. Heavy sorrow seemed to lie upon her bosom and to struggle in despair in all her voices. But as the day wore on, the aspect changed. First there was a dull and watery sun and then the heavy mists went rolling upward; the light shone and birds began to sing. So in the afternoon came warmth and beauty, and in the beauty a softness and mystery that never would have fallen upon the land but for the dreary vapors of the morning.

Brethren, have you ever noticed in the Psalms a progress like that of our hills? Have you ever noticed how often they begin cheerless and tearful and with a shrouded sun? And then have you noticed how, as they proceed, they break into the light of joy and trust, a light that is made more beautiful and tender by its trailing and misty fringes of the morning. Such is the little Psalm before us here. It begins with a cry out of the very depths. It ends with the sunshine of the glad assurance, "Thou shalt deal bountifully with me."

First, then, let us examine some of the times in which our spirit is overwhelmed within us. And may I ask you to note the word the psalmist uses? "My *spirit*," he says, "was overwhelmed within me." Now, in the Old Testament whenever that word *spirit* is used, it carries the suggestion of activity. There is another passage in which the psalmist says, "When my *heart* is overwhelmed within me, lead me to the rock that is higher than I." But the overwhelming of the heart is a little different from the overwhelming of the spirit. The heart is the inward nature of the man viewed passively as the groundwork of his character. The heart is the soil from which the actions spring, white as the lily or black as the night. But the spirit is the action and the energy, the manhood rising up to face its duty, the treasury of life, if I may put it so, out of which all our conduct draws supply. And when the spirit is overwhelmed within us, there will always be one sign of that dejection. It is the sapping of the springs of energy, the heaviness and the weariness of duty. The hands grow weak, the knees become feeble; power and hope die down. The spirit hears the call but cannot rise to it—as the psalmist puts it, it is overwhelmed.

Now one of the seasons when this is likely to happen is the season when troubles are multiplied. A single problem we can generally handle; it is when problems are multiplied that we fail. Now you may always be certain that where you find a proverb, it voices a pretty general experience. If a proverb is not generally true, men have no use for it and it dies. And one of the proverbs that has survived the years and grown familiar to every one of us is that troubles never come singly. Why, think of Job when a messenger came running to tell him that his oxen and asses had been stolen; and while he was yet speaking came another to tell him that his camels were gone. And while he was yet speaking another hotfooted in with more trouble, and I say that that is the experience which humanity corroborates. Had Job been written by some hermit scholar, he would have put an orderly space between the messengers. But whoever wrote that book knew human life well when he hurried the messengers on one after the other. Isn't that how troubles often come, thronging together, following one another, blow after blow in shattering succession? Now it is just that relentlessness that is so prone to overwhelm the spirit. "Innumerable evils have compassed me about; therefore my heart faileth me," says David. If a single wave were to dash against us, we would have power to resist the shock. It is when "*all* thy billows are gone over me" that the spirit is so near to being overwhelmed.

Another time when we are likely to faint is when we feel ourselves unequal to our difficulties. When the tasks of our appointed calling overwhelm us, then often our spirit is overwhelmed too. There comes times to every one of us when our courage melts, when tasks appall us, and doubts and fears rush in like the tide. It may be all a matter of our health, for body and spirit are in close union. It may be that our work becomes more difficult through competition or altering conditions. Or it may be that there is trouble somewhere that cannot be eradicated so that a person is unable to give himself to a task that calls for quiet or concentration. It is in such time that even the most valiant are in danger of an overwhelmed spirit. The knees become weak; the hands hang down; strong men bow themselves and the keepers tremble. One cannot look upon the golden bowl but he shudders lest it be broken at the fountain.

Such mysteries do not only crush the heart, they do far more; they overwhelm the spirit. You know how hard it is to be a faithful servant if you are serving an unreasonable master. Nothing so crushes the spirit out of service as to be at the sport of whim and of caprice. But, on the other hand, nothing is more effectual in making our service one of joy and steadfastness than just to know that the master whom we serve is a perfectly just and reasonable man.

You can crush the spirit of a child by cruelty and by terrorizing its imagination. But remember, there is another way that may be quite as fatal in the after-years. It is bringing the child up under the growing sense that in the conduct of the home there is no justice, that there is nothing over it from day to day but the foolish whim of affection or of temper.

Brethren, we are all children in this world, and we know that in heaven is our Almighty Father. And it isn't His chastisements that try our spirit, although His chastisements are often hard to bear. It isn't even what we cannot fathom—for who are we to comprehend the Infinite? It isn't what we cannot comprehend, but what we cannot reconcile. We do believe that God is perfect wisdom and perfect justice and all love. And it is when we meet with mysteries that we cannot reconcile with justice or love or wisdom that our spirit—our power for reasonable action—is likely to be crushed into the very dust. Why should one who would not harm a creature be bowed for years in acute pain? Why should a mother lose her one and only child? Why should the reprobate live for many years and be useless to all and a misery to many; and some precious life be terminated in the morning when its influence was so needed in the world?

By and by it will all be plain to us, for now we know in part and see in part. Blessed are they that having not seen, yet believed. Shall not the Judge of all the earth do right? Yet compassed as we are by clouds and darkness and confronted by the mysteries of providence, have we not all had times like the psalmist's when our spirit was overwhelmed within us?

Isn't it a mark of our overwhelming hours that our pathway seems to stop or disappear? Like the children of Israel on the banks of the Jordan, we are confronted by a swollen river. Our path seems to suddenly reach some chasm or ravine, and on the edge it disappears. How often we have taken a path across the fields that seemed to lead in the way we wished to go. For a little while it was plain beneath our feet, and then it grew fainter and became divided, until at last, perhaps when the sun was setting and the shadows of evening were falling on the valleys, the path we followed just disappeared. It is always so in overwhelming hours. We lose our peace because we lose our path. Our plans are crushed; our prospects are destroyed. We seem like helpless wanderers in the twilight. And it was then that David comforted his soul with the assurance that was given him from God, that all the time although he couldn't see it, there was a pathway for his weary feet. He was not an aimless wanderer in the dark, the result of an accident or chance. His feet were moving on a prepared path through light and shade to a prepared end. Let him go forward trusting Jehovah—*that* was his duty if the path were there, and by and by it would lead him from the valley and bring him to the waters of repose.

And then the psalmist had this other comfort: not only was there a pathway, but God knew it. As he reviewed his overwhelming hours, he saw it clearly—*"then* thou knewest my path." The Thou is emphatic—the accent is on Thou. I did not know my path—but *Thou* didst. Of that the psalmist could never be in doubt when he surveyed the way he had been led.

Brethren, where the Scripture says "God knows," it means far more than bare words convey. *Our* knowledge is often useless and inoperative, but the knowledge of God is always full of action. He knows us, and therefore He will help us. He knows our path, and therefore He will guide us. When my spirit was overwhelmed within me, the Lord was my shepherd and I did not want. Let us hold to that confidence whenever, like the psalmist, we are crushed in spirit. Clouds and darkness are around His throne, and yet He knows and is very merciful. And then at last, when the dayspring has arisen and the mystery has passed away forever; when the book is opened in which He keeps our wanderings, then we shall look back upon it all with all its happiness and all its heartbreak and say, "When my spirit was overwhelmed within me, then thou knewest my path."

When the Spirit Is Overwhelmed

My spirit is overwhelmed within me; my heart within me is desolate.—
Ps. 143:4

There are some natures more prone than others to this overwhelming of the spirit, but it wouldn't be true to say that the peril is limited to temperament. Some of the last persons one would ever dream of are prone to this hopeless sinking of the heart. I would expect it in Jeremiah, that most tremulous of all the prophets; but in Elijah—that man of iron will—I would scarcely anticipate finding it. Yet in the life of Elijah came an hour when, plunged into the deeps, his prayer was that God would let him die. There are few things that men hide so well as this inner desolation.

Sometimes such an overwhelming feeling comes for reasons that are purely physical. This is the body of our humiliation, and we are fearfully and wonderfully made. I asked a friend only the other evening if she ever experienced an overwhelmed spirit, and she answered, "When I am very, very tired." Nothing is more delicate and subtle than the interaction of the body and the soul. Lack of faith is sometimes related to lack of health which should make us very tenderhearted and forbearing in judgment towards those who are never really well.

Sometimes we become overwhelmed through simple failure to do our duty. To shirk our God-appointed task is to court the presence of despair. When Christian and Hopeful were on the King's Highway, Giant Despair was never encountered. But when they got into By-path Meadow, *then* they fell into the giant's clutches. And whenever anybody leaves the King's Highway, sooner or later, but inexorably, "melancholy marks him for her own." To omit the task we know we ought to do, to shirk the duty of the hour and shun the cross, to refuse to lift the burden and put selfishness in place of service—all this, in this strange life of ours, is to head straight for the overwhelmed spirit.

I should like, too, to add here that we should never pass judgment in overwhelming hours. Let a man accept the verdict of his Lord, but *never* the verdict of his melancholy. Hours come when everything seems wrong and when all the lights of heaven are blotted out, and how often, in such desolate hours, do we fall to judging the universe and God! It is part of the conduct of the instructed soul to resist that as a temptation of the devil. Such hours are always unreliable. The things that frighten us in night are the things we smile at in the morning. We are like that traveler who in the fog through he saw a ghost; when it came nearer, he found it was a man; and when it came up to him, it was his brother. Overwhelming times are times for leaning; God does not mean them to be times for judging. They are given to us for trusting; they are not given to us for summing up. Leave that till the darkness has departed and the dawn is on the hills, and in His light we see light again.

Indeed, the great need in overwhelming hours is the old, old need of trust in God. It is to feel, as the hymn has it, that we are "safe in the arms of Jesus." To be assured that God is love and that He will never leave us nor forsake us; to be assured that He knows the way we take and that His wings are folded over us all the time, *that* is the way to keeping a brave heart when everything is dark and desolate. Plunged into such depths, there is something even deeper. There is the love of God commended in the cross. *Underneath* are the everlasting arms. So we endure as seeing the invisible, and then (and often sooner than we expect) the day breaks and the shadows flee away.